PRISONERS OF PROGRESS

PRISONERS

American Industrial

Macmillan Publishing Co., Inc.
NEW YORK

Collier Macmillan Publishers
LONDON

OF PROGRESS:

Cities 1850–1920

by MAURY KLEIN and
HARVEY A. KANTOR

FOR *Cathy* AND *Jayne,*
who know why . . .

Macmillan Publishing Co., Inc.
866 Third Avenue, New York, N.Y. 10022
Collier Macmillan Canada, Ltd.

Library of Congress Cataloging in Publication Data

Klein, Maury.
    Prisoners of progress.

    Bibliography: p.
    Includes index.
        1.   Cities and towns—United States—History.
2.   Urbanization—United States—History.   3.   United
States—Industries—History.   I.   Kantor, Harvey A.,
joint author.   II.   Title.
HT123.K55   301.36′3′0973   76-12528
ISBN 0-02-563880-7

FIRST PRINTING 1976
Printed in the United States of America

Contents

TABLES

Preface

THIS BOOK IS about two of the most dominant forces of our age, industrialization and urbanization, as they occurred in the United States between 1850 and 1920. Unlike most other books on these subjects, which tend to deal primarily with one or the other, we have tried to give both equal weight. Our assumption is that the two are inextricably bound together in the American experience, and that the relationship between them holds the key for understanding their historical development. We live in a society that has become overwhelmingly industrial and urban, and our history of the past century suggests we have had no little difficulty in coming to terms with that kind of society. Most people would agree that we have yet to understand, much less master, these complex forces that govern our lives. For these reasons, it is important that we try to comprehend their origins, character, and lines of development.

Since writers wish to be read by everyone, it is always difficult to select a particular audience at which to aim. We have intended this book primarily for the interested general reader and the student. In doing so, we have assumed no background in the subject on the reader's part. Nor have we included the usual scholarly paraphernalia of footnotes and bibliography. This is an interpretive history drawn from a wide range of primary and scholarly sources. Historians who specialize in these areas should easily recognize most of the sources; the general reader, on the other hand, is seldom interested in the details of a book's pedigree. Thus, the list of sources for each chapter is in no way comprehensive, but includes only works quoted or used in some manner in that chapter. The photographs are intended both to illustrate points discussed in the text and to stand on their own as a pictorial essay.

Like all writers, we have incurred more debts of assistance than we can possibly repay or even acknowledge. Staff members of the University of Rhode Island library, the Library of Congress, National Archives, Kansas City Public Library, Gary Public Library, Oak Park Public Library, the Chicago Historical Society, New-York Historical Society, Rhode Island Historical Society, Museum of the City of New York, and many others were uniformly generous and cheerful in the aid they rendered. Our three typists, Debbe Carter, Kathy Hendry, and Betty Hanke, deserve special merit badges for heroism under fire. The patience and encouragement of our wives is duly recorded in the dedication.

Usually the writing of a preface is a joyous task, a celebration for the end of a long and arduous project. But these words are dipped in sorrow for my co-author and friend, Harvey Kantor, who died of leukemia on February 18, 1975. He was thirty-one years old, a kind and gentle man whose infectious laughter and warmth infused everyone who had the privilege of knowing him. He had known of his condition for some years and fought its advance with a cheerfulness and determination that was awesome to those of us who were but helpless spectators. Only a few of his friends even knew of his illness until very near the end.

Much of the last year of Harvey's life went toward completion of this book, which meant a great deal to him and which he wanted very much to see in print. It grieves me deeply that he has been denied that moment of fulfillment.

I have never understood, and probably never will, why death seems always to claim first those to whom life means the most. I know only that he is gone, that our loss is great, and that we are thankful for even the brief time we had him. Wherever his spirit resides, this book salutes its memory and its inspiration.

Kingston, R.I.
February 24, 1975

MAURY KLEIN

Introduction

THERE WAS A TIME not so long ago when the tenor of American
life was very different from what it is today. Looking back a century
and a half, life seems to have been simpler, and indeed it was—if we
are careful not to confuse "simpler" with "better." The structure of life
seemed clearer, all experience more direct and absolute, and the pace
of living less hurried.

Compared with our own age, life appeared to be more orderly and
settled. Men still attached great importance to religion and organized
their values and lifestyles around their creed. They moved more slowly
and solemnized every event from birth to marriage to death. Even
smaller incidents were cloaked in formality. A journey transcended
mere travel to become an experience worth describing in great detail to
friends and family; a visit or social outing was prefaced by careful
preparations; every family activity, such as attending church or eating
dinner, was ritualized.

Men seemed closer to nature a hundred and fifty years ago. Their struggle with the elements was immediate and perpetual. Most families still
wrested their living from the soil, and for many it was a bitter and
exhausting struggle. Their lives marched not to the ticking of a clock
but to the timeless rhythms of sun and season. They worked for themselves, toiling long hours, sometimes helped by a hired hand or two if

the family could afford it. To them Nature was both opportunity and enemy. Those who lived on the land and drew their livelihood from it were prisoners of the harsh and fickle limitations imposed by climate and soil.

That fact alone sharpened the contrasts between every emotion and sensation. Lacking all modern conveniences, our ancestors felt more keenly the differences between warmth and cold, light and darkness, pain and pleasure. So simple a thing as noise was an event to them, for in the stillness of the countryside every sound had a meaning and none went unnoticed. They knew silence as we cannot. The extremes of sickness and health, joy and sorrow, happiness and despair, were more direct and intense with them. In simpler times there is more a quality of mystery to life, and with it a keener sense of excitement.

The contours of daily routine a century and a half ago were elemental and unsubtle. Work occupied the central part of most people's lives. Most men worked for themselves rather than for wages and saw the fruit of their labor directly, whether it be wheat, fish, boots, or a piece of furniture. Work was important to them because it was both their subsistence and the measure of their talent and skill. Most work was still manual. While machines entered early onto the American scene, the vast part of productive energy still came from animal and human muscles.

Compared to today, the majority of working people were far less specialized in both training and occupation. The requirements for most professions were modest and obtained with little difficulty. In their pursuit of success, men did not hesitate to change careers as often as they changed clothes, or to do several things at once until they found the one that appeared most promising to their future. They viewed America as an open society in which new opportunities beckoned everywhere and demanded versatile men unfettered by past experience or failures.

Nor did men often compete directly with each other for jobs or markets except at the local level. Local competition might sometimes be intense, but it was always mitigated by the lure of new possibilities elsewhere.

This promise of distant opportunities and the willingness of Americans to pursue it made our ancestors a restless and mobile people. Even though Americans were constantly on the move, the places where they lived and the details of their lives were similar in many respects. The vast majority lived in the country or in small villages. Even those who lived in cities had lives much different from modern city-dwellers.

In the early nineteenth century, American cities were much smaller (in 1850 there were only sixteen with as many as 25,000 people and four with more ·than 50,000) and more intimate. They tended to be communities in both spirit and character. People of all classes lived among each other rather than in neighborhoods separated by economic and social class. Bankers, fishermen, jewelers, blacksmiths, and mechanics were acquaintances, if not intimates. All tended to live near their work. Business and manufacturing firms were usually small enough for wage earners to know their employer personally and deal directly with him. People of all classes attended the same churches, sent their children to the same schools, took part in local politics, and shared the same community activities. While every town had its elite or "best people," they were not isolated or even much segregated from those beneath them on the social ladder. If they did not mingle freely, at least they crossed paths frequently.

The basic conditions of life were different in both rural and urban America. Huddled near the water lanes which were their source of existence, cities were often little more than outposts set amidst the wilderness. Primitive forms of transportation made travel slow and difficult. So, too, with communication: a message could go from one place to another only as fast as someone could carry it by horse or boat. Goods could not be moved long distances in great quantity except by water. Most producers therefore catered to local markets. People tended to grow or make most of the things they needed at home, and what they could not make for themselves, they bought from local merchants (usually a general store) or from itinerant peddlers who roamed the countryside. Luxuries usually required a long journey to the nearest city.

The social order was simpler and more of a whole piece in both cities and villages. Most of the population came from like ethnic origins. There were, of course, many races and nationalities already in America, but the tidal wave of immigration had not yet crashed its great sea of ethnic diversity down upon our shores. Government was simple, direct, and often informal. Men of every class followed its course and took some part; in many areas, the town meeting had not vanished from the scene.

Religion and the family remained the twin pillars of the social order everywhere in the land. For most Americans they were the fountainhead of learning, leisure, and moral instruction. The family unit served as work force, school, recreation group, and civilizer. To a large extent, church and family reinforced each other's work; they were the bulwark of social stability and order.

This portrait of a bygone world is a static one, a still life that does not take into account the tremendous forces of change pressing against it. It is not intended to depict a "better" or "happier" time, but only a different one that was already passing out of existence before the Civil War. We may call it a still life of preindustrial America. In little more than a generation after the Civil War it would be gone, vanished as completely as the world found in the fading photographs of an old family album.

Both the extent of change and the speed with which it occurred were so startling that few Americans could comprehend it all. They saw their world dissolving and re-forming about them, but were slow to grasp the sources of this great transformation. Small wonder that they were perplexed, for they were engulfed by the most sweeping revolution in all human history, one that has continued with undiminished fury into our own time.

Consider just the bare outline of this revolution. Within little more than half a century, the machine replaced manual labor as the dominant source of energy and productivity. The output of goods and services multiplied as the factory system supplanted the house shop and "putting-out" system. Machines also moved onto the farms, enabling fewer people to produce more food. Large factories and plants, built to process raw materials and manufacture finished products, drew millions of people from the farm and from abroad in search of jobs. Others came to operate related businesses or provide services for the growing industrial network.

These enterprises and their satellite concerns tended to cluster together in strategic locations where they had access to sources of power, raw materials, and markets. In these favored spots, small towns or even wilderness were transformed into great cities which became the heart of economic and commercial activity. Ambitious men and women, seeking great fortune, a fresh start, or simply a bare livelihood, flocked to them. Steadily the nation's population shifted from the country to the cities. By 1900 there were 160 cities with a population of 25,000 or more, and nearly 40 percent of all Americans lived in towns of 2,500 or more people.

Economic miracles were occurring within these sprawling cities. The railroad, the telegraph, and the telephone revolutionized transportation and communication. Goods and materials could be shipped nearly anywhere in the country from the point of manufacture. Food, building materials, tools, machinery, and other necessities could be brought into the cities to supply the thousands of people living there. Urban America grew utterly dependent upon its rail arteries for survival, just as the railroads depended upon the urban market for their economic well-being.

The transportation network fostered the rise of regional and national markets. Since products could now be sold anywhere in the land, it was possible for firms to produce in great quantity and compete for distant markets. The size of corporations grew rapidly, and so did the fierce competition among them. As small businesses evolved into giant enterprises, they became impersonal bureaucracies employing thousands of persons. They commanded vast wealth and resources, to say nothing of immense economic and political power. Their actions affected the destinies of millions of people everywhere. In little time they exceeded the ability of society to restrain or control them.

The great corporations became the dominant institutions in American life. Alarmed by their sudden rise, Americans reacted by attempting to meet power with power. They increased the size and scope of their governments, devised new agencies, and gradually created a public bureaucracy no less complex and imposing than that of the business and financial communities.

Every aspect of American life grew more complex and confusing. Working people lost their independence as more and more of them took jobs in factories and plants. The proportion of wage earners to self-employed persons increased every year. The factory system drew women and children into its work force as well, and forced everyone to toil long hours under wretched conditions for meager wages. The old personal relationship with the boss was severed by the growth of firms into giant concerns; in its place came a hierarchy of shop stewards, foremen, and supervisors.

Jobs became more specialized and less satisfying. Few people worked on a whole product from beginning to end, and fewer still felt any personal attachment to or pride in the product of their labor. The factory system compelled them to discipline their lives to the inexorable ticking of the clock. Periodic cycles of depression made job security nonexistent. Low pay and uncertain employment left most families with no margin for disaster and little opportunity for advancement. Long working hours and boring repetitive work left little time or energy for leisure, recreation, or self-improvement. Unable to improve their lot individually, workers turned to collective action. They formed unions to counter the superior power of their employers with a united front. Sometimes they were successful; more often they were not.

The landscape was no less ravaged than its inhabitants. Americans have never treated the land or its creatures gently; every generation from the earliest settlers despoiled the forests, slaughtered game, and exhausted the soil with callous indifference. In the New World waste and destruction went hand-in-hand with progress. Industrialization spurred this profligacy to new dimensions. Smokestacks rose to belch the by-products of success into the atmosphere. Natural hills, bluffs, and ravines were gouged and stripped to make room for the iron horses of progress. Whole mountains were catacombed with mine shafts or leveled to extract their treasure of ore. Rivers, lakes, and streams became dumping grounds for industrial wastes. Foul-smelling clouds of smoke hovered above most large cities. "Industrialism," Lewis Mumford observed, "the main creative force of the nineteenth century, produced the most degraded urban environment the world had yet seen."

Living conditions changed no less drastically. The quality of urban life deteriorated steadily for all but the well-to-do. While rural and village life was never the pastoral idyll imagined by later nostalgists, it did have certain advantages: fresh air, sunlight, clean water, trees, grass, plenty of living space, and sources of healthful recreation. The farm and village were not models of hygiene or sanitation, but they were usually isolated enough to escape the spread of the epidemic diseases that ravaged nineteenth-century America.

City dwellers were not so fortunate. The lower classes were crowded into grim, unimaginative housing where such necessities as air, light, heat, and toilet facilities became precious luxuries. The urban ghettos overflowed with human misery. They reeked of filth and foul odors and were ravaged by disease. The lack of space gave rise to tensions and periodic outbursts of violence. In these dismal hellholes the struggle for existence wore down the endurance of even the most ambitious newcomers. Some escaped to a better life, but the vast majority were doomed to pass their entire lives in this bleak setting.

The upper and middle classes fared better. They had access to better housing and facilities, and many escaped to the suburbs or to the ultimate retreat, a house in the country. For nearly everyone, however, city life underwent a radical transformation: it ceased to be a community in spirit or structure. The business district now swarmed with faceless people ever in motion. As the population swelled, business and personal relationships diminished in both quality and duration. Increasingly people found themselves doing business with strangers and confining their social activities to family and a small circle of intimates.

Successive waves of immigration induced people to retreat steadily into association with "their own kind." Both the concept of community and any semblance of a unified social order were shattered by the growing diversity of racial and ethnic groups. Bewildered by alien tongues and customs, people of common origins and status tended to cluster together. Neighborhoods became segregated by race or nationality as well as by social and economic class. So, too, did churches and schools. Even as the public school system expanded to embrace the flood of newcomers, a parallel network of private schools developed to educate the children of upper-class families. Clubs, lodges, parishes, gangs, and other forms of association became the center of social life for every class. These were largely neighborhood organizations, and their emergence reflected the shrinking domain of urban dwellers. As the city grew larger, its occupants were cut off from close contact with all but their own limited territory.

Government grew no less specialized as each class or ethnic group organized its own base of power. Politicians became specialists whose art lay in putting together successful coalitions of diverse groups to obtain control of urban government. Politics became a profit-oriented business for many of its practitioners. As political machinations grew more complex, the opportunities for corruption multiplied. Fewer people participated directly in the political process, except passively as voters. Most were too busy pursuing their own ambitions while the "better people"— the class that traditionally governed—were either jostled aside or confined themselves to denouncing the decaying morality of civic life.

Family life was no less buffeted by the shock waves of change. Among the lower classes every traditional function of the family was strained as women and children were forced to take jobs. The middle and upper classes escaped this plight but faced situations no less novel. Men devoted an ever-increasing share of their time to work and so were absent from the home most of the time. Children were sent off to school and found more of their leisure and recreation outside the home.

Urban women (middle- and upper-class) confronted a confused situation. On one hand, their domestic duties were lightened by the availability of cheap servants and a rising store of labor-saving devices for the home. On the other hand, they were shut out of meaningful roles in business and politics. In a sense, they occupied a social vacuum that forced many to seek new roles and activities. Women had long dominated the tastes and temper of American culture; they continued to do so, but a few pursued careers as artists. Some struggled to breach the barriers in business and politics while others campaigned militantly for women's rights. Still others developed full- or part-time careers in social work, charities, and a variety of organizations.

The whole structure of American family life was changing. All its internal relationships—between wife and husband, parent and child, brother and sister—were losing their traditional cohesion. So, too, were the ancient bonds between the nuclear family and the extended family. Religion no longer played a dominant or even active role in the lives of many people. The old verities no longer seemed sure guides to behavior; often they seemed irrelevant or inapplicable to the realities of daily life. The inner world of Americans was in no less a state of flux than their outer one.

In broad terms, what was happening can be put simply: a society of individuals was giving way to a society of organizations—and often giant organizations at that. The main source of this transformation was that complex of forces we call the Industrial Revolution. This was surely the most far-reaching revolution in all human history, and everywhere it was accompanied by the rise of great cities unlike any the world had ever known. There were bigger cities and towns, and more of them. Their nature and functions changed, as did the composition of their populations. They came to assume a more important—and ultimately dominant—role in national life.

Eventually urbanites adapted to their new roles, and for them the city became a familiar landscape. Organizations filled the vacuum created by the powerlessness of individuals. Specialized expertise substituted for the artisan's creativity. Group identification eased the wounds of fractured personal relationships. Skyscrapers permeated the consciousness as church steeples had once done, to provide a sense of place. The noise and bustle of the city became as familiar a background as the quiet of the countryside.

Still the pace of change accelerated. This organized urban society, coupled with the technology of mass production and the automobile, reshaped the city into a regional metropolis just at the time people were coming to grips with the industrial process. Because this transformation, which took place after 1920, came so quickly on the heels of large-scale industrialization, and because the underlying forces of the private marketplace were never sufficiently altered, American notions of urban living remain out of step with the realities of the metropolis.

Only now, with the tools of historical and social science research and the potential of federal help, do urbanites have the opportunity of regaining the harmony of people with environment which industrialization destroyed. Because industrialization and urbanization were inseparable, and because these forces play so vital a role in the modern world, it is crucial to understand the relationship between the two, which is the essential purpose of this book. Our analysis is confined to the American experience, but it may also shed light on the European experience. At the least, it seeks to acquaint readers with the origins of those forces that govern the society and the milieu in which they live.

PRISONERS OF PROGRESS

CHAPTER 1

The Industrial Revolution

In proportion as the principle of the division of labor is more extensively applied, the workman becomes more weak, more narrow-minded, and more dependent. The art advances, the artisan recedes. On the other hand, in proportion as it becomes more manifest that the productions of manufactures are by so much the cheaper and better as the manufacture is larger and the amount of capital employed more considerable, wealthy and educated men come forward to embark in manufactures, which were heretofore abandoned to poor or ignorant handicraftmen. . . . Thus at the very time at which the science of manufacturers lowers the class of workmen, it raises the class of masters. . . . In a short time the one will require nothing but physical strength without intelligence; the other stands in need of science, and almost of genius, to ensure success. This man resembles more and more the administrator of a vast empire; that man a brute. The master and workman have then here no similarity, and their differences increase every day.

—ALEXIS DE TOCQUEVILLE
Democracy in America (1835)

IF THERE IS one great event that divides American history into two distinct eras, it is not the Civil War but the Industrial Revolution. For Americans, as for people everywhere, industrialization involved nothing less than a revolution of their total experience. It transcended ideologies, ignored moral dictums, defied the strictures of politics, overturned social orders, and unraveled the fabric of tradition. Even in the smallest details of their daily routines, men were separated from the past with a finality that bewildered them.

To understand the impact of industrialism, one must recognize that it held the potential to solve one of humanity's oldest and most pressing problems. From the dawn of his earliest history man's condition has been one of material want and scarcity. His struggle to survive was a constant quest for the bare essentials of life—food, water, clothing, shelter, heat, protection from nature and from his enemies. The struggle was long and harsh. Through the centuries great civilizations rose and flourished, but none managed to solve the problem of economic scarcity.

There were in truth two aspects to the problem: one concerned production and the other distribution. Every society had its own philosophy or system of distribution, and these varied widely from one people to another. In simple terms the problem of scarcity is that there are not enough goods and services available to satisfy the demand of those who want them. Obviously, the system of distribution deeply influences the level of individual scarcity. The more equitable the distribution of goods and wealth, the greater the share of every person. An inequitable distribution meant that the privileged few lived well while the rest had to content themselves with what was left over. But no system of distribution could enlarge the total store of goods and resources; only an increase in productive output could do that.

Throughout the preindustrial era, productivity remained the chief barrier to material progress. Two difficulties compounded the problem, one quantitative and one qualitative. The first concerned the growth of population. Little progress could be made if the level of productivity did not increase faster than the number of people clamoring for its fruits. There were many checks to the growth of population, nearly all of them related to some aspect of scarcity: famine, disease, and war, to name but three. The life span of most individuals was short because the conditions of life were harsh and the struggle for survival wore people out at an early age. While this issue is a complex one, it can be said that conditions of scarcity operated as a check upon population growth. The more these conditions were alleviated, the more populations increased and thereby put added pressure on the productive system.

The qualitative difficulty was more subtle, and has to do with what we now refer to as "standard of living." A rise in productivity created the *potential* (depending on the system of distribution) for more people to live more comfortably and securely than before. But as the level of material well-being rose, so did the level of expectations among all classes. The wealthy expected to indulge their advanced tastes on a more lavish scale. Those directly beneath them on the economic pyramid wished to move beyond mere comfort to the realm of luxury. Those at the bottom demanded at least to be rescued permanently from their bitter struggle with privation. Unfortunately, expectations could always be manufactured more quickly than the goods needed to satisfy them. As a result, improvements in productivity did not relieve the problem of scarcity, but often actually intensified it.

The discovery of the New World excited people's imaginations largely because it seemed to offer some escape from the bonds of scarcity. Early explorers looted the civilizations of America and returned home with staggering loads of booty. While these treasures greatly increased Europe's store of wealth, there was a limit to the amount of spoils even captive peoples could yield. In the long run it was not the riches of the Aztecs or Incas that whetted Europe's appetite for gain, but rather the possibilities of the continents themselves.

To the settlers of North America, the most stunning reality of the New World was its overwhelming abundance. America seemed to have a boundless supply of everything Europe lacked: land, resources, water, trees, and freedom. It was a virgin continent stretching out beyond anyone's ability to measure or even imagine it. There existed no political or social structures to restrict exploitation of its resources. Everything was there for the taking if men would work to extract it. Virgin continents have not come along very often in history, and the colonists were determined to seize their golden opportunity. Thus arose the image of America as a land of plenty for all. Enthusiasts in both Europe and America waxed eloquent over the promise of America, but none captured its appeal so well as Hector St. John de Crevecoeur, a Frenchman who had settled in Orange County, New York:

There is room for everybody in America: has he any particular talent, or industry? he exerts it in order to produce a livelihood, and it succeeds. Is he a merchant? the avenues of trade are infinite; is he eminent in any respect? he will be employed and respected. Does he love a country life? pleasant farms present themselves; he may purchase what he wants, and thereby become an American farmer. Is he a labourer, sober and industrious? he need not go many miles, nor receive many informations before he will be hired, well fed at the table of his employer, and paid four or five times more than he can get in Europe. Does he want uncultivated lands? thousands of acres present themselves, which he may purchase cheap. Whatever be his talents or inclinations, if they are moderate, he may satisfy them. I do not mean, that every one who comes will grow rich in a little time; no, but he may procure an easy, decent maintenance, by his industry. Instead of starving, he will be fed; instead of being idle, he will have employment; and these are riches enough for such as come over here.

Crevecoeur's last point is well taken. In the excitement it was easy to forget, then as now, that America offered not wealth but the *potential* for wealth. To extract its promise required hard work under the rugged conditions of an alien environment. The struggle wore out our ancestors and sent many of them to premature graves. Much of their energy went to learning the art of survival. Few of them got rich or even well-to-do. Many died from disease or at the hands of Indians, and all endured hardships we can scarcely conceive. We look back upon them as people of incredible courage and determination. So harsh was their lot that we might just as easily call them damned fools.

It was their vision of a better life that drove them to suffer these privations. To vast throngs of people, America opened doors that Europe had long since closed. Life in America was better than life in Europe even if it was no paradise on earth. By the early 1800s the young nation offered most people a higher standard of living than they could find anywhere else in the world, but it had by no means solved the problem of scarcity.

On the eve of the industrial era, then, the western world found itself nowhere near a solution to the problem of economic scarcity. It may be true that more people enjoyed a higher standard of living than ever before, though even this is denied by some scholars, but for the great masses of people life remained, as Thomas Hobbes put it, "solitary, poor, nasty, brutish, and short." All of man's ancient enemies—hunger, cold, disease, poverty, misery, ignorance—stalked him everywhere. Earthly life remained a millstone of suffering and deprivation, an exhausting ordeal that wore down even the hardiest. Under these circumstances it is hardly surprising that men sought refuge from the pain of this world in the promise of a better life in the next. Religion girded the spirit to endure, for it seemed that nothing short of a miracle could bring the body comfort and material ease.

Yet it was precisely this miracle that the Industrial Revolution was to accomplish; that is what makes it the most significant and far-reaching revolution in all human history. It offered the potential for solving the problem of scarcity. From modest beginnings it rushed onward like a juggernaut until it had achieved a fantastic increase in productive output. And it did more: it created nothing less than a new basis for human life, a new order for human society. Industrial society was the true New World, one more vast and mysterious, filled with more promise and perplexity, than that dark continent Columbus bumped into while searching for the fabled riches of the East.

The Factors of Industrialization

Industrialization is a phenomenon more easily measured than defined. We may assemble volumes of statistics, charts, and graphs to indicate the terrific growth in output; these are indeed informative, and we will have to resort to them here. But figures alone will not tell us *what* happened or, more important, *how* it happened. We have used the term "industrialization" deliberately. For our purposes, the *process* of industrialization is no less crucial than the thing itself. The modern industrial city is the product of several forces and factors coming together at a certain time in a unique way. To understand the product, we must investigate the processes that shaped it.

The dictionary defines industrialism as "the organization of society built largely on mechanized industry rather than agriculture, craftsmanship, or commerce." But how does this take place, and what factors are involved? Let us consider the second question first. In the American industrial experience there are ten developments that may be isolated as key factors. These are outlined below in no particular order:

1. Power-driven machinery replaced hand tools and animal or human muscle as a source of energy and productivity.
2. Production came to be centered in large factories, which transformed not only the techniques of production, but also the whole basis of labor relations.
3. A full-blown market economy emerged as markets extended beyond the local to the regional and national levels.
4. There occurred a revolution in transportation as the development of railroads fostered the growth of a national transportation network.
5. New forms of communication (notably the telegraph and telephone) were developed to speed up the flow of information.
6. Technological innovations proliferated at an accelerating rate and penetrated every area of economic activity, creating new mental patterns concerned with problems of technique.
7. An organizational revolution occurred in which economic activity came increasingly to be dominated by large enterprises.
8. Specialization began to characterize every aspect of economic activity.
9. Population increased at a rapid rate.
10. The proportion of Americans living in cities and towns increased steadily.

This list is by no means comprehensive, but it is complete enough to illustrate the pattern of industrial development. Before taking up these items in more detail, a word of caution is needed. It would be misleading to think of them as "causing" the Industrial Revolution. There is no single "cause" or set of "causes" of industrialization—indeed, the word "cause" is best omitted from the discussion. American industrialization was the product of all these factors interacting with and reinforcing each other. The crucial point is not the individual factors but the nexus of relationships among them. They are so thoroughly intertwined that it is difficult even to discuss them in isolation.

And the process was always a dynamic one. Over the years these interactions intensified steadily, as did the scale on which they operated. The result was an expanding industrial system with no simple or direct lineage. In short, American industrialization was not the offspring of one or even several factors or forces; rather, it evolved through a complex process of interaction and accretion. It has no "causes," only sources. Some of these sources will be examined in this chapter, the rest in Chapters 2 and 3.

The Advent of Machinery

The New World abounded with the basic elements for material success: land, resources, and unfettered opportunity. So vast were its holdings that they overwhelmed the sparse white population. In such a setting there seemed always too much work to do and not enough hands to do it. Economic prosperity on a large scale demanded some solution to this labor shortage. A system of indentured servants was tried with little success. The South, with its great staple crops, seized upon slavery as the answer to its labor problem, but slavery created more difficulties than it solved. In time, the Americans found their solution by emphasizing mind over muscle. They resorted to a variety of inventions, gadgets, devices, and contraptions known to later generations as machines.

A machine is literally an apparatus with interrelated parts that work together to perform some kind of work. All sorts of machines had been devised long before the Industrial Revolution, but their usefulness was limited in one important way: their source of power had to be supplied either by human or animal muscle or by nature (usually water power). Only when new sources of energy were invented did machines come to play a major and ultimately dominant role in productivity.

That was the significance of the steam engine. Thomas Newcomen, an Englishman, produced the first commercially successful steam engine in 1706. It was introduced five years later and was perfected by 1720. Further improvements were made over the next half century, culminating in the work of a brilliant English scientist, James Watt. In 1775 Watt formed a partnership with Matthew Boulton, a prominent manufacturer, to produce Watt's improved engine. After a struggling start the venture prospered. In Boulton's words, people seemed to be going "steam-mill mad." Most of the firm's engines went to mines or waterworks for use as pumping units. Then in 1782 Watt perfected a rotary engine which could supply power to a wide range of manufacturing activities, notably the textile, iron, and mining industries.

From these modest origins the machinery revolution surged forward as fast as imaginative inventors and businessmen could carry it. New machines were devised to perform with ease tasks that had once been laborious and time-consuming. The textile industry was among the first to be radically transformed. Most of the early innovations were English but soon found their way to America: the spinning jenny (1764) which enabled one operator to handle 30 spindles at once, the water frame (1769), and the mule (1779). During the late eighteenth century, textile mills sprang up throughout the United States. By 1815 there were 213 mills in operation, most of them in New England where water power and cheap labor were both plentiful.

These early mills were limited to the spinning of yarn. But in 1814 Francis Cabot Lowell of Boston, an astute student of English textile mills, devised a power loom and found a mechanical genius named Paul Moody to build it. Lowell and some fellow capitalists erected a large mill at Waltham to house the new loom. There, for the first time, machines did both spinning and weaving in one factory. The Boston Manufacturing Company, as the company was named, became an immediate success and long remained the leader in its field. The factory built its own machinery and in 1817 began to sell its machines to other factories. For several decades the firm prospered both as a textile manufacturer and producer of textile machinery. By 1845 its machine shop was the largest and best known in the country.

The use of machinery and steam power spread quickly to other areas. Every stage of farming and agriculture felt the influence of "creeping mechanization." The production of cotton—the raw material for the textile mills—was revolutionized by Eli Whitney's invention of the cotton gin in 1793.* The first cast-iron plow was patented in 1797; a seeding machine was invented two years later. In 1819 Jethrow Wood of New York created a three-piece cast-iron plow with standardized interchangeable parts. A major breakthrough in farm machinery came during the early 1830s when Cyrus McCormick and Obed Hussey, working separately, invented the first reapers. Over the next three decades there appeared the first crude thresher (1837–40), steel plow (1837), revolving disc harrow (1847), binder (1850), twine knotter (1858), and checkrower corn planter (1864).

During the 1780s Oliver Evans, a Delaware farmer, created an automatic flour mill which cut the labor needed by half. Steam power was

---

* Whitney later pioneered the concept of mass production when he successfully utilized the principle of interchangeable parts to fill a government contract for muskets.

introduced into sawmills in 1798 and its use spread quickly. Transportation especially underwent a startling change. The first steamboat appeared in 1786 but lacked sufficient power to be practical. Then in 1802 John Stevens invented the screw propeller, and five years later Robert Fulton launched the first successful steamboat. This new craft revolutionized river transportation. It meant that boats were no longer prisoners of the current but could travel both upstream and downstream.

The greatest advance, however, came not in water but in land transportation. John Stevens devised the first locomotive with multitubular boiler in 1826; four years later Peter Cooper built the first American locomotive. The next decade witnessed a steady parade of mechanical breakthroughs in rail transportation. By 1840 Americans everywhere were busily engaged in constructing railroads. The steam-powered locomotive, even more than the steamboat, freed man from the limitations imposed by nature upon the movement of goods and people. As we shall see, the railway era revolutionized not only travel and shipping but the whole fabric of American life.

Well before the Civil War, Americans established themselves as masters of machinery. Borrowing ideas from everywhere and adding their own genius to them, Americans poured out an endless procession of practical devices. Some of these included a machine to cut and head nails in one operation (1790), the revolver (1835), sewing machine (1846–54), rotary printing press (1846), shoe manufacturing machinery, locks, vulcanized rubber, rope spinners, food canning, power tools, machines for tile cutting, sand sifting, and cask making, and the first crude electric motors.

A swelling stream of new inventions poured forth from the workbenches of American tinkerers. The average number of patents granted each year soared from about 600 in the mid–1830s to nearly 5,000 by 1860. While some were important innovations, the vast bulk achieved instant oblivion. A few gained publicity as curiosities, like the flying machine of Jacob F. Hestor in which, according to the August 1841 issue of *American Magazine*, "the aeronaut is to be put into a kind of garment or bag, and suspended to a balloon, then wings are to be used, by means of which he is to mount upward." Americans from every walk of life tried their hand at invention. Young Jay Gould, later to become Wall Street's most notorious financier, took the old adage to heart and tried to win his fortune by literally marketing a better mousetrap. The reverence of Americans for machines knew few bounds. "There appears to be something in the pursuit of mechanical invention which has a reaching up after our divine title, 'lords of the creation,'" commented a writer in *Scientific American.* "It is truly a sublime sight to behold a machine performing nearly all the functions of a rational being."

Especially did Americans excel at the invention and production of machine tools. These ranged from measuring instruments of all sorts to machines that performed every kind of basic precision work. The first screw-cutting machine appeared in 1809, the circular saw in 1814, the profile lathe in 1818, and the turret lathe in 1854. The Brown and Sharpe Company of Providence, Rhode Island, produced the first commercial vernier caliper in 1851 and quickly developed an international reputation for its precision tools, instruments, and clocks. Even before the Civil War, metals and machinery were themselves becoming a major industry, and their size and importance grew steadily throughout the nineteenth century.

The iron industry, perhaps the key sector of an expanding industrial system, underwent a striking transformation during the first half of the nineteenth century. Prior to the 1830s, iron works tended to be small and widely scattered. Much of their crude iron went to village blacksmiths or artisans who shaped it into tools, wire, spikes, hoes, rakes, shovels, spades, axes, knives, horseshoes, anvils, anchors, plows, stoves, kettles, and other products. Forges were often separate works from furnaces, and charcoal was the fuel used for smelting.

Then in rapid succession a series of innovations occurred. Two of them were borrowed from the British: the rolling mill, a machine which reduced the labor needed to refine and shape the iron into bars, and the "puddling" process for refining pig iron in open forges without bringing it into direct contact with the heat. The puddling process enabled iron works to manufacture on a greater scale and allowed the possibility of using cheaper mineral coal as fuel instead of charcoal. The possibility became a reality when, in the early 1830s, the huge anthracite coal fields of Pennsylvania were opened up.

The presence of this high-quality fuel may have been the spark that touched off a rapid expansion of American industry. Anthracite provided clean, cheap fuel for steam power. It also enabled the iron industry to transform its scale and scope of operations. In 1840 David Thomas of Connecticut devised a hot blast furnace for anthracite, and within the next few years machines for breaking, crushing, and rolling coal were invented. During the 1850s William Kelly of Kentucky and Henry Bessemer of England developed similar methods of converting pig iron into steel. The age of iron and steel had dawned. The main thrust of American economic expansion was becoming grounded in metals and machinery. Iron and steel were the backbone of that industrial sector, and anthracite coal became the fuel which spurred the production of iron and steel in unprecedented quantities. The use of anthracite spread rapidly to other industries; by the 1850s it had become the staple of America's industrial and household fuel needs.

By that time the nation was well on its way to becoming an industrial society. Every stage of that journey was marked by increased reliance upon machines. But machines were not the only source of that development. In literal terms machines are labor-saving devices—they enable fewer people to produce more things of consistent quality at a faster rate. They can create products superior to those produced by manual labor, and in some cases not even possible by manual labor. But to achieve these miracles machines must be utilized effectively. To be efficient they require a radically different organization of the productive process than that used for hand or simpler machine production. That is why the growing dependence upon machines was accompanied by the emergence of the factory system.

The Factory System

The term "factory" has several meanings. A "factory" is a place, the "factory system" is a method of organizing production, and we may refer to the "factory stage" as one level of industrial development. Perhaps the best approach is to break the factory system down to its separate components, examine each one, and observe the process by which they came together. To do that we need first to consider how production took place during the preindustrial era.

In the beginning, the United States was overwhelmingly a nation of self-employed farmers. Most farm families owned their land and worked for themselves, although they might have hired hands if they were prosperous; planters, of course, relied upon slave labor. Beyond the farm, a wide variety of people worked for themselves and often by themselves: artisans, craftsmen, professional men, shopkeepers, small businessmen, merchants, traders, bankers, trappers, hunters, cobblers, blacksmiths, curriers, hatters, tailors, weavers, and many others.

What kind of jobs paid wages to those not fortunate enough to work for themselves? In addition to farm hands there were sailors, fishermen, boatmen, dockmen, lumberjacks, miners, journeymen, apprentices, clerks, servants, laborers of all sorts, and those who worked in mills, factories, foundries, and other establishments. In most cases the work force in any one firm was small because production was modest and limited to local markets. Many manufacturing enterprises were located in the country close to the raw materials they required. These ranged from iron works and sawmills to distilleries, sugar mills, salt works, tar kilns, paper mills, potash plants, and brickyards.

As late as the War of 1812, household manufacture (goods made in the home mainly for family use) remained the staple of American industry. Over the next four decades, however, household manufactures steadily lost ground (except in the area of food production) to three different forms of organized productivity: handicraft production, the domestic or "putting-out" system, and the factory system. This transition is significant, for all three of these systems produced not for home use but for market sale. They differed from each other radically in their means of production, but all three arose in response to a growing market demand for manufactured goods.

The simplest of these three forms—handicraft production—evolved from the ancient practice in which a craftsman made an object and sold it to a buyer. The process was largely an informal one. The craftman's home served as both shop and "store," and he tended to produce only on order. This meant that he created his wares not for sale in an impersonal market but for a particular customer. He owned his tools, ran his own business, and worked his own hours.

As a market demand for their goods developed, many craftsmen began to produce for market sale. This shift changed the entire situation. Since quantity of output grew more important, the craftsman concentrated upon production. His home ceased to be a store. He no longer sold directly to customers, but rather to a merchant, who might also supply the craftsman with the raw materials he required. The craftsman probably hired apprentices and journeymen to increase output. At this stage he became less a craftsman and more a supervisor directing the work of others. How far all of these changes were carried always depended upon the kind of wares he produced, the market in which they were sold, and his own ambitions.

The domestic system carried this transformation even further. Merchant capitalists took the initiative in organizing production, furnishing raw materials to people who worked on them in their own homes. Sometimes these workers turned out finished products; often, however, they did only what amounted to piecework. The merchant collected the goods and had them assembled or completed in a central shop. The finished wares were then sold, often in places quite distant from where they were manufactured. A wide variety of products were made in this way, including woven cloth (cotton and woolen), boots and shoes, buttons, horse whips, suspenders, and some types of hats.

Both these systems appear to presage the factory system, yet it is hard to generalize about the connection. Obviously each system suited the manufacture of some items well and others poorly. Few industries evolved from one system to the next in any logical pattern. Everything depended upon the amount of demand for the product, the capability (human and mechanical) of producing it in quantity, and the ability to get it to markets beyond the immediate locale.

Notice that both the handicraft and domestic systems tended to decentralize production by scattering it in homes throughout the countryside. This was a deceiving trend. The factory system proved to be the wave of the future, and it went in exactly the opposite direction. The heart of the factory system was the way in which it brought all the basic factors of production together in one place.

This last point suggests a general description, if not a definition. The factory was an enterprise organized by one or more businessmen seeking profits by producing something on a large scale. It was usually located on a site convenient to sources of power, raw materials, a labor force, and access to markets. The organizers of the enterprise erected the buildings and installed whatever machinery was needed in them. They hired labor by paying money wages. If the enterprise was large enough, they might hire supervisors, clerks, bookkeepers, and even managers to help run the operation. They furnished all the raw materials and arranged for sale of the product. They produced for the market and in quantity. In skeletal form these are the essential characteristics of the factory system. By the 1850s it had become the dominant form of industrial enterprise; between 1860 and 1900 it expanded so spectacularly as to dwarf everything that had gone before.

What forces brought the factory system into being? The only satisfactory answer would be a detailed account of the interaction among all the factors we have listed for industrialization. Without going into them all, we can list one or two examples to suggest what was happening. The growing use of machinery provides a good insight. Machines were expensive and usually immobile. They could not be farmed out to workers or purchased by them from their own meager funds. To operate efficiently, machines must produce in quantity. That requires a steady supply of raw material, a large and reliable labor force, regularized production procedures, standardization of goods, quality control, and reliable sources of capital to keep the enterprise going.

None of these conditions could be met by individual craftsmen working separately. Someone had to organize the enterprise, raise the money, and bring everything together in one central location to insure maximum output and efficiency and to reduce operating costs. In a sense, then, we can say that the advent of machines compelled the rise of some form of centralized production. The form that developed is what we have come to call the factory system, but its emergence depended in turn upon other factors such as the growth of a market demand to justify production on a large scale, access to those markets through improved transportation, and the availability of reliable sources of labor and raw materials.

The particular structure of the factory system in the United States derived largely from the model provided by the Boston Manufacturing Company mentioned earlier. So successful was this textile enterprise that its methods were widely copied by other industries until the final product came to be known as the "American system." The important point about the Waltham approach is that it was a *system*. As Gilman Ostrander has observed, "The originality of Waltham lay on its overall conception rather than in specific methods, which were largely adaptations of English methods. The Waltham method was characterized by an overriding emphasis upon standardization, integration, and mechanization of the processes."

Yet the specific components of the Waltham method are vital to understanding the system as a whole. Most of them should sound familiar at this point: Every aspect of cotton cloth production was done in a single plant under one management; strong financial backing provided enough capital for both continuous operation and expansion; supervision of the process was carried out by men who were not technical experts but capable general executives; the plant concentrated upon cheap coarse cotton fabrics for which the market demand was soaring; the company sold its product through a single marketing outlet instead of relying upon various jobbers and commission agents;* the standardized coarse cloth that Waltham specialized in could be produced by relatively unskilled (and therefore cheap) labor; and the factory conducted its large-scale operations with a work force of young women recruited from the New England countryside and installed in special dormitories near the plant.

The last two items point to one of the most significant influences of the factory system: it revolutionized not only the methods of production but also the basis of labor relations. This was an ironic twist that illustrates the manner in which economic development often thwarted and even perverted the best of social intentions. Some inventors of machines, and even a few early factory owners, were no less idealistic than other

---

* See Chapter 3.

people. They viewed their work as a salve for the lot of working people. Machines were, after all, labor-saving devices which enabled a person to produce more with less effort. A factory could be seen as a source of secure employment and, if organized and run properly, a sort of benevolent working community in which employer and employees labored in harmony for their common good. Robert D. Owen, an ardent utopian and founder of New Harmony, Indiana, declared, "I can make manufacturing pay without reducing those whom I employ to misery and moral degradation."

These were noble and stirring ideals, but they went the way of all utopias. The unhappy fact was that idealism did not square with the profit motive, and in that contest ideals never had a chance. If a new machine or an improved version of an older one enabled a worker to produce the same output in half the time, it also allowed him to produce twice the output in the same time—and even more, if he were made to toil longer hours. It happened, too, that the better the machine, the easier (and therefore more tedious) it was to operate. A declining skill level in the factory meant lower labor costs to the owners but more dreary and monotonous tasks for the workers. It also meant less job security, for low-skill workers were much easier to replace than skilled ones. Few employers were likely to choose the road that led away from increased output, lower costs, and greater profits.

Of course, the employer could ameliorate the worker's plight by offering improved working conditions. He could shorten the number of work hours and provide a cheerful, sanitary factory environment. He could build pleasant housing, make good meals or food available at reasonable prices, and install facilities for recreation and self-betterment along with the leisure time to take advantage of them. Some like Lowell tried to do these things, but they were few in number and their ranks dwindled steadily. The harsh truth was that benevolence cost money. It was a luxury that profit-oriented, expense-conscious employers could ill afford.

Once established, factories in nearly every industry found themselves competing bitterly with other firms for markets. In that competition victory went to the firms that could sell the most goods at the lowest prices. A factory is an expensive proposition that cannot easily be dismantled and converted into some other business. Once built, it must make money or its owners will lose their investment. In a competitive market, therefore, cost becomes crucial and leaves little margin for investment in benevolence. In fact the opposite trend develops—the worker becomes one more resource to exploit, an input to production that must be obtained as cheaply as possible. In this manner the quest for increased profit and production absorbed all other considerations. As Ostrander put it, "the factory, operating in a fiercely competitive system, tended to determine the conditions under which it would run—and a concern for human happiness was not one of its attributes." The tendency to sacrifice all consideration of the worker to the larger goals of profit and productivity was seldom based upon malevolence or even greed. Rather it was an impersonal and detached decision usually attributed to "sound business principles," a phrase that in American business history was to cover a multitude of sins.

These developments profoundly altered the pattern of labor relations in America. During the preindustrial era, the journeyman or apprentice saw himself and his employer or master linked by a common bond. They worked together and shared a community of interest. The journeyman worked with his own tools at his own pace to create a complete product which he sold. Even mechanics and other skilled workers were paid more for the product they made than for the time they spent at it. No deep antagonism infected the relationship between employer and employee, capital and labor.

The factory system changed all that. Factories employed semiskilled or unskilled workers, paid them a fixed daily wage, compelled them to work a specified number of hours (and therefore to order their entire existence around that schedule), and reduced them to performing one or more tasks instead of making a complete product. As the factory grew, workers were separated from the owners and supervised instead by salaried foremen and officers. Management and labor became clearly separate entities, and their relationship grew ever more impersonal. This new impersonal wage system demanded a constant increase in efficiency and productivity, which in turn meant longer hours, the lowest possible wage, the speeding up of every work function, and no money wasted on frills like improved working conditions.

As the factory system took root, it changed the composition of the labor force. Most factories drew their workers from the farms; like some great vacuum they sucked up men, women, and children, whole families, from the countryside. The early cotton mills especially relied upon women and children for cheap labor, while some heavier industries required men or at least teen-aged boys. Gradually the work force was swelled by successive waves of immigrants seeking jobs and willing to endure anything for a fresh start in life. As factory working conditions grew more brutalized, they strained the family structure of their work force.

To country folk in general, and naïve young girls in particular, the textile mills were a terrifying experience at first. The general process was much like the production of cloth done on the farm except that it was broken down into several specialized steps. Once the cotton bales were opened, cleaned of dirt and seeds, and separated by grade, the cotton was shoved through a "lapper" to flatten it into sheets and wind it around a cylinder. It then went through the carder, which drew the fibers straight and eliminated knots, whereupon it was put upon a drawing frame to pull the fibers together and twist them up. After being wound on cylinders again the cotton went to the spinning room, where it was pulled out in strands and twisted into thread. Some thread was placed on spindles and made ready for the woof, while other thread had to be brushed and sized before it could be sent to the weaving room.

What made this long and tiresome but familiar process so alien to country girls was the machinery used in the process. Everything moved rapidly, at an unfamilar pace. One factory girl's experience at Lowell was described this way:

> She felt afraid to touch the loom, and she was almost sure she could never learn to weave; the harness puzzled and the reed perplexed her; the shuttle flew out and made a new bump on her head; and the first time she tried to spring the lathe she broke a quarter of the threads. . . . The overseers watched every motion, and the day appeared as long as a month had at home. . . . At last it was night. . . . There was a dull pain in her head, and a sharp pain in her ankles; every bone was aching. . . .

Slowly but inexorably American wage earners slid downward into that abyss of misery and despair once reserved for the working classes of England. There developed an implacable hostility between labor and capital which soon found expression in outright rebellion and attempts to organize unions. Not even skilled workers escaped the impact of the factory system, for often, like the weavers, they found themselves displaced by machines which did their work more cheaply and efficiently. The overall result was intense economic and social dislocation, and a future characterized by strife and bitterness. The triumph of the factory demonstrated convincingly that the price of economic progress was too often paid in the coin of social instability and upheaval. And, in the long run, the price proved steeper than anyone suspected.

The Market Economy

We have used the term "market" several times already without bothering to define it. Actually, we will need more than one definition to clarify the concept and our particular use of it. A market is simply a meeting place for exchanging goods for money or other goods. Sometimes it literally refers to a specific place where buying and selling occur, such as a farmer's market, neighborhood grocery, or stock exchange. More often the term is used as an abstraction—even a metaphor—to describe all persons engaged in transactions over some particular item. Thus economist Robert Dorfman defines a market as "a group of people and firms who are in contact with one another for the purpose of buying and selling some commodity." That contact need not be direct and often is not. Transactions in securities, land, agricultural commodities, and many others are arranged by brokers or other middlemen for buyers and sellers who never meet. In this same abstract sense we can speak of the "market" in wheat or oil or automobiles. Notice that this mythical market includes persons, place, and process in its definition.

Markets serve the important function of determining price levels for all commodities through the process of buying and selling. Prices result from the interplay of that oldest of economic axioms, the law of supply and demand. A subsistence economy, where people produce only for their own use, has no need of a market system. But when economic activity rises beyond subsistence, when men produce more than they consume and sell or exchange the surplus for other goods, some method of determining prices becomes necessary. In most economies isolated markets tended to emerge at the local level on a random, piecemeal basis. As the economy grew more complex, the number of markets proliferated. Historically, then, the growth of a market system has always been closely linked to the process of economic development. Especially did it become identified with the process of industrialization. One scholar, Karl Polanyi, declared this to be the essential feature of the Industrial Revolution. In the following passage, notice how he interrelates several of our factors:

But how shall this Revolution be defined? What was its basic characteristic? Was it the rise of factory towns, the emergence of slums, the long working hours of children, the low wages of certain categories of workers, the rise in the rate of population increase, or the concentration of industries? We submit that all these were incidental to one basic change, the establishment of market economy, and that the nature of this institution cannot be fully grasped unless the impact of the machine on a commercial society is realized. We do not intend to assert that the machine caused what happened, but we insist that once elaborate machines and plant were used for production in a commercial society, the idea of a self-regulating market was bound to take shape.

To understand what Polanyi means by "self-regulating market" requires a brief outline of how it came into existence. Here we can draw upon the previous sections on machinery and the factory system. In a preindustrial society, agriculture and commerce dominate economic activity. Even much of the commercial trade has to do with buying and selling farm goods. Nonfarm industries of all kinds exist, of course, but they produce in relatively small quantities and sell to local markets.

As we have seen, the advent of machinery radically alters that pattern. Mechanized production can be introduced into this structure only by subordinating it to the process of buying and selling. According to Polanyi, the merchant alone commands enough capital to undertake this venture: "He will sell goods in the same manner in which he would otherwise sell goods . . . but he will procure them in a different way, namely, by not buying them ready made, but by purchasing the necessary labor and raw material. The two put together according to the merchant's instructions, plus some waiting which he might have to undertake, amount to the new product."

The consequences of this development are sweeping. The merchant becomes a manufacturer, the shop or home enterprise a factory, and the independent worker a wage earner. Specialization seeps into every aspect of production. And there is more. Since machine production is expensive, it is not feasible unless two conditions prevail: goods must be produced in large quantities, and a steady flow of raw material must be assured. As Polanyi emphasized, this means that *all* factors needed for production must be available for sale in quantity to anyone prepared to buy them; otherwise investors would hesitate to risk their money in expensive machines.

The problem is that these conditions do not naturally exist in an agricultural society. They must be created, and though the process of creation occurs gradually, the effects amount to no less than a new framework for economic activity. Polanyi summarizes the changes this way:

The transformation implies a change in the motive of action on the part of every member of society: for the motive of subsistence that of gain must be substituted. All transactions are turned into money transactions, and these in turn require that a medium of exchange be introduced into every articulation of industrial life. All incomes must derive from the sale of something or other, and whatever the actual source of a person's income, it must be regarded as resulting from sale. No less is implied in the simple term "market system," by which we designate the institutional pattern described.

The close tie between industrial development and the emergence of a market economy should now be obvious. Industrialization expands both the volume of production and the degree of specialization within the economy. This expansion tends to organize every factor into markets. Not only do the number and size of markets increase, they become more interconnected as well. Eventually this interdependence proves decisive. As the industrial economy matures, these countless, once isolated markets coalesce into what Polanyi calls the "One Big Market," a full-blown market economy.

Once established, the market economy tends to become self-regulating and self-adjusting. Prices regulate themselves and profits are at the mercy of market fluctuations. All factors are converted into commodities and find their own price level within the system. Markets develop for every element of industry: goods and materials are sold at commodity prices, labor for wages, services for salary, fee, or commission, land for rent, and money for interest. That is the essence of the market economy. Whatever noneconomic qualities its factors possess come to be subsumed by their market definition as mere commodities to be bought and sold. The significance of that development is enormous, for, as we shall see later, the market economy eventually created a market society subordinate to its needs. According to Polanyi, this marked the first time in human history that an economic system dictated the structure of a social system. While that observation may be somewhat exaggerated, it is clear that the market economy marked the dawning of a new and complex stage of economic and social institutions, the implications of which we have yet to fully grasp.

There is no law of God or nature which decrees that markets *must* be self-regulating. Markets and prices may be regulated in several ways, the most obvious of which is through government policy. The American economic system was shaped by a collection of ideas and beliefs that embraced—even venerated—the notion of self-regulating markets. At some point, probably around 1830, our economic ideology became firmly committed to the principle of noninterference. That concept was the cornerstone of the "free enterprise" or "laissez-faire" system which dominated the American economic mind throughout the nineteenth century. Gradually its ideas were frozen into dogma that still retain a hallowed niche in our national ideology.

The story of how this system of thought developed and triumphed in America is too involved to tell here. Its origins trace back to the writings of various English and Continental theorists, most notably Adam Smith, Thomas Malthus, and David Ricardo. During the nineteenth century its tenets were elaborated and reinforced by American scholars. During the industrial era, its principles were reasserted within a new framework formulated by Herbert Spencer and his American disciples. Both the economic liberalism of Adam Smith and Spencer's Social Darwinism were used by Americans to rationalize their economic experience because the concept of a self-regulating market economy nicely suited American needs and demands. It squared with the principle of maximum individual liberty and provided a system for the working out of individual economic aspirations. In short, it met the requirements (at least in theory) of a people who believed in freedom from restraint, equal economic opportunity, and all the virtues of rugged individualism. In time, changing circumstances would erode that ideology to the point where it no longer accurately described the realities of industrial society, but so devoted were Americans to its precepts that they clung tenaciously to them despite all evidence to the contrary.

The ultimate outcome of a growing market economy was the emergence of regional and national markets. Once goods are produced in mass quantity, they outstrip the needs of local markets and must seek customers in distant locales. The search for fresh outlets led first to the surrounding region and eventually to the nation as a whole. Obviously access to such a vast market encouraged a manufacturer to produce infinite quantities of goods if he could capture buyers for them. The rise of national markets, therefore, had terrific implications for the whole industrial system, not the least of which were a growing emphasis upon techniques of marketing and a new form of competition on a grand scale. Before any of this could occur, however, the problem of getting products to distant markets had to be solved.

The Transportation Revolution

The transportation revolution illustrates the headache of trying to disentangle the prime factors from one another. Their connections are continuous and resist efforts to sort them out. We might, for example, relate them in the following manner: without a developing market economy there could be no large-scale factory system; without efficient transportation there could be no market economy; without the rapid growth of railroads there could be no efficient transportation system; without the advent of machinery and an increase in population and the rise of cities there could be no railroads . . . and so on to infinity. Or simply reverse the chain or shuffle it into any order and start again. Either way, the chain of connections seems hopelessly circular, tempting one to take two aspirin and turn in relief to a novel or magazine.

Yet the chain is not so much circular as it is a spiral in which the factors reinforce one another and gain momentum as they move through time. In that onrushing spiral the role of transportation and railroads in particular was critical. The transportation revolution did not "cause" industrialization, but in many ways it holds the key for understanding how that process occurred. The railroads became the vital arteries that linked the other factors to one another and accelerated their interaction. One historian, Edward Pessen, states flatly that "the transportation revolution and the *de facto* single national market it helped create made possible and indeed decisively fostered great increases in profit-making opportunities even before victory of industrialism. . . ."

Major improvements in transportation occurred even before the appearance of the railroad. By 1815 improved roads, new bridges, and the growing use of riverboats were already driving down the cost and time of transportation. During the next two decades a craze for constructing turnpikes and canals swept the nation. Huge sums of money were poured into these projects by both governments and private citizens; by 1840 New England's investment in turnpikes totaled about $6,500,-000, while Pennsylvania alone spent $6,000,000 by 1822. Most turnpikes were conceived as toll roads expected to pay for themselves in time, but that hope proved illusory. While the turnpikes did expedite the movement of goods and people, only a handful earned even their upkeep, much less a profit. Numerous bridges were also built on the toll principle and proved more successful. A mania for constructing toll plank roads to connect shorter routes developed during the 1840s but petered out before the Civil War.

The canal craze was ignited by completion of the 364-mile Erie Canal between Buffalo and Albany in 1825. This great engineering triumph, achieved against enormous obstacles, connected Lake Erie to the Hudson River and thus to New York City and the Atlantic Ocean. By far the longest canal in the world, the Erie excited imaginations everywhere about the possibilities of inland water transportation. Nor was the Erie's financial success overlooked, for traffic increased so rapidly that the canal had to be enlarged only ten years after it opened. Fired by this vision of progress and profits, enthusiasts in every state with a river or two busied themselves with plans. Dozens of projects grand and small were designed, start-up capital was raised, and the frenzy of digging commenced.

George Rogers Taylor has estimated that between 1816 and 1840 some $125,000,000 was spent to construct 3,226 miles of canal, a distance exceeding that between New York and Seattle. Numerous projects floundered into financial difficulty and were never completed. Of those that were finished, several proved successful and profitable. None equaled the spectacular record of the Erie, however, and the majority failed to repay their investment. Huge construction costs undid most of the canals and drove some states, which had provided much of the funding, to the brink of bankruptcy. There were other reasons for the financial failure of canals, including high upkeep costs, poor management, and inadequate traffic to pay for such expensive projects. Moreover, by 1840 the canals were being challenged by a new form of inland transportation, the railroad.

Yet the importance of the canals and of water transportation in general should not be minimized. Water shipping dominated American transportation until the Civil War and, to a lesser extent, well into the 1870s. Flatboats, keelboats, and barges all played major roles in this traffic, but after 1815 it was the steamboat that became what Taylor termed "the most important agency of internal transportation in the country." Steamboats first captured the bulk of river traffic and then penetrated steadily into lake, bay, and ocean shipping. But even at its zenith water transportation had some serious shortcomings. The most obvious drawback was that boats could go only where there was navigable water. Even steamboats did not travel very fast (seldom more than 15 miles an hour), and they had to follow the long, tortuous meanderings of the rivers. The rivers themselves were filled with snags, sandbars, and other hazards. Northern rivers and lakes iced up for several months during the winter and were closed to traffic.

Railroads possessed none of these drawbacks. They were faster, more flexible, and could run according to regular schedules. Rails could be put down nearly anywhere and in a comparatively direct line. Trains could operate all year round and could tailor their equipment and schedules to the needs of their customers. For these and other reasons, the railroads cut steadily into the waterway traffic. By the Civil War, they were already shifting the flow of the great midwestern grain traffic from its north-south Mississippi River axis to an east-west overland axis. After the war, the nation exploded into a frenzy of rail construction. In 1860 the United States possessed 30,626 miles of railway; that figure soared to 93,262 by 1880 and 193,346 by 1900.

What function did the railroads perform? As already noted, they opened new markets and developed existing ones. The expanding rail network hastened the settlement of vacant or thinly-settled areas such as the vast Plains region between the Mississippi River and the Rocky Mountains. Once assured of access to markets, the most remote territory could become populous and productive. Industry, agriculture, and commerce all rode the rails to prosperity and new heights of activity.

Railroad connections turned sleepy hamlets into booming commercial centers and created cities where none had existed before. Atlanta was perhaps the most conspicuous example. Prior to the railroad era, the site of modern Atlanta was but a remote outpost known as East Point. As late as 1848 it was little more than a scrubby village of shacks and shanties. But Atlanta lay precisely at a point where two strategic trade routes intersected: a northwest-southeast route from the Ohio Valley to the Atlantic seaboard and a southwest-northeast route running roughly from New Orleans to Richmond and Washington. By 1860 it was a bustling commercial city on the verge of becoming the distribution center for the entire Southeast. Within twenty years after the Civil War, Atlanta had become the leading city of the South.

Similarly, Birmingham did not even exist prior to the 1870s. Because northern Alabama contained fabulous deposits of high-quality iron ore and coal, the Louisville & Nashville Railroad joined forces with Alabama promoters to complete a rail line between Nashville, Tennessee, and Montgomery, Alabama. Some of the promoters bought huge tracts of land at a point along the line rich in mineral deposits. Envisioning a great industrial center like Birmingham, England, they adopted the name for their fledgling village. The depression of 1873–79 delayed their plans, but by the late 1880s Birmingham had become the outstanding industrial city of the South.

Trains routinized transportation as no other form ever had. They regularized the shipment of goods, materials, and people. They hauled large volumes of more kinds of things at greater speeds than any other method of transport known to man. By lowering the cost of inland transportation, they rendered distant markets not only accessible but economically feasible. Within an amazingly short time, the rail system became the lifeline of industrial and urban America, a network of steel tentacles pushing into every corner of the Republic.

But the railroads were more than just reliable transportation. They were themselves a vital market for other major industries, notably iron and steel, coal, lumber, and heavy machinery. Without the railroad as its primary customer, it is doubtful that the iron and steel industry could have developed so rapidly. A host of other industries owed their growth to the railroads' constant need for equipment and supplies. And, as Alfred D. Chandler has emphasized, the railroads were the nation's first big business. They pioneered in new methods of finance and new forms of organization. Their complex and far-flung operations required elaborate administrative structures, professional managers, more so-phisticated accounting, and other business techniques. In these and

other areas, the railroads furnished blueprints for corporate operation
that later industries would draw upon as they grew larger. In form as
well as travel the railroads were innovators.

Modern patterns of labor relations developed first on the railroads with
their large and sprawling labor force. The railroads were the first major
industry to be unionized and the first to be regulated by government.
As the first giant corporations, the railway companies introduced Americans to the wide range of problems wrought by unrestrained big business. In all these areas the railroads were innovators not out of genius but
out of necessity. No other business matched their capitalization, their
investment in plant and equipment, their operating expenses, the size
of their labor force, or the complexity of their logistical problems. They
became the model upon which giant corporate enterprise in America
was fashioned.

The Communications Revolution

Innovations in communication paralleled those in transportation. They
were similar, too, in their dependence upon power to do their job. Where
the railroads moved commodities and people, the new communication
gadgets moved information. The growth of big business and a national
market would have been stunted, possibly prevented, without a radical
speedup in the flow of information. No industrial system could proceed
on horseback, especially that of the United States with its far-flung
continental marketplace. Yet before the telegraph was invented, no
message could travel long distances faster than the man or beast
carrying it.

The telegraph removed that limitation. Introduced first in America
during the 1840s largely through the efforts of Samuel F. B. Morse, the
magnetic telegraph spread like a prairie wildfire. By 1860 nearly 50,000
miles of line had been installed, and a year later the first transcontinental
wire was completed. Telegraphic communication was used extensively
during the Civil War and, along with the railroad, helped revolutionize
the logistics of warfare. The new device also fostered the development
of large railroad systems. Without some form of instant communication
it would have been difficult if not impossible to dispatch large numbers
of trains running at high speeds on regular schedules on the same tracks.
So, too, with businesses of every kind. The larger and more centralized
corporations grew, the more dependent they became on information
flowing in from the hinterland.

After the Civil War, the Western Union Company, through bitter struggles with rival firms, established its supremacy over the national telegraphic network. Its growth was astounding. In 1870 it owned 112,000 miles of wire, operated 3,972 offices, and handled 9,158,000 messages. By 1900 the company controlled 933,000 miles of wire, 22,900 offices, and handled 63,168,000 messages. By 1900, too, the wireless telegraph, an invention of Guglielmo Marconi, had appeared and was being used on ocean liners. Once perfected, the wireless would open new possibilities for the telegraph. The telegraph had been an important breakthrough in communications, but on its heels came yet another new device destined to overshadow its achievements: the telephone.

Alexander Graham Bell patented his brainchild in 1876, but at first the device was regarded as little more than a novelty. The earliest models were admittedly crude instruments. Arthur M. Schlesinger described the experience this way: "To use it a person, after briskly turning a crank, screamed into a crude mouthpiece and then, if the satanic screechings and groanings of static permitted, faintly heard the return message." There was another problem, this one of custom: how did one adjust to using the instrument? Operating a machine was one thing, talking to it quite another. "The dignity of talking consists in having a listener," one contemporary article observed, "and there seems a kind of absurdity in addressing a piece of iron."

For a time Bell was reduced to touring the country exhibiting his telephone like a sideshow curiosity. But the tide of opinion soon turned in his favor. He won a crucial victory in 1879 when the Western Union Company, which had waged a fierce battle against Bell's telephone as a threat to the telegraph, relented and sold its own telephone interests to Bell's group. A host of mechanical improvements soon transformed the telephone into an efficient communications device. The first central switchboard was installed in 1878 in New Haven; a year later, L. B. Firman devised the multiple switchboard. The way was open for a rapid expansion of service.

Still there remained serious problems, many of them unique to the telephone. Businessmen had to be convinced that the gadget was useful, if not indispensable, to their operations. The public had to overcome its prejudice against speaking with disembodied voices. More important, there existed no centralized communications system to connect all telephone users, and the creation of such a system required the kind of monopoly that was anathema to most Americans. It would also cost a lot of money. There was considerable risk in the investment because the Bell patents expired in 1893, and no one could predict what would happen after that.

Under the vigorous leadership of Theodore Vail, the Bell Company met each of these problems successfully. Vail worked tirelessly to extend the company's lines, improve the quality of service, and promote technical and mechanical advances. He made the crucial decision to lease rather than sell the equipment to insure uniformity and control. When public clamor arose over the growing jungle of overhead wires, he pushed research for a wrapped cable that could be buried underground. His enthusiasm for copper wire in place of iron led to experiments that demonstrated its superiority. This was a significant innovation, for copper could conduct sound over long distances and therefore connect telephones in scattered cities. In 1885 Vail organized the American Telephone and Telegraph Company to build and operate long-distance lines throughout the country. Vail and his associates had another objective in mind: to bring all telephone service in the United States under the control of one company.

Eventually AT&T did become the parent holding company for all the Bell systems. By 1893, when the patents expired, that system operated 266,000 telephones or an average of 3.9 instruments per 1,000 population. The system was handling an average of 1,872,000 local and 34,000 toll calls every day. But it failed to achieve a monopoly; after 1893 small independent companies began to appear, especially in small midwestern towns left untouched by the Bell system. By 1900 these independent companies were operating some 520,000 telephones, only about 20,000 of which connected with the Bell system. Despite this drawback, the smaller companies were handling an average of 2,916,000 local and 44,000 toll calls daily. Of course, the Bell system had also expanded during these years. In 1900 it operated 836,000 phones with a daily average of 4,773,000 local and 149,000 toll calls.

In one generation the telephone had advanced from a mere toy to a necessity of American life. Over the next few decades the rate of expansion would be astronomical. The existence of a central telephone network was to exert a vast influence upon the growing industrial system which, as it grew larger, depended increasingly upon its lines of communication. Toward that end even that old standby, the postal system, made new contributions. The rate for single letters was lowered in 1883, and a special-delivery service was added. Four years later, free delivery was extended to include all towns of 10,000 or more people. Perhaps the greatest innovation came in 1896, when rural free delivery was introduced. This service helped transform the retail buying habits of rural America by fostering the growth of the great mail-order houses such as Montgomery Ward and Sears, Roebuck. Once again, standardization, centralization, and volume, coupled here with improved mail service, worked to undermine small merchants and local firms by diverting their market elsewhere.

For all the fancy new gadgets and services, the post office still bore the major burden of communication in America. The number of post offices jumped from 18,417 in 1850 to 76,688 in 1900, when these offices handled more than 7,000,000,000 items of mail, a volume nearly twice what it had been only fourteen years earlier. And, with some exceptions, the mail was moving faster, if only because most intercity letters went by train and the trains were getting speedier. By the century's end the communications revolution had imposed striking changes on the American lifestyle. It had also created new industries, some of them giants even among the giants.

The Technological Revolution

It might be thought that our earlier discussion of machines was sufficient to dispose of this subject, but in fact it only scratched the surface. Technology embraces far more than machines, though it begins with them. Machines do not suddenly knock at society's door and ask to be put to work, nor can they be ordered to their tasks like obedient serfs. Their presence in large numbers, and their increasing productivity and sophistication, required dramatic changes in the whole structure of the economic system. These changes in turn affected the noneconomic institutions of society as well. In time no area of life was left untouched by the impact of machinery.

From this interaction between men and machines emerged a new mindset, a different way of looking at the world. This new ethic of the machine age embodied the deeper meaning of technology: an overriding concern with technique. Jacques Ellul, a French sociologist who has been a close student and harsh critic of the technological revolution, defines technique as "the translation into action of man's concern to master things by means of reason, to account for what is subconscious, make quantitative what is qualitative, make clear and precise the outlines of nature, take hold of chaos and put order into it." To this, Robert K. Merton adds, "Technique refers to any complex of standardized means for attaining a predetermined result. Thus, it converts spontaneous and unreflective behavior into behavior that is deliberate and rationalized. . . .

The Technical Man is fascinated by results. . . . Above all, he is committed to the never-ending search for 'the one best way' to achieve any designated objective."

To some extent, the advent of machinery compelled this sort of thinking by forcing men to rearrange their economic system around the capacities of each new mechanical marvel. Seen in this light, the machine was an agent of both progress and disruption. Ellul put it this way:

> The machine took its place in a social milieu that was not made for it, and for that reason created the inhuman society in which we live. . . . Technique integrates the machine into society. It constructs the kind of world the machine needs and introduces order where the incoherent banging of machinery heaped up ruins. It clarifies, arranges, and rationalizes; it does in the domain of the abstract what the machine did in the domain of labor. It is efficient and brings efficiency to everything.

The key to understanding the role of technique lies in the terms "efficiency" and "the one best way." Industrialism is above all a *system* of production. To operate properly and profitably it must find the most efficient means (i.e., one best way) of carrying out every function from the broadest strategy to the smallest operating detail. It is hardly surprising that industrial man became engrossed with technique—indeed, many of the great American businessmen regarded it as the fountainhead of success.

As the industrial era unfolded, this passion for technique and efficiency took some peculiar twists. One of them was a tendency for the distinction between means and ends to get lost in the shuffle. Technique originated as a means for achieving some end; it was a tool and nothing more. As the industrial system matured, however, technique gradually became an end itself. It became a field of study, a sort of science of technique, a specialty to which men devoted much time and resources. In less obvious fashion it shifted the emphasis from "why" something was done to "how" it could best be done. This shift is crucial because a technical or "how to" decision is quantitative; it shirks the broader moral and philosophical issues involved. The objective of finding the "one best way" acquires a narrow definition: "best" comes to be equated with "most efficient" to perform the task at hand without inquiring into the broader consequences or even whether the task needs to be done at all. Through this subtle process technique gives rise to what we refer to these days as the "engineering mentality."

The influence of this passion for technique was first and most deeply felt in the economy, which in the industrial age required a steady diet of planning and efficiency. But even before the nineteenth century expired, the gospel of technique was fast spreading into other realms of American life. Especially were many of the Progressive reformers imbued with this outlook. In place of corrupt legislatures and graft-riddled city machines they demanded governments that were not only honest but also efficient. Businessmen advanced the argument that government should be run like a well-managed corporation (many business leaders were willing to apply this analogy to any social institution).* Conservationists pleaded their cause partly on the grounds that the nation could no longer afford to waste its resources or utilize them inefficiently. Educators called for reforms that would enable schools to augment their curriculums with more practical "how to" courses. Education itself, like other professions, became increasingly absorbed with matters of technique. The twentieth century would witness an astonishing extension of this concern for technique into every area of personal life. The "how to" mania seized everything from salesmanship to personality development, from home repair to tennis strokes to techniques of lovemaking.

One important source of the gospel of technique was the growing influence of science upon American thought. By the late nineteenth century, Americans in virtually every profession proclaimed their intention of making a "science" of their field or taking a "scientific" approach to their work. This attitude was reflected in the growing number of occupations and services that became "professionalized." What was a professional but an "expert" trained in a particular skill who performed his specialty better and more efficiently than the untrained amateur? To cite but one example, social work evolved from a field ruled by altruistic amateurs to one dominated by trained professionals intent upon systematizing their work. Much of this concern with scientific method was in fact a concern for technique, a quest for the "one best way." The fast-growing cult of expertise was in part a reflection of the new faith in efficiency.

Much of the late nineteenth-century American experience could be used to illustrate this trend but nothing quite typifies it or the era like "Taylorism," the scientific management system pioneered by Frederick W. Taylor. Born into a comfortable Philadelphia family, Taylor eschewed college for factory work. He began as a journeyman machinist with the Midvale Steel Company, and within six years rose to the position of chief engineer. As an engineer Taylor enjoyed a successful and inventive career. Perhaps his most notable achievement came in

* See Chapter 11.

1902 when he and his associates, after much experimentation, helped revolutionize the field of cutting machinery by developing a new form of high-speed tool steel.

But it was as a theorist that Taylor won his greatest acclaim. In mind and spirit, Taylor embodied many of the conflicting currents swirling through the nineteenth century. He subscribed to all the verities of the Protestant ethic, especially the doctrine of hard work, but he filtered these traditional American tenets through a mind trained in the practical science of engineering and fascinated by the problem of technique. What emerged was a residue of moralism mixed with scientific method. As Gilman Ostrander put it, "Scientific management, as developed by Taylor, was intended as the means of applying the Protestant ethic with mathematical precision."

Early in his career, Taylor became engrossed by the problem of inefficiency of production, much of which he attributed to the careless and slovenly work habits of factory hands. At Midvale, and later at Bethlehem Steel, he undertook an analysis of the whole productive process, breaking it down into its simplest components. His study led to the publication of several widely read papers and culminated with his classic work, *The Principles of Scientific Management* (1911). Taylor's findings startled those industrial managers who read them, for they described a management system that called for not just new policies but a complete reorganization of the shop, changed roles for both managers and workers, and no less than a "mental revolution." In return, Taylor offered the promise of greater output, lower costs, higher wages, and with all this a new area of harmony in management-labor relations.

How were these miracles to occur? Largely by applying scientific techniques to the entire work operation. To do this, management must first make careful studies of every aspect of every phase of production. Once this information was gathered, each task could be timed to determine a standard level of performance for it. Each job was to be broken down into separate stages and workers would be trained to handle each one of these tasks. The labor force thus became piece-workers of the highest order, and wages would be geared to the standard performance level as determined by the objective studies. In this manner the rate of output became a product of scientific technique rather than a "guesstimate" devised by foremen or supervisors.

With such a standard, managers could ascertain whether their people were working at maximum efficiency. Each worker would earn a base pay rate based on the standard performance, but this rate, according to Taylor, was a "figure which will allow the workman to earn scarcely an ordinary day's pay when he falls off from the maximum pace." To it would be added an incentive rate for workers whose output exceeded the norm. This incentive rewarded superior workers for their skill and ambition. It would stimulate everyone to give their best, and above all it would increase output and lower costs. To attain these goals, management had to display initiative and intelligence by organizing its shop to speed the flow of work, eliminate all wasted energy and motion, and run its machinery at peak efficiency.

The essence of Taylorism was the principle that "scientific" production norms could be established, that standards of performance could be measured, and that employers could objectively calculate and therefore insist upon a specific rate of output for every worker. If successful in practice as well as theory, the implications would be far-reaching. Not only would men be perfectly integrated with machines, they would themselves be operated like individual machines. That such a system would chain a worker to the same specialized task day after day did not bother Taylor, who praised the "real monotonous grind which trains character." In this attitude he found support from another innovator, Henry Ford, who observed, "I have not been able to discover that repetitive labour injures a man in any way. . . . The average worker, I am sorry to say, wants a job in which he does not have to put forth much physical exertion—above all, he wants a job in which he does not have to think."

Taylorism drew a hail of criticism from both within and without the business community. Some resented its dehumanizing implications, while others simply shrugged off the results as not worth the bother they entailed. Like most ideal systems, it never achieved the purity of its theories in practice. Several of the attempts to implement it were made piecemeal, while others were simply botched. With charming naïveté, Taylor assumed that employers would dutifully collect all the necessary data, implement all the necessary changes in organization and operation, and refrain from manipulating the objective data to suit their own purposes (such as speeding up the performance standards). But rarely were these conditions met. Like most prophets, Taylor was too often betrayed, even caricatured, by his followers and practitioners, to say nothing of his critics.

Nevertheless the broad import of his ideas was to have considerable influence upon American industrial development, especially after World War I. The devotion to technique, the search for the "one best way," the integration of man and machine, and the disciplined work force required by such specialization all found their fullest expression in the development of a new mode of production—the assembly line. From

Henry Ford, the pioneer of this new production technique, came a clear signal of the direction in which American industrialization was tending:

The discipline throughout the plant is rigid. . . . We expect the men to do what they are told. The organization is so highly specialized and one part is so dependent upon another that we could not for a moment consider allowing men to have their own way. Without the most rigid discipline we would have the utmost confusion. I think it should not be otherwise in industry.

CHAPTER 2

Harnessing Leviathan:
The Organizational Revolution

> But the flames of a new economic revolution run around us and
> we turn to find that competition has killed competition, that cor-
> porations are grown greater than the State and have bred indi-
> viduals greater than themselves, and that the naked issue of our
> time is with property becoming master instead of servant, property
> in many necessaries of life becoming monopoly of the necessaries
> of life.
>
> —HENRY DEMAREST LLOYD
> *Wealth Against Commonwealth* (1894)

"IN NO COUNTRY has the principle of association been more successfully used or applied to a greater multitude of objects than in
America." With this observation, written in the early 1830s, Alexis de
Tocqueville coined a major prophecy of his century. It should be clear
from the previous chapter that industrialization compelled radical
changes in the institutions of economic activity. Even this was but a
prelude to an organizational revolution which gained momentum so
rapidly that in the half century between 1880 and 1930 it transformed
the whole structure of American civilization. During those years, a
society of individuals metamorphosed into a society of organizations. The
"principle of association" was, in fact, the genesis of a new age in
human history. For that reason it deserves more detailed examination
than the other factors.

This revolution proceeded on two levels. On one, existing organizational forms were radically altered and new ones devised; on the other,
the principles of organization were extended into every area of human

activity as it became clear that the older casual ways of doing things could no longer be applied to a complex industrial society. The new order simply could not function on the freewheeling basis that characterized most early American development. This discovery shocked and confused our ancestors. Improvisation was a talent they had elevated to an art form, but it had little place in an industrial system. The larger and more specialized activities became, the more planning and coordination they required to operate properly. Once that truth became clear, improvisation gave way to systematization and integration.

Most Americans foresaw none of this. The organizational revolution occurred through a process of drift rather than design, and it was fashioned out of necessity rather than desire. It originated in the private sector and was at first confined to the economy. The industrial system was built by ambitious men pursuing their private interests with little restraint from government. It was therefore not a product of planning or design but of accretion, the accumulation of thousands of decisions made and actions taken by individuals who gave no thought to the broader effects or implications of their work.* The entrepreneurs who by their energy and imagination established successful enterprises found it increasingly difficult to administer what they had built. They were a bold and expansive breed, and the grander their visions, the greater was the need for better ways of organizing the resources to fulfill them.

In solving these problems they unwittingly revolutionized the structure of economic institutions in America. But that was only the beginning. The economic order, awesome in its size and power, was found to be incompatible with traditional social institutions. Industrialization disrupted the social order as no other force of change ever had. Staggered by successive shock waves of tension and conflict which threatened to rip the social fabric apart, Americans reorganized their social system around the demands of the economic system that had sprung so suddenly into existence. In this manner the market economy formed the emergence of a market society which found its fullest expression in the spectacular growth of cities.

---

* This is only to say that there was some design in the parts but not in the whole. A single firm like Standard Oil, and even entire industries, might be models of planning, but not the industrial system as a whole and certainly not the social order. These "larger" orders were undesigned and unintended wholes, the sum of diffuse, often contradictory parts.

The Corporate Economy

We have already observed how industrialization concentrated production into factories and plants utilizing large aggregates of capital, labor, raw materials, and machinery. Before the nineteenth century had ended, transportation, commerce, distribution, banking, and marketing underwent a similar process of growth and centralization. As individual firms grew bigger, they encountered problems of administration which traditional forms of organization could not solve. These growing pains demanded innovations in the forms of business organization, the most important of which proved to be the corporation.

So spectacular was the corporation's development that by 1900 it had become the dominant institution in the economy, if not the whole society. So complete was its triumph that we often refer to modern American civilization as the corporate society. Obviously, then, the corporation looms large in the history of the organizational revolution. To understand the process by which it gained ascendancy, we can first construct a simple scenario to serve as a model for the general pattern. Then we will explore the nature of the corporate form and its effects upon economic activity.

Our model begins with an individual who comes up with an idea that might make money. The idea might be a new invention (telephone), an improved machine (automatic printing press), some different or improved process (Bessemer process for making steel), a new product (artificial teeth, ready-to-wear clothing), or some innovation in production, distribution, or marketing techniques. In short, the idea may be something entirely new or simply a better way of doing something that is already being done. Once the individual decides to organize a business around the idea, he becomes its promoter or entrepreneur.

His first problem is to raise money for the venture. Some men might already have enough cash, but most do not. Probably our entrepreneur will borrow some or most of it. He may acquire supporters or partners to share the burden and help develop the enterprise. Beginning on a small scale, the partners have to do everything themselves. They must figure out how to make their product as cheaply and efficiently as possible. They must determine how to sell it, to whom, and at what price. Gradually they work out the major questions of finance, production, technology, and marketing among themselves. Their organization is small and flexible, their methods of operation loose and informal. Everyone has several jobs to do, and much of their work is improvised because they are new at it and have few precedents to go by. The partners keep much of the vital information in their own heads and operate out of a small office or even their own homes. Along the way they make mistakes and, if they are alert, learn from the experience.

Once past the initial problems, the product is made and offered for sale. If it is poorly received, the enterprise fails. The partners chalk it up to experience and turn to some other scheme. But if it is a success, they think at once of expanding production. Expansion will require more capital, some of which may come from profits and some from borrowing. If they wish to produce on a grand scale, they will probably form a corporation to raise the money they need and to hedge their personal losses should the venture turn out badly. Shares are sold to the public (the partners retaining a majority for themselves), and the partners become managing officers in the new company.

Immediately, expansion changes the way in which they operate. The partners buy new machinery and equipment, hire more people to tend them, and install the whole enterprise in a large new building. Quickly it becomes clear that the business can no longer be kept in their heads or run casually out of their desks. To cope with the new problems that appear, each partner assumes some particular responsibility and men are hired to assist them. A managerial staff begins to emerge, arranged in a hierarchical chain of command which separates the partners and their subordinates from the workmen in the plant. Every member of the staff assumes some specialized function. All procedures (such as accounting, purchasing, marketing) are formalized and systematized; otherwise it proves impossible to keep track of everything as the scale of operation increases.

If success continues, the business grows still larger and more complicated. Output of the original product increases and new lines of products are added. These may require separate divisions or even separate corporations to administer them. More plants are built and competing firms are bought out and added to the complex. The labor force swells steadily and grows restive. The amount of capital invested reaches astronomical figures. The company becomes a national concern with salesmen opening up markets across the continent and perhaps overseas as well. As the economy expands, so does the company. Divisions beget more divisions, each of which may acquire several subsidiaries. An organizational monster now stands astride the shoulders of the original idea.

By this time, the original partners are long past the point where they can do or even oversee everything. They retreat to formidable offices attended by an army of secretaries, clerks, typists, messengers, and junior officers. Relieved of the details of production, they confine their energies to broad questions of policy and strategy while lesser minions handle the routine work. The partners can no longer even promote new ideas by themselves; they are too busy administering their empire. Every aspect of the operation falls prey to creeping specialization. Some officers (and their staffs) devote their entire attention to financial matters, while others tend strictly to production, marketing, technology, transportation, purchasing, research, and eventually personnel, labor relations, and public relations. The company may even hire specialists or experts to study its administrative structure and production methods to improve their efficiency. It recognizes that at every level coordination and planning are essential if the whole operation is to function smoothly. Yet those objects become more difficult to attain as growth continues.

Already in their twilight years and contemplating retirement, the partners may reflect upon what has happened to their original idea. They have nourished it to a destiny undreamed of at the start. The enterprise has assumed a life of its own, one that transcends the individuals who serve it. No longer is it dependent upon any one person or group of persons. When the founding partners die or retire, their departure will be mourned and their accomplishments celebrated, but company operations will scarcely feel their absence. Handsome portraits of them will be hung in the company's office, where they will gather dust and occasional glances from people of a generation too far removed from their achievement to understand what it was or what it meant.

Like any model, our scenario may not fit the exact history of any particular firm, but it does depict the general process by which small companies were transformed into giant organizations. In this transformation the corporation played a crucial role because it could solve problems that earlier forms of organization could not. This fact becomes clear if we look briefly at these earlier forms and their inherent limitations. They may be divided into three general types:

1. *The proprietorship*: one individual owning and managing the entire business.
2. *The partnership*: Two or more individuals each owning some share of the business, contributing some part of its assets, and usually managing some aspect of its operations.
3. *Unincorporated shareholder company*: a private organization based upon a written agreement in which individuals owned shares and from which one could withdraw by selling his shares. The shareholders often hired managers to run the business, but the company had no legal status beyond the private written agreement by which it was founded.

These were all simple, direct, and personal arrangements. The same persons both owned and directed the business except in some shareholder companies. Since their self-interest was directly at stake, it was presumed that they would conduct their affairs with care and vigor. Such uncomplicated forms were adequate for firms operating in a small-unit economy and servicing local markets. As a basis for large-scale enterprises, however, they had serious defects. Few individual entrepreneurs or even partnerships possessed the resources to finance or manage a giant company by themselves. They could not easily raise the large amount of capital needed for industrial or transportation enterprises. The death of a partner dissolved the firm and required new arrangements, as might a serious falling-out among them. Moreover, the partnership had unlimited liability, which meant that each partner was personally liable, to the full extent of his fortune, for all the firm's debts. This fact alone caused men to hesitate before plunging into a large and risky undertaking.

In short, a partnership made no legal distinction between the business and its owners. Neither did the shareholder company, which went beyond the partnership but did not escape most of its shortcomings. The shareholders also had unlimited liability, though they could retire from the company without dissolving the firm. But its legal status hinged upon private agreement and left ample room for disagreement among the shareholders. In addition, large sums of money could not be raised without bringing in so many shareholders that direction of the business risked becoming a sort of management-by-town-meeting.

The corporation solved all these problems. Since corporations were founded upon charters secured from the state, they had both a clear legal status and a separate identity from the persons who organized them. Through these charters the state might impose restrictions upon a company's powers, but it might confer special privileges as well.* As a creature of law, the corporation outlived its founders and was unaffected by their demise. Ownership was easily transferable through the buying and selling of shares without affecting the company's operations. Large amounts of capital could be raised by selling shares in the company or by issuing bonds against its property. In theory, at least, the corporate form allowed unlimited growth and specialization of function. Taken together, these attributes fashioned the corporate form into a supreme instrument for planned, rational economic enterprise on a large scale.

---

* Several early railroads, for example, were given tax exemptions for a period of years to encourage their construction.

Historically the corporation traced its roots to England. Originally conceived as an instrument of mercantilist policy, it was designed to achieve goals of broad public policy by granting special privileges in unusual instances. For a time this approach prevailed in America. Only a handful of business corporations were granted charters prior to 1775, most of them for such public services as waterworks and wharves. Between 1775 and 1801, states granted 326 corporate charters, nearly all devoted to public works. Of these, Curtis P. Nettels has calculated that 207, or 63 percent, went to bridge, turnpike, or canal projects, 34 to banks, 33 to insurance companies, and only 8 to manufacturing enterprises. After 1800 the number of charters increased steadily. More important, the general attitude toward the purpose and function of corporations underwent a radical shift. By the Jacksonian era, the granting of corporate charters had boiled up into a fierce political controversy.

Hitherto corporate charters had been granted as a restricted privilege to individual projects. By the 1830s, however, ambitious entrepreneurs, restrained from embarking upon large-scale projects by their lack of capital, seized upon the corporate device as a solution to their problem. They demanded that it be transformed from a limited privilege to a universal right. Instead of being chartered by special act of the legislature, they insisted that the right of incorporation be made available to anyone paying a reasonable fee and satisfying some minimal requirements.

Some Americans opposed any liberalizing of incorporation laws during the Jacksonian era. While their reasons varied, most critics denounced corporations as a tool of moneyed interests and therefore a menace to democracy. Daniel Raymond, a lawyer and economist, argued as early as 1820:

The very object . . . of the act of incorporation is to produce inequality, either in rights or in the division of property. They are always created for the benefit of the rich, and never for the poor . . . . The rich have money, and not being satisfied with the power which money itself gives them, in their private individual capacities, they seek for an artificial combination, or amalgamation of their power, that its force may be augmented.

Others voiced alarm at the ethical implications of the corporation. William M. Gouge, writing in 1833, warned that "As directors of a company, men will sanction actions of which they would scorn to be guilty in their private capacity. A crime which would press heavily on the conscience of one man, becomes quite endurable when divided among many." His fears were seconded by a wealthy Bostonian, Peter C.

Brooks, who stated bluntly that "Corporations will do what individuals would not dare to do." The very impersonality of corporations made them handy solvents for dissolving individual responsibility. It encouraged a split ethic which applied one set of standards to business matters and another to noneconomic affairs. A sense that this was occurring probably lay behind the admonition of Amos Kendall in 1840 that "there is but one code of morals for private and public affairs."

To the modern reader these criticisms ring prophetic. At the time, they proved little more than straws in the wind. The movement for more liberal incorporation laws grew to irresistible proportions. Not only the wealthy but those on the make threw their weight into the fight. In the struggle they even advanced the corporation as a democratizing force which would sharpen the competitive sword. The results of their campaign were both successful and ironic. In the pungent words of Arthur M. Schlesinger, Jr., "The general laws sprinkled holy water on corporations, cleansing them of the legal status of monopoly and sending them forth as the benevolent agencies of free competition."

Connecticut responded first by passing a general incorporation act in 1837. By the 1850s most states had followed suit. Massachusetts had already written the principle of limited liability into law in 1830 and was soon followed by other states. Gradually the corporation evolved from a guarded instrument of public policy into a general vehicle for private enterprise. Nearly half of all the corporate charters granted prior to 1860 were issued during the 1850s. Gradually, too, the use of the corporate form spread from transportation and banking to manufacturing enterprises. It was not a sudden or dramatic transition, but it was decisive, even though most American manufacturing was done by unincorporated firms well into the late nineteenth century. Most firms continued to be incorporated by special legislative acts rather than by the general statutes because more liberal charters (and often special privileges) could be obtained that way. But in general, the ideal prevailed that incorporation was little more than a public licensing function. Clearly the balance of decision-making power within the American economy had shifted from the public to the private sector. As Rowland Bertoff observed, "Incorporation came to seem not so much a privilege granted in the public interest as a private right to be protected by the state."

On the eve of the Civil War, then, the corporation had firmly established itself as a form of business organization. Within the next half century, it became the structural norm for large enterprise in the American economy because it could operate efficiently on a scale that would have swamped even the most intelligently managed partnership. In conquering the problems of size and longevity, the corporation had simply transcended human limitations. That was the essence of corporate innovation and, indeed, of the organizational revolution.

The implications of this fact were startling. As our model suggests, the corporation was originally an extension of individual efforts to organize business enterprises on a larger scale and overcome limitations of resources. It accomplished that purpose only too well. In time this creature of ambitious entrepreneurs grew into a leviathan that dwarfed its creators and assumed a life, a character, and an identity of its own. Conceived as a servant of men, its spectacular growth compelled men to serve its needs and redefine their own visions along lines dictated by the necessities of corporate development.

Therein lay a bitter irony of the industrial era: men pursuing their individual economic visions created organizational monsters that destroyed the system which spawned them. To most people the corporation was an enigma—neither fish nor fowl, but some new impersonal entity. It was created and managed by men, but it was something more than men. "A great business is really too big to be human," Henry Ford admitted. "It grows so large as to supplant the personality of man. In a big business the employer, like the employee, is lost in the mass." And the larger it grew, the more men puzzled over its inner nature and ultimate effects upon their lives. A popular phrase of the era betrayed this uneasiness by complaining that a corporation possessed neither a soul to damn nor a body to kick.

But no one forced businessmen to form corporations. Why, then, did the corporate form become so popular during the late nineteenth century? Size (or growth) is certainly part of the answer; it explains, for example, why railroads became the first major industry to be organized almost entirely in corporate form, and it accounts for the early organization of some other kinds of enterprise such as canals, banks, insurance companies, and even some manufacturing firms. Yet size alone does not tell the whole story. The fact is that most industrial and manufacturing enterprises began as some kind of noncorporate venture and only later reorganized in corporate form. Why the switch? And why did so many new giant corporations appear during one particular time period, 1890–1910? To some extent, growth accounts for both the conversion and the timing, but there was another equally important factor: the problem of competition.*

---

* There is a third major factor besides size and competition that accounts in part both for the proliferation of corporations and for the trend toward combination discussed

As observed earlier, the preindustrial American economy, with its small-unit production geared to local markets, fostered little serious competition. In an agrarian economy farmers are the major producers, and they do not compete with each other in any meaningful sense. They may vie for land and might even sell in the same market, but their "competition" is seldom direct or personal. The number of producers is virtually limitless, fluctuating, and therefore unpredictable. Moreover, individual farmers do not possess the means to determine or even influence such crucial factors as output, price, costs, and market demand. They are basically individual producers struggling not against each other but against the uncertainties of a common environment. The success or failure of any one farmer will not affect the position of other farmers.

In manufacturing and industry the reverse is true. Producers can determine their output and to some extent their costs, prices, markets, and other factors. Given enough capital, machines, raw materials, labor, an efficient organization, and decent transportation, production can be expanded tremendously. The problem then becomes one of finding markets in which to sell this outpouring of goods. Once regional and national markets arise, it is possible for all producers of the same product (and substitutes for it) to compete with each other if they can muster the resources and organization to do so. Competition then becomes more direct and intense because some companies might grow powerful enough to shut rivals out of markets and monopolize or dominate an entire industry. Thus both the possibilities and pitfalls of business enterprise are multiplied.*

The possibilities of expansion intoxicated American entrepreneurs. Farmers and some kinds of businessmen were immune to this lure simply because it was not possible for them. No individual or group, however clever or efficient, could supply the entire demand for wheat or control the market for it. But the production of steel or locomotives

---

later in the chapter. This third factor might be called the manipulative or speculative factor. Financiers quickly discovered that the intricacies of corporate structure offered lucrative possibilities for profits achieved through the manipulation of securities and other complex transactional maneuvers. While these "transactional" profits were an undeniably important force behind the mania for creating new corporations, the subject lies somewhat outside the mainstream of our analysis and so is not discussed here.

* For example, local butchers in a city or town might compete with each other, but not with butchers from other communities. And in fact they rarely competed with butchers outside their neighborhood in a large town. But once meatpacking grew into a giant industry, the large firms like Swift, Armour, Morris, Wilson, and Cudahy competed with both local butchers and each other in hundreds of places all over the nation.

or whiskey or most manufactured goods could be dominated by some central organization. It would be a gigantic undertaking, far beyond the capacity of individual proprietors or partnerships. Only the corporation as an organizational form could attempt such a feat because it could command resources and conduct operations on a scale unprecedented in all human history.

Few entrepreneurs looked this far ahead. More often the growth of corporate enterprises evolved out of the conditions of industrial competition. In the early stages of most industries firms were small and catered to local markets. Since the start-up costs were usually low at this stage, many players could afford to enter the game. The contest was open to all comers, each hoping to prosper and expand. The competitive situation, therefore, tended to be one of many small companies servicing nearby markets. As the demand for goods increased and improved transportation allowed access to more distant markets, ambitious firms endeavored to extend their share of the market.

As long as the market kept growing, it could absorb the industry's total output. This favorable condition lured more firms into the industry and encouraged those already there to increase their output. Eventually, however, production capacity outstripped the market's ability to absorb goods. One famous producer, John D. Rockefeller, defined the general problem clearly for his own industry. Noting that the refining of oil offered large profits for a relatively small investment (which was a major reason why he got into the business), he observed that "Naturally all sorts of people went into it; the butcher, the baker, the candlestick maker began to refine oil, and it was only a matter of time before more of the finished product was put on the market than could possibly be consumed."

At that point the industry entered a stage of furious competition. Sensing the threat to its future, every company redoubled its efforts to seize the largest possible share of the existing market. This could be done only by shutting out competing firms. In the heat of combat every company sought some telling advantage over its rivals. Costs could be lowered by more efficient production methods or by introducing new technology. These same steps might also produce higher-quality goods. Raw materials might be obtained more cheaply; wages might be lowered. Transportation might be secured at lower rates through natural advantages of location or through secret and often illegal agreements. A company might develop superior marketing arrangements or more reliable sources of capital. Any of these advantages might enable some firms to undersell their rivals or drive them out of markets by more devious means.

But victory was seldom quick or cheap or complete, for competitors rarely quit the field without a desperate fight. Whether that fight was a pitched battle, a siege, or a series of flanking maneuvers, one outcome was certain: the industry was plunged into turmoil.

This sort of chaos was intolerable to most industrialists. Instability penalized the most efficient producers because it upset all their calculations. They could not estimate their share of the market or compute their costs with any accuracy. Price wars frustrated their need to be sure of the price at which their product would be sold. Rate wars and such practices as rebating unsettled the cost of transportation and disturbed marketing arrangements. Sources of raw materials, which often became choice prizes, were rendered insecure by the contest over them. The impact of new technology and patents could not be predicted. Labor disturbances posed another threat as workers rebelled against their dismal lot.

There were political and legal problems as well. Companies often required charters, rights-of-way, and other kinds of privileged legislation. Wherever these could be obtained through bribery and other corrupt means, companies fought bitterly to buy the services they needed and to prevent rival firms from doing likewise. More than once, the future of an enterprise hinged upon the outcome of these dubious battles.

All these uncertainties threatened the well-being of everyone and drove most businessmen to a common conclusion: cutthroat competition was anathema in industry. It was fine in theory but ruinous in practice. It bred waste, inefficiency, and instability. As a form of industrial warfare it too often brought Pyrrhic victories. It was far too rugged a form of individualism. To survive, much less to prosper, businessmen had to eliminate or at least minimize competition in their industry, though of course they might continue to extol its virtues for other industries.

The most obvious way to eliminate competition was to eliminate competitors. The strongest firms simply bought out or crushed their weaker rivals. In part, then, growth became a by-product of the competitive struggle: the weak succumbed to the strong and were absorbed by them. But growth was also a product of superior efficiency, resources, and organization. In many industries, the strongest firms were those which best pruned waste from every phase of their operations. They made a good product at the cheapest possible cost, sold it at the lowest price, and streamlined the whole enterprise. Then they could use this leverage to drive competitors to the wall and force them to sell out or quit. Their methods were often ruthless—even vicious—but they worked.

In this manner order gradually replaced chaos in most industries. As competitive wars winnowed out the weaker firms, a handful of larger companies emerged to dominate the industry. This stage of the contest compelled some smaller survivors to seek refuge in size. Individual entrepreneurs or small companies discovered they could not compete with giant corporations unless they, too, combined on a scale that enabled them to command equal resources and leverage. The emergence of a giant or two in a given industry soon forced competing firms to follow suit. In economic life the race for success boiled down to an inexorable maxim: organize or perish.

The legendary industrial pioneers—the Rockefellers, Carnegies, Havemeyers, Swifts—understood this trend perfectly. It was no coincidence that these great economic individualists were also great organizers; in many cases that proved to be their supreme talent. "Take from me all the ore mines, railroads, manufacturing plants and leave me my organization," boasted Carnegie, "and in a few years I promise to duplicate the Carnegie Company." The genius displayed by these men and the success of their organizations deeply impressed (and alarmed) their contemporaries, who were quick to learn the proper lesson. As Samuel P. Hays wrote:

Businessmen, farmers, and workers individually could not cope with the impersonal price-and-market network, but they soon discovered that as organized groups they could wield considerable power. Individual economic enterprise, therefore, gave way to collective effort. . . . It revealed the degree to which industrialism had shifted the context of .economic decisions from personal relationships among individuals to a struggle for power among well-organized groups.

The race toward organization on a large scale had several significant effects, one of which was the closing of whole industries to new competitors. The capital investment required to enter the iron and steel, oil, meatpacking, foundry, or other major industries in 1890 was enormous compared to what it had been in 1860. Occasionally some extraordinary event, like the fabulous Spindletop oil strikes of 1901 in Texas, thrust new firms into the competitive picture. Occasionally, too, a group of smaller firms would combine into a larger corporation. But these were giants mobilizing to join other giants. The scale of operation and increased use of machinery rendered start-up costs prohibitive for newcomers, except in relatively undeveloped or localized industries or unexplored areas.

A second effect was the devastating blow dealt to small local firms when corporate giants invaded their markets. Local butchers and slaughterhouses could not compete against the Chicago packing-houses, nor could the general store match the prices or diversity of a Sears or Montgomery Ward catalog. In communities throughout the land, the small businessman, long the bulwark of our national economic ideology, found himself besieged by mass producers, chain stores, mail-order houses, department stores, and other forms of large enter-prise.* Everywhere local economies were becoming more centralized and standardized, their businesses dominated by distant corporations.

The emergence of large corporations in several key industries marked the dawn of a new stage in the organizational revolution. The age of entrepreneurs gave way to the age of managers as individual companies were transformed into giant bureaucracies with hierarchial pecking orders. This came about partly because businessmen discovered that competition among corporations was quite a different beast from competi-tion among individuals. Since the stakes of the game had been hiked considerably, the sheer scale of corporate warfare made cutthroat compe-tition intolerable not only to the firms involved but to society itself.

Here, too, the relationship between size and competition made the difference. In the preindustrial economy, where competition was mini-mal and none of the firms were very large, victory or defeat affected few people beyond the contestants. Since the economic system was not yet tightly interlocked, the failure of any particular company seldom changed the overall competitive situation or had much impact upon the general business climate. But in an industrial economy organized around large corporate enterprise, the situation changed entirely. As the economy shifted from random isolated markets to a national inter-dependent system, competition became more direct and intense, and its destruction spread across a broader terrain.

The experience might be compared to the transition from limited war to total war. Suddenly the combat zone widened to embrace those noncombatants who had previously escaped the horrors of battle and its wholesale destruction. The clash of arms within the industrial arena reverberated throughout the economic system. The failure of any major corporation was an infection that might spread quickly to other sectors. Thousands of men could be thrown out of work. Subsidiary firms, sup-pliers, jobbers, retailers, even transportation companies were adversely affected. Security prices might drop and the money market tighten. The wave of contraction launched by a single major failure could buffet banks and brokerages and thereby crash down upon seemingly distant

* See Chapter 3.

businesses and industries. One fearful shudder of collapse might trigger a panic or recession and even signal the onset of a major depression.*

In short, an enlarged scale of operations multiplied the impact of both success and failure upon the entire system. The diverse elements of the industrial economy grew so intertwined that any major disturbance invited disaster. Unrestrained competition thus menaced not only businessmen but society, which recoiled from the fallout produced by corporate warfare. At this point, the role of competition in the American economy came full circle. Direct competition was largely the offspring of industrialization in its early stages. As the industrial system expanded, it bred intense competitive struggles which in turn bred size for some companies, failure for others. Size demanded stability and harmony of interest, which decreed an end to cutthroat competition.

This last point becomes clear if we consider the advantages and disadvantages an industrial corporation derives from size. In the previous chapter we touched upon some of the advantages. The company's plants can produce more goods with greater efficiency at lower cost. Elaborate machines, too costly for a small enterprise, can be employed. Raw material, transportation, and other factors of production can be procured more cheaply in quantity than in smaller lots. Specialization increases the efficiency of workers and managers alike. Large firms can raise capital and exert political leverage more easily than can smaller companies. They can afford to invest money in research, hire technicians, buy or develop patents, and develop new product lines.

But if Goliath is strong, he is also vulnerable. As the enterprise grows larger, communication and coordination become more difficult. Management finds it harder to maintain efficiency and impart a clear sense of direction throughout the whole organization. These problems are but the familiar headaches of any bureaucracy. Moreover, a large operation requires an enormous capital investment, most of it in fixed costs such as plant and machinery. Fixed costs, unlike variable costs (such as labor, raw materials, and transportation) must be paid regardless of whether or not the company sells any goods. If business is slow, management may cut back production and lay off workers, but it cannot lay off rent, utilities, interest charges, or taxes. In other words, fixed costs continue despite changes in output or sales. And as the units of production grow larger, the proportion of fixed costs to variable costs rises steadily.

* In the period from 1850 to 1920, there were two major depressions, the first lasting from 1873 to about 1879 and the second from 1893 to 1897. There were also severe panics in 1857, 1884, and 1907, and two recessions, 1913–1916, and 1920–1921. In addition, there occurred numerous lesser panics, slumps, and crises.

To maximize profits, the company must produce its wares constantly and as near full capacity as possible since most of its costs continue anyway. If large-scale operations promise great profits, they also threaten great losses if all does not go as planned. Once fixed costs assume so large a share of total costs, regularity of output becomes as important as efficiency of output. This necessity to produce creates in turn a necessity to sell *regardless of whether or not there exist enough buyers to take the entire output*. If the demand is not there, it must be generated; if the market is not sufficient, it must be developed. This necessity works strange wonders on the fabled law of supply and demand. No longer does demand coax out enough supply to fill its needs; instead, the capacity to supply in extraordinary quantities fosters an urgent need to stimulate a demand equal to output.

This was no mean task. It was a new dilemma, little known in the early stage of American industrialism when producers were struggling to meet a swelling demand for goods and services of every kind. By the 1870s, however, productive capacity was beginning to exceed demand in several key industries. There followed recurring cycles of depressions and recessions, price declines and fluctuations, overproduction and growing surpluses. Many firms found it increasingly difficult to produce at full capacity, which meant that a growing proportion of plant and equipment stood idle or worked part-time while fixed expenses continued.

No industry could ignore the dangers posed by a saturated market. The first response of many companies was to slash prices to get whatever business they could on the premise that it was better to sell at a low price (even a slight loss) than to sell nothing at all. This was the heyday of cutthroat competition. Railroads especially got embroiled in vicious rate wars, but price slashing infected the petroleum, iron and steel, and many other industries. Small firms loathed this type of combat because they lacked the resources to sustain the fight. But even large enterprises could not long endure this condition because of the waste and uncertainty it bred. A clear axiom of the corporate economy asserted itself: the larger the capital investment at stake, the more intolerable competition and instability became. To eliminate these evils, both the industry and the market it serviced had to be organized on some cohesive basis.

From these seeds of turmoil rose the neatly ordered garden of the corporate economy. Two general approaches were developed: collusion and combination. The first involved attempts to create stability through agreements among the major competitors in an industry. Collusive agreements assumed many forms, most of which were secret pacts among two or more competitors. The best-known of these devices was the industrial pool. While the main object of most pools was to maintain prices at profitable levels, some were used to divide markets on a prorata basis, control output, restrict patents, consolidate sales agencies, or combine services. Some pools went competely public and established formal organizations; most were private and informal. First introduced by the railroads, which made the most extensive use of it, the pool was later employed by such diverse industries as rope, wallpaper, and whiskey.

The pool was a nice halfway house between individual competition and cooperation, but it never worked satisfactorily. Since pools lacked any sanction in common or statutory law, they could not really be enforced. They were in effect gentlemen's agreements, and businessmen were not generally known to be gentlemen. Usually pool members did not hesitate to scuttle the pool or violate its provisions if it served their own interests to do so. This was especially true in hard times, when desperate firms needed business more than they needed harmony and stability. "A starving man will usually get bread if it is to be had," declared railroad magnate James J. Hill, "and a starving railway will not maintain rates."

It soon became clear that the pool was no solution to the problem of stability. Like most forms of collusion, it ran afoul of laws governing restraint of trade, and Congress explicitly outlawed pooling in the Interstate Commerce Act of 1887. By then many businessmen had already discarded the device and turned to combination as a surer road to stability.

Combination or integration could proceed in two directions: a company might reach backward to control its suppliers and forward to dominate finishing processes or distribution outlets (vertical integration) or it might seek to acquire or merge with direct competitors (horizontal integration). In the first case, a refining company like Standard Oil might move to acquire oil fields, pipelines, warehouses, barrel manufacturers, transportation and docking facilities, retail outlets, and other businesses related to the production and sale of oil. In the second case, Standard Oil might simply acquire control over as many other oil refineries as possible.

Vertical integration could help stabilize a company's whole production process. It assured a steady flow of raw materials at predictable prices, guaranteed regular transportation connections, and provided a reliable network for distributing and selling the finished product. If every stage of the production process were controlled, the company could function like a well-oiled machine and minimize the danger of interruption or breakdown. And vertical integration could produce real economies, greater efficiency, better quality control, and more dependable production schedules.

Horizontal integration was quite another matter. When carried off successfully, it stabilized not only the firm's position within the industry but also the industry itself. The object was not to improve efficiency but to maintain and control prices by eliminating competition. If one corporation could dominate an industry, it could set price levels and control markets. Competition would not be entirely eliminated; no American corporation ever obtained a complete monopoly in a major industry. There were always numerous small fry to joust with the giants, but they posed no serious threats; in fact, their presence helped preserve the illusion of a competitive system. While horizontal integration might impose stability upon an industry, it had little effect upon efficiency of operations. It could not solve the problem of excess capacity. A company might be converted from a rival to a subsidiary, but it still had to produce. It could be shut down or run at a loss, but neither of these alternatives attacked the central problem.

The quest for stability drove American businessmen relentlessly down the road of combination and merger. In their search for a more perfect order, they devised two new forms of organization: the trust and the holding company. Both were legal innovations that revolutionized the structure of American business. They were the product of efforts to extend and unify control over an entire industry, and their appearance reflected the changed conditions of business enterprise in America.

After Standard Oil pioneered the trust device in 1879, other firms quickly adopted it. Within a decade, an impressive variety of industries seemed to be dominated by trusts: oil, sugar, whiskey, lumber, meatpacking, salt, lead, copper, iron and steel, farm machinery, elevators, chemicals, paper, cottonseed oil, tobacco, and cordage, to name but a few. By 1890 alarmed critics were pinning the label to every giant enterprise and using it as a loose synonym for monopoly. By that date, however, the trust as an organizational form had already outlived its usefulness. It possessed serious structural drawbacks and was being assailed in the courts for restraint of trade. After the years 1889–1896, when New Jersey greatly liberalized its incorporation laws (other states soon did likewise), large enterprises turned to the holding company as a more flexible form of organization.*

* A holding company differs from an operating company primarily in that it does not produce any goods or perform any services. Rather it owns securities of all types, mostly stocks and bonds, in other companies and thereby centralizes the control of several companies in one separate corporate entity. For example, if a holding company

New Jersey's legal innovations were an important milestone in the organizational revolution. They signaled the emergence of a corporate economy and confirmed the new structural realities of American business. The law placed few restrictions upon corporations. It allowed them to capitalize at any amount and still limit stockholder liability. It permitted them to own property and conduct operations in other states and to own stock in other corporations. These provisions made New Jersey an attractive haven for any corporation seeking to unify many far-flung firms into one giant empire. Throughout the nineteenth century, the dominant trend in American law had been to broaden and extend the range of individual freedom; now it was granting the same privilege to corporations as well.

The consequences were swift and sure. In less than a generation, the basic structure of the American corporate economy was fixed for a century to come. Between 1890 and 1910, the trickle of combinations swelled into a raging stream. The previous twenty years of corporate warfare had produced spectacular growth by individual companies but only twelve real giants, whose combined capitalization was less than $1,000,000,000. During the decade 1895–1904, according to Ralph L. Nelson, there occurred 319 mergers with a total capitalization of $6,030,000,000. Of this figure, $2,410,000,000 (40 percent) was accounted for by only 29 mergers (9.3 percent) involving new corporations with capitalizations of $50,000,000 or more. One new colossus alone—United States Steel—was capitalized at $1,370,000,000, or 23 percent of the total. The average capitalization of all the merged firms was $2,100,000.

Plainly this decade was midwife to the era of giant enterprise in America. Its first few years saw a frenzy of consolidation—several large and small firms uniting into one huge corporation. During the decade, an average of 301 companies disappeared every year, swallowed by some greater entity; in 1899 alone, 1,028 companies vanished in this manner. Once this basic pattern was established, further growth was characterized more by acquisition of independent companies than by the continued merger of smaller firms into large companies. Nelson calculated that such acquisitions accounted for only 16.5 percent of net firm disappearances between 1895 and 1904. In later years, when the steam had gone out of the merger movement, the figure rose to 47.5 percent for 1905–1914 and 65.5 percent for 1915–1920.

---

holds a majority of stock in numerous other companies, one can gain control over all these companies simply by gaining control over the holding company. There are many other advantages to the holding company—and many dangers as well.

Contemporary observers were flabbergasted by these developments. John Moody, editor of *Moody's Manual of Corporation Securities,* tried earnestly to measure the dimensions of this trend toward consolidation. In his book *The Truth About the Trusts* (1904) Moody listed 440 industrial, franchise, and transportation "trusts" which possessed an aggregate capital of $20,400,000,000 and controlled a total of 8,664 plants, transportation lines, and utility franchises. Of the industrial trusts, the seven largest alone were capitalized at $2,700,000,000 and controlled 1,528 plants.* Some 298 "lesser industrial trusts," capitalized at $4,000,000,000, operated 3,426 plants.

Among the franchise trusts, Moody found eight telephone and telegraph corporations with 136 plants and a combined capitalization of $629,000,000, and 103 gas, electric, and street railway companies with 1,336 franchises capitalized at $3,700,000,000. The railroads were even more impressive, for next to farming they comprised the largest single type of business enterprise in the country. Moody discovered that the American railway network had been consolidated into six gigantic alliances dominated by the six interest groups which together controlled 790 railway lines with 164,586 miles of track and an aggregate capitalization of over $9,000,000,000.** This left only about 250 lines with 39,500 miles of track and a combined capitalization of $380,000,000 still "independent," but nearly a third of this mileage was strongly influenced by one or another of the titans.

Recent studies have confirmed most of Moody's findings. The pattern was unmistakable: the age of enterprise had created an age of organizations. The saplings of individual initiative had grown into a mighty forest of corporate bureaucracies whose towering presence left little ground or sunlight to nourish ambitious young sprouts. The demonic energy of countless entrepreneurs had wrought an economic revolution, one which was fast dooming their breed to extinction. The most famous among them, John D. Rockefeller, grasped this truth clearly. Commenting on the trend toward combination, he observed:

This movement was the origin of the whole modern economic administration. It has revolutionized the way of doing business all over the world. The

---

* These seven giants were United States Steel, Standard Oil, American Sugar Refining, Amalgamated Copper, American Smelting and Refining, Consolidated Tobacco, and International Mercantile Marine.

** These interest groups were listed, somewhat inaccurately, as the Vanderbilt, Pennsylvania Railroad (closely allied to the Vanderbilt), Morgan-Hill, Gould-Rockefeller, Moore, and Harriman-Kuhn, Loeb groups.

time was ripe for it. It had to come, though all we saw at the moment was the need to save ourselves from wasteful competition. . . . The day of combination is here to stay. Individualism is gone, never to return.

The Corporate Society

The organizational revolution was by no means confined to the economic sphere. In time its influence spread to the social system and helped create a corporate society in which every aspect of human activity found expression through organizations. What is significant about the corporate society is that it arose in response to the forces and needs of the corporate economy. The sequence here is important, for the origins of the corporate society explain much about its character.

To understand how the corporate economy gave rise to a corporate society, we must recall the unique properties of the corporation. It is a planned and rational enterprise usually blessed with remarkable clarity of vision and narrowness of purpose. It has an efficiency of organization that can harness vast resources in pursuit of its goals. To that same end, it can exert terrific economic and political leverage over an indefinite length of time. In short, the corporate enterprise knew what it wanted, where it was headed, and why it was headed there; it needed only to discover how best to get there.

No other institution, certainly nothing in the public sector, could match these qualities. Since the American people had long made economic development the nexus of their civilization, it was no surprise that economic institutions formed the vanguard of the organizational revolution. Nor was it much of a surprise that economic power and decision-making was to a great extent concentrated in the private rather than the public sphere—though the *degree* of this concentration later came as an unpleasant shock to many Americans. This was, after all, the main purpose of the free enterprise system: to enable individuals to pursue their self-interest and fulfill their private visions free of undue legal or governmental restraint.

The most striking consequence of this open system was that it divorced economic power from social responsibility. Within the limits of law (and the law itself was often an ambiguous and inadequate set of boundaries), the individual had few obligations to society beyond those imposed by his own conscience. He could amass wealth and property as best he could in whatever manner he chose, do whatever he pleased with it, and let the broader consequences of his actions fall where they may. Even in a preindustrial society, this laissez-faire ethic gave rise to serious social problems; in the industrial era it threatened to destroy the very foundations of society.

Within this framework the corporation evolved into the most powerful institution in the country. Although a kind of mutant with qualities radically different from those of individual enterprises, it operated within a social and economic system geared to the maximization of individual freedom. We have already noted how Americans, rather than adjusting their ideology to fit this novel intruder, tried at first to fit the corporation into their prevailing ideology. The Supreme Court, in a series of cases beginning in 1873, adopted this view by ruling that corporations were individuals in the eyes of the law and therefore entitled to the protection guaranteed individuals under the Fourteenth Amendment. By writing myth into law, the Court sidestepped the unique nature of the corporation and its devastating impact upon American society. Yet the Court faced a genuine dilemma: to have ruled otherwise would have forced the justices to revise much of what Americans had long held sacred in their ideology, especially the prevailing concept of property rights and the proper role of government in economic matters. That was far more than the Court was prepared to undertake.

The result was a rapid development of corporate power within the individualist framework. The corporation, like any private enterprise, was free to use its awesome resources in any manner it chose with little or no concern for the broader consequences of its actions. Of course the scale of its effects upon society far exceeded that of smaller enterprises, but the difference was more than one of scale. If the corporation lacked a body to kick or a soul to damn, so, too, did it lack a conscience to prick. As an impersonal organization it was dedicated to the single purpose of making money. Individuals within the corporation might be sensitive to social needs or feel some twinge of social responsibility, and on occasion they might even attempt to formulate policy with these nobler ends in mind. More likely they discharged their consciences in private acts of charity outside the company. The business of the corporation was business. It had little room for sentiment, and whatever social benefits it conferred were by-products of the relentless quest for profits.

This enormous concentration of economic power (and the political influence it could muster) within the private sector, coupled with the separation of power from social responsibility, threw the entire social system out of balance. No area of American life escaped its demoralizing effects. So shattering was its impact that many thoughtful Americans feared for the future of the Republic. Grim visions of apocalypse surfaced everywhere: in literature, in newspapers and magazines, in coffee-house and drawing-room conversations, in the fertile soil of political oratory. The traditional American attitudes of optimism and faith in progress continued to assert themselves, but for the first time they were joined by a serious counterpoint of pessimism and despair. Beneath the swelling tide of material progress there ran a powerful undertow of confusion and dislocation, a sense that society was changing too rapidly, careening down an unknown road towards an uncertain destiny with no clear way of restraining its pace or deflecting its course.

It is impossible to describe all the sources of this discontent here, but we can suggest some of its roots. In the economy, the steady advance of corporate power threatened to close off the open system and its traditional avenues to success. That menace outraged Americans who had long regarded the open system as the nucleus of their ideology. The promise of American life had always rested upon the wide field of opportunities it offered the enterprising individual; without an open system, many believed the entire scaffolding of democratic society would collapse. Theodore Roosevelt merely echoed the sentiment shared by most citizens when he declared in 1910 that

> Our country—this great republic—means nothing unless it means the triumph of a real democracy, the triumph of popular government, and in the long run, of an economic system under which each man shall be guaranteed the opportunity to show the best that is in him. . . . In every wise struggle for human betterment one of the main objects, and often the only object, has been to achieve in large measure equality of opportunity.

Woodrow Wilson put the case even more forcefully. During the campaign of 1912, he posed the ideal and the harsh reality that threatened to extinguish it in succinct terms:

> And this is the country which has lifted to the admiration of the world its ideals of absolutely free opportunity, where no man is supposed to be under any limitation except the limitations of his character and of his mind; where there is supposed to be no distinction of class, no distinction of social status, but where men win or lose on their merits.
>
> I lay it very close to my own conscience as a public man whether we can any longer stand at our doors and welcome all newcomers upon those terms. American industry is not free, as once it was free; American enterprise is not free; the man with only a little capital is finding it harder to get into the field, more and more impossible to compete with the big fellow. Why? Because the laws of this country do not prevent the strong from crushing the weak. That is the reason, and because the strong have crushed the weak the strong dominate the industry and the economic life of this country.

Wilson's words may smack of campaign rhetoric, but a large number of Americans could verify the truth of what he said from their personal experience. In the corporate economy the independent operator, the legendary "little man," found his chances to be anything but equal. As the economic system became more integrated, the range of individual opportunities narrowed. Men might strive to attain a high place within the great business organizations, but they found it tough going to start up and maintain their own business outside the corporate realm. The corporate economy encouraged men not to carve out a place for themselves, but rather to find their niche within the existing scheme of things.

Those who attempted to go their own way were usually locked into a perpetual struggle for survival. Small businessmen complained that corporations used a variety of unfair practices to squeeze out their smaller rivals or leave them very little room in which to operate. The impersonality of corporations and the mysterious ways in which they exerted such vast power also drew criticism. A man could resist a tyrant or fight a competitor, but how was he to combat the oppression of a system? How was he to track down the ultimate source of his grievances, and to whom should he complain? "The truth is," Woodrow Wilson observed, "we are all caught in a great economic system which is heartless."

Moreover, the fabulous wealth produced by industrialization proved a mixed blessing because it was distributed so unevenly. Nothing in the new order of productive miracles required an equitable distribution of its fruits. In fact, the opposite was true: both the ethic of individualism and the concept of private property guaranteed men full possession of whatever fortune they could acquire as a just reward for their initiative. And if the enormous profits of industrial enterprise accumulated unchecked in the hands of those privileged few who controlled the instruments of economic power, the result could only be even greater extremes of wealth and poverty.

And that is precisely what came to pass. While the material lot of society as a whole improved slowly but steadily, the gaps between different classes widened into unbridgeable chasms. Some men amassed huge personal fortunes and bequeathed their families a legacy of privilege. Wealth brought with it all the trappings and luxuries of the socially elite. There had always been people with money in America, but never so many of them with so incredibly much of it. The age of enterprise was giving birth to a new and powerful moneyed aristocracy.

While the rich got richer, the ranks of the poor swelled into an army of misery. For every person who profited from the new industrial order, thousands more slipped beneath the wheels of progress and were crushed by their weight. The grotesque contrast between the rich and the poor punctured the cherished myth of America as a classless society. As the maldistribution of wealth worsened, there emerged instead a dark vision of society divided into a ruling plutocracy above and a demoralized working class below, both of them pressing hard against the fast-growing but bewildered middle class. In 1879 Henry George sounded the alarm that was to echo throughout the next century when he exclaimed:

But just as . . . a community realizes the conditions which all civilized communities are striving for, and advances in the scale of material progress . . . so does poverty take a darker aspect. Some get a better and easier living but others find it hard to get a living at all. The "tramp" comes with the locomotive, and almshouses and prisons are as surely the marks of "material progress" as are costly dwellings, rich warehouses, and magnificent churches. . . . It is as though an immense wedge were being forced, not underneath society, but through society. Those who are above the point of separation are elevated, but those who are below are crushed down. . . . This association of poverty with progress is the great enigma of our times.

The specter of a ruthless plutocracy grinding the working class into ever greater depths of misery and intimidating the middle class into submission haunted the imaginations of concerned Americans. Nor was this all. This same concentration of economic power perverted the democratic political system into a caricature of its ideals. Grasping the essential forces of his age, reformer Henry Demarest Lloyd warned that "Liberty produces wealth, and wealth destroys liberty." He proved too fine a prophet. Corruption and scandal tarnished every level of government in America as well as the electoral process itself. Politicians bought votes and sold favors to whatever interests required them and were willing to pay for them. This was especially true in the cities, where the political machines quickly became the symbol for everything that was wrong with American democracy.

In urban America political office was a negotiable asset. Mayors, aldermen, councilmen, judges, policemen, and others peddled their services or used their positions as levers for personal gain. State legislators were no less immune to bribery, boodling, and back-scratching, and too often the sewer of corruption backed up into the lofty chambers of national government. It had long been a favorite national pastime to snigger at the pompous, dawdling antics of Congress. In the industrial era, however, the dreary, unending procession of scandals soured laughter into a black humor of cynicism and despair. Americans of every party and ideology denounced politics as a sordid travesty on the democratic process. While critics varied widely upon their remedies, they agreed upon the primary source of evil: the growing political influence of business interests in general and corporations in particular.

Society, too, was strained to the breaking point by the runaway momentum of industrialization. As the pace of change accelerated, it disrupted traditional patterns, habits, values, and institutions. Americans had always been a people who accepted—even welcomed—change as a sure sign of progress, but in the industrial era they were simply overwhelmed by its dimensions. As the forces behind the corporate economy intruded upon their lives and altered the familiar landmarks by which they measured their roots and their identity, people of every class feared that they were losing control over their lives and their destinies.

Physical growth, exploding like a chain reaction, further unsettled the social order. Wilderness mushroomed into villages, villages into towns, towns into cities, and cities into sprawling metropolises. Rural folk, displaced by machinery or disenchanted with the narrowness and monotony of farm life, flocked to the city in search of opportunity and adventure. There they collided with waves of immigrants equally bewildered by the strangeness of their new surroundings. In small town and city alike, old-stock Americans, the "best people," cringed at the foreign rabble crowding into what they considered to be their private domain. Many felt jostled by the changing ethnic composition. More than that they feared that this influx of alien peoples, ideas, and cultures challenged the sovereignty of white Anglo-Saxon Protestant culture, which had long dominated American civilization and of which they were the proud custodians.

Society was becoming atomized and fragmented. The sense of homogeneity and community that had given preindustrial America some semblance of identity and cohesion was dissolving. In its place came a social order tormented by extremes, dazed by the accelerating pace of change, and maddened by accumulating tensions which often erupted into violence. Amidst the opulence of its material furnishings, the stage of American civilization was being stripped bare of its spiritual props.

This transformation did not occur overnight, and certainly not everywhere at once. For a time rural America, and to a lesser extent small-town America, preserved their customs and social order reasonably intact. People adhered to the old verities and life went on pretty much as before, with only an occasional hint of the storm of change raging beyond the horizon. But in the cities it was a different story. Urban America was a maelstrom of change, swirling in many directions at once and catching up more and more people in its violent currents. In time no area of America, however remote, would escape its pull.

How did Americans respond to this shifting environment? In most cases they discovered that the old reliance upon individual action was inadequate to the problems at hand. The doctrines of rugged individualism and self-help were of little use in an age when men no longer had control over their economic destinies. In the corporate economy, individual action could scarcely dent, let alone deflect, the course of events; the centers of power were organizations. The sources of political corruption and social dislocation were either organizations or a set of forces too vast for individuals to oppose and too complex for their sources to be clearly traced. Yet they oppressed the human spirit and the social system no less brutally than the cruelest despot. If concerned individuals could not get at them directly or resist them alone, then they must band together in concerted resistance. They must fight fire with fire. From this realization flowed a massive surge toward organization that was the genesis of the corporate society.

This surge assumed many forms, Some groups organized to protect their private interests against the power wielded by corporate enterprise. These included labor unions, some business organizations, farm organizations, and professional organizations. A second type consisted of organizations formed to advance some broad public interest or to attack some problem within society. These covered an incredibly wide range: reform groups, consumer leagues, charitable or philanthropic organizations, and an assortment of groups dedicated to fighting some particular problem. A third type included organizations that arose primarily for social, charitable, recreational, or cultural purposes: YMCA's, lodges, clubs, fraternal organizations, athletic teams, literary guilds, ladies' clubs, symphony orchestras, and countless more. One might include as a fourth type existing institutions which were compelled by the changing times to expand greatly to meet new needs and provide new services. The most obvious example here would be all levels of government, but even such private institutions as the educational system and religious organizations pursued a similar course. No doubt some organizations straddled these categories while others fell somewhere between them. What they all shared was the belief that only through organization could they achieve their purposes or make their voices heard.

Once again the business community blazed the trail. Businessmen realized earlier than most groups the need for different kinds of organizations to protect and extend their interests. As a result, they devised an elaborate network of organizations beyond the corporate level. Perhaps the most significant of these was the trade association. Once the firms within an industry recognized their common interests and mutual dependence, they formed associations first at the regional and later at the national level. These associations dealt with a variety of matters. They exchanged information about costs, prices, orders, and inventories, and sometimes represented the industry in matters relating to the outside world. In some cases this led to collusive practices, especially in pricing. The range of industries that created trade associations is remarkable. A random sample might include the American Iron and Steel Association, American Brass Association, National Association of Stove Manufacturers, National Association of Wool Manufacturers, National Erectors Association, National Millers Association, and National Metal Trades Association. Thomas C. Cochran has estimated that about a thousand of these associations existed by the end of World War I.

The trade association remained a creature of particular industries. On another level, businessmen founded organizations to pursue interests beyond their own bailiwick. These included the National Chamber of Commerce, National Association of Manufacturers, National Board of Trade, and National Council of Trade, all of which had similar origins: they began as local groups which joined together into state or regional associations and later formed national organizations. In addition there arose several groups devoted to specific issues, such as the American Protective Tariff League, American Anti-Boycott Association, National Business League, and American Manufacturers Export Association—the last two being concerned with widening overseas markets.

Predictably, the rapid organization of business interests compelled workers to adopt the same tactic. As the number of wage earners in the employ of large companies soared, a radical shift in management-labor relations occurred. One of the first casualties of size was the old personal association—or at least acquaintance—with the boss typical of firms earlier in the century. The corporate form transformed the "boss" into an abstraction: a hierarchy of salaried managers (foremen, supervisors, inspectors) who derived their authority from distant sources. This arrangement shattered the illusion of management-labor relations as a partnership working in harmony for their mutual benefit. Within the corporate economy the "community of interest" ideal quickly became an endangered species.

It is easy to see why this happened. Though sometimes tinged with an aura of paternalism, the new business bureaucracies were impersonal and largely indifferent to individual needs and problems. Their concern was with profit and efficiency, not human welfare. They embodied the final triumph of a market economy in which management-labor relations (the phrase itself was an invention of the era to describe a newly formalized relationship) were stripped of their social aspects, and labor was reduced to a commodity to be bought and sold. Moreover, the era of large firms destroyed whatever contractual balance once existed between employer and employee. No worker could bargain with a corporation on even remotely equal terms; he was compelled to accept the going wage or seek work elsewhere. He had no voice in the conditions of his employment, nor could he take a grievance directly to the owner. On every front the individual worker found himself isolated and helpless.

Unfortunately, this loss of influence occurred just when influence was most needed. American plants and factories had become hellholes in which to work. The advance of industrialism reduced the skill level of workers, depressed wages, lengthened the workday whenever possible, and fostered the rise of dreary and unhealthy work environments. To this were added the tedium of most jobs and an incessant cry from employers for a faster work pace. Numbed by fatigue and boredom, workers often lapsed into reveries of carelessness and were maimed by the machines they tended. Accurate statistics on the number of fatal or crippling accidents in American industry prior to 1920 do not exist. The impressionistic evidence suggests that it was appallingly high, and the individual accounts that survive leave the modern reader horrified and heartsick. A serious accident cost the victim more than a limb or some fingers; frequently it destroyed his capacity to earn a living and threw his entire family into the abyss of poverty.

Mutilation or crippling injury was by no means the only threat to job security. The waves of immigrants from abroad and from the farms, coupled with an increasing use of women and children, created a labor pool (often a surplus) that drove wages even lower. Recurring cycles of recession and depression threw thousands of people out of work and kept the wolf of insecurity lurking at the door of those who managed to retain their jobs. Age, sickness, or simple prejudice on the part of a supervisor was enough to cost a person his job without warning. In the industrial army the privates had few privileges and fewer rights. All these factors combined to undermine the bargaining position of the individual worker and to demoralize the working class as a whole.

Many wage earners responded to their harsh lot in a logical manner: they sought salvation through organization. Like their employers, they came to recognize that unity might accomplish what individuals could not achieve alone. Like their employers, too, they began to perceive common interests and needs and realized that these could best be attained through cooperation rather than competition. It is true that the origins of unionism in America extend back into the preindustrial era, but both the character and scale of unions underwent a profound change in the industrial age. It is significant that both the emergence of big-business enterprise and a phenomenal expansion of unionism took place during the same period, the decade of the 1880s.

The long, bloody, and uphill struggle to unionize American workers is too complex a saga to relate here. For our purposes it is enough to observe that by 1900 unions had become a fact of economic life even though the right of collective bargaining was not written into law until the New Deal era. By 1900, too, the mainstream of the labor movement had shifted from what Gerald Grob has called "reform unionism" to trade unionism. Where reform unionism (such as the Knights of Labor) had advocated a wide range of social reforms on the grounds that the working man's lot could be bettered only by improving the social system in which he lived, trade unions (the American Federation of Labor, for example) confined their energies to bread-and-butter issues that directly affected their members. Gradually the triumph of trade unionism defined the labor movement as one more organized interest group within the corporate economy seeking to attain its private objectives with little concern for the broader consequences of its activities.

Farmers followed the same path in hopes of rescuing their declining position in American society. Traditionally farmers were regarded as the most stubbornly individualistic and conservative of people, but under the duress of changing conditions they were quick to seek relief not only through political movements like the Greenback and Populist parties but also through a variety of interest group organizations. Some of these include the granges (local, state, and national), the Alliances, local clubs, state and county agricultural societies, a host of cooperative ventures, and less well-known regional groups like the Farmer's League in the Northeast. After 1900, as agriculture came increasingly to be dominated by large enterprises that resembled (and sometimes were) corporations, agrarian interests turned to organizations that functioned more as tight-knit pressure groups. Of these, the American Farm Bureau Federation, National Farmers Union, and to a lesser extent the American Society of Equity proved the most effective. Through these organizations farm interests made far greater gains in the twentieth century than their more diffuse political movements achieved in the nineteenth.

The fever of organization infected the professions no less than it did wage earners and farmers. By 1920 virtually all the professions had formed their own organizations, including doctors, lawyers, educators, architects, social workers, and musicians. As education became professionalized and more specialized, scholars banded together in organizations reflecting their common discipline such as the American Economic Association, American Historical Association, and American Sociological Association. Perhaps the most powerful and effective organization belonged to the bankers, who erected the American Bankers' Association upon a foundation that included forty-five state groups as well as numerous local clearinghouses.

Several factors spurred professional people toward organization. The professions were becoming more specialized and complex. Pre-industrial society had valued the jack-of-all-trades. People moved easily from one occupation or profession to another because none of them required extensive training and few possessed rigorous standards of certification for their practitioners. Such versatility was in fact honored as a hallmark of true democracy. Industrial society, with its rapid expansion of technical knowledge and increased specialization, reversed this attitude by emphasizing the importance of skills that could only be acquired through extensive training and education. An ill-prepared or self-taught doctor could no more cope with new advances in medicine than a country lawyer could master the intricacies of corporation law. As a result, both the professions and the training required for them grew increasingly organized and systematized.

Through this process each profession formalized standards for its discipline. Some kind of organization was required to formulate, test, and enforce these standards. This necessity, coupled with a growing awareness of their common identity and mutual interests, impelled doctors, lawyers, educators, and others to establish ties with their peers through organizations: American Medical Association, American Bar Association, American Association of University Professors, and countless others.

The power and influence of these groups varied widely, as did the functions they performed. All enabled members to establish contacts and exchange information. Most worked actively to protect and advance the interests of the profession. Many, by creating standards of training and conduct, cast amateurs and ill-prepared practitioners into disrepute. The emphasis upon standards served two purposes: it protected the public from charlatans, and it enabled many professions to set their own criteria without outside interference. The organization could thereby invest its members with the cloak of professional legitimacy and in some cases regulate the number of authorized practitioners in order to prevent excessive competition among them.

In broader terms, professional organizations helped confirm the personal identity of their members in an age when traditional sources of self-identity were crumbling. To a greater degree than ever before, people in the corporate society defined themselves according to their economic function. The customary inquiry of "Who are you?" was replaced by "What do you do?" As work became more specialized every profession acquired an air of mystery, a meshwork of technical complexity unfathomable to laymen outside the field. The mystique of professionalism was quickly embraced by other occupations and soon became a characteristic attitude of the corporate society.

The age of the specialist or "expert" had dawned, both as a fact of economic life and as a frame of mind, yet expertise proved a two-edged sword in the corporate society. "Professionalism" offered people a badge which identified their function to themselves and to others, but it also separated them from one another by burning important social and intellectual bridges over which people had communicated in an earlier, simpler era. Experts found it difficult to talk about their work with anyone except their colleagues, a fact which alone tended to narrow not only their intellectual but also their social circles. In general, specialization tended to isolate social and economic classes from each other. By narrowing the range of social contacts and forcing social relationships into new channels, it added another element of instability to an already volatile social order.

All these groups—businessmen, wage earners, farmers, professional people—sensed in the corporate economy some threat to their well-being and took refuge in organization. The general character of their organizations resembled the corporate model in that they were formed as private entities to protect and extend the self-interests of their members. Some performed valuable public services, and most at least paid lip service to the ideal of public responsibility. But in practice most were self-serving organizations whose service to society, like that of corporations, was incidental to this primary function. Thus did the corporate society embody that fateful principle of the corporate economy: the divorce of power from social responsibility. Like corporations, these interest organizations tended to adopt a relatively narrow viewpoint and to interpret the problems of the larger outside world through a prism colored by their own needs and values.

But of course there was more to the corporate society than organizations based upon class or economic interests. Much of the organizational revolution occurred in reaction to the social turmoil wrought by industrialization. Any inventory of the evils which plague modern society reveals that most of them have deep roots in that turbulent era when the corporate society was taking shape. A partial list would include destruction of the natural environment, waste of resources (human and material), poverty, slums, rampant crime, racial and ethnic strife, political corruption, and that vast array of social problems which our forefathers lumped together under the general rubric of the "Social Question."

Concerned individuals, overwhelmed by the enormity of these issues, found themselves powerless unless they banded together with others who shared their feelings. As a result, reformers, philanthropists, radicals, activists of every type created organizations to carry out their objectives. The number and diversity of these groups were fantastic: civic leagues, reform clubs, settlement houses, charitable associations, investigatory commissions, the Anti-Saloon League, Consumers' League, National Civic Federation, National Conservation Association, Federation of Good Government Clubs, National American Woman Suffrage Association, National Child Labor Committee, National Federation of Settlements, the Communist and Socialist parties, Municipal Voters' League, and the Salvation Army, to name but a few of the hundreds formed to deal with the social fallout of industrialization. These groups, like those discussed earlier, tended to spring up first at the local level and gravitate toward state and national organizations. Nearly all were private organizations formed to deal with public problems.

Meanwhile, what of the public sector itself? The duress of change prodded government at every level to enlarge its size and scope. Power within the corporate economy had become concentrated within the private sector, and a relatively narrow circle of that sector. Sensing that life in an industrial society was too complex to be left at the mercy of private interests, Americans sought to restore balance to their economic and social system through an expansion of public power as well as through organizing their own interest groups.

To match the power of private interests, government had to fight size with size. To provide new services and expand old ones required more staff, more money, and an enlarged structure. Between 1880 and 1920 the federal government established such new agencies as the Departments of Agriculture (raised to cabinet level in 1889), Commerce, and Labor, Division of Forestry (within the Department of Agriculture), Bureau of Corporations, Civil Service Commission, Federal Reserve Board, Interstate Commerce Commission, Federal Trade Commission, Federal Power Commission, Children's Bureau, and a plethora of special commissions to study particular problems. In addition, many existing departments and agencies were assigned new responsibilities which en-

larged their personnel and budgets. In 1881 the federal government had
100,020 paid civilian employees. That figure rose to 239,476 by 1901
and 655,265 in 1920. And the expansion of government was expensive:
federal expenditures increased from about $268,000,000 in 1880 to
$6,403,000,000 in 1920. To help fund this swelling budget, the Six-
teenth Amendment, providing for a federal income tax, was ratified in
1913 after a long and bitter struggle.

With this burst of growth, the federal government took its first
lumbering steps down the road to bureaucratic giantism. The pace of
that journey has quickened to the point where government has assumed
a dominant role in many areas of American life once untouched by its
presence. This transition of the federal government from a passive to a
more active role, along with its growth from a relatively small organization to a sprawling bureaucracy, was yet another major characteristic of
the corporate society. It occurred largely in response to the welter of
social problems produced by industrialization and the emergence of a
corporate economy. In a sense, the expansion of government parallels
the corporate model in its growth from a "firm" of modest size to a
mammoth organization.

State and municipal governments followed this same course and, in
fact, usually blazed the trail. Most social problems surfaced first at the
local level and had to be dealt with there. Frequently this could be done
only by expanding the powers of government and extending the range
of its services. When the dimensions of a problem overwhelmed
municipal authorities or reformers, they sought help from the state
legislature, where much of the power for governing cities resided anyway.* In the industrial society, however, the knottiest problems, such
as the regulation of railroads and big business enterprises, factory conditions, social welfare issues, child and woman's labor, and the purity of
food and drugs, transcended state boundaries. Once reformers recognized
the state's impotence in solving these issues, their eyes turned toward
Washington. Here, too, the principle of osmosis was at work.

In the industrial age, then, all roads led to organization. As the
contours of the corporate society gradually emerged from the fog of
social dislocation, Americans could extract some harsh but inexorable
truths from their experience. The first and most obvious of these was
that power could be obtained only through organization. While the
individual still counted for much, and while individualism remained the
most prized virtue of our folklore, he was in reality no longer the decisive

---

* See Chapter 10.

element in the social system. In the corporate society, the individual became less a prime mover and more a part of some greater whole, a cog in social machinery that was itself growing ever larger and more elaborate.

A second axiom followed from the first: if individual goals were best achieved through combined effort, then those groups which organized most effectively did far better than those which did not or could not. Organization was an instrument of power, a means to some common end. It happened that within the American framework private interests could be organized far more easily and efficiently than public interests. Here a third axiom surfaced: in general, the tighter the organization, the narrower its aims, and the greater the resources at its disposal, the more likely it was to achieve its purpose.

It was the *combination* of these factors that rendered success probable. Thus corporations, lobbies, political machines, and similar private interests used their superior resources, efficient organization, and clear sense of purpose to gain power at the expense of consumers, workers, reformers, and the disorganized mass of people like the poor who lacked comparable resources, could not easily be organized, and were usually divided among themselves over what they wanted and how best to obtain it. Skilled workers unionized far more effectively than the unskilled; the superior farm organizations belonged to the large agrarian interests not the dirt farmers. Doctors and lawyers defended their interests far better than did teachers. Government could command enormous resources but lacked any unity of purpose or direction. Too often it was made to serve the will of those private interests powerful enough to get what they wanted from it. In that sense, the public sector, however big it grew, still functioned largely as an adjunct of the private sector.

The pattern for the future was clear, though later generations would challenge it: the corporate society remained a private society. The vision of a balanced society, in which power was shared at least to some degree by all the groups within it, continued to hover out of reach like a mirage upon the desert horizon. Real power remained firmly entrenched in the hands of private interest groups reluctant to accept or acknowledge responsibility for the social consequences of their activities.

CHAPTER 3

Industrialization and Urbanization

The modern city marks an epoch in our civilization. Through it,
a new society has been created. Life in all its relations has been
altered. A new civilization has been born, a civilization whose identity
with the past is one of historical continuity only. . . . the modern
city marks a revolution—a revolution in industry, politics, society,
and life itself. Its coming has destroyed a rural society, whose making
has occupied mankind since the fall of Rome. It has erased many of
our most laborious achievements and turned to scrap many of our
established ideas. Man has entered on an urban age. He has become
a communal being.

—FREDERICK C. HOWE
The City: The Hope of Democracy (1905)

THREE OF OUR key factors remain to be explored: population,
specialization of function, and urbanization. By placing this trio
in a separate chapter, we do not mean to isolate them from the other
factors or imply that they have some special relationship. By now it
should be apparent that our ten factors form a seamless web in which it
is impossible to talk about one without touching upon the others. Our
separation of them is artificial, a device resorted to out of expediency. In
previous chapters we have mentioned all three of the remaining factors;
here they will claim center stage.

Here, too, we come to the main concern of this book: the relationship
between industrialization and urbanization. That relationship is as difficult to define as it is important to comprehend. For one thing, there is no
automatic connection between the two developments. As David Ward
reminds us, "Historically there are examples of urban growth without
industrial development and of productive innovations in distinctly rural
settings, and even today rapid urbanization is taking place in many

parts of the underdeveloped world, accompanied by little advance in per capita productivity." Having issued that caveat, Ward then continues: "But in the economically advanced world, despite considerable differences in timing, the acceleration in urbanization and increases in productivity occurred almost simultaneously."

Whatever the case elsewhere, the American experience is overwhelmingly of the latter type. The central theme of our book is that the spectacular growth of American cities was largely the product of their interaction with the forces of industrialization. Since urbanization was both a key factor in the industrial process and a phenomenon of it, we must discard the easy premise that one "caused" the other and instead view their relationship as dynamic and reciprocal. Both the industrial system and its cities developed through a process of accretion in which each fed upon and reinforced the other.

Even a brief survey of this relationship illuminates much about its effects upon American life. We exaggerate little in saying that urban America was the central stage upon which the great drama of industrialization was played out. What we have called the corporate economy was born and nourished in the industrial city. Nearly all the social problems associated with industrialization arose first in the city. In its response to these problems, urban America brought to pass much of what we have called the corporate society.

As the cities were to discover, the role of pioneer is never an easy one. Urbanites became a microcosm of the American response to industrialization. Battered by successive waves of economic expansion and social change, city dwellers turned to organization in a desperate attempt to stabilize their volatile environment. The result was nothing less than the formation of a new social system in which the city emerged as the nerve center around which the rest of society would be ordered. In the strengths and weaknesses of that model would rest the future of American civilization.

Population and Occupation

A later chapter will examine the composition of the urban population. Here we are concerned with developments in two broader areas, the national population and that part of it which comprised the labor force. Important trends in the population of the United States between 1850 and 1920 can be quickly summarized: it was increasing rapidly, it was becoming more ethnically diversified, it was becoming more urbanized, its center was shifting steadily westward, and its median age was rising consistently.

The most striking fact about the American population during the period 1850–1920 is its sheer growth. The following table gives the figures for each decade and the annual rate of increase within each decade:

TABLE 1

SIZE AND GROWTH OF UNITED STATES POPULATION 1850–1920

YEAR	POPULATION	AVERAGE ANNUAL RATE OF INCREASE BETWEEN DATES (%)
1850	23,191,876	3.6
1860	31,443,321	3.6
1870	38,558,371	2.7
1880	50,189,209	2.6
1890	62,979,766	2.6
1900	76,212,168	2.1
1910	92,228,496	2.1
1920	106,021,537	1.5

SOURCE: Edward G. Stockwell, *Population and People* (Chicago: 1968), p. 178.

This phenomenal growth record becomes even more impressive when compared with figures for the entire globe. Between 1850 and 1920 world population increased about 55 percent while United States population increased about 357 percent. Of course, this gain did not come entirely from natural reproduction; much of it involved the flood of immigrants pouring into America. During these years, 31,746,135 people migrated to the United States, 14,549,768 of them after 1900. By 1920 slightly over a third of the people living in the United States were either foreign born or the children of at least one foreign-born parent.

Shifts in the sources of immigration were no less significant than its weight of numbers. Prior to the Civil War the bulk of immigrants (nearly 90 percent) came from Great Britain, Ireland, and Germany, and therefore possessed an ethnic stock, cultural background, and language similar or at least familiar to most native white Americans. Except for the Irish, these immigrants were assimilated into the American social system with relative ease. After the Civil War, the pattern underwent a striking change. The proportion of total immigration coming from the three countries listed above dropped from nearly 90 percent in the 1860s to 63 percent in the 1880s to a low of 14 percent in the 1910s.

The new immigrants came primarily from Italy, Poland, Russia, and the Baltic states, which together accounted for an average of more than 41 percent of all immigrants entering the United States between 1890 and 1920. Being "foreign" in every respect, they were not so easily assimilated. They brought with them to America strange cultures and customs to which they clung fiercely. They were slow to understand or appreciate American traditions. They spoke alien tongues and harbored alien ideas which many Americans considered dangerous. To many genteel natives, the unwashed rabble were more than unsightly intruders; they were a positive menace to the future of the Republic. Unlike their predecessors, they seemed too remote from the mainstream of American culture ever to become a part of it. Their presence drove many old-stock Americans from their neighborhoods and spurred the partitioning of urban society into a maze of subcultures. The dark fears and emotions aroused by this clash of cultures cannot be overstressed. A surprising number of genteel Americans echoed the bitter complaint of a character in Henry Blake Fuller's novel, *With the Procession*:

It is not the old public I used to know twenty years ago—it has changed a good deal. It is better organized against us—a banding together of petty officials with their whole contemptible following: steerage-rats that have left their noisome holds to swarm into our houses, over them, through them, everywhere—between the floors, behind the wainscoting—everywhere.

Urban America was the battlefield for these clashes. As the population grew it also piled up in the cities. In 1800 the inhabitants of urban places (those with 2,500 or more people) numbered 322,371 or about 6 percent of the total population. By 1860 those figures had increased to 6,216,518, or nearly 20 percent of the population. Even this was but a prelude to the phenomenal expansion of the next sixty years. In 1920 urban dwellers totaled 54,157,973 and comprised more than 51 percent of the national population. During that same period, the number of urban places jumped from 392 to 2,722 and the roster of cities containing 50,000 or more people from 16 to 144. The growth rate of the urban population averaged about 48 percent each decade, compared to about 24 percent for the whole population.

At the same time the population was concentrating in urban areas, its center was moving steadily westward. In 1800 the center of population was located eighteen miles west of Baltimore, Maryland. Sixty years later it had shifted to a point twenty miles southeast of Chillicothe, Ohio, and by 1920 it rested in Owen County, Indiana, some eight miles southeast of the town of Spencer. Curiously, the center moved westward on a relatively straight line, never fluctuating more than thirty miles north or south of the 39th parallel. Finally, it is worth noting that the median age of the population advanced steadily throughout the period. In 1820 the median age (usually a year or two younger than the average age) stood at 16.7 years; it increased to 18.9 years by 1850 and to 25.3 years by 1920.

If the population grew larger and more diverse, so did the labor force. Here the trends clearly reflect the impact of industrialization, for in the century between 1820 and 1920 there occurred a profound transformation in the ways Americans earned a living. The most striking change was the steady shift of the labor force from farming to nonagricultural pursuits. In 1820 roughly 70 percent of the labor force was engaged in agricultural occupations; by 1920 the figure had dwindled to about 27 percent. A second trend, less obvious but no less significant, concerns the relationship between property and income. While the data is scant for the earlier period, it has been estimated that in 1820 about 80 percent of all Americans owned the property from which their livelihood was derived. They were, in other words, independent and self-employed. Seventy years later the figure was reversed: in 1940 only about 20 percent earned a living from their own property. The remainder of the work force depended upon wages or salaries for their support.

This estimate suggests sweeping changes in both the nature of work and the status of workers. Even a bare sketch of these changes requires a closer look at the labor force* of the industrial era. According to census figures, in 1870 there were about 12,925,000 "gainful workers" above the age of nine. This amounted to approximately 44 percent of the

---

* The term "labor force" is used here in a general sense. In technical terms, the data used refer to "gainful workers" rather than the "labor force." The difference has to do with the definitions used by the Bureau of the Census in compiling their data. Under those definitions, the labor force consisted of "the sum of the employed and the unemployed. It is confined to persons 14 years of age and over, since labor market participation by persons under that age is relatively small."

By contrast, "the primary purpose of the gainful worker statistics was a count of occupations. The data were based on a question relating to occupational status and not to employment status. . . . Thus, census enumerators were instructed to find and enter the occupation of each person 10 years of age and over who followed an occupation in which he earned money or its equivalent, or in which he assisted in the production of marketable goods. In sum, gainful workers were people for whom a gainful occupation was entered in response to this question."

Since we are concerned with trends in occupation rather than employment, the latter concept is obviously more useful. The term "gainful worker" is rather clumsy, however, so we have chosen instead to use the phrase "labor force" with the understanding that it is purely descriptive.

total population. In 1920 the figures stood at 42,434,000, or about 51 percent of the population. During the industrial era, then, a growing proportion of the population became a part of the labor force. Nor did this trend reverse itself over the next half century of rapid technological change and declining immigration, for in 1950 the figure stood at 52 percent. One other characteristic deserves mention: the proportion of women in the labor force rose from about 15 percent in 1870 to 21 percent in 1920. Here, too, the upward trend continued; by 1950 women comprised 27 percent of all gainful workers.

Of far more significance were changes in the kinds of work Americans did. Once again, the data before 1920 is sketchy and must be handled with caution. But even if the available statistics are somewhat imprecise, they still reveal some unmistakable trends. Two American scholars, Lewis Corey and C. Wright Mills, working independently of one another, analyzed occupational trends during the period 1870–1940. Their findings agreed at several points, the most important of which was the emergence of a new salaried middle class as the fastest growing of all occupational groups. Some of Corey's results are summarized in Table 2, on the following page.

If these figures are correct they reveal a startling fact: even by 1870 a majority of the labor force worked for someone else. By 1920 three-fourths of all workers depended upon wages or salaries for their living; if we include tenant farmers who do not own the land they cultivate and therefore work for someone else, the figure reaches 81 percent. Even with a liberal margin for error, the conclusion is inescapable: for the vast majority of people, economic opportunity in the industrial society lay not in going one's own way but in finding a place within the existing scheme of things. C. Wright Mills put the matter bluntly: "For them [the new middle class], as for wage-workers, America has become a nation of employees for whom independent property is out of range. Labor markets, not control of property, determine their chances to receive income, exercise power, enjoy prestige, learn and use skills."

A closer look at the data suggests that the new middle class rose to prominence between 1870 and 1910, a period of intensive industrialization and urbanization. This is no coincidence. The new middle class was overwhelmingly urban, and its growth reflected an economic system in which every component was becoming increasingly specialized. To clarify that point, we can extrapolate from some other tables in Corey's article.

First, the number of independent enterprises increased sharply in absolute terms even though they declined as a relative portion of the

TABLE 2

OCCUPATIONAL COMPOSITION IN THE UNITED STATES, 1870–1940

(Figures show percent of all gainful workers for each group and subgroup)

GROUP	1870	1920	1940
I. FARMERS	27	16	10
1. Owners	20	10	6
2. Tenants	7	6	4
II. WAGE EARNERS	52	55	57
1. Industrial Workers	28	37	31
a. Manufactures	16	23	18
b. Mining	2	2	2
c. Transportation	4	6	6
d. Construction	7	6	6
2. Farm Laborers	13	5	4
3. Other Workers	11	13	21
III. MIDDLE CLASS OCCUPATIONS	20	29	32
1. Independent Enterprises (Old Middle Class)	13	8	7
a. Business	11	7	7
b. Professional	1	1	1
2. Salaried (New Middle Class)	7	20	25
a. Managerial-technical	1	4	4
b. Professional	2	4	5
c. Clerical	1	7	8
d. Sales people	2	5	6
e. Public service	.4	1	1

NOTE: Figures do not always add up to 100 because of rounding.
SOURCE: Compiled from data in Lewis Corey, "Problems of the Peace: IV. The Middle Class," *Antioch Review* (March 1945), p. 68.

total labor force. Their ranks more than doubled between 1870 and 1910, going from about 1,532,774 to 3,261,631. Such enterprises included building and manufacturing companies, mining firms, wholesale and retail establishments, cleaners, dyers and laundries, entertainment operations of every kind (theaters, resorts, race tracks, etc.), livery stables (later garages), and all kinds of general services (hotels, restaurants, saloons, barber shops, etc.). Professional people and artisans who worked for themselves also fell into this category. Obviously, the independent or self-employed operator was not disappearing from the American landscape, but he was becoming a shrinking minority in the labor force.

Second, the professions, managers, technicians, and white-collar workers, which comprised the bulk of the middle class, all underwent a terrific expansion during the period 1870–1910. In raw numbers, the middle class nearly quadrupled, jumping from about 2,289,000 in 1870 to 8,870,000 in 1910. Between 1870 and 1940, the number of wage earners increased eight times, while the new middle class alone multiplied sixteen times. And with growth came diversification. More people flocked into the traditional occupations, but at the same time many of the latter specialized to a point where they subdivided into several fields. Moreover, the corporate economy brought into existence a variety of new occupations. Within this general pattern each of the groups mentioned above followed a course of development that varied in degree but not in kind.

The number of professional people increased from about 332,480 to 1,546,074, about 366 percent. While the traditional professions like medicine, law, and the clergy grew apace, the most striking gains occurred in less obvious fields. Table 3 gives some random examples.

TABLE 3

GROWTH OF SELECTED OCCUPATIONS BETWEEN 1870 AND 1910

OCCUPATION	1870	1910
Actors	2,066	28,297
Architects	2,039	17,444
Artists	4,120	34,094
Designers and Draftsmen	1,291	47,449
Musicians	16,170	139,310
Photographers	7,652	31,775
Reporters and Editors	5,375	34,382
Teachers and Professors	128,265	614,905
Trained Nurses	1,204	82,327

SOURCE: Corey, "The Middle Class," pp. 74, 79.

In addition, some new professions emerged, most notably accountants, librarians, and social workers. In 1870 there existed no formal occupation of accountancy (though there were of course bookkeepers and clerks), largely because financial record-keeping lacked any semblance of standardization. As the financial paperwork of the corporate economy grew more complex, it required not only routinized practices using standard forms, but also specialists adept at the wizardry of figures. From this need evolved a new profession which numbered over 39,000 practitioners by 1910. The accountants held but one of several new specialized occupations wrought by industrialization. So great an expansion of professions reflected a maturing economy wealthy enough to devote more resources to education, the arts, recreation, and leisure. A growing majority of professional people were salaried rather than independent operators. Some 76 percent of this number worked for someone else in 1910, compared with about 61 percent in 1870.

Managers and technicians might properly be thought of as professional people, too, but both groups have special characteristics that warrant treating them separately. Perhaps more than any other groups, managers and technicians signal the emergence of a maturing corporate economy. Managers are the officer corps of bureaucracy; their ranks multiply when institutions expand in size and complexity and must break their structures down into more specialized units. Similarly, technicians are the offspring of an advancing technology which becomes too sophisticated to be entrusted to persons not formally trained for the task. In effect, technical progress calls into being its own hierarchy of specialists. Some devote their careers to consolidating the gains already made and applying them to new uses, while others concentrate upon research. In the industrial era, discovery, invention, and innovation became increasingly institutionalized.

By Corey's estimates, the number of people employed in management positions soared from 121,380 in 1870 to 893,867 in 1910. Of the latter figure, 587,741, or 65 percent, worked in manufacturing, transportation, mining, communication, and construction industries. Another 45,274 (5 percent) were engaged in trade and 56,059 (6 percent) in banking. By 1910 the group was large and varied enough to be divided into "upper" management (executives, officers, managers) and "lower" management (foremen, overseers, supervisors, inspectors). In 1910, of the 633,015 people categorized in this manner, 391,990 (61 percent) belonged to lower management and 241,025 (39 percent) to upper management. Virtually all management people were salaried employees.

So were technicians, who increased from about 8,118 in 1870 to 109,198 in 1910. The bulk of these (88,600 or 81 percent) were engineers; the rest included chemists, metallurgists, assayers, and various kinds of laboratory technicians and assistants. Like other professions, engineering was bitten hard by the bug of specialization. In 1870 some 7,094 people listed their occupation as engineer, with no breakdown by area of specialty. By 1910 there were civil engineers, electrical engineers, mechanical engineers, and chemical engineers. To this list would soon be added mining and industrial engineers.

Thanks to the work of C. Wright Mills and others, white-collar workers are in the popular mind more closely identified with the new middle class than any other group. It should come as no surprise that this group underwent a phenomenal expansion from 374,433 in 1870 to 3,221,647 in 1910, by which time white-collar workers comprised more than a third of the middle class. Within another twenty years, the group would more than double its ranks and constitute about 45 percent of the middle class.

White-collar workers were the foot soldiers of bureaucracy, the rank-and-file of the corporate economy: bookkeepers, clerks, stenographers, typists, store clerks and salespeople, drummers and other commercial travelers, sales agents (insurance, real estate, etc.), telephone and telegraph operators, and many more. It is not difficult to account for their proliferation. The jobs they filled required less training and education than the professions or other middle-class occupations. Most of the positions were accessible to people from the working class who regarded them as a step upward from the drudgery and squalor of the factory. While the work hours were often equally long and the pay equally meager, white-collar jobs offered better working conditions, more cheerful surroundings, some measure of prestige, greater security, less exhausting toil, and the possibility (often illusory) of further advancement. Small wonder that working-class people prized them as an entrance into worlds that once seemed out of reach. For those whose future was a closed book, even a morsel of hope went a long way.

White-collar workers toiled entirely for salaries or commissions. Like other middle-class groups, the vast majority of them lived in urban areas. Like the others, too, their amazing growth betokened an economic system that was becoming ever larger and more specialized.

Specialization

The theme of specialization drifts through this book like a *leitmotif*. We have already noted its role in the broad areas of productivity, organization, technique, and labor. The time has come to examine its nature and influence more closely. Let us admit at the outset that the subject is somewhat slippery in that specialization tends to operate on several levels at the same time. To minimize confusion, we will limit our analysis to a few basic principles and illustrate them with historical examples.

It should be apparent by now that specialization is a key factor in the process of industrialization. Simple logic, confirmed by the American historical experience, shows why this is so: in describing the industrial order as a *system*, we mean that it is a combination of separate parts which together form a complex and unified whole. For that whole to function properly each of its components must perform its particular (i.e. specialized) role.* Eric E. Lampard has defined that role in this manner:

The object of specialization, therefore, is a greater economy of time, effort, and resources—the sources of higher productivity and material advance. . . . The very circumstances and incentives which make for specialization in the first place will, other things being equal, tend to foster its cumulative development. Specialization tends to breed specialization. It develops furthest where it is most prized; where socio-economic institutions are best adapted to its forms.

In these few lines Lampard advances two important principles: that specialization tends to produce even greater specialization, and that, like most things, it flourishes best in a congenial environment. By a congenial environment we mean, among other things, a society dedicated to economic growth and eager to discover new ways of increasing productivity. It is hard to find a historical milieu better suited or more committed to these principles than nineteenth-century America.

Four broad trends, all of which bore the imprint of "creeping specialization," characterized the maturing industrial economy. Two of them involved the labor force. On one hand, the proportion of the labor force engaged in industrial and other nonagricultural pursuits increased steadily. As the figures in Table 2 indicated, the percentage of gainful workers employed in agriculture dropped from about 40 in 1870 to 21 in 1920. On the other hand, there occurred a steady shift within the labor force from primary (i.e. production-oriented) to secondary (service-oriented) occupations. Third, markets for both goods and services shifted from rural to urban areas. Finally, the institutional structure of economic activity was becoming more centralized and diversified.

The last trend may seem contradictory at first glance, but in fact centralization and diversification were complementary developments. As enterprises grew larger, they tended to concentrate several functions and stages of economic activity within one organization. At the same time, the central organization tended to expand its activities, to do more things

---

* Since any system is by definition composed of specialized parts, one may be tempted to conclude that systemization breeds specialization. But the implied cause-effect relationship is by no means so clear-cut. Does systemization (which involves increases in both size and complexity) produce specialization, or is it the other way around? We are back to the "chicken-egg" dilemma, and the best answer seems to be that systemization and specialization arise through a process of continuous interaction with one another. They are inseparable aspects of the same phenomenon. This conclusion is not so much a standoff as it is a point of departure. It emphasizes the fact that both industrialization and specialization are historical processes which evolve over time.

than its original components had previously done. To oversimplify what was taking place, we might describe it as a tendency to centralize organizations and diversify the activities in which they were engaged.

Earlier we observed how both productivity and labor underwent a process of constant division and subdivision. These developments were classic examples of the tendency toward *specialization of function*. But the impact of specialization extended beyond the realms of productivity, machinery, and jobs to such areas as commerce, distribution, finance, and retailing. It is in these areas that the principles of centralization and diversification help illuminate the process by which such activities grew more specialized.

Methods of distribution and retailing underwent a metamorphosis during the nineteenth century. During the early decades, agricultural commodities were the nation's main product. They found markets either locally or abroad, which meant that distribution beyond the local level consisted of getting the products to the seaboard for export. Most manufactured goods were imported from abroad and therefore required a more elaborate arrangement. In an era dependent upon waterways for transportation, all trade routes led to the seaboard, and coastal cities emerged as the primary centers of distribution. Located upon some navigable river system, each major port serviced a sizable hinterland and became a clearinghouse for goods flowing in both directions.

Within this framework of seaboard-dominated markets arose a complex and rather cumbersome system of distribution. The functions it performed fall into two categories: wholesaling and retailing. At the wholesale level, several different kinds of middlemen appeared: importers, shipping merchants, commission merchants, jobbers, brokers, and auctioneers. While each of these was a distinct type, the services they provided often overlapped and varied according to the kinds of goods they handled and the nature of their customers.

Importers often conducted both wholesale and retail operations. They received goods from abroad and sold them to retail merchants from the interior who replenished their stocks by making one or two buying trips a year to the seaboard. Most importers handled a general business until about the 1830s, when some began to specialize in particular commodities. At first their specialization was confined to broad categories of goods, the most typical of which were groceries, hardware, dry goods, and housewares. By the 1850s, however, some importers were limiting their trade to cottons or woolens or goods from a particular locale such as England, India, or the Orient.

Shipping merchants differed from importers in several respects. They usually restricted their business to wholesaling and usually owned all or part of the ships carrying the goods they handled. Like importers, however, they gradually shifted their business from a general line of goods to more specialized stocks. This development complicated the lives of those interior merchants whose businesses were too small to specialize in only one or two kinds of goods and who therefore had to make the rounds of several importers and shipping merchants to get everything they wanted.

This inconvenience led to the emergence of the jobber, who acted as a sort of middleman between the retail merchants and other middlemen. Jobbers bought several kinds of goods from the more specialized wholesalers and resold them to retailers. In this way they performed two useful functions. They enabled visiting merchants to obtain most of what they needed in one place, and they allowed merchants to purchase stocks in smaller or "broken-lot" quantities than were usually available from the larger, more specialized wholesalers. For many country merchants, often operating on a shoestring budget, this last point was a godsend.

Of all the wholesalers, the commission merchants (also known as factors) ranked first in both numbers and importance. Acting as agents for both foreign firms selling goods in the United States and for Americans buying imported products or selling their own products overseas, commission merchants performed a remarkable variety of functions. For foreign companies they handled, sold, and distributed goods, took care of all the financial transactions involved, and offered advice on market conditions. For American planters, they sold cotton, sugar, tobacco, and other crops abroad, purchased supplies of all kinds, and handled financial matters. They performed similar services for textile companies and other manufacturers seeking wider markets. In the realm of finance, they made advances, collected due payments and other debts, and handled bills of exchange, among other services. Commission merchants often took care of transportation as well, buying or selling or chartering ships, outfitting vessels, gathering freights, and arranging for insurance. It was a busy profession, full of subtle pitfalls for the inept and lucrative rewards for the adept. Small wonder that an impressive roster of American business titans began their climb to success as commission merchants.*

---

* Commission merchants derive their name from the fact that they charged a commission for each of the various services they performed. They were therefore independent operators working for a fee, much like a doctor or lawyer. The size of their commissions varied with the particular service and the difficulty of the work

Brokers were middlemen in the most literal sense. They did not personally buy or sell goods, but rather brought buyers and sellers together for a fee. More than any other type of middlemen, brokers were the product of advancing specialization in that the nature of their work inclined them to concentrate upon one commodity. Since an agricultural economy has little need for specialists, brokers were a rare species early in the century. However, their ranks increased steadily during the early industrial period, and by the 1850s they were already clustering in those cities which established formal commodity exchanges.

Auctioneers were more commonplace than brokers, especially in the early 1800s. The auction was in fact a hoary American institution. In olden times it was a favorite means of selling off goods acquired second-hand, under court order, or from bankruptcies. Shortly before 1800 the auction was bent in a new direction—the quick disposal of imported goods in large lots to visiting buyers or local retailers. Auctions gained popularity because they were speedy and convenient for buyers and sellers alike. No permanent establishment was required, overhead costs were minimal, and a wide variety of goods could be handled. They also provided a handy vehicle for unloading end-of-season stocks, outmoded styles, and goods that were moving slowly.

In contrast to this maze of wholesalers, retailing stayed reasonably simple. Some of its forms—the public market, the fair, peddlers and drovers—were legacies of medieval, even ancient times. While these could be found all across the land, they lost ground in the nineteenth century to a relative newcomer, the over-the-counter store. The most common type of establishment, especially in rural areas, was the legendary general store. No institution ever lived up to its name so well. Totally unspecialized in both function and commodities, the general store carried an incredible diversity of hard and soft goods selected by the proprietor on his buying trips to the seaboard. In the hinterland that was its market, the general store possessed a retailing monopoly Standard Oil might have envied. Since farmers rarely had much cash in their pockets, credit was usually liberal and interest rates high. Proprietor and customer still haggled over prices, and the buyer's only guarantee was the reputation of the storekeeper. It was a simple, even primitive business, which ebbed and flowed with the cycle of the crops.

For much of the nineteenth century, the general store dominated American retail enterprise. Yet even while it clung to its modest and

---

involved. Usually the range extended from 1 percent to 5 or 6 percent, with 2.5 percent being the figure for many of the services.

isolated monopoly, specialization was infiltrating city stores. As towns grew and with them the volume of retail trade, stores began to concentrate upon particular lines. At first their specialities revolved around the familiar categories of drygoods, hardware, groceries, and housewares, but further growth soon brought even more subdivisions. Even before the Civil War, any large city or town had shops selling books, cutlery, boots and shoes, china and glassware, tobacco, clothing, millinery, and a host of other items. Since urban retailing fostered not only specialization but also competition among stores selling similar goods, merchants devised new practices to capture customers. These included the one-price system, return privileges, free delivery, special sales, advertising, and catchy displays.

The preindustrial system of distribution may be summarized as follows: It was oriented to the seaboard and dominated by the wholesalers. Several layers of middlemen separated the producer of goods from the consumer, and these layers possessed no coherent order or clear relationships among themselves. Most retailers were independent operators who catered to a local market. Firms tended to specialize in either wholesaling or retailing, but seldom both. Urban shops moved steadily toward specialization by commodity, while the general store maintained its monopoly over the rural hinterland and continued to stock everything in sight. Neither type developed any real specialization of function; rather, their proprietors bought and sold their wares, arranged transportation and storage for them, handled their own financing, gauged the market in which they sold, judged the quality of the goods they bought, and bore all the risks at every stage.

As the reader might suspect, this was not a terribly efficient system; in fact, it was not much of a system at all. It was slow, costly, and cumbersome, but it suited an environment characterized by local or at best regional markets, low domestic industrial output, water transportation, and slowly rising demand. Once industrialization began to alter these conditions, the old system could not long endure. The rising productivity of American factories led to a sharp expansion of domestic output and a parallel decline in dependence upon imported goods. The result was a terrific growth in the volume of domestic trade.

The transportation revolution was crucial to this process. Railroads, canals, and turnpikes erased the boundaries of local and regional markets. By opening up the interior, they helped create new inland distribution centers and thus destroyed the primacy of the seaboard. As new marketing arrangements became possible, they fostered two broad trends: markets became national in scope (diversification), and they concentrated ever more in urban areas (centralization). Productivity shifted from home to factory, leaving in its wake the old tradition of self-sufficiency. As Bernard Weisberger observed, "In a generation the country moved from a homemade to a store-bought society."

Industrialization spurred the development of a new distribution system. As the volume of domestic trade expanded, it propelled merchants steadily down the road to specialization. Already urban stores had become specialized in activity (wholesale or retail) and commodity, but after 1870 they grew increasingly specialized by function as well. This occurred because other specialized agencies and institutions emerged to relieve the merchant of peripheral responsibilties and allow him to devote his full attention to merchandising. Among these new institutions were common carriers, like the railroad, operating on regular schedules; freight forwarding agencies; public warehouses; improved banking and credit facilities; better insurance arrangements; a variety of new publications providing regular information on the market; a relatively stabilized monetary system; improved communications; and the advent of professional promotional and advertising firms.

Like other revolutions, that in distribution did not progress without incurring casualties. Foremost among them were the wholesaler and the general store. Both were victims not only of the trend toward greater specialization, but also of corollary tendencies toward increased. centralization and diversification.

From the start, industrialization rendered the wholesaler an endangered species. As the industrial system grew larger, it could no longer tolerate the old clumsy labyrinth of middlemen. The wholesaler's turf was invaded from two directions. On one side, producing firms marched into the realms of distribution and marketing; on the other, retailing underwent a series of innovations, one effect of which was a drive to insure greater control over the supply of goods than could be achieved by working through a hodgepodge of middlemen. The ultimate result was to squeeze out many of the wholesalers and forge direct links between producing companies and retail outlets.

The story of the producers has already been told in a different context. Beset by the problems of size and competition, manufacturers required a more sophisticated system of distribution. In their quest for assured markets, reduced costs, and economies of scale, they could leave nothing to chance. The logical step for large firms was extending their control forward to the retail outlet through vertical or horizontal integration. In the first, an individual company established its own branch plants, warehouses, wholesale supply system, and retail outlets. The horizontal strategy, resorted to more frequently, differed from the vertical primarily in that several large companies joined forces for marketing. Firms pursuing one of these courses included Standard Oil, United States Rubber, Singer Sewing Machine, American Tobacco Company, Swift & Company, National Biscuit Company, International Harvester, and International Paper.

By their entry into marketing, these corporate giants virtually eliminated the independent wholesalers from their domains. In their place came an army of hired agents: sales managers, supervisors, drummers, and others. Integration also allowed the corporations greater control over standardization of products and prices. Moreover, they could tie products to the parent firm through the use of brand names. Once consumers were trained to purchase a product on the basis of its brand name, advertising and promotion became powerful instruments for spurring sales. The quality of an item came to be identified not with the merchant who sold it, but rather with the company that produced it. "Recognized" brands reshaped consumer tastes and buying habits. Even before 1920, Americans everywhere ate Quaker Oats or Grape-Nuts, munched Uneeda Biscuits, drove a Studebaker Six, Mercer, Ford, or Packard, smoked Pall Malls or the more exotic Turkish Murads, drank Knickerbocker or Pabst beer, listened to Victor Records, wore Arrow shirts, struggled into Gossard or Bon Ton corsets, and washed with Ivory or Palmolive soap.

Innovations in retailing also eclipsed the role of traditional wholesalers and destroyed the splendid isolation of the general store. Here the primary agents of change were the department store, the mail-order houses, and the chain stores. All three reflected trends in retailing parallel to those occurring in production: through a process of growth, consolidation, and integration, large corporate enterprises replaced or overshadowed small individual establishments. The organizational revolution worked its miracles in the store no less than in the factory.

The department store led the charge. It was, in fact, the first institution to employ the techniques of mass selling, which might be thought of as the retailers' version of mass production. Such an approach could be attempted only in large cities where there existed a large consumer market. The basic principles behind the department store were simple but farsighted: offer customers a wide selection of goods within a single store so they don't have to wander from one store to another to do their shopping; develop customer loyalty by assuming full responsibility for all merchandise; and put one price on every item to eliminate haggling and expedite the turnover of goods in large quantities. While other refinements were added over the years, these policies remained the formula for success.

Although the department store evolved after the Civil War, A. T. Stewart of New York had already demonstrated the possibilities of large-scale retailing during the antebellum period. Stewart confined his business to dry goods and did not organize his store along departmental lines, but his imaginative techniques and large sales volume made him a millionaire and an inspiration for other merchants. His pioneering efforts were soon followed by the men who created the modern department store: Rowland Macy, the Gimbel brothers, Ebenezer Jordan, Marshall Field, and John Wanamaker. Like Stewart, each of these men began as either a wholesaler or a small retailer in dry goods, and one of them, Marshall Field, maintained a wholesale business which for years outstripped his department store in sales volume.

Relying heavily upon advertising, department stores rose to prominence between 1870 and 1900. Once having lured urban shoppers away from specialty shops, their sales and profits soared until the onset of depression in 1930. So phenomenal was their success that most were able to finance expansion entirely from accumulated earnings. In most cases ownership remained firmly in the hands of the founding family.

During these golden years, the big department stores perfected the techniques of centralization and diversification. Within one central building they housed a broad variety of merchandise broken down into individual departments. For the whole enterprise to succeed, each department—or at least most of them—had to outsell the leading specialty shops in their line of goods. Once it became apparent that volume sales and cost efficiency held the key to victory, market trends and customer preferences had to be read carefully and anticipated.

Volume sales were achieved through several devices. The one-price system—and usually a low price at that—was coupled with a return privilege on defective or unsatisfactory merchandise. Special sales were created to stimulate business during normally slack periods such as January and August. New advertising techniques were coined, often by professional agencies or copywriters, including the use of bold-type ads covering several columns and featuring vivid descriptions of the merchandise. Fresh promotional gimmicks were employed on special occasions. Nearly all of these techniques required resources beyond the reach of most specialty shops.

Cost efficiency, too, utilized techniques on a scale smaller shops could not match. Department stores kept wages abysmally low and bought goods in volume from a wide variety of sources. Some stores made private contracting arrangements directly with manufacturers or even integrated backwards into wholesaling and manufacturing. Both practices eliminated middlemen and assured a reliable supply of goods. Wherever possible, the large stores utilized the internal efficiencies and economies of scale.

Where department stores undermined urban specialty shops, the mail-order houses struck at the rural general store. In this instance, the principles of centralization and diversification were applied in a different but no less effective manner. The mail-order houses were a kind of long-distance department store made possible by the growing railroad network and such improvements in the mail system as the creation of special postage rates for catalogs and magazines in 1873, the establishment of rural free delivery in the 1890s, and the addition of parcel post service in 1912.

The pioneers in the mail-order business are familiar names: Aaron Montgomery Ward and Richard W. Sears. It was Ward who founded the first mail-order house in 1872 in hopes of tapping the ripe but hitherto isolated rural market. Through use of a catalog distributed by mail and bolstered by an endorsement from the National Grange, Ward tried to lure the farmer out of his traditional buying patterns. He was successful enough to attract numerous competitors to the field, including such department stores as Macy's and Wanamaker's. Although Montgomery Ward & Co. remained the leading mail-order firm until the 1890s, it was soon eclipsed by the spectacular rise of Sears, Roebuck.

The career of Richard Sears was a classic chapter of the "rags-to-riches" saga. A native of Minnesota, he quit school at sixteen to help support his family. His youth was spent in a variety of jobs which brought him into close contact with farmers and gave him a thorough grasp of their habits, tastes, and ways of thinking. Bright and ambitious, Sears was forever alert to fresh opportunities. The turning point in his life came in 1886 when he seized upon a chance to sell some watches that had been refused by a local merchant. From that modest incident, he nursed a small mail-order watch business into a successful enterprise. In 1889, at the tender age of twenty-five, he sold his watch company for $72,000 and moved to Iowa to take up banking. But banking proved too tame for his restless energy, and before long he returned to the retailing of watches and jewelry.

For a few years, Sears alternated spurts of furious and profitable activity with retreats into retirement. Then in 1893 he joined with two friends to form Sears, Roebuck & Company, a mail-order firm offering several lines of goods besides watches and jewelry. Housed in Chicago, Sears aimed to capture the sprawling rural market. To succeed, he had to persuade farmers to revamp not only their buying habits but also their prejudices. Always short of money and slow to part with it, farmers were apt to distrust any scheme that asked them to buy goods sight unseen from unknown merchants in distant cities. While suspicious of city slickers, farmers also bore no great attachment to the general store that charged them high prices and even higher interest rates.

In his campaign to disarm the farmers' suspicions, Sears made the catalog his chief weapon. Issued twice a year, the catalog was a masterpiece of sales propaganda which in time became an American classic. Drawing upon his sure grasp of the rural mind, Sears crafted his catalog with loving artistry. In cheerful, homespun prose he described his wares, invited the folks to come visit his Chicago plant, and hammered home his policies: low prices, high quality, and guaranteed satisfaction or money cheerfully refunded. Every item was described in appealing and rarely understated terms. In addition, Sears blanketed the farm magazines with advertisements for his catalog. His aim was twofold: to break down buyer resistance and to make the name Sears a household word. He succeeded in both tasks.

The result was a prolific increase in sales, a frenzy of hostility from rural storekeepers who saw their future threatened, and a financial crisis caused by Sears's tendency to expand faster than his resources would permit. To cope with the last problem, Sears took a momentous step in 1895: he bought out his unnerved partner Roebuck's interest in the business for $25,000 (in a short time that share would be worth millions) and formed a new partnership with two men, Julius Rosenwald and Aaron Nusbaum. The new partners reorganized the company and launched a rapid-fire expansion program. A clash of personality led to Nusbaum's departure shortly after 1900. Sears himself retired in 1908, leaving the company under the brilliant leadership of Rosenwald, who remained its president until 1921.

By 1908 Sears, Roebuck had become a mammoth organization and a public corporation. Where Sears had been a consummate salesman and promoter, Rosenwald displayed a genius for management and administration. As the company steadily expanded its line of wares, it integrated backward to control the supply of key products. The company owned all or part of nine factories in 1906, over twenty in 1908, and more than thirty by 1918. A buying office was opened in New York in 1902 and a branch mail-order house in Dallas four years later. A second branch house (Seattle) was added in 1910 and a third (Philadelphia) in 1920. Sales volume passed that of Montgomery Ward by 1900 and reached $42,000,000 by 1907. Within another decade, the gap between the two houses widened to a chasm; in 1917 Sears, Roebuck sales totalled nearly $166,000,000 to about $73,500,000 for Montgomery Ward.

Having captured a lion's share of the rural market, the mail-order houses turned their attention to the urban arena. By the 1920s Sears, Roebuck had, in Alfred Chandler's words, "worked out a centralized, functionally departmentalized structure for its mail-order business." But times were changing. People were still moving into cities, the automobile was already transforming shopping habits, and the rise of chain stores posed a serious threat. Confronted by these and other pressures, Sears responded by plunging directly into the retail business. Montgomery Ward followed suit, and by 1929 each house owned several hundred retail outlets.

Although the mail-order houses pioneered the retail revolution, they were not the wave of the future because rural America was not the wave of the future. That honor belonged instead to the chain stores, which first appeared in the 1870s but only became a major force after the turn of the century. By the 1920s the chain stores were well on their way to establishing a pattern of retailing which prevails to this day. Their evolution displayed yet another version of the principles of centralization and diversification.

The chain-store formula for success was a blend of the policies utilized by mail-order houses and department stores. Working within the same framework, they put the pieces of the commercial puzzle together in a different but no less effective way. They bought in quantity directly from the manufacturers wherever possible. Instead of a high markup on goods, they relied upon a high volume of sales at low prices and a fast turnover of merchandise. For this approach to succeed, they had to solve several key problems involving markets, cost efficiency, and organization. The first men to tackle these questions were F. W. Woolworth, who opened his first variety store in 1879, and George F. Gilman and George H. Hartford, who expanded their coffee and tea business into a chain operation in groceries under the name Great Atlantic & Pacific Tea Company. Their efforts laid the foundation for later chain enterprises.

Obviously, a strategy based upon high sales volume and small profit margin required a large and expanding market. Thus chain stores catered almost exclusively to urban areas, but they used different tactics to pursue that common strategy. Some, like A&P, Woolworth's, and the early drugstore chains, concentrated at first upon large cities and medium-sized towns while others, notably J. C. Penney & Company, went after the small-town trade. To maximize their impact, most of the early chains carried a wide variety of goods, but eventually the chain method was adapted by such specialties as men and women's clothing, shoes, tobacco items, and theaters.

Like the mail-order houses and department stores, the early chains attacked the problem of cost cutting with ruthless efficiency. They sold only for cash to eliminate the expense of credit; this was a feasible policy for urban operations, but not for the rural general store whose customers were always starved for coin. They paid the lowest possible wages on the simple premise that, as Woolworth explained it, "We must have cheap help or we cannot sell cheap goods." Above all, they strove to eliminate middlemen and the expense they entailed. Both Gilman and Woolworth went at this work with a vengeance, and both encountered desperate opposition from the wholesalers. After bitter struggles, both managed to destroy the old distribution arrangements and make their own contracts directly with manufacturers. Unlike the mail-order houses, however, the chain stores rarely went into manufacturing.

Hard-pressed by these innovations in retailing, the ranks of the wholesalers dwindled steadily. It was not that middlemen were in danger of becoming extinct, but rather that their functions had changed. The old independent importers, commission merchants, shipping merchants, and jobbers gave way to a variety of specialists in purchasing, marketing, and advertising, most of whom were salaried employees. The distribution revolution consolidated the steps between producer and consumer; the new retail system shortened the time lag between manufacture and market, reduced costs all along the line, and gave producers a more immediate feel for trends in style and taste. It enabled retailers to handle a larger flow of goods with greater efficiency.

Like the production process, distribution was becoming relentlessly systematized. In both areas, specialization brought increased standardization of goods and services. For producers, standardization took the form of factory-packaged, brand-named products that could be marketed nationwide. For distribution, it meant brand-name retail institutions that provided the same products and services on a national basis. Implicit in this new arrangement were promises of consistent quality, guaranteed satisfaction, and reliable performance. To its creators the new system was a stunning blend of art and science. In singing its praises, John Wanamaker observed:

The comfort and convenience enjoyed by the public in shopping, the saving of wear and tear of body and mind, the educating power of well-displayed collections of products of the fine and useful arts are incidents in the system of modern retailing that will go far toward justifying its present phase of development.

But no hymn to progress is without its sour notes. The various middlemen and small retailers displaced or threatened by the new order lashed out at what they considered to be its inequities: it crushed the small businessman, destroyed individual initiative, encouraged monopoly, depersonalized the relationship between retailer and customer, and did not really lower prices all that much. While these charges were debated in numerous public forums, two more serious accusations were levied which were to reverberate throughout the twentieth century. These concerned the use of advertising and the mass distribution of adulterated or defective goods.

In the growing consumer economy, advertising emerged as the prime weapon of commercial warfare. Critics charged that much of it was deceptive and fraudulent and that lavish use of it by the great retail houses was merely a higher form of the sharp practices used by merchants to victimize gullible customers. In addition, many prepackaged products were denounced as inferior at best and positively harmful at worst. This complaint was aimed especially at the food and patent-medicine industries, but was by no means limited to them. Several shocking exposés, including Upton Sinclair's horrifying account of the meatpacking industry in his novel *The Jungle* (1906) and the scandals surrounding canned food purchased by the government for soldiers in the Spanish-American War, verified the problem. Some thoughtful critics connected the two problems by noting that in the new impersonal marketplace extravagant advertising could be used to sell the most inferior product no less effectively than the superior one.

While these debates led to strenuous efforts at reform, few of them were successful. Meanwhile the new system entrenched itself ever more firmly into American society. As production and distribution grew more specialized, they became more interdependent as well. To a lesser extent, the same pattern occurred in the neighboring realm of banking and finance. Every aspect of the financial system—banks, brokerages, stock and commodity exchanges, the money market, finance companies—crossed the great divide from small, individual, often casual operations to larger and more formal institutions. Bankers, brokers, and other financial agents gradually abandoned a general business to concentrate upon some narrower field.* In finance as in manufacturing and distribution, there appeared elaborate pecking orders within and among organizations.

For banks, organization was in fact the primary problem. To underwrite the growth and consolidation of the industrial economy into giant enterprises, banks needed strong central institutions capable of servicing large territories. According to Fritz Redlich, there were nearly 16,000 banks in the United States by 1905. Of that number, about 6,000 were national banks; the rest included state banks, private banks, and trust companies. The average bank was modest in size, had a working capital of $25,000 to $300,000, and served a limited area. In smaller towns the bank was often owned by the proprietor of the dominant local industry and run as an adjunct to it. The world of small banks, like that of small businesses, was a precarious one characterized by slender profits and a high death rate.

The major banks lived in quite another world. The larger cities—especially New York and Philadelphia—had always been the centers of American finance. Industrialization only magnified the dominant position of the large urban banks and enabled both commercial and investment firms to reap enormous profits and pay astronomical dividends to their stockholders while understating their true assets and funneling large sums into hidden reserves. The powerful First National Bank of New York, for example, listed its working capital at an incredibly low $500,000 until 1902, while accumulating a surplus of more than $11,600,000 or 2,100 percent of its capital. Numerous other banks differed only in degree.

To achieve these impressive gains, banks had to organize in a way that would allow them to do business on a larger scale. Several went the route of centralization and diversification. Centralization could be undertaken in several ways: new banks could be founded; existing ones could be enlarged by plowing profits back or by raising additional capital through issuing securities; or a giant new organization could be created through consolidation and merger. After 1900 banks, like industrial corporations, tended to favor diversification. Led by the great investment bankers—especially J. P. Morgan—the banking communities in New York, Chicago, and Philadelphia steadily consolidated their interests

---

* On this point two of our themes intersect: the declining role of commission merchants and the rising importance of investment bankers. A surprising number of the most prominent investment bankers got their start in business as commission merchants. Over the years they shed their merchant functions and devoted full attention to the banking end of the business.

through mergers, interlocking stock ownership, and interlocking direc-
torates.*

By 1910 alarmed critics could speak of the "Money Trust" as posing
a grave threat to the future of the Republic. Since the bankers had
themselves authored and managed most of the industrial and transportation consolidations, the mounting centralization in their own ranks was
in effect a combination of the combiners. Louis D. Brandeis, a brilliant
corporation lawyer and later Supreme Court justice, described the effects
of banking concentration in ominous tones:

> The dominant element in our financial hierarchy is the investment banker.
> Associated banks, trust companies and life insurance companies are his tools.
> Controlled railroads, public service and industrial corporations are his subjects.
> Though properly but middlemen, these bankers bestride as masters America's
> business world, so that practically no large enterprise can be undertaken
> successfully without their participation or approval. . . . The key to their
> power is combination—concentration intensive and comprehensive. . . .

In banking as in distribution, centralization also meant territorial
extension. Branch banking emerged as a common device for gaining a
foothold in suburban areas or the hinterland. The first American to
create a statewide branch banking system was Amadeo Giannini, who
expanded his Bank of Italy into the dominant financial institution in
California.** Branch banking aroused fierce opposition, especially among
small local bankers, and was outlawed in several states. Wherever
branching was denied, centralization was achieved through chain banking, whereby a group of bankers obtained control over several banks
within a region. This could be done either by individuals owning stock
in other banks, or by several major bankers establishing a separate
holding company which in turn controlled other banks.

As the larger banks centralized, they also diversified their activities.
Commercial banks established bond departments, went more heavily
into the call loan business, undertook trust work, and loaned money to
consumer-credit agencies. Investment banks were slow to follow suit
until after World War I, when their dominant role in underwriting
industrial expansion and consolidation declined sharply. Yet even be-

---

* At this same time the leading investment bankers, especially Morgan, gained
control or considerable influence over the major insurance companies. As heavy buyers
of securities, the giant insurance firms provided bankers with a captive market for their
underwritings and thus became a primary source for capital.

** Giannini's bank later changed its name to the Bank of America.

fore the war many large American banks were, in Fritz Redlich's words, "well under way toward what came to be called department-store banking in the 1920s."

Most of our examples in this section have concerned a growing specialization of function. Yet that is only part of the story, for the period 1870–1920 also witnessed a powerful tendency toward specialization of area or location as well: specialization became characteristic not only of *what* was being done but also *where* it was being done. Efficiency is a matter of geographical as well as functional organization; its spatial dimensions are no less important than its structural or managerial ones.

Seen in this light, urbanization is itself a form of specialization, and a crucial one at that. Eric Lampard pinpointed the connection by declaring that "the growth of the modern city and the march of the industrial revolution are joint products of the same cultural strand—specialization." This states the case too baldly by implying a clear cause-effect relationship, but Lampard went on to clarify the connection between specialization and urbanization:

Specialization of function makes inevitably for specialization of areas: it prompts a territorial division of labor between town and country and differentiates town from town. A real differentiation is, in fact, the spatial corollary of functional specialization and logically serves the same end— economy. The closer integration of interdependent functions means that less of a community's limited stock of energy and material need to be devoted to overcoming the various disutilities of distance. Local concentration of specialized activities is thus an ecological response to certain technical and cost considerations which impel a more selective use of space, a more efficient pattern of land-use. . . . From a socio-ecological standpoint, city growth is simply the concentration of differentiated but functionally-integrated specialisms in rational locales. The modern city is a mode of social organization which furthers efficiency in economic activity.

With these principles in mind, we are ready to consider urbanization as a factor in industrialization.

Urbanization

In a sense the remainder of this book discusses this factor, or at least that phase of it we call the Industrial City. Here we are concerned with the general phenomenon of urbanization and its relationship to the other factors of industrialization. As noted earlier, urban growth proceeded on two levels: cities got bigger, and there were more of them. Historically their pattern of growth may be separated into three broad stages: the commercial or preindustrial city, the industrial city, and the metropolis. There is nothing original in these categories; for more than fifty years scholars have used some version of them to describe the growth of cities.

Obviously these stages characterize urban growth primarily in economic terms. That is entirely fitting, for the American city was essentially a creature of economic forces. There is probably no single fact more important for understanding its nature. When we say that economic factors were the dominant forces in shaping urban development, we do not mean they were the *exclusive* forces. Other factors were important, but not as much so. And in the end economic factors exerted a profound, even decisive influence upon the noneconomic aspects of city life.

Shifting patterns of trade and industry determined the character, the structure, the "personality," even the very location of American cities. Business was the lifeblood of every urban center. Its presence nourished growth and prosperity, sometimes to fabulous dimensions; its absence drained the vitality and ambition of the entire community. Commerce and industry shaped the rhythms of the city's inner life, transformed it into an arena where enterprising people battled tirelessly to realize their visions of success. As Thomas C. Cochran and William Miller have observed, the city became the lodestar of American civilization:

And in so far as American culture has been a business culture it has found its most profound expression in the cities. American farmers have lived off its markets, American workers have lived off jobs in the cities, American factories have found their labor and their leaders there, and American artists of every kind, when they have found patronage, have found it in the cities. . . . The intelligent and ambitious of every culture have come to seek their fortunes there. In industrial America they made the city a symbol of intense competition, of heightened individualism in business matters and uniform failure in most aspects of community life.

The reader should bear in mind that our three stages are artificial constructs. Not all cities passed through every stage or displayed all the characteristics listed for each one. And since cities tended to follow their own timetables of growth, the dates given are rough estimates. Our schema is nothing more than a simple working model designed to portray broad trends and general principles. Like all models, it is not the biography of any one city, but it should illuminate the history of many cities.

The Commercial City

In the United States, the commercial city flourished roughly between 1800 and 1870. During that period industrialization was still in its infancy though spreading rapidly. Except in textiles and iron, mechanized production had not yet made a great impact. Wind, wood, and water remained the principle sources of power, hand tools and craftsmen the major agents of production. Agricultural commodities dominated the economy and were the chief source of wealth. Most towns were trade centers servicing a rural hinterland and feeding upon the commerce generated by it. Few urban economies relied upon industry or manufacturing to any great degree. In 1860, according to Lampard, only five of the nation's fifteen "leading" cities had more than 10 percent of their labor force engaged in manufacturing. Although some smaller towns—especially New England mill towns—were more heavily involved in manufacturing, most cities depended upon trade and commerce for whatever growth and prosperity they achieved.

But changes were clearly in the wind. The use of machinery and steam power increased rapidly, especially during the 1850s, when stationary steam engines were devised for mechanized production. The factory system spread beyond textiles into other industries. Markets expanded as transportation improved. The combination of these forces revolutionized domestic manufacturing in general and the transportation, textile, iron, and machine-tool industries in particular.

Technological and organizational change swept across the commercial cities and transformed many of them into industrial centers. Wherever its impact was felt, urban growth occurred, often in quantum leaps. By creating important new sources of centralized economic activity, it doomed the purely commercial city to extinction or at best obscurity. Urban areas still serviced the commercial and financial needs of their rural tributary, but now they began to *produce* for that hinterland—and more distant markets—as well.

Production still catered primarily to the rural market and hewed closely to the basic needs of food, clothing, housing, transportation, household necessities, and tools. Leading items included farm implements, sewing machines, textile goods, stoves, lamps, boots and shoes, wagons and buggies, clocks, flour and meal, clothes, and leather goods. Even in factories where the division of labor was most advanced, there was little that resembled the modern assembly line. Machines were large, often unwieldly, and usually performed only one or two functions;

human labor had to supply the rest. Steam power had worked miracles in transportation but had not yet penetrated deeply into factories, where water power still prevailed. But transportation was indeed critical, for as domestic manufacturing surged upward, enterprising men worked furiously to extend their city's connections to distant markets. Early in the game they accepted as gospel the maxim that cities built railroads and railroads built cities.

Not even the interruption of a civil war could stay the momentum of urban growth, which by 1870 was plainly on the threshold of a new era. The larger cities were fast diversifying their economic base into a mixture of manufacturing, commercial, distributive, and financial activities. Smaller cities and towns were already exhibiting distinct signs of economic specialization. The New England mill town was the most conspicuous example of this tendency, but by no means the only one. As one early student of the New England economy put it:

In 1840 it would have been difficult to find 50 out of 479 townships in Southern New England which did not have at least one manufacturing village clustered around a cotton or a woolen mill, an iron furnace, a chair factory or a carriage shop, or some other representative of the hundred miscellaneous branches of manufacturing which had grown up in haphazard fashion in every part of these three states.

These forces were harbingers of a future that would wrench urban America into a new and difficult stage of development. Before passing onto it, let us first sketch a bare still-life of the commercial city. It was a relatively small place nestled against some navigable waterway which, along with turnpikes or country roads, formed its only connection with the outside world. Business revolved around the individual enterprise or partnership, while production was centered in the home shop and retailing in the home store. The general store still held sway in smaller towns, but elsewhere was supplemented or replaced by a sprinkling of specialty shops. Most of the labor force was directly involved with producing goods rather than services. A high proportion of workers, perhaps nearly a third, were skilled or semiskilled.

The commercial city was a walking city. It was small enough for people to reach most places on foot; otherwise they resorted to carriages or an omnibus. The population tended to be ethnically homogeneous. Class barriers existed, but were not so high as to wall off contact between people of different classes. Most neighborhoods were mixed in two senses of the term: people tended to live near where they worked, and people of various classes lived in the same area. No rigid separation between business and residential districts had yet appeared; neither had segregation by class or ethnic group advanced very far. For visitors, transients, and the unmarried, there were inns and boardinghouses.

Since the workday was usually long and society still relatively simple, families spent much of their leisure time together. The church provided an outlet for both religious faith and socializing. Beyond home and church, there were a variety of community socials, festive celebrations like the Fourth of July, park concerts, and in larger cities a few commercial entertainments such as theater. Traveling shows, touring artists, lecturers, and occasional religious revivals were treats which usually aroused great local enthusiasm. And for those so inclined, there was that ancient source of social roistering, the tavern.

The technology of the commercial city, like its pleasures and its social organization, seems simple in retrospect. Hand tools and simple machines did most of its work; wood, water, coal, and animals furnished most of its power. Homes, shops, and other buildings seldom rose above one or two stories and were constructed of wood, stone, or brick. Most foods were prepared at home (many houses had their own garden and often a cow or two). Clothes too were usually homemade from cheap coarse fabrics, brightened by such store-bought frills as buttons, ribbons, and lace. However, traditional habits of diet and wardrobe were fast being altered by the rise of commercially prepared items.

For the wealthier class, urban life moved on a different plane. Although few in number and not yet isolated from those of lesser means, the rich often possessed fortunes equal to the holdings of upper-class Europeans. While some wealthy Americans made a virtue of living on a modest scale despite their means, others invested in the trappings of splendor. They lived in magnificent houses filled with elegant furnishings (imported from Europe) and staffed with an army of servants. They ate the finest foods, drank the best wines, and wore the finest clothes. They entertained lavishly and fled on schedule to the cultural sanctuaries of Europe. In short, they cultivated a lifestyle that can only be described as aristocratic. Yet even its worst excesses pale in comparison with the bloated extravagances indulged in by the postwar nabobs of industrialism.

For people of all classes, the commercial city still possessed at least some sense of community. It was a strange but not yet alien environment, familiar enough to achieve a measure of self-identity but large enough to satisfy an urge for change of station or expansion of possibilities. The pace of life was quickening but not yet furious. It was a kind of twilight zone between the small rural community and the bustling industrial center in which most of the familiar social and cultural landmarks fell victim to the relentless quest for economic progress.

The Industrial City

"The United States in 1870," writes Sam Bass Warner, "could be said to be an integrated national economy organized around its major city markets. The entire economy, however, was as yet only partially organized on a national basis because manufacturing had not yet settled into a pattern whereby each specialty located in its best site, and from such a single base or cluster of bases sold its products throughout the nation."

The industrial city was the product of this tendency toward the creation of a specialized base or cluster of bases which proceeded at a rapid rate between 1870 and 1920. It signified a specialization of area that complemented the growing specialization of function so characteristic of the industrial system. The result was not merely larger cities, but a new kind of urban environment with radically different economic, political, and social relationships from those found in the commercial cities. Since the later chapters will examine these aspects of the industrial city in detail, we will limit our concern here to its general economic characteristics.

The forces that induced firms to locate in a particular area and to specialize in a particular product or line of products have already been mentioned. They include access to raw materials, power sources, markets, a reliable labor supply, and sources of capital. Sometimes other factors, such as climate, land and labor costs, transportation arrangements, the attitude of local government, or technological considerations, played an important role. In retrospect it appears that the choice of site for a given industry was often a blend of rational calculation, intuition, and blind chance. The element of chance should not be overlooked, for there is more than a dash of serendipity in the history of American economic development.

Upon these chosen sites the industrial city rose and flourished. All the familiar forces of industrialization converged into a torrent of growth. Small factories became large plants and attracted subsidiary businesses to manufacture tools, parts, and other equipment for the primary industry. Transportation and distribution facilities were expanded to handle increased output, and these, too, required equipment, machine shops, storage and warehouse facilities, and a wide range of services.

More banks and other financial institutions were needed. Since growth expressed itself most obviously in new and larger buildings, the construction industry became an important part of the urban economy.

As large industrial complexes emerged, armies of workers flocked to them in search of jobs. As the stream of humanity pouring into the industrial cities widened, a larger share of them found work in secondary occupations. A multiplying population had to be fed, housed, clothed, and provided with goods, services, and amusements. These needs attracted a seemingly endless procession of grocers, butchers, blacksmiths, merchants, mechanics, barbers, doctors, dentists, druggists, ministers, saloonkeepers, craftsmen, artists, and entertainers, to say nothing of the countless jobs open to unskilled workers.

The most striking feature of industrial cities was the extent to which their civic vitality hinged upon the performance of their primary industry or industries. This was especially true for the smaller towns which had literally sprung up around a central plant or mill or business. But not even the economies of larger and more diversified cities could escape the gravitational pull of their primary industry. It was a sun around which all other economic affairs rotated as satellites and upon which all depended for life and sustenance.

Unfortunately, it was a universe which too often moved in erratic orbits. The industrial city, with its domino-like interdependencies, caught up all of society in its economic vacillations. We need only consider the reverberations of failure to glimpse its broader effects. If a plant declined or failed, stockholders lost money, managers were fired, and workers were laid off. Subsidiary industries suffered a drop in orders and tightened their own belts. Railroads, warehouses, and other service industries soon felt the pinch. Everyone from the grocer to the barber lost business. As unemployment spread and incomes declined, people confined their spending to the bare necessities, setting off a wave of contraction among merchants. Defaults on mortgages and loans brought foreclosures and a reluctance on the part of banks to lend money. Local tax revenues dropped and municipal services suffered accordingly. Unless the cycle was reversed by a renewal of industrial activity or an infusion of new business, the town was likely to stagnate. There might follow an exodus of people seeking better prospects in more thriving communities.

Prosperity, of course, had exactly the opposite effect. In both cases the industrial city exhibited a degree of economic specialization and interdependence unlike anything found in preindustrial towns. To that extent it marked a radical departure from past urban experience. For that reason it is helpful to attempt some measurement of just how far this pattern of specialization had advanced by 1900. The figures given below are intended to be indicative rather than comprehensive, and they approach the problem from two different angles. The first concerns broad correlations between population, urbanization, and manufacturing output; the second examines the degree of industrial specialization within particular cities.

Throughout this book we have assumed certain basic correlations between population, urbanization, and industrialization. In particular we have developed two themes: that as the population increased, a larger portion of it resided in urban places, and that the great bulk of industrial activity was located in urban areas. The data in Table 4 support these assumptions and allow us to carry them a bit further.

TABLE 4

RANK OF SELECTED STATES IN POPULATION AND
MANUFACTURING TOGETHER WITH NUMBER OF
PRINCIPAL CITIES IN EACH STATE IN 1900

STATE	POPULATION RANK	GROSS MANUFAC- TURING RANK (a)	NET MANUFAC- TURING RANK (a)	NO. OF PRINCIPAL CITIES (b)
New York	1	1	1	20
Pennsylvania	2	2	2	20
Illinois	3	3	3	11
Ohio	4	5	5	12
Missouri	5	7	8	5
Texas	6	23	23	7
Massachusetts	7	4	4	25
Indiana	8	8	7	8
Michigan	9	10	10	7
Iowa	10	17	16	8
Wisconsin	13	9	9	6
New Jersey	16	6	6	13
Percent of National Total	56%	70%	70%	67%

NOTES: (a) Based upon value of products.
(b) A principal city is defined as one with a population of 20,000 or more. In 1900 there were 209 principal cities in the United States.
SOURCE: Compiled from data in *Twelfth Census of the United States, Vol. 7: Manufacturers, Pt. 1* (Washington: 1902).

The correlation between population and urbanization is obvious. The twelve states listed comprise little over a quarter of the total states, but contain 56 percent of the nation's population and 67 percent of its principal cities. Even the simple figures in Table 4 suggest clearly what closer investigation would verify: the most populous states in 1900 were also the most urbanized and had the lion's share of principal cities. That comes as no surprise. Urban populations are high-density populations, and one would expect to find that the most populous states have more areas of high population density.

Yet it is a useful starting point for grasping the correlation between urbanization and manufacturing. Notice that this same list of twelve states embraces not only the ten most populous states, but also the ten leading states in terms of both gross and net value of products manufactured. In other words, we need add only two states to the population leaders to encompass the leaders in manufacturing as well.* Notice also that all but three of the twelve states lie east of the Mississippi River and north of the Mason-Dixon line. The broad tier of states between Illinois and Massachusetts formed the heartland of urban industrial America.

These generalizations assert but do not measure the degree to which industry was concentrated in urban areas. To do that we must go beyond the data in Table 4. In 1900 no less than thirty-four of the forty-four states produced more than 50 percent of their manufactured goods in urban rather than rural areas. Of that number, the proportion for eighteen states exceeded 75 percent, and five of these were above 90 percent. The most intense concentration was in New England, where 296 cities contained over 75 percent of the region's population. These cities harbored 81 percent of the region's manufacturing establishments, which together accounted for 90 percent of all goods produced (in terms of product value) and paid 91 percent of all wages. The middle Atlantic states were not far behind. There 293 cities held 62 percent of the population and 73 percent of the region's manufacturing establishments which produced 84 percent of all goods and paid 87 percent of the region's wages. The figures for the north central or midwestern states are even more revealing. In that region 459 cities contained only 39 percent of the population and 60 percent of the manufacturing establishments. Nevertheless these firms managed to account for 84 percent of manufactured product value and 86 percent of wages paid. Of the 100 leading manufacturing cities in the United States, only 32 lay outside these regions, and most of them were well down the list.

No parade of statistics can tell the whole story, but these figures do suggest that by 1900 the industrial city had become a distinctive entity

---

* Of the two most populous states not among the manufacturing leaders, Iowa ranked first and Texas fifth in gross value of agricultural products.

if not the archetype of urban America. Indeed, the term "industrial city" is not used here merely as a handy label; it describes that crucial stage of urban history in which the two developments—industrialization and the rise of the city—are no longer separable from one another. On this point, too, the data are impressive both in the aggregate and for individual cities. The aggregate figures refer to 73 selected industries which include every major sector of the American industrial economy. In 1900 the 209 principal cities (see Table 4) accounted for 67 percent of total product value, 64 percent of the capital invested, and 64 percent of the wage earners employed in these 73 industries. In short, nearly 66 percent of the nation's primary industrial activity was located in these cities.

The figures are no less revealing for individual cities. Here the problem is best attacked from two different angles. One concerns the degree to which particular industries were concentrated in one or more cities; the other involves the degree to which the economies of individual cities were engaged in one industry. Both are revealing measures of specialization. The first is expressed in terms of product value, the second in both product value and the proportion of a city's wage-earners employed in the specified industry. Table 5 gives some selected data

TABLE 5

Selected Data on Localization of Particular Industries in Individual Cities in 1900: Listed in Descending Order of Concentration

INDUSTRY	CITY	PERCENT OF NATIONAL PRODUCT VALUE IN CITY NAMED
Collars and Cuffs	Troy, N.Y.	85.3
Oysters, canned and preserved	Baltimore, Md.	64.4
Coke	Connellsville, Pa.	48.1
Brassware	Waterbury, Conn.	47.8
Carpets and Rugs	Philadelphia, Pa.	45.6
Gloves	Gloversville, N.Y.	38.8
Silverware	Providence, R.I.	36.3
Slaughtering and Meatpacking (Wholesale)	Chicago, Ill.	35.6
Jewelry	Providence, R.I.	27.4
Agricultural Implements	Chicago, Ill.	24.5
Silk and Silk Goods	Paterson, N.J.	24.2
Tobacco Products	St. Louis, Mo.	22.7
Corsets	Bridgeport, Conn.	21.7
Worsted Goods	Lawrence, Mass.	20.5

source: Same as Table 4.

on the concentration of individual industries within a handful of cities.

This list is by no means comprehensive. It includes only those industries in which at least 20 percent of the total national output came from a single city. While these figures indicate the most conspicuous examples of localized industries, they reflect only the tip of the iceberg. Countless industries were dominated by a relatively small circle of urban centers, yet this tendency of industries to localize in one or more cities was far surpassed by the tendency of cities to specialize in one or more industries. Thousands of cities and towns moored their economic fate to some specific industry, even though their output might comprise only a fraction of the national total. For that reason, our second approach offers even more striking evidence of urban industrial specialization. The data are assembled in Table 6.

Only three of the cities listed produced more than 10 percent of their special industry's national total in terms of product value; yet in all but one of them, the special industry generated well over 50 percent of the city's total industrial output and employed more than 50 percent of its labor force. If the sample were greatly enlarged, it would reveal a pattern of which only the barest contours emerge in Table 6: a distinct correlation between size and degree of specialization. The smaller the town, the more specialized its industrial economy. Conversely, the larger the city, the more diversified its industrial economy is likely to be.

This is a logical, even predictable pattern. After all, urban economic growth proceeds in one of two ways: either the special industry simply keeps getting bigger, or new industries come in to broaden the local economic base. In most cases there are inescapable limits upon the ability of the special industry to grow. Foremost among these is the market for the goods produced, but even if the market demand exceeds the industry's ability to supply it, competing firms in other cities are always eager to capture a larger share. The most common pattern, therefore, was for urban economic expansion to occur through an inflow of new industries to supplement the primary one. When this happened, it did not mean that the primary industry declined. In fact, it might well continue to expand, but its *relative* share of the city's total product grew smaller, and the city became less dependent upon the single industry for its economic welfare.

None of this is meant to suggest that all industrial cities were alike. Every city had its own personality, its own character and style, which was a blend of its unique traditions and customs. That personality mainly influenced the noneconomic aspects of urban life but frequently it spilled over into material affairs as well. What these cities shared was a common

TABLE 6

SELECTED DATA ON DEGREE OF INDUSTRIAL
SPECIALIZATION WITHIN INDIVIDUAL CITIES IN 1900

CITY	INDUSTRY	PERCENT OF NATIONAL TOTAL PRODUCED BY CITY	PERCENT WHICH LISTED INDUSTRY FORMS OF CITY'S TOTAL INDUSTRY	PERCENT OF CITY'S WAGE EARNERS EMPLOYED IN INDUSTRY LISTED
Springfield, Ohio	Agricultural Implements	5.2	41.3	35.6
Brockton, Mass.	Boots and Shoes	7.6	75.2	77.4
Haverhill, Mass.	Boots and Shoes	5.8	61.1	69.6
Troy, N.Y.	Collars and Cuffs	85.3	47.7	68.7
Warwick, R.I.	Cotton Goods	1.3	71.2	78.7
Fall River, Mass.	Cotton Goods	8.6	68.2	80.4
New Bedford, Mass.	Cotton Goods	4.9	65.2	74.9
Lewiston, Maine	Cotton Goods	1.4	54.0	64.3
Bethel, Conn.	Fur Hats	3.5	79.7	86.0
Danbury, Conn.	Fur Hats	18.0	69.4	72.5
Orange, N.J.	Fur Hats	9.0	53.7	55.2
Millville, N.J.	Glass	2.9	62.0	63.9
Tarentum, Pa.	Glass	2.0	57.7	81.1
McKeesport, Pa.	Iron and Steel	4.3	92.6	88.8
Youngstown, Ohio	Iron and Steel	3.5	81.0	72.6
Johnstown, Pa.	Iron and Steel	2.2	79.1	63.3
North Attleboro, Mass.	Jewelry	6.0	69.8	71.7
East Liverpool, Ohio	Pottery, Terra-Cotta	9.3	75.2	87.4
West Hoboken, N.J.	Silk Goods	3.7	72.1	76.2
South Omaha, Neb.	Slaughtering and Meatpacking	9.7	96.3	89.9
Kansas City, Kansas	Slaughtering and Meatpacking	10.5	88.4	72.7

SOURCE: Same as Table 4

experience with industrialization which gave them similar economic characteristics we have used to identify a pivotal stage of urban growth. These characteristics have to do with such things as the level of industrial activity, patterns of organization, and technological developments, all of which were discussed earlier. They are pulled together here to form a sort of composite portrait of the primary factors of production within the industrial city.

In most industries, the factory system had become predominant. Its techniques were refined and its organization made more efficient. Production proceeded on an in-line basis and was fully mechanized in some larger factories. Although a version of the modern assembly line had made its appearance in the shops of that brash pioneer, Henry Ford, widespread use of it still lay over the horizon. Corporate giantism was firmly entrenched in the industrial city. Whether owned by founding families or far-flung shareholders, large enterprises were fast becoming the centers of power and leadership. This held true not only in manufacturing, but also in banking, distribution, insurance, utilities, and transportation. The national railroad system reached its zenith in 1916 and provided access to every corner of the nation. In some cities it was supplemented by electric street railways, interurbans, and subways. Motorcars were on the streets, too, the first trickle of what would soon swell into a flood of automobiles and trucks.

Technological innovations poured forth in a steady stream, transforming old industries and creating new ones. Perhaps the most important of these concerned a revolution in sources of power. The rapid development of electricity as an energy source was already reshaping the face of cities and their industries. The sheer dimensions of this change are amazing. Between 1870 and 1920, American consumption of energy of all kinds increased about 440 percent. It has been estimated that in 1870 wood was the source for about 73 percent of the total energy consumed in the United States, and that only about 20 percent of all energy was used for industrial purposes. As Table 7 indicates, the sources of power shifted drastically over the next half century.

From the figures in Table 7, electricity does not appear to have made much of an inroad by 1920. This is somewhat misleading, since a great deal of electric power was produced by burning some other fuel, usually coal. In 1920 hydropower accounted for only about one-fourth of all electrical energy produced. As a source of power, electricity was growing at a far faster rate than any of its rivals. We must remember how recent an innovation it was. The nation's first electric power station was installed in 1879. Twenty years later there were 2,250 stations, and by

TABLE 7

SPECIFIC ENERGY SOURCES AS PERCENTAGES
OF TOTAL ENERGY CONSUMPTION, 1870–1920

YEAR	WOOD	COAL (a)	OIL	NATURAL (b) GAS	HYDRO-POWER (c)
				(d) /	
1870	73.2	26.5	.3	na	—
1880	57.0	41.1	1.9	na	—
1890	35.9	57.9	2.2	3.7	.3
1900	21.0	71.4	2.4	2.6	2.6
1910	10.7	76.8	6.1	3.3	3.3
1920	7.5	72.5	12.3	4.0	3.6

NOTES: (a) Includes both anthracite and bituminous
(b) Includes both natural gas and natural gas liquids
(c) Defined as electricity generated by waterwheels
(d) Not available

SOURCE: Drawn from Sam H. Schurr, Bruce C. Netschert et al., *Energy in the American Economy, 1850–1975* (Baltimore: 1960), 36.

1920 the number stood at 3,831. Between 1902 (the first year for which there is reasonably reliable data) and 1920, the generation of electricity soared from 5,969,000,000 to 56,559,000,000 kilowatt hours, an increase of 847 percent. By comparison, total energy consumption for that same period rose 126 percent.

While these figures are impressive, the true significance of electricity becomes apparent only when we look at the *uses* of power rather than its sources. Commercial and residential customers consumed nearly 20 percent of the electricity generated in 1920. These uses included lighting, street railways, and the operation of water pumps, elevators, refrigeration units, ventilation devices, and appliances. The availability of electric power in great quantity and at relatively low cost marked the dawn of a new and fateful era in American life. It spearheaded a chain reaction of technological innovations which would eventually transfigure the whole structure of American life and society. Even before the 1920s were gone, the electric life-style had captured the cities and was fanning out into the hinterland. Life in the Electric Age proved a severe jolt to many Americans. For all its gadgets and conveniences, it was yet another force that wrenched them from their past experience and habits. Like the other fruits of industrialization, it was a form of progress with which they were unprepared to deal; they hailed its blessings even as they floundered in the confusion it wrought for their lives.

Electricity had no less decisive an impact on industry. Here, too, its usage increased at an astounding rate. No reliable figures on total industrial consumption are available prior to 1912, when industry used about 11,200,000,000 kilowatt hours. By 1920 the figure reached 31,500,000,000 kilowatt hours, and during the next decade it would double again. Especially did the use of electric power take hold in the factories. According to one estimate, electric motors furnished only 4.8 percent of the total mechanical horsepower used in manufacturing in 1899. Within a decade, electric motors supplied 25.4 percent of total horsepower, and by 1919 the figure had jumped to 55 percent. Still the trend surged upward until it reached 82.3 percent in 1929. Some of the industries relying heavily upon electric power included paper, chemicals, mining and extracting, metals, textiles, and meatpacking.

Electricity revolutionized the basis of industry no less than it did the structure of society. Its effects went far beyond providing a new and cheap source of power. The mechanical motors used in many plants were large, unwieldly creatures with miles of belting wrapped around drive shafts and pulleys. Electric motors were smaller, occupied less space, and could easily be shut off when not in use. Best of all, electricity was more flexible than any other source of power. It could be transmitted long distances over power lines, which meant that plants need no longer be located at their source of power.

It was this development that reordered the industrial process. Not only did it free plants from their power source, it also allowed them to rearrange their internal organization. Hitherto every factory, large or small, drew its mechanical power from one prime source. Since that source was unmovable, the entire plant literally had to be designed around it. Usually the machines requiring the most power were placed nearest the prime source; those facilities needing little or no power were then located in the remaining space. Obviously this limitation bred inefficiency and inconvenience. It forced upon factories a distorted inner logic whereby operations were organized not around the production process, but around the power source. The sequence of steps in a production line demanded one arrangement of machines and facilities, the source of power another; and rarely did the twain meet.

Electric power dissolved this limitation. It allowed each machine to have its own motor and be placed anywhere in the plant with little or no power lost in the distance between the machine and its energy source. Factory design could then devote its attention to maximizing efficiency and convenience of operations. Whole new realms were opened up in the areas of industrial economics and scientific management.

In more ways than one, the power revolution marked the threshold of a new era. The Electric Age plunged both industry and society into the icy rapids of technological change and swept them with gathering speed into a world they never envisioned. For urban America, that epochal journey was embodied in the transition from industrial city to metropolis.

Metropolis

Most urban growth after 1920 assumed one of two forms: the enlarged industrial city or the metropolis. Since both fall out of the time span of our study, we will do little more than sketch their general characteristics. Both types of cities grew upward and outward. Upward growth, symbolized by the skyscraper and high-rise hotels and apartments, was a legacy of the industrial city. It meant a great density of buildings and people packed into the relatively limited downtown area. Outward growth was more a product of the new age with its sweeping technological advances, especially in transportation. It was most commonly expressed in the headlong flight by industry and people out of the central city and into new industrial parks and suburbs that semed to spring up overnight.

The essential difference between the two types of city concerned their pattern of economic development. In general, the industrial city remained specialized while the metropolis grew more diversified. The city based its growth upon the expansion of its primary industry, the metropolis upon a proliferation of industrial activities. In reality, of course, the distinction between the two forms was more a matter of degree than a sharp separation, since no enlarged industrial city was entirely dependent upon just one industry.

Early in the twentieth century, the factory system took a giant step forward with the introduction of a new mass-production technique. Known popularly as the assembly line, it wrung maximum use from the old principle of standardized interchangeable parts. It appeared first in the automobile industry, where Henry Ford was its chief author and messiah, but other industries were quick to grasp its possibilities for their own plants. By integrating men and machines with clockwork precision, the assembly line fulfilled the fondest hopes and deepest fears about the factory system. To many observers it was Taylorism writ large upon the industrial landscape. How fitting it was that the carmakers pioneered its development, for their industry was destined to dominate the American economy and revolutionize our transportation system, demography, landscape, and lifestyle in the twentieth century no less completely than did the railroad in the nineteenth.

The assembly line, along with some related innovations, pushed the industrial city to its fruition. Huge industrial complexes were concentrated in one area to the extent that some cities (Detroit being the most conspicuous example) remained heavily dependent upon one industry for their economic well-being no matter how large they grew. Like other industrial cities, Detroit developed its own economic solar system with a large assortment of industrial satellites revolving around its automotive sun. These included metal alloys, rubber, glass, electrical equipment, chemicals and electrochemicals, petroleum products, parts manufacturers, and a variety of other suppliers and subcontractors. From this concentration of factories, firms, specialists, services, technicians, and a standing army of workers arose an industrial complex awesome in size and ominous in its utter dependence upon the parent industry. The Detroit of the 1920s posed a striking contrast to the Detroit of 1900, in which the leading industries were foundry and machine-shop products, druggists' preparations, tobacco products, iron and steel, and slaughtering and meatpacking.

Of course, the industrial city could not keep on growing to infinity. Even a booming industry like automobiles had upper growth limits. Moreover, by the turn of the century, many cities were already choking on their own congestion. Upward growth aggravated rather than relieved this problem. To survive the crush, cities had to expand outward. As the inner city became unbearably crowded, its land overpriced, and its neighborhoods decayed, the city limits pushed steadily into the neighboring countryside in search of cheaper land for industrial and residential use. The combination of industrial diversification and physical expansion were the primary forces behind the rise of the metropolis. This was a new entity, rather than an exploded version of the industrial city. As Sam Bass Warner observed, "The industrial metropolis was not just the nineteenth-century big city grown larger; neither was it today's megalopolis constricted. It had a unique social and spatial organization."

The larger cities had already reached or were fast approaching the metropolitan stage before World War I. Even in 1900 their economic power and diversity was awesome. In that year, fourteen cities outranked at least half the nation's states and territories in the value of their manufactured products. New York City outproduced every state except its own and Pennsylvania. Chicago outproduced forty-seven states, Philadelphia forty-five, and Boston, Pittsburgh, and St. Louis thirty-seven each. The diversity of their industrial economy is illustrated in Table 8 (pages 112–113), which lists the leading industries in ten major cities.

Warner singled out two distinctive aspects of what he called the industrial metropolis: "its organization of most of the population into work groups and its widespread use of residential segregation." Both were also characteristic of the industrial city, but not to the same degree or on so grand a scale. In this sense the metropolis carried tendencies already present to their logical fulfillment.

The metropolis bore the stamp of an advanced industrial society. It was a highly specialized and distended social order in which every element of daily life had become more organized, commercialized, and depersonalized. Most metropolitan working people held jobs within some organization, whether it be a plant, corporation, department or other retail store, bank, government post, school, construction company, or business office. Corporate giantism was firmly entrenched in the metropolis, along with all the other great companies that catered to national markets.

The metropolis harbored a tremendous variety of business enterprises which were no longer confined to the downtown business district. As congestion and decay worsened in the inner city, plants, retail outlets, and business offices raced their employees to the suburbs in search of new homes. Just as electric power gave industry more flexibility of location, so did transportation innovations, especially the automobile, enable people to work in one place and live in another. The true sprawl of every metropolis was measured not only by its advancing city limits but also by its widening ring of "bedroom suburbs." Commuting became a way of life as each year more workers traveled greater distances to reach their jobs.

Suburbs were but one aspect of a broader pattern of residential segregation in the urban metropolis. Where people lived was determined largely by their income and their racial and ethnic origins. Since the inner city offered the cheapest and least desirable housing, it became a refuge for the poor, the unskilled, the elderly with modest means, and those held prisoner by racial or ethnic discrimination. Beyond these densely packed ghettos lay clusters of working-class and middle-class neighborhoods, and beyond them the more costly and roomy enclaves of the well-to-do.

While this outward progression from one income or ethnic group to the next was seldom direct or symmetrical, the isolation of each group from the others was fairly complete. Segregation fastened itself upon metropolitan life as much through a process of drift as by design. It was, in fact, a characteristic of the industrial city which was accelerated by the outward expansion of the metropolis. For most metropolitan dwellers, life revolved around an island community with its own schools, churches, stores, and social organizations. One suburban island was as remote from another as both were from the downtown ghettos or the aeries of the rich. Privacy and the amenities of a better life were achieved at the cost of extreme social separation. The sense of community became no less narrowly specialized than other aspects of urban life.

Every element of metropolitan living was organized on a more formal and impersonal basis. Standardization of goods, tastes, and styles advanced rapidly. Brand names knew no boundaries, and in that respect at least urban dwellers were truly metropolitan. They wore the same clothes, drove the same cars, ate the same foods, and used the same appliances. Pleasure, too, was prepackaged. For amusement they watched the same films, listened to the same radio shows, and cheered the same athletic teams. Politics still remained the property of urban machines which had long since turned government into a lucrative business. While community politics occasionally aroused interest and ignited passions—especially in matters of education, zoning, or taxes—the broader arena of metropolitan government was usually left to the professionals.

It should be apparent that the primary forces behind metropolitan growth were centrifugal and atomistic. Cities were spreading across ever greater areas. The larger they grew, the more insulated each of their sections became. Most people no longer lived near where they worked. More than that, their lives were becoming ever more compartmentalized and dependent upon sources outside the home for everything from sustenance to entertainment. Cut off from all but superficial contact with those different from themselves, they lost their sense of a larger community beyond the neighborhood. In this ironic fashion the metropolis developed its own strain of parochialism. The larger the city grew, the more restricted were the horizons of its inhabitants.

Not that the opportunities for cultivating a truly metropolitan outlook were lacking. Obviously the giant cities contained a diversity of peoples and possibilities not available to those who lived in small towns or rural communities. But metropolitan life simply was not arranged in such a way as to encourage people to explore experiences beyond their own bailiwick. Urban life offered enormous opportunities for individuals to expand their visions and enrich their lives, but they were exploited mostly in a marginal and haphazard fashion. For too many people, life in the metropolis turned out to be less an open door than an isolation booth.

TABLE 8

RANK OF 6 LEADING INDUSTRIES
OF 10 MAJOR CITIES IN 1900

CITY	1ST INDUSTRY	2ND INDUSTRY	3RD INDUSTRY	4TH INDUSTRY	5TH INDUSTRY	6TH INDUSTRY
New York (a)	Women's Clothing	Men's Clothing	Printing and Publishing (b)	Masonry, brick & stone	Tobacco Products	Wholesale Slaughtering
Chicago	Slaughtering & Meatpacking	Foundry & Machine Shop	Men's Clothing	Iron & Steel	Agricultural Implements	Railroad Cars
Philadelphia	Foundry & Machine Shop	Sugar & Molasses, Refining	Carpets & Rugs	Carpentering	Men's Clothing	Woolen Goods
Brooklyn	Sugar & Molasses, Refining	Foundry & Machine Shop	Coffee & Spices Roasting & Grinding	Malt Liquors	Bread & Bakery	Carpentering
St. Louis	Tobacco Products	Slaughtering & Meatpacking	Malt Liquors	Foundry & Machine Products	Carpentering	Boots & Shoes

	1	2	3	4	5	6
Boston	Sugar & Molasses, Refining	Printing & Publishing (b)	Foundry & Machine Shop	Men's Clothing	Book & Job Printing, Publishing	Malt Liquors
Pittsburgh	Iron & Steel	Foundry & Machine Shop	Electrical Apparatus & Supplies	Ornamental Ironwork	Carpentering	Malt Liquors
Baltimore	Men's Clothing	Canning & Preserving Fruits & Vegetables	Tobacco Products	Foundry & Machine Shop	Tin & Copper Smithing, Sheet-iron Ironworking	Slaughtering & Meatpacking
Cincinnati	Men's Clothing	Foundry & Machine Shop	Slaughtering & Meatpacking	Distilled Liquors	Boots & Shoes	Malt Liquors
Cleveland	Iron & Steel	Foundry & Machine Shop	Slaughtering & Meatpacking	Women's Clothing	Malt Liquors	Men's Clothing

NOTES: (a) Borough of Manhattan and Bronx only
(b) Newspapers and Periodicals
SOURCE: Same as Table 4

Clearly, in metropolitan America a new pattern of living was emerging based upon the realities of an age where organization and specialization reigned supreme. It is a pattern all too familiar to Americans who live or have lived in the modern city. Although that pattern came to full flower in the metropolis, its roots are embedded deep within the industrial city. To understand these roots and the hold they still have upon our lives today, we must explore the sources that nurtured them in more detail.

CHAPTER 4

The City as Marketplace

This town of ours labors under one peculiar disadvantage: it is the only great city in the world to which all its citizens have come for the one common, avowed object of making money. There you have its genesis, its growth, its end and object; and there are but few of us who are not attending to that object very strictly. In this Garden City of ours every man cultivates his own little bed and his neighbor his; but who looks after the paths between? They have become a kind of No Man's Land, and the weeds of a rank iniquity are fast choking them up. The thing to teach the public is this: that the general good is a different thing from the sum of the individual goods.

—Henry Blake Fuller
With the Procession (1895)

In the previous chapters, we have analyzed the basic factors of industrialization and examined their relationship to urbanization. The following chapters will survey in detail that stage of urban growth we have called the industrial city. Before doing so, however, we need to explore the character or spirit of the industrial city. Since these are intangible and therefore elusive qualities, any approach to them must be impressionistic. Even so, the "soul" of urban America is no less important than its material aspects and cannot be neglected simply because it is hard to get at. What follows, then, is an attempt to interpret the character of the industrial city.

The Ultimate Marketplace

As a stage of urban growth, the industrial city marked an important departure from its predecessor. For one thing, it represented a distinct break with the tradition of city or town as community. As towns grew into cities, their sense of community withered. Growth radically altered social and geographical relationships, stretching the community's ability to maintain close and enduring personal ties beyond its capacity. It quickened the pace of change and thereby destroyed the sense of stability and continuity vital to an ongoing community. The industrial city was larger, faster, and more impersonal; its institutions were more specialized, its population more mobile and less stable, its social contacts narrower. From this cauldron of urban change emerged nothing less than a full-blown market economy which in turn spawned a full-blown market society.* The industrial city became the ultimate marketplace where relationships of every type, noneconomic as well as economic, were reduced to a transactional basis. For that reason it is an ideal laboratory for examining the strengths and weaknesses of the market society.

What made the industrial city so perfect a microcosm of the market society? Obviously part of the answer lies in the close relationship between industrialization and urbanization. By 1900 cities had become the heart of industrial society. Within their relatively compact confines could be observed all the factors of the industrial process interacting with and reinforcing one another. Given the intimacy of this relationship, it is hardly surprising that the industrial process tended to mold cities in its own image.

Part of the answer, too, has to do with the effects of growth. As the industrial system expanded, so did the size and number of its cities. For both, the impact of growth was qualitative as well as quantitative. It subsumed social relationships to economic considerations, to a point where the social were virtually trampled underfoot by the economic. While all cities are both social and economic entities, it is the relationship between the two aspects that is crucial. American cities have always been centers of important economic activities, but in the industrial era the balance shifted even further in that direction.

This is why we have defined the stages of urban growth primarily in economic terms. Especially during the industrial era did the forces of economic development shape the growth of cities. In bald terms, people came to the industrial city to make money. That single fact overrode all other considerations and probably does more to explain the essence of urban growth than any other factor.

Money lay at the heart of the matter even when urbanites expressed their ambitions in other terms. Some may have come to the city to taste

---

* To recall the nature of the market system and its role in the process of industrialization, see the discussion in Chapter 1.

adventure or sample its unique pleasures, but adventure and pleasure cost money. Others with loftier visions sought fame or power or glory, but in urban America these required fortune as a starting point. Whatever their dreams or urgings, newcomers to the city quickly learned that the task of earning a livelihood took priority over everything else. The well-to-do sought vast undertakings, the impecunious greenhorns a bare living. In the market economy, money was king. It was the fuel of ambition and the yardstick of success in any endeavor.

The industrial city became the ultimate marketplace because everything was for sale there and anything could be had for a price. Not only its economy, but also its society and its culture, were organized around the dollar sign. Its inhabitants measured not only the business acumen of their peers but also their human worth by their financial assets. In the industrial city every person was both producer and market and little else to anyone beyond the circle of his immediate family and friends.

Size and impersonality were not so much "causes" of this new order as reflections of it. While urban growth naturally rendered relationships of all kinds more impersonal, it did not automatically put them on a market or transactional basis. There were several possible ways in which a city might have cast its relationships, ordered its values, and organized its internal affairs. But if the possibilities seem limitless in theory, they were in reality limited by the historical setting in which they evolved. Since history never operates in a vacuum, we must look not only at the industrial city itself but also at the traditions and institutions that gave rise to it.

Much of the latter has already been discussed and needs only to be tied more specifically to the industrial city. Within the complex urban organism, specialization and impersonality emerged as the chief characteristics. All economic activity was organized around what Adam Smith called the "propensity to barter, truck and exchange one thing for another." Labor was bought and sold like any other commodity in transactions stripped of social obligations. Land was commercialized in a variety of new ways and put to work by the highest or cleverest bidder for its services.

Elaborate mechanisms and institutions were devised to expedite the process of exchange itself. Money and credit, in all their many forms, became a business to which large numbers of men and organizations devoted their entire attention. The apparatus of banking and finance assumed an elephantine scale and Byzantine complexity, as did the stock and commodity exchanges which sprang up in several major cities. Although the New York Stock Exchange dominated trading in stocks and the Chicago Board of Trade that in commodities, they never had a monopoly. By 1900 there were twelve regional and numerous local stock exchanges and no less a variety of commodity exchanges. Insurance companies also became an important source of investment funds. The awesome power commanded by these financial institutions rested firmly upon the base of a maturing market economy centered in the cities.

Within these cities the market system extended beyond economic matters into every aspect of urban life. In small communities where relationships were not yet so impersonal and transactional, citizens furnished a variety of necessary services, ranging from political leadership to police and fire protection, on a relatively informal and often voluntary basis. Real power usually belonged to a controlling elite who administered it in a personal, casual manner. Within these communities, economic, political, and social power were inseparable; they tended to belong to the same group.

The size and complexity of the industrial city demanded a more formal and permanent arrangement. Growth destroyed both the small town's narrow leadership base and its unity of purpose. In a sense, every urban dweller became a specialist peddling his skills. Workers sold their labor and lawyers their acumen; politicians bought votes and sold influence; city governments collected taxes and dispensed social services; newspapers sold information, teachers education, and revivalists salvation. Every person, whether doctor or drummer, policeman or prostitute, banker or barker, found his livelihood, his pleasures, and his possessions in the marketplace.

Within the urban job market, the possibilities seemed limitless. Opportunity beckoned to the unskilled greenhorn no less than to the talented professional or eager speculator. The whole range of urban services—police, fire, sanitation, utilities—evolved into formal professions out of necessity. Pleasure and entertainment, too, developed their own professionals and formal establishments. For the price of admission one might attend a concert, recital, lecture, play, vaudeville show, nickelodeon, dance hall, amusement park, or any number of other pleasure palaces. One could buy or rent another person for simple companionship or sexual gratification. The variety of personal services for sale in most industrial cities often surprised even the jaded urban roué and positively benumbed raw newcomers.

Even the legendary comforts of home and hearth had their substitutes or at least imitations in the city. For the large transit or floating population there were institutions which furnished (for a price) food, lodging, and sometimes even a semblance of companionship or fellow-

ship. These included hotels, restaurants, boardinghouses, YMCA's, social clubs, missions, and flophouses. Their quality varied from plush
grandeur to filthy hovel, according to their clientele's ability to pay.

These facilities were, for Americans in motion or simply adrift, a home
away from home or a home in lieu of a home. They were hired substitutes for what roots and family and sense of place once provided.
Their very impersonality suited those who wished amenities without
entanglements. But these establishments could not satisfy the urge for
more than a place to eat or sleep and some casual companionship. To
the lonely, they offered shelter but seldom comfort. And most bore a distinct air of unreality. Their society was gay but artificial, as if it were
suspended in time and detached from the harsher world outside with
all its pressing cares. This was especially true of hotels, the most elegant
and fanciful way stations of a transient people. No one understood this
better than Henry James, the expatriate novelist whose sensibilities were
alternately jarred and bewitched by the customs and antics of his country-
men. In *The American Scene* (1907) James mused upon the "hotel-
spirit":

. . . you are in presence of a revelation of the possibilities of the hotel—for
which the American spirit has found so unprecedented a use and a value;
leading it on to express so a social, indeed positively an aesthetic ideal, and
making it so, at this supreme pitch, a synonym for civilization, for the capture
of conceived manners themselves, that one is verily tempted to ask if the
hotel-spirit may not just *be* the American spirit most seeking and most
finding itself. . . .

There are endless things in "Europe," to your vision, behind and beyond
the hotel, a multitudinous complicated life; in the States, on the other hand,
you see the hotel as itself that life, as constituting for vast numbers of people
the richest form of existence.

No aspect of urban life escaped the magnetic pull of the marketplace,
and few resisted the tug toward specialization and impersonality. Well
before 1920 the city had become for many Americans not only an alien
place but a place of alienation. Few urbanites, let alone rural dwellers,
could comprehend that peculiar paradox whereby the crowding together
of people in one small area produced not familiarity but anonymity; not
intimacy but estrangement; not mutual cooperation but conflict. Through
this weird social alchemy, the city provoked a mixed reaction; like most
things alien, it both fascinated and repelled. In time Americans would
seize upon it as an emotion-charged symbol for modernism in all its many
and conflicting facets.

Above all, the industrial city became the ultimate marketplace because it developed entirely within the individualist tradition. Its destiny, character, organization—even its very face, like that of America itself— was shaped not by rational planning or unified purpose but by the process of drift and default. Its history was no well-wrought story but the accumulation of countless private sagas of individuals eager to advance their personal interests and unconcerned with the larger consequences of their actions.

In urban America even more than the nation at large, power gravitated to the private sector. All the important decisions were made there. Public policy was either emasculated or harnessed to the private engines of politicians and their henchmen. Municipal and state governments, infested with corruption and graft, could do little to promote the general welfare or ameliorate the harsher aspects of urban society. In most cities, the "best people" fled public service in disgust or floundered uncomfortably among enlarged constituencies they no longer knew or understood. Their replacements, disciples of the new order in urban politics, knew little of genteel integrity but were well schooled in the art of accommodation. Large numbers of public servants served no public but the special interests that installed them in office or purchased their services.

The result was predictable. There developed that separation of power and responsibility which characterized the larger society. Power accrued in the private sector where those wielding it bore no responsibility to anyone or anything but themselves and their clients. Local government, the traditional repository of social responsibility, was usurped by vested interests and made to serve those who could and would pay for what they wanted.

Once government was reduced to simply another business, an adjunct of the private sector, the triumph of the market society was assured. Real power resided in private hands which used it almost exclusively for economic purposes. Local government abdicated any semblance of broad social responsibility, which fell by default to private organizations and charities ill-equipped to handle so great a burden. Neither law nor the political process exercised any effective restraint upon individual action, becoming instead commodities to be bought and sold by those requiring them as vehicles to further their schemes.

Freed from the shackles of law and custom, enterprising men poured their energies into the quest for profit. This release of individual ambition took priority over all other needs in the industrial city. Social questions, the quality of life itself, were left to one's own resources. Freedom proved to be a two-edged sword: men were liberated not only from the restraints of strong public policy, but also from its protection. To most men, the advantages of the first far outweighed the hazards of the second. In their pursuit of fortune they were willing to risk everything, and their dedication to this task was both impressive and all-absorbing. "I do not love the money," Philip D. Armour, the meatpacking magnate, exclaimed. "What I do love is the getting of it. . . . What other interest can you suggest to me? I do not read. I do not take part in politics. What can I do?"

This Hallowed Ground

Land has both a social and an economic function, as do the buildings put upon it. Rarely can a given parcel of land fulfill both functions, since using it for one purpose usually precludes using it for another. To exploit land for economic gain means to deprive it of any social function, as a park or forest or wilderness or just plain scenery. In a crude sense, then, every society must choose how much of its land is to be used as an economic resource and how much as a social resource. The decisions may not be conscious or planned, but in the end the land gets put to one use or another. What results is both a historical pattern of land use and an insight into the society's hierarchy of values.

Of course, the matter is by no means this simple. Much depends upon the amount of land available to the society; much, too, depends upon who owns it or has access to it and can therefore decide what shall be done with it. Even the question of power goes beyond mere ownership to the way in which land is conceived. Is land to be regarded in narrow terms as simply property, or in broader terms as a social resource? The answer to this question may well determine not only who may own land, but also what they may do with it. Obviously the first approach conceives of land primarily in economic terms, and the second primarily in social terms.

With minor exceptions, the American response to this question has always followed the first approach. From the earliest colonial days, the private ownership of land was regarded as an individual right, one which lay at the heart of the passion for freedom and independence. In an agricultural society land was both home and livelihood to an individual. Possession of it freed him from dependence upon or obligations to those of higher rank or station. For these reasons, the New World was settled on the basis of private individual ownership. Every attempt to organize settlements along other lines—most of them feudal in origin—failed miserably. Even in the colonial era, individual ownership of land became indelibly associated with personal freedom. The rights of private property assumed the status of a civil liberty no less revered than those pertaining to freedom of speech, worship, or assembly. Most of the lingering vestiges of feudal custom were swept away by the American Revolution.

What made all this possible of course was the abundance of land in America. This vast domain enabled Americans to base land ownership upon the fee-simple principle whereby land was bought or sold or rented for cash or goods, with no further obligations or services other than to pay taxes upon it. After the Revolution, Americans planted the fee-simple principle firmly into law. Both the Northwest Ordinance and the Constitution adopted it as the basis by which all lands west of the Allegheny Mountains would be disposed of. There would be no feudal estates in America.

These distant events largely fixed the destiny of land ownership and use in America. The principle of fee-simple tenure enabled men to buy, sell, rent, and bequeath land with great ease and a minimum of interference. To operate successfully, it had to restrict the extent to which public agencies could step between a man and his property. For the most part, then, government land policy concentrated mainly upon finding the most equitable procedures for releasing land into the hands of private citizens. And once having delivered land into private hands, government was not likely to interfere with it again except under the most compelling of circumstances.

All this guaranteed that Americans would have, in Sam Bass Warner's words, "the freest land system anywhere in the world." It also insured that each individual would decide the use to which his land would be put. In effect, land came to be conceived of not only as property but as *private* property. The contrary notion of land as a social resource weakened steadily until it came to be defined largely in private and individual terms. So long as land remained plentiful, the socially harmful effects of individual land use were ignored or played down. When public and private interests clashed, the law tended to protect individual property rights above nearly all other considerations. This narrow partiality betrayed not a class bias so much as the fervent belief of Americans in the principle of private property as a mainstay of their social system.

The American approach to land had another fateful consequence: it released most land to the free play of the market. All one needed to obtain land was money, which meant that those with capital got most of the land and the best of it. Land speculation became a national mania that has never lost its grip upon Americans. Every historian of the westward movement acknowledges the pivotal role played by speculators who bought huge tracts of land and sold them off slowly to profit from rising land values. Often speculators dominated the political and financial life of the regions they purchased. Their influence went beyond local boundaries; it is likely that the lion's share of American fortunes in the early nineteenth century were grounded in land and real estate speculation.

What has all this to do with the industrial city? It forms the tradition within which urban America was settled and organized. Like many other traditions, the American approach to land use passed unchanged from the preindustrial into the industrial era. But industrialization and urbanization worked strange wonders upon the hoary practices of the past. Land in the city turned out to be quite a different thing from land in the country, and its uses soon disclosed a horde of anomalies and anachronisms.

The land question illuminated yet another aspect of the city as ultimate marketplace. Traditional policy assumed an abundance of land, but this premise evaporated in the heat of urban development. There might be plenty of land in and about the city, but location became quite as important as quantity. In most urban industrial centers the general principle held sway that the nearer land was to the center of town, the more valuable it was. Distance meant increased travel costs, transportation and communication delays, lost time, and other complications. As a result, urban land acquired a curious aura of scarcity: there might be plenty of land around, but only a limited amount in the right place. Since every city possessed only a given quantity of "prime" land, the competition for it was apt to be savage.

From this condition flowed an inexorable chain of consequences which ultimately shaped the physical arena of the industrial city. Given the scarcity of prime land, it could not easily be used for both economic and social purposes. Agricultural America avoided the worst dilemmas posed by this conflict through sheer quantity of land and wide dispersal of settlement. A nation of relatively self-sufficient farmers required few public facilities and had ample land for social needs. Even small towns and commercial cities were not large enough for the space problem to reach crisis proportions.

But in the industrial city conflict ran rampant. Land sought by industrialists for factories or offices could not be set aside for parks or schools. Waterfront properties might offer gorgeous scenery and lovely settings for public or private facilities, but they were also demanded for wharves, refineries, warehouses, and other facilities requiring access to water travel. Wide boulevards and landscaped arcades might expedite the flow of traffic and render the urban scene more pleasant and attractive, but they consumed valuable ground coveted by railroads, manufacturers, retailers, and real estate speculators. The simple necessities of light and air could be obtained only through a judicious use of space, but space was precisely the commodity most in demand within the city. Like parks or boulevards, light and air produced no income; they were social amenities to be shared by all the city's inhabitants. Only government could provide them by setting aside land for just such purposes and by regulating the uses made of land in private hands. But that course of action ran contrary to traditional land practices. Where land was left to the whim of the marketplace—and that was everywhere—investors quickly snatched up the prime real estate for their own purposes.

Municipal governments were slow to grasp the notion that they had a vital role to play in the use of land. Even when the light finally dawned, knowledge was not power. The most vigorous city officials found it difficult to assert the primacy of public interest over the ancient rights of individual property owners. And the truth was that in most cities vested interests of all kinds dominated municipal governments. Businessmen could usually get the favorable legislation or services they required if they had the money to pay for it.

The outcome for most cities was a common pattern of land use that favored economic development at the expense of almost everything else. Once again it was the market mechanism that organized the process. Where land was available to the highest bidder, it went to those economic interests best equipped to exploit it. As the city grew, the demand for prime downtown land intensified. Land values soared until only larger interests could afford the price; small proprietors and residents fled to cheaper land around the urban core. In short order, the downtown area of most industrial cities evolved into specialized business districts dominated by offices, banks, hotels, restaurants, theaters, and retail establishments.

The conversion of downtown areas into specialized business districts flowed naturally from the practice of determining patterns of land use by the free play of the market. But the same economic forces imposed a like pattern of rigid segregation upon the rest of the city as well. Neighborhood segregation was, after all, merely a form of specialization by area. As people and businesses found land that suited their needs and means, there arose a variety of uniform districts. Industrial, factory, warehouse, mill, refinery, and waterfront sectors encircled the central business district along with clusters of residential neighborhoods that included inner city ghettos, lower-class tenements, lower-middle-class homes, tidy middle-class houses, and spacious upper-class manors.

With surprising speed, most industrial cities developed along the lines of what has been called the sector and ring pattern. Most business activities concentrated into narrow sectors that pushed out along steadily widening lines from the city's inner core, while residential sections circled the central city in large uneven rings, segregated from one another by class and ethnicity. In retrospect, the sector-and-ring pattern has a logical and systematic appearance which obscures the fact that it arose not by planning but by accretion. It emerged not from the drawing board but from the market, the product of decisions made and actions taken by thousands of individuals seeking nothing more than to fulfill their own private interests. Once the basic pattern was fashioned, however, it could not easily be undone. It imposed a structure upon urban life and shaped the city's inner dynamics as surely as if it had come from some grand blueprint.

Growth merely reinforced this pattern and enlarged the scale upon which it operated. Industrial cities experienced similar cycles of expansion because they were influenced by the same kinds of forces. The basic cycle was that familiar pattern of interaction mentioned earlier. As large numbers of people poured into a given area, the demand for water, gas, electricity, and other services soared. More transportation arteries were routed into the area to move people and goods. As general facilities improved, more businesses streamed in to take advantage of them. Congestion increased to the point of overtaxing available land and facilities.

The process did not always follow this exact pattern. Sometimes the population arrived ahead of the facilities, and sometimes facilities were installed to lure customers. In either case, facilities and services cost money. They were paid for through higher taxes if public agencies furnished them, or through service charges if private companies provided them. Higher costs caused land values to soar, which in turn drove out those unable to afford the expense of maintaining a business or residence on this rising scale. Those who remained responded by finding ways to exploit the land at their disposal more intensively. As we shall see, this usually meant the construction of larger and higher buildings to produce a greater return. For businesses the result was an outcrop of skyscrapers; for residences, a profusion of apartment buildings and tenements.

As the cycle progressed, prime downtown land was surrendered entirely to business or industry or tenements. Eventually, however, these

activities spread outward to nearby residential neighborhoods where
the cycle repeated its inexorable course. Single-dwelling neighborhoods,
overrun by rising land values and soaring costs, were converted into
multi-family units or were replaced by factories or warehouses or loft
manufacturing. Their less affluent inhabitants were shoved into other,
often cheaper neighborhoods while the middle class and well-to-do fled to
more distant havens where land was still relatively cheap and such
amenities as air, light, grass, trees, and fresh water were still available.

The sheer momentum of this cycle did much to shape the pattern of
rigid urban segregation. After 1900 the rise of zoning ordinances helped
ossify the patterns that had already been established. Zoning traced its
origins to two diverse sources: the desire of Californians to keep the
Chinese penned up in their own neighborhoods and the fear of New
Yorkers that multi-storied buildings would destroy traditional land-use
patterns. In both cases, the central thrust was to preserve the existing
character of neighborhoods. New York's experience proved to be the
more influential, for it produced the New York Zoning Law of 1916,
which became a model for similar statutes adopted by hundreds of cities.

Zoning was conceived as an instrument for preventing unscrupulous
speculators or real estate operators from destroying the integrity of a
neighborhood by acquiring parcels of land within it and using them for
whatever function would fetch the greatest profit. Thus a factory might
be plunked down in a residential area, or multi-family units within a
neighborhood of single dwellings, or "undesirable" races or ethnic groups
invited into an area where the residents resented their presence. To
prevent these conflicts, most zoning laws divided the city's private land
into numerous areas or zones. The landowners in each zone were in
effect empowered to determine what could go into their neighborhood
and on what terms. This was done by listing specific restrictions within
each zone for such things as the height and size of all buildings, the
number of floors they might have, the uses to which they might be put,
the minimum size of lots and the amount of each lot that the building
might occupy, the amount of open space, and the number of people
that might inhabit the building.

At first glance, the early zoning ordinances appeared successful in
preventing the worst abuses of predatory real estate operators. But they
did so at the terrific social cost of confirming patterns of segregation and
imposing uniformity upon neighborhoods not only at the time, but for
generations to come. That was precisely their intent, but the property
owners who turned so eagerly to zoning never anticipated the broader
social ramifications of their actions. As Warner observed, "the rationale

of zoning was aimed not at disturbing existing conditions but at projecting current trends into the future and perpetuating them."

In this manner the industrial city was fashioned. Its contours and inner structure were left to the caprice of the market where, as usual, victory went to the biggest battalions. Those who forged its geography and its functions were motivated by the quest for profit rather than the desire to create a decent place in which to live. The industrial city was a creature of economic forces because it reflected the aspirations of its authors. As private individuals, they bore no responsibility for anything beyond themselves. If their economic enterprises made the city a hellhole in which to live, they discovered early that men of means could escape its ugliness and unpleasantness by living somewhere else. For them, as for large companies, the city became less a home than a home base.

The City as Buildings

The same forces that shaped the uses made of land also determined what was put upon it. Since those forces were overwhelmingly economic rather than social, the industrial city tended to be a commercial success and an architectural disaster. Its face wore a dull, drab expression of uniformity seldom relieved by charm or distinction, the natural result of having been sculpted by businessmen instead of artists. Everywhere the aesthetics of the urban landscape, both in its buildings and in its layout, owed more to the cash register than it did to taste or imagination.

To some extent, tradition bore a share of the blame. The federal survey system, established in 1785, had a profound influence upon the mapping of nearly all the territory west of the Allegheny Mountains. In particular, the survey conceived of townships as square plots of land six miles long on each side subdivided into 36 square-mile lots or sections each containing 640 acres. From this tidy system emerged the grid pattern that organized the physical arrangement of most American cities and towns. To the surveyor, the grid pattern produced a logical and orderly layout; to the eye, it produced an eternity of unbroken squares and rectangles which made one town indistinguishable from another.

This drab uniformity imposed by the grid pattern led Lord James Bryce, after visiting numerous American towns, to complain that "their monotony haunts one like a nightmare." Nearly every town had its town square and its unending procession of streets bordered by rows of shade trees met at right angles by other streets. Since buildings and houses lined both sides of most streets, the visual effect was a "tunnel" to the distant horizon. Most streets of most towns and even many cities shared this pattern, which rendered one street visually indistinguishable from another in the same or different towns. Even in larger cities, where buildings soared to great heights, there were few interruptions to sight lines down the canyon between the buildings.

The influence of the grid pattern went even further. If it was logical to organize a township in terms of squares, it was no less logical to sub-divide the sections into squares or rectangles. As towns grew into cities, the pressures mounted to partition land into regular-sized units con-venient for selling and reselling. From this crossbreeding of tradition with economic need emerged the standard-sized lot, a piece of ground of uniform size, usually 20 or 25 feet wide and 100 feet deep. Despite the rapidity with which the standard-sized lot became the dominant land unit in urban America, it was less an offspring than a mutant. In the words of Lewis Mumford, "The rectangular parceling of ground pro-moted speculation in land-units and the ready interchange of real property: it had no relation whatever to the essential purposes for which a city exists."

That position is not entirely correct. The adoption of standard lots was in fact another illustration of the extent to which economic forces were the primary considerations behind the American city's existence. Here, too, the market reigned supreme. The grid system imposed a uni-formity upon urban land that ignored both the peculiar contours of the terrain and the diversity of uses to which land might be put. Nature had not based its designs upon a blueprint limited only to squares and rectangles; nor had human activities, economic or otherwise, evolved within so limited a geometry. Nevertheless, in urban America, the pre-vailing grid system with its standard-sized components dictated that most structures and functions proceed within these restricted physical dimensions.

In retrospect, the consequences seem as inevitable as they were un-fortunate. As urban land values soared and property owners sought maximum profits from minimum investment, the temptation to exploit every inch of ground proved irresistible. Businessmen or speculators snatched up land needed for social purposes—be they parks, playgrounds, or sheer breathing space—and utilized it for income-producing enter-prises. To insure the greatest possible return, most of them erected struc-tures that covered all the land at their disposal. Within every industrial city block after block filled up with unbroken rows of stores, offices, businesses, brownstones, and tenements. Even single-family residences were constructed from uniform designs upon uniform lots to expedite quick sale and turnover.

This hunger for profit overran nearly every effort at intelligent land use or long-range planning. Since the dimensions of any building had to conform to the size of the lot on which it was placed, the uniformity of standard lots impelled a certain uniformity of architecture. To this was added the economic pressure of erecting buildings as cheaply as possible. It was, of course, within the power of architects and owners to design buildings even for standard lots that differed strikingly from one another. All that was needed was the willingness to invest the time, money, and imagination to produce variety, distinction, and a pleasing aesthetic effect. But such efforts were expensive, and neither variety nor aesthetic effects brought financial returns.

"With five or six exceptions," complained Lord Bryce, "American cities differ from one another only herein that some of them are built more with brick than with wood, and others more with wood than with brick. In all else they are alike, great and small." That harsh judgment fit most industrial cities only too well. Each had its straight and narrow streets flanked by unbroken rows of offices, shops, and stores; its tenements and apartments which formed solid walls down both sides of the streets; its small private dwellings with postage-stamp lawns, tiny rear yards, and narrow side ways. Seldom did variety, in the form of a park or playground or open space—or simply a curved avenue or irregular street pattern—intrude upon the monotony of the grid pattern and its unexceptional structures.

Why the wholesale failure of American architecture in the age of the industrial city? The answer lies in a peculiar combination of drift and design. Neither architects nor their clients showed much interest in seeking new forms that would capture and express the business culture of industrial America. Both, in fact, went entirely in the opposite direction: they tried to conceal the vitality of that culture by cloaking its structures in styles borrowed from ancient and medieval history which were wholly at odds with the actual function or purpose of the building.

The result was a bizarre procession of structures in which form either ignored function or parodied it: railroad stations disguised as Gothic cathedrals, banks as Greek temples, and commercial buildings as medieval fortresses. Even the homes of the rich were cast in overblown imitations of French chateaus, Italian villas, or English country manors. Every era of history was ransacked to supply forms and tastes for an age apparently helpless to create its own.

For the client, this failure was largely a matter of economy, lack of taste and imagination, and indifference. The architect's shortcomings went much deeper. With few exceptions, American architects either missed the spirit of their age or cringed from its boundless energy and rampant materialism. Where entrepreneurs overflowed with imagination and daring, architects seemed timid and uncertain. Repulsed by the vulgarity of the industrial city and unnerved by the constant turmoil of change it embodied, they retreated behind a belief that American society was too young and too plastic to possess a tradition and character of its own, and must therefore draw its inspiration from other times and other places. This inability to come to terms with urban industrial society plagued American artists in general. In *The Architecture of America,* Albert Bush-Brown and John Burchard observed:

> No American musician . . . no significant painter had yet seen the beauty in technology and industry and their potentials for humanity. The question for architecture was whether it too might have a Whitman. No influential architect was prepared for the role; nor did society clamor that any one should essay the part.

Technology opened up a vast array of fresh possibilities for architects. A bare list of innovations prior to 1900 would include structural steel, new foundation techniques, electricity, elevators, extensive use of glass, fireproofing, plumbing, and the various communications devices. All these offered new dimensions of freedom in design and structure, but their implications fell upon barren ground. Few American architects displayed the imagination to grasp their import or the courage to explore their revolutionary potential.

Of the major figures, only two broke significantly with the past. Henry H. Richardson drove his extraordinary talents from their mooring in conventional forms to a brief frenzy of pioneering that culminated with a dazzling masterpiece, the Marshall Field wholesale warehouse in Chicago. But Richardson died in 1886 at the age of forty-eight, cut down at the height of his powers. And there was Louis Sullivan, a stubborn, erratic genius who pointed the way to a new era in architecture. Through his writings and a series of startlingly original buildings, Sullivan tried to jar his peers out of their complacency. He left an impressive legacy, not the least of which was his influence upon Frank Lloyd Wright. But among his fellow architects, Sullivan was more admired than copied. He died a bitter man, alone and impoverished, while his peers prospered through their clever imitations of antiquity.

Ultimately most architects shrank from all the vital elements of the new era. They distrusted the new technology and held even less esteem for engineers and engineering. Instead of flocking to new techniques, they either shunned them or tried to disguise what use they did make of them. Steel frames, for example, freed architects from the necessity of massive pillars for carrying weight. Their use not only permitted much higher buildings, but also radicalized design by using stone or brick to form curtain walls and help fireproof the metal instead of serving as heavy support bases. Engineers jumped at the new idea, but architects held back. Except for Sullivan and a few others, most architects employed steel frames to create taller buildings, but continued to encase them in heavy concrete settings. Through this device they managed to make the new look very much like the old.

So, too, with electricity. Artificial light opened a world of new possibilities for both interior and exterior design which few architects bothered to explore. If anything, they regarded technological innovations as conveniences at best and positive nuisances which intruded upon aesthetic considerations at worst. "That's all a building is nowadays," cried an architect in Henry Blake Fuller's *The Cliffdwellers* (1893), "one mass of pipes, pulleys, wires, tubes, shafts, chutes, and what not, running through an iron cage of from fourteen to twenty stages. Then the artist comes along and is asked to apply the architecture by festooning on a lot of tile, brick, and terra-cotta."

For the most part, architects considered themselves tastemakers for a culture that lacked a suitable style or spirit of its own. To fill that void they looked to Europe, for if nothing else, Europe had a surplus of history and tradition. Imitation Gothic was the first fruit of this craze for cultural cross-pollination. Applied first to educational and religious edifices, it was soon extended to banks, office buildings, and railroad stations, and reached its apogee with the Woolworth Building in New York.

Alongside the Gothic wave went a revival in Renaissance forms. While Renaissance styles were especially prized for the palatial residences of the rich, they were also applied to commercial buildings with incongruous results. Classical Greek styles also dominated the work of several influential architects. The fabulous "White City" of Chicago's Columbian Exposition in 1893, which drew huge crowds from all over the nation to gawk at its splendors, stood as the grandest monument to the classical school's devotion to antiquity.

The problem went beyond the conviction that industrial America had no spirit or character worthy of its own style. Many architects displayed little interest in the types of buildings that dominated the industrial scene or organized urban life. "The significant generalization about American architecture of 1860–1885," concluded Bush-Brown and Burchard, "is that the most needed building types of the period, that is, the factory and its supporting housing, were excluded from architecture altogether." On the whole, the same generalization may be extended to the era between 1885 and 1920.

Nor was this failing confined to factories and housing; it embraced most other kinds of structures as well as amenities like parks and playgrounds, which served no economic function. The urban landscape was conspicuous for what it lacked as well as for what it contained. Fountains, for example, abounded in European cities but were absent from most American cities. Their presence broke the monotony of urban thoroughfares, gave a pleasing aesthetic effect, and offered urbanites a respite from the city's incessant bustle and noise. A 1901 editorial in *Scribner's Magazine,* calling upon "beneficent societies" to undertake a program of fountains, asked, "why go on building miles of stone thoroughfares in our great towns without so much as a spray of water, in any part of them, to make rainbows in the sun, and to cause our spirits to take wings a little at the sight?"

The answer was, of course, that fountains produced no return and therefore held no interest for private investors. Such amenities were provided only if private groups or individual philanthropists (often dubbed rich eccentrics) waged a determined crusade for them. Even if municipal government threw its weight behind a campaign, the outcome remained in doubt. Amenities required precious land and invariably aroused the opposition of real estate operators or other private interests who wanted the area for their own uses. Parks, too, encountered the same pressures. Kansas City managed to construct an elaborate system of parks and boulevards which covered about 45 miles of avenues and 2,100 acres of parkland. The system cost about $10,000,000 and was paid for by assessments against adjoining properties. This approach succeeded because the open space increased property values. As George Kessler, the city's landscape architect, explained, "It was found that wherever parks and boulevards were established, the character of the neighborhoods at once improved."

But the Kansas City approach was not applied in many other places. So long as the private market governed the disposal of land and the kinds of buildings put upon it, both remained firmly in the hands of economic interests. The businessman was concerned with return on investment, and he wanted an architecture consistent with that purpose. On that score architects served him only too well. The vast majority of buildings in industrial cities occupied as much vertical and horizontal space as possible with little concern for style or order of living or working conditions. That is why so much of the city's face seemed, then and now, nondescript and jumbled, as if everything had been piled up and thrown together.

Design played a larger role in major buildings, but here, too, its purpose was economic rather than aesthetic. Most skyscrapers were essentially giant commercials, designed to symbolize the power and wealth of their occupants and to attract new customers. Banks needed to appear solid, stores open and attractive, offices formidable, hotels luxurious, and theaters exotic. For such purposes, radical or experimental designs would not do. The image of a building had to fit existing expectations; anything else amounted to an expensive gamble in re-educating public tastes. In short, a major commercial building had to attract attention without inviting ridicule. Obviously this was a severe limitation upon those architects whose vision and imagination outran the conventional wisdom. It helps explain why men like Louis Sullivan and Frank Lloyd Wright found it difficult to get major commissions.

Similar thinking carried over into housing. Since housing was a function of the market (i.e., people bought the type and amount of housing they could afford), it also served as a barometer of class status and tastes. Most residences, be they tenements or mansions, advertised the economic and social standing of their inhabitants. For the lower and middle classes, this fact, coupled with the desire of developers to turn out a maximum of product at minimum cost, resulted in neighborhood after neighborhood filled with uniform and unimaginative housing. The modern plat house or "ticky-tack" has strong roots in the early industrial city. Then as now, people bought houses because they were like houses owned by other people, and differences in detail seldom obscured their general sameness.

Not even the rich escaped this fate. They spent far more money and built on more lavish a scale. Often they went to great lengths to outdo one another in grandeur or distinction of design. But the mansions of the rich were seldom original. Like commercial buildings, most of them were derived from European models, but on an oversized scale that caricatured the model. Usually they combined styles, tastes, furnishings, and details from so many sources and periods as to resemble nothing of the originals so much as some unidentifiable mélange. In this manner, every mansion achieved the originality of a picture puzzle with all its pieces put together in the wrong way.

The great mansions were not intended to be lived in so much as to be shown off. They were spectacular advertisements for affluence in which taste was coined not in style or comfort but in the sheer weight of contrived magnificence. Their thick walls became garish storehouses for the priceless treasures of Europe. Paintings, tapestries, furniture, carvings, pedestals, implements, musical instruments, fireplaces—sometimes whole rooms or buildings—were carted off from France or Italy to be reinstalled in Newport or New York or some other fashionable spot. Perhaps nothing expressed the confusion and pretensions of the era so well as the huge "summer cottages" built in Newport at a cost of millions of dollars by people who occupied them only a few weeks each year.

In the end, American architects achieved little rapport with industrial urban society. Even the most advanced practitioners showed little interest in the city's social problems. The slum, the tenement, the factory, the choking congestion of downtown—all these remained outside their attention as well as beyond their power. The face of urban America became an ugly blight not through conspiracy but through indifference, and the accretion of thousands of decisions made by private individuals who had other things in mind.

The principle upon which Louis Sullivan hoped to base a distinctly American style of architecture was embodied in the oversimple expression that form must follow function. The reality of urban America, underlying the buildings which filled its landscape, betrayed a somewhat different and harsher truth: form followed the marketplace.

The City as Arena

The metaphors of the industrial city are those of speed and action, noise and violence. Every account depicts it as a place of extraordinary energy and vigor. In this fact rests the primary explanation for the widening gulf between urban and rural America. Industrialization accelerated the rate of social change, and its driving forces were centered in the city. There was nothing tranquil or static about the urban landscape; it was constantly in motion, a relentless engine of change. To feel its power we must turn to the novelists, a whole generation of whom were fascinated or repelled by the city's dynamism. Here is a description of Chicago taken from *The Pit* (1903) by Frank Norris:

The Great Grey City, brooking no rivals, imposed its dominion upon a reach of country larger than many a kingdom of the Old World. For thousands of miles beyond its confines was its influence felt. Out, far out, far away in the snow and shadow of Northern Wisconsin forests, axes and saws bit the barks of century-old trees, stimulated by this city's energy. Just as far to the southward pick and drill leaped to the assault of veins of anthracite, moved by her central power. Her force turned the wheels of harvester and seeder a thousand miles distant in Iowa and Kansas. Her force spun the screws and propellers of innumerable squadrons of lake steamers crowding the Sault Sainte Marie. For her and because of her the Central States, all the Great Northwest roared with traffic and industry; sawmills screamed; factories, their smoke blackening the sky, clashed and flamed; wheels turned, pistons leaped in their cylinders; cog gripped cog; beltings clasped the drums of mammoth wheels; and converters of forges belched into the clouded sky their tempest breath of molten steel.

What fueled these mighty engines? The visions and aspirations of thousands of men seeking opportunities and fortunes. American individualism found its ultimate expression in the industrial city, which provided men with a grand arena in which to exhibit their talents. It was a lake for fish who had outgrown their native ponds. The possibilities for profit were limitless—production, professions, commerce, construction, finance, speculation, services, franchises, boodling, and hundreds more. The roads to success ran in many directions and encountered few obstacles.

Those who traveled farthest and fastest down these roads were the great warriors of business. The urban arena rang with the din of their combat. In their fierce battles for success, they asked no quarter and gave none. Victory required daring and foresight, unswerving dedication, ruthlessness, unflagging energy, some measure of talent, and a little luck. If the ordeal imposed stiff demands and the fight often seemed cruel or even vicious, the rewards it promised were fabulous. The scale of profit in industrial society soared to heights that dizzied the imagination.

Obtaining those treasures required ceaseless devotion to the battle. The contest pitted raw power against power, cunning against cunning, sometimes with whole empires at stake. Men struggled not only against each other but against the marketplace itself, the impersonal nexus of economic relations and interests, parts of which might combine at any time to crush some individual scheme or punish an interloper for his brashness. It was no place for the timid or the squeamish. Recoiling from this primitive spectacle, a character in *The Pit* murmurs:

There is something terrible about it . . . something insensate. In a way, it doesn't seem human. It's like a great tidal wave. It's all very well for the individual just so long as he can keep afloat, but once fallen, how horribly quick it would crush him, annihilate him, how horribly quick, and with such horrible indifference! I suppose it's civilisation in the making, the thing that isn't meant to be seen, as though it were too elemental, too—primordial; like the first verses of Genesis.

Clearly the industrial city was fertile soil for the individualist ethic. Here, too, it is pointless to debate the cause-effect relationship between the individualist tradition and the urban environment. What matters is their continual interaction which bred a virulent new strain of rugged individualism fiercer and more intense than its precursor.

Part of the explanation lay in the changing role of competition. In agrarian America, men pitted themselves more against nature than against each other. Some fought Indians and some fought one another on occasion; but economic competition was seldom direct, rarely vicious, and never on a grand scale. Within the urban industrial setting, this situation underwent a dramatic reversal: competition was less against nature and more head-to-head. Much of it remained indirect and, through the marketplace, was fought against unseen or unknown opponents, but it was still between individuals or groups grasping for the same prizes. One man's victory usually meant another man's setback. Direct competition was more intense and kept constant pressure upon everyone in the game.

The competitors felt that pressure keenly. The documents of the era—letters, diaries, newspapers, magazines, speeches, novels—offer eloquent testimony on that point. Rich and poor alike viewed themselves as being caught in a struggle not only for success but for survival. Since the competitive race bred both opportunity and insecurity, moods shifted with the circumstances, plunging from exhilaration to despair. Some were broken on the rack of failure, while others found that success only increased the pressure to maintain or improve their position. For victor and vanquished alike, the ordeal was often exhausting and self-defeating over the long haul. A character in William Dean Howells's *A Hazard of New Fortunes* (1890) expressed this weariness when he complained bitterly:

It ought to be law as inflexible in human affairs as the order of day and night in the physical world, that if a man will work he shall both rest and eat, and shall not be harassed with any question as to how his repose and his provision shall come. . . . But in our state of things no one is secure of this. No one is sure of finding work; no one is sure of not losing it . . . and so we go on, pushing and pulling, climbing and crawling, thrusting aside and trampling underfoot, lying, cheating, stealing; and when we get to the end, covered with blood and dirt and sin and shame, and look back over the way we've come to a palace of our own, or to the poorhouse, which is about the only possession we can claim in common with our brother men, I don't think the retrospect can be pleasing.

The emergence of a corporate society did not alter this condition so much as enlarge the scale on which it operated. Competition within organizations was no less fierce than that between rival businessmen. As the social structure evolved into one based upon organized interest groups, power relationships were formally placed upon an adversary basis. In many ways conflicts of interest among groups proved more intense than those among individuals, and the outcome of their clashes tended to affect far more people. Moreover, the rise of corporate power added a lethal new dimension to economic rivalries. The protagonist in Robert Herrick's novel, *The Memoirs of an American Citizen* (1905), says of a great meatpacker, "He's the biggest dog, and it's dog eat dog in our business as all over nowadays." When pressed on the point, he adds, "There's a change coming over business, and you feel it the same as you feel a shift in the wind. It's harder work fighting to live now than ever before, and it can't go on like this forever. The big dog will eat up the rest."

In their efforts to comprehend this new state of things some Americans found a perfect metaphor in the tooth-and-claw jungle ethic of Social Darwinism as propounded by Herbert Spencer. While the metaphor may be apt, it is also misleading and its influence upon American thought easily exaggerated. In retrospect, businessmen may appear to have been acting out the great Darwinian struggle for survival in their economic affairs, but precious few of them were aware of that fact. Most businessmen read little beyond the financial news and the daily papers; they were not students of Social Darwinism so much as unwitting caricatures of it.

The source of their inspiration lay rather in the venerable axioms of individualism and self-reliance. To these were added two other themes: the "get-rich-quick" spirit which had burst forth during the expansive Jacksonian years, and the "rags-to-riches" ideal which was already popular before the Civil War but found its most classic expression in Horatio Alger's novels after the war. The intermingling of these themes produced a curious but potent ideology for success in the competitive urban arena.

The cornerstone of this ideology was the self-reliant rugged individual. His quest for success required certain tools of character including industry, perseverance, frugality, and sobriety—not just with drink but in all personal habits and traits. His origins could be humble; in fact, the ideology romanticized "good" rural poverty, properly shaped by a devout mother and poor but hard-working father, as a virtue. Genius was not needed and might even be an obstacle; what mattered most were not the qualities a man inherited, but those he cultivated through dedication and diligence. Indeed, the march of the self-made man to his just rewards was largely an extended act of will, the triumph of character over circumstance. On this point the ideology was adamant: the gladiators of business who ventured forth in the urban arena had to be both physically and morally fit. Anything less would doom them to failure or taint whatever success they achieved.

Through this emphasis upon character and self-development, the success ideology fastened upon an individual the full responsibility for his own success or failure. It ignored environment as a decisive factor in character formation, conceding its importance only as the source of circumstances which tested one's character and nourished its growth. In short, environment was merely arena, the battlefield for the struggle of life in which inner strength counted far more than outer forces. Thus was the self-made man truly self-made according to the ideology of success; and thus, too, was the ne'er-do-well fully a product of his own hand and therefore deserving of his wretched lot. Poverty was the fitting reward for those who had done nothing with their lives. Society might provide (in miserly fashion) for the handicapped, the feeble, the sick, or the insane, but not for the poor who lacked such excuses. They were regarded at best with pity, at worst with contempt.

It should be apparent that success tended to be defined in material terms. Most Americans simply equated success with making money. While the cash nexus had always been held in high esteem, it became a national obsession in the industrial era. A character in Robert Herrick's *The Common Lot* (1904) captured the prevailing mood when he declared that "What men respect in this town is money—first, last, and all the time. So it's only natural for a man, whether he is a lawyer or anything else, to do as the other Romans do."

Herrick was by no means alone in recognizing money's powerful hold on people's minds. The avid pursuit of wealth, the mania to make as much money as possible as fast as possible, dominated the literature of the era. The success ideology did not deny the nonmaterial aspects of life so much as subsume them to the material. Money could not buy happiness, but it could buy much that made a person happy. It gave one the means to fulfill the other areas of his life. In social terms, it defined one's status and, implicitly, his worth. A prosperous man was assumed to be a happy and most likely a humane one. Contentment sprang from economic security and the possession of property.

Moreover, the pursuit of wealth was itself noble and exciting. It gave life a sense of purpose and direction. Several observers viewed the American businessman as a warrior who loved the fight far more than the spoils of victory. "That the American, by temperament, worked to excess, was true," Henry Adams noted sourly; "work and whiskey were his stimulants; work was a form of vice; but he never cared much for money or power after he earned them. The amusement of the pursuit was all the amusement he got from it." This sentiment was echoed by novelist Henry Webster, who described a character in his *The Banker and the Bear* (1900) this way:

> Melville Sponley and others like him are the soldiers of fortune of today. . . . whatever their ability, whatever their weapons, daggers, or collateral securities, they are all alike in this: that not having, but getting, is their purpose; it is not the stake but the play that interests them.

How and where did the successful warriors acquire their money? We have already noted that most fortunes great and small were made in urban areas and often in ways directly connected to the city's growth. In 1892 the *New York Tribune* attempted to compile a list of all the millionaires in the country, along with the primary sources of their wealth. While the results included many errors, they remain the most accurate information we have on the subject. The final list contained 4,047 names, of which 3,137 or 78 percent lived in the states listed in Table 4. In fact, 1,103 or 27 percent of them lived in New York City alone.

About three-fourths of the millionaires made their fortunes in predictable areas: trade, transportation, manufacturing, and finance. But the matter is not quite so simple because many of the fortunes came from several sources and no exact division by source is possible. Despite that limitation, it is clear that land—or real estate, as it came to be called in the city—played a key role. Of the 4,047 millionaires, real estate was listed as one source of their fortune for 1,260, or 31 percent; and of that number, 347, or 8 percent, were based chiefly or entirely upon real estate. If anything, these figures are conservative, for several fortunes were attributed in part to "investments" which probably included real estate. Rare was the urban man of means who did not at least dabble in land.

Even in urban and industrial America, land remained a primary source of wealth, but in new ways. Some people simply bought land and held it through several generations while it climbed steadily in value. Several wealthy families owed their entire fortunes to the foresight of their forebears and were content to live off the proceeds. Others speculated actively in real estate, either as a sideline or as their whole concern. Both were old practices, but the intensity of the urban land market surpassed anything that had gone before it. Other sources of wealth—franchises, transportation, industry—also brought businessmen into the land market, often on a large scale.

For the ambitious hustler, the city offered many roads to riches, but the journey took a terrible toll on the travelers. Those who sought the prize of success willingly paid the price only to discover that it was much steeper than they had anticipated, or that the prize brought them less pleasure or fulfillment than they had expected. There are few more common or classic literary themes than that of men neglecting all else in life to pursue what William James called the "bitch-goddess SUCCESS" only to come up spiritually empty amidst their fame and fortune. The price of their dedication to ambition was usually twofold: what they lost along the way in their narrow-minded pursuit and what they failed to gain from the material success they achieved.

The persistence of these themes in post-Civil War literature, and the variety of situations in which they were set, suggests that they were firmly grounded in the realities of American life. It is a topic worth a book of its own; we can only hint at its bare contours here.

Especially in urban America did the race for success absorb the principal attention and energies of most men. It led them to divide their lives into distinct spheres. Where once work had been only part of the larger organic whole of human activity, it now assumed primacy and subsumed other areas of life. The devotion to what men called "practical affairs" became obsessive and reflexive. Family life revolved around the work schedule and centered ever more upon economic concerns. Religion took a back seat to secular matters and was often confined to churchgoing or neglected entirely. Culture was shunted into the hands of women or a meager band of artists and professional aesthetes. Spiritual concerns—the larger questions of the heart—were detached from the realm of practical affairs and treated as isolated if not unreasonable intrusions upon the work at hand.

In essence, Americans developed a split personality, and with it a split ethos. Like war, the urban arena developed its own rules; and like soldiers, its warriors lived by their own code. There was business and there was life. Instead of making life their business, many men made business their life. In this manner, men found themselves prisoners of their routines like David Marshall in Fuller's *With the Procession*:

Why did he go to bed at half-past nine? In order that he might be at the store by half-past seven. Why must he be at the store by half-past seven? Because a very large area to the west and northwest of the town looked to him for supplies of teas, coffees, spices, flour, sugar, baking-powder; because he had always been accustomed to furnish these supplies; because it was the only thing he wanted to do; because it was the only thing he could do; because it was the only thing he was pleased and proud to do; because it was the sole thing which enabled him to look upon himself as a useful, stable, honored member of society.

This went beyond a question of priorities; it reflected a growing schism within the inner man. The ethical standards and code of conduct of the business world contrasted sharply with those governing noneconomic affairs. Behavior that might outrage social relations was condoned in the business world with little complaint. Practices that might be denounced as sharp or unethical in the society at large passed muster in the business arena with the curt explanation that they were "a matter of business." That telling phrase, eloquent in its brevity, identified business as a world unto itself.

The moral implications of this schism were tremendous. If business was life, everything else could be reduced to weapons in commercial warfare. Values and institutions—to say nothing of other people—could be viewed as mere instruments for those who knew how to manipulate them. No writer grasped this point more clearly than Theodore Dreiser, whose Frank Cowperwood may be the best-drawn business character in American literature. In *The Financier* (1912), Cowperwood muses upon the law and lawyers:

Law . . . was an unholy and unsatisfactory disrupting and delaying spectacle, a painful commentary on the frailties of life, and men, a trick, a snare, a pit and gin. In the hands of the strong, like himself when he was at his best, the law was a sword and a shield, a trap to place before the feet of the unwary; a pit to dig in the path of those who might pursue. It was anything you might choose to make of it—a door to illegal opportunity; a cloud of dust to be cast in the eyes of those who might choose, and rightfully, to see; a veil to be dropped arbitrarily between truth and its execution, justice and its judgment, crime and punishment. Lawyers in the main were intellectual mercenaries to be bought and sold in any cause. It amused him to hear the ethical and emotional platitudes of lawyers, to see how readily they would lie, steal, prevaricate, misrepresent in almost any cause and for any purpose. . . . Still he used law as he would use any other trap or weapon to

rid him of a human ill; and as for lawyers, he picked them up as he would
any club or knife wherewith to defend himself. He had no particular
respect for any of them. . . .

Some were strong and ruthless enough to accept the jungle ethic or
even thrive upon it. Others grew weary of the incessant struggle or
found their lives blighted by its effects. In the end, none survived with
their sensibilities intact and all experienced a chilling sense of loss that
bordered on despair. Few writers drew the moral of the success saga
more bluntly than Howells in A Hazard of New Fortunes. "I can't see
as we've got a bit more comfort in our lives, Jacob, because we've got
such piles and piles of money," wailed the wife of a businessman named
Dryfoos. "I wisht to gracious we was back on the farm this minute."
Of Dryfoos himself, Howells rendered a succinct verdict:

His moral decay began with his perception of the opportunity of making
money quickly and abundantly, which offered itself to him after he sold his
farm. He awoke to it slowly, from a desolation in which he tasted the last
bitter of homesickness, the utter misery of idleness and listlessness. When he
broke down and cried for the hard-working wholesome life he had lost, he
was near the end of this season of despair, but he was also near the end of
what was best in himself.

Howells colored his account with a romantic view of the virtues of a
simple country life. Nevertheless, Dryfoos was a reasonable archetype
for hundreds of men who could be found in every industrial city stalking
their destiny like some rare and elusive prey. The point is not whether
Howells's judgment is right or wrong, or even whether his portrait, or
similar portraits by numerous other writers, is accurate. The point is
that millions of Americans in city and country believed that the portrait
was accurate and the judgment sound. Howells had but given literary
expression to what was fast becoming the American morality play: the
way in which the quest for success made good men do evil things,
perverted their character, wore them out, destroyed their sense of values,
and left them spiritually bankrupt within the prison of their earthly
treasures.

This morality play served as counterpoint to the myth of success and
the image of the self-made man. It was the underside of the Horatio
Alger legend and had a strong following among those who had failed,
faltered, or grown disillusioned with the chase or simply tried to stand
aloof from its corrosive influence. Together they form yet another of the
many paradoxes that make American history so complex an enigma.

The industrial city left a deep imprint upon all its inhabitants, not only upon their souls but etched into their countenances. That was part of what Henry James meant when he observed, "No impression so promptly assaults the arriving visitor of the United States as that of the overwhelming preponderance, wherever he turns and twists, of the unmitigated 'business man' face, ranging through its various possibilities, its extraordinary actualities, of intensity."

The urban arena was the ultimate marketplace for talent as for everything else. Its record in the realm of human affairs was no less skewed and haphazard than its handling of other commodities. In the end it proved no less inadequate as a mechanism for ordering the complex interrelationships of urban life. If the industrial city became the ultimate marketplace, it also emerged as the most striking evidence against continued reliance upon the market to regulate human affairs in industrial urban society.

CHAPTER 5

The Treadmill of Progress:
Technology and Physical Growth

> That a city had any other purpose than to attract trade, to increase
> land values, and to grow is something that, if it uneasily entered
> the mind of an occasional Whitman, never exercised any hold
> upon the minds of our countrymen.
>
> —LEWIS MUMFORD
> *Sticks and Stones* (1924)

To THE MODERN URBANITE the industrial city seems a quaint, almost
primitive place. Its sights and smells bear a strong flavor of nostalgia:
streets lit by gas lamps and filled with carriages, drays, and streetcars;
sidewalks bustling with gentlemen in tall hats or derbies, wearing high,
starched collars; ladies in long dresses with parasols resting on their
shoulders; workmen dressed in cheap drab shirts and pants, brightened
by gaudy bandanas tied about their neck or head; messenger boys
dashing from one office building to another; deliverymen straining
beneath their blocks of ice, kegs of beer, or racks of clothing; sidestreets
filled with peddlers' carts loaded with wares of every kind, their cries
intermingling in a cacophony of confusion; sidewalk markets bulging
with fresh fruit and produce, tiers of fish or slabs of meat, all picked
over by swarms of shoppers; strolling policemen with bright brass buttons
and fat nightsticks; and ragged newsboys trumpeting the day's headlines
above the din of the street traffic.

The wistful flavor of this scene is deceptive. While its pace and tumult may appear tame to people in a high-speed, computerized, automated society, contemporaries regarded the city as an engine of progress in which everything seemed constantly on the move. In this feeling, that generation was no less correct than our own; the difference lay largely in the level of technology achieved by each era. To an amazing degree advances in technology shaped the growth, appearance, and pace of the industrial city. Then as now, cities could expand only by discovering new techniques for moving people, goods, and information. New machines, materials, and designs revamped the city's face and accelerated its inner rhythms. Urban growth was therefore both a function of technology and a reflection of its pervasive influence.

Yet technology, even in its most imaginative forms, did not solve problems so much as recast them. Rapid growth strained the city's ability to perform such elementary functions as transporting, feeding, and housing people, protecting them from fire and crime, educating their children, and providing a healthy, attractive environment in which to live. It complicated every aspect of urban life and fragmented urban society. Almost every industrial city endured a phase of madcap expansion during which its distended social system threatened to collapse beneath the weight of increased demands for services and accumulated social tensions.

To solve the physical problems created by rapid growth, most cities resorted to sophisticated technology and techniques. But every "solution" unmasked a tangle of new problems which in turn called for still more sophisticated hardware. Thus the electric trolley and elevated railway moved more people at greater speed than the omnibus, but both presented problems unforeseen in the heyday of the horse and buggy. The result was a vicious circle, a kind of "Catch-22" in which every new stage of technological advance proved less a gateway into some new golden age than a harbinger of fresh difficulties.

Nor was this all. The vicious circle traced by the interaction between technology and growth uncovered a deeper contradiction in the American notion of progress. Americans had always tended to equate progress with growth. During the industrial era, progress came increasingly to be defined in material and mechanical terms. This faith in the notion that "bigger is better" assumed that quantitative growth would improve the quality of life. Since technology was a primary instrument in quantitative growth, Americans logically turned to it as a means for resolving the perplexities of industrial society.

Urban growth especially fed upon advances in technology. In quantitative terms, that growth proceeded at breakneck pace and reached gigantic proportions. But the industrial city turned out to be something less than the promised land. For all the splendors of its swelling statistics, it never became a pleasant or even decent place in which to live for a majority of its inhabitants. Too late city-dwellers discovered that their faith in technology had been misplaced; that mere quantitative growth did not automatically bring qualitative improvement. In their quest for a better life, urbanites had created not a road to utopia but a treadmill which they labeled "progress."

Mass Transit and Mass Exodus

Just as the railroad affected the locations and functions of cities on a national scale, the street railway shaped their internal growth. From its crude beginnings with horse-drawn omnibuses to steam-power trolleys and later the electrified lines, mass transit moved urbanites faster and more efficiently. Every advance in transportation technology quickly outmoded its predecessor only to create new problems in construction, congestion, and pollution.

The most important effect of mass transit was its expanding the physical limits of the city. The street railway destroyed the compact "walking city" of colonial and preindustrial towns. Prior to about 1850 most towns were still intimate locales where street congestion involved nothing more than people on foot, on horseback, or in carriages. Most people lived near their place of work and could reach nearly any spot in the city in a thirty-minute walk. Few towns extended farther than two miles from their core, which usually nestled against some waterway.

During the 1820s the omnibus emerged as the first urban passenger carrier. Initially little more than enlarged hackney coaches, these wagons later resembled boxes on wheels with two lengthwise seats holding twelve to twenty people. They appeared first in the larger cities—New York, Boston, Philadelphia, New Orleans, Washington—where small businessmen, usually those already in the livery or freight business, seized the initiative in establishing omnibus lines to tie the two most traveled parts of the city together.

For a five- or ten-cent fare, a passenger on the new urban transit line was treated to a slow ride which lurched through frequent stops, bumps, and jerks. He sat on unpadded benches and enjoyed little protection from the elements. Even though the fare was too steep for the masses, omnibuses drew heavy patronage from small businessmen and clerks, many of whom still went home for lunch. By the 1840s Boston had eighteen omnibus lines, of which twelve extended to outlying suburban communities. Despite its limitations, the omnibus speeded up the tempo of life, regularized transportation patterns, and launched the outward migration of wealthier people from the center of the city to the suburbs.

The era of the omnibus lasted scarcely a generation before the horse railway surpassed it in the 1850s. The horse railway, too, resembled a stagecoach, but utilized flanged wheels operating on iron tracks. The pioneer run of a horsecar in New York in 1836 also made history as the first horsecar accident. When its brake failed to catch, the second car smacked into the first car filled with city dignitaries. Fortunately, neither dignitaries nor horses were injured. Undaunted by the mishap, Mayor Walter Browne applauded the run as an event which "will go down in the history of our country as the greatest achievement of man."

Other cities soon followed New York's lead. By the 1850s Boston, Philadelphia, Chicago, Baltimore, St. Louis, Cincinnati, Newark, and Pittsburgh all had laid horsecar tracks and were extending their boundaries. Iron rails allowed horsecars to reach speeds of six to eight miles per hour, about one-third more than the omnibus could muster. Reduced friction did more than add speed. It provided a smoother ride and increased the number of passengers that could be hauled.

Iron rails also increased costs. Inevitably the horsecar companies required a greater capital investment than the omnibus lines. As expenses mounted, financing became more feasible through incorporation rather than individual ownership. Sometimes local businessmen lacked the capital or imagination to organize large transit enterprises, and sometimes promoters from elsewhere sniffed the profits to be made from such ventures and scurried to obtain a franchise. Whatever the case, ownership of transit facilities fell increasingly into the hands of outside entrepreneurs who neither knew the local scene nor cared about how cities developed. Each phase of technological innovation made urban transportation a bigger business than it had been. By the end of the nineteenth century, transit or "traction" enterprises held the nexus of political and economic power in most major cities.

The new horsecar lines also affected the social behavior of their passengers. As the cars grew larger, more people were packed into them. Those who bemoan modern-day subway crowding and defacement will find no golden age in the horsecar era. Straphangers were already commonplace and one observer likened the riders to "smoked hams in a corner grocery." The New York Herald of October 2, 1864, described a ride on mass transit as an experience in "martyrdom" and claimed that "the discomforts, inconveniences, and annoyances of a trip on one of these vehicles are almost intolerable." A British traveler to the city in the same year verified the *Herald*'s account and concluded that "the street cars with their impudent managers, are always crammed and uncomfortable."

The horsecar had another unsavory effect upon the urban landscape: it added to the piles of horse manure littering the streets. Lest we forget that pollution comes in many forms, it is well to heed Joel Tarr's reminder that the automobile was once hailed as the savior of the city from animal waste. "In a city like Milwaukee in 1907," he wrote, ". . . with a human population of 350,000 and a horse population of 12,500, this meant 133 tons of manure a day, for a daily average of nearly three-quarters of a pound of manure for each resident." For New York and Brooklyn in the 1880s, with a total horse population of around 150,000, the problem was much worse. Carcasses of dead horses sprawled in the streets added to the sanitation nightmare.

This contemporary image of mass transit as a crowded, unsafe, unpleasant, and polluting form of transportation sounds hauntingly familiar to the modern ear. Moreover, the horsecar had inherent limitations as a form of transportation: it could go no faster than the horse pulling it and could not increase its passenger load without adding more horses, which posed other difficulties. To growing cities, these became intolerable drawbacks. The obvious solution was to devise a transit system that utilized mechanical rather than muscle power. By the 1860s the search for alternatives was well underway. Louis Ransom of Akron, Ohio, advocated adopting his Ransom Steamer to iron rails. George Clark of Cincinnati promoted a system of compressed-air cars, while a New Orleans firm experimented with a car propelled by ammonia gas.

The most successful of the early mechanically-powered cars was the cable car, which operated by hooking onto a rotating underground cord. In 1873 Andrew Smith Hallidie, a Scottish immigrant, tried out his invention on the steep hills of San Francisco. When Hallidie perfected his system several years later, it featured a grappling device which attached to an endless underground cable powered by a stationary steam engine. Hallidie found the ideal locale for his cable car in San Francisco, where Nob Hill and other steep grades taxed the endurance of the strongest horse. Yet Chicago, Philadelphia, Seattle, and twenty other cities also employed cable cars during the 1880s. Once the cable car's disadvantages surfaced, however, its popularity waned quickly. These shortcomings included high installation costs, breakdowns which affected the entire line, inability to make up lost time, and an unvarying travel speed during the rush and slack hours. Only San Francisco retained Hallidie's invention, primarily for nostalgia and tourism.

While some cities were installing underground cables, others built elevated transit lines. By 1879 cars pulled by steam-powered cables on elevated lines operated along both Sixth and Ninth Avenues in New York. These lines hauled over 175,000 passengers a day. Brooklyn and Kansas City quickly followed suit, but it was Chicago which instituted the most complex arrangement in its Loop area. Early trips on the "els" crackled with amusement-park excitement as passengers thrilled to the adventure of high speeds on high rails.

But elevateds were very expensive and found backing only in the major urban centers. Although they contributed some architectural monuments to the city in the form of elaborate Gothic stations, the els for the most part had a disrupting effect on the streets. An English visitor to New York in the late 1870s capsuled the disenchantment with the els when he described how "the nineteen hours and more of incessant rumbling day and night from the passing trains, the blocking out of a sufficiency of light from the rooms of houses, close up to which the lines are built . . . the frequent squirtings of oil from the engines" disconcerted those unfortunates who lived or worked alongside the tracks. The expense, dirt, noise, and spewed ashes and oil all helped restrict expansion of the els. Yet despite their drawbacks and inconveniences, the elevateds created a powerful urban image which John Marin captured effectively in his Ashcan School painting, "The Sixth Avenue El" (1906).

No innovation in urban mass transit rivaled the application of electrical power. Oddly enough, the pioneer projects developed in the least urbanized area of the nation. James A. Gaboury, the owner of an animal traction line in Montgomery, Alabama, witnessed a demonstration of an electrical car at the Toronto Agricultural Fair in 1885 and determined to adopt the method to his system. In 1886 Montgomery's Court Street line became the first in the country to offer a citywide system of electric transportation. Several years later, Frank J. Sprague, a naval engineer who had worked for Thomas Edison, formed his own company and secured a contract to build a line in Richmond, Virginia. The success of his project spurred the construction of electrical transit lines elsewhere.

The electric cars moved along iron tracks in the street, drawing current from a central power source passed to the trains through overhead wires. The effect of a wire leading a car resembled that of a "troller"; soon the corruption of the word became universal and the new vehicles were dubbed "trolleys." Trolleys displaced horses so rapidly that by 1900 only 2 percent of the lines were horse-drawn, compared to 70 percent a decade earlier. By 1895, 850 lines embraced over 10,000 miles of electrified track. The new trolleys speeded up travel service to about twelve miles per hour and more in less congested areas. Their overhead wires cluttered the streetscapes of American cities and wreaked havoc during high winds and storms.

Frank Sprague made a second major contribution to transportation systems. He designed an electrical multiple-unit control system which allowed each car to be independently powered, lighted, heated, and braked. These cars did not require a locomotive since they possessed their own power source; yet they could be controlled by a master switch located in any one of them. At one stroke Sprague removed the major obstacles to constructing underground railways. Automated electric cars could operate without the accumulation of smoke, gas, and dirt discharged by steam-powered cars. Between 1895 and 1897 Boston built a mile-and-a-half subway at a cost of $4,000,000. Immediately after the turn of the century, New York constructed a route from downtown City Hall to 145th Street. Within a few days after opening in 1904, it "began to show signs of crowding during the rush hours." Since then the crowd has seldom let up. The popularity of the subway, coupled with the city's extreme congestion, led New York to take the lead in underground transportation. Moreover, its hard-rock geological formation could support the construction of tall buildings above ground and tunnels below.

All these achievements in the technology of transportation affected the physical growth of cities. The rural ideal retained its hold upon Americans even in the city, where its influence drove people toward the suburbs. Prior to the advent of mass transit lines, however, only the wealthy could maintain houses on the outskirts of the city. Once the pedestrian confines were broken in the 1850s, an outward migration commenced. Warner has painstakingly traced the development of Roxbury, West Roxbury, and Dorchester as bedroom satellites of Boston. Every stage of suburban development expanded the physical limits of Boston to house wealthy, middle-class, and lower middle-class expatriates from the city. Since all of the transit lines were privately built, the new suburbs alongside their tracks were the product of individual decision-making rather than coordinated social policy.

Other cities followed similar patterns. Milwaukee, for instance, began its outward sprawl in the 1880s after the introduction of new transit lines. Swallowing up older villages like Humboldt, Milwaukee's upper crust abandoned the city's central core. In 1880 34 percent of its population lived within one mile of the business center at Third and Wisconsin streets; by 1900 it had dropped to 17 percent. Cincinnati's physical area jumped from six square miles in 1850 to 23 square miles in 1880 and over 50 square miles in 1910.

Traction entrepreneurs enthusiastically promoted the flight to the suburbs. They found support among those who regarded the exodus as a boon for relieving congestion in the city's inner core. Adna Weber, the leading student of American cities in the nineteeth century, stated flatly, "it is clear that we are now in the sight of a solution of the problem of concentration of population." Weber advocated the extension of electrified transit lines and cheap fares because he saw in the rise of the suburbs "the solid basis of a hope that the evils of city life, so far as they result from overcrowding, may be in large part removed."

Unhappily, things did not work out that way. While upper- and middle-class urbanites left for greener pastures, the poor remained packed together in the central city, where they shared space with businesses and industries. Mass transit promoted this pattern of segregation within the city. More than any other factor, it transformed the diversified walking city into a central urban core of poor people and businesses surrounded by successive rings of surburban neighborhoods.

In fact, mass transit failed even to relieve population congestion. Transit lines did not scatter people about so much as cluster them in dense communities wherever transportation was available. New housing developments pursued every new construction or extension and quickly overflowed its service. As one alert observer wrote in an 1896 *Harper's Weekly*, "the trolleys seem to have created a new patronage of their own. Travel has been stimulated rather than diverted." Instead of thinning out settlement, mass transit created corridors of dense groupings alongside their lines. This magnetic pull pleased the traction promoters immensely. It was great for business; its effect upon the city's already strained social structure was quite another matter.

Many Rivers Crossed

Technology extended the city's boundaries in another important way. Innovations in bridge-building made it possible for the first time to span the widest rivers. The implications of this breakthrough for urban growth were enormous: waterways ceased to be an obstacle to physical expansion. More important, it allowed traffic to flow in and out of the city with ease. Just as railroads dissolved limitations upon land travel, so the new bridges banished the fickle vagaries of waterways. Small wonder that to many Americans the Brooklyn Bridge and other mighty spans became the supreme symbol of American civilization.

American bridge-builders had always displayed a genius in the construction of wooden spans, but they could not overcome the inherent limitations of the material. Timber trusses set upon masonry pilings could not bear heavy loads across long spans, and they posed a serious fire hazard. Industrialization aggravated these shortcomings even while it devised the means to remedy them. The expanding railroad system demanded longer and sturdier bridges to handle longer and heavier trains; the emerging iron and steel industry provided new materials with which to build them.

Iron surpassed wood in strength, durability, and resistance to fire. Unlike stone masonry, it possessed high tensile strength and elasticity. It also had serious liabilities which American engineers were slow to grasp. After the first iron railroad bridge appeared in 1845, the ensuing decades were marred by a dismal trail of accidents, disasters, and trial-and-error learning. Within a decade after the Civil War, some engineers were experimenting with steel as a more durable alternative to cast and wrought iron. Bridge trusses designed by Thomas Pratt and Squire Whipple were used throughout the country and later adapted to longer spans.

While engineers groped toward a mastery of these practical tools, urban entrepreneurs were quick to glimpse their possibilities. City fathers, boards of trade, chambers of commerce, and other business groups worked feverishly to span nearby rivers in hopes of increasing trade by luring railroads to their city. The Ohio River emerged as a principal testing ground for new truss developments when early railroad bridges were constructed at Steubenville (1864), Cincinnati (1867), and Louisville (1870). But the boldest leap in bridge design and urban imagination took place at St. Louis on the Mississippi River.

The business community of that thriving river town was engaged in fierce competition with its upstart rival Chicago for supremacy in midwestern trade. Eager to secure through rail connections to the East, St. Louisans had explored the prospects of bridging the Mississippi even before the Civil War. After rejecting several early projects, the city accepted a proposal by James B. Eads in 1867. Eads proposed to span the most majestic and dangerous river in America with a double-decked steel-arched bridge. It was an audacious plan, made all the more remarkable by the fact that it came from a man who had never built a bridge in his life.

Eads had made a fortune by inventing a diving bell which he used to salvage sunken steamers and by establishing a glass factory in St.

Louis. He possessed an intimate knowledge of the river, and he was a superb organizer. Surrounding himself with first-rate engineers, Eads and his staff labored on the project for seven years. Despite floods, ice storms, tornadoes, and technological difficulties, he completed the span in 1873. The task claimed twelve lives and crippled two men, but the finished product won Eads an international reputation and solidified St. Louis as the gateway to the West.* The first major steel-arched bridge in the country, Eads's span brimmed with structural and architectural innovations. A century later it still carries vehicular and railroad traffic across the Mississippi.

Despite his magnificent achievement, Eads never won the public recognition he deserved. His classic span was soon eclipsed in the popular imagination by one of the finest symbols of the industrial era: the Brooklyn Bridge. Throughout the early nineteenth century, various schemes had been advanced for connecting New York City with the "bedroom" community of Brooklyn ("a kind of sleeping place for New York," Charles Dickens had called it). Regular ferry service—primarily to Fulton Street—discouraged bridge construction, but in the mid–1860s severe storms curtailed services. The inability of many New York businessmen to get to work helped spur the drive for a bridge to regularize the Brooklyn-Manhattan commuter traffic.

The task fell to John Augustus Roebling, a German-born engineer who had come to the United States in 1831 and founded a steel cable factory in Trenton, New Jersey. After pioneering in the manufacture of wire-rope cable, Roebling turned to building suspension bridges which utilized his own cable. After some minor successes in the 1840s, he established a reputation as America's foremost bridge builder on the strength of two spectacular projects: a double-decked suspension bridge above Niagara Falls (1855) and a magnificent suspension bridge over the Ohio River at Cincinnati (1867). In 1867 these stunning accomplishments won him the commission to do the East River bridge.

It was an enormous undertaking. The East River, wide and deep with swift, turbulent currents, proved a treacherous adversary. The work claimed its share of lives, including Roebling himself. A tugboat rammed into a piling on which the engineer was standing and crushed his foot. The subsequent amputation led to a tetanus infection from which Roebling died on July 22, 1869. His son Washington replaced him as

---

* By the turn of the century, St. Louis had become the second largest rail center in the United States.

chief engineer, but he, too, was crippled on the job and had to supervise the remainder of the work with a spyglass from his Brooklyn Heights home.

Fourteen years passed before the final sections of the 3,455-foot, $17,000,000 bridge were put into place. On May 24, 1883, Queen Victoria's birthday, a grand celebration marked the opening of the world's largest bridge. Shopkeepers proudly displayed signs in their windows that read: "Babylon had her hanging gardens, Egypt her pyramid, Athens her Acropolis, Rome her Athenaeum; so Brooklyn has her bridge." President Chester A. Arthur attended the ceremony as tugboats sprayed streams of water, bands played, cannons fired, and firecrackers exploded. An engineering and architectural masterpiece, the bridge did not win unqualified acceptance. Some New Yorkers viewed the two giant granite towers and suspending cables as a monstrosity. One critic labeled it "arrogantly ugly, a defiant celebration of the raw, crude American civilization."

Yet the Brooklyn Bridge has stood the test of time. Hailed by Lewis Mumford as "the first product of the age of coal and iron to achieve a completeness of expression," the bridge remains an enduring symbol of New York City. Solidifying the relationship between Manhattan and Brooklyn, ultimately leading to their consolidation as the Greater City in 1898, the bridge stands, in the words of architectural critic Montgomery Schuyler, as "one of the great and most honorable works of engineering."

Like mass transit, the great bridges dissolved obstacles to the city's outward growth. But to what purpose? Thoughtful critics wondered whether expansion solved the problems spawned by urban congestion or simply spread them across a larger territory. One veteran urban reformer, Jacob Riis, made no effort to conceal his disillusionment with the results of urban growth. Writing in 1910, he recalled:

Then, was our answer some years ago, we must have bridges, subways; we must burst the barriers that fence us in. We have done it. We have built bridges and subways, but ahead of the surging crowd that seeks the open, is the r.e. [real estate] speculator, buying up the land and building tenements where there should be no tenements and is no need of them other than that which proceeds from his own greed.

Sticks, Stones, and Steel

As mass transit and great bridges expanded the city's outer limits, innovations in building forms lifted its inner face. Like bridge-building, the new age of construction dawned with the shift from wood to iron and steel. Preindustrial cities were filled with two- or three-story buildings, shops, warehouses, and row houses made of timber. Government buildings, merchant exchanges, and athenaeums comprised the major public buildings; the church spire still dominated the skyline.

The industrial city presented a radically different scene. Multi-story buildings filled with corporate and professional offices stretched high into the sky. Cast-iron and sash-steel factories housed long ranks of machines whose operators lived in tall brick tenements. New kinds of buildings—railroad terminals, department stores, theaters, apartments—ornamented the urban landscape. The transition from church spire to skyscraper signified a revolution in construction techniques and in the way city-dwellers identified with their surroundings.

Great movements often hinge upon small details. In construction it was the lowly nail that boomed residential building and urban expansion. Prior to the 1820s home-building in America copied the English method of using heavy beams shaped at the ends to fit into slots in adjoining beams. If there was tension on the two beams, a hole was augured and a wooden peg fitted into place to hold the stress. This mortise-and-tenon method required skilled craftsmen. Houses built in this manner were sturdy but expensive.

The mass production of iron nails in the 1820s liberated builders from the English method. With these inexpensive joining devices, houses could be built in the skeleton form still common today. The "balloon frame," as it was called, consisted of thin plates and studs (usually 2″ x 4″) "nailed together in such a way that every strain went in the direction of the wood (i.e. against the grain)." The first balloon-frame building appeared in Chicago, where in 1833 a carpenter named Augustine Deodat Taylor built the city's first Catholic church in three months at a cost of only $400.

With that simple edifice, Chicago commenced its long career as a pioneer in urban design. Balloon-frame structures sprang up all over the city, and the popularity of skeleton construction survived even the Great Fire of 1871. Other young western towns like San Francisco, Denver, and Seattle adopted the balloon-frame form, as did the more established cities of the East. Although attacked by contemporaries as shoddy and tasteless, the balloon frame proved irresistible to the urban market with its insatiable appetite for cheap housing. Once transit lines made commuting feasible, developers and speculators bought large tracts of farmland adjacent to the city, carved them into lots, and threw up whole neighborhoods of houses modeled upon a common design.

Like another simple innovation, Eli Whitney's cotton gin, the balloon frame energized an entire industry. It put single-unit dwellings within the reach of many people once unable to afford such a luxury. Home construction soared in every major industrial city and fueled the exodus to the suburbs. Once this pattern of settlement emerged, most cities hastened to annex the new subdivisions that dotted their perimeters. Urban boundaries marched steadily into the surrounding countryside in random fashion, and new towns sprang up everywhere. As Carl W. Condit noted, "Within a generation the balloon frame dominated the West. . . . Without it the towns of the prairies could never have been built in the short time that saw the establishment of rural and urban society in the region."

Commercial buildings underwent no less drastic changes in design and construction techniques. Preindustrial cities utilized wood or bulky masonry for all their buildings. In downtown areas, where buildings were packed closely together, the inhabitants lived in constant fear of fire. The search for stronger, less inflammable materials began as early as the 1820s when two American architects—John Haviland and William Strickland—experimented with iron supports on some of their buildings. Iron found its most ardent disciple in Daniel Badger, the owner of a foundry in New York. Convinced that iron was the answer to every problem, Badger set out to popularize its benefits. It was strong, cheap, durable, provided more light and open space, and was relatively fireproof. But Badger did more than simply promote iron. In 1857 his company built the five-story Haughwout Building (still in use) in New York under the supervision of architect John Gaynor.

Badger's achievement was surpassed by his better-known contemporary, James Bogardus, an imaginative mechanic and inventor. Bogardus constructed the first wholly cast-iron building in New York at the corner of Centre and Duane Streets. The cast-iron design immediately showed its value. It eliminated the thick, space-consuming masonry columns in the interiors, thereby offering more room to economy-minded occupants. Iron buildings went up quickly and could be disassembled quickly if the need arose. For two decades cast-iron dominated the construction of warehouses, department stores, and office buildings in American cities. There remains in New York City a compact area south of Houston Street which preserves the beauty of cast-iron construction. This community, now known as So-Ho, intersperses artists' lofts and galleries with light manufacturing and includes such classic buildings as the Haughwout, the Singer Building, and Griffith Thomas's original Lord and Taylor Building. The ability of cast iron to reproduce elaborate details

as decorations at low cost gave five- or six-story buildings a unique flavor
of elegance in the 1850s and 1860s.

Yet cast iron's primacy lasted only two decades before steel replaced
it as the leading construction material. Steel was more durable and
stronger for both tension and compression and, unlike cast iron, did not
melt when fire reached it. It allowed architects and engineers to raise
their structures higher, a compelling feature at a time when downtown
land values were soaring. By the 1890s steel framing had converted most
major architects through its ability to provide added height and more
flexible interior space.* The mass production of plate glass gave architects a material for large windows strong enough to withstand wind and
stress at high altitudes. This combination of steel framing and plate
glass laid the foundation for skyscraper construction in the twentieth
century.

William Le Baron Jenney is credited with constructing the first
steel-frame skyscraper. In his ten-story Home Insurance Company in
Chicago (1885), Jenney employed an internal skeleton of steel and
"curtain" walls. For four years Jenney's fellow architects clung stubbornly to their old reliance upon iron and masonry; then abruptly they
converted en masse to the new methods. Between 1890 and 1893, a
host of steel-framed skycrapers rose in Chicago. The architects who added
their own innovations became widely known as the "Chicago School."
The prolific architectural firm of John Holabird and Martin Roche
introduced the riveted skeleton in their Tacoma Building (1889). Two
of Chicago's most influential architects, Daniel Burnham and John
Wellborn Root, produced the second Rand McNally Building in 1890.
With these structures the modern skyscraper came of age in Chicago.

The leaders of the Chicago School—Jenney, Holabird and Roche,
Burnham and Root—vigorously boosted their city as the leader of modern
design in skyscrapers. Burnham especially succeeded as a promoter
because his values reflected those held by his businessmen clients.
"My idea," he once said, "is to work up a big business to handle big
things, deal with big businessmen, and to build up a big organization,
for you can't handle big things unless you have an organization." Part
of the Chicago School's boosterism bore ironic fruit in the Chicago
World's Fair in 1893, the architecture of which was dominated not by
the Chicago School, but by more prestigious and conservative easterners.
Instead of modern design, the Exposition was swathed in dazzling
monuments to the classical style.

* It is worth noting that the first structure in New York City (other than a bridge)
to use steel framing was the Statue of Liberty, completed in 1886.

Nevertheless, as Burchard and Bush-Brown point out, "the greatest buildings of the Chicago style were built *after* the Exposition." In this work it was not Burnham or one of his colleagues but the maverick genius Louis Sullivan who blazed the trail. More of a personal and romantic architect than his fellows, Sullivan sought not merely to let form follow function, but also to fuse visual purpose and drama with function. The skyscraper was, after all, a novelty on the American landscape, one which symbolized a radically different social and economic order. "How," he demanded, "shall we impart to this sterile pile, this crude, harsh, brutal agglomeration, this stark, staring exclamation of eternal strife, the graciousness of those higher forms of sensibility and culture that rest on the lower and fiercer passions?"

Sullivan answered his own question by declaring that the skyscraper "must be every inch a proud and soaring thing, rising in sheer exultation that from bottom to top it is a unit without a single dissenting line." In his work Sullivan practiced exactly what he preached. His Transportation Building (1893) for the World's Fair broke utterly with the classical design of the other buildings. His first skyscraper, the Wainwright Building (1891) in St. Louis, unabashedly revealed its skeletal structure. Later projects like the Guaranty Building (1895) in Buffalo, the Gage Building (1898) in Chicago, and the Bayard Building (1898) in New York all stressed vertical piers to accentuate height and loftiness.

But it was in his Carson, Pirie, Scott and Company building (1906)— a department store rather than a skyscraper—that Sullivan produced what Carl Condit called "the masterpiece of the Chicago School and America's greatest work of commercial architecture." In this structure, according to Condit, "the neutral cage of iron and steel is transformed into fine architecture through Sullivan's unerring sense of proportion, his ornamental skill, and his exact calculation of depth of the window . . . [gives] maximum power to the elevation." The store was Sullivan's last major commission, though he lived until 1924. His later work centered entirely in small midwestern towns where he found more congenial clients than the conventional-minded businessmen of Chicago. Known as the "father of the skyscraper," Sullivan feared that his new form was "profoundly antisocial." He died a broken and neglected genius.

Other large industrial cities, like Minneapolis with its Metropolitan Building (1890), followed the lead of the Chicago School, but nowhere was the building mania greater than in New York. Constricted in its amount of downtown space and growing at a phenomenal rate, New York embraced the skyscraper as its salvation. But it was not love at first sight. As in Chicago, it took a strenuous courtship to woo architects and clients to tall buildings. The five-story Equitable Building (1870) marked the beginning of New York's high-rise skyline. Other buildings followed but, except for George B. Post's eight-story Produce Exchange (1884), few contributed structural innovations.

Even the Chicago system met resistance in New York. Bradford Gilbert was the first to employ the steel interior framing and curtain walls in his eleven-story Tower Building (1889). In adopting the Chicago system, Gilbert acted out of necessity. The building stood on a narrow lot; to have used thick masonry walls would have left only enough room for a hallway on the first floor. For his daring Gilbert paid dearly in aggravation. He got a building permit for the project only after a long struggle. When the building was completed, he found few customers eager to rent space in it. "So wary were New Yorkers of a building whose walls were supported by a metal frame, rather than vice versa," wrote one historian, "that Gilbert had to reassure them by occupying the topmost offices himself."

For several years architects and engineers tinkered with mixtures of iron, steel, and masonry. Finally New York departed from the past in a succession of structures beginning with the seventeen-story Manhattan Life Insurance Company Building (1894) and including the twenty-story American Surety Building (1895), the twenty-six-story St. Paul Building (1896), the thirty-story Park Row Building (1898), and Sullivan's Bayard Building. All these buildings used iron and steel framing to sweep upward to unprecedented heights. The frenzy of construction culminated in 1913 with the competion of the awesome Woolworth Building.

Designed by Cass Gilbert, the Woolworth Tower's fifty-five stories soared 760 feet into the air. Its ground area of 30,000 square feet provided more usable floor space than any other building then in existence. The majestic tower, rich in ornamental detail, cost $7,500,000, but Woolworth considered it money well spent. He had frankly wanted an edifice that would attract international attention, and that was precisely what he got. On April 24, 1913, thousands of people gathered around City Hall Park to witness the official opening of the behemoth. At the prescribed moment President Woodrow Wilson pressed a button in the White House which lighted 80,000 electric light bulbs in the building. The crowd gasped, then roared their approval. Few doubted that Gilbert's work would stand for some time as the tallest building in the world. Critical opinion divided sharply, with detractors dismissing

it as the ultimate collage of bad taste in American architecture. Upon
one point all parties agreed: the Woolworth Building deserved its
epithet as the "Cathedral of Commerce."

In addition to the techniques of steel framing, other innovations,
such as hollow tile for fireproofing, spurred the high-rise boom. Obviously
engineers could not have built bigger buildings without better elevators.
Elisha Graves Otis, a Vermont-born inventor, worked out the basic
model of the first passenger elevator while trying to perfect an automatic
safety device to prevent the fall of hoisting machinery. After demon-
strating his invention in 1853 in New York's great cast-iron structure,
the Crystal Palace, Otis installed his first elevator in 1857 in the Haughwout Building. Intended as a convenience for the department store's
customers, the new lift rose so slowly that according to one scornful
observer, "the aged or infirm or fatigued, or even lazy occupants of the
cage were easily distanced by the circumambient athletes who continued
to prefer the enclosed staircase."

Known originally as the "vertical screw railway," the primitive lift
worked on the principle of an artesian screw threaded into a groove in
the car. The Equitable Building in New York was probably the first
structure designed to hold an elevator, and its success triggered a move
to abandon the five-story maximum on buildings. Otis built a company
around his invention, which progressed gradually from pulley power to
hydraulic power and gearing techniques in the 1870s to electrical power
in the 1880s. By that time the elevator had won wide acceptance and
Otis made a fortune.

The skyscraper mania was not without its detractors. In 1896 the
New York Chamber of Commerce declared that tall buildings were "not
consistent with public health and that the interests of the majority of
our citizens require that the height should be limited." That same year
The New York Times warned that "the time is evidently near when
it will be necessary to proceed in the public interest against the excesses
of selfishness." The major complaints were that the tall buildings
exacerbated the already crowded conditions of most downtown areas,
cut off sunlight to adjacent structures and sidewalks, and were basically
unsafe. Completion of the Woolworth Building sparked the drive to
limit building heights. In 1916 New York City adopted its comprehensive zoning law which included a restriction on height. But architects
deftly circumvented the provision by utilizing the "wedding cake" design and skyscrapers continued their upward spiral.*

* The "wedding cake" design involved setting each five or ten stories back from
those beneath it. The effect resembled the layers of a wedding cake. It is a classic

The application of new technology to building design and the record heights achieved by skyscrapers reinforced the dilemma posed by mass transit. New technology, designed to improve urban activities, often aggravated the very conditions it attempted to alleviate. Just as new transit lines generated additional traffic and congested surburban corridors, skyscrapers increased the density of inner-city population. A product of efforts to wring maximum use from expensive downtown land, skyscrapers in turn pushed land values even higher and thereby created a perpetual spiral of rising heights and rising values.

Chicago succumbed early to this spiral because Lake Michigan, the River, and the Loop's railroad system all blocked outward expansion of its downtown business district. Once the technology of steel-frame construction and the elevator were perfected, the obvious solution was to build upward. Moreover, the new skyscrapers, or "cloudscrapers" as some called them, quickly became commercial status symbols. Older, smaller buildings began to lose corporate tenants who scurried to find space in the newest "tallest building in the world." The prestige of a skyscraper address encouraged other firms to invest in high-rise construction, which in turn caused land values to skyrocket.* In his study of Chicago land values, Homer Hoyt concluded that "the advent of the skyscraper was responsible for a marked increase in ground values in the central business district of Chicago from 1889–1891." Although the twenty-five or so buildings which rated "high-rise" status occupied only about 7 percent of the total downtown area, other land owners revalued their lots on the basis of their being potential skyscraper sites. The cry in Chicago became "tear down the old rat trap and erect a sixteen-story building."

Only one other edifice rivaled the skyscraper as the supreme monument of the industrial age: the railroad terminal. Like the city itself, terminal architecture progressed rapidly from makeshift shack to palatial mansion. In growing industrial centers, railroad officers and city fathers alike attached great importance to the terminal as both a symbol and an advertisement. The train station had replaced the gate and the port as the entranceway to cities; it gave visitors their first impression of the place. Determined to make that impression a memorable one, cities everywhere tried to outdo one another in the magnificence of their

---

illustration of how businessmen could twist reform legislation to their own purposes without actually breaking the law.

* This competition over prestige continues even today, with the old rivals, New York and Chicago, still in the forefront of the race. Both cities are constructing gigantic new skyscrapers.

transportation temples. Most terminals were built by the railroads, though some municipalities offered direct aid or at least indirect assistance.

Influenced more by the classical Beaux-Arts tradition of the Chicago World's Fair than by the functionalism of the skyscraper, terminal architecture often seemed at odds with the steam-puffing machines it housed. Locomotives projected an aura of power and energy that reflected the very essence of the industrial era. Disdaining the implications of that image for their own work, most architects chose instead to encase trains in imitation white Pantheons or heavy stone Gothic castles.

New York predictably seized the lead in the terminal race by constructing two major train stations. To house the trains of his powerful company, Alexander J. Cassatt, president of the Pennsylvania Railroad, went to one of America's foremost architects: Charles F. McKim of McKim, Mead and White. Legend has it that Cassatt and McKim conceived of the Pennsylvania Station at Delmonico's Restaurant, over a bottle of Madeira wine. Whatever the case, McKim accepted the commission and completed the structure in 1910.

Located on Seventh Avenue, the Pennsylvania Terminal awed visitors with its colossal scale. The grand vaulted glass-and-steel skylights over the main concourse freely exhibited the building's construction lines. The interior featured a grand staircase leading to a great hall modeled upon an imperial Roman bath. Beyond the great hall lay a second huge area which abandoned Rome for a more modern decor. Filled with stands and entrance gates to the tracks, this second area betrayed the extent to which form seemed out of tune with function in the great terminal. Nevertheless, it achieved instant status as a showcase for New York. Unlike the great temples of antiquity, however, Pennsylvania fell victim to rising costs and declining traffic in the 1960s and was torn down to make way for a sports and office complex erected in the valuable air space above the railroad tracks.

Fortunately, Grand Central Station, New York's other main terminal, managed to sell its air rights and survive intact. Completed in 1913, Grand Central remains perhaps the nation's greatest monument of the railroad age. It possessed several unique features, including two separate levels of track which segregated suburban from interurban traffic, a loop design which allowed trains to turn around without reverse movement, complete electrification, and a system which enabled trains to move in both directions on all four approach tracks. In both architectural and engineering terms, Grand Central was a marvel of daring and ingenuity. Done in French Baroque style, the station featured a statue of Mercury, the deity of business, whose upraised hand welcomed visitors to the city.

Whatever their architectural or aesthetic merits, the two New York terminals represented a stupendous engineering feat. Carl Condit has called them "the most extensive and most impressive civic projects in the United States built by private capital." No other terminal in the world matched them in size or grandeur. Both applied design on a grand scale to the solution of pressing urban problems, and both succeeded in their goals. By placing rail facilities underground, they reclaimed precious land needed for other purposes. By centralizing and integrating rail traffic, they reduced urban congestion and expedited the flow of people to and from the city. But, of course, their triumph was a fleeting one; the efficiency of their operation only invited still greater congestion that eventually overtaxed the new facilities.

Other cities followed New York's lead on a more modest scale. Daniel Burnham designed classical stations for Washington and Pittsburgh, and Jarvis Hunt did likewise for Kansas City. Chicago, Cleveland, and Cincinnati all erected new stations as part of a broader concept of civic design. Chicago's huge Union Station, located next to the Chicago River, remains an impressive example of the terminal as Greek temple; few stations equaled its purity of classical expression. Both Louisville and Nashville, on the other hand, opted for Gothic designs replete with towers and turrets. Atop the 219-foot central tower of Nashville's Union Station (1900) stood a 20-foot statue of the ubiquitous Mercury.

Whether cast as Greek temples or Gothic cathedrals, the rail terminals of industrial cities were fitting monuments for their age. Like the skyscraper, they invoked a sense of majesty and grandeur. Like skyscrapers, too, they advertised the immense wealth and power of their occupants. In their imitation of antiquity, they betrayed the extent to which business had become a religion in the industrial city.

Utilities and Disutilities

The physical strain wrought by urban growth involved more than land and buildings. Expanding populations required not only housing but water, gas, electricity, and sewer lines. Better and wider streets were needed to handle the city's heavier traffic. Small cities suddenly grown large found themselves called upon to provide more utilities and services than ever before. Once again municipalities sought refuge in new technology and techniques, and once again every solution gave rise to new problems. As with mass transit, "progress" brought fewer benefits to the public than to the corporate interests that owned the utilities and charged exorbitant rates for their services. Utility franchises, paving contracts, street cleaning, garbage hauling, and maintenance work all reaped financial windfalls for the contractors and politicians in charge of dispensing contracts or fulfilling them.

The importance of streets to urban growth and commerce is so obvious that it needs no elaboration. Yet the history of their construction and care is a dismal chapter in the conflict between public and private interest. Streets in most American cities took a terrific pounding and most were in wretched condition. Any city-dweller who ventured beyond his front door understood that fact only too well. When civic-minded individuals complained about the scandalous condition of their town's thoroughfares, the lament usually fell upon deaf ears. A first-rate street system required a large capital investment, which meant higher taxes. Many other services were also clamoring for more funds even while urbanites protested against more taxes. The result was a pattern of benign neglect in which streets got a relatively low priority in the municipal budget. On one hand, few cities allocated sufficient funds for street construction and care; on the other, graft, inefficiency, and lack of planning sapped the effectiveness of the funds that were allocated.

When it came to paving, for example, most city governments agreed to it only as a last resort, and then tried to do the job as cheaply as possible. Streets were extended long before money was available to pave them. When they were finally paved, the contractor concentrated on the surface rather than the foundation. As a result, few streets enjoyed a long or happy life. Repairs were frequent and recurring; besides disrupting traffic and inconveniencing travelers, they cost a lot of money in the long run. But if this "pound-foolish" economy did not serve the public well, it proved a boon to politicians and their friends who discovered that paving contracts were lucrative plums for "friendly" contractors.

Conditions were even worse in the West, where new towns usually relegated street paving to the bottom of the improvements list. Ladies wishing to cross the street had to hop across stones planted in the mud. In Abilene they still tell the tale of the stranger who jumped off his horse and disappeared—except for his hat. The larger midwestern cities like Chicago and Detroit commonly laid down boards over large cedar blocks. To many observers the effect was only a marginal improvement over the mire. As late as 1890 the *Detroit Journal* grumbled that cedar blocks furnished the city with "150 miles of rotten, rutted, lumpy, dilapidated paving." In that same year, according to Arthur M. Schlesinger, "only 629 of Chicago's 2,048 miles of streets were paved at all, about half with wood block, the rest with macadam, gravel, stone block, asphalt, cinders or cobblestones."

The most common surfacing used in the late nineteenth century was cobblestone. Large cities such as Philadelphia, New York, and especially Baltimore favored these large durable stones, which provided the bumpiest, noisiest rides found anywhere. Urbanites benumbed by the din of modern traffic would find no relief in the industrial city with its horses' hooves and wagon wheels clattering on cobblestones, trolleys clanging down the middle of the street, and trains roaring on the elevated lines. Eastern cities used cobblestones because they were readily available; most came over as ballast in ships. Granite blocks were also used.

The erratic surfaces of most American streets provoked much consternation as traffic increased. In the 1880s Washington, Buffalo, and Philadelphia adopted the European practice of paving with asphalt. Although it refracted the heat and tended to be slippery, asphalt did provide a quiet surface. Usually it was laid in the suburbs and new sections of town. For the central business district, which required a stronger material, bricks became common in the 1880s, particularly in cities like Philadelphia, Des Moines, Columbus, and Cleveland, which manufactured them.

But American streets did not improve appreciably until builders got beneath the surface of the problem. A substantial and well-drained foundation reduced the amount of surface material used and provided a longer-lasting road. Once cities and their contractors took the trouble to prepare the roadbed, macadam soared in popularity. Cheap stones crushed and mixed with oil, then placed in a well-laid foundation, became the standard paving practice in many cities during the 1880s and 1890s. Sacramento was an early user of this method, along with New York, Buffalo, New Bedford, and Los Angeles. By the century's end, cities could lay their streets with a reasonably cheap, durable, quiet surface, and macadam joined asphalt as the leading pavement in suburban and residential developments.

If street care often languished from neglect, it also suffered from spurts of municipal zeal. Technological innovations never operate in a vacuum. Progress toward solution of one problem often had unfortunate repercussions elsewhere. In this case, cities found it necessary to rip up their streets to install pipes, tubing, or cables for utility services. Sewer lines especially took their toll on streets because, once in widespread use, they went down in nearly every neighborhood. Growing cities produced a mountain of human, animal, and industrial waste, the disposal of which defied the capacities of government and private citizen alike. Few problems dogged the industrial city so persistently or outran new solutions so rapidly. Nor has the modern city improved much upon this legacy of failure.

Most cities handled the problem by simply dumping their waste in the nearest body of water. New York, Boston, and Chicago, which in 1856 built the first comprehensive sewer system, installed underground conduits to carry wastes into the nearby sea. By 1916 New York City alone was dumping close to 500,000,000 gallons of raw sewage a day into her rivers. Smaller towns relied upon village depositing techniques which held little value for the congested city. In 1877 Philadelphia had 82,000 private vaults and cesspools; Washington, 56,000; and Chicago, 30,000. The inadequacy of this ancient arrangement impressed itself upon the eyes and nostrils of every city-dweller. One citizen echoed a familiar complaint of the era when he reported that in Philadelphia and "numerous other cities of eastern Pennsylvania the pedestrian along the streets was continually stepping over a little stream of soapy water flowing in channels across the sidewalk from the house to the street gutters."

Discontent brought action but little relief. In 1887 Los Angeles built a sewer farm to make use of its sewage while Baltimore covered its open gutters and constructed an underground system which connected to each of its 125,000 dwellings. Chicago's experience offers the most instructive example of the waste-disposal treadmill. Realizing even in the 1870s that the city's waste was ruining Lake Michigan, city officials struck upon an audacious plan to reroute the flow of deposits: they would reverse the flow of the Chicago River away from Lake Michigan and allow the river to carry waste downstream where ultimately it would reach the Mississippi River. After considerable effort and the expenditure of $80,000,000, which included the construction of six pumping stations to keep the flow moving, this was accomplished.

To its chagrin, Chicago discovered that it had not solved the problem so much as compounded it. The new system inflicted Chicago's wastes upon distant rivers where it spoiled the water of downstream towns. Moreover, the drainage system backed up into Chicago and Lake Michigan during heavy rains. The waterways around Chicago and heavily industrialized Gary went on accumulating waste, and regional pollution continued to run rampant.

Well might Chicagoans have regarded "progress" as a costly and bitter joke, but other cities fared no better. No combination of civic energy, money, and new technology seemed capable of containing the flood of waste materials that resulted from rapid growth. The same held true for garbage disposal. Major ports like New York and Boston early adopted the practice of towing their garbage out to sea in scows and dumping it on an outgoing tide, thus making a gift of their refuse to other shores and other places. During the 1880s some cities, especially in the land-locked Midwest, erected furnaces to burn their garbage. This practice spread quickly and endured for decades. As modern urbanites know, the burning of refuse merely converted solid waste into a less visible but no less distressing form of pollution.

While accumulation of waste and garbage threatened to bury the industrial city, their presence also menaced its water supply. Nearly every major city drew its drinking water from the same area where it dumped waste. Chicago, for instance, built pumps to discharge waste far out into the lake to minimize pollution closer to the shore. Still the water was unfit to drink without adding tons of chemicals, and the chemicals did nothing for the taste. Well before 1900 naturally pure water had become extinct in most sizable cities.

The use of technology to increase the supply of pure water illustrates again the manner in which technology failed to satisfy the appetites of its recipients and merely stimulated the demand it was intended to quell. As Lewis Mumford put it, "the most characteristic technical achievements of the big city are those that further congestion; and the first of these is the canalization of water into storage in reservoirs, its transmission through vast mains, tubular rivers, from the open country to the heart of the city."

Philadelphia pioneered in public water systems soon after the yellow fever epidemic of 1793. Engineer-architect Benjamin Henry Latrobe devised a plan for steam pumps to gather the water and a system of wooden pipes and street hydrants to distribute it. The entire operation went into effect in 1801, but was quickly outgrown, whereupon the city decided in 1819 to build a dam across the Schuylkill River along with a series of water-powered pumps to draw the water up Fairmount Hill. There the water would be stored in large reservoirs and fed by gravity down to the city. The Fairmount system and the open space surrounding it evolved into the nation's first major urban park by 1844.

Other municipalities envied the Philadelphia plan, and New York moved first to copy it. In 1842 it completed the 34–mile Croton aqueduct, which prompted one visitor to the city to declare that "a work more akin in magnificence to the ancient and Roman aqueducts has not been achieved in our times." But New York's population doubled during the 1840s and quickly outstripped the capacity of this engineering marvel. Between 1885 and 1892 the city erected a second aqueduct, the New

Croton, which carried four times the amount of water (approximately 300,000,000 gallons a day) provided by the original Croton. When even that did not suffice, New York was obliged to build 100 miles up the Hudson River to the Catskills to tap a new water source, which doubled its supply at a cost of $180,000,000. In the water-starved West, some cities went even farther afield. Los Angeles traveled 250 miles to the Sierra Mountains to get water for its swelling population. The Los Angeles water system used enough cement to build a wall around Manhattan Island ten feet thick and forty feet high.

Most cities in the 1870s and 1880s constructed major waterworks but the inability to keep up with spiraling demand caused many places to experience "water famines." And the water that did come was virtually untreated. In 1870 no city had a filtration system, and by 1900 only 6 percent of the urban population received filtered water. Pittsburgh, which deposited its industrial waste into and drew its drinking water from the Allegheny River, waited until its death rate from typhoid fever reached four times the national average before constructing a filter system. Between 1908 and 1914, the city installed pumping stations along the Allegheny to filter the water through sediment, whereupon the death rate promptly dropped. Yet even after the improvements, the city's typhoid death rate, although only about half the American average, remained twice that of major European centers.

By 1920 a majority of large American cities possessed filtration and treatment plants. Jersey City pioneered in chemical treatment with a plant built in 1908. But everywhere the surge of population growth pressed hard upon the ingenuity of engineers and resources of municipal governments. The passing decades have brought no solution to the water dilemma; on the contrary, it has reached crisis proportions in many modern cities. Even a century ago it often seemed that in the complex urban environment the most basic needs were the hardest to fulfill satisfactorily.

Technology had another curious effect upon the urban environment: it transformed innovations into necessities of life. The advent of electric energy illustrates the process by which technological breakthroughs generate on a colossal scale demands which had never before existed. Electricity touched every aspect of the city's life—it powered machinery, ran trains, lifted elevators, and lighted streets and homes. To some extent, electricity merely replaced other sources of power and performed old functions in a new way. But once its versatility was recognized, new inventions utilized it for an incredible variety of purposes which urbanites by 1920 accepted as indispensable to their life-style. No one grasped the impact of the dynamo, the means for converting mechanical energy into electric energy, more surely than Henry Adams. "Among the thousand symbols of ultimate energy," he concluded, "the dynamo was not so human as some, but it was the most expressive."

Forty-five years after British scientist Michael Faraday discovered the principle of the dynamo in 1831, the American Centennial Celebration in Philadelphia proudly displayed several generators. The first practical use of the dynamo for urban purposes came through the work of Charles F. Brush, an Ohio engineer who in 1887 applied the current of a dynamo to an arc lamp. The electrical current in Brush's lamp passed between two slightly separated sticks of carbon and the burning of the carbon produced a sputtering bluish-white arc flame. Brush's lamps, introduced first in Cleveland and then in San Francisco and Wabash, Indiana, soon illuminated every main thoroughfare in the country. Although some women complained that the lamps cast a ghastly pall upon their complexions, carbon arcs proved vastly superior to the older city lamps flamed by a petroleum derivative called gas oil. They were brighter, cheaper, and easier to maintain.

Electric lighting took its most significant step forward when it moved off the street and into the home. No truly satisfactory form of interior lighting existed until Thomas A. Edison invented the electric light bulb. Working in his Menlo Park, New Jersey, laboratory in the late 1870s, Edison tested thousands of materials to find one that would act as a long-burning filament in a sealed vacuum bulb. When he patented his incandescent lamp in 1880, it caught the imagination of the American public as few inventions ever had.

The new lamp excelled the older gas models in every respect. It was safer, burned brighter and more steadily, and gave off less heat. Edison also found a way to switch individual lamps off without affecting others on the same circuit. Huge crowds gathered at his showroom on Fifth Avenue to gaze at the new marvel. On December 31, 1889, the Pennsylvania Railroad ran a special train to Menlo Park from New York City just so people could view Edison's bulbs displayed in his laboratory.

While Carl Auer van Welsbach's invention of the "water gas" mantle lamp in 1885 gave the gas light a new lease on its diminishing life, the future clearly belonged to electricity. In 1882 the Edison-designed Pearl Street Power Station opened in New York. The first central power station in the country, it sent direct electrical current to eighty-five buildings. New electric companies sprang up everywhere; in Chicago alone, eleven firms appeared by the mid–1880s and multiplied their business tenfold by 1893. That same year a successful exhibition of electric lamps at the Chicago World's Fair aroused great enthusiasm. In the two decades after the Fair, production jumped thirty times; and architects Louis Sullivan and Charles F. McKim used electric lighting exclusively in their new structures, including the Chicago Auditorium and Boston's Symphony Hall.

Hotels also switched to electricity. In 1882 the Hotel Everett in New York became the first urban hotel to be lighted with electricity. Later the same year Chicago's famous Palmer House built its own generator for ninety-six incandescent lamps in two dining rooms. James Hood Wright of Fort Washington, New York, won acclaim in December, 1881, as the first citizen to light his house by connection to a central power station. Cornelius Vanderbilt and J. P. Morgan enjoyed the amenities earlier than Mr. Wright by installing power plants in their mansions.

The zeal with which Edison promoted his direct current system could not conceal the fact that it possessed serious limitations. It could not transmit current farther than a mile or two from the power source, which meant that a large city like New York would require about sixty separate power stations each equipped with small engines and generators. During the mid–1880s a different system based upon alternating current —devised by a Frenchman named Gaulard and developed in the United States by George Westinghouse—challenged Edison for the American market. The superiority of alternating current lay primarily in its ability to send current over long distances.

The ensuing struggle plumbed depths of ferocity unusual even in the tradition of cutthroat competition. Scientists in both America and England opposed alternating current on the grounds that it was dangerous. Those interests who had invested heavily in the direct-current system fought desperately against the threat of ruination. Edison himself, who savored his reputation as a pioneer in technology, found himself in the uncomfortable role of resisting technical innovation with all his might. The whole affair led Westinghouse to observe with fair accuracy that "the struggle for the control of the electric light and power business has never been exceeded in bitterness by any of the historical commercial controversies of a former day." But in the end Westinghouse and alternating current prevailed.

Even more than gas lamps, electric lighting transformed the city into a twenty-four-hour place. The pace of urban activities livened as night-life entertainment was extended, people were able to get around more freely and safely, and the evening hours began to attract rather than discourage walkers. Merchants extended their hours, and some industrialists kept their factories running longer. New lighting inspired aesthetic adornments for the city like well-designed lampposts and illuminated monuments, statues, and fountains. The whole atmosphere of city streets seemed cleaner and whiter, a bit like the "Great White City" of the Chicago Fair which had impressed visitors so deeply. It was as if someone, by turning on these electric wonders, had caused urbanites to take a closer look at their cities, and to extract from the shadows a new sense of the degree to which the magic of technology had altered their lives.

Clockwork Efficiency

As new inventions changed the outward appearance of the industrial city, so did they improve its inner efficiency. The telephone and telegraph were but two of the most conspicuous examples. Bell's "talking box" maintained business communication lines which both outward and upward growth threatened to disrupt. Not only could companies spread across the continent without losing touch, they could also occupy several floors of a skyscraper with no sacrifice of instant contact. The telephone also provided jobs for newly arrived farm women who manned the switchboards as the famous "Hello Girls." By the 1890s more than 800,000 phones were in service, more than twice as many as in all of Europe.

A host of new machines invaded the office and revamped business procedures. The "ticker tape," patented in 1867, originated in the need for quick communication between brokers and exchanges. Its mechanical alphabet and number wheels replaced the ten or fifteen boys a brokerage house once employed to watch its special commodities. By the 1870s every major banking and financial institution—and numerous individual investors—possessed a ticker tape to scan fluctuations in stock prices. In time it became a symbol (and not always a benign one) for Wall Street, for speculation, and for capitalism.

Where the ticker tape confined its presence to the financial arena, the typewriter penetrated every imaginable type of business office. Patented in 1868 by Christopher L. Sholes and immediately placed on the market, the new machine with its precise and uniform lettering won converts with a speed that revivalists might well envy. Like so many other machines, it was both a labor-saving device and an instrument of social change. According to the Department of Labor, the typewriter could produce a thousand-word document in 19.8 minutes, whereas a hand copyist required 74.8 minutes for the same work. It also contributed to the broader trend in which women replaced men in secretarial positions. The typewriter occupies so familiar a place in the modern office that it is hard to recapture how deeply its efficiency impressed contemporaries. S. M. D. North of Utica, New York, the first businesman to adopt the typewriter to his office operation, reflected years later: "I have often wished that I had kept that original machine for it would have illustrated better than any other mechanism . . . the marvellous rapidity with which American ingenuity advances to the point of perfection any labor-saving instrument."

Edison's mimeograph machine (1876), along with the cash register (1876), the stenotype (1876), the adding machine (1888), and the spring-weighing scale (1895), combined with the telephone and typewriter to indicate how far business operations had come from the quill pen, letter book, musty ledger, messenger boy, and hand copyist of an earlier era. Yet none of these equaled another instrument as the supreme symbol of the industrial order: the mass-produced watch.

The hand watch embodied both the genius of American inventiveness and the spirit of the age of mechanization. Fittingly enough, machine watchmaking developed during the 1850s, the same decade in which the preindustrial walking city was giving way to the industrial city. Aaron Dennison's factory in Roxbury, Massachusetts, was the first to manufacture a watch with interchangeable parts in large quantities. Dennison removed his factory to Waltham, Massachusetts, and with Edward Howard formed the American Watch Company which anticipated Henry Ford's assembly line production by fifty years.

Waltham quickly emerged as the center of America's watchmaking industry. By 1900 the factories there averaged 250 watches a year per worker, while Swiss watchmakers could manage only 40. The spectacle prompted a British visitor to remark, upon leaving the Waltham factory, that "the manufacture of watches on the old plan was gone." But Waltham did not long keep the field to itself. By the late 1870s watchmakers in Waterbury, Connecticut, were producing timepieces at a price the masses could afford. In 1900 a mass-produced watch, complete with a year's guarantee, sold for a dollar. The dollar watch offered tangible benefits and some intangible liabilities. On one hand, the workingman owned a fine timepiece to slide in and out of his pocket; on the other hand, he could no longer plead ignorance or poverty as an excuse for being late to work.

While it still took nine months to produce a baby, nearly everything else in the city quickened. As never before, time became a commodity to be arbitrarily divided and put to its most efficient use. The old adage "time is money" acquired new meaning for employer and worker alike. Despite its vaunted reputation for efficiency, the American industrial order operated at a level well below its potential throughout the nineteenth century. Problems of organization, scheduling, technology, and above all the work habits of its labor force plagued firms in every industry.

As Herbert G. Gutman has pointed out, nineteenth-century workers, whether displaced artisans, recruits from the farm, or newly arrived immigrants, belonged to cultures whose work habits clashed sharply with those required for factory work. They lacked the kind of discipline needed for industrial work, were accustomed to working their own hours, chafed at subordinating their social pleasures to the work routine, and resented the novel demand that they report for duty every day. Of course a little time in the industrial trenches trained many workers to the industrial grind, but many industries relied upon unskilled labor, and the turnover rate in such factories was appallingly high. Even those who reported for work regularly could not always be made to apply themselves unsparingly to the task at hand. Few problems vexed efficiency-minded businessmen more than the fickle vagaries of their work force.

Seen in this light, the clock vastly transcended its immediate function of telling time. It symbolized the concerted attempt to harness the raw material of labor to the iron regimen of American work habits. Workmen predictably resisted the efforts as best they could, but the odds turned against them. As immigration swelled the labor force, it created a surplus which heightened the competition for jobs, especially in hard times. However distasteful the factory routine, it was preferable—even inviting—when starvation seemed the only alternative. Gutman cites a verse by Yiddish poet Morris Rosenfeld which vividly portrays the clock as oppressor:

> The Clock in the workshop,—it rests not a moment;
> It points on, and ticks on: eternity—time;
> Once someone told me the clock had a meaning,—
> In pointing and ticking had reason and rhyme. . . .
> At times, when I listen, I hear the clock plainly;—
> The reason of old—the old meaning—is gone!
> The maddening pendulum urges me forward
> To labor and still labor on.
> The tick of the clock is the boss in his anger.

The face of the clock has the eyes of the foe.
The clock—I shudder—Dost hear how it draws me?
It calls me "Machine" and it cries [to] me "Sew"!

As urban man grew more apart from his rural cousin with every passing year, nothing separated them more than the clock. While the farmer measured his life by the organic rhythms of seasonal change, of sunrise and sunset, the urbanite chained himself to the "tyranny of time." Trains ran on schedule and were expected to be "on time"; work proceeded with "clockwork efficiency"; mechanical processes were geared "according to the clock"; novels gave way to "periodicals"; and when electricity was mated with the clock in plants, workers had to "clock in." "With the sense of the passage of time felt by everyone under the prevalence of time machines," historian Roger Burlingame has written, "the old easy-going days were over. Lateness at work, school, business appointments was no longer tolerated. . . . As factory work became more exacting, time schedules played an important part in production." Once established, the industrial pattern surged forward on its own momentum; there could be no turning back. What the future held in store for cities would be built upon the precedents already set, not upon some idealized version of what once was or might have been.

Technology powered the city, expanded it upward and outward, provided its water, lighted it, carried its wastes, and organized its work patterns. It did much of this crudely, inefficiently, and at great human sacrifice, but Americans had always been slow to reckon the social cost of "progress." More important, it fixed the destiny of the industrial city. Future change or improvement would center upon more sophisticated technology, more prudently applied. No amount of daydreaming or wishful thinking could banish or reverse the technological presence.

The industrial revolution changed the physical city into a larger, more congested, more polluted place. But it had done so under man's guidance. Blind faith in mechanical progress as human progress and the unfettered power of the profit system left little room for pondering the larger ramifications of success. By World War I the industrial city was the dominant urban form which the legacy of unbridled technology willed to the twentieth century.

CHAPTER 6

Peopling the Cities:
The Clash of Cultures

The first visit to New York is always productive of a singular
sensation—a realization of your utter inconsequence in the world;
a feeling that everyone who swells in the crowd and rush of
Broadway is of infinitely more importance than yourself, and that
you are as much out of your sphere as though some mighty occult
force had suddenly transported you to a strange planet, the inhabitants of which were rushing about in their efforts to destroy
themselves and every world in the infinite firmament.

—JAMES W. BUEL
Mysteries and Miseries of America's Great Cities (1883)

FOR MUCH OF the nineteenth century, millions of men, women, and
children streamed into American cities to operate the machines of
the new age. Drawn from the countryside, the small towns, and foreign
lands, newcomers swelled the population of established cities and created
new ones overnight. To their adopted city they brought a wildly mixed
baggage of cultures, languages, customs, dress, and ideas. Their presence
strained every facility the city offered. Housing, never plentiful, vanished entirely; trolley cars bulged with riders, schoolrooms overflowed;
and drinking water, toilets, and hospital beds became scarce. In every
city the crowded ethnic enclaves had the highest crime rate, the lowest
health standards, and the worst educational record.

More subtly, however, the "greenhorns" changed the temper of the
city. Their presence transformed cities into more complex and cosmopolitan places filled with strange sights, sounds, and smells. They were
strangers in a strange land, but ironically they helped make the city an
alien place even to those who had always lived in it. Neither native nor

newcomer felt entirely at home in the unfamiliar milieu of the industrial city. Social confusion led to social conflict which often exploded into violence. Throughout the period 1850–1920, the vision of a stable—let alone integrated—social order hovered tauntingly beyond the reach of most American cities.

Draining the Countryside

The reasons people came in such large numbers have already been noted. Jobs were the main impetus. Factories, foundries, steel mills, oil refineries, slaughterhouses, and construction firms, among others, required a constant flow of skilled and unskilled labor. Moreover, job opportunity in the cities was coupled with declining opportunity in the country. In part, the city lured young people because the farms no longer needed them, or offered them a pallid future at best. This situation stemmed directly from the effects of industrialization upon rural life. After the Civil War farming shifted from self-sufficiency to commercial productivity. No longer content to produce for themselves and barter for what else they required, farmers turned to cash crops and found themselves wedded to regional, national, and even international markets.

The transition was deceptively easy. The West offered endless acres of fertile land, railroads provided access to urban markets, improved farm implements and farming techniques made large-scale productivity possible, and growing cities demanded food in huge quantities. All the ingredients were there to transform the farmer into a businessman. For those who took the leap, and there were many, the perils often outweighed the prospects. Competing for a share of expanded markets required heavy investment in land and machinery. Seldom long on capital, farmers resorted to borrowing large sums at exorbitant interest rates. In 1860 the value of farm machinery in the United States totaled $246,000,000. It jumped to $750,000,000 by 1900, then skyrocketed to $3,595,000,000 by 1920. Land prices rose sharply, and the cost of transportation fluctuated at the whim of the railroads, who favored large shippers and were not above resorting to such practices as rebates and long- and short-haul discrimination. Most agrarians echoed the lament of Dyke, the hops farmer in Frank Norris's novel, The Octopus (1901): "He remembered he had once said the great trust had overlooked his little enterprise, disdaining to plunder such small fry. He should have known better than that. How had he ever imagined the Lord would permit him to make any money?"

Many farmers proved poor businessmen. The huge debts they incurred, coupled with falling prices, robbed them of any chance for sizable profits. Many went broke, defaulted on the mortgage, and either left for the city or became tenants on the land they once owned. Inevitably the scourge of hard times drove farmers to seek relief first in politics and then in organization. From this effort evolved the Granger movement, the Alliances, the Populist party, and ultimately the national farm organizations of the twentieth century.

Mechanization of the farm increased crop yields and reduced the manpower needed to produce it; that bare fact does much to explain the exodus to the city. In 1880 the rural population of the country constituted 71.4 percent of the total population; by 1920 the figure dropped to 48.6 percent. Not only young people but some of their parents gave up the struggle and moved to town.

The reasons for their departure are not hard to discover. Beyond the eternal struggle to make ends meet, farmers had to combat nature's own calamities. Droughts, dust storms, snowstorms, frosts, and floods plagued the farmers as did attacks of insect pests like the cinch bug, the boll weevil, and the corn bore. Disease ravaged livestock and crops, while overworking the land led to graver problems of soil exhaustion and erosion. Ole Rölvaag described the terror unleashed by an onslaught of grasshoppers in his *Giants in the Earth* (1927), perhaps the finest novel written about farm life on the prairie after the Civil War:

The ominous waves of cloud seemed to advance with terrific speed, breaking now and then like a huge surf, and with the deep, dull roaring sound as of a heavy undertow rolling into caverns in a mountain side. . . . But they were neither breakers nor foam, these waves. . . .

And now from out the sky gushed down with cruel force a living pulsating stream . . . it flared and flittered around them like light gone mad; it chirped and buzzed through the air; it snapped and hopped along the ground; the whole place was a weltering turmoil of raging little demons. . . . They whizzed by in the air; they literally covered the ground; they lit on the heads of grain, on the stubble, on everything in sight—popping and glittering, millions on millions of them. . . . The people watched it, stricken with fear and awe.

Beyond these travails the desolation of the farm and rural village stifled restless young people who doubted that tedium was a just reward for the hardships of farm life. Through the railroad, the telegraph, the enchantments of the Sears catalog, and the stories of traveling salesmen or other strangers a picture of the outside world filtered into the countryside. Frederic Howe wrote in his autobiography, "At Chatauqua I heard some lectures on political economy by Richard T. Ely, of Johns

Hopkins. They made men want to know more about the world outside of my little town." Visions of the city's excitement, the adventures and opportunities it offered, threw the drab monotony of farm life into bold relief. Those who aspired to something more than slopping pigs, milking cows, and wrestling with nature—all for a modest place in calico society—cast their lot with the city.

Hamlin Garland caught this sense of a stillborn future in his collection of stories entitled *Main Travelled Roads* (1891). Having escaped the rural hardships of his youth for a literary career in Boston, New York, and Chicago, Garland returned to the prairie and was shocked at what he saw. In his introduction he depicted the despair born of the contrast between city and farm:

The farther I got from Chicago the more depressing the landscape became. It was bad enough in one farmer's home in Mitchell County, but my pity grew more intense as I passed from northwest Iowa into southern Dakota. The houses, bare as boxes, dropped on the treeless plains, the barbed-wire fences running at right angles, and the towns mere assemblages of flimsy wooden sheds with painted-pine battlement, produced on me the effect of an almost helpless and sterile poverty.

And Garland was not alone. The magazines of the era were filled with such articles as "The Drift to the Cities," "The Doom of the Small Town," "The Isolation of Life on Prairie Farms."* Even while these laments poured forth, a procession of homesteaders trekked overland to find land in the Far West. Those who endured the sufferings and hardships settled the West but did not win it. Victory went instead to those who possessed the means to exploit the West's resources: railroads, mining companies, lumber interests, large corporate ranching and agricultural companies, and land speculators. On the whole, the number of homesteaders was a mere trickle compared to the flood of settlers accumulating in the cities.

The exodus to the city drained the countryside of more than bodies. It removed those with youth, vitality, and ambition—in short, the generation's movers and leaders. Their departure drained rural America of the fresh blood it needed to infuse village life with a new sense of purpose and vigor. The growing population imbalance also inflamed the emotions of those who feared the effects of urban imperialism upon rural life. Some lashed out at the city itself. A contributor to *Atlantic*

---

* One recent author, Michael Lesey, was so overwhelmed by the prevalence of despondency, suicide, and insanity in the small towns of Wisconsin that he entitled his pictoral study *Wisconsin Death Trip*.

Monthly in 1899 proclaimed that "Boston is to blame for Belchertown and its decadent tributaries. The country has made the city. All that you boast of courage and vigor and dauntless progress,—have we not suffered a loss for every gain you have won?" Others reacted with fulsome rhetoric extolling the moral superiority of agrarian life: "Work in a factory, and what are you? A dolt and a stupid drudge. Man has made the machine, and the machine has unmade man. Work on a farm and what are you? Ah, thank God, you are the lifter, and the wiser, and the brim fuller of versatile, polytechnic resourcefulness every day of your rustic life."

Such pieties, however, did not jell with reality and they did not stem the tide. The city had too much to offer, whether one left the farm for the big city or, as was more often the case, stopped first in some smaller town. In seeking a fresh start, most unskilled newcomers accepted the lowest and grimiest jobs. Blinded by the glitter of the American Dream, they endured the harshest of circumstances in the belief that it marked the first step of their climb to the top. That unique process which urged farm boys to emulate the success sagas of the tycoons fed upon such claims as appeared in a small Missouri newspaper in 1915: "When Wall Street wants good business men she usually goes back to the soil to get them." The adventures of Horatio Alger's characters, the admonitions of Russell Conwell's lectures,* and the exaggerated tales of former farm boys returning home for visits, fueled the rush to metropolis.

Sheer adventure and escape from boredom added spice to the quest for economic opportunity. The crowds, color, and variety of the city along with its big buildings, hotels, saloons, schools, and museums bedazzled rural folk. William Allen White, leaving Emporia for a visit to Kansas City in 1891, bought a suit, went to a concert, heard a poetry reading, and came home proclaiming that "life certainly was one round of joy in Kansas City." Hamlin Garland described his heroine's reaction to the city in *Rose of Dutcher's Coolly* (1895): "This was to her like entrance into war. It thrilled and engaged her at every turn. She was the center of human life. To win here was to win all she cared to have." A Connecticut farm girl reported, "When I was in Hartford, I seen a man that seen a man that said he seen the devil." Such titillations hardly discouraged those contemplating a move to the city. While more staid guardians of decency fulminated against what G.S. Dickerman, in a 1915

---

* In a characteristic exhortation from his immensely popular "Acres of Diamonds" lecture, Conwell affirmed that "I say again that the opportunity to get rich, to attain unto great wealth, is here in Philadelphia now."

Atlantic Monthly article, called the "indescribable allurements to vice" in the city ("What wonder that so many city boys grow up with disordered appetites and depraved tastes!"), it was precisely those allurements, among others, that attracted many people.

We know precious little about native white Americans after they got to the city. Immigrants and native blacks attracted more attention at the time they came to the city and have been the focus of many more specific studies ever since. But details about white farmers, "hillbillies," "crackers," and "buckwheats," are scarce for the industrial period. Native whites blended into the urban population and left few traces of their trials in adapting to the city.

We do know that native whites who migrated to cities did much better than immigrants or blacks. Mobility studies indicate that native Americans adapted more easily because they did not have to fight for political or civil liberties, because they had no language barriers, and because they were white. William Miller has pointed out that 30 percent of the railroad leaders of the Gilded Age were the sons of farmers. Many rural people had skills—blacksmithing, toolmaking, carpentry—which could be adapted to industrial work or odd jobs. While distinctions clearly existed between urban and rural people, the United States never developed the type of peasantry found in Europe, and its farm folk adapted more easily to urban life. Typical rural apprehensions of city living—fear of anonymity, specialization, and severe class distinctions—existed in the minds of natives, but not in so virulent a form as in the minds of foreigners.

Nevertheless, a sense of strangeness weighed heavily upon those fresh off the farm. Their country dress, awkward manner, and stumbling unfamiliarity with urban conditions made them the butt of ridicule and the helpless prey of "city slickers" who exploited their ignorance. Perhaps nothing suggests the metamorphosis in American life more vividly than the changed image of the farmer. In little more than a generation, he had toppled off the pedestal upon which Jefferson had enshrined him as the proud yeoman of the soil and plunged steadily toward the less noble characterization of hayseed, hick, or country bumpkin.

Dreams of Gold, Years of Dross

However painful the discrimination faced by rural natives, it never matched the gross inequities that confronted newcomers from abroad. Native immigrants had their detractors when they came to the city, but they also had well-wishers. The "rags-to-riches" success myth possessed strong rural roots. It ennobled the virtues of honest poverty and toil in the background of those who had left the farm to win fame and fortune in business. Most Americans shared the sentiments of an 1895 *Forum* article which stressed the common bonds held by all Americans: "We in the United States cherish a deep love for the farms and villages from which most of us háve sprung."

No such bond salved the ordeal of the foreign-born who swelled the population of industrial cities. While America had always recruited its citizenry from abroad, the post-Civil War influx represented a radically different ethnic grouping which soon led native Americans (i.e., those who had been here for a time) to distinguish between "old" and "new" immigrants. As noted earlier, the new breed hailed from the great peasant stocks of sunny Mediterranean lands like Italy and Greece, the patchwork of Balkan states, the Austro-Hungarian Empire, and the enclaves of eastern Europe. From 1880 to 1900 the proportion of immigrants from Italy leaped from approximately 5 percent to 23 percent. While most previous decades had received between 500,000 and 3,000,000 foreign newcomers, the 1880s saw the figure jump to an unprecedented 5,000,000. The figure dipped during the depression-ridden 1890s only to surge after the turn of the century when 8,000,000 arrived in the first decade and over 6,000,000 in the second decade.

The demand for cheap unskilled labor drew these new immigrants to the cities. They endured the wrenching experience of leaving home for an uncertain journey to a strange land partly because there was nothing to keep them at home. A future which promised only poverty, misery, despair, and sometimes even religious or political persecution, snapped even the strongest cords of sentiment. As one Italian laborer admitted. "Italy is for us whoever gives us our bread."

Overblown tales of America with its "streets paved in gold" and boundless economic opportunities enticed even the fainthearted. Sometimes this hyperbole was only the innocent exaggeration of returnees from America or excited letter writers. "As a boy of nine, and even younger," reminisced one immigrant from eastern Europe, "in my native village of Blato, in Carniola—then a Slavenian duchy of Austria and later a part of Yugoslavia, I experienced a thrill every time one of the men of the community returned from America."

Other encouragements were less innocent. Speculators, colonization societies, and steamship lines promoted distorted tales of economic plenty to increase their own business. As Philip Taylor chronicled in *The Distant Magnet*, "Steamship advertising reached every corner of Europe. Posters from North German Lloyds could be found ornament-

ing cottages in Bohemia. Agents cover Italy as the locusts covered
Egypt! Advertisements could be found in Greek coffee shops and
grocers' shops." While some immigrants warned of the harsh conditions
in American industrial plants ("Here in America we must work for
three horses"), the song of opportunity drowned out more dissonant
tunes. Some large companies actively promoted immigration. Sylvester
Stevens has recounted the recruiting efforts of Andrew Carnegie's steel
empire:

The factories, the mills and the mines were in need of cheap, unskilled
labor. Searching for it, agents of Carnegie and Frick combed the villages of
the Old World, luring the peasants of Hungary, Slovakia and Poland to
the mines and mills of Pittsburgh. Those who responded signed contracts
(not until 1885 did Congress outlaw the contract labor system) that secured
them passage. Carnegie placed a value of $1800 on each adult because "in
former days an efficient slave sold for this sum."

   Political and religious persecution also drove Europeans to seek a
better life in America. The sheer joy of escaping oppression in their
native land led some refugees to exaggerate the blessings of their new
home. One newcomer enthused that "It is wonderful to live in a free
country where the rights of men are upheld, one weighing as much as
the next in the scales, with no difference between rich and poor." A
Norwegian satisfied himself that religious equality existed in America
because "the minister dress just like members of the congregation. He
wears no cassock in church, as in oppressed Europe, to call attention to
differences in station in society."
   While experience might later temper such remarks, it seldom disturbed the conviction that conditions in the United States were far
superior to those in the old country. Polish peasants who could not afford
the rent on their unproductive land left for America. Russian Jews,
feeling the brunt of brutal government-inspired pogroms, fled to
America. Italians, Greeks, and Slovaks who had made heroes of their
departed fellow villagers realized they, too, should go to America. Improved ocean transportation, promises that immigrant welfare societies
would meet the ships arriving in New York, and knowledge that millions
of their fellows were embarking on similar journeys, made it easier to
sever lifelong ties in the mother country. Moreover, there was always
the hope—often fulfilled—that many of those ties would be resumed in
the United States.
   The majority of the "new" immigrants came from agricultural backgrounds. Most of them assumed they would continue to work the land,

and some did make the trek by wagon or rail into the interior. Scandinavians dotted the Minnesota and Dakota frontier; Ukrainians settled in Kansas and Czechs in Nebraska. Far more numerous, however, were the former peasants who stayed in urban areas.

Immigrants congregated in the cities for diverse reasons. Some viewed factory work as only a way station to a plot of land on the western frontier, but financial hardship kept immigrants in the factory longer than they expected. To put a 160-acre farm into production required an average investment of $1,500. Few newcomers could accumulate that much capital on a daily wage of $1.50, and none could do it very quickly. Since most of them arrived in the major ports of New York, New Orleans, and Boston, sheer inertia or convenience, bolstered by encouragement from immigration societies, kept them in the cities where they landed. The arrival of so many immigrants in a few central locations gave rise to ethnic communities which served as beachheads of familiarity and assistance for each succeeding batch of arrivals. For people already traumatized by a sudden break with their past, this prospect of clinging to some sense of their old identity and customs overrode the urge to venture further in search of opportunity.

Prior to 1850, most immigrants wound up in the cities of the east and north central regions. The Irish comprised the largest immigrant group in 1850, and about one-fifth of them lived in New England, mainly in Boston, Lawrence, and Fall River. A second major group, the Germans, trekked inland by steamship to north central cities like Cincinnati, Cleveland, and Milwaukee. After the Civil War the West attracted some Germans, mostly in Denver and San Francisco, and Scandinavians, who filled Minneapolis and St. Paul. One group, the French Canadians, got no farther from home than New England, except for those who settled in Louisiana.

Already by the 1890s the tendency of the "new" immigrants to cluster in cities was apparent. The census of 1920 confirmed this fact by revealing that 80 percent of all Hungarians, Poles, Italians, and Russians lived in cities. Jews concentrated especially in New York, along with the Italians, many of whom also settled in Newark and Providence. Slavs and Poles, while drawn to eastern cities like New York, Buffalo, Bridgeport, and Newark, also found their way to interior cities such as Chicago, Cleveland, Milwaukee, and Pittsburgh. Southern cities drew the smallest number of immigrants.

The mass influx of foreigners into industrial cities had a profound effect on every facet of urban life. At first native Americans feared the economic competition of the newcomers; certainly the presence of so much cheap labor threatened to depress wages, create unemployment, and undercut attempts to unionize. On the other hand, foreigners nearly always got the least desirable jobs and thereby allowed native workers to move up the occupational scale. As one observer wrote in 1892, "When the foreigner came in, the native engineered the jobs, the former did the shoveling." The "new" immigrants possessed fewer skills than the Germans, English, French, and Belgians of the pre-Civil War years, who had come far more prepared to take a position in the industrial system than had the peasants of southern and eastern Europe.

By 1880 immigrants from northwest Europe were well represented in most industrial jobs. In New York foreigners comprised well over half the carpenters, masons, bricklayers, domestic servants, and common laborers. Germans predominated as carpenters and tailors, Irishmen as draymen, servants, and laborers. Pittsburgh's iron and steel mills had more foreign than native workers, while Chicago, Boston, and other large cities had a preponderance of German and Irish workers among their draymen, masons, and tailors. Although it is true that some immigrants—including Adolph Ochs, the Lehman brothers, Carl Schurz, and Henry E. Steinway—achieved spectacular success, the occupational census indicates that most immigrants found jobs that did not require them to master the language, business skills, or proper dress and manners.

After 1890 the children of these Germans, Englishmen and Irishmen advanced a step or half-step up the occupational ladder as more recent arrivals took the unskilled positions. While it is difficult to generalize about the kinds of work done by the "new" immigrants, some occupations did attract higher proportions of particular nationalities. By 1910 Eastern European Jews had captured New York's garment industry as well as the tobacco and fur trades. Jews found a haven in the garment industry not because they possessed experience in the trade—indeed, only about 10 percent of them had done similar work in Europe—but because it offered access to commercial activities. They toiled at the sewing machines and presses of the huge garment factories in hopes of gaining enough capital to open a retail operation for themselves or their children. Few other industries offered so ready an entrance into wholesaling or retailing than the manufacture of clothing.

The Italian, described in patronizing tones by Jacob Riis as "gay, lighthearted and, if his fur is not stroked the wrong way, inoffensive as a child," found employment to a large extent in construction work. Then as now, the American city resembled an enormous construction site, one forever being built, enlarged, torn down, and rebuilt. Houses, office buildings, streets, subways, and public works all generated work for large numbers of Italians. Some had engaged in similar pursuits in Italy, but most sought the unskilled trades in construction simply because jobs were plentiful. Carl Wittke has described this tendency well:

In New York, he crowded out the Irish and Poles in the building of subways and streets. In Philadelphia, he joined the street-cleaning force. In Chicago and Kansas City, he went into the stockyards. In New Jersey, he went into the silk mills; in New England, into the textile towns; and in Pennsylvania, into the mines and steel mills. Kansas City, St. Louis, and Cleveland have their "Little Italies"; in St. Louis, "Dago Hill" is near the clay pits and brickyards where the Italians worked. Utica, Schenectady, and Reading have large Italian colonies, and there is a large community of Italian cigarmakers in Tampa, Florida. Large numbers entered the garment trades where they crowded out the Jews, or became stone and cement workers.

Other Italians, along with Slavs, Poles, Croats, Serbs, and Hungarians manned the blast furnaces and meatpacking plants in Pittsburgh, Chicago, Buffalo, Cleveland, Youngstown, and Gary. These occupations attracted highly mobile Eastern European men who were still single or had not yet sent for their families in the old country. Accustomed to seasonal work in Europe, the move to America represented for them a difference of degree rather than kind. At first they regarded low-paying factory jobs as a temporary expedient. But as conditions improved or their surroundings grew more familiar, they summoned their families and resigned themselves to life in the plants.

The Czechs who came to America after 1870 possessed more skills than most other immigrants. Bohemians settled in Chicago, New York, St. Louis, and Cleveland, where they worked as artisans, particularly in the building trades. Slovaks, on the other hand, having few skills, dominated the steel, coke, and coal industries in Pittsburgh, Youngstown, and Bridgeport. Pennsylvania had the highest concentration of Slovaks because of its heavy industries. Poles, too, found employment in heavy industry and "pick and shovel" labor. Replacing the Irish as street workers, they also toiled in textile mills, stockyards, packinghouses, and sugar refineries. By 1920 Poles constituted 26 percent of the foreign-born population of Buffalo, 21 percent of Milwaukee, 20 percent of Detroit, and 17 percent of Chicago. Hungarians went into commercial activities as well as industrial work. Magyars in New York, Cleveland, Chicago, Detroit and Akron opened shops, restaurants, and cafés which served not only their ethnic brethren but the city at large. Other groups took the nearest work at hand. French-Canadians who moved southward into New England entered the textile mills of Fall River, Lewiston, and Woonsocket because jobs were plentiful there. Long familiarity with the work beckoned Portuguese to the fishing fleets and Greeks to the breweries.

As immigrants concentrated in particular occupations, they also separated into particular neighborhoods. This tendency to congregate in enclaves or ghettos gave the industrial city both a distinctive structure and a diversity unmatched by earlier towns. According to Jacob Riis, a map of New York City in 1890 "coloured to designate nationality, would show more stripes than on the skin of a zebra, and more colours than any rainbow." To emphasize the significance of this mixture, Riis also calculated that New York had "half as many Italians as Naples, as many Germans as Hamburg, twice as many Irish as Dublin, and two and a half the number of Jews as Warsaw."

As ethnic groups divided into their enclaves, and even subdivided along finer regional or village distinctions, they lent an international flavor to the city as a whole. Although fear, hostility, and general wariness kept groups apart, the ethnic boundaries were never so rigid as to disallow some mingling. Young Jewish boys cultivated the pleasures of Italian cuisine while the Italian could savor a knish sold by a Jewish peddler. Pockets of Ukrainians, Serbs, or Croats were not so isolated that the strange newspapers, speech patterns, foods, music, and religion of one entirely escaped the notice of the others. Even the monolithic mother church tailored its brand of faith to Irish, Polish, or Italian parishioners. Synagogues, too, drew distinctive character from the congregations that supported them.

Enclaves were set and boundaries delineated on a block-by-block basis, but the patterns of segregation could not wall out the sights, sounds, and smells of adjoining areas. The ghetto was a place, a territory, a way of life; but it was not an iron curtain. Its inhabitants understood themselves to be one piece of a larger international mosaic that was the city. Even if lines were crossed only en route to work, or, much worse, for purposes of fighting, immigrant groups recognized the presence of strangers about them whose very unfamiliarity made them familiar. The transformation of the city into a polyglot of ethnic mixtures insured that urban life would never be the same again.

Every city had neighborhoods in which one particular nationality predominated, but only in the largest—New York, Chicago, Philadelphia —were ghettos confined by strict geographical boundaries. Howard Chudacoff has pointed out that in some medium-sized cities (Omaha, Kansas City, Des Moines) ethnic neighborhoods harbored a mixture of nationalities even on the same block. It is important, therefore, to realize that the term "ghetto" can refer to both physical and psychological separation. In large cities it meant both; in smaller ones the psychological isolation was probably more significant for newly arrived immigrants.

Ghettoization also rearranged the city's geography. While preindustrial cities contained pockets of ethnic concentrations, they were nowhere as large or distinct as those found in the industrial city. Early American cities were basically homogeneous places until the twin forces of mass transit and mass immigration partitioned the city into specialized neighborhoods. As David Ward has noted:

Before the Civil War, Irish and German immigrants concentrated in central locations abandoned by more prosperous residents, but this source of housing served only a small part of the total influx. Others had to seek accommodation and employment in almost every section of the city, and many squatted in peripheral "shanty-towns," which were displaced only after the Civil War when street-car systems opened new areas to middle-income development.

Once this displacement took place, new arrivals to the city crowded into the area next to the central business district. Lack of means to buy houses in new developments and the absence of inexpensive rentals in expanding neighborhoods forced immigrants into areas within walking distance of work. Since the real estate market catered to high- and middle-income groups and government declined any role in providing housing, immigrants had no choice but to content themselves with the dregs of the private market. They jammed into recently vacated buildings or obtained apartments in tenements designed expressly for them. In block after block, the tenements stood shoulder to shoulder, every apartment of every building stuffed to overflowing with humanity. One 32-acre section of New York, where congestion was worst of all, crammed 30,000 people into a five- or six-block area. That averaged out to about 986 persons per acre compared to 485 in Prague, the worst slum in Europe, or 760 in Bombay, the most densely populated slum found anywhere in the world outside of New York. The teeming ghetto was a spectacle that appalled social reformers and gratified slum landlords, many of whom earned profits as high as 40 percent on their properties.

Immigrants piled into the residential fringe of central business districts because wealthy and middle-income native Americans abandoned those areas for homes in new suburban neighborhoods. Landlords converted their empty houses into multi-family dwellings and filled nearby alleys and vacant lots with cheap new buildings. Large homes were partitioned into separate rooms and made into boardinghouses for unmarried professionals, clerks, transients, and newcomers to the city. Eager to capitalize on the housing squeeze, landlords pressed every available inch of space into use.

If the immigrants chafed under their miserable living conditions, they endured them because they had no choice. Crowding and squalor reinforced the enclave pattern and even intensified it. The ghetto represented a haven in which ethnic groups could live with their compatriots. Most of them grafted village lifestyles onto their urban neighborhoods. Little Italies, Warsaws, and Hungaries sprang up everywhere. Jane Addams's description of the area surrounding Hull House in Chicago in the early 1890s reflected this kaleidoscope of neighborhoods:

Between Halsted Street and the river live about ten thousand Italians: Neapolitans, Sicilians, and Calabrians, with an occasional Lombard or Venetian. To the South on Twelfth Street are many Germans, and side streets are given over almost entirely to Polish and Prussian Jews. Further south, three Jewish colonies merge into a huge Bohemian colony, so vast that Chicago ranks as the third Bohemian city in the world. To the north-west are many Canadians—French, clannish in spite of their long residence in America, and to the north are many Irish and first-generation Americans.

In this manner the village-like atmosphere of the old country also pervaded the new and turned the sprawling industrial city into a crazy-quilt of diversity. Ethnic enclaves acted as buffers against the pressures of the larger alien society beyond its boundaries. They also resisted the tendency of the urban experience to erode the old ways and customs. The result was a continuous conflict of values which strained the social fabric of every ethnic neighborhood. Young people in particular felt little urge to cling to the customs of a society they had never known or could not remember. Despite the terrific pressures of change, most ethnic groups did remarkably well at preserving their ancient heritage. To that extent the industrial city was not a faceless mass at all, but rather a cluster of individual neighborhoods, each of which embodied a distinctive culture and lifestyle.

The Italians in particular had strong family and village ties which bound them together. Expecting aid from relatives or from their *paisani* (people of their same region), Italians grouped together in the Mulberry Street area of New York, in Boston's West End, and in similar communities in Chicago, St. Louis, and Providence. Within these communities could be found regional subdivisions in which an Italian might continue to think of himself as a Calabrese, a Veneziano, an Abruzzese, or a Siciliano. Each block or district possessed its own regional flavor, its distinctive customs and dialect.

Besides strong family and village ties, the *padrone* system concentrated Italians into tight communities. The *padrone* represented many things to many people, but essentially he was a sort of Italian boss who acted as a broker to bring the unskilled *contadini* in contact with an employer who needed labor gangs. Naturally the *padrone* profited handsomely from such transactions and exercised a good deal of power in the community. Critics of the system have denounced it as a form of slavery; but while the system possessed many unsavory features, it also performed an important function. In the market society, where individuals got little or no assistance from public agencies, it operated as an ad hoc system which serviced genuine needs. Like the political boss, the *padrone* ministered to a constituency that had nowhere else to turn. Like the political bosses, too, *padrones* exacted a high price for their services and were prone to abuse their power. They spoke the newcomer's dialect and above all could find jobs for men who did not know how to do so on their own. In the words of one immigrant: "Signorino, we are ignorant and do not know English. Our boss brought us here, knows where to find work, makes contracts with companies. What should we do without him?"

Strong family and cultural ties also bound Jewish immigrants together in ethnic communities. Viewing the family as the nucleus of society and primary agent for teaching the Torah, Jews congregated on the Lower East Side of New York and in similar ghettos in Boston, Philadelphia, Detroit, Rochester, and Chicago to preserve their ethnic and religious heritage. Although sharp distinctions existed among German, Polish, and Russian Jews, the commonality of religion lumped them together in the eyes of the larger society.

The Jewish immigration of the 1880s and 1890s touched off a resurgence of religious orthodoxy which further aided concentration. The need to be near the synagogue and to have the children attend services and *cheder* (the afternoon religious training) tightened Jewish community ties. Then, too, the growth of *landsmannschaften*—the groups that made the transition from Old World study and social circles to New World fraternal orders—provided newcomers with a familiar landmark and imparted to Jewish ghettos a strong sense of the *shtetl*-type life that had been left behind.

The same forces that led Italians and Jews to form tight communities also affected most other immigrants. At the heart of the matter lay a longing for something familiar in a strange land with its strange ways, whether it involved gaining access to a job, preserving family and religious ties, or simply seeing a familiar face and hearing a familiar tongue. Once this longing drove ethnic groups together in tight island communities, they acted as both beacon and haven for the next wave of arrivals. Institutions arose to ease the transition from Old World to New. Whether it was the Orthodox Church in the Greek communities, the freethinkers' societies in the Czech communities, the "sokols" for physical training in the Slovak communities, or the scores of mutual benefit societies among Hungarians, Poles, or Lithuanians, these organizations smoothed the trauma of adjustment by offering some sense of continuity between what had been and what was yet to be.

Restless Natives

As might be expected, native Americans reacted violently to the presence of so many foreigners. No ethnic group escaped the scourge of nativist prejudice during the nineteenth century, but even the opprobrium heaped upon the Irish paled in comparison to that leveled at the "new" immigrants. While Americans preached the gospel of equality and went so far as to plant a gigantic statue in their major harbor proclaiming welcome for "the huddled masses yearning to breathe free," they shrank in horror from the invasion of alien peoples, customs, tongues, and ideas.

The sheer size of the immigrant flood appalled nativists; the concentration of ethnic groups into tight-knit communities positively frightened them. Charges of clannishness, ignorance, immorality, and radicalism gave rise to the specter of a strong nation diluted by a mongrel people. Some feared the economic competition of the immigrants; yet the brunt of the attack came from those who had few economic worries. It was rather the threat to America's racial purity and cultural integrity which alarmed them.

Nativism means literally a policy of protecting the interests of a nation's inhabitants from those of immigrants or outsiders. According to John Higham, "Nativism . . . should be defined as intense opposition to an internal minority on the ground of its foreign (i.e., "un-American") connections. . . . While drawing on much broader cultural antipathies and ethnocentric judgments, nativism translates them into a zeal to destroy the enemies of a distinctively American way of life." In *Strangers in the Land*, Higham identified three distinct strands of

American nativism which he labeled anti-Catholic, antiradical, and anti-racial. The first two trace their roots well back into the formative years of the Republic (anti-Catholicism goes back even further); the third arose during the industrial period and focused upon the "new" immigration.

Nativist thought presumed the existence of a distinctive American way of life. What that was depended, of course, entirely upon who was defining it. To the extent that such a thing existed, it consisted of those values, attitudes, beliefs, and customs popularly known as White Anglo-Saxon Protestant culture. Obviously not all Americans or even most of them subscribed to the tenets of WASP culture or qualified for membership in its nebulous congregation. Nor could its self-appointed spokesmen always agree upon exactly what they were defending from outside encroachment. Nevertheless the belief circulated widely that a distinctive American way of life existed, and that it must be preserved from corrosion by foreign influences.

It is pointless to dwell upon the illogic and inner contradictions of nativist thought. A more fruitful approach is to suggest that nativism was a force propelled by emotional rather than logical fuel. Whatever the source of their arguments, nativist movements emerged during periods of extreme social tension. In broad terms, their purpose was to ferret out disturbers of the social order and exorcise them from the community. For those who sought simple explanations for complex events, immigrants offered a choice target. Some foreigners served better than others for this discharge of wrath. Nativists found the Irish especially objectionable because they were both Irish and Catholic. Prior to the Civil War, anti-Catholic sentiment boiled up into a political movement which resulted in the Know-Nothing (later the American) party.

The Civil War stifled the Know-Nothing insurgency against Catholicism, but antiforeign sentiment revived quickly once immigration stepped up in the 1880s. Spawned by the dislocations of industrialization, the postwar nativist upsurge lashed out against the most visible agents of social change: the industrial city itself and the alien racial or ethnic composition of the "new" immigration. The inseparability of the two phenomena made it all the easier to link them to a common pattern. Strange peoples poured into the cities, huddled together in their own neighborhoods, and infused urban life with a babel of foreign tongues, ideas, and practices. From this mixture emerged a potent brew of nativist hysteria and reaction.

Americans steeped in the rural tradition had always harbored dark suspicions of urban life. The growth of cities during the industrial era only inflamed this distrust. Critics decried the loss of agrarian virtues when rural folk moved to the city, and attributed congestion, ill-health, moral decay, potential radicalism, and other sins to urban civilization in general. Benjamin O. Flower, the muckraking founder of *The Arena,* characterized the city as "civilization's inferno" and viewed it as "a world of misery, where uninvited poverty abounds: a commonwealth of victims whose wretchedness fills the heart with mingled sorrow and indignation." Along with this antiurban bias went the feeling that the influx of so many foreigners gravely worsened matters.

No one articulated the nativist position more forcefully than the Reverend Josiah Strong. In his popular and influential book, *Our Country: Its Possible Future and Its Present Crisis* (1885), Strong stated flatly that "the typical immigrant is a European peasant, whose horizon has been narrow, whose moral and religious training has been meager or false, and whose ideas of life are low." Immigration, he added, "not only furnishes the greater portion of our criminals, it is also seriously affecting the morals of the native population." In his catalog of perils to American civilization, Strong began with immigration and proceeded to show its pernicious influence upon most of the others, including Catholicism, intemperance and the liquor traffic, socialism, and the city. In ominous tones Strong concluded that "immigration complicates our moral and political problems by swelling our dangerous classes."

At the same time, Strong singled out the city as the stage upon which immigration played out its evil drama:

The city has become a serious menace to our civilization because in it, excepting Mormonism, each of the dangers we have discussed is enhanced, and all are focalized. It has a peculiar attraction for the immigrant. . . . Because our cities are so largely foreign, Romanism finds in them its chief strength. For the same reason the saloon, together with the intemperance and the liquor power which it represents, is multiplied in the city.

Socialism, too, flourished in the city:

Here is heaped the social dynamite; here roughs, gamblers, thieves, robbers, lawless and desperate men of all sorts, congregate; men who are ready on any pretext to raise riots for the purpose of destruction and plunder; here gather foreigners and wage-workers who are especially susceptible to socialist arguments. . . .

In masterful fashion Strong intertwined immigration and the city into a common strand of menace to American civilization. His work reflected the racist elements present even among those who claimed humanitarian motives and espoused "liberal" theology. Numerous other commentators followed the trail blazed by Strong, and some had long since taken up the cry. Charles Loring Brace's *The Dangerous Classes of New York and Twenty Years' Work Among Them* (1872) deplored the social effects wrought by the presence of large, impoverished foreign populations in the cities:

Thousands are the children of poor foreigners, who have permitted them to grow up without school, education, or religion. All the neglect and bad education and evil example of a poor class tend to form others, who, as they mature, swell the ranks of ruffians and criminals. So, at length, a great multitude of ignorant, untrained, passionate, irreligious boys and young men are formed, who become the "dangerous" class of the city.

A New York judge put the case less charitably when he observed that "there is a large class—I was about to say a majority—of the population of New York and Brooklyn, who just live, and to whom the rearing of two or more children means inevitably a boy for the penitentiary, and a girl for the brothel."

The strident fears expressed by Strong and Brace helped pave the way for more sophisticated presentations of the antiforeign position. Edward A. Ross, Prescott F. Hall, and even the progressive John R. Commons scarcely concealed their racist ideology behind a thicket of academic jargon. Perhaps the apotheosis of racism came in 1916 with the publication of *The Passing of the Great Race* by Madison Grant, a conservative lawyer and head of the New York City Museum of Natural History. Professing scientific detachment on the subject, Grant warned that the "new immigration"

contained a large and increasing number of the weak, the broken and the mentally crippled of all races drawn from the lowest stratum of the Mediterranean basin of the Balkans, together with the hordes of the wretched, submerged populations of the Polish ghettoes. Our jails, insane asylums and almshouses are filled with this human flotsam and the whole tone of American life, social, moral and political has been lowered and vulgarized by them.

The reaction against foreigners went beyond rhetoric to organized social and political action. The American Protection Association, a secret organization founded in 1876 and composed primarily of midwesterners, led the anti-immigrant crusade. Building on the anti-Catholicism of the pre-Civil War years, the APA advanced a lethal mixture of stereotypes about radicalism and criminality combined with more practical fears of economic competition. Rumors were spread about papal plots, Italian criminality, Oriental cunning, and Jewish banking conspiracies. John Higham cites newspaper editorials which assailed the "invasion of venomous reptiles" and "long-haired, wild-eyed, bad-smelling, atheistic, reckless foreign wretches, who never did an honest hour's work in their lives."

While editors vented their spleens and demanded that the authorities "do something," calmer voices pursued the more basic argument of economic competition. Francis S. Walker, a census bureau chief in 1870 and later president of M.I.T., charged that immigrant workers undermined the position of native American labor by their willingness to work for cheap wages. The economic duress of the 1890s, with its widespread unemployment and episodes of industrial unrest like the march of Coxey's Army, the Pullman strike, and the violent Homestead strike, heightened these fears. Alarmed by the depth of the depression and the mounting crescendo of social disorder, protectionists swung into action. In 1896 Henry Cabot Lodge introduced a literacy test bill in Congress. After vigorous debate the bill failed, partly because immigration had slackened during the depression years.

But the seeds had been sown and the positions staked. For the next two decades the campaign continued, led by the Immigration Restriction League and congeries of New England Brahmins, Southern aristocrats, and Progressive intellectuals. The United States Immigration Commission of 1907–11, known as the Dillingham Commission, gathered statistics to reinforce the notion that cheap foreign labor depressed the wages and working conditions of American workers. Racial and ethnic incidents flared everywhere. The sensational Leo Frank murder case in Atlanta (1911) merely reflected in grotesque fashion the social and economic discrimination heaped upon Jews. Italians were mobbed in New Orleans in 1891, while southerners continued to maim and lynch hundreds of blacks every year. Less spectacular episodes of discrimination marred the everyday routine of foreigners and blacks everywhere as America erupted into a cauldron of racial and ethnic antagonism. Novelist Kenneth Roberts, his pen dripping venom, echoed a popular sentiment when he wrote: "If a few million members of the Alpine, Mediterranean, and Semitic races are poured among us the result must inevitably be a hybrid race of people as worthless and futile as the good-for-nothing mongrels of Central America and southeastern Europe."

Despite this backdrop of popular hysteria and social violence, the drive for restrictive legislation stalled in Congress. The return of prosperity, the determination of big business to maintain an unbroken supply of cheap labor, the pressure exerted by ethnic lobbying groups, and the outbreak of World War I combined to thwart restriction efforts. Once the war ended, however, the drive gained fresh momentum. In the disillusioned, tension-wracked postwar atmosphere, the philosophy of racial purity which had developed over the years won new adherents. The downturn of the economy in 1921, the fear of Bolshevism inspired by the Russian Revolution, and a general reaction against things foreign opened the way for passage on February 22, 1921, of a major immigration restriction act.

The act limited the number of aliens admitted from any European country to 3 percent of the natives from that country residing in the United States at the time of the 1910 census. This was considered a temporary measure, but restrictionist sentiment found congenial soil in the social anxieties of the 1920s. A permanent restriction bill passed Congress in 1924 which, after modification in 1929, reduced the total annual flow of immigrants to 150,000. The new act limited admission from any European nation to 2 percent of its natives living in the United States at the time of the 1890 census. The switch in census base figures reflected a desire to favor immigrants from northwestern Europe at the expense of those from southern and eastern Europe.

Senator David Reed of Pennsylvania hailed the passage of the 1924 bill as a victory for his "grandchildren," who would now be able to live in a "more homogeneous nation, more self-reliant, more independent, and more closely knit by common purpose and common ideas." The *Baltimore Sun*, however, lamented that "the United States abandons definitely and perhaps finally that old and admirable tradition that this land was to serve as a refuge for the oppressed of all nations." The *Sun* proved a better prophet than Senator Reed. A corner had been turned in American history: the era of massive immigration was over.

Protectionist propaganda, coupled with prejudice on a local everyday level, did more than help close the gates to new immigrants; it also hampered the assimilation process for those already here. It was difficult enough for foreigners to adjust from a preindustrial to an industrial society, and in most cases from a rural to an urban environment, in a strange land. To undergo this transformation in the face of constant discrimination and hostility taxed the emotional stamina of the hardiest individual. It was, in fact, a cruel paradox that confronted the immigrant. In most cases, he had come to America believing that assimilation was possible. Having swallowed the American Dream whole and digested its possibilities eagerly, foreigners wanted not merely to live in their adopted country, but to become a part of it. Yet they encountered on one side an ideology which stressed equality and opportunity, and on the other a people bristling with hostility. The experience could only leave deep scars upon those already disoriented by the ordeal of midpassage. This is precisely what made the ethnic ghetto so important to greenhorns. It created islands of familiarity within the industrial city where inhabitants preserved their identity within the vast impersonal urban setting.

Yet isolation could never be complete; quarantine was not possible in so large and dynamic an environment. Contacts with other people, however cursory or unpleasant, nonetheless occurred. The boss had to be talked to, directions solicited from the trolley conductor, landlords and merchants haggled with—all of which necessitated learning the language, picking up the native customs, adopting new attitudes. These brushes with the outside world pushed the psychological limits of the ghetto outward and subtly transformed the immigrant into a different person, one with roots in both the old world and the new but belonging entirely to neither.

Assimilation extracted a cruel toll from those who struggled to achieve it. Few survived the transition with their ideas and culture intact. Those who failed found the grave an escape from a career of poverty, disappointment, and suffering. Those who succeeded sometimes found themselves spiritually trapped in midpassage. Such a fate befell the hero of Abraham Cahan's novel, *The Rise of David Levinsky* (1917), perhaps the best novel on the immigrant urban experience in American literature.

In the novel Levinsky migrates to America from Russia, bringing with him little more than a passion for learning, nourished by the Talmudic seminary at which he studied, and a deep attachment to the verities of orthodox Jewish culture and family life. Once in America, he gradually sheds his old identity and strives desperately to Americanize himself. Through a subtle but inextricable process, the drudgery of earning a living first subordinates and then extinguishes his past intentions. He drifts into the garment trade, prospers at it, and becomes a millionaire. In doing so he shaves his beard, changes his eating and dressing habits, learns English, and gradually abandons both his religion and his customs.

From this experience Levinsky emerges rich beyond his wildest dreams, but spiritually isolated. Outwardly he has become completely Americanized; inwardly he cannot shake free of his old identity which has been stifled and warped in his new world. Caught up in the rhythms of American life while still clinging to the values of his childhood, he has lost all sense of inner unity or harmony. He belongs to neither world, but occupies a painful social and spiritual vacuum between them. Success has brought no solace to his spirit; it has left him hungry and yearning. Aware that his career has been a success and his life a failure, he utters a poignant lament doubtless shared by some of his fellow immigrants:

Am I happy?
There are moments when I am overwhelmed by a sense of my success and ease. I become aware that thousands of things which had formerly been forbidden fruit to me are at my command now. . . .
My sense of triumph is coupled with a brooding sense of emptiness and insignificance, of my lack of anything like a great, deep interest.
I am lonely. . . .
I give myself every comfort that money can buy. But there is one thing which I crave and which money cannot buy—happiness. . . .
I often long for a heart-to-heart talk with the people of my birthplace. I have tried to revive my old friendships with some of them, but they are mostly poor and my prosperity stands between us in many ways. . . .
There are moments when I regret my whole career, when my very success seems to be a mistake. . . .
I can never forget the days of my misery. I cannot escape from my old self. My past and present do not comfort well. David, the poor lad swinging over a Talmudic volume at the Preacher's Synagogue, seems to have more in common with my inner identity than David Levinsky, the well-known cloak-manufacturer.

Chains of Color

Difficult as assimilation to life in the industrial city was for immigrants, it shrank before the obstacles that confronted native black Americans. While Negroes had never found cities to be a haven of freedom, even in the North, the pressures of industrialization, competition with the various ethnic groups, and rigid strictures imposed by native whites made their position more precarious than ever before. The combination of intense competition and belligerent racism relegated blacks to the poorest jobs and most squalid housing the city had to offer. Yet not even these discouragements kept blacks from flocking to urban centers in large numbers.

In the antebellum South, slavery operated in the city no less than on the plantation, but it did not flourish there. Blacks manned the iron and tobacco factories in Richmond, the gasworks in New Orleans, and did industrial labor in Montgomery, Mobile, and elsewhere. However, the concentration of slaves in an urban setting made effective control difficult if not impossible. Secret and informal associations among slaves, the lack of surveillance over "hiring out" and "living out" arrangements, and the sabotage of plant machinery by slave workers all threatened to crumble the system. After the war blacks migrated in large numbers to southern cities. Zane Miller has attributed this movement to

the insecurity of life in the isolated countryside, the desire to authenticate freedom by exercising the right to such opportunity where they might, the knowledge that before the war conditions in the cities had been better than in rural regions, and the attraction of urban educational and welfare facilities.

Whatever the motivation, the move to the city usually netted the same results: racial segregation and hostility. In general, the story of blacks in the cities parallels that of Reconstruction as a whole. After about twenty years of futile effort to forge a new black-white relationship in the South, the full weight of white supremacy came crashing down upon black attempts at accommodation. Through violence, economic coercion, social repression, and control of the political and judicial machinery, whites succeeded in restricting urban Negroes to the status of second-class citizens. Although numerically strong (in 1890, for instance, Charleston was 56 percent black, Mobile 44 percent, and Memphis 45 percent), the black population lacked political experience and organization. Dispersed among the worst slums of the cities, they were hard to unify into a cohesive power base. Moreover, black leaders disagreed among themselves over what tactics to use to improve their lot. Whites suffered from no such divisions. United on the basic concept of Negro inferiority, they maintained "Jim Crowism" through both formal legislation and informal repression.

Conditions in the North differed little. Nearly every large northern city had a significant class of black small-businessmen who ran barber shops, catering firms, restaurants, drugstores, and photography studios; black craftsmen who did tailoring, printing, carpentry, and shipbuilding; and black professionals—lawyers, doctors, teachers—who worked primarily in black neighborhoods. This nucleus of middle-class strength exceeded its counterpart in the South and tempts one to conclude that blacks fared better in the North. Perhaps they did in some small ways, but in the areas that count, the difference between North and South was more of style than of substance. In both places white society placed economic, social, and political constraints upon the black community and denied it access to dominant institutions. In fact, the subtle brand of racism practiced in the North proved harder to fight than the more forthright southern version.

Industrialization offered hard-pressed blacks little economic relief and may, in fact, have worsened their position. While the number of available jobs rose sharply, so did the competition for them. Rural immigrants and foreigners grabbed the best and even many of the worst positions; it was already an axiom that blacks got jobs no one else wanted and got paid less than whites doing the same or similar work. These tended to be menial positions—as pullman car porters or handymen, in domestic service, shining shoes, and in the foulest of industrial work—like some types of packinghouse jobs.

Part of the problem lay in the fact that northward migration of southern blacks occurred under the worst of circumstances. Immediately after the Civil War the flow amounted to little more than a trickle, but it surged steadily toward floodtide by World War I. Between 1916 and 1918 alone about 500,000 Negroes moved north. Some blacks left the South to escape the abysmal poverty that was their fate there; others responded to the encouragement of relatives who had already gone or to the blandishment of northern companies seeking cheap "union proof" workers. In times of industrial strife some firms imported barge-loads of blacks as scabs to break strikes, thereby grafting racial tensions onto economic conflicts. Ignorant of the role in which they found themselves, blacks often paid dearly in the form of violence and bloodshed. Labor unions, too, resented the aspirations of Negroes and usually followed policies no less lily-white than those of the larger society. Their discrimination forced blacks to create their own organizations.

Most of the black migrants went to the industrial cities of the Northeast and Midwest. During the decade 1910–1920, the Negro population of Gary increased 1,200 percent; Detroit, 620 percent; Cleveland, 308 percent; and Chicago, 148 percent. In raw figures, Chicago's black population jumped from 6,500 in 1880 to more than 100,000 in 1920. Border cities like Baltimore, Louisville, and Washington, which had received only a few blacks after the Civil War, were 15 to 25 percent black by 1900. Alarmed by the scale of this migration and fearful that more would follow, urban whites worked feverishly to confine Negroes to particular neighborhoods and limit their economic and social mobility. A new wave of racial antagonism, often tinged with violence, swept through northern cities.

From this northward migration and the reaction to it emerged the black ghetto which remains a familiar landmark of all northern cities. New York's experience illustrates how the ghetto evolved into an urban institution. Gilbert Osofsky has traced the kindling of racial antagonism in New York directly to the growing migration. Rising numbers made

Negroes more visible and therefore more vulnerable. Churches which once allowed integrated services began pushing out their black congregants. Employers used blacks as strikebreakers in labor disputes and diverted the wrath of workers into racial hatred. The pressure for additional housing created a real estate boom in the upper West Side neighborhood of Harlem as blacks began pouring into that previously all-white area. The high price of rentals coupled with the low wages of tenants quickly led to deteriorating physical conditions. Manipulative real estate agents carved the residences of departed whites into small makeshift apartments and packed them with people. As if by magic, private dwellings turned into tenements.

The congestion and squalor grew steadily worse because the tenants themselves, unaccustomed to city life, knew nothing about how to survive in their new environment. Many lacked jobs and most lacked even the barest rudiments of health and sanitation. There was little in the routine of the cropper's shack that prepared blacks for tenement living. Deteriorating conditions led to landlord indifference, and by the 1920s the vicious cycle of ghetto life—physical decay, high rents, low wages, poor health, social demoralization, high crime rates, and a powerful sense of frustration and hopelessness—congealed as a way of life.

The pattern bore a depressing similarity everywhere: Harlem and San Juan Hill in New York, the Seventh Ward in Philadelphia, State Street in Chicago, the Northwest Neighborhood in Washington, the Druid Hill Avenue section in Baltimore. Whatever its local tag, "Bucktown," "Nigger Row," "Smoketown" or "Black Bottom," the ghetto became a fixture of the city. Once scattered in neighborhoods throughout the city but especially on the periphery, blacks now collected in the inner city. In a curious sense, they exchanged places with the middle-class whites fleeing to the outskirts of town.

Physical segregation had far-reaching effects upon blacks and whites alike. The black ghetto differed strikingly from the ethnic ghettos. Foreigners endured many hardships and much discrimination, but never so rigid a separation as that imposed upon blacks. They could view the ghetto as a temporary way station to further assimilation, whereas the blacks entertained few illusions about the possibilities open to them. Barring unforeseen miracles, they were in the ghetto to stay. No group encountered more systematic exclusion from employment opportunities than blacks, and poor wages were the crux of ghetto life. Of all the differences that set minorities apart from the social mainstream, none loomed so large as color.

Nativist groups who opposed foreigners concentrated their efforts upon closing the gates of entry. Since this approach could not be applied to incoming blacks, racists resorted instead to internal restraints. When racial tensions exploded, blacks suffered brutal reprisals for their un-wanted presence, as the East St. Louis Riot of 1917 and the Chicago Riot of 1919 demonstrated. Gradually the black ghetto became not only a haven of safety and familiarity with brethren, but a way of life stand-ing outside the mainstream of white urban society. A culture of destitu-tion, the ghetto life-style became institutionalized and endured far longer than most transitory enclaves of the white ethnics.

The critical factor of race also fixed the destiny of Orientals who entered the United States. Although migrating from abroad like the white ethnics, Orientals encountered a degree of hostility and discrim-ination previously reserved for blacks and American Indians.

While Chinese immigrants reached the West Coast as early as the California Gold rush of 1849, the tide of newcomers did not peak until 1882 when 40,000 arrived. Most came to work in the mines and to help build the great transcontinental railroads. At first the Chinese lived in the camps and temporary towns of these industries, but after the railroad work tapered off, they began settling in Pacific Coast cities like San Francisco, Seattle, and Tacoma. In the cities they found work as domestics, operators of independent laundries and restaurants, gar-deners, and laborers in shirt, cigar, and shoe factories. By 1890 there were 107,488 Chinese in America, half of them located on the West Coast.

Like other immigrant groups, the Chinese clustered in tight neigh-borhoods among their own kind. The small Chinatowns that developed created a reaction far beyond their size. "Anticoolie" activity developed as early as the 1850s and intensified in the 1870s as many workingmen blamed Chinese immigrants for their difficulties during the depression years. State and local officials passed restrictions on Chinese businesses, levied occupational taxes solely upon Orientals, and imposed a variety of social discriminations.

Nativists objected to the Chinese on both economic and social grounds. Accustomed to living on a shoestring, the Chinese worked for lower wages than whites, yet still managed to accumulate savings from their meager pay. For this offense, which earlier generations had hon-ored as the virtues of thrift and frugality, they were accused of taking jobs from white citizens who needed them and lowering the standard of living. More than once this animus erupted into violence in both cities and mining camps. A series of riots broke out in the 1870s. The first major one occurred in 1871 in Los Angeles, where fifteen people were hanged and six shot as the "Pick Handler's Brigade" declared war on the Chinese. Similar incidents occurred in Rocky Mountain mining communities as labor organizations across the West denounced Chinese "coolie" workers as a "curse upon the land."

On both the East and West Coasts, social discrimination spread rapidly upon wings of public hysteria. The campaign went beyond the usual desire to segregate the Chinese from association or competition with whites; it launched a frontal assault upon the Chinese community itself. Most nativists regarded Chinatown as an unspeakable den of iniquity to which the inscrutable Chinese lured innocent white girls, addicted them to opium, and reduced them to drugged servitude or forced them into white slavery. The vivid image of the "opium den" unleashed every primal instinct and repressed passion of native whites. From a generation reared upon the discreet axioms of Victorian prudery it provoked an emotional reaction that often surpassed anti-Negro fulminations.

To sense the potency of this image, one need only to read the chapter on Chinatown in Jacob Riis's classic *How the Other Half Lives* (1890). Normally an astute observer of ghetto life, Riis apparently let moral fervor cloud his reporter's eye when it came to the Chinese. There was little he found attractive in them except their neatness. After indulging in a parade of stereotypes which portrayed Chinese as mercenary, irreligious, stealthy, secretive, dissipated, and, of course, inscrutable, he described the "opium dens" in lurid colors:

> The Chinaman smokes opium as Caucasians smoke tobacco, and apparently with little worse effect upon himself. But woe unto the white victim upon which his pitiless drug gets its grip! . . .
>
> From the teeming tenements . . . come the white slaves of its dens of vice and their infernal drug. . . . There are houses, dozens of them, in Mott and Pell Streets, that are literally jammed, from the "joint" in the cellar to the attic, with these hapless victims of a passion which, once acquired, demands the sacrifice of every instinct of decency to its insatiable desire. . . . the women, all white, girls hardly yet grown to womanhood, worshipping nothing save the pipe that has enslaved them body and soul.

Riis did not invent these overdrawn stereotypes so much as confirm what many whites already believed. Once nativists mobilized alarm into action, they gained results with surprising ease. The Chinese were in fact the most vulnerable of all the new urban minorities. Unlike other immigrants, they belonged to a different race from the whites, and unlike the blacks, they were foreigners whose entry into the country could be restricted. Convinced that public opinion shared Riis's conclusion "that the Chinese are in no sense a desirable element of the population, that they serve no useful purposes here . . . ," nativists moved to bar further immigration.

In August of 1882, the same year in which Chinese immigration reached its peak, Chester A. Arthur signed into law the Chinese Exclusion Act which suspended Chinese immigration for a period of ten years. The first of a series of restrictive acts, it gave the Chinese the dubious honor of becoming the first target of anti-immigration legislation. By 1924 all Oriental immigration had been shut off and would not be resumed. Already by 1920 the total Chinese population in the United States had dwindled to 61,639, most of whom settled into a pattern of developing institutions within their communities which mirrored the larger white society.

Chinatowns still exist in New York, Boston, San Francisco, Los Angeles, and elsewhere, as reminders of the queer tendency of American cities to espouse assimilation and promote fragmentation. The experience of Japanese, Mexicans, Puerto Ricans, and other nonwhite groups who followed the blacks and Chinese to the cities, differed in degree rather than in kind.

The saga of migration and immigration thus remains a bitter paradox. Industrialization promoted large-scale population movements which drew rural natives and foreign immigrants to the cities. By the end of World War I, when the massive influx from abroad had ended, the city accepted its new arrivals with mixed emotions—welcoming their labor, despising their customs, and dreading their impact upon the racial and cultural purity of the Republic. Amidst the contradictory patterns of acceptance and rejection, assimilation and segregation, open arms and shut gates, accommodation and violence, all sides grappled desperately for some basis upon which to reconcile their differences and erect a stable social order. Their failure to find that better way has been matched only by our own. Perhaps the divisions and atomization that rent the American social order ran too deep to heal quickly or at all. Several generations have struggled with the problem only to admit defeat and await a better day. The paradox of that unhappy legacy is embodied in the ill-chosen metaphor of the melting pot. In the final analysis, the American experience resembled not a melting pot but a salad bowl, in which all the ingredients got tossed and mixed and piled on top of each other, but nothing ever quite came together. The result was a society in which the parts somehow never added up to a whole.

CHAPTER 7

Life at the Top: The Urban Elite

There's just one thing about this; either they accept us or they don't. If they don't, well and good; we can't help it. We'll go on and finish the house, and give them a chance to be decent. If they won't be, there are other cities. Money will arrange matters in New York—that I know. We can build a real place there, and go in on equal terms if we have money enough. . . . Don't worry. I haven't seen many troubles in this world that money wouldn't cure.

The wife of Anson Merrill, the great dry-goods prince, . . . was eastern-bred—Boston—and familiar in an offhand way with the superior world of London, which she had visited several times. Chicago at its best was to her a sordid commercial area. She preferred New York or Washington, but she had to live here. Thus she patronized nearly all of those with whom she condescended to associate, using an upward tilt of the head, a tired droop of the eyelids, and a fine upward arching of the brows to indicate how trite it all was.

—THEODORE DREISER
The Titan (1914)

AMERICA HAD COME a long way in the nineteenth century. For some people who retained hazy memories of the "good old days," it had come too far and too fast for comfort. "Progress" came in many sizes, shapes, and flavors, not all of them well-fitting or sweet-tasting. It took Finley Peter Dunne's irrepressible "Mr. Dooley" to put the era in proper perspective. Musing in 1897 on the Diamond Jubilee of Queen Victoria, Dooley imagined what the queen's reflections about England might be and then offered his own estimate of America's performance in the Victorian years:

While she was lookin' on in England, I was lookin' on in this counthry. I have seen America spread out from th' Atlantic to th' Pacific, with a branch office iv th' Standard Ile Comp'ny in ivry hamlet. I've seen th' shackles dropped fr'm th' slave, so's he cud be lynched in Ohio . . . an' Corbett beat Sullivan, an' Fitz beat Corbett. . . . An' th' invintions . . . th' cotton-gin an' th' gin sour an' th' bicycle an' th' flyin'-machine an' th' nickel-in-th'-slot machine an' th' Croker machine an' th' sody-fountain an'—crownin' wurruk iv our civilization—th' cash raygister.

In one deft stroke, Mr. Dooley laid bare the two rawest nerves in American society: the mixed track-record of "progress" and the national obsession with money. Neither was new to the American experience, but both assumed new roles in the industrial social order.

To grasp this fact, one must recall how novel this new milieu was. Life in the industrial city differed sharply from anything America had experienced before. Rapid growth jolted the social order out of its traditional channels and swept natives and newcomers alike across unfamiliar ground. Those accustomed to rural or village life floundered desperately in the cold, swirling currents of urban society; those who had always lived in cities scrambled to keep afloat as the flood tide of change swept away familiar landmarks which had ordered their lives. It was as if the old city and its ways lay drowned beneath the rising waters of strange faces and voices, new machines, expanding businesses, different things to do, and different ways of doing old things. In this sense, the city deserved its reputation as an alien place; it resembled nothing its inhabitants had ever known.

Nor did it stand still long enough for its face to become familiar. Growth not only altered the patterns of daily life and reshaped the city's face, it also separated people from one another and drove them into new kinds of relationships. This process of atomization destroyed whatever sense of community urban dwellers once possessed. No industrial city could function as a community in the true sense of the term. Its citizens lacked a common heritage, lineage, or even culture. They did not share the same principles of politics, religion, or economics. They did not even speak the same language, and their customs and moral standards clashed sharply. The most striking characteristic of the urban population was its incredible diversity. If Americans had esteemed diversity as a social asset, it might have provided the foundation for a mature social order based upon mutual tolerance and respect. But most Americans regarded diversity as a social liability if not an outright threat. Some saw urban society as a salad bowl and determined to keep the tomatoes segregated from the radishes or cucumbers. Others viewed it as a melting pot and despaired over the mongrelized amalgam that stewed within it.

City dwellers had little in common beyond the accident of similar location and a hunger for self-betterment. Neither of these could act as a mortar to hold urbanites together in a stable social order. Within the industrial city, the marketplace molded society in its own image. In the market society, tradition had limited cash value and intangibles like customs, ideals, values, or sense of community fetched no premium. As other social currencies fell by the wayside, wealth became the handiest medium of exchange. It measured not only success in business but social standing and even personal worth as well.

Wealth and status had always gone together in America but never so exclusively or on so grand a scale. There had never been so much money, so many people with it, and so much clamor to translate wealth into social standing. While earlier generations had displayed great zeal in amassing wealth, even their worst excesses paled before the rampant materialism of post-Civil War America. The spectacle involved more than neglect of those spiritual or cultural qualities which could not be measured by the appraiser's cold eye; nor was it just the crass veneer of nouveau riche society. Rather it lay in the growing belief that the nation had lost touch with its roots, that somehow its noble ideals and sense of purpose had been perverted into a prescription for fortune hunting.

If the quest for wealth united Americans, the acquisition of it separated them as nothing else could. Even more than in 1860, America was a house divided: by class, by race and nationality, by customs, and by experience. Nowhere did these divisions assert themselves more prominently than in the industrial city. Their presence defeats any effort to draw a composite picture of urban life. The diversity of urban experience demands several different pictures to show different modes of living. Since economic status was the single most important factor in determining how city dwellers lived, it is the logical window through which to glimpse their lifestyles. For convenience we have divided the urban social structure into three broad groups: the upper, middle, and lower classes. The first will be taken up here, the others in succeeding chapters.

Wealth, Power, and Status

While Americans might argue over whether or not wealth brought "real" happiness, everyone agreed that it was far more pleasant to be rich than to be poor. A fortune meant more than mere possessions or luxuries; it conferred power and status as well. In typical fashion, America defined its elite through the mechanism of the marketplace. While the democratic tradition spurned any notion of formal aristocracy, it tolerated a privileged class based upon wealth.

Cynics might dismiss this as meaning only that the children of the American elite inherited money instead of titles. Nevertheless, the distinction between a hereditary and a moneyed aristocracy is an important one. It implies an elite that was fluid, informal, and above all accessible, in which the worth of a person depended mainly upon how much the person was worth. To some extent, this image was deceiving. The American aristocracy was never so casual or so open to newcomers as popular myth averred. Recent studies have confirmed that most of those at the top started near the top. In practice, the moneyed elite exercised as much power as traditional elites—and sometimes more. Their dominance of economic, political, and social affairs was no less complete because they had no royal titles, less exalted bloodlines, a slimmer gallery of family portraits, and family crests of dubious origins.

Yet the myth of the open system persisted despite the accumulation of evidence to the contrary. The new avenues to wealth and status opened by industrialization strengthened the belief in social mobility and the competitive system. Buoyed by the faith in progress shared by most Americans, urbanites regarded the city as the optimum environment for economic success. The released energies of the urban economy triggered a mad scramble for position on the economic and social ladder. Not surprisingly, the fiercest competition involved those seeking a place on the top rungs.

The behavior and values of metropolitan elites during the industrial period reveal much about the dynamics of urban life. At once the most revered and despised element in the community, they fought savagely among themselves for supremacy but closed ranks when challenged by upstarts from outside the charmed circle. In exercising leadership within the city, their own intense struggles for greater wealth and prestige influenced the destiny of the entire community. As social leaders they established tastes and patterns and indulged in a lifestyle that was admired, envied, ridiculed, hated, and, above all, aped by those beneath them. Despite the popular disdain for hereditary titles and elites, Americans habitually deferred to people of wealth and status. More than that, they conceded to people of means other qualities that had little to do with the ability to amass riches. Since America's Calvinist climate stressed character as the prime prerequisite for moneymaking, the possession of a fortune legitimized its holder's character and conferred upon him a special status.* It elevated him to the rank of authority upon all matters

* The equation that tied wealth to good character was severely shaken by the intricacies of fortune-seeking in the industrial era. Yet the myth survived even the

from education to politics. In early America, society placed its faith in
the leadership of those who had proven successful in the marketplace.
James Henretta concluded in his article on early Boston social structure:

> By the third quarter of the eighteenth century, an integrated economic
> and political hierarchy based on mercantile wealth had emerged in Boston
> to replace the lack of social stratification of the early part of the century
> and the archaic distinctions of power and prestige of the religious community
> of the seventeenth century. All of the important offices of the town govern-
> ment, those with functions vital to the existence and prosperity of the town,
> were lodged firmly in the hands of a broad elite, entry into which was
> conditioned by commercial achievement and family background.

In Boston as in most places, material wealth brought political leadership and social status. Commercial success, primarily in shipping and
trading, established political and social hegemony. Merchant "princes"
and river "lords" reigned over their urban habitats. Firmly entrenched in
the dominant enterprises of the city, the leading families fashioned a
social hierarchy in which they chose the most desirable homesites on the
hill or town square, built the most gracious houses, and set the tastes in
private and public entertainment. Often solidifying their business and
social prominence through intermarriage, this early elite insured that the
commercial city remained in the hands of those with the greatest "stake
in society."

And indeed their stake was great. In pre-Civil War Brooklyn, which
ranked as one of the nation's leading commercial centers, the men who
controlled the waterfront also controlled virtually everything else. Edward Pessen calculated that eighty families—1 percent of the total population—controlled over 42 percent of the city's wealth. Men like Jacob
Hicks, Tunis Joralemon, and Hezekiah Pierrepont seized the pinnacle
of the merchant economy and turned the nation's seventh largest city
into their personal fiefdom.*

Even in the expanding West, where social democracy presumably
flourished, the new river cities which arose after the Revolution quickly
evolved social hierarchies dominated by the merchant. Migrating along
the Ohio River, ambitious men with little capital invested in town lots
and started trading enterprises. If their gamble paid off, if their location

---

well-advertised excesses of that period. It is perhaps a tribute to the tenacity of American
mythology that the outrageous antics of the so-called "robber barons" provoked much
public outcry but did not destroy the general belief that character was the handmaiden
of wealth.

    * It is perhaps fitting that these names are preserved today as streets in Brooklyn
Heights, the most fashionable area of Brooklyn.

garnered enough of the river traffic, a bustling commercial center sprang up around the town lots and assured their owner both wealth and social prominence. Early families like the Leavys, Trottes, and Clays in Lexington; the Piatts and Longworths in Cincinnati; and the Chouteaus, O'Fallons, and Von Phuls in St. Louis purchased large tracts of land both near the water and on the outskirts of town at cheap prices. Commercial prosperity attracted more people to these young towns. Since growth tightened the ratio of land to people, those who had come first benefited most from rising land values and also got the choicest parcels.

The "first families" worked hard to cement their newly won dominance. Through an elaborate ritual of social activities tied to parties, balls, and "privileged assemblies," they strove to set themselves apart from their fellow townfolk. An early commentator on Louisville society remarked:

There is a circle, small 'tis true, but within whose magic round abounds every pleasure, that wealth, regulated by taste can produce, or urbanity bestow. There the "red heel" of Versailles may imagine himself in the emporium of fashion, and whilst leading a beauty through the maze of a dance, forget that he is in the wilds of America.

Every town had its "circle" to which lesser social lights looked as a beacon of guidance. While some people merely worshiped their social betters from afar, the more ambitious among them sought to emulate these lofty tastes and habits. This could prove a costly indulgence, even in a small town. In Booth Tarkington's novel *The Magnificent Ambersons* (1918), set in a small midwestern town, a character observes in a curious mixture of pride and complaint that "This town never did see so much style as Ambersons are putting on these days; and I guess it's going to be expensive, because a lot of other folks'll try to keep up with 'em."

The establishment of early elites seldom strayed from this pattern. Since waterways flowed at the heart of every new American city, most of the "first families" made their fortunes in water-related commercial activities. Success at commerce, coupled usually with choice holdings of local real estate, guaranteed economic prominence which in turn led to social and political prominence. Once in this commanding position, families were likely to remain entrenched for decades, unless ambition drove them to try their luck in some larger city or unless some improvident progeny squandered the family fortune.

Industrialization broadened the realm of economic opportunities and complicated the lives of those who had already established themselves as a commercial elite. Both as capitalists and as community leaders, they

faced tough economic decisions which affected their private fortunes and
the future of the entire town. Should they hew closely to the tried-and-
true ways of commerce or should they expand (or even switch) their
investments into some sort of industrial enterprise? The response to this
challenge varied. The tiny villages that dot the New England coast, like
Marblehead, Massachusetts, and Stonington, Connecticut, speak to a history of decision-making that stayed with the fortunes of the sea rather
than investment in landed industry. Other towns like Gloucester and
New Bedford, Massachusetts, tied their destinies to large-scale commercial
fishery and thrived on the favors of the cod and the whale.

Still other towns chose to mix their economic base. Newburyport,
Massachusetts, illustrates one approach to blending industry with commerce. In this case, the impetus for change came not from the local elite
but from a newcomer. When Charles T. James moved to Newburyport
in the 1840s, his bubbling enthusiasm for steam-powered textile mills
shook the town from its commercial lethargy. James won the confidence
of Newburyport's "staid old capitalists" and persuaded them to invest
large sums in textile manufacturing. Within a decade, the sleepy fishing
town turned into a thriving textile center with five mills that employed
1,500 persons. The population nearly doubled, new buildings went up
everywhere, cultural amenities appeared, and the old commercial elite
basked in the bounty of newly swollen fortunes.

Not all towns enjoyed Newburyport's success, but most opted for some
type of mixed economy. No major American city ignored the trend toward
industry. In some places, members of the established commercial elite
initiated the change; in others, they dawdled until new men charged forward, carried the rest of the town with them, and thereby won themselves a place in the "circle." Acting consciously or by chance, in groups
or alone, entrepreneurs everywhere played the game of city building.
Their activities betrayed the extent to which the destinies of most towns
were inextricably tied to the achievements of their prime movers.

The Case of the Hub City

Among larger cities, Boston offers a good example of how elite decision-
making contributed to urban growth. In that great seaport, the early commercial elite built their fortunes upon shipping, regional trade, and foreign trade, especially with Calcutta and Canton. Once Boston's merchant
capitalists recognized what Jefferson's embargo and the War of 1812
meant to their trading operations, they went into manufacturing to take

up the slack. The most notable venture was the Boston Manufacturing Company,* formed by Francis Cabot Lowell, his brother-in-law Patrick Tracy Jackson, and new arrivals Nathan Appleton, Amos Lawrence, and his brother Abbott Lawrence.

The Boston Associates, as they came to be called, prospered in the textile industry and consolidated their position through a labyrinth of intermarriages and close contacts in the social and cultural spheres.** The towns of Waltham, Lowell, and Lawrence, which emerged under their aegis, transformed Boston's agricultural hinterland into the nation's first successful urban manufacturing region. During the 1840s and 1850s the city's commercial families extended their investments beyond textiles to railroads, machine-tool manufacturing, and other enterprises. They had therefore responded to a commercial crisis by redirecting their energies and investments into the industrial sphere. In so doing they revitalized Boston's economy and solidified their own position of leadership. Thus could Frederic Jaher acknowledge that "Pre-Civil War Brahmins were, for the most part, a group of self-assured entrepreneurs secure in their social status and proud of their role in the community."

But then a curious fate befell the Boston elite. Having met the challenge of industrialization and preserved their status, they found themselves overwhelmed by the very forces they had set in motion. With industrial success came pressures for expansion, for increased production and efficiency, which demanded closer attention to business detail at the expense of politics or society or other interests. As Boston's expanding economy attracted new entrepreneurs to the city, business competition stiffened. Thousands of workers flowed in to fill the mills and factories, and the city added new buildings and remodeled old ones to cope with its soaring population.

Economic success had in fact recast the comfortable environment of the elite. Unfamiliar faces appeared at the business table (including some who were not married or otherwise related to members of the first fami-

* See Chapter 1.
** To impress upon the reader the extent of this inbreeding we can do no better than quote the following explanatory footnote from Arthur M. Johnson and Barry E. Supple, *Boston Capitalists and Western Railroads* (Cambridge, 1967): "Francis Cabot Lowell was related directly to the Cabots through his mother, to the Higginsons through his father, and to the Jacksons and Tracys through his wife. His wife's sister married Henry Lee, and his brothers-in-law Patrick Tracy Jackson, Charles Jackson, and James Jackson cemented the Jackson-Cabot alliance by marrying Lydia Cabot, Fanny Cabot, and Elizabeth and (a second marriage) Sarah Cabot, respectively. Fanny Cabot was Charles Jackson's second wife—his first was Amelia Lee!"

lies) and alien voices were heard in the streets. Neighborhoods changed
their character as the city sprawled into the hinterland, swallowing up
suburbs on every side. This new environment posed another challenge
to the Brahmins, one far more subtle and complex than the earlier commercial crisis.

Their responses varied. Some simply abandoned trade and manufacturing altogether, retiring upon handsome incomes derived from their real
estate and securities. Inheriting a distaste for the vulgarity of business
matters along with the family fortune, the children of these blueblood
families—men like Brooks and Henry Adams, Charles Eliot Norton, and
James Russell Lowell—denounced the excesses of materialism and devoted
themselves to culture and society. Norton spoke for the others when he
once defined the ideal community as "New England during the first
thirty years of the century, before the coming in of Jacksonian Democracy, and the invasion of the Irish, and the establishment of the
system of Protection."

Some Brahmins pointedly urged their children to shy away from mere
money-grubbing in favor of a career in the church or university. Others
tried to straddle the dilemma by remaining in industry while assailing the
changes taking place in both society and the economy; that amounted to
little more than denouncing the behavior of one's own shadow. Yet the
practice of cursing those who followed in one's footsteps evoked more
than irony; it reflected the curious process in America which transformed
aggressive entrepreneurs into established wealth, speculators into cautious
trustees of property.

On this point as elsewhere, the Boston elite helped establish the pattern that would occur in cities throughout the land. The Brahmins considered themselves successful because they earned their fortunes skill-
fully and honestly, exercising their power with taste and restraint. A
generation or so of wealth sprinkled the family tree with a liberal dusting
of education, culture, family tradition, social leadership, and civic responsibility. Once anointed into this higher realm of civilization, the
Boston elite naturally wished to shield themselves from brash interlopers
with their own urgent ambitions.

It required only about one generation of wealth to separate the cultivated from the barbarians. But as the upstarts laid siege to the bastions
of wealth and social respectability, they split the once-solid upper class.
On one hand, their presence could not be tolerated; on the other, their
financial credentials could not be denied. The only recourse left to many
Brahmins was to denounce the newcomers as shifty, irresponsible, vulgar
nouveaux riches and retire from the financial arena to their cultural and

social strongholds. In their retreat, they heeded the admonition of George W. Curtis: "Commercial prosperity is only a curse if it be not subservient to moral and intellectual progress, and our prosperity will conquer us if we do not conquer our prosperity."

Not all the heirs of early Boston money were content to live on the dividends of their fathers' enterprise. A few like Charles Francis Adams III, Godfrey L. Cabot, and James Jackson Storrow took a stab at business careers, but they were exceptions to the rule and were considered by some of their peers as traitors to their class. For the most part, early financial success bred a strain of conservatism among the elite which made it difficult for them to compete in the freewheeling industrial era. Family money went not into building factories, but into trusts designed to provide income for future generations. This emphasis upon stable and secure investments eliminated much of the "old" money as working capital for the risky ventures of the industrial era, and incidentally made Boston, rather than New York, the capital of trust banking.

Brahmins shrank from the business practices of the postwar era no less than from its investments. Their value system, which linked fortune to a strict sense of social responsibility, disclaimed the stock manipulations and financial legerdemain of men like Daniel Drew, James Fisk, and Jay Gould. Frederic Jaher, historian of the proper Bostonians, summed up their plight:

Vulgarity and corruption had become, at least to some figures, more horrendous than missed opportunities, surrender of economic hegemony, or even bankruptcy. . . . The Brahmins, having established ascendency in social as well as economic affairs, manifested traits of a hereditary aristocracy. Unlike family merchants in early nineteenth-century Boston, they were responsible for a legacy of values and customs. Brahmin businessmen could no longer evaluate new methods or new products solely in terms of counting-house rationality.

The loss of economic hegemony by the Brahmins paralleled the decline of Boston's potential as a national city. New York emerged as the dominant economic center in the East, leaving Boston to cling to its supremacy in New England.

While the Brahmins recoiled from the excesses of the countinghouse, they also faced rejection at the ballot box. Unlike the pressure of economic competition, which came from interlopers seeking a place at the top, the political challenge arose from those near the bottom. Irish immigrants pressed for political recognition and developed effective organizations to get it. The prospect of catering to ethnic constituencies soured the taste of elective office for most Brahmins; nor did Irish voters seem anxious to keep the "bluebloods" in high places.

The rise of ethnic political machines, coupled with the tainted atmosphere of politics during the years of the Grant administration, compelled the elite to protect their moral integrity by withdrawing from public service. Henry Adams, who was fond of writing lengthy epitaphs for the American political system, needed only a few lines to expose the raw nerve that pained Brahmins most. In his novel *Democracy* (1880), the central character, Mrs. Lightfoot Lee, muses; "Why was it, she said bitterly to herself, that everything Washington touched, he purified, even down to the associations of his house? and why is it that everything we touch seems soiled? Why do I feel unclean when I look at Mount Vernon?"

Only in cultural and civic affairs did the Brahmins maintain their leadership. Heading church, museum, hospital, and charity organizations, they also helped establish the Boston Public Library, the Boston Museum of Fine Arts, and the Boston Symphony Orchestra. But these missions, however noble or gratifying, seemed only a shell of the power they once wielded in the city. Bruised by change, the old elite lapsed into nostalgia. In the words of Oscar Handlin:

Depressed by the ugliness of industrialization and by the vulgarity of its new wealth, the proper Bostonians wished to think of themselves as an aristocratic elite rooted in the country, after the English model. They moved out to the rural suburbs of Brookline and Milton and resisted proposals to annex those towns to Boston. They sent their children to private schools and found self-contained satisfaction in their gentlemen's clubs.

By this retreat to independent suburbs, the old elite formally abandoned Boston to a new generation of leaders and acknowledged their own loss of prestige. Like all displaced royalty, they fed thereafter upon a diet rich in tradition and memory.

This brief survey of the Brahmins points up four important aspects of elite behavior. First, the decisions made by a powerful urban elite had great ramifications for the entire community. Second, the economic success of an early elite often led them into a financial conservatism which crippled their ability to respond to newer stages of economic growth. Third, by not moving into new investment areas, the old elite lost their economic hegemony when more aggressive entrepreneurs—men on the make—challenged their business leadership. While it is quite likely that, in the expansive urban economy, this challenge would have come anyway, the Brahmins hastened its triumph by declining to fight in so vulgar an arena. They had, in short, lost their taste for economic combat and thereby forfeited their chance of retaining some measure of dominance except in the areas of banking and railroad investment. Finally, the decline of an elite which conceived of its power as deriving from both wealth and a sense of community spirit created a vacuum in urban politics. A new type of leader rushed to fill this vacuum, one quite different from the civic-minded, noblesse oblige type of gentleman.

Public Interest, Private Interest

The fall of the old elite destroyed the unity of economic and political leadership they had imposed upon most cities. In their place came a new breed of leaders who carved out separate spheres of power within the industrial city. Early American cities were governed by individuals who integrated their personal values, business activities, and official positions into a single vision of social responsibility. It was not that the ruling elite made no distinction between public interest and private interest, but rather that they saw no serious conflict between them. So long as they wielded power in both the economic and political spheres, and so long as conscience and sense of duty prodded them to view their own interests within the larger context of the public good, the elite provided the city with strong, unified leadership.

Of course, those exalted standards of leadership carried more than a tinge of antidemocratic bias; and like all ideals, they were realized only imperfectly by imperfect men. In the long run, however, rapid growth doomed this model of urban leadership by making cities too large and diversified to operate on so narrow a power base. Once the dominance of the old elite splintered, as it did in Boston, the city suffered in two ways. First, civic affairs no longer attracted the close attention of its richest and often most talented citizens. The wealthy did not have to rule, but their interest and participation were vital if the city were to forge a stable social order. By retreating to the suburbs and shedding their concern for municipal affairs, they handed urban rule over to men who lacked their broad sense of public responsibility.

The city suffered, too, from the character and values of its new leaders, who differed markedly from the old elite. They were in no way a unified ruling class. The diversity of their origins mirrored the transition from the relatively homogeneous preindustrial town to the heterogeneous industrial city. Like the industrial city itself, the new leaders possessed no common core of culture, nationality, or tradition. They shared little beyond their mutual ambition to achieve wealth, status, and power. To reach that intersection of goals, they traveled separate avenues and used many different vehicles.

Lacking unity among themselves, the new leaders could scarcely impart any unified vision to municipal affairs. Few of them viewed the city as anything more than an arena for advancing their private interests. In short, they were the first generation of urban leaders to conceive of the city as marketplace instead of community. While that transition had long been in the making, it burst forth only after the forces of change and growth destroyed the monopoly of power held by the old elite. The new leaders did not simply replace the old elite in positions of power, nor did they inherit the kingdom intact. The change in personnel reflected a more basic force at work: the fragmentation of municipal power into distinct spheres of interests presided over by separate groups whose activities seldom strayed beyond their own bailiwicks.

The urban economy fell increasingly into the hands of the entrepreneurs who controlled the city's factories, banks, utilities, and traction franchises. Sometimes these magnates were local men; often they lived elsewhere and ruled their business domains as absentee landlords. In both cases their primary interest lay in profit making rather than in broader issues of civic affairs. When, as often happened, their pursuit of profits conflicted with public interest, they used every means at their disposal to gain their objectives regardless of the social consequences. Most entrepreneurs displayed little interest in politics and took no part in governing the city. When they required political favors or legislation, they bought what they needed much as they purchased raw materials or any other resource. Otherwise they left urban government to a separate group of ambitious men who had acceded to power in most cities.

The new breed of politicians rose to prominence in the same manner as other businessmen—by creating an efficient organization and utilizing it to advance their own interests. They viewed municipal office not as a public charge or civic duty, but as a golden goose to be plundered and exploited. Most urban bosses never even bothered to hold office, but were content to run their machines from the shadows. The business of politics revolved around a simple formula: The boss bought votes from the poor and sold favors to the rich.* He was, in the words of Cochran and Miller, "the man who set the prices for special favors, sold the franchises, and guaranteed a controlled electorate. He was the man who made it possible to conduct government in the interest of the upper middle class in spite of a great lower class electorate."

---

* For a more detailed analysis of urban politics, see Chapter 10.

This separation of political and economic power reduced urban leadership to a shifting coalition of interests, a complex mosaic of self-serving men who fought, bargained, and schemed their way to positions of control and influence. They were the new elite: a loose collection of businessmen and politicians who felt no deep attachment to the city itself and were unhampered by the restraints of culture and tradition. Their ascendance completed the divorce of power from social responsibility. Under its new leaders, the industrial city became a private city in which the public interest was conceived as the aggregate of individual private interests, rather than something apart and above them.

Sam Bass Warner has detailed the evolution of this pattern in Philadelphia.* While proper Philadelphians never displayed quite the same zeal for public life as their Boston counterparts, they did pay heed to their city's development prior to industrialization. Then a new view of the city appeared among its leaders during the industrial period. Warner uses Jay Cooke, the noted banker, to exemplify the change:

> The city of Philadelphia did not serve [Cooke], as it had served for previous generations, as an important frame through which he saw the world and out of which he took action upon the world beyond. No deep knowledge of, or concern for, the general welfare of his city informed Cooke's business, politics, or philanthropy.

All the world was not Philadelphia for Cooke, because it had never been so. He was not a product of the city, and his business concerns rested primarily in the area of national finance.

This indifference prevailed among the Civil-War generation of business leaders. The old elite simply abandoned their former roots in the city; the new elite rarely bothered to put any roots down. For them the city became little more than home base, the place one happened to have his headquarters: "The new habits of business taught the mid-nineteenth-century Philadelphia businessman that the city was not important to their daily lives, and in response these business leaders became ignorant of their city and abandoned its politics." The departure of the old elite from Philadelphia's politics coincided with their physical removal to the suburbs, an increased specialization of local government leaders, the growing influence of ethnic politicians in public affairs, and the rising strength of political machines.

Robert Dahl found the same pattern operating in the politics of New Haven, Connecticut, and defined it more rigorously as a "triple dynasty" cycle. The election of a carpet manufacturer as mayor in the 1840s broke

* It is worth noting that Warner entitled his book *The Private City*.

the "patrician" phase of elite rule and ushered in a long line of businessmen in office:

The emergence of the new (but assuredly not idle) rich as occupants of
public office reflected an important splitting off of wealth and political influence from social standing and education in New Haven. With the growth
of manufacturing a new kind of man rose to the top in the local economic
order. . . . He was, in short, the epitome of the self-made man.

Yet by 1900 the rising strength of ethnic voting eclipsed the businessmen
as well. The assumption of political control by immigrants, or "ex-plebes"
as Dahl called them, completed the patrician-businessman-immigrant
dynasty cycle. Although the pattern varied in detail from place to place,
the weight of competition from other businessmen and the numerical
strength of ethnic electorates combined to destroy the political power of
the old elite even before the Civil War.

Of the cities about which we know a good deal, Springfield, Massachusetts, presents a striking exception to this triple-cycle pattern. Michael
Frisch, in his study of that key city on the Connecticut River, found that
an older elite never really jelled there. A wide range of economic opportunity, a relatively open social system, and a high degree of geographic
mobility hindered the formation of a closed aristocratic leadership. When
the Civil War encouraged investments in munitions, no "old guard"
existed to resist the move. Indeed, old wealth joined with young entrepreneurs to spark an industrial boom which drew national attention.

As Springfield grew, its new economic elite moved into the political
arena. Governing Springfield through the late 1860s and early 1870s,
they seemed, like the old elite, able to combine the notions of "private"
and "public" interests which had been split in the larger cities of the East.
But when the Panic of 1873 and the subsequent depression shattered this
ideal, the ruling elite began "wondering whether their position meant
very much, given the chaos they saw around them. They wondered
whether the forces they had set in motion were proving too powerful, and
running out of control." They reacted to the crisis by advocating retrench-
ment and efficiency as the best means for riding out the depression,
whereupon the electorate quickly ousted them from office.

The Springfield case suggests that once urban problems boiled into
crises, governing elites could no longer comfortably submerge their private interests beneath the public. At that critical point they retired from
office voluntarily or were thrown out by the voters. In their place came
the new breed who made no pretense of separating private gain from the
public weal.

In city after city a similar pattern unfolded. Old families, new men on the make, or both, made decisions which industrialized their communities. Economic growth spawned urban problems of such vast dimensions as to defy every effort of the old leadership to deal with them. Having changed their communities into cities, the elite, like parents of some strange mutant, fled in horror from their progeny. If, as in the case of Springfield, they attempted to stay on and apply solutions that had worked in the past, they were usually ejected by their constituents. In the unflattering words of Howard Mumford Jones, "the old aristocracies in Boston, New York, Philadelphia, Charleston, St. Louis, Natchez, New Orleans, and other centers steadily declined into islands of genteel obsolescence."

Having renounced their interest in the city and its government, the social aristocracy rechanneled its energies in two directions. On one hand, it devoted more time to the making of money and especially to the spending of it. No longer obliged to temper their wealth with civic responsibility, many of the old elite indulged themselves in an orgy of extravagance barely more refined than that practiced by the nouveaux riches they scorned. From this bent emerged a panoply of social ritual and display. On the other hand, the elite lent their patronage to a myriad of social, cultural, charitable, and recreational institutions. In so doing they altered the nature of urban life and culture. The dual roles of spendthrift and philanthropist were not mutually exclusive among the elite. In the end, however, it was the image of self-indulgent hedonism and wanton excess that lingered most vividly in the minds of future generations when they recalled the urban elite of the industrial era.

"Mrs. Astorbilt"

Sooner or later, those who amassed a fortune in the industrial era or inherited one from their forebears had to confront the delicate question of what to do with their money. It was a question that tortured a small but growing circle of Americans, for by the 1880s the nation possessed a sizable upper class, most of whom resided in urban areas. Every industrial city had a millionaire or two, the larger cities boasted whole collections, and New York positively overflowed with them. And beneath those who had passed the magic million mark swarmed an impressive array of merely well-to-do urbanites.

Never in the history of the Republic had so many people possessed so much money. For some it was a tool for obtaining still greater wealth, a yardstick for measuring success in the great game of business. For others it served as a lever for some other objective such as political power. Some hoarded it and reveled in its steady accumulation, while others immersed themselves in the possessions and pleasures it brought them. There were even men who regarded wealth as little more than a by-product of their life's work and who took little interest in what it could buy or bring them.

Whatever its function, money obsessed most inhabitants of the in-dustrial city. In that fluid social environment where traditional measures of self-identity and social status lacked firm roots, money was above all an expression of personal success. Those who did not have it counted for little in the eyes of those who did. Society—no less than personal worth—was a creature of the marketplace. While money could not buy immediate social status, it served as the bridge upon which the newly rich or their children eventually crossed into the promised land of social acceptance.

The proliferation of wealth in the industrial era produced a crisis in upper-class society. In most cities, the old elite had long ruled the social roost as they had economic and political affairs. To themselves, and to the rest of the community, they were the "best people." Time and a stern sense of the proprieties had dignified their wealth with the trap-pings of family tradition and prestige, education, taste, and culture. Their dominance of society rested not merely upon the size of their fortunes, but upon the manner in which they lived—the elaborate system of social rituals and values which set them distinctly apart from the rest of the community.

As custodians of high society, the old elite admitted few newcomers to their charmed circle. They tended to marry their own kind and vigilantly resisted attempts by "new money" to penetrate their ranks. Ob-viously the key to social acceptance lay not in wealth alone, but in hereditary wealth. The original source of the money did not matter; it might come from butchering cattle or butchering competitors in busi-ness or on the stock exchange. The point was that an inherited fortune allowed its possessor the time and leisure to acquire the breeding and habits necessary for proper society. In most cases it required only a generation to convert a parvenu into a family accepted as being to the manner born.

The crisis came when the flush industrial economy produced a bumper crop of nouveaux riches who flocked eagerly to the portals of high so-ciety and demanded entry. Their problem was to find some alchemy which converted instant wealth into instant social acceptance. Their first impulse was to attempt to buy the respectability it had taken the old elite decades to accumulate. Unhampered by any guise of the social restraint, devotion to tradition, or cultivation of taste which characterized much of the country's old wealth, the new industrial tycoons ushered in an era of reckless spending and social excess. Not only did this parvenu extravagance offend the sensibilities of older wealth like the Boston Brahmins, it also raised the price of high society. Ward McAllister, the high priest of fashionable New York society, described the transition into what he called the "Era of Extravagance":

We here reach a period when New York society turned over a new leaf. Up to this time [about the 1880s], for one to be worth a million of dollars was to be rated as a man of fortune, but now, bygones must be bygones. New York's ideas as to values, when fortune was named, leaped boldly up to ten millions, fifty millions, one hundred millions, and the necessities and luxuries followed suit. One was no longer content with a dinner of a dozen or more, to be served by a couple of servants. Fashion demanded that you be received in the hall of the house in which you were to dine, by from five to six servants, who, with the butler, were to serve the repast. The butler, on such occasions, to do alone the headwork, and under him he had these men in livery to serve the dinner, he to guide and direct them. Soft strains of music were introduced between the courses, and in some houses gold replaced silver in the way of plate, and everything that skill and art could suggest was added to make the dinners not a vulgar display, but a great gastronomic effort, evidencing the possession by the host of both money and taste. . . .
Our forefathers would have been staggered at the cost of the hospitality of these days.

The most conspicuous display of wealth was the great mansions. Every city had an enclave in which the rich secluded themselves from the rest of society. On upper Fifth Avenue in New York, the Gold Coast in Chicago, Nob Hill in San Francisco, Euclid Heights in Cleveland, the industrial barons erected residential monuments to their affluence. Juxtaposed against the wretched tenements of urban slums and the dreary sameness of middle-class housing, the mansions evoked in city dwellers a peculiar mixture of awe and resentment. As visual images of success they served their owners well.

The example of Potter Palmer is instructive, if not typical. A Chicago businessman who had made his fortune in dry goods, State Street real estate, and the luxurious hotel which bore his name, Palmer commissioned a new mansion in the mid–1880s. Built on the North Side, the stone-turreted Gothic castle featured every modern convenience except knobs on the outside doors—this to prevent unwanted callers from intruding unless screened first by a servant. According to Ray Ginger, a visitor to the house presented his calling card which "had to pass through the hands of twenty-seven servants before a decision was made whether he would be seen. Mrs. Palmer's best friends were required to write for appointments."

Some entrepreneurs, like Marshall Field, built on a less ostentatious scale, but they were exceptional in their restraint. Harold McCormick, the heir to another great Chicago fortune, erected a mansion at 1000 Lake Shore Drive that rivaled the Palmer castle. Completed in 1912, the place attracted so much attention as to be featured in an article entitled "The Renaissance Villa Developed into a Complete Residential Type for Use in America." As a detail of elegant living, the McCormick household preceded every meal with a printed menu—in French.

The homes of Mark Hopkins, Leland Stanford, and Charles Crocker on Nob Hill; Daniel Clemson's residence in Pittsburgh's East End; the Vaile mansion in Independence, Missouri; Henry Clay Frick's stately edifice in New York; and hundreds more all followed the same mold. None generated more excitement than William H. Vanderbilt's block-long, triple brownstone mansion at Fifty-first Street and Fifth Avenue in New York.* Styled after the Italian Renaissance, the sprawling mansion cost about $3,000,000. While every room harbored its own treasures, the elegance of Mrs. Vanderbilt's bedroom led one visitor to rhapsodize that

In this exquisite room, where silver toilet services, embroidered silks, and delicate hangings vie with masterly paintings to refresh the attention, it would seem that dreams must be propitious, and the waking pleasant. Among the fragile glitter of the upholstery, where everything seems to start bright and crisp from the hands of the artifice, there is one worn-looking object, and only one. it is the little Bible.

At least Mrs. Vanderbilt permitted herself the luxury of sleeping amidst the magnificence. Mrs. Stuyvesant Fish, another socialite, commissioned the creation of a Gothic bedroom which so enchanted her tastes that she left it unsullied and moved her bed to an adjoining dressing room.

By 1900 Fifth Avenue boasted a long phalanx of mansions which housed, among others, the Huntingtons, Morgans, Goulds, Sages, Astors, Harrimans, Carnegies, Whitings, and Phippses. But the rich did not confine themselves to dwellings in the crowded city. To escape the press of urban life many families had summer places or "cottages" which

---

* Mansions owned by members of the Vanderbilt family dominated Fifth Avenue from Fifty-first to Fifty-eighth streets.

often exceeded the city manor in gargantuan size and splendor. Those without a summer place flocked to fashionable resort towns like Narragansett Pier, Rhode Island; Saratoga Springs, New York; Bar Harbor, Maine; and Hot Springs, Virginia. In 1890 the *New York Tribune* regularly published eight full columns of summer resort notices.

The exodus of the fashionable to these otherwise sleepy towns did wonders for local economies. Urban elites came to indulge themselves by spending their money freely, and spend it they did. Anson Phelps Stokes led the Berkshire Mountain boom by constructing a 100-room granite castle in the capital of that social belt, Lenox, Massachusetts. The Stokeses were not above a little entertaining but even aristocracy had its limits. On one occasion in 1896 young Stokes wired his mother that he planned to bring ninety-six of his classmates home to "Shadowbrook" only to receive the reply, "MANY GUESTS ALREADY HERE. ONLY HAVE ROOM FOR FIFTY." Lenox regarded itself as the crossroads of the East. So frenetic was social life there that when Grover Cleveland died in 1908, the local editor, unwilling to believe the former president had never visted Lenox, published the headline "PRESIDENT DEAD" with the hopeful subhead, "MAY HAVE FISHED HERE."

Opulent as these summer havens were, none could rival the social or architectural majesty of Newport. Once a major port and slave-trading center, Newport experienced a social and economic revival when the wealthy seized upon it as a playground. Situated on Aquidneck Island at the mouth of Narragansett Bay, the town offered stunning cliff walls and striking views of the Atlantic. Along Bellevue Avenue and Ocean Drive went up the nation's grandest assortment of summer "cottages," many of which are still preserved for public inspection. While "The Elms," "Chateau Sur Mer," "Rosecliff," "Champ Soleil," and others strove to outdo one another in palatial splendor, it was left to the Vanderbilts to build the two most imposing edifices. William K. Vanderbilt constructed the magnificent "Marble House" for his wife with rare marble imported from Africa and a ballroom paneled in gold.

Not to be outdone, Cornelius Vanderbilt II chose the most beautiful seafront site and erected his enormous Renaissance palace, "The Breakers," at a cost of several millions. Filled with art treasures, priceless furnishings, a breathtaking assortment of marbles from many lands, and every modern convenience, the huge mansion required a live-in staff of forty, exclusive of gardeners, groundsmen, grooms, and stable hands. Every room was a masterpiece of elegance and opulence. Throughout the manor could be found two of the Vanderbilt family emblems, the porpoise and the acorn cluster; and above the fireplace in the library, beneath a ceiling of rich gold-inlaid walnut, hung the old Commodore's motto, "Little do I care for riches."*

Both "The Breakers" and "Marble House," as well as William Vanderbilt's Fifth Avenue mansion, were the handiwork of Richard Morris Hunt, an architect who established a reputation as "chateau builder" for the wealthy and collected many fashionable commissions, especially from the Vanderbilts. Hunt's professional philosophy expressed both his client's desire for opulence and the undisputed triumph of money over aesthetics. On choosing designs for the rich Hunt observed to his son, "The first thing you've got to remember is that it's your client's money you're spending. Your business is to get the best results you can following their wishes. If they want you to build a house upside-down standing on its chimney, it's up to you to do it, and still get the best possible results."

The grandiose palaces of the industrial titans stood as physical monuments to a social philosophy that replaced civic concern with unabashed self-indulgence. Going far beyond the limits of useful space or ornamentation, the gaudy edifices offended virtually every canon of taste and sensibility. But they reflected the purpose for which they were built. Bigness connoted not only success but, hopefully, permanence as well. In the shifting sands of American society, insecurity bred architectural overkill. Imitation castles and extravagant imports from exotic places were substitutes for personal taste that did not exist. For those in whom breeding and education had not produced dignity, it was thought that money could buy it. Finally, gargantuan size, like that of feudal castles, represented a retreat, a barrier to the outside. The absence of doorknobs stated bluntly what all the mansions implied more discreetly: a social philosophy of segregation from and indifference to the mundane, clamoring needs of the industrial city.

The social whirl inside these lavish homes embodied this same philosophy. Within their own aeries, the elite shut themselves off from the outside world by concocting elaborate social rituals of their own. Most flung themselves into the whirligig of society with cheerful abandon. There emerged a complex pecking order within the social set which maintained rigid standards of acceptance for advancing from one level to the next. Exclusiveness was cherished, as if isolation itself somehow bred status. Thus, what appeared to the untrained eye to be the solid

---

* Both "The Breakers" and "Marble House," as well as many of the other mansions named, are available for public tours thanks to the work of the Newport Preservation Society. No description of these mansions can compare with an actual visit to them. The impression they leave upon the visitor may give far more of a sense of the era than any number of books can.

pyramid of elite society proved upon closer inspection to be teeming with fine gradations, subtle nuances, and minute distinctions.

In a circle where everyone had money, the criteria for acceptance went beyond mere wealth to matters of blood, breeding, and respectability. Touchstones of approval were established in clothes, exotic possessions, exquisite parties, balls, and dinners, and above all the willingness of one socialite to suffer the company of another upon some festive occasion. Access to a higher level of society usually came in the form of an invitation to some social event or simply to call. Within the uppermost ranks of society, the guest lists for important events excited the sort of rumors, speculation, flights of hope and despair usually reserved for treaties, elections, or major scandals. "Making it" in elite circles also meant being listed in the Social Register. The very institution of a Social Register, begun in 1887 by Louis Keller, suggests a compelling need for recognition, as if status were confirmed or made "real" by being written into the public record.

The man who furnished wealthy families with the proper social hierarchy they craved was Ward McAllister, the greatest social arbiter America has spawned. Called "the world's greatest dude" and the "autocrat of the drawing room," McAllister devoted his life in New York to the promotion of heraldry, genealogy, court etiquette, gourmet cuisine, fine wines, balls, parties, and guest lists. Fashion was for McAllister an end in itself, and for two decades he reigned supreme over New York's high life.

McAllister organized High Society by reviving the old concept of the elite assembly. In 1872 he formed the "Patriarchs for the Association," a group of men including names like Astor, Livingston, Phelps, Post, and Rensselaer, who "had the right to create and lead Society." Invitations to balls, dinners at Delmonico's, and parties given by the Patriarchs were deemed especially important by McAllister because "the social life of a great part of our community, in my opinion, hinges on this and similar organizations, for it and they are organized social powers, capable of giving a passport of society to all worthy of it."

During the heyday of McAllister's control over New York society, those striving to gain acceptance coveted an invitation subscription to one of the Patriarchs' events. McAllister tantalized those aspiring for recognition by establishing a mythical figure of "400" to encompass the true inner circle. Speculation as to who belonged on the list, who was about to make it, who might be sliding off, engrossed socialites throughout the 1880s. Not until immediately before Mrs. William Astor's great ball of February 1, 1892, did McAllister finally release to

The New York Times the names of the fabled "400." The list reflected the social organization McAllister sought to promote for New York: a combination of old family wealth with new fortunes made in iron, copper, railroads, real estate, investments, and banking. McAllister's power in social arbitration offered a striking example of the need felt by the rich for tangible recognition of their status among their peers.

The emphasis placed upon social standing promoted a lifestyle dedicated to stalking the goals of recognition and acceptance. The result was a kind of social warfare in which ambitious hostesses alternately laid siege, launched frontal assaults, or conducted flanking maneuvers against the bastions of higher respectability. Their chief weapons were indefatigability and a certain ingenuity in devising forms of entertainment that attracted even their social superiors. "You don't give parties to enjoy yourselves," remarked a bachelor at a particularly exhausting affair in Newport, "but to advance yourselves."

To Mrs. William K. Vanderbilt, wife of the Commodore's grandson, belonged the supreme victory of that frantic decade. For all their wealth and trappings of magnificence, the Vanderbilts had not penetrated the topmost roost of New York society presided over by Mrs. William Astor. Once installed in a Fifth Avenue chateau, Mrs. Vanderbilt threw down her gauntlet to the Astors: she announced her intention of giving the most magnificent ball in the annals of New York society. The news flooded society columns and whipped up a froth of excitement that permeated even the thick portals of the Astor mansion. Twelve hundred persons were to be invited, the selection of whom, according to *The New York Times*, "disturbed the sleep and occupied the waking hours of social butterflies, both male and female, for over six weeks."

Caught up in the fever of anticipation, Mrs. Astor at length let the word out that she and her daughter would honor the ball with their presence if invited. But even that remarkable concession was not enough for the strong-willed Mrs. Vanderbilt. For years she had smarted at being ignored when invitations to the Astor Ball went out, and now she demanded unconditional surrender. Through emissaries she expressed her desire to invite the Astors but wondered if it was possible since Mrs. Astor had never honored her with a formal call. The surrender took place at the Vanderbilt mansion a few days later when an Astor footman, liveried in blue, delivered to a Vanderbilt footman, dressed in maroon, a white flag in the form of Mrs. Astor's calling card.

Mrs. Astor received her invitation and the Fancy Dress Ball, if those present and the newspapers can be believed, fulfilled every expectation. The *New York World* estimated sourly that the affair cost about

$250,000 for the costumes, catering, food, champagne, and the decorations, which included converting the second-floor supper room into a tropical forest replete with potted palms and countless orchids. Wall Street broker Henry Clews, who was there, conceded that the ball fell short of Alexander the Great's feast at Babylon and perhaps a few of the entertainments given by Cleopatra and Louis XIV but added, "taking into account our advanced civilization, I have no hesitation in saying that the Vanderbilt ball was superior to any of those grand historic displays of festivity and amusement. . . ." More important, the ball "seemed to have the effect of levelling up among the social ranks of upper tendom, and placing the Vanderbilts at the top of the heap, in what is recognized as good society in New York." The new social union atop New York society inspired one disenchanted critic a decade later to give all ambitious hostesses the tribal name of "Mrs. Astorbilt."

The same pattern unfolded elsewhere on a less spectacular scale. The extent to which those who played for high social stakes absorbed themselves in the game lent a special flavor to every American city, each of which touted its own version of the "400" (in Denver, it was the "Sacred Thirty-Six"). Those who retained lavish inner-city dwellings were caught up in a constant round of party-going, opera attendance, luncheons, formal calls, soirees, or patronizing of fine salons in exclusive shopping districts. Edith Wharton, in her classic novel of American manners, *The House of Mirth* (1905), captured the breathless tempo of upper-class society in one marvelous paragraph:

Meanwhile, the holidays had gone by and the season was beginning. Fifth Avenue had become a mighty torrent of carriages surging upward to the fashionable quarters about the park, where illuminated windows and outspread awnings betokened the usual routine of hospitality. Other tributary currents crossed the main stream, bearing their freight to the theatres, restaurants, or opera; and Mrs. Peniston from the secluded watch-tower of her upper window, could tell to a nicety just where the chronic volume of sound was increased by the sudden influx setting toward a Van Osburgh ball or when the multiplication of wheels meant merely that the opera was over or that there was a big supper at Sherry's.

The upper class, with their constant striving toward greater social heights, set their own style for the city. It was a style by which some people lived and of which all were aware. Fashionable inner-city enclaves, isolated suburban retreats, country clubs in the outskirts of town, select shops and restaurants, exclusive clubs, and private schools were the provinces of the privileged alone; but they permeated the consciousness of everyone.

Yet in many ways the style and flair of the fashionable belied their inner tensions. The pace they maintained was arduous and often self-defeating. Having created elaborate social rituals to set themselves apart from the vulgarity of the world beyond, some of the elite came to feel imprisoned by their own exclusiveness. Having fashioned for themselves a narrow life, the more restless began to wonder if there were not more to life. So fierce was the struggle to preserve social standing at the uppermost level that it reduced many of those in the race to measuring their personal worth by the ostentation of their mansion, an inventory of their possessions, a head count of their servants, the number and quality of invitations they received, or their standing on the most recent exclusive list. This reliance upon outward manifestations of wealth brought the ethic of the marketplace full circle. It boiled everything—self-worth, family honor, community recognition—down to its dollar value. As Pemburton, a character in Robert Herrick's *The Common Lot*, observed, "Men were content to take part of their pay in honor and respect from the community. There's no denying that's all changed now. We measure everything by one yardstick, and that is money."

For some, the vicious circle of social ritual produced a deep sense of ennui which sank steadily into decadence. The quality of elite society, despite its glitter, harbored more than its share of fool's gold. Not even the most ornate setting or elaborate entertainment could conceal the fact that many wealthy persons, like many ordinary folk, were dull people with narrow interests. Lloyd Morris depicted this shallowness in unsparing terms:

At Mrs. Astor's dinner parties, as at really all others, little was done for the entertainment of guests beyond providing them with a large amount of elaborate food. There were seldom fewer than seven courses, accompanied by many varieties of wine, with a Roman punch in the middle of the meal to stimulate flagging courage. One was rarely amused by one's table-companion. New York did not run to good talk. "Society" was given to a deplorable habit of tête-à-tête prattling. People felt that saying anything to their neighbor was more polite than listening to anyone else. Under a convention that no pauses must occur, the art of conversation had been lost. The general effect was flat and arid. "Society" was a Sahara without oases, without lions, and certainly without lion hunters. The Four Hundred would have fled in a body from a poet, a painter, a musician, or a clever Frenchman.

Moreover, the escalation of social display drove the more jaded participants beyond weariness to perverse caricatures of their own rituals. In search of a remedy for boredom, Mrs. Stuyvesant Fish adopted the cynical Harry Lehr for her court jester and fashioned entertainments around a program of pointed insults, vicious practical jokes, and sophisticated malice. On one occasion Mrs. Fish hosted a formal dinner party at which the guest of honor was someone's pet monkey dressed in white tie and tails. Another wealthy animal lover gave a banquet for his pet dog, who received a $15,000 diamond collar. One New Yorker entertained his guests with a "poverty special" dinner at which everyone ate on wooden plates and drank from rusty tin cans. In 1897, during the depression, Mrs. Bradley Martin gave a lavish ball at the Waldorf which cost an estimated $250,000. Eight years later James Hazen Hyde, heir to an insurance fortune, enlisted the talents of architect Stanford White to re-create a court ball in the style of Louis XIV at which guests and attendants alike wore period costumes and the state suite of Sherry's restaurant was converted into a replica of the salons of the Grand Trianon.

These expensive fantasies provoked public outrage at their callow excesses, tastelessness, and indifference to conditions outside the ballroom. They also suggest the bankruptcy of spirit and imagination which had seized the idle rich. It remained for Thomas Beer, writing in 1926, to dismiss this lifestyle with the most contemptuous blast of all:

The Four Hundred, the balls of some man named Bradley Martin, Pink Teas and the attempt of youngsters to wear silken knee breeches at dances— all these matters were copied from paper to paper and delighted lumberjacks in Oregon. The timid ostentations of a possible three thousand men and women living in cramped, airless houses between two polluted rivers were advertised as though an aristocracy moved proudly through some customary ritual.

The Haunts and Habits of the Rich

Among the wealthy the yardstick of status was by no means confined to homes and home entertainment. Every aspect of upper-class life— whether it be distinction of dress, leisure-time activities, social haunts, transportation—raised the cutting edge of exclusiveness. Often there occurred the familiar clash between new money and old, pitting awesome magnificence against quiet, tasteful dignity. But the lines of snobbery were not always so clearly drawn, the gradations so clearly defined. Whatever the intricacies of rank and rancor among the "ins," no one could fail to see the grand demarcation of status that separated them from the "outs."

The social club epitomized this demarcation. A bastion of exclusiveness, it was patronized by men of means and prestige who had the leisure time to enjoy its plush, dignified atmosphere. The Union, the Knickerbocker, the Racquet, and Metropolitan in New York, the Philadelphia Club, the Chicago Club, the Pacific Union in San Francisco, the Denver Club, the Boston Club in New Orleans, the Metropolitan in Washington, and the Maryland Club in Baltimore were but some of the more renowned institutions found in every city. Enclosed in grand brick designs, these urban retreats became the focus for lunchtime activity, after-work discussion, and leisure hours. Featuring stately reading rooms, the finest food, wine, and cigars, well-schooled servants, and quiet, elegant decors, the clubs catered to a well-bred class that cultivated a private lifestyle and desired to be with their own kind. As Dixon Wecter wrote, the gentleman's club was "his peculiar asylum from the pandemonium of commerce, the bumptiousness of democracy, and the feminism of his own household."

The rich also sought distinction in the sports they patronized. Disdaining the organized mass sports that were becoming popular in the late nineteenth century, most wealthy individuals indulged themselves in diversions which required money, such as horse racing and yachting. Both sports removed their participants from the city and demanded costly facilities. Horse breeding needed wide expanses of pasture and well-kept stables; yachting required a fine-rigged ship and often a large crew. Rivalries abounded in racing and in the splendor of the animal or craft.

While the horses nibbled bluegrass in Kentucky and the yachts tacked in the balmy winds of the Atlantic, the social aspects of the two sports thrived among their partisans in the city. Jockey clubs sprang up everywhere, the oldest of which included the Pioneer Jockey Club in San Francisco and the Louisville Jockey Club. For racing devotees, the major races formed a fashionable social circuit: one went to Louisville for the Derby, to Baltimore for the Preakness, and to Saratoga Springs for the Travers. The whirl of gaiety climaxed with the National Horse Show in Madison Square Garden where bejeweled ladies and tuxedoed gentlemen in top hats filled the boxes to watch the judging of their prize stock as if the verdict were being rendered upon their own breeding.

Yachting, too, boasted its corps d'elite. "You can do business with anyone," J. P. Morgan insisted, "but only sail with a gentleman." And Morgan, no less than his peers, practiced what he preached. Few haunts of the rich presented more impeccable credentials or demanded more imposing criteria for membership than the New York Yacht Club, the

Southern Yacht Club in New Orleans, the Seawanhaka Yacht Club in New York, the San Francisco Yacht Club, and others of their ilk. Perhaps the most signal honor to befall the yachtsman was the privilege of joining the syndicate to finance the ship to defend the America's Cup against challengers from Europe in a series of races held in the waters off Newport. More than one titan of industry or finance was denied admission to this reserved circle.

In the final analysis, however, the mainstay of urban elite society was not the gentleman but his wife. The fact was that most men were deeply involved in their business affairs and had little time for amusements or interest in the social whirligig except as prisoners of their wives' ambitions. While an occasional group like the Patriarchs spent time erecting social guidelines, and while heirs of old money cultivated lives of studied leisure, those men actively engaged in business were conspicuous by their absence from social rituals. It was the women who filled the society columns (and who read them avidly), and followed the vibrations of every social happening. As the visitor in William Dean Howells's utopian novel, *A Traveler from Altruria* (1894) observed, "I understand that in America society is managed even more by women than it is in England." The response to his comment was accurate and succinct:

"It is entirely in their hands," I said with the satisfaction we all feel in the fact. "We have no other leisure class. The richest men among us are generally hard workers; devotion to business is the rule; but as soon as a man reaches the point where he can afford to pay for domestic service, his wife and daughters expect to be released from it to the cultivation of their minds and the enjoyment of social pleasures."

The reasons for feminine domination of society are not hard to understand. Relieved of the burdens of household routine and unencumbered by any domestic responsibility except childbirth, upper-class women found time heavy upon their hands. The very indolence of their schedule acquired an aura of status, a form of what Thorstein Veblen called conspicuous consumption, no less symbolic of wealth than the extravagance of their expenditures. Locked out of business, politics, and other "men's work" by Victorian barriers, and locked out of their households by their own affluence, many women found refuge in the machinations of society.

To that endeavor they devoted a prodigious amount of time, energy, and talent. Their whims piloted the course of society. Every nuance of their tastes and behavior aroused envy or relish and above all imitation or counterattack. The rivalries among society's grandes dames assumed legendary proportions not only in the fashionable East but also in the raw communities of the West. In Denver, for example, society had jelled sufficiently by the 1880s to sport a fashionable clique comprised of the wives of the "Bonanza Kings." When this Sacred Thirty-Six resisted the efforts of Margaret Tobin Brown, wife of upstart silver tycoon "Leadville Johnny" Brown, to enter their charmed circle, that indefatigable lady departed for Europe to entertain on her own. Having survived the sinking of the Titanic and created a social sensation on the Continent, Margaret won her place in the hearts if not the drawing rooms of Denver and earned her reputation in more recent times as the "Unsinkable Molly Brown."

In striving to retain their hegemony over society, women followed their husbands' lead in establishing social clubs. The Vincent Club in Boston and the Colony Club in New York epitomized these feminine bastions of selectivity. Hoping to remain the bulwarks of a truly "American" elite, some upper-class women also banded together on a national level to establish native social groups. The Colonial Dames and the Daughters of the American Revolution, both founded in 1890, and the Daughters of Cincinnati (1894) served to confirm real or fancied pedigrees. In 1901, with the formation of the Junior League, the organizational spirit dipped down to embrace aspiring younger socialites. Disguised as a social-service unit for debutantes, the Junior League quickly caught on in the major cities of the East. During the 1920s it spread into the Midwest and became the leading arbiter of social status. In cities like Indianapolis, Kansas City, Omaha, Milwaukee, and Des Moines, the Junior League roster functioned as a social register for young women with impeccable credentials. Membership was tantamount to social acceptance.

By the late nineteenth century, upper-class women stood astride the social arena. In that position they accepted their role as social arm of the family. The prevailing cliché of upper-class family life became that of the hard-driving businessman relegating the tasks of leisure, culture, and social proprieties to his wife. As financier Russell Sage confessed, "Work has been the chief, and you might say, the only source of pleasure in my life." The miserly Sage, in fact, worked so hard and clutched his riches so tightly that it was only after his death at the age of ninety that his wife could do anything with his money. She promptly poured $35,000,000 of it into a philanthropic enterprise, the Russell Sage Foundation.

To women fell the responsibility for presenting the proper family image to society and protecting its good name. Some pursued the role so vigorously as to forge a stereotype of the domineering female forcing her reluctant husband into the rigors of the social circuit. Charles Dana Gibson, the illustrator of the "400" and originator of the chic Gibson girl, often drew scenes of huge matrons herding their wan spouses to the next ball. In one Gibson cartoon, a despairing industrialist, slouching in his tuxedo at a fancy party, dreamed wistfully of a distant bucolic retreat.

Making It

However much businessmen enjoyed their image as prisoners of the social whirl, they relished even more the notion that success derived from hard work pursued for moral, religious, or familial gains. The pose of the wealthy industrialist as self-made man, risen from boyhood poverty through tireless exertion and the support of his loyal wife, dominates the popular mythology of the industrial era. In reality, the success saga of most tycoons diverged sharply from the legendary pattern but did not shake the hold of that pattern on the popular mind.

The success myth found its ideal stereotype in the Horatio Alger image of poor boy rising to millionaire. From schoolhouse primers to graduate seminars in political economy, apostles inculcated the concept that business success could be attained through hard work and skill. As Alger himself wrote at the conclusion of one of his 135 novels, "So closes an eventful passage in the life of Luke Larkin. He has struggled upward from a boyhood of privation and self-denial into a youth and manhood of prosperity and honor. There has been some luck about it, I admit, but after all he is indebted for most of his good fortune to his own good qualities." This theme, that honest struggle against poverty and temptation brought fame and fortune, infused nearly all the Alger novels and encouraged the estimated 50,000,000 readers of the books.

And indeed there were titans who seemed cast from precisely that mold: Andrew Carnegie, John D. Rockefeller, Jay Gould, and George F. Baer, to name but four. While the purity of their methods might be suspect, their impoverished origins could not be denied. Nor were those who had risen from humble station hesitant to offer themselves as shining examples of the rewards produced by hard work. The success myth propelled employees toward greater productivity, reinforced their faith in the existing order, and obscured the harsh fact that opportunities for making it big were limited. It was, in short, an ideal defense of the status quo of the industrial social order.

Some industrialists—Carnegie, in particular—took great pains to weave the loose fabric of the success saga into a social philosophy. Carnegie viewed his life as the essence of the American experience. Born into a humble family in Scotland, he emigrated to the United States, charted his goals, impressed his superiors, stuck to his task, labored tirelessly, and built an empire in iron and steel. It all seemed clear to Carnegie, who prescribed a similar course for everyone. Poverty steeled a man to adversity and goaded him to improve his station; those who had the misfortune to be born rich labored, in Carnegie's eyes, under the curse of indolence and ease. Of poor but ambitious boys, he said:

They appear upon the stage, athletes trained for the contest, with sinews braced, indomitable wills, resolved to do or die. Such boys always have marched, and always will march, straight to the front and lead the world; they are the epochmakers.

Carnegie's gospel of success fell upon responsive ears. The litany of opportunity, coupled with the expanding economy, imbued millions with visions of grandeur. There existed a sufficient crop of self-made men to make the gospel credible, and the press diligently fed the hunger for details upon the rich and how they made it. In 1891 the *Forum* published a widely discussed article, "The Coming Billionaire" by Thomas G. Shearman, which calculated that the nation already possessed 120 men worth at least $10,000,000.

Even more than press notices, the presence of genuine self-made men in every city whetted the appetite for success. In Cleveland it was Rockefeller; in Pittsburgh, Carnegie; and Denverites turned to the storybook career of William Larimer. A Pennsylvanian who went broke in the 1850s, Larimer went West seeking a fresh start and settled at the mouth of Cherry Creek in Colorado.* Recalling that "Everything was open to us," Larimer developed the virgin spot into the city of Denver. As the city expanded into the Queen City of the Rockies, Larimer piled up a fortune and a reputation as the eastern knockabout turned spectacular promoter in the West.

The Larimer story was repeated many times over. Although many more failed or went nowhere, people chose to identify with those who bore out the "rags-to-riches" myth. In Cincinnati two men—William Proctor and James Gamble—pooled their resources of $7,500 in 1837 and went into the soap business. In 1879, when they began mass producing the world's first floating soap, they were well on their way to

---

* It was a characteristic of many wealthy businessmen to have failed at one or more ventures before attaining success.

becoming millionaires. In Kansas City, Thomas H. Swope, James F. Homes, and Kersey Coates joined the economic elite by virtue of modest investments in real estate which grew as their town grew.

The rags-to-riches saga comprised only one side of upper-class mobility in the industrial period. While it contained a germ of truth, local success tales should not obscure the fact that the late nineteenth century witnessed the formation of a national urban elite whose wealth and power in banking, industry, and commerce dwarfed that of local leaders. Some of these men rose from humble origins, but they were exceptions to the more general rule that those at the top started near the top.

A good deal of research sustains this conclusion that mobility was considerably more limited among national leaders than among local scions. In studying the careers of the industrial elite in steel, textiles, and railroads in the 1870s to determine their social origins, Frances W. Gregory and Irene D. Neu concluded by asking:

Was the typical industrial leader of the 1870's, then, a "new man," an escape from the slums of Europe or from the paternal farm? Did he rise by his own efforts from a boyhood of poverty? Was he as innocent of education and of formal training as has often been alleged?

Their answer painted a drastically different portrait from that found in the literature of success:

He seems to have been none of these things. American by birth, of a New England father, English in national origin, Congregational, Presbyterian, or Episcopal in religion, urban in early environment, he was rather born and bred in an atmosphere in which business and relatively high social standing were intimately associated with his family life.

The point was inescapable. In the real world outside Horatio Alger's novels, breeding, family, and wealth counted far more than pluck, hard work, ingenuity, or purity of character. William Miller found a similar pattern among business leaders at the turn of the century. So limited was upward mobility, he concluded, that one could "look almost in vain" for men who had struggled upward from modest beginnings. Only a handful of "working class or foreign origins" reached the highest levels in finance or manufacturing. It was no accident that those at the top bore familiar names like Lowell, Perkins, Drexel, or Morgan. They were the heirs of privilege who had utilized their advantages and in turn passed them on to their children.

For all the vicissitudes of changing fortunes, the American elite possessed a surprising degree of continuity. It was stable enough to survive the explosion of fortunes during the industrial era and its dynamic layering of new wealth upon old. By that time the upper class had solidified enough for social tensions to rub the one against the other, yet it was fluid enough to accept new money by filtering it through a generation or two of social ritual. The recognition that riches could still be had and could buy one's access into "proper" society continued to excite many Americans. In changed form and under changed circumstances, the success myth endured.

Those individuals who vaulted to the top of urban society entered a world sealed off from the masses. Hardening class lines disjointed the social structure of the industrial world both between and among classes. The old families of wealth slid unobtrusively into "islands of genteel obsolescence," while the new families basked in the pleasures of conspicuous consumption. In the acid words of Thorstein Veblen, the leisured elite consumed "freely and of the best, in food, drink, narcotics, shelter, services, ornaments, apparel, weapons and accoutrements, amusements, amulets, and idols or divinities." Yet even within this rarefied atmosphere, the elite paused occasionally to enrich the city with cultural or educational contributions.

Spreading the Manna

Two basic considerations impelled the upper class to endow their city with new agencies of culture and learning. The first involved a peculiar philosophy of social responsibility which influenced numerous wealthy people to bestow large chunks of their fortune upon "worthy" causes. The second evolved from a need among the rich to surround themselves and their cities with the trappings of what they believed to be "culture." From this impulse flowed the founding of innumerable libraries, schools and universities, museums, art galleries, theaters, operas, and symphony orchestras.

Urban philanthropy combined the old sense of noblesse oblige with a layer of guilt or at least uneasiness over so much money amassed at the expense of so many others. It was not the possession of vast wealth but its disposition that bothered industrial titans. Under the American individualist ethic, they need not account for how large a fortune they accrued, but great interest arose over what they did with it. Gradually there evolved a twofold criteria of personal worth: a man was successful if he accumulated wealth; he became a good man as well only if he disposed of or utilized his riches wisely. This growing sense of accountability surfaced in the remark of wealthy industrialist Mark Hanna who,

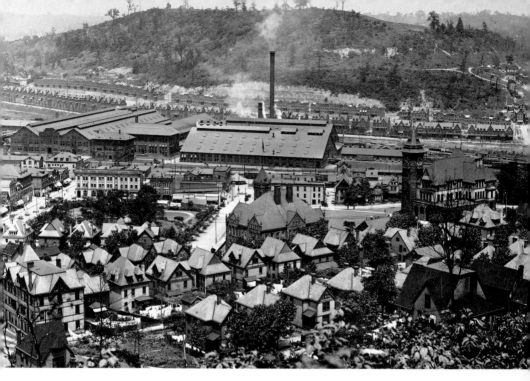

Two types of industrial cities: the company town and the emerging metropolis. (*Above*) The Westinghouse Air Brake Company plant in Wilmerding, Pa., 1905. Note the ranks of houses that surround the plant. (*Library of Congress*) (*Below*) New York City, looking east from the Singer Building, 1900s. Note the complete lack of open space and the rigid grid pattern of the streets. (*Library of Congress*)

Monuments of industrial magnificence. The transformation of American architecture can be observed in these four buildings. (*Above left*) The Philadelphia City Hall, 1900s, an edifice described by one critic as "projected on a scale of magnificence better suited for the capitol of an empire than the municipal buildings of a debt-burdened city." (*Library of Congress*) (*Below left*) William LeBaron Jenney's Home Insurance Building (1885), the first steel-frame skyscraper. (*Chicago Historical Society*) (*Above right*) The technique of steel framing can be clearly observed in this view of the Flat Iron Building under construction in New York City, 1900s. (*Library of Congress*) (*Below right*) Between 1885 and 1913 the skyscraper race soared from Jenney's 10-story Home Insurance Building to Cass Gilbert's awesome 55-story Woolworth Building. (*Library of Congress*)

Cathedrals of Commerce:
(*Above*) The Arcade in Cleveland, Ohio, 1900s, one of the several such
masterpieces constructed while wrought iron was in fashion. (*Library of
Congress*) (*Right*) The interior of Pennsylvania Station, 1900s, modeled
upon an imperial Roman bath. No visitor ever saw the great hall empty
of people. (*Library of Congress*)

Housing in the industrial city varied as widely as incomes. Among the wealthy some chose to install themselves in mansions like the Potter Palmer residence in Chicago (*above*), while others were content with more modest quarters like those along fashionable Fifth Avenue in New York (*below*). (*Library of Congress*) An increasing number of middle- and upper-middle-class urbanites moved into apartments like this unit under construction in Boston during the 1890s (*above right*). (*Library of Congress*) For the working class, or at least those who scrimped together a down payment, there were standard frame houses like these being constructed for workers flocking to the new industrial city of Gary, Indiana, in the early 1900s (*below right*). (*Gary Public Library*)

The raw materials of industrialization. (*Above*) A boatload of immigrants, about 1890, making the crossing. Their faces seem to reflect a mixture of anticipation and anxiety over what awaits them at journey's end. (*Library of Congress*) (*Above right*) This picture of a Boston machine shop, 1890s, suggests the mechanical partners that awaited the newcomers, most of whom were destined to become cogs in the rapidly expanding industrial machine. (*Library of Congress*)

(*Below right*) Workers engulfed by the endless forest of belts, pulleys, and gears in the machine department of National Cash Register Company, Dayton, Ohio, about 1900. (*Library of Congress*)

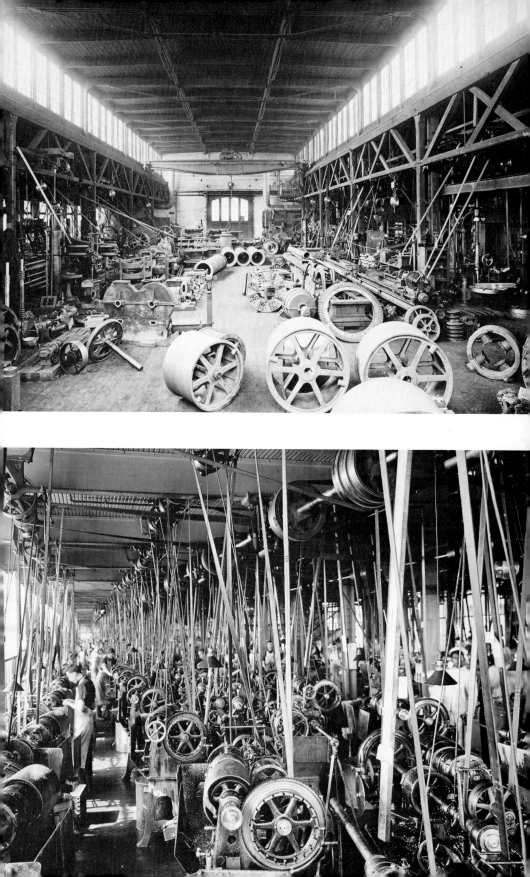

(*Above*) A glimpse of white collar workers and the endless
sea of paperwork in a large, unidentified office about 1900.
Notice that several women are included among the work
force. (*National Archives*)

(*Right*) Midnight breadlines of
the unemployed at the Bowery
Mission, January 1908.
(*Library of Congress*).

(*Above*) Striking workers pack Union Square in New York City, 1913. Note the signs in many languages. (*Library of Congress*)

eft) Cities responded to the ten-
ns created by capital-labor conflicts
building enormous armories to
use the National Guard formed to
down social and labor unrest.
is armory in Buffalo, New York, is
one of several throughout the
ntry. These armories were among
best examples of imitation Gothic
hitecture in America.
brary of Congress)

(*Below*) Looking across the Brooklyn Bridge into
Manhattan Island, obscured by smoke, 1903. In this picture
can be seen all the principal modes of urban transportation
except the subway: the interurban train, the streetcar,
the horse-drawn wagon and, of course, the pedestrian.
(*Library of Congress*)

(*Left above*) When the trolley comes, can urban sprawl be far behind? This picture of Madison Street in Oak Park, Illinois, 1903, captures the early stages in the growth of a Chicago suburb. The transportation arrived in 1890, the power lines were installed, and the lots were laid out. After a slow start, they filled up rapidly. (*Oak Park Public Library*)

Contrasting lifestyles I. (*Left below*) Collingwood Avenue in Toledo, Ohio in the 1900s, a quiet, tidy, suburban neighborhood. (*Library of Congress*) (*Below*) A teeming side street on the Lower East Side, 1900s, filled with market wagons and peddlers' carts. Note the wrought-iron balconies on which tenement inhabitants often slept in the summer to escape the suffocating heat inside. (*Library of Congress*)

Contrasting lifestyles II. (*Above*) The parlor or sitting room of an upper-middle-class Boston home, 1890s. Arthur Schlesinger described the parlor as "a sort of mortuary chapel for the reception of guests." (*Library of Congress*) (*Below*) A dilapidated tenement room around 1900, blessed with a window, if nothing else. It is impossible to tell whether the sink on the right still brought forth water. (*Library of Congress*)

upon being introduced to a man reputed to be worth $200,000,000, snapped, "Yes, and what the hell else is he worth?"

It remained for Andrew Carnegie to weave a diffusion of religious and social pronouncements on the responsibilities of the rich into a cohesive creed, the Gospel of Wealth. Although the Gospel drew upon many sources, especially the Protestant notion of stewardship, Carnegie acted as its most articulate spokesman and indefatigable proselytizer. Not only did he practice what he preached (he gave away over $350,000,000 of his $380,000,000 before his death), he also influenced some of his fellow titans to do likewise. When Carnegie said that "the problem of our age is the proper administration of wealth, so that the ties of brotherhood may still bring together the rich and the poor in harmonious relationship," others of his class listened.

Many industrialists—like John D. Rockefeller, Ezra Cornell, and Peter Cooper—reached the same place by their own route and without bothering to explain their philanthropy with a full-blown exegesis. Nearly all operated on the same basic premises. They felt a duty to assist the lesser privileged in improving themselves and thereby moving up the economic ladder. They dismissed outright charity as patronizing and pernicious in that it merely supported the idleness and vicious habits of the lower classes. The point was to proffer opportunity to those with ambition and energy enough to seize it. Carnegie insisted,

"The duty of the man of wealth . . . [is] to produce the most beneficial results for the community—the man of wealth thus becoming the mere agent and trustee for his poorer brethren, bringing to their service his superior wisdom, experience, and ability to administer, doing for them better than they would or could do for themselves."

That was the concept of stewardship in a nutshell, and it had important effects upon city life.

Nothing better illustrates this viewpoint or Carnegie's devotion to it than his mania for libraries. Beginning in the 1880s, Carnegie offered to build a library for any city that would provide a suitable site, buy books, and maintain the operation. Libraries fit Carnegie's requirements perfectly. They did not provide food, clothing, or shelter; they offered only food for the mind. They did not relieve the misery of the poor, but rather provided a tool by which the strong could lift themselves from their lowly station. By 1910 Carnegie had donated $32,000,000 toward establishing 2,800 free libraries. So vigorously did he pursue this endeavor that he fell prey to the stinging pen of satirist Finley Peter Dunne and his popular character, Mr. Dooley:

"Has Andhrew Carnaygie given ye a libry yet?" asked Mr. Dooley.

"Not that I know iv," said Mr. Hennessy.

"He will," said Mr. Dooley. "Ye'll not escape him. Befure he dies he hopes to crowd a libry on ivry man, woman, an' child in th' counthry. He's given thim to cities, towns, villages, an' whistlin' stations. They're tearin' down gashouses an' poorhouses to put up libries. Befure another year, ivry house in Pittsburg that ain't a blast-furnace will be a Carnaygie libry. In some places all th' buildin's is libries. If ye write him f'r an autygraft he sinds ye a libry. . . ."

Through the efforts of Carnegie and local patrons like Enoch Pratt in Baltimore the number of volumes in urban public libraries jumped from 12,000,000 in 1875 to 47,000,000 in 1900. The New York Public Library consolidated in 1895, the same year that the Boston Public Library opened its new Roman Renaissance building on Copley Square. A host of innovations expanded the educational services of libraries: Boston pioneered the branch system in the early 1870s; Pawtucket, Rhode Island, the first children's reading room; Cleveland the open shelf in 1890; and Buffalo, Chicago, and St. Louis the adult education class. In this manner the library both fulfilled the need of elites to serve their community and offered the city a truly democratic cultural asset. It served every class of urbanite while preserving the Social Darwinist credo of its donors, expressed in the maxim carved on many libraries, "You cannot push any one up a ladder unless he be willing to climb a little himself."

Colleges and universities also attracted the patronage of the wealthy. Peter Cooper, the New York industrialist, founded his Cooper Union in 1859 to offer free courses in practical subjects for the working class. In 1868 Ezra Cornell supplied a major gift to establish the university bearing his name in Ithaca, New York. Indeed, tycoons everywhere seemed intent upon endowing some institution with their money and, hopefully, their name as well. In 1876 Baltimore merchant Johns Hopkins, who made his fortune in the Baltimore & Ohio Railroad, founded his university, which became the nation's first major graduate research institution. Jonas Clark, a rich merchant and real estate speculator, endowed Clark University in Worcester, Massachusetts. A sample of other institutions would include the Carnegie Institute in Pittsburgh, Drexel Institute in Philadelphia, Stanford University, Vanderbilt University, and Duke University. John D. Rockefeller contributed heavily to the establishment of the University of Chicago, as did the Candler family of Coca-Cola fame to Emory University in Atlanta.

While these contributions triggered a renaissance in higher education, they had their drawbacks. Thorstein Veblen, in *The Higher Learning in America* (1918), chastised the "intrusion of business-like ideals, aims, and methods" in many universities, arguing:

Through indoctrination with utilitarian (pecuniary) ideals of earning and spending, as well as by engendering spendthrift and sportsmanlike habits, such a business-like management diverts the undergraduate students from going in for the disinterested pursuit of knowledge, and so from entering what is properly university work. . . .

No benefactor took quite so regal a position toward the object of their endowment as Mrs. Leland Stanford, who in 1893 officially listed the faculty of the Palo Alto campus as her "personal servants" for probate court purposes.

The arts also benefited from the largesse of the urban elite. During the 1870s the Centennial Exposition in Philadelphia catalyzed local efforts to encourage the arts. William W. Corcoran had already established a major gallery named after himself in Washington, D.C. in 1869, and the Centennial helped to precipitate similar action in other cities. Philadelphia itself added a new gallery to the Pennsylvania Academy of Fine Arts, the Peabody Institute in Baltimore acquired a permanent collection, and in 1876 Boston opened its Museum of Fine Arts. New York could not long ignore the competition to promote the arts, and in 1880 dedicated a new building in Central Park to house its nine-year-old Metropolitan Museum of Art. Buffalo, St. Louis, Kansas City, Portland, and others followed suit.

The establishment of civic museums nearly always depended upon the initiative of upper-class citizens. In Cincinnati, for instance, Joseph Longworth, the grandson of Nicholas Longworth, led the drive to set up an art school attached to the Cincinnati Museum. In Chicago, Charles L. Hutchinson, "a banker who had inherited a fortune from a father who was known as a rowdy trader on the wheat exchange," and Martin A. Rysson, "a lawyer by profession and a man of wealth by inheritance," spearheaded the movement for the Chicago Art Institute. In Milwaukee it was Frederick Layton, a wealthy meatpacker; in Indianapolis, John Herron, a leading real estate dealer; and in Pittsburgh, Carnegie himself supplied the resources to establish a fine art gallery.

The museum and art gallery movement settled into a familiar pattern. Once spurred by a significant event—in this case the Centennial Exposition—the wealthy leaders of a community vied with other cities to back a civic enterprise that would enhance the prestige of their locale. During the 1870s and 1880s these urban boosters promoted the fine arts much like the wares they pushed during business hours. By the time the Chicago World's Fair of 1893 rolled around, Americans were far more familiar with public museums than they had been in 1876. The fair had the effect of directing attention toward public art away from museums and out into the entire city. Concerned individuals formed municipal art leagues eager to beautify their cities with sculpture, statues, parks, and other public displays.

Richard Morris Hunt, the architect of the elite, assumed leadership of New York's public art movement by launching the Municipal Art Society in the early 1890s. In other cities, local art societies received and approved countless designs for park statues, benches, municipal lampposts, bridges, and buildings according to their aesthetic quality. The import of the municipal art movement was to project a greater concern for the physical appearance of the city and ultimately to encourage urban planning. But because the upper class dominated the movement—pure aesthetics had, after all, a very limited popular appeal—only a scattering of monuments, statues, and benches in most American cities resulted.

The upper-class mania for collecting art also redounded to the benefit of many cities. The acquisitive habits of Henry Clay Frick, Henry E. Huntington, and J. P. Morgan led to the establishment of galleries which the public now enjoys. The private collection of Andrew W. Mellon provided the nucleus for the National Gallery of Art in Washington, D.C. The competitive and hoarding instincts of the rich in the realm of art treasures amused Mr. Dooley, who attributed it to a thirst for prestige rather than a genuine love or knowledge of art. "Ye see, Hinnissy," he pointed out, "whin a man gets hold iv a large hatful iv money, wan iv th' first things he does is to buy some art." In the end, however, many of these priceless collections found their way into public galleries, usually by donation, where a wide audience could savor them.

Music no less than art furnished status to and drew patronage from urban elites. Opera enjoyed the most impressive backing. On October 2, 1854, when the Academy of Music opened in New York, it ushered in an era that linked social standing to presence at the opera. Fashion did not require that one understand or even enjoy the musical spectacle—indeed, some wealthy patrons, like Jay Gould, were so tone-deaf they could barely distinguish between *Aida* and "The Star-Spangled Banner"—but only that one attend the event, preferably upon the gala opening night. The New York scene witnessed a particularly bitter competition for the opera house's limited number of boxes. By the early 1880s the Academy's scant eighteen boxes—clutched firmly by old New

York blueblood families including the Livingstons, Schuylers, Bayards, and Beekmans—proved inadequate to the demand by new arrivals.

A social crisis ensued. The newcomers, led by the Vanderbilts, offered as much as $30,000 for boxes in the dress circle, but the old guard flatly refused to taint their exclusivity with nouveaux vulgarians. Banker August Belmont stepped forward with a tactful proposal to add twenty-six new boxes to the dress circle. To this the Vanderbilt camp objected, saying they wanted places in the original boxes. If something new were required, they averred, it would not be a few contemptible boxes, but a whole new opera house. From that slight arose the most famous opera house in America, the Metropolitan. At its opening-night performance on October 22, 1883 (the opera performed was Gounod's *Faust*, if anyone noticed), the boxes overflowed with Vanderbilts, Goulds, Rockefellers, Morgans, Drexels, Whitneys, Bakers, Huntingtons, and others. Two rows of boxes known as the Diamond Horseshoe enclosed titans worth an estimated $540,000,000.

Quick to grasp the significance, the newspapers covered the event with their music critics, society editors—and financial reporters. "The Goulds and the Vanderbilts and people of that ilk," sniffed one displeased journal, "perfumed the air with the odor of crisp greenbacks. Their tiers of boxes looked like cages in a menagerie of monopolists." The event was an undeniable success.* Within a decade, the parvenu Metropolitan brought the older Academy to its knees and scored a social victory for the nouveaux riches. Flushed with success, the Metropolitan reduced its boxes from seventy to thirty-five—the fabled Diamond Horseshoe—and raised the ante to $60,000 a box.

No other city quite matched the vituperative squabble in New York's opera circle, but elites elsewhere erected opera houses and patronized them with no less devotion to social ritual.** The gold kings of San Francisco opened their house in 1854, while in Chicago, Ferdinand Peck, son of a self-made millionaire, led the reorganization of that city's opera after the Great Fire. In 1917 Atlanta received the great

* With all this glamor it is sad to report that the Metropolitan, despite its well-heeled backers, still managed to lose $600,000 in its first season.
** The grand opening of Denver's Tabor Opera House in September, 1881, produced an incident indicative of social strivings in that Rocky Mountain city. When patron Tabor arrived for the opening, he called the manager aside and asked:
"Whose portrait is that?"
"Why, it's Shakespeare's, sir."
"Who is he?"
"The greatest author of plays in history."
"Yes, but what has he done for Denver? Take it down and put mine up."

Caruso and, according to one account, "the benign gentry sat in their boxes during intermission sipping bottled Coca-Cola through a straw." Nor was the opera craze confined to the large cities. Central City, Colorado, was but one of several bonanza mining towns to erect its own opera house, and many a midwestern whistle stop boasted an "opry" house that seldom saw an opera.

Instrumental music also received a boost from the wealthy. The New York Philharmonic Society began as early as 1842, but a chain reaction ensued after Leopold Damrosch formed the New York Symphony Orchestra in 1878. Henry Lee Higginson, a Boston blueblood, founded the Boston Symphony Orchestra in 1881 and paid all its debts from his own pocket for nearly forty years. There followed a series of new orchestras in Chicago (1891), Cincinnati (1895), Pittsburgh (1896), Philadelphia (1900), Minneapolis (1905), St. Louis (1907), and San Francisco (1911).

The cultural fads and fancies of the rich showered the city with a fallout of artistic and musical delights; their value to urban cultural life quickly obscured their dubious origins. That the Metropolitan Opera arose because old New York money snubbed new did not detract from its cultural impact upon the city. While the rich indulged themselves in amassing private art hoards or sponsoring lavish balls, they also embellished city life. Although the cynical tongue of Mr. Dooley and other critics lashed tartly at such blatant excesses, others dreamed less of dispossessing the wealthy than of joining their ranks. For these dreamers, the extravagances of the upper class merely fueled their ambitions. Cynics and radicals saw different uses for money thus spent, arguing that the poor needed food and housing more than music or art.

In any case, most American cities owed their cultural institutions in large measure to the clawing rivalry of social one-upsmanship. But the random application of money to aesthetic pursuits, however munificent or well-intentioned, proved a hollow endeavor. A museum, a library, an orchestra, even a college could not compensate for the withdrawal of urban elites from meaningful roles in urban life. No barricade of gifts could cover their retreat from social and civic responsibility. In the end, the elite remained conspicuous not for their contributions to the city but for what they failed to contribute.

CHAPTER 8

Life in the Middle:
The Urban Middle Class

> My father was one of the sixteen or seventeen children of a
> pioneer farmer of eastern Canada, who drove west with his wife
> in a wagon to Illinois, where he bought, cleared, and worked his
> piece of wilderness, raised his big herd of tall boys and strong
> girls, and, finally, died in 1881, eighty-one years of age. . . . Because
> my father . . . was small and not strong, his father . . . told him
> he probably would not live; and when he did live, the old man
> said that, anyhow, he was no use on a farm. He let him, therefore,
> do what he wanted to do: go to town, take a job in a store and
> courses in two commercial colleges. Working by day and studying
> at night, my father got his education and saved up enough money
> to go west. . . .
> He joined a wagon train. . . . When the wagon train broke up
> and scattered, he went on to San Francisco. He was not seeking
> gold or land but a start in business, and in San Francisco he found
> it (Sept. 1862) as bookkeeper in the firm of Fuller and Heather,
> importers and dealers in paints. That was his job when he married
> and I was born. But soon thereafter he was offered a quarter interest
> in a branch store which the firm was establishing in Sacramento.
> He went there. . . .
> My father's business seems to have been one of slow but steady
> growth. He and his local partner, Llewelen Tozer, had no vices.
> They were devoted to their families and to "the store," which
> grew with the town. . . .
>
> —LINCOLN STEFFENS
> *Autobiography* (1931)

AMERICA HAS ALWAYS been a middle-class society. Commentators
on the American scene from Crevecoeur to David Riesman
have stressed the importance of that broad range of the populace in the
center of the social scale. Nurtured on democratic politics, social egali-
tarianism, and an unshakable faith in economic progress, the middle
class grew strong and influential. Whether the freeholder in Puritan
New England, the Jacksonian Democrat, the sod-house settler on the
frontier, the frame-house dweller on Main Street, or the Levittown
suburbanite, somehow the middle class or "middle America" represented what the country was all about.

In part, this view stemmed from the tradition which identified the
middle class as custodian of society's values. "Solid" and "respectable"

were the adjectives most often used to describe its members. The rich might fritter away their status on self-indulgence, and the poor might wallow in misery or rumble about revolution, but the middle class could always be counted upon to preserve the social order. Within its ranks could be found that model citizen whom William Graham Sumner, long before Franklin D. Roosevelt, called the "Forgotten Man":

Who is, then, the Forgotten Man? He is the clean, quiet, virtuous domestic citizen, who pays his debts and his taxes and is never heard of out of his little circle. . . . He works, he votes, generally he prays . . . his name never gets into the newspaper except when he gets married or dies. He keeps production going on. He contributes to the strength of parties. . . . He is a commonplace man. He gives no trouble. He excites no admiration. . . . Therefore, he is forgotten. All the burdens fall on him, or on her, for it is time to remember that the Forgotten Man is not seldom a woman.

In this essay Sumner expressed what many Americans had long believed, that the middle class was the anchor of American civilization. Against its weight the ship of society could not drift far into uncharted waters. Through its conservative influence the middle class assumed the mantle of social arbiter—the definer of respectability, common decency, and proper taste. For much of American society, the effect was to set standards from the center out.

This function as social caretaker did not meet with universal approval. While some admired the middle-class anchor for its stabilizing effects, others cursed it as a drag upon social and cultural advancement. The controversy is an old one, going back several generations before H. L. Mencken popularized it. Critics charged the middle class with stifling creativity, diluting culture, and reducing tastes and standards to a common denominator. As custodians they had achieved stability at the cost of imposing a drab uniformity and oppressive dullness upon American life. The epithets coined by scorners were bitter and unsparing: repressive, dull, hypocritical, shallow, mean, narrow-minded, and shortsighted.

Of all the stereotypes applied to this inchoate swath of American society, one missed the mark badly: the lack of diversity among its members. An incredible variety of people regarded themselves as belonging neither to the elite nor to the dregs. Part of the mystique of the middle class lay precisely in the fact that it embraced everyone between the recognizable extremes of society. The Hungarian baker in Buffalo, the Connecticut farmgirl who became a nurse, the piano teacher in Mason City, the shopkeeper in Little Rock, the young corporation lawyer in Springfield, the policeman, the minister, the school-teacher, the architect—all differed in sex, geography, background, and ambition. There were countless crosscurrents of status and ethnic resentments, education gaps, differences in customs and manners which rubbed the one against the other in the wrong way.

Yet each of these individuals held in common a value system which Americans regarded as the bedrock of their society. No matter how recently one had climbed into these ranks or how desperately one wished to escape them, these people straddled a common if vague social ground between the rich and the poor. This shared notion of a common value system and the knowledge of a center position in the social order cut across ethnic, occupational, and status differences. They jelled men and women, however tenuously, in the shaky mold known as the middle class.

The value system binding the middle class together underwent a complete overhaul during this period. Shaken by the tremors of institutional giantism, it faced new challenges at every turn. But through a process of refashioning beliefs, the middle class emerged from the industrial period stronger in numbers and influence throughout all the city's institutions.

A powerful nostalgia clouds any contemplation of late-nineteenth-century middle-class life. To modern eyes those years seem infinitely simpler and more appealing than our own. People grow sentimental about strong family ties grounded in the eternal verities which gave one strength to face the outside world with confidence. Even the century's last decade—a period riddled with social dislocation, strikes, war, a seething discontent among all classes, and the worst depression experienced by Americans up to that time—has somehow been translated to the modern generation as the Gay Nineties! This rose-colored hindsight is revealing not because it distorts the hard times people experienced, but because it demonstrates how successfully they met these challenges. Asserting their muscle in the economy, the schools, the churches, and in politics, the middle class adapted to change not by discarding old values but by reshaping them to fit "modern" conditions. The result—although considerably different from what existed before—contained enough of the old to remain acceptable.

Having weathered the industrial storm, the middle class succumbed in the 1920s to an orgy of self-indulgence. The twenties marked the apotheosis of middle-class dominance. Yet, while everyone conceded the power it now wielded, this recognition also prompted the most virulent opposition to the middle class yet heard. Mencken unleashed his acerbic observations on the ruling "boobocracy." Sinclair Lewis dissected the cultural vacuities of Main Street. More important, provincial America erupted in resentment over the new urban middle-class ways. The revulsion against alcohol, flapper morality, and Al Smith's Catholic candidacy represented a last desperate effort to stem the swift tides of change. A nerve-racked minority objected to what had happened to the triple pillars of middle-class life—the family, education, and religion—but they remained an unheeded voice in the rural and small-town wilderness. For most people the new society seemed bountiful, and they busied themselves with harvesting its fruits.

The Expanding Job Market

Before examining the family, school, and church, it is important to understand the kinds of work middle-class urbanites did and what ramifications it had on their lives. In Chapter 3 we noted that the middle class had increased tremendously because of an upsurge in the types of employment considered middle-class work. Independent businessmen increased, but far more significant was the proliferation of managers, technicians, and white-collar clerks who filled the corporate and government bureaucracies. The ranks of professional people swelled; there were more professions and more people working in them. From these sources emerged the "new middle class."

The way in which this new bureaucratic corps multiplied is not difficult to comprehend. A sort of Parkinson's Law operated, for which the urban housing field offers a good model. The city presented acute problems of overcrowding. Middle-class people—clergymen, social workers, public health officials, journalists—perceived the problem, studied it, and searched for remedies. In 1901 New York's municipal government took concrete action by passing the first major regulatory act dealing with tenement conditions. Immediately a new agency was created to implement the act; in the first twelve years of its existence, the New York Tenement House Commission employed 165 inspectors and 200 other people to handle the paper work involved in processing over 500,000 violation complaints. Thus, between 1901 and 1913, one municipal government added over 350 new white-collar employees to handle just one area of concern.

Multiply this example by the number of other cities, corporations, schools, libraries, laboratories, etc., which handled a myriad of other problems and the dizzying spiral of white-collar employment becomes clear. Population growth created a need for more teachers, doctors, and other service workers. An increase in government services meant more people on the city's payroll. The rise of new industries and rapid growth of some old ones (such as insurance) also generated new jobs. With these shifting occupational patterns came important changes in the tenor of American life. The new middle class, uncertain at first of its weight on the social scales, gradually evolved a pattern of action which gave it enormous influence over the direction of society.

In general, this pattern was identical for all occupations. First, as in the housing field, a problem was perceived: in public health, it might be cholera or tuberculosis epidemics; in sanitation, the issue was waste disposal; and in social work, family disintegration. Once identified, the problem had to be studied. Commissions were appointed (or undertook on their own) to examine the matter in microscopic detail. These earnest, "fact-minded" bodies filled bulging volumes with statistics on every aspect of the problem. They surveyed crime-to-population density figures, faculty-student ratios, the diets of poor children, the working and living habits of prostitutes, manufacturing and sweatshop productivity, and an endless variety of other questions where insight seemed accessible through statistical or "scientific" analysis. The *Pittsburgh Survey*, a multi-volume study of social conditions in that industrial city in 1907–1908, was perhaps the most ambitious of these projects.

Once the data were accumulated, conferences were held and communications directed to those working on similar problems in other cities. Journals were begun to stir debate and national organizations formed to thrash out ideas and formulate answers. Finally, when solutions were agreed upon, the respective groups pressed for action and usually hired a professional staff to implement the guidelines. But implementation meant expertise, which required training; the final step in the process of professionalization, therefore, became education. Graduate and professional schools were founded and standards were established to train people for a particular vocation.

Whatever the field of endeavor—public health, law, social work, urban planning, teaching—it followed some variant of this pattern. Aspiring professionals went to schools with similar curriculums, passed examinations based on national standards, read national journals, and belonged to national organizations. From this process emerged a professional cadre of middle-class people in the industrial city. The old schoolmarm who taught several grades in one classroom from her general knowledge gave way to the professional teacher who went to college, practice-taught in a particular grade, got a job in a school system, and belonged to the National Education Association. The change did not occur overnight and, of course, it did not affect everyone in the profession. It was a trend, but one which gained momentum with every passing year.

Beyond the expertise, education, and specialization required of the new middle class, a subtle change took place in how they viewed their jobs. Because they were tied together on a national scale, certain occupations came to represent strong communities of interest. People identified with others doing the same things. This identification manifested itself in large national organizations and unions. Professional occupations became a way in which people defined their self-worth as other such touchstones eroded. As Robert Wiebe described this phenomenon:

> These men and women communicated so well in part because they were the ones building a new structure of loyalties to replace the decaying system of nineteenth-century communities. As members of the new middle class found their rewards more and more in the uniqueness of an occupation and in its importance to a rising scientific-industrial society, the primary differentiators of the nineteenth century weakened proportionately. They lost that appreciation for fine gradations in wealth and its display, that close emotional involvement in differences between English and Irish, Swedish and Bohemian. . . . Joining an occupational organization was a defining as well as an identifying act. Just as a political party had once done, now the occupational association supplied many answers, hopes, and enemies far beyond the range of their immediate experience.

The growing influence of middle-class work and the rising status (often self-generated) that attended it attached this important group to the American social order. Loath to rebel against the existing social order anyway, middle-class people realized that through organized power they could modify the system to fit themselves more snugly into it. Marxists who believed industrialization would produce a propertyless class that would eventually reign supreme overlooked the force which a professional bureaucratic middle class could exert. This propertyless group found status and wealth within the growing technological bureaucracy and saw no reason to oppose a system that was good to them. Technicians, managers, professionals, petite bourgeoisie, although traumatized by industrialization, found niches in the new order, viewed it as an ever-expanding process which allowed upward mobility, and so were disinclined to disrupt it. This ability to adapt characterized the middle class in all facets of its existence. And a valuable ability it was, because the volatile forces of upheaval left adaptation as the most painless means of survival.

The Closing Family Circle

So committed are Americans to the family as the nucleus of social structure that we forget how relatively new an institution it is. According to Philip Aries, a French historian whose *Centuries of Childhood* was a pioneer work in this neglected field, the modern family did not emerge until around the sixteenth century. William L. O'Neill has summarized part of Aries's findings in succinct form:

In the sixteenth and seventeenth centuries, the modern conjugal family began to emerge in consequence of the discovery of the child. Once it was established that the primary obligation of the family was to train and nurture children, the apprenticeship system was gradually replaced by formal education. As family life became progressively more oriented around the child, privacy and domesticity increased and the family commenced to lose its old public character. . . . Among the middle classes the conjugal family became the normal type, formal visiting was introduced in place of the old casual social relations, and the home came to be marked by the modern characteristics of comfort, privacy, isolation, and domesticity.

In America the family has always stood at the pinnacle of middle-class life. Once having embraced the conjugal family as their model, Americans somehow convinced themselves that it had always existed. As O'Neill observed, "What seems to have happened was that an idealized version of the contemporary middle-class family was created and then pushed back in time until it became a universal norm to which all existing discrepancies could be invidiously compared."

Whatever its origins, the preindustrial middle class cherished the family as a divine institution for which marriage was but an instrument, and child rearing its primary goal. Within this compact cell lived father, mother, and children in mutual aid. Nature formed the unit and economics held it together. Living together, working together, cultivating crops or operating a business, doing chores, going to church, sitting around the fire, wove a web of tight and warm relationships. Each knew his or her place with the others and drew security from this knowledge. So went the image of the early American family.

A seventeenth-century Bostonian maintained: "Such as Families are, such at last the Church and the Common-wealth must be," and most Americans throughout their history agreed. They viewed the family as a vital transmitter of cultural values. While an occasional dissenter like a character in Nathaniel Hawthorne's *The House of the Seven Gables* (1851) might urge that "Once in every half-century, at longest, a family should be merged into the great, obscure mass of humanity, and

forget about its ancestors," the middle class valued the continuity provided in family living and clutched it as a bulwark of order and
stability. Within this archetype, the father stood as undisputed master
of the realm. He was the prime mover, the maker of decisions, the director of the family's labor, and the final voice in all family matters. Law
and custom alike confirmed his unquestioned authority over his brood.

The mother usually held a more subtle leadership role. Assigned a
secondary position in the family hierarchy, she nonetheless rendered
judgments—both explicitly and by evocation of mood—which influenced
decisions. A mother's sigh of disapproval or calming hug often meant as
much as a father's declaration from on high. In daily routine the mother's
tasks were less subtle: cleaning, cooking, preserving, clothes mending,
animal tending, gardening, child rearing, crafts, and a variety of other
chores. For husband and wife alike the hours of toil were long and un-
remitting.

Children also had specified roles. Obviously subservient, they generally served as apprentices, aiding their parents in daily routines, knowing that someday they would hold identical positions in their own family.
In the hours away from school or play, the son helped his father harvesting or fence building while the daughter sewed or cooked along with her
mother. All youthful frolicking ceased when work had to be done;
children were expected to pull their own weight in the family economy.
Families tended toward large numbers of children, for each new mouth
to feed was also another pair of hands in the family labor force.

Many preindustrial families included an additional member or two:
an itinerant uncle who showed up for six months every year, an aunt
who never married and taught school or took in sewing, a widowed
grandparent—all added a dash of wisdom, humor, or mystery to the
household. Here, too, economics as well as blood ties helped explain
their presence. The lighthearted aunt or garrulous grandfather might
add extra warmth, the finicky grandmother might aggravate everyone,
or the ne'er-do-well uncle might undermine family standards, but their
presence generally aided the operation of the household whatever their
virtues or faults.

Life in the preindustrial era was never idyllic. Every family suffered
the terror of disease, the fear of early death, the ravages of crop failures,
or the boredom of routine. Insanity, crime, dissension, insecurity, or
melancholy touched some corner of every household. But the family did
offer comfort. Tradition bred security and closeness; familiarity, laughter,
and warmth eased the trials of daily life. These virtues, along with economic necessity, meshed individuals into a family unit. As industrializa-

tion knocked the economic prop out from under the family pedestal, its members clung ever more tightly to the virtues they cherished.

Samuel Slater, the father of the textile industry in the United States, recognized the strength of the family unit and tried to bring it intact into his mill. But this brief experiment, at best a half-step, crumbled beneath the factory's demand for the most efficient labor force regardless of familial ties. The factory system wrenched the artisan from his home workshop and splintered the family into diffuse parts. Having ceased to be an integral economic unit, the family began to specialize like other components of the industrial order. Working-class families were hit hardest, but none escaped the impact. Middle-class men removed to the factory for skilled positions or took salaried jobs in the growing industrial bureaucracy. This shift weakened the male's traditional dominance of the family. Arthur Calhoun, an early historian of the family, referred to this trend as the "passing of patriarchism":

Men are increasingly absent from home whether as commercial travellers, trainmen, commuters, or mere laborers and business men at work some distance from the place of abode. The pressure of businesses and labor gives man small chance to keep up with the new thought outside his own vocation. . . . Only in out-of-the way places can the archaic patriarchism maintain itself.

Removed from the household for a good part of the day, the father began to measure his success not in family but in individual terms. The industrial economy forced the male to work not as senior partner of the family firm but as its leading financial supporter. His personal rewards and satisfaction came from a job which, being detached from the family context, competed with the latter for his time and attention. It was a subtle but dramatic shift. Work took place somewhere else; success had to be achieved there. The family became a responsibility—not an economic asset, as it had once been. American men "will work longer and harder for happiness of wife and child," two English commentators recorded in 1869. "The husbands are content to slave in business in order that their wives and families may live in affluence." And as men increasingly viewed their success in occupational terms, their families reacted in kind. Esteem previously gained from cooperation became respect for a job well done. Family emotions remained warm and close, but shaded toward formality.*

* Marx described this change in more blunt language: "The bourgeoisie has torn away from the family its sentimental veil, and has reduced the family relation to a mere money relation."

As the male worked harder on the job to provide for his family, the control he exercised over it declined. The female, ostracized from many occupations by tradition, prejudice, and the duties of child rearing, was left in charge of the home. Freed of many time-consuming chores, the urban middle-class "housewife" spent more time on herself, her children, and her home. Modern conveniences wrought by new industrialism lightened the burdens of cooking and housekeeping. Packaged cereals like Quaker Oats and Wheatena, available on the grocer's shelves, replaced more time-consuming breakfast foods like cornmeal mush. Commercially prepared breads eliminated the need for home baking, while a variety of canned fruits and vegetables relieved women of the need for keeping a garden or doing their own preserving. Iceboxes, bread toasters (which sold for 20¢ in the Sears, Roebuck catalog), and coffee grinders all sold rapidly as labor-saving kitchen devices. Historian James McGovern has observed how advertising vigorously promoted the new image of the gadget-laden housewife. "Generally speaking," McGovern wrote,

women depicted in advertising in or around 1900 are well rounded, have gentle, motherly expressions, soft billowy hair, and delicate hands. They are either sitting down or standing motionless; their facial expressions are immobile as are their corseted figures. After 1910, they are depicted as more active figures with more of their activity taking place outside their homes.

An advertisement in a 1915 issue of *Collier's*, McGovern found, featured one woman saying to another on the telephone, "Yes, drive over right away—I'll be ready. My housework! Oh that's all done. How do I do it? I just let electricity do my work nowadays." Vacuum cleaners allowed women to "Push the Button—and Enjoy the Springtime!" Van Camp claimed it could save "100 hours yearly" with its "Pork and Beans." Campbell's soups, Wizard Polish, Minute Tapioca and Gelatin all made similar promises to ease the housewife's burden. And what electricity or processed foods could not accomplish, a servant could. Rare was the middle-class budget that did not provide for a servant, usually an immigrant who worked for a few dollars a week.

When not in the kitchen, the woman of the household usually spent her hours in her bedroom—a combination boudoir and workroom. Amid porcelain jars of shell hairpins and perfume atomizers, the lady found quiet retreat to pamper herself with a wide variety of new commercial hair preparations, cold creams, powders, and other beautifiers, or to attend to family correspondence at her writing desk. Sewing supplies, including a Singer machine, occupied a corner by a window; but more and more, needlework became a decorative hobby rather than essential household manufacturing.

Most clothing was becoming store-bought. The ready-made apparel business enlivened the fashion consciousness of most women. "Women are harder to sell to than men because as a rule they have, or think they have, more time to shop than men do," Professor Paul Nystrom wrote in his *Economics of Retailing* (1915). Shopping became a favorite pastime of middle-class women when, for the first time, they could indulge in the pleasures of fashion.

And indulge they did. By the turn of the century the corset companies alone were doing a $14,000,000 annual business with Warner Brothers Company leading the field. (This represented a high point for the foundation business as women, after being laced and squeezed breathless, began their century-long discarding of rigid undergarments). Chiffons, satins, velvets, and silks were purchased by the bolt to make dresses, blouses, handbags, hats, and underwear. The bonnet, garnished with lace, ribbons, bird feathers, or imitation fruits and vegetables, enjoyed great vogue; women paraded in them through A.T. Stewart, Jordan Marsh, Wanamaker's, Macy's, Shillito's, and other downtown department stores. The thrifty-minded shopped for material and went home to sew their McCall or Butterick patterns, but for the most part, store buying prevailed. Women gobbled up the clothing produced by immigrants in the garment factories of New York. "There is no place in the world," one female commentator noted, "where such dainty machine-made garments of all sorts can be found as in American department stores." The ready-to-wear business in effect allowed women to use the time once spent in making clothes to shop for them. Most considered that a wholesome exchange.

The rise of ready-to-wear clothing actually reached men before it did women. Until the 1920s women in the upper middle class still patronized their favorite seamstresses who fashioned apparel distinctive to each customer. While women resisted the trend toward "pre-made" clothes, men succumbed rapidly to it. The Civil War, with its huge demand for uniforms, had led to the discovery that clothes manufactured in a range of standard dimensions or "sizes" would fit the majority of men. This revelation, coupled with increased commercial use of sewing machines, precipitated the rise of a large clothing industry. "As late as 1880 less than half of men's clothing was purchased ready-to-wear," wrote Daniel J. Boorstin. "But by the beginning of the twentieth century it had become rare for a man or boy not to be clothed in ready-made garments.

Now even the wealthy, who had once employed tailors, were buying clothes in the better shops."

The urban world did provide opportunities for women seeking work, usually in secondary jobs such as store clerks, telephone operators, and secretaries. Clerical work in particular abounded after the typewriter secured its place in offices. The real leap forward in women's employment came in the first decade of the twentieth century. The percentage of women between the ages of sixteen and forty-four gainfully employed rose from 21.7 percent of the American work force in 1890 to 23.5 percent in 1900, and 28.3 percent in both 1910 and 1920. It is doubtful that many of these working women belonged to the middle class. Of those who did, most were probably daughters able to work at prevailing low wages because they lived at home and were still largely supported by their parents. Women forced to support themselves entirely from working found survival a grueling ordeal at going wages. As Dorothy Richardson, a middle-class girl compelled to make her own way, complained in her book *The Long Day* (1905): "Work was plenty enough. It nearly always is so. The question was not how to get a job, but how to live by such jobs as I could get." Few survived the grind intact. The fortunate escaped through marriage or some stroke of luck; the less fortunate slid downward into the lower classes, a journey chronicled in brutal detail by David Graham Phillips in his long and powerful novel, *Susan Lenox* (1917).

Single women filled most of these clerical and stenographic jobs. Married women, barred by class and status restraints from working, chose club activities to fill their idle hours. Organizations sprang up everywhere, their interests ranging from azaleas to Dante to temperance. One writer declared, "We have art clubs, book clubs, dramatic clubs, poetry clubs. We have sewing circles, philanthropic organizations, scientific, literary, religious, athletic, musical, and decorative art societies." Some observers like Edward Bok, the feisty editor of the *Ladies' Home Journal*, chastised women's groups for lacking "a more intelligent conception of its trusteeship." But whether engaged in social reform, neighborhood improvements, or an exchange of tastes in flowers, books, or recipes over afternoon tea, the social club afforded middle-class women a chance to leave the house and develop a sense of camaraderie with others. A small minority even gained national prominence as their activities challenged existing social and political institutions.

For the majority, though, the structure of urban industrial life placed women in a precarious bind that still exists in many middle-class homes. In effect, "progress" stripped women of their traditional functions without providing other meaningful outlets for their energies and talents. The industrial economy filled the home with conveniences which transformed the housewife's role from producer to consumer. A generalist by trade, she found herself surrounded by specialists whose separate activities usurped the tasks she had once performed. She spent most of her time in the house, but had less to do there. Labor-saving devices gave her unaccustomed leisure time and created a new sense of freedom, but social custom severely limited the uses to which these could be put.

Because the larger society blocked access to most meaningful jobs, and because Victorian taboos on child rearing restrained many women from trying to open new doors, an ominous mood of ennui developed. In every sense, the middle-class housewife was a woman all dressed up with no place to go. The Industrial Revolution had forged a new kind of household, yet custom dictated that the housewife preside over its operation in the old manner. Some women accepted this mandate with aplomb: they transformed their homes into models of scientific management and made the task into a full-time career. But for others, the house became a trap: a labyrinth of dull routine, a museum of unfulfilled emotions. A few women broke the chains and fought for something better; most resigned themselves while groping for some activity that would alleviate their distress and sense of emptiness. As children they had been taught that the family was a woman's ultimate fulfillment, and many turned to their families. But in squeezing their husbands and children more tightly, they only tied themselves closer to the household. This ordeal became even more frustrating as the larger society began wrenching children from the family to provide the education once considered the supreme task of parents.

For children, this socialization of training and schooling represented the most important change wrought by the urban industrial era. Previously assigned apprenticeship roles under a parent or relative, they increasingly found outside adults in charge of guiding them. The industrial society, unwilling to tolerate haphazard personal upbringing, consigned the training of children to specialists and institutionalized every aspect of the educational process. The details of this trend in public education will be covered elsewhere; the point here is that middle-class children lost their economic function in the family. The move from farm to city, from an agrarian to an industrial setting, lessened the need to put children to work at an early age.* The immediate effect of this change was a sharp drop in the size of families. One found few broods of ten or

---

* Of course, this did not hold true for children of the lower class. See Chapter 9.

fifteen children in the city. In 1900 the average number of children per
family stood at 4.5; by 1920 the figure had fallen to 2.8.

Socialized training eroded the pedestal upon which the father of the
family once stood. As Calhoun put it, "children are taught to aim higher
than their father's career and are scarcely likely to think him a great
man." Increasingly occupied with the strains of business, fathers had
less time to spend with children and gradually their authority weakened.
Their word was no longer absolute law, their example no longer the
automatic model upon which sons built their own ambitions. The result
of this declining patriachy was a rising filiarchy. Children became less
the disciples of parental guidance and more the products of outside
stimuli. Parents encouraged this tendency; anxious to provide the best
possible advantages for their offspring, families became more child-
centered. Emerson reflected upon this change when he noted in 1880
that "Children had been repressed and kept in the background; now
they were considered, cosseted, and pampered."

The prevailing influence of Social Darwinism reinforced this discovery of the child. The notion of progressive evolution encouraged
parents to see to it that their children did better than they had done.
Children's success reflected favorably upon parental efforts, even though
parents were having less direct influence upon the training behind that
success. Heated debates flared over progressive child-rearing and education, but as early as 1871 the Dr. Spock of the post-Civil War era
sanctified the children-first philosophy. In his work *Gentle Measures in
the Management and Training of the Young*, Jacob Abbott proclaimed
that growth should take place "in harmony with the structures and
characteristics of the juvenile mind." Upbringing had to consider
the child's personality and talents rather than molding young people
to age-old guidelines.

The world of urban middle-class children swirled with new delights.
Relieved of the routine drudgery that characterized farm life, they had
more time to play, to learn, and to sample the experiences city life offered.
Their schedules grew attuned to the school calendar rather than to the
farmer's almanac. After-school hours, vacations, and summers belonged
largely to play and not to chores. Occasionally the rigors of Victorian
discipline upset this new world, but by 1900 it can be said that the child's
special existence within the family had been established. Tasks like table
cleaning and bedmaking barely interrupted the activities reserved for the
young. A carnival of games filled city streets and yards: stickball, kite
flying, mumblety-peg, one old cat, hide and seek, kick-the-can, roller
skating, stilt walking, jump-rope, jacks, dolls, and marbles "for keeps".

As one fad in the neighborhood waned, another captured undivided attention for a month or so.

Like modern-day record companies and clothing manufacturers, turn-of-the-century businessmen recognized the growing influence of young people. Cigarette makers plastered the faces of baseball stars on cardboard and hoped to increase their sales by appealing to the fanaticism of ten-year-old trading-card hustlers. William Randolph Hearst parlayed his newspaper sales into record figures with the addition of a new youth-oriented feature, the comic strip. After their initial introduction in 1896, the comic antics of Happy Hooligan, The Captain and the Kids, and later Buster Brown and his dog Tige, captivated the children of urban middle-class homes. No one enjoyed greater success than Frank Merriwell, who emerged full-blown in the dime-magazine medium catering to youth. Outflanking other ten-cent heroes like Fred Fearnot and Bowery Bill, dashing Frank became the idol of 125,000,000 readers. The editors of *Time-Life* explained his appeal this way:

First at Fardale Academy, then at Yale College, and later during world-wide adventures, the magnetic Frank Merriwell accomplished every task with perfect ease. Time and time again, he won the day in boxing, baseball (he possessed a pitch that curved in two directions), football, hockey, lacrosse, crew, track, shooting, bicycle racing, billiards, and golf. He outwitted Chinese bandits, Texas rustlers, and urban thugs. In addition to his feats of brain and muscle, he was good. When classmates stole a turkey from a farmer as a prank, Frank stayed behind to pin a five-dollar bill to the roost. He loved his mother, his alma mater and his country; he abhorred poor sportsmanship, drinking and bullies.

Young people had more to read and fantasize about than the adventures of Frank Merriwell. The late nineteenth century marked a golden age in children's literature. Boys and girls could lose themselves for hours in the adventures of *Little Women* (1869), *Little Men* (1871), *Alice in Wonderland* (1865), *The Prince and the Pauper* (1882), *Treasure Island* (1883), *The Wizard of Oz* (1900), *Little Black Sambo* (1900), *Black Beauty* (1890), and in what Gilman Ostrander called "by far the most influential in its import upon child care," Frances Hodgson Burnett's *Little Lord Fauntleroy* (1886). This outpouring of literature represented the most lasting contribution toward the catering, the sentimentalization—indeed, the worshiping—of childhood. Some like Daniel Beard, the author of *American Boys Handy Book* (1890), feared what city life would do to boys, and in 1910 he helped found the Boy Scouts in hopes of preserving the outdoor skills and closeness to nature of a rural childhood. But such back-to-nature schemes, although success-

ful, became extracurricular activities that embellished but could not replace the excitement of city life.

So far did the enshrinement of children go that some critics credit it
with sterilizing the whole of American literature. It was the middle class
that bought most of the books, magazines, and periodicals, and their
delicate sensibilities imposed restraints upon reading matter which forced
American writers either to launder their language and subject matter
or else go underground in search of publishers for their "prurient" material. The desire to let nothing unseemly pass before the eyes of the
young reduced the level of literature to a standard acceptable to children.
As Larzer Ziff has said:

The price paid by society for treating its young people in this fashion was
that of keeping itself in a public state of total innocence so that nothing
would offend or corrupt the young person. Sexual experience was forced to
remain a secret matter; publicly all was virginal because the public submitted
to the standard of its youngest member. A writer who assumed a young-girl
audience, then, was not writing down to one snowy element of his society
but was, quite simply, addressing all the intelligent readers of his society
on the only assumption which would gain him an audience.

Other family members did not adjust to the city as easily as did the
young. The "extra" members—those outside the nuclear family—especially
suffered from the move. In the competitive world of the city, where work
took place outside the home, fewer families welcomed the presence of
an additional relative or boarder. With living space at a premium and
fewer chores to perform, an aunt or grandparent often found themselves
little more than an extra mouth to feed. Their presence meant an extra
burden on the family and a painful effort on their part to make themselves useful.

Elderly relations posed a special problem. With values and traditions
changing so swiftly, there appeared little need to cater to the aged or to
learn the wisdom of outmoded folkways. As living space grew tighter
and family attachments looser, older people were shunted aside, isolated
in a world of their own kind. So began that separation of the aged into
lonely enclaves within the city. Boardinghouses, retirement houses,
cheap tenements, or run-down city hotels became the haunts of the
elderly. By dispatching their elders, Americans cut themselves off
from their own roots. In a society obsessed with the present and geared
to calculating self-worth in monetary terms, those too old to work held
little value. After a lifetime of struggle, many old people suffered a fate
that amounted to exile.

The middle-class family in the industrial city thus bore little resemblance to its preindustrial counterpart. It was smaller and more compact—"little islands of propriety," to use Dreiser's phrase. Both men and women tended to marry later and to have fewer children; between 1860 and 1920 the national birthrate declined from 44.3 to 27.7.* The average time spent by a woman in having children declined from 17 to 9.7 years in the nineteenth century. While women in 1800 were apt to be about sixty years old when their last child left the nest, they would be in their mid-fifties around 1900. As the time spent in having and rearing children dropped, the average duration of marriage increased from 30.4 to 35.4 years in the nineteenth century and then leaped above 40 years in the 1920s.

More time spent together and less time raising children did not necessarily mean closer marital relationships. Men worked harder on the job, and women, freed of many household duties, looked for outside interests. Both situations created additional tensions for husbands and wives. As David Potter has written:

By diffusing the focus which the family had given to social organization, the new economy made status a matter of several fragments—a man's status among his fellow employees, his status in his neighborhood, his status at the bank—rather than one of a single, homogeneous social relationship. In this case the original whole was far greater than the sum of the subsequent parts.

For the woman the same type of dilemma arose: how to find personal identity or self-worth in her changed situation.

These kinds of tensions contributed to what many feared might be the end of the family altogether. As industrial output soared, so did the divorce rate. Since the city happened to be the locale for most divorces, blame was heaped upon it as a wellspring of corruption. To a society which had enshrined the family as the bulwark of civilization, a rising divorce rate seemed the first symptom of a degenerating social order. Of course, the issue was by no means so simple or clear-cut. Numerous factors accounted for the increase in divorces, some of which were peculiar to urban conditions and some of which were not.**

* These figures mean approximately 44 and 28 births per each 1,000 of population.
** While space does not permit a detailed discussion of this point, an excellent analysis may be found in William L. O'Neill, *Divorce in the Progressive Era* (New Haven, 1967). O'Neill argued persuasively that, contrary to the alarums of contemporary critics, the rising divorce rate signaled not the death of the conjugal family but a strengthening of it through the creation of an important safety valve. "The rising divorce rate was a real social change of considerable importance," he declared. "But

In 1870 nearly 11,000 divorces were granted in the United States. Although this might seem an impressive number, many Americans even in large cities did not know anyone who had ever broken the sacred vows. Mabel Dodge Luhan, in her memoirs of early childhood in Buffalo, recounted the experience of her neighborhood's first divorcée in the 1880s:

People didn't divorce in those days. We knew only one woman who had ever done so, and when she reached the pinnacle of resolution that enabled her to jump off into the uncharted realm, she was without guide in the conduct that was required, so she had to invent her procedure. What she did was to put on deep mourning and, ordering a closed carriage, she drove from house to house announcing her divorce to her friends and showing her papers.

Such formality waned as the occurrence became more commonplace. The number jumped to 19,633 in 1880, 55,751 in 1900, and 167,105 in 1920. Between 1860 and 1900 the divorce rate per 1,000 marriages increased from 1.2 to 7.7. Put another way, by 1900 one marriage in twelve ended in divorce; no other country matched this rate. Forty percent of these people divorced after having children, and the average length of marriage before separation was nine years.

The response to this upsurge in marital dissolutions was predictable. Clergymen attacked society's sins which tempted the weak to break the bonds of marital bliss. A National Divorce Reform League began in 1881. The Federal government launched a study in 1887 to collect information, and unequal state laws—which ranged from South Carolina's denial on any grounds to Washington's "any other cause deemed by the court sufficient"—bore the brunt of stinging criticism. The mounting statistical tally prompted guardians of morality to seek underlying causes. Caroline Grimsby of the Chicago Court of Domestic Relations reasoned in 1913 that lack of money undermined the family system:

The husband works for a small wage. When he comes home tired at night he hasn't the home he wants, because his wife hasn't the money to make it comfortable. The wife is unattractive. She has no money to buy pretty clothes and no time to make the best of herself.

Arthur Calhoun pointed to the psychological problems created by economic prosperity which "keyed up the nervous system, thus unsettling

---

whatever its other implications, it did not signal the impending destruction of the family. Rather it constituted nothing more than a modification of the conjugal family system that had become general only in the nineteenth century."

the equilibrium of the home." In particular he singled out the problems of the female:

Modern industrialism has developed a pathological parasitism of the female which makes her little more than a vendor of sex services or a vehicle of advertisement. She sells herself to the highest bidder and passes into a lifelong prostitution accredited with respectability. Under such conditions the probability of happiness is slight and a divorce scandal in high life is more intrinsically normal in many cases than was the forging of the bond that made it necessary.

The changing relationships within the family wrought by industrial society jangled the chains of many marriages; liberalized divorce laws, changing social attitudes, and a variety of other factors increased the willingness of more couples to break them.

People had fretted over the family's future for a long time. In 1868 the author of a book on the subject maintained that "the sense of the sacredness of the marriage tie is unquestionably declining." By 1900 the "home is in peril" theme ran rampant through popular and scholarly literature. Rising divorce rates, the growing number of women with jobs, increasing permissiveness between the sexes, and parental loss of control over their children's behavior all seemed to foreshadow the family's doom. Dorothy Dix was moved to comment in 1913 that there had been "so many changes in the conditions of life and point of view in the last twenty years that the parent of today is absolutely unfitted to decide the problems of life for the young man and woman of today."

Yet the family survived and even flourished in the industrial city. Dramatically altered, roles shaped anew, reduced in size, it nonetheless remained the primary goal to be sought by middle-class citizens. Some gushing commentators even interpreted the family's transformed nature as harbinger of a new freedom of expression. Freed from its old basis in economic necessity, they reasoned, the modern family could now be planted in the more hospitable soil of love.

Courtship, as the term implies, had always been an upper-class phenomenon, but in industrial America it passed into the hands of the middle class. Romance magazines and novels flourished; their success was symptomatic of a growing belief that mating should be based upon mutual passion rather than the traditional mechanism of parental match-making. Few, however, realized the consequences of this shift. While the prospect of a marriage based upon love seemed one of the few bright spots in the family's future, the emphasis upon love beginning in the early twentieth century set into motion the paradox whereby romantic courtship climaxed in the moral, upright, and proper state of matrimony. And as later generations would discover, marriages based upon individual choice rather than social design proved less enduring. Passion and personality were less stable, more susceptible to change, than a belief that marriages were made in heaven and were, above all, a social duty.

Home, Cluttered Home

The middle-class home environment changed no less than its occupants. Houses shifted from spare raw-looking abodes to crowded, comfortable nests harboring the latest conveniences of industrial progress. Cluttered and elaborately decorated, middle-class homes had a warm, almost stuffy atmosphere throughout the industrial period.

The paragon of middle-class housing, the goal toward which all aspired, was the single-family dwelling. Indeed, the acquisition of one's own home became more than a symbol for success; it also inferred moral rectitude. Russell Conwell, the proselytizer of success, emphasized this point in "Acres of Diamonds":

My friend, you take and drive me—if you furnish the auto—out into the suburbs of Philadelphia, and introduce me to the people who own their homes around this great city, those beautiful homes with gardens and flowers, those magnificent homes so lovely in their art, and I will introduce you to the very best people in character as well as in enterprise in our city, and you know I will. A man is not really a true man until he owns his own home, and they that own their homes are economical and careful, by owning the home.

"Suburbs" stand as a key element in Conwell's formula. Middle-class people from the 1850s onward abandoned the inner city for the "crabgrass frontier," as Kenneth Jackson called it. Committed to cities for economic reasons, people in search of a bucolic home site viewed the suburbs as an ideal middle ground between city and countryside. Hoping to escape tawdry inner-city housing, filthy air, and what they thought were equally shabby neighbors, the middle class aspired to a patch of green in newly opening suburbs all about the city.

Those who remained found their familiar surroundings becoming daily more alien. The Marshall family in Fuller's novel *With the Procession* illustrates these pressures perfectly. The Marshall house, built at the opening of the Civil War "as far 'out' as seemed advisable for a residence of the better sort," had plenty of yard space and was surrounded by countryside. But over the years Chicago's sprawling growth bore down relentlessly upon the Marshall homestead. The shrubbery was the first to feel the change: "the atmosphere had years ago become too urban for the poor cherry-tree, which had long disappeared . . . and the last of the currant-bushes, too, were holding their own but poorly against the smoke and cinders of metropolitan life." Strange neighbors and buildings crowded in on every side:

But the day came when the church jumped from its old site three blocks away to a new site three miles away. And by that time most of their old neighbors and fellow church-members had gone too. . . . Then business, in the guise of big hotels, began marching down the street upon them, and business in all manner of guise ran up towering walls behind them that shut off the summer sun hours before it was due to sink; and traffic rang incessant gongs at their back door, and drew lengthening lines of freight-cars across the lake view from their front one; and Sunday crowds strolled and sprawled over the wide green between the roadway and the waterway, and tramps and beggars and peddlers advanced daily in a steady and disconcerting phalanx, and bolts and bars and chains and gratings and eternal vigilance were all required to keep mine from thine; until, in the year of grace 1893, the Marshalls had almost come to realize that they were living solitary and in a state of siege.

The first suburban houses built in the 1850s and 1860s reflected a transition in architectural style from earlier urban modes. Usually mixing older styles like colonial or classical revival with newly popular forms of mansard roofs and bay windows, these homes took on a curious air of appearing neither urban nor rural. By the 1890s the shingle style dominated, and middle-class owners adorned this basic mode with columns, pilasters, towers, turrets, gables, and eaves. While exterior lines took various turns reflecting the flexible interior space designed for the use of a particular family, the houses remained basically similar in their shingled sidings, prominent sides facing the street, front porches, and hedges or fences precisely defining property lines.

Inside, homes tended to be dark, cluttered, and comfortable. Most families stuffed their house with prized possessions, heirlooms, photographs, knicknacks, and the ever-present piano. But no matter how individualized these treasures were, the presence of so many of them gave homes a remarkably similar character. The interiors of middle-class homes of the late nineteenth century have been alternately described by Arthur M. Schlesinger as resembling a "reign of terror" and a "museum of aesthetic horrors." Massive furniture, lace doilies over every table top and chair arm, dark heavy rugs, stuffed animals, wax flowers, china statuettes, Japanese lanterns, bamboo stands, and easels, reinforced in the 1870s by cheap linoleum and wallpaper with gaudy prints, made central rooms an impenetrable jungle of possessions.

Interior design improved toward the end of the century. When English furniture designers—particularly William Morris—fashioned a cleaner line for tables and chairs, manufacturers in Grand Rapids, Chicago, and New York brought imitations to retailers at lower mass-produced costs. The Philadelphia Centennial of 1876 and the Columbia World's Exposition in 1893 promoted more aesthetic considerations in home decoration. Far more important was the publication of the *Ladies' Home Journal* (1883) and *Good Housekeeping* (1885), which brought displays of more tasteful room arrangements into many American homes.

Schlesinger has itemized the major changes inside houses that made them brighter and more appealing. The parlor, that "ceremonial room which, darkened with drawn shades and closed doors" had "served as a sort of mortuary chapel for the reception of guests," disappeared. Larger windows, and more of them, allowed sunlight to spray into rooms. Lighter wallpaper designs went up over the darker, gaudier prints. Carpets continued to be popular, but rugs were used increasingly as a matter of simple convenience and because floors tended to be smoother and more even. All of these improvements, impressed upon housewives by popular magazines and domestic science propaganda, lifted household interiors out of their cluttered Gothic gloom into a brighter, more spacious atmosphere that has remained in favor ever since.

Technically household interiors improved a great deal. Wood-burning and Franklin stoves, along with fireplaces, became secondary heating agents as base burners gained popularity. By 1900 middle-class families could afford furnaces which forced hot air or steam heat through heavy pipes to iron registers on the upper floors. Central heating proved far superior to the older localized sources and also reduced the hazards of fire. Indoor plumbing, too, gradually became standard fare for most urban middle-class housing after the Civil War. Throughout the 1880s city and state health officials pressed for statutes to improve domestic sanitary standards. New technology solved part of the problem. Noxious sewer odors were alleviated by improved plumbing. By the late 1880s the lavatory had become a welcome addition to middle-class homes. As this room became liberated, more attention was directed toward design of plumbing fixtures. White enamel and porcelain tubs replaced the old tin or zinc-lined wooden ones. In time the bathtub became the central fixture in this once-dismal little room, and Americans were on occasion inclined to measure the splendid progress of their civilization by its advances in the technology of indoor plumbing.

Perhaps the most striking feature of urban housing—besides the suburban boom—was the introduction of apartment living to middle-class people in the city. As with most trends in home improvements, the apartment style began with the wealthy and filtered down to the middle class. Innovations came quickly after Richard Morris Hunt built the first modern apartment house in 1870 at 142 East Eighteenth Street in New York City. Modeled after the "French flats" popular in Paris, Hunt's building featured all the conveniences and luxuries of home living tailored to high-rise structures. High land costs and multiple rental incomes inspired construction not only of luxury apartments, and of course low-income tenements, but also of apartments within the reach of middle-income groups.

For children, apartment living meant playing on concrete; for women, it meant stairs to climb after grocery shopping; and for everyone, it meant less privacy and a tighter allotment of living space. But the conveniences the apartment offered in access to work and ease of maintenance appealed to those who enjoyed city living or who had not yet accumulated a down payment for their dream castle in an outlying neighborhood.

Reading, 'Riting, 'Rithmetic, and Rote

Besides family and home, the school stood as the second pillar of urban middle-class life. A citadel of the values most middle-class people wished to inculcate into their children, the schools became engulfed in controversy when those values underwent repeated challenges. This lengthy debate sometimes obscured the most significant fact: most children were in school, and public education now undertook much of the socialization a child previously received from his parents, church, and community.

Public education ranked as the era's greatest revolution in child upbringing and urban youth were in the vanguard of that upheaval. The rise of public education in America closely parallels that of urban growth. Cities alone had the concentration of population which made mass education socially desirable and the resources to make it economically feasible. Public schools therefore grew as rapidly as did the cities themselves, and often with equal lack of direction and foresight.

After the Civil War, and after the path-breaking work of Horace

Mann and Henry Barnard, universal public education was enacted through city and state compulsory attendance laws. As late as 1870, the average American received only four years of schooling, but the figure went up rapidly. Attendance in public schools increased from 6,800,000 in 1870 to 10,000,000 in 1880 and 15,500,000 in 1900, a growth rate which outstripped that of most cities. National expenditures for education rose from $63,000,000 in 1870 to $145,000,000 in 1890 and $234,-000,000 in 1902. One immediate result, as educators noted proudly, was that the illiteracy rate dropped by nearly half between 1870 and 1900. In 1907 the Commissioner of Education included these interesting figures in his annual report:

The plant used for formal education is valued at 1 per cent of our entire national wealth, or twice the value of our telephone system, or ten times the value of our Pullman and private cars, or one-tenth the value of our railroads. The number of teachers is approximately that of the clergymen, engineers, lawyers, and physicians together, five times that of the regular Army and Navy and about twice that of the saloon keepers and bartenders and their assistants.

That same year the total annual expenditure on education, excluding that spent on physical plant, stood at twice that expended by the War and Navy Departments.

This outlay of funds for public education spawned complex bureaucracies to preside over it. The federal government established a national Bureau of Education in 1869 but it served an informational rather than a supervisory function. State governments also set up agencies, primarily to establish standards and evaluate criteria. The cities themselves were responsible for the creation and operation of public education. Looking to the factory as a model, they established school systems divided into districts headed by boards and superintendents, with principals in charge of individual schools. City systems varied widely in philosophy and competence; but increasingly the community of educators organized, met at annual meetings, read the same official reports and professional journals, and thereby moved toward standardizing their systems.

The education bureaucracy enjoyed some major successes, and innovations in one city were quickly imitated elsewhere. High schools in particular prospered; by 1900 the number of secondary institutions had risen to 6,000 from a meager 100 in 1860. Friedrich Froebel's idea of the kindergarten found acceptance in William T. Harris's school system in St. Louis in 1873, and within two decades most urban systems operated kindergartens. Francis W. Parker, the superintendent in

Quincy, Massachusetts from 1875 to 1880, introduced art and manual work into his curriculum to stimulate creativity. Harris and Calvin M. Woodward in St. Louis, Parker in Quincy, Edward A. Sheldon in Syracuse, and Edward J. Wand in Rochester all achieved national recognition for promoting innovations in the public school system.

Overshadowing these accomplishments, however, stood a tendency within public education to veer toward dullness and routine. The problems inherent in growth and size beset public education no less than other institutions; in fact, urban schools looked a good deal like counterpart organizations in business. Stress fell on efficiency, specialization was encouraged, and standardization inevitably resulted. To process their large clientele, school officials gradually adopted theories and practices that centered upon the mediocre student at the expense of those above and below his abilities. In effect, the public school—especially the high school—became an institution of the middle, by the middle, and for the middle student.

Not only social and educational philosophy but also logistical problems brought about this result. Sheer numbers alone demanded control and efficient organization, but the growing bureaucracy lagged hopelessly behind skyrocketing enrollments. This inadequacy was aggravated by the sharp diversity which existed among the student body. The heterogeneity of the city's population spilled over into the classroom, where both teachers and administrators were inundated by a myriad of tongues, habits, and conceptions of learning. Confronted with this sea of strange faces and alien tongues, educators resorted to their most powerful resource—authority. If the threat of chaos in the schools demanded authoritarian control, the inexperience of most educators virtually compelled it. Faced with unprecedented conditions and entrusted with large amounts of money and property, most school administrators lacked training or experience in creative management. Fearing that powers so recently gained would be removed or curbed, they discovered that strict control pleased their external constituents whatever its effect might be on their pupils. Both logistics and politics dictated that order come first and education after.

The impulse toward control had several results. The generalized one-room schoolhouse concept was abolished as unsuitable for organizational and educational needs. A graded system emerged which ranked students according to age. Along with it came a standardized curriculum with uniform textbooks and grading criteria. Administrators hoped to regulate a student's growth by standardizing the hurdles he was required to pass at prescribed junctures in his career. Selwyn Troen has cited a

late-nineteenth-century superintendent who had fully imbibed the doctrine of the educational assembly line and envisioned that "The program
of one school shall be the program of all, the same grade shall recite in
the same study at the same hour all over the city."

The district plan also emerged from the need for control. By reducing
the area of supervision, the district tightened administrative handling
of school records. School districts tied to neighborhoods determined
where a student should go, lessened his mobility throughout the system,
and also reinforced patterns of neighborhood homogeneity which hopefully would lessen tensions created by mixing ethnic groups. To an era
that regarded ethnic and other differences as a threat rather than a virtue,
social segregation seemed an indispensable policy for control.

The quest for control and efficiency took physical shape in the uniform architectural design of school buildings. Most city schools followed
the same format: drab, depressing brick structures surrounded by concrete moats designated as "playgrounds," featuring classrooms of uniform
size and sterility, usually with a number or a compass direction in place
of a name. Inside these dreary buildings was an educational system
based upon rote and frequent examinations which stressed proper de-
portment and equated learning with recitation. But the controls so
desperately sought never really settled over the urban school system.
Instead, the city schools remained a cauldron seething with discontent
and barely repressed energies while harassed teachers and administrators
grappled with problems too deep and divisive to yield easy solutions.

The influx of foreign immigrants launched tortuous debates over the
questions of foreign language and religious training. Hoping both to
accommodate ethnic diversity and to bring immigrant children into the
mainstream of American culture, schools searched futilely for some
means to resolve these contradictory goals. St. Louis reached one compromise settlement when its decision to teach German in the public
schools attracted the children of that ethnic group. Cincinnati, on the
other hand, established a separate system for its German students.
Neither city was entirely happy with the results of its decision.

Foreign influences affected the curriculum, too. The traditional
methods of American education, which stressed the three R's and demanded strict discipline and memorization, seemed inadequate to the
changed conditions of schools in the industrial city. After Victor Della
Vos, director of the Russian Imperial Technical School, impressed American educators with the value of manual training, Calvin M. Woodward
of St. Louis quickly grasped the benefits of such work and in 1880
opened a Manual Training School. Educators in Baltimore, Chicago,

Philadelphia, and Cleveland soon followed suit; a number of American city schools began offering courses in carpentry, metalwork, sewing, and the manual arts. Such programs nicely suited the needs of an industrial society and won enthusiastic support from businessmen. Educators, too, realized that workbenches substituted for desks might siphon off the energies of youngsters with little interest in book learning.

Parents also gave warm support to manual training. Those skeptical of abstract learning saw practical advantages, while others viewed the school shop as a substitute laboratory for skills once learned at home. Labor leaders, fearing a deluge of competition for their jobs and distrustful of business support for the plan, objected strongly to the innovation. One union leader denounced such programs as "breeding schools for scabs and rats." By 1900, however, most unionists had come to accept high school manual arts training.

Curriculum changes veered in other directions. During the early 1890s Joseph M. Rice conducted a survey of American schools. Visiting 36 cities and interviewing 1,200 teachers, Rice concluded that public schools were sorely deficient. His results, published in nine articles in the *Forum*, found "public apathy, political interference, corruption, and incompetence" rampant. Rice's exposés, along with the criticisms of settlement house workers against the city schools, stirred a national debate on the issue.

John Dewey, a professor at the University of Chicago, synthesized the debate and became its major spokesman. Concerned with the problems of the young and how suited they would be for the world after leaving school, Dewey was greatly impressed by Francis W. Parker's experimental school in Chicago. Parker's philosophy—that the school should be "a model home, a complete community and embryonic democracy"—motivated Dewey and his wife in 1896 to form the Laboratory School to implement these tenets. Three years later, in *The School and Society*, Dewey rocked the educational establishment with his theories and activities.

Stressing a pragmatic approach, Dewey believed schools had to break out of their tradition of rote memorization and strict routine. Education had to be instructive in many different ways. Dewey was among the first to understand the school's role as substitute for the family. He urged an atmosphere of "embryonic community" to fill this gap. Curiosity had to be tapped and imagination stimulated. Curriculums should stress creativity, go beyond narrow academic subjects to concerns of citizenship and exploration of what was possible in the adult world. To Dewey the schools represented a vital agent of social reform as well as a transmitter of skills and culture.

The School and Society, along with other writings of Dewey, launched a vigorous campaign for "progressive education." Reformers attacked traditional teaching techniques and strove to make the classroom less coercive and more spontaneous. The reliance of teachers upon discipline ("How can you learn anything with your knees and toes out of order?" insisted one teacher) was condemned; progressives encouraged educators to act more as guides than as taskmasters. As the Dewey philosophy stressed creativity over routine, new ideas filtered into the classroom. Handicrafts, personality fulfillment activities, citizenship training, and personal hygiene joined grammar, mathematics, and the ubiquitous McGuffey's reader.

For all the hoopla raised by progressive education, it never shook the basic sameness of urban public education. Outlooks did broaden somewhat, but the ideal of creativity never overcame the reality of conformity. City schools became brighter and less repressive places, but Deweyism did not eradicate the bureaucratic necessity for authority and control that is the industrial era's legacy to modern public education. And in time Dewey's philosophy was itself distorted by overzealous and unimaginative disciples into a caricature of its original intents.

Perhaps the most interesting aspect of Dewey's progressive movement was its reflection of middle-class values. Dewey, a small-town boy who had become an academic professional, wished to preserve the basic values he saw vanishing in the industrial urban society. Disturbed by the declining influence of family and community, he wished to transform the school into an adequate substitute. His label as a progressive obscured a nostalgic commitment to the values of citizenship and good work which he considered the hallmarks of an earlier America. The industrial city was an alien place that activated a strong sense of loneliness and anomie, a social and spiritual vacuum which the school might fill by restoring in part a sense of community he felt urban America had lost.

Though Dewey and his followers were harbingers of the twentieth century, culturally their roots lay in the nineteenth. Like many progressives, they attempted the formidable task of trying to look forward and backward at the same time. They hoped to impose their ideal of a small, virtuous middle-class community upon urban school systems which had passed into the hands of bureaucrats whose main objective was social control. The revolt of the progressive educators was, in part, a lashing out of the middle class against the massive engines of industrialism which put their children in city schools and tried to educate them with techniques borrowed from the assembly line. Having surrendered their children to the schools, they tried to compel the schools to stress the values they could no longer teach within their own households.

This reaction on the part of the middle class was indicative of their behavior throughout the industrial period. Faced with radically changed circumstances in some area of their life—in this case, their children's education—they adjusted to new conditions while conceding little of their own values. In this fashion, older agrarian ideals were grafted onto the new industrial setting and thereby helped accommodate the middle class to it. The price paid for this adjustment was a tendency to avoid confronting changed conditions on their own terms. Instead they were glossed over with nostalgic palliatives which made them bearable but never got at the heart of the difficult problems they spawned.

That New-Time Religion

In ordinary times, the church offers a refuge for people buffeted by the forces of social change. But in the industrial era, this third pillar of middle-class society offered little comfort. As people moved to the city and struggled to gain their bearings, they found that the church they had known so well in their small town or village had become a strange sanctuary. The sense of belonging had changed; fellow congregants looked different; ministers espoused unfamiliar philosophies. As people adapted to the urban church, the relationship of church to worshiper took on new forms. The church, no less than the family and school, was transformed by its industrial surroundings.

Most churches regarded the sprawl of urban growth around them with distaste. Ministers were quick to interpret the new forces as hostile and issued shrill warnings from their pulpits. Josiah Strong, one of the most prominent in this regard, reminded his congregants in Cincinnati (and the readers of his books) that: "The first city was built by the first murderer, and crime and wretchedness have dwelt in the city ever since." The titles of several books published in the late nineteenth and early twentieth century repeated this warning: *The Challenge of the City, The Redemption of the City, If Christ Came to Chicago,* and *Christianity's Storm: A Study of the Modern City.*

The causes of this storm are not difficult to discern. Most inner-city churches, usually the "First Church," found themselves suddenly stranded in a sea of foreign newcomers. Their once-nearby congregation, which formed a close-knit community in preindustrial times, had moved to the suburbs, abandoning their ministers and building to a neighbor-

hood now filled with businesses or tenements. Most middle-class clergymen, ill equipped to deal with uprooted natives or foreigners, turned
their empty halls into a fortress and bewailed the loss of once-happy
surroundings. Some attempted to convert their facilities into the leading
"cathedrals" of their denomination replete with fine music, distinguished clergymen, and an elite congregation. Large downtown churches
came to represent a closed society to most new urbanites and in a few
cases, most notably Trinity Church in New York, incited antagonisms
by becoming owners of slum properties.

Downtown churches, the major congregations of most American cities,
fell victim to changing neighborhood patterns after the introduction of
mass transit. Ignoring their new neighbors, most churches pursued their
middle-class congregants to the suburbs. Seventeen Protestant congregations in lower Manhattan alone left for more congenial surroundings
between 1869 and 1888. Such moves usually broke up the large church
into a scattering of smaller units. Robert Cross observed this tendency in
mid-nineteenth-century Springfield, Massachusetts: "those who thought
of themselves as Congregationalists but did not wish to journey into
the center of town to 'Old First Church' founded successively a North
and South Congregational Church, a Faith Church, a Hope Church,
until more than a dozen neighborhood churches had been created."

This splintering pattern not only boosted the number of churches of
a particular denomination, but it changed the nature of church life in
general. Where the concerns of the old congregation were citywide,
members of the newer churches saw little beyond the bounds of their
neighborhood. "Each new congregation," Cross noted, "tended to be
markedly segregated, and thereby highly susceptible to a very specialized
notion of the nature of the Church and its proper relations with the
World." Neighborhood churches mirrored the segregated, stratified nature
of middle-class living patterns and thereby reflected the social fragmentation of the industrial city.

The suburban churches accommodated those with means enough to
live in those areas. Some Protestant clergymen began realizing, however,
that the unreached masses in the inner city could not be ignored forever.
The response to this dawning awareness led to one of the most vibrant
crusades ever to shake American Protestantism. Urban revivalism began
when Charles G. Finney shifted the focus of his emotional preachings
from the "burnt-over district" of rural New York to the cities. During
the 1830s his evangelical message stirred the residents of New York,
Cincinnati, and other major cities. By the 1850s revivalism was a common

feature of Protestantism and enjoyed a vogue in Boston, Hartford, Buffalo, and Detroit as a means of whipping up religious fervor.

Revivalism seemed the perfect answer to the new urban conditions. Transplanted rural folk especially welcomed it as a buffer against the unfamiliar city scene. Even before a newcomer had joined a neighborhood church, it provided a feeling of continuity with his past religious experience. Clergymen favored revivalism because it seemed as logical an approach for saving souls in the "city wilderness" as it had been on the frontier. Cities provided a unique arena for mass meetings, and the revival brought diverse peoples together in a common bond. Finney regarded the city population as a strong challenge. "See how crazy those are who are scrambling to get up," he chastized, "enlarging their houses, changing their styles of living." Revivalists also received strong backing from conservative businessmen in the city who endorsed their positions on morality and the status quo. With these forces behind it, revivalism prospered in industrial America apart from particular congregations and denominations.

The master of the trade in the post-Civil War city was a gargantuan 300-pound bearded firebrand named Dwight L. Moody. Heir to Charles Finney and ancestor of Billy Sunday and Billy Graham, Moody perfected the revival style for urban audiences. A converted businessman from Boston, he applied businesslike techniques to his crusade. His sessions were carefully planned, well-financed, adequately staffed, and highly advertised. His music man, Ira D. Sankey, warmed his audience for Moody's presence, which carried a simple down-home exhortation to embrace Christianity and be saved. This no-nonsense approach fit Moody's belief that "The Bible was not made to understand."

Never ordained as a minister, Moody did not permit tradition or ritualistic niceties to interfere with his work. As befit the urban marketplace, he once sold "stock certificates" to investors who could watch a Sunday School group study. An independent force, Moody aroused high enthusiasm with his simple message in mass meetings which warmed the souls of his middle- and lower-middle-class audiences. As William McLoughlin described the carnival-like atmosphere:

The crowds, the hymnbook and photograph vendors, the singing, the general hubub and excitement encouraged many to come to the warm, friendly meetings for a free evening of entertainment which bordered on the secular and yet which was good for the soul. For many regular churchgoers the meetings were social occasions for meeting friends and brightening drab lives. Moody wisely insisted that the advertisements for his meetings be placed on the amusement pages of the newspapers.

The Moody message failed to reach the masses of urban poor, but for thousands of city dwellers, his heavenly refrains were joyous relief from the uncharted wilds of urban life.

The volatile atmosphere of urban religion that allowed revivalism to flourish also spawned one of the few indigenous American religions—Christian Science. Inspired by a frail Massachusetts woman named Mary Baker Glover Patterson Eddy, Christian Science offered salvation through mind over matter training. Mrs. Eddy had experienced conversion at the hands of a Portland, Maine, healer named P.P. Quimby. After Quimby relieved her spinal problems, Mrs. Eddy founded the Massachusetts Metaphysical College in 1881 in Lynn and led whoever would listen to the belief that ailments could be cured by working in harmony with the Eternal Mind as revealed through Jesus Christ.

The positive thinking of Christian Science appealed to the "can-do" Horatio Alger mentality of industrial America. By 1890 over 200 Christian Science groups totaling nearly 9,000 members attested to Mrs. Eddy's inspirational and organizational skills. In 1895 she founded the "Mother Church"—the First Church of Christ Science—and was well on her way to becoming a major religious force. She died fifteen years later, but her church and its primary credo of pain and disease overcome in "the ratio you expel from mind a belief in the transmission of disease" survived her.

The rise of Christian Science was indicative of the search many urban Americans underwent in hopes of finding meaning for their lives. As Robert Cross has noted, "Most of the members had not long before been members of the older Protestant churches; most were middle or upper middle class; almost all were living in cities; the preponderance of women members was exceptional, even for the American churches." Christian Science burst forth as an adaptation of traditional Protestantism to convert thousands of middle-class urbanites looking for new hope in a new environment.

Revivalism and the formation of new sects such as Christian Science were but two of Protestantism's adaptations to the industrial city. A third took place within the established churches themselves as an attempt to become more responsive to the needs of industrial society. The impetus for this movement, known as the social gospel, came from the recognition that city churches were not reaching the lower classes. In 1896 Washington Gladden, a leader in the movement, summed up his fears of what the city was doing to the social order:

So it is great gain to humanity to have industry specialized if the unity of the spirit is not broken in the process. But this calamity, unhappily, is precisely what we are suffering. The forces that divide and differentiate have not been balanced by those that unite and integrate. Therefore we are driving toward chaos. . . . How can all these competing tribes and clans, owners of capital, captains of industry, inventors, artists, farmers, miners, be made to understand that they are many members but one body. . . .

Having pinpointed the disruptive forces of the industrial city, Gladden and others of similar insight attempted to bring the church around to a position where it might work to heal these wounds.

By 1900 the social gospel had made a significant impact upon Protestant churches in the cities. Clergymen preached a doctrine of social concern and urged their followers to get involved in solving urban problems. The movement jolted the churches out of their smug defense of the status quo and exhorted them to work for a "Kingdom of God" on earth rather than merely endure the harshness of this world as preparation for the blessings of the next. The social gospel clergy were instrumental in guiding the middle class toward a concern for social problems.

One practical consequence of the social gospel was the formation of what became known as the institutional church. Downtown churches, which tended to be Episcopalian or Congregational, began programs to aid people in the surrounding community. St. George's Episcopal in New York, Congregationalist Berkeley Temple in Boston, People's Temple in Denver, and Fourth Church in Hartford were prime examples of the institutional church, but Russell Conwell's Grace Baptist in Philadelphia grew to be the largest. Conwell came to Grace in 1882 and began a vigorous building program that resulted in the Samaritan Hospital, the Baptist Temple (which formed the nucleus for Temple University), and a broad range of recreational and social clubs. Some preachers, like William S. Rainford of St. George's, incurred the wrath of wealthy members like J. P. Morgan and Alfred Mahan, but the institutional church survived as a form of religious practice which included participation in the social welfare of the outside community.

The Protestant churches were basically middle-class institutions which had to respond to the changing life patterns of both their constituents and the people immediately surrounding them. The other two major denominations—Catholicism and Judaism—were shaken by the large influx of immigrants and poor who dramatically increased their ranks in the late nineteenth century and will be considered in the next chapter. The Protestant majority, its churches set adrift by the forces of urbanization and industrialization, went in several directions: some splintered apart and cloistered themselves in the suburbs; some found refuge in the emotional upsurge of revivalism which catered to recently uprooted farm folk; some turned to new sects like Christian Science; and others joined with their clergy to bring their church into a new harmony with the changed realities of their surroundings. Like the family and the schools, Protestant churches by World War I looked much different from the way they had half a century earlier. But through all the buffeting currents of change, the middle class clung dearly to their traditional values and grafted them onto the emerging institutions of the industrial city.

The City as Playground

The ways in which the middle class played during the industrial age changed as much as their work did. Both recreation and culture appealed to spectator audiences on a mass basis. Entertainment specialized and professionalized as people began watching those trained and paid to do what everyone once did merely for fun.

Sports offer the best example of what happened to entertainment in this age. Baseball rushed to the heights of a national pastime through organization, professionalization, and intercity rivalry. Once a twilight release of energy for hundreds on city sandlots, baseball became a business—a national operation that enshrined leading practitioners in its own Hall of Fame. Like other businesses, baseball began at the local level and through vigorous organization transformed itself first into a regional and then a national enterprise. As it did so, the sport was refined into a business operation with a formal governing structure and a system of territorial and talent monopolies that other industries might well envy. By 1920 baseball, like other businesses, was ready to go big-time.

After the Civil War, cities began forming teams to play squads from neighboring cities. In 1869 Cincinnati fielded the nation's first professional team, the Red Stockings, a club which traveled over 11,000 miles in winning a phenomenal fifty-six games while losing none and tying one. Two years later the National Association of Professional Baseball Players was founded with nine charter members. The league played several seasons but lost public confidence when bribery and gambling infiltrated its operations.

This loss of confidence prompted businessman William A. Hulbert and others to found a new league in 1876. Called the National League, the new body featured tighter organization and a higher caliber of players, many of them lured from the old National Association. The organizers standardized the rules of the game, improved equipment, forbade gambling, and designed uniforms for the players. Growing crowds and enthusiatic newspaper coverage rewarded their efforts. When the new league enjoyed success, a group of dissonant interests formed a rival league, the American Association, in 1882. The result was a classic fight for the business market. After a vicious round of player raids, ticket price slashing, and other competitive differences, the two leagues signed an agreement in 1883, and their champion teams played a post-season series in 1884. An attempt to form still another new league, the Union, embroiled baseball in competitive wars again. The imbroglio led to the creation in 1885 of the Brotherhood of Base Ball Players, the first modest attempt at unionization by professional athletes.

By the 1890s the American Association, the Union League, and the Brotherhood had all folded and the National League reigned supreme. But rivals threatened on all sides. In 1900 sportswriter Byron Bancroft "Ban" Johnson took a minor league, the Western Association, and transformed it into a major circuit—the American League. The smug Nationals tried to ignore the upstarts but their hauteur lasted only three years. Unwilling to lose its monopoly and wounded by player raids, the older league came to terms. On October 1, 1903, the Boston Red Sox and Pittsburgh Pirates, champions of the two leagues, met in the first World Series. New disputes canceled the series the next year, but by 1905 the marriage between the rival leagues was finally consummated. Though new challengers were to appear, notably the Federal League in 1914, the arrangement has remained intact to the present day.

The first World Series, which opened at Boston's Huntington Avenue grounds, attested to baseball's growing hold on the popular mind. The third game had to be halted when unruly Boston fans swarmed the field. After patrolmen cordoned off the crowd with a rubber hose and officials instituted the ground rule of awarding two bases for a ball hit into the crowd, the game proceeded. A total of 100,429 people watched the Red Sox take the Series in eight games. The Series culminated a hectic summer schedule which saw two major and a host of minor leagues playing before enthusiastic crowds. Civic pride soon appeared in another guise—the construction of facilities. When Chicago opened a new ball park in 1892, it fired the first modest salvo in a competition for the finest stadium that has escalated steadily over the years.*

The recent upsurge in the popularity of professional football has led many fans and commentators to dismiss baseball as a nineteenth-century relic. Slow, deliberate action filled with dramatic pauses, wide-open

---

* One need only examine the colossal Superdome in New Orleans to see how far this rivalry has advanced.

spaces, the ritualistic nature of the game all remind people of an earlier, simpler America; this characterization reveals how clichés that lean heavily toward nostalgia distort reality. Baseball is a slower and less brutal sport than football, but its rise to national prominence in the late nineteenth century carries a different message about that era. First, money had to be directed to the game. In the industrial age, for the first time, a mass entertainment sport became a profitable business. Owners invested in players, uniforms, equipment, and physical plants. They organized teams as they would any other business because there now existed a large urban market for their product. Second, the game became national in scope because national transportation links made intercity competition possible. And finally, baseball's emergence reflected the growth of a middle class with time and money to spend on an afternoon of leisure. Far from representing a simpler era, baseball stands as a monument to a modern America—professional, specialized, profit-oriented, and national in scope. The pinstriped mustachioed executors of Abner Doubleday's rulebook share more with contemporary America than they do with their preindustrial counterparts.

It is significant that the sport most city dwellers indulged in themselves relied upon a new machine—the bicycle. First exhibited at the Philadelphia Centennial and later mass produced by a Boston entrepreneur named Colonel Albert A. Pope, the bicycle became a national rage. "There is a psychic and moral void in city life which 'the bike' goes farther toward filling than any other single institution," proclaimed *Scribner's*, and Americans took to wheels to test the notion. Some 10,000,000 riders were estimated during the 1890s, for which Pope's Company produced "a cycle a minute." Races and touring clubs sprouted up in every town, prominent people were photographed struggling to keep their equilibrium, and cycling literature filled the newsstands. The Sears catalog of 1908 devoted ten pages to its line of bicycles, accessories, and equipment, topped by the 1908 Peerless offered at $17.95.

The cycle craze of the 1890s again suggests that the urban industrial nation was tied closely enough together that a truly national sports phenomenon could develop. Men and machines united in fun and healthful recreation; city folk could tour the secluded outskirts of their towns, go on picnics, or even ride to work. In the halcyon days before the automobile, the bicycle represented freedom and mobility at low cost.

The enthusiasm for cycling and other sports like football, cricket, golf, tennis, and croquet meshed with other concerns for more breathing space in the city to emphasize the need for parks and playgrounds. Frederick Law Olmsted and Calvert Vaux's triumphant plan for Central Park in

New York during the 1850s offered a classic model that others sought to emulate. Prospect Park in Brooklyn, Fairmount in Philadelphia, Lincoln in Chicago, Forest in St. Louis, Swope in Kansas City were but a few outstanding examples of green space reserved for the pleasure of city dwellers. Beginning with Chicago in 1868, cities built zoos to provide weekend and holiday recreation. Throughout the late nineteenth century, cities acquired pieces of real estate for conversion into play areas for both adults and children. By 1910, according to Blake McKelvy, eighty communities boasted public playgrounds and a hundred more had private ones.

Urban dwellers also began supporting the theater during the industrial age. Patronage increased because Saturdays became holidays (or half holidays) for most middle-class people, because improved transportation encouraged traveling companies and offered better fare for most cities, and because electric lighting upgraded theater interiors. As a result, theaters grew and added large numbers of "plebian" seats to hold the masses now attracted to their productions.

New York captured the lead in theatrical excellence early in the nineteenth century with houses in the Bowery, Astor Place, and Union Square. The 1880s marked the period of greatest expansion in the legitimate theater. Entrepreneurs like Augustin Daly, Lester Wallach, Steele MacKaye, and A. M. Palmer dominated the business and formed stock companies which offered highly sophisticated performances. Mac-Kaye in particular put his imagination to work. In 1884 he built an elevator stage in the Madison Square Theater and in 1893 planned a huge facility for the Chicago Fair. The 10,000 seat "Spectatorium," with movable stages and water tanks for ships to be floated, ran afoul of financial difficulties and was never completed. MacKaye's reputation went down with his project; he never received the acclaim his bold schemes deserved.

During the 1890s the early actor-manager types gave way to a monopoly group known as the Theatrical Syndicate. This powerful group headed by Charles Frohman, Marc Klaw, and others dominated most of the "first-run" theaters in the country. Gradually, however, a resourceful competitor, David Belasco, started organizing the independents. Belasco, along with Sam, Lee, and Jacob Shubert, began backing "second-rate" products and their popularity broke the stranglehold of the syndicate group.

New York retained its preeminence in the field; by the turn of the century "Broadway" was a term synonymous with excellence in theater. Other major cities—Chicago, Boston, San Francisco, New Orleans—built lavish theaters, but usually featured road companies of Broadway performances after the New York run had been completed. A network of smaller cities like New Haven, Providence, and Rochester emerged as a testing ground for productions before they opened in New York.

Teddy Roosevelt, Admiral Dewey, and Thomas Edison were the most famous Americans in the early years of the twentieth century, but increasingly names associated with recreational activities (like Tinkers, Evers, and Chance in baseball) rose to national prominence. Performers such as Annie Russell, David Warfield, Maude Adams, Julian Marlowe, and Ethel Barrymore also captured wide public acclaim. When Richard Mansfield starred in *Cyrano de Bergerac* at the Garden Theater in New York in 1898, one critic applauded it as "the most successful play that has ever been produced at any time in the history of drama." Actors and actresses, previously regarded as disreputable figures of traveling companies, were now respected artists, or at least renowned personalities in the "legitimate" theater.

The popularity enjoyed by stage performers paled in comparison to the attention lavished on stars like Rudolph Valentino and Clara Bow in the 1920s. But the medium which catapulted these individuals to stardom was only a flickering, stilted black-and-white image in 1900. Moving pictures slowly infiltrated the urban entertainment arena after the first motion picture show opened at the Koster and Bial Theatre in New York on April 27, 1896. Like most movie houses, this Twenty-third Street establishment was only a converted store with crude seats and a ticket booth.

Elaborate movie houses did not appear until around 1910. By that date the Edison Company, the Vitagraph Company of Brooklyn, and others had built studios sophisticated enough to produce feature-length films. With the growing interest in the new media, the *Independent* magazine could report in 1908 that "moving picture theaters or exhibition halls have opened in nearly every town and village in the country and every city from the Klondike to Florida and from Maine to California supports from two or three to several hundred."* After 1915, when D. W. Griffith made a quantum leap forward with the release of his twelve-reel epic, *The Birth of a Nation*, the future of the motion picture as a mainstay of the urban entertainment scene was assured.

* It is interesting to note that by 1910, when films began to be regularly shown in cities, censorship had already reared its righteous head. A San Francisco board of censors rejected thirty-two films on the grounds that they were "unfit for public exhibition." Those getting the ax included "Saved by a Sailor," "In Hot Pursuit," "The Black Viper," and "Maggie the Dock Rat."

During those same years the meteoric rise of Charlie Chaplin helped establish the "star" system in film on a level of extravagance unmatched by the theater.

In 1912 *Variety*, the bible of the entertainment industry, reflected on the growth of the field. With George M. Cohan's wealth estimated at $1,500,000, David Belasco's at $1,000,000, and Maude Adams's at $225,000, it was apparent that entertainment had become a major industry. Americans had the money, time, and the desire to invest in amusements. A cursory glance at the entertainment scene in 1912 suggests the variety of available pleasures. That year saw Leopold Stokowski appointed musical director of the Philadelphia Orchestra; offered 175 stage productions in New York City alone, including *Little Women* at the Playhouse, *Hamlet* in a record-breaking engagement at the Garden, and the realistic Belasco production of *The Governor's Lady* at the Republic; hailed the enterprising Florenz Ziegfield's seven-year-old *Follies* at the Jardin de Paris; and watched the film industry capture the stage's leading lady, the "divine" Sarah Bernhardt, in *Queen Elizabeth*. Nineteen-year-old Mary Pickford did her first full-length feature, appropriately entitled *Her First Biscuit*, and Douglas Fairbanks signed his first contract. And all the while Mack Sennett convulsed audiences with the delightful mayhem of his Keystone Company.

The entertainment industry, the rise of national sports, and even crazes like bicycling all relied heavily upon advertising and coverage in city newspapers. The urban press not only served as the source of information on the fortunes of the home team or the scheduled appearance of the next traveling show, but also was widely regarded as the most important single influence upon public opinion in the community. Only the newspaper, whose circulation skyrocketed in the industrial city, could cover every area of urban life. As cities grew larger and more complex, newspapers enlarged their coverage and added new departments to keep pace with changing conditions. They aroused public interest, whipped up civic pride, raked up political and social scandals, and molded opinion. The urban press in the industrial age served a dual function: it encouraged civic betterment while recording the foibles of men and women struggling with life in the city.

The number of newspapers in the United States jumped from 4,500 in 1870 to 7,000 a decade later. By 1914 there were 2,250 dailies, 13,000 weeklies, and 400 semiweeklies blanketing the country. New machines, including the linotype, the high-speed power press, the typewriter, and the telephone, helped spur this proliferation. Apart from technology and sheer numbers, the new strength of the newspaper lay in two familiar realms: a more sophisticated brand of journalism and the application of organizational techniques to the industry. By 1920 the average metropolitan daily had been transformed into a corporate enterprise no longer dominated by the personality of a single individual and often part of a chain of papers. Personal journalism had largely given way to corporate journalism, in which news reporting and most other aspects of the paper had become largely standardized in method and format.

Charles A. Dana helped set the tone for late-nineteenth-century journalism when he purchased the *New York Sun* in 1868. Introducing the "human-interest" story, Dana covered a good deal of crime and scandal but insisted upon high writing standards from his staff. Horace Greeley's (later Whitelaw Reid's) *Tribune*, William Cullen Bryant's *Evening Post*, and James Gordon Bennett's *Herald* were New York's other leading dailies after the Civil War. They were joined in 1896 by a German immigrant who migrated north from Chattanooga, Tennessee, and bought the failing *New York Times*. Adolph S. Ochs dedicated his new enterprise to extensive coverage, a conservative format, and a motto of "All the News That's Fit to Print," and built his paper into an international institution.

Other cities boasted their own journalistic entrepreneurs. George W. Childs and Francis A. Drexel bought The *Philadelphia Public Ledger* in 1862 and built its circulation up to 90,000. Henry W. Grady became part owner of the *Atlanta Constitution* in 1880 and earned the epithet "the voice of the South" before his premature death in 1889. His influence in the South was exceeded only by "Marse Henry" Watterson, editor of the *Louisville Courier-Journal*. Melville E. Stone and William Dougherty began the *Chicago Daily News* in 1876; by 1888 Stone had increased its circulation to 200,000. In Kansas City William Rockhill started the *Star* in 1880 to "boost Kansas City" and became a powerful force for civic betterment in that fast-rising midwestern city.

But New York claimed the two most famous newspapermen of the era: Joseph Pulitzer and William Randolph Hearst. Pulitzer, a poor Hungarian immigrant, came to America in 1864 and fourteen years later founded the *St. Louis Post-Dispatch*. After guiding the *Post-Dispatch* to national prominence, he went to New York and bought the moribund *World*, for which he outlined his intentions this way:

There is room in this great and growing city for a journal not only large but truly democratic—dedicated to the cause of the people rather than to that of the purse potentates—devoted more to the news of the New World than the Old World—that will expose all fraud and sham, fight all public evils and abuse—that will battle for the people with earnest sincerity.

Pulitzer's *World* and *Evening World* dedicated itself to hard-nosed reporting spiced with games, crusades, illustrations, and strong editorials that became the envy of the profession.

Hearst did more than envy Pulitzer; he copied him. His *San Francisco Examiner* and later *New York Journal* swashbuckled with sensationalism and perfected what had become known as "yellow journalism." Churning out "scare" headlines, fake news, and outlandish editorials, Hearst outdid himself in publicizing the events which led up to the Spanish-American War. "You get me the pictures, I'll get you the war," he reputedly told one of his photographers. His erratic blend of brilliance and antics boosted circulation enormously and made Hearst a national sensation.

More responsible editors sent out energetic reporters like Jacob Riis, Charles E. Russell, Ida Tarbell, Lincoln Steffens, and David Graham Phillips to investigate America in the raw and report evidence of scandal and misdeeds. Their findings often led to reformist crusades. The muckrakers vied for attention in the newspaper's columns with specialized sports and entertainment pages, women's news, puzzles, and bedtime stories for children. The lovelorn were assuaged by features like Marion Harland's "Helping Hand" and Laura Jean Libbey's "First Aid to Wounded Hearts." And, of course, the funnies captured everyone's rapt attention. When "The Yellow Kid" made its appearance in 1895, creator R. F. Outcault became the first cartoonist producing a daily strip. The "Katzenjammer Kids" by Rudolph Dicks, Outcault's "Buster Brown," "Happy Hooligan," and "Mutt and Jeff" rapidly followed.

The multiplication of newspapers throughout American cities paralleled a similar trend in the magazine field. Older respected journals like the *Nation, Harper's,* and the *Atlantic Monthly* were joined by new weeklies and monthlies carrying fiction, analytical reporting, and commentary. *Scribner's Magazine, Century, American Review of Reviews,* Edward Bok's *Ladies' Home Journal, McClure's, Cosmopolitan, The New Republic,* and others surveyed the American scene more thoroughly than ever before. Those preferring pictures could turn to *Frank Leslie's Illustrated Weekly.* Through their newspapers and journals, as well as through their fiction, some of which dug deeply and candidly into the problems of urban life, Americans received a vivid panorama of themselves and their nation. Through these pages they read about the experiences of hundreds of their contemporaries; they were exposed to faraway places which expanded their horizons; they learned about the activities of their political leaders at home and in Washington. Much of what they read excited them; some of the reporting they found strange and bewildering. With the constant barrage of slum portraits and exposés of business and political corruption, with the news that two brothers had lifted a fragile contraption into the sky over Kitty Hawk, North Carolina, in 1903, with the automobile chugging impudently down city streets, and with the ghastly photographs of trench warfare in Europe, most Americans realized that the forces of change which had bombarded them for the past half century were far from spent.

America's industrial and technological might would speed them on toward even more chaotic social change. But for all the uncertainties facing them, most middle-class Americans still exhibited great confidence in the future. It was a confidence grounded in the knowledge that long-standing values had been twisted and bent by the industrial experience, yet had remained surprisingly durable. Middle-class urbanites knew their lives had changed and become far more complex, yet their faith in these values had enabled them to weather every storm. More prosperous than ever and astride the saddle of altered institutions, they looked toward the emerging metropolitan giantism of the twentieth century with a confidence born of trials successfully met.

CHAPTER 9

Life at the Bottom:
The Urban Lower Class

In Sutherland, where the best off hadn't so painfully much more
than the worse off, and where everybody but the idle and the
drunken, and even they most of the time, had enough to eat, and
a decent place to sleep, and some kind of Sunday clothes—in
Sutherland the poverty was less than in Cincinnati, infinitely less
than in this vast and incredibly rich New York where in certain
districts wealth, enormous wealth, was piled up and up. So evidently
the presence of riches didn't help poverty but seemed to increase it.
No, the disease was miserable, thought Susan. For most of the
human race, disease and bad food and vile beds in dingy holes and
days of fierce, poorly paid toil—that was the law in this hell of a
world. And to escape from that hideous tyranny, you must be
hard, you must trample, you must rob, you must cease to be human.

—David Graham Phillips
Susan Lenox (1917)

IN 1903 JACK LONDON went off to England to investigate London's
notorious East End. From that experience he wrote *The People of
the Abyss,* a searing account of life among the English lower classes.
That this same misery existed at home he knew well from his own
bitter childhood which, at age fourteen, found him working ten hours
a day in a jute mill for a penny an hour.

London did well to choose the image of an abyss in depicting
lower-class existence. Like other chroniclers of the poor, he recognized
that social structure in America was not a ladder with regularly spaced
rungs. The gaps between top, middle, and bottom were far too great
to be negotiated by short, even steps. In the industrial city, the middle
class occupied a plateau—a tableland perched between two extremes.
On one side lay the mountains where high above the clouds dwelled
the rich, the well-born, the powerful. Ascent was possible, but the
climb was steep and the footing treacherous. On the other side lay a
deep canyon in whose dark depths dwelled the poor and the wretched.

Among the middle class there was no greater fear than that circumstances might conspire to push them over the edge and down into that bottomless maw from which return seemed all but impossible. To reach the plateau, those in the depths had to scale the steep, sheer face of adversity. They harbored no greater ambition than to escape their mean existence, but the climb was rugged and the footholds few. The mere struggle for survival at the bottom sapped the energies of all but the hardiest and most determined.

Poverty took on a darker aspect in the city than it had in the country. In preindustrial times a mythology had arisen to invest what Lincoln, quoting Thomas Gray's "Elegy in a Country Churchyard," called "the short and simple annals of the poor" with a sense of dignity. The gap between the rich and poor was not yet so wide; most people lived between the extremes of wealth and poverty. Only in the cities could one find paupers, and they were relatively few in number compared to the industrial era. Country folk might be poor, but rarely did they lack the means to sustain a decent if unadorned existence. The work might be hard, the hours long, and the routine stultifying, but the land yielded the essentials of life—food, clothing, shelter—and sometimes a bit more.

Industrialization changed all that. It transformed native immigrants and European peasants into proletariat. As newcomers streamed into the cities to meet the mechanical partners awaiting them, they became a new phenomenon of the industrial era: wage earners. By going to work for others, they lost control over their economic destiny and surrendered their fate to the erratic rhythms of the industrial system. As the cheapest and most expendable commodity in the urban marketplace, they became grist for the mill of industrial progress. They took the meanest jobs, worked exhausting hours, occupied the dingiest housing, ate the most unsavory foods, and endured unspeakable hardships.

Unlike what Michael Harrington called the "invisible poor" of modern America, the impoverished of the industrial city were highly visible. Attired in the garb of many lands, speaking a cacophony of tongues, the lower classes splashed the urban landscape with color and vitality. Squatting in shantytowns on bare hills or packed into tenements, they poured into the streets to work, talk, celebrate, or brawl. Neighborhood segregation isolated much of the stench, disease, and crime associated with poverty, but people throughout the city saw and felt the presence of the lower class.

Relations between the working class and their "betters" deteriorated steadily during the late nineteenth century. As social tensions mounted, this shifting, formless mass of humanity, swarming like caged animals in the slums of every large city, evoked cries of alarm—even hysteria—from the upper classes. Shuddering at the memory of violent strikes and haunted by the twin specters of anarchism and socialism, factory owners grew uneasy at the sight of so many men assembled in one place. Even practical men—hardened warriors of the business arena—feared that closeness bred unionism—perhaps even revolution—in which the lower class would topple the existing social structure by sheer weight of numbers.

The middle class shared this vision of impending apocalypse. They interpreted the rumblings from below not as discontent bred by misery and stifled ambitions, but as an ominous threat to their own hard-won place in the social order. In the slums they saw constant violation of those moral values esteemed by respectable people. Shocked by the spectacle, they seldom bothered to look beneath the surface or inquire into larger causes. From the sanctuary of their cluttered parlors, they were content to denounce the unwashed rabble as a rising tide which, if not contained, might swamp everything they held sacred.

There were legitimate grounds for fear. Between 1870 and 1914 the industrial city smoldered with social tension and class conflict. Long and bitter strikes punctuated the entire period. The Tompkins Square Riot (1874), the Molly Maguire riots (1875), the railroad strikes of 1877, the Union Pacific strike (1884), the Wabash strike (1885), the strike against Jay Gould's southwestern railroads (1886), the Haymarket riot (1886), the Homestead strike (1892), the Coeur d'Alene strike (1892), the Pullman strike (1894), the coal miners' strike (1902), and the textile strikes in Lawrence, Massachusetts (1912) and Paterson, New Jersey (1913) were only the most conspicuous markers of the undeclared war between capital and labor. At Homestead an anarchist tried unsuccessfully to shoot Henry Clay Frick, the hard-nosed industrialist who had fought the strikers with every means at his disposal. Assassins gunned down two Presidents of the United States, James A. Garfield and William McKinley. The march of Jacob Coxey's ragtag army on Washington (1893) inflamed fears of a wholesale insurrection while the depression-riddled decades of the 1870s and 1890s drove even farmers into open revolt.

The lines of conflict were drawn in words as well as deeds. On one side, defenders of the status quo sternly reminded the lower class that higher powers had determined their lot in life. "God has intended the great to be great and the little to be little," declared Henry Ward Beecher. Conceding that wages of a dollar a day would not "support

288 PRISONERS OF PROGRESS

a man and five children if a man would insist on smoking and drinking beer," he asserted that "the man who cannot live on bread and water is not fit to live." Beecher left no doubt as to the cause of poverty:

There may be reasons of poverty which do not involve wrong; but looking comprehensively through city and town and village and country, the general truth will stand, that no man in this land suffers from poverty unless it be more than his fault—unless it be his *sin*.

Samuel C. T. Dodd, a brilliant corporation lawyer who served Standard Oil long and well, echoed this sentiment when he attributed poverty to the fact that "nature or the devil has made some men weak and imbecile and others lazy and worthless, and neither man nor God can do much for one who will do nothing for himself."

At the opposite pole, radical theoreticians peddled inflammatory rhetoric on the evils of industrial capitalism and grimly awaited fulfillment of their doctrines. A small circle of dedicated terrorists succeeded in making anarchism the great bogeyman among the upper classes. While neither anarchism nor communism gained much of a following, socialism set down firm if modest roots in the political system. A medley of radical groups and organizations converged in 1901 to found the Socialist Party of America. Eugene V. Debs, its perennial presidential candidate, polled over 400,000 votes in both 1904 and 1908 and received 897,000 votes, or 6 percent, of the popular vote in 1912. Milwaukee's Victor Berger and New York City's Meyer London won seats in Congress. In 1911 some 73 cities, including Milwaukee, Schenectady, Berkeley, California, Butte, Montana, and Flint and Jackson, Michigan, elected socialist mayors, while 340 cities and towns elected about 1,200 socialists to lesser offices.

In the years prior to World War I, it appeared that socialism was becoming a permanent feature on the political landscape. Not only workers but some middle-class people, journalists, educators, lawyers—even a handful of millionaires and society figures—avowed their faith in socialism. And the socialists were by no means alone on the left. Henry George's *Progress and Poverty* (1879) had aroused widespread interest in his "single tax" panaceas; in 1886 George himself ran second to businessman Abram S. Hewitt in New York's mayoralty race. Similarly, Edward Bellamy's *Looking Backward* (1888) spawned a network of Nationalist clubs dedicated to realizing the socialist principles depicted in the novel. Further to the left were two groups that struck terror into the hearts of respectable people: the small but vocal Communist parties and the International Workers of the World, a militant labor organization.

Radical literature circulated everywhere, and in the war of words the leftists had much the better of it. Muckrakers like Upton Sinclair, Charles E. Russell, and Lincoln Steffens, all of whom became socialists, wrote scathing exposés of the industrial and political systems. A flood of utopian novels portraying socialist republics drowned contrary efforts like *The Scarlet Empire* (1906), a feeble caricature of an egalitarian society written by businessman David M. Parry, onetime president of the National Association of Manufacturers. Against the eloquent perorations of conservative ministers and business apologists, radical authors hurled an outpouring of tracts, pamphlets, and articles. Two gory dystopian novels, *Caesar's Column* (1891) by Ignatius Donnelly and Jack London's *The Iron Heel* (1907), presented chilling visions of a future in which the struggle between rich and poor culminated in uprisings drenched in blood and butchery.*

In these troubled times, and especially during episodes of violence when social tensions ran high, the nightmare of impending revolution haunted the upper and middle classes much as the fear of slave revolts had preyed upon slave owners in the Old South. Yet despite the fertile circumstances, the violence, the inflamed rhetoric and interminable social crises, the revolution never came. The different classes never lived in anything close to harmony—they fought, mocked, cursed, even killed one another—but the social structure remained intact. The maturing capitalist industrial order proved a durable foe.

Even more, it proved a clever seducer. Those who wallowed in the depths of economic deprivation clung fiercely to the traditional ambition of the upward climb. Among the newcomer and the downtrodden, no vision of socialist utopia or class solidarity captured their hopes as fully as did the siren's song of the American dream, the gospel of success, the Horatio Alger rags-to-riches myth. Faith in the individual's ability to claw his way to the top remained stronger than any dream of a better world built by collective effort. No real class consciousness ever developed in America at the time when it seemed most likely. Native and immigrant poor alike shared only a common sense of lowliness and a fervent belief that someday this would change if they worked at it hard enough.

---

* London's remarkable novel, too often neglected or dismissed because of its literary defects, is a fascinating document of the period. In mood and theme it foreshadows George Orwell's *1984*.

Life of Labor

The expanding industrial system created thousands of new jobs. Some required a skilled hand or a trained eye but most demanded only the brute force of a shoulder or forearm. Most work was routine with little chance for creativity or individuality. Amidst the stench of the slaughtering room, the roar of blast furnaces, the whirring of bobbins, the flying shavings of optical glass, or the stifling inferno of a sweatshop or laundry, employers required not artisans but durable time-motion human automatons. Men, women, and children alike trooped to the factories with the rising sun, worked an exhausting sixty to seventy hours or more, and collected their wages with only a day to rest before the cycle began again.

The factories themselves were raw, cheerless places lacking even the bare rudiments of health, safety, or comfort. Their oppressive atmosphere, coupled with the monotony of the work itself, numbed the sensibilities of the hardiest worker. Most newcomers learned their task quickly and performed it in a mental fog, their thoughts drifting to past memories or fantasies of a future where things would be different. Stephen Crane, in his novel *Maggie: A Girl of the Streets* (1893), captured this sense of stupor as his heroine toils in a clothing factory:

The air in the collar-and-cuff establishment strangled her. She knew she was gradually and surely shrivelling in the hot, stuffy room. The begrimed windows rattled incessantly from the passing of elevated trains. The place was filled with a whirl of noises and odours. She became lost in thought or she looked at some of the grizzled women in the room, mere mechanical contrivances sewing seams and grinding out, with heads bent over their work, tales of imagined or real girlhood happiness, or of past drunks, or the baby at home, and unpaid wages. She wondered how long her youth would endure.

Work drained most people of strength and left time for little else than to eat, sleep, and take those pleasures nearest at hand. Fatigue demoralized the industrial army, filling its ranks with pale faces, expressionless eyes, stooped bodies, and blighted spirits. The grind of production became the human grind. One suspects the revolution never took place because people were just too tired.

If life was grim in the best of times, the slightest change in circumstances could plunge whole families into a desperate struggle for survival. Hard times or seasonal layoffs snapped the economic lifeline and threw everyone into a frenzied search for work. Sickness meant a loss of income, and prolonged illness a loss of position. Industrial accidents crippled and maimed thousands of workers every year. A disabling injury turned the family breadwinner into a burden overnight. In *The Jungle*

(1906), Upton Sinclair depicted the sense of dread that seized Jurgis Rudkus when he injured his ankle in a Chicago packinghouse:

They were in for a siege, that was plainly to be seen. Jurgis had only about sixty dollars in the bank, and the slack season was upon them. Both Jonas and Marija might soon be earning no more than enough to pay their board, and besides that there were only the wages of Ona and the pittance of the little boy. There was the rent to pay, and still some on the furniture; there was the insurance just due, and every month there was sack after sack of coal. It was January, mid-winter, an awful time to have to face privation.

Nor could those who survived the gauntlet of their working years rest easy. Before them loomed the specter of old age. No longer able to work and bereft of pensions or savings, they were thrown upon the mercy of relatives or charities. Lacking these, the aged had recourse only to what most regarded as the final humiliation and degradation: the poorhouse. The pitiful scene of elderly folk abandoned to their fate became a familiar sight to social workers. Jane Addams described one "tottering old lady" brought to Hull House by a young boy:

The old woman herself said absolutely nothing, but looking on with that gripping fear of the poorhouse in her eyes, she was a living embodiment of that dread which is so heartbreaking that the occupants of the County Infirmary themselves seem scarcely less wretched than those who are making their last stand against it.

The industrial army may be broken down into three distinct groups. Its sergeants and corporals were the skilled workers. Usually natives or English-speaking immigrants, they were respected by management and fellow workers alike. Some considered themselves middle class; often they held semi-management positions. Of all workers, they had the most comforts and the strongest identity with the values of the factory-owner class. Skilled workers were the hardest workingmen to replace and the easiest to unionize along trade lines. Possession of a skill gave them added leverage in dealing with employers; it also separated them from other workers and made the organization of unions by industry rather than trade a difficult task. In this way the trade union movement undermined efforts to create class solidarity among all workingmen.

The second group consisted of semiskilled and unskilled workers. As industrial foot soldiers, they formed the largest group and held the most tenuous positions. So long as a plentiful supply of cheap labor continued to pour into the city, the semiskilled and unskilled found it hard to improve their lot or obtain work benefits. Job security was non-existent in those industries where one pair of hands could do the work as well as another. The fact that unskilled laborers could be replaced so easily also made attempts at unionization a discouraging business. For workers in this group, the struggle for better wages, shorter hours, and improved working conditions was a long and bitter ordeal.

Transients formed the third group. Within the industrial army they were the irregulars, the militia. Sometimes working, sometimes panhandling, their ranks included a motley assortment of down-and-outers who had suffered a run of bad luck, could not shake a drinking habit, or had simply failed to make the transition to the city. They drifted from city to city, job to job, street corner to street corner. Every village had a few such characters, usually called the "town drunks" or "village bums," which the community took care of in some fashion. But in the city, where they gathered by the thousands and where community spirit had vanished, they were dismissed as derelicts or loafers, the dregs that collected at the bottom of the urban barrel. They were the lost souls of the industrial city, wandering aimlessly through its slum districts with unshaven faces, tattered clothes, and vacant expressions in which the fire of ambition had long since burned out.

While it is very difficult to generalize about how the majority of working-class people lived in the industrial period, a few observations can be made. Most industrial workers improved their lot from 1850 to 1920. Real wages rose roughly 10 to 20 percent in the 1870s and another 25 percent in the 1880s alone. Skilled workers were the primary recipients of these gains, while women and children received lower wages than adult males. But the working class came nowhere near gaining a fair share of the economic benefits of industrial growth.

Within the confines of these generalizations a good deal of variance existed. As in every age, different families could do different things with the same amount of money. As John Garraty points out:

Early social workers who visited the homes of industrial laborers in this period reported enormous differences in the standard of living of men engaged in the same line of work, differences related to such variables as the wife's ability as a homemaker and the degree of the family's commitment to middle-class values.

One Illinois social investigation found a family of five living frugally but decently in 1883 on $250 a year. Many families lived carefully enough to save money from an income of $400 or $500 a year.

Other investigators found less cheerful results. Carroll D. Wright, chief of the Massachusetts Bureau of Labor Statistics, after studying the textile industry in 1882, maintained that "A family of workers can always live well, but the man with a family of small children to support, unless his wife works also, has a small chance of living properly." The variables were infinite: the industry, the job, the national economic cycle, the region, the number of children, personal habits, and many more. Those who made it rarely climbed far above the margin. Toiling long hours, they scrimped and saved for a better future that seldom arrived. For the poor, a decent life required not only good habits but good luck.

Despite an ample supply of both workers and grievances, labor organizations progressed slowly in the United States. The American working class shared neither an ideology nor a common ground of circumstances upon which to forge a bond of unity. Craft divisions, regional differences, ethnic and cultural diversity, and lack of a strong radical tradition were but a few of the obstacles to organization. Those who did form unions were usually the skilled workers such as railroad men, miners, and ironworkers. By 1870 about 300,000 men belonged to unions and a national federation, the National Labor Union, appeared in 1866. Politically inept and unresponsive to its membership, the N.L.U. lasted only six years.

In 1878 the colorful Knights of Labor, founded in 1869 as a union of garment workers, reorganized as a national union. Under the flamboyant but erratic leadership of Terence V. Powderly, the Knights attempted to become the one great union of the working class. It welcomed all workers, men and women, white and black, skilled and unskilled, and won immense prestige in 1884 with a successful strike against Jay Gould's Southwestern railroads. Two years later, membership in the Knights peaked at more than 700,000. But a flair for secret ritual, fuzzy philosophy, internal dissension, and an exaggerated reputation for violence drove the Knights to extinction by 1900.

The future of the national labor movement lay not with the one great union but with the trade union movement. The American Federation of Labor, organized in 1886 by Adolph Strasser and Samuel Gompers, gained support because it was conservative, stressed "bread and butter" issues instead of broad reforms, and stayed out of politics. In effect, the A.F.L. organized its member unions as a pressure group, a kind of labor corporation, to achieve its goals. Over the years the A.F.L. under Gompers used its muscle against not only management but rival labor organizations as well. It has been said that the A.F.L. improved the lot of its members at the expense of the labor movement as a whole. Certainly it dominated the labor scene until the unskilled workers shunned by the A.F.L. began to organize in the twentieth century.

More important, its approach dominated the attitude of American labor. Despite the efforts of radical and militant groups like the I.W.W., most union men accepted the prevailing wage system and were content to seek moderate gains within it.

Behind this conservative impulse among the working class lay an almost mystical faith in the open system. In America, unlike other industrial nations, the dream of obtaining a satisfactory place in the capitalist system overcame most opposition to it. Workers desired not to overthrow the existing order but to win a higher place within it. So long as the desire remained, and so long as they believed it possible to attain, they were immune to schemes for reorganizing the system along different principles. While few men rose from the plant to the board-room, enough did to sustain the faith. Even if one advanced only a few feet up the cliff of success, a foothold had been gained from which one's children might proceed even further.

It is difficult to gauge why the success myth remained so strong in the United States. Even though workers continued to improve their positions (and their children usually made a further advance), the distance between rich and poor widened steadily. By 1900 distribution of wealth had become, in Harold Faulkner's words, "shockingly un-equal." One publicist figured that in 1889 "200,000 people controlled 70 percent of the nation's wealth. Seven-eighths of the families of the country, on the other hand, controlled only one-eighth of the national wealth in 1890." Faulkner maintained that "it is safe to conclude that 80 percent of Americans lived in 1900 on the margin of subsistence while the remaining 20 percent controlled almost the entire wealth of the country." The lower class did not need statistics to acquaint them of the distance between themselves and the rich. They needed only to walk past the mansions of Fifth Avenue or to admire the finery in shop windows. The trappings of wealth were visible to the poorest inhabitant of the industrial city.

Herbert Gutman, working with mid-nineteenth-century census statistics, has recently offered another answer why workers acquiesced in the growing gap between the rich and the poor. His survey of locomotive, iron, and machinery manufacturers in the growing industrial community of Paterson revealed that enough working-class people became owners to keep the vision of success burning brightly. Gutman concluded:

The rags to riches promise was not a mere myth in Paterson, New Jersey between 1830 and 1880. So many successful manufacturers who had begun as workers walked the streets of that city then that it is not hard to believe that

others less successful or just starting out on the lower rungs of the occupational ladder could be convinced by personal knowledge that hard work
resulted in spectacular material and social improvement.

Gutman's conclusion runs counter to most other studies. If the Paterson case is accurate, workers could see in their own community enough
people who had made it to nourish their hopes. The problem is that we
do not know if the Paterson example is a general one or if, as Gutman
cautions, it is a "mutant." In a much more extensive study of Newburyport, Massachusetts, during the same period, Stephan Thernstrom
found almost no "rags-to-riches" cases. Few unskilled workers made it
past the ranks of the semiskilled, and their sons did no better. "The
barriers against moving more than one notch upward were fairly
high," he declared. Yet, Thernstrom concluded, even this modest advance upward was enough to keep the workers of Newburyport hard at
work, scrimping and supporting the social structure which had given
them a morsel of success and might someday yield a banquet.

More studies like those on Paterson and Newburyport are needed to
resolve the question of social mobility in the industrial age. For now it
would be accurate to say that most industrial workers made some progress
up the social scale but the distance they had to travel continued to increase. For most, however, movement rather than distance was the important thing. Whether goaded by propaganda from above or inspired by
local success stories, American workers stuck to their routine and rejected
radical upheaval because their lot kept improving a little at a time.

The Bowery, the Back-of-the-Yards, the Bottoms

If the domestic side of middle-class life seemed cluttered and comfortable, that of the lower class was spare and spartan. Most workers
lacked the means to buy a single-dwelling house or to stuff their homes
with possessions. Long working hours left little time or energy for
domesticity, especially when the wife also worked. The physical aspects
of lower-class housing have been discussed in Chapter 6. Native and
foreign-born workers in the central city lived in segregated neighborhoods which took on the ethnic character of their inhabitants. The poor
districts looked different in various cities: run-down row houses in
Philadelphia and Baltimore; two- and three-decker frames in Boston,
Newark, Chicago, and St. Louis; tall barracks-like buildings in New
York City. Sometimes the tenements were once-elegant townhouses
abandoned by the well-to-do and partitioned into apartments. These older

dwellings tended to be more solid than buildings thrown up hastily to profit from the pressing demand for housing.

In any large city, the lower-class district was an overpowering collage of sights, sounds, and smells whose vitality mystified—even frightened— respectable folk. Lacking the privacy and quiet of suburban neighborhoods, ghetto society held court in the streets. To newcomers the first impression was that of noise and movement, a cacophonous ballet of people milling on sidewalks, hanging out windows, and chatting on stoops or fire escapes; the cries of children dodging in and out; the clatter of wagons and carts; the yells of peddlers hawking their wares; strains of distant laughter and argument; and sometimes even music, a song or accordion rising above the din.

Unlike more genteel neighborhoods, the ghetto wore its emotions close to the surface. The temper of the neighborhood spilled into the streets, ebbing and flowing with the circumstances. Paydays, holidays, a wedding, or a celebration charged the atmosphere with gaiety while hard times, a strike, layoffs, or a death hung like a sullen pall. In the streets of lower-class districts, silence was so unnatural as to be a dangerous omen. Life was far more casual and elemental there. Moods shifted quickly, excitement boiled up into violence. To the passerby or visitor, it was life in the raw, stripped of the frills and refinements with which middle and upper-class people concealed their passions.

Some thrived on this environment; others were worn down by the constant pressure of making ends meet and repelled by the squalor and stench and overcrowding. Whatever their feelings about the neighborhood, almost everyone dreamed of the day when they could leave it for their own house in a respectable suburb.

Many reformers considered the tenement districts to be the major urban evil. City after city appointed investigating commissions which studied the slums, decried their horrors, and then did nothing. As early as mid-century, this had become standard operating procedure for state and municipal governments. Most of these reports followed the tone of an 1857 New York state study of how tenements evolved in New York City:

At first the better class of tenants submitted to retain their single floors, or two and three rooms, at the onerous rates, but this rendered them poorer, and those who were able to do so, followed the example of former proprietors, and emigrated to the upper wards. The spacious dwelling houses then fell before improvements, or languished for a season, as tenant houses of the type which is now the prevailing evil of our city; that is to say, their large rooms were partitioned into several smaller ones, (without regard to proper light or ventilation) the rates of rent being lower in proportion to space or height from the street; and they soon became filled, from cellar to garret, with a class of tenantry living from hand to mouth, loose in morals, improvident in habits, degraded or squalid as beggary itself.

The cry against housing conditions echoed through the latter half of the nineteenth century. Fanned by these official reports, by muck-raking journalists, and by the earnest sermonizing of the clergy, the "tenement problem" with its attendant evils of crime, disease, and moral decay came to be regarded as "civilization's inferno." One wonders if the clamor ever reached the residents of these neighborhoods who, for all their deprivation, still considered their house a home. A moving example of this inner view appears in Stephen Crane's novel, *George's Mother* (1896). Crane depicts how much a building which most people would consider abominable meant to one of its occupants:

Bleecker lived in an old three-storyed house on a side street. A Jewish tailor lived and worked in the front parlour, and old Bleecker lived in the back parlour. A German, whose family took care of the house, occupied the basement. Another German, with a wife and eight children, rented the living-room. The two upper floors were inhabited by tailors, dressmakers, a peddler, and mysterious people who were seldom seen. The door of the little hall bedroom, at the foot of the second flight, was always open, and in there could be seen two bended men who worked at mending opera glasses. . . . Each part of the woodwork was scratched and rubbed by the contact of innumerable persons. In one wall there was a long slit with chipped edges celebrating the time when a man had thrown a hatchet at his wife. In the lower hall there was an eternal woman, with a rag and a pail of suds, who knelt over the worn oil-cloth. Old Bleecker felt that he had quite respectable and high-class apartments. He was glad to invite his friends.

Bleecker's pride notwithstanding, the statistics and reports on tenement life paint a dismal portrait. Slums have always existed in cities; even colonial Americans knew their miseries. But during the industrial era, they spread so rapidly as to become landmarks in every city. Housing operated on a free-market basis and was always in short supply. For property owners, the magic profit formula was high density, high rent, and low maintenance. Hard-pressed families met their rent by taking in boarders or by sharing quarters with another family. They paid dearly for wretched housing in which the owner invested little for upkeep or improvements because his tenants had nowhere else to go. Like the slave-ships of old, tenement districts packed their human cargoes into every available inch of space. Some reformers calculated that if the density rates of the most congested ghetto blocks were applied world-wide, the earth's entire population could be crammed into an area about the size of Delaware.

The handsome return on tenement properties induced men of every class to brush aside the stigma "slumlord" and get into the business. Some of America's first families drew part of their fortune from these properties, as did ambitious newcomers whose notion of success was to move up from tenant to landlord. "One of the most discouraging features about the present system of tenement houses," complained Jane Addams, "is that many are owned by sordid and ignorant immigrants."

As tenements multiplied, so did the reaction to them. As early as 1837, economist Mathew Carey studied 64 Philadelphia tenements containing 92 families totaling 473 inhabitants and found that "there are THIRTY TENEMENTS containing FIFTY-FIVE FAMILIES and TWO HUNDRED AND FIFTY-THREE INDIVIDUALS that have not the accommodations of a privy for their use!!" This recognition of blight in Philadelphia was matched in other cities. Citizen investigators combed the tenement districts for shocking statistics; public opinion, although blaming the residents themselves for their plight, eagerly awaited each new report. "Facts, facts piled up to the point of dry certitude, was what the American people then needed and wanted," said journalist Ray Stannard Baker of the huge muckraking volumes on housing. A new profession—social work—evolved out of the collecting, sorting, and arranging of dismal data on urban housing. Historian Robert Bremner has collectively referred to the social workers, muckrakers, clergymen, economists and others who looked at the tenement situation as "the factual generation." The studies produced by this factual generation included Robert A. Woods's *The City Wilderness: A Settlement Study, South End, Boston*; Robert Hunter's *Tenement Conditions in Chicago*; W. E. B. DuBois's *The Philadelphia Negro*; Emily W. Dinwiddie's *Housing Conditions in Philadelphia*; and Edith Elme Woods's *The Housing of the Unskilled Worker*. All painted a grim picture which indicted municipal inactivity and private profiteering for the wretched state of lower-class housing.

The most significant study of housing took place in New York City under the direction of a wily and erratic housing expert, Lawrence Veiller, and his patrician partner in social reform, Robert DeForest. Using a state tenement house commission appointed by Governor Theodore Roosevelt as their medium, Veiller and DeForest gathered important sociological data and in February 1900 prepared one of the most successful public exhibitions on slum life ever held. Exhibitions were a popular tool of social workers to raise public awareness, but Veiller outdid all others with his elaborate displays of photographs, maps, statistical graphs, and models displaying the hardships of tenement life. The Veiller Exhibition helped prompt the passage of the 1901 New York City Tenement Reform Bill, the most significant piece of housing reform legislation during this period. The bill prohibited the narrow dumbbell shaft in all new tenement construction. Besides creating dark inner rooms, the shaft caught and spread the noises, smells, and diseases of the building. The bill also required bathroom facilities in all apartments and instituted stiff fire-safety measures. It soon became a model for other cities.

One of Veiller's other major achievements was his compilation of a report entitled *The Tenement House Problem* (1903). Coedited with DeForest, the report ranks as a classic of the factual generation. In two volumes the editors amassed data on the lighting, ventilation, sanitation and fire dangers of the tenements and itemized a long list of proposed improvements. Veiller wisely observed that the tenements housed not only the "drunken, the dissolute, the improvident, and the diseased," but also "the great mass of respectable working men" and therefore deserved vigilant attention. *The Tenement House Problem* and the Housing Bill of 1901 made Lawrence Veiller a prototype of municipal reform—a man who steeped himself in the facts of the problem and worked tirelessly to find solutions.

As a giant in the field of social research, *The Tenement House Problem* was matched only by the *Pittsburgh Survey*, begun in 1907. Pittsburgh proved fertile ground for investigation. As center of the iron and steel industry, its belching smokestacks, choking pollution, giant corporations, restless labor force, and polyglot population formed the setting for the ambitious social workers who endeavored to diagnose what made Pittsburgh run. Headed by social worker and journalist Paul U. Kellogg and financed by the new Russell Sage Foundation, the *Survey* probed deeply into the relationship between labor and capital. Wherever they looked, as historian Roy Lubove has written, the investigators found the same picture: "a startling contrast between the dynamic, planned industrial sector, and the bumbling, archaic mix of governmental institutions that failed, literally, to safeguard human life." Back-breaking physical labor, wages geared to the individual and not his family, work injuries, long hours, and environmental filth were all catalogued in the *Survey*'s volumes.

This massive study, which ranged over seven years, was the culmination of the first systematic effort of reformers to deal with lower-class improvement. In Lubove's terms the *Survey* stands as a

unique experiment in American social and community analysis. Never before had so many specialists been drawn together to explore so many facets of a community's life. . . . The Survey was equally distinctive in its effort to explore a wide range of social, industrial, and civic issues, and relate them to each other. It differed, in this respect, from earlier but more limited investigations of housing, health, cost of living or vice in American cities. . . . The Survey, focusing upon the wage-earning population, attempted to "reduce conditions to terms of household experience and human life," to put institutions to the "test of a distinctively human measure." It achieved, in this connection, an impressive synthesis between the statistical, empirical perspective of the census report, and the vivid, personalized touch of the journalist.

The *Survey* epitomized the finest in social investigation in the industrial age. Unfortunately it also stands as a precursor of the many incisive but neglected reports of our own day.

Tenement living received the greatest attention because it affected so many poor people; yet other urban indigents had to make their way in even shabbier surroundings. As industrial sprawl gobbled up every available inch of room, the space behind buildings sprouted with jerry-built housing. Alleys became the dwelling spots for thousands of the poorest. Blacks in particular were forced to carve out space in these dank back ways. Shanties with wood stoves and the crudest appurtenances served as households near the industrial heart of Chicago, Cincinnati, Cleveland, and even under the shadow of the national capitol in Washington, D.C. Roving animals and uncollected trash filled the alleys and shantytowns which stood beyond the pale of municipal caretaking and outside the glaring spotlight of the muckrakers.

Tramps, beggars, paupers, and criminals preyed on the alleyways and shantytowns. If the growing army of vagrants who pestered people on street corners, invaded parks, and slept or passed out in doorways had confined themselves to the alleys, they would have been ignored; but their appearance throughout the city made them a "public nuisance." Tramps frightened people because they seemed to be everywhere, a swelling legion of parasites in search of handouts. A few ragged bums were at worst an annoyance; a large number might become a menace to social order. Private groups attacked the problem first. In New York patrician reformer Josephine Shaw Lowell led an investigating committee which spurred the establishment of soup kitchens and lodging homes. The Mills Hotel on Bleecker Street in New York offered rooms

(*Above*) The court of the Palace Hotel in San Francisco, 1904. Of the "hotel-spirit" among Americans, Henry James wrote: "There are endless things in 'Europe,' to your vision, behind and beyond the hotel; in the States, on the other hand, you see the hotel as itself that life, as constituting for vast numbers of people the richest form of existence."
(*Library of Congress*)

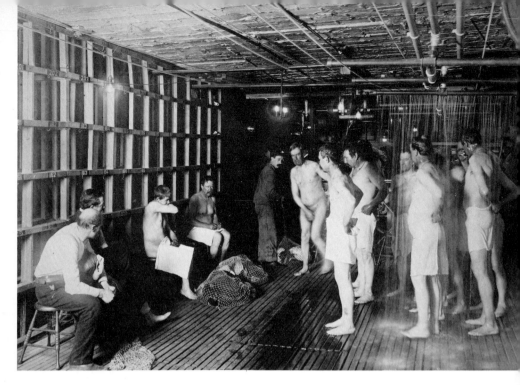

(*Above*) Bathing and fumigating the lodgers and their clothing at a municipal lodging house in New York City, 1908. (*Library of Congress*)

(*Below*) A Jacob Riis photograph of the condemned Essex Market School in New York City, 1902. Note the open gas jets and the iron stove in the corner. (*Library of Congress*)

(*Above*) A Lewis Hine photograph of "breaker boys" at the Pennsylvania Coal Company, South Pittston, Pa., 1911. (*Library of Congress*)
(*Below*) Street hazards I. A group of children playing on the curb show more interest in the photographer than in the body of a dray horse awaiting removal on a New York City street, 1900s. (*Library of Congress*)

(*Left*) Street hazards II. The Great Blizzard of 1888 paralyzes New York City. This is New Street looking towa Wall Street. (*Museum of the City of New York*) (*Below*) Saviors of the streets. Waring's White Angels parade down Fifth Avenue, 1913. (*Library of Congress*)

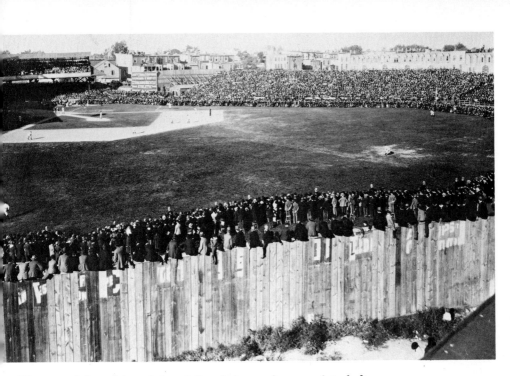

Pleasures of the unleisured class. (*Above*) An overflow crowd, including fence sitters and rooftop spectators, watches Boston play Baltimore, 1897. (*Library of Congress*) (*Below*) New York City's Coney Island, shown here in 1905, was only one of the many amusement parks that lured urbanites to outings of fun and fantasy. This pavilion was known as Dreamland and included among its exhibits the "Fall of Pompeii" (left) and "Fighting Flames" (right). Note the bathing pavilion at lower right. (*Library of Congress*)

Imprint of reform. (*Right*) Mulberry Bend, the most notorious slum in New York, around 1890. (*Museum of the City of New York*) (*Below*) A reform crusade led by Jacob Riis and others finally succeeded in having the tenements on Mulberry Bend demolished and replaced by Columbus Park, shown here in 1905. The Bend is at the upper right. (*Library of Congress*)

(*Below, right*) Part of the White City of the Columbian Exposition, which gave inspiration and impetus to the city planning movement. This view includes the west end of the Main Basin and shows the Obelisk and MacMonnie's Fountain, 1893. (*Chicago Historical Society*)

(*Above*) Outside the White City, in downtown Chicago, life went on as usual. This
monumental traffic jam occurred at Dearborn
and Randolph Streets, 1905.
(*Chicago Historical Society*)

at modest fees while the Salvation Army and Volunteers of America maintained soup lines, rescue missions, lodging homes, and shelters of all types.

When municipal governments got around to dealing with the tramp question, they too favored lodging homes. To make this form of welfare palatable to the public, work-incentives were often instituted. This modified version of outdoor relief pleased many people; *The Outlook,* a socially conscious journal, declared that "the work test is the best and only antidote for vagrancy pure and undefiled." In the summer of 1902 Philadelphia opened its new Wayfarer's Lodge No. 1, which was described as

a substantial four-story red brick structure whose construction and equipment are of modern and durable description, special emphasis being placed on four things—ample bathing and disinfecting facilities, thoroughly good ventilation, plenty of cubic air space for each sleeper (there are no double-deckers) and every precaution against fire. . . . The working arrangements are practical in the extreme. A large wood-yard is an essential part of the institution, the labor being wholly provided by the lodgers, who pay in this way for their meals and bed. One day's board and lodging can be earned in three or four hours, leaving a good part of the day free in which to look for other work.

Despite a concerted effort by most cities to deal with vagrants, the problem never vanished. Cities still shelter the dregs of society, bums, winos, down-and-outers, and street people who scrounge as best they can to survive, picking from garbage cans, panhandling, and pilfering incessantly. Massive programs have been launched against the problems of health, crime, and housing, but the urban arena still harbors its armies of lost souls. Everywhere slums have been razed; everywhere slum life goes on.

Home, Bittersweet Home

Contemporary accounts of living conditions among the working and indigent poor are so dismal that it is difficult to envision what kind of home life went on inside. Consider this brief description of Chicago's Halsted Street area:

Little idea can be given of the filth, and rotten tenements, the dingy courts and tumble-down sheds, the foul stables and dilapidated outhouses, the broken sewer pipes, the piles of garbage fairly alive with diseased odors, and of the numbers of children filling every nook, working and playing in every room, eating and sleeping in every window sill, pouring in and out of every door, and seeming literally to pave every scrap of "yard."

Similar reports from other cities, repeated again and again, have shaped our impression of lower-class life in the industrial period.

One leading progenitor of this image was the master journalist Jacob Riis. Sometimes called the American Dickens, Riis was himself a Dutch immigrant whose writings often smacked of middle-class resentment toward the immigrants whose plight he portrayed so vividly. Riis spent years combing the streets of New York City as a police reporter. His investigations were fertile groundwork for his classic *How the Other Half Lives*. Published in 1890 (the same year, ironically, as Ward McAllister's *Society as I Found It*), Riis's volume had the same impact as John Steinbeck's *The Grapes of Wrath* and Michael Harrington's *The Other America*. Although skimpy in places, it was the first popular account of urban poverty. Riis followed with several more books including *The Battle with the Slums, Children of the Tenements, A Ten Years' War,* and *Out of Mulberry Street.* In his works Riis sounded the alarm for the problems within the houses of the poor. A *Forum* article entitled "The Tenement: The Real Problem of Civilization" (1895) described the drift toward urbanization and asked "whether or not the readjustment from the old plan to the new, in which the city home is to be the central fact can be made safely; whether in it *the home* can be protected." If not, he warned, "then this is but the beginning of far greater changes to come. The state-society itself, as we know it—is not safe. It has had its day and must yield to the forces attacking it."

Other observers of lower-class lifestyles emphasized their effects on family structure. A reviewer of the *Pittsburgh Survey* saw the "destruction of family life, not in any imaginary, or mystical sense, but by the demands of the day's work, and by the very demonstrable and material method of typhoid fever and industrial accidents." Riis reinforced this notion of the crumbling lower-class family with his vivid portrayals of tenement life. Of one family on Elizabeth Street in New York, he said:

They cooked, I suppose, at the stove in the kitchen, which was the largest room. In one big bed we counted six persons, the parents and four children. Two of them lay crosswise at the foot of the bed, or there would not have been room. A curtain was hung before the bed in each of the two smaller rooms, leaving a passageway from the hall to the main room. . . . They were sweater's tenements. . . . There had not been water in the tenements for a month.

Reformers warned that such conditions bred degeneracy; that prostitution, gambling, heavy drinking, drugs, incest, and other vices flourished within the tenement. To some extent it was true. Parents knew little of what went on in the household during their absence. When they were not working, children were easily enticed by street life. Drunkenness and violence were no strangers to the tenements, nor were other vices in an area where the struggle for survival was most desperate. John Spargo, another journalist, catalogued the misfortunes of poor young people and by implication the ruin of lower-class families. His book, *The Bitter Cry of the Children* (1906), depicted a way of life that deprived children of childhood. Of child labor he wrote:

In the sweat shops and, more particularly, the poorly paid home industries, the kindergartens are robbed to provide baby slaves. I am perfectly well aware that many persons will smile incredulously at the thought of infants from three to five years old working. "What can such little babies do?" They ask. Well, take the case of little Anetta Fachini, for example. The work she was doing . . . wrapping paper around pieces of wire, was very similar to the play of better favored children. . . . She was compelled, however, to do it from early morning till late at night and even denied the right to sleep.

Life in the industrial city did strain working-class families. Yet the wonder is not that some broke under the stress, but that so many remained intact. Although some changes in values and attitudes occurred, by and large the family endured.

Few lower-class people left written accounts of their lives. Beyond the descriptions provided by commission reports, novelists, social workers, and investigators like Riis, little else is known about the domestic life of lower-class families. In recent years historians have begun investigating census reports of the period to see what data they can uncover on the subject. Some early findings suggest a remarkable stability in working-class families despite all the obstacles they faced. Herbert Gutman, for instance, has suggested that "it is time to discard the notion that the large-scale uprooting and exploitative process that accompanied industrialization caused little more than cultural breakdown and social anomie. Family, class, and ethnic ties did not dissolve easily."

Here, too, Gutman drew upon his study of Paterson, an industrial and basically immigrant working-class city. In surveying sixteen census enumeration districts in Paterson for 1880, Gutman found a large majority of households "intact," that is, with two parents at the head of the household. Virginia Yans McLaughlin, who studied patterns of work and family organization among Italians in Buffalo, also found few signs of disintegration. At one point she concluded, "Buffalo Italians, then, endured two conditions commonly associated with family breakdown and female domination—irregular male employment and temporary absence of the father from the household." Elizabeth Pleck's recent study of Boston found the basic family unit among blacks holding up well despite the ordeal of migration northward. Pleck discovered that "the most typical black household in late nineteenth-century Boston included the husband and wife, or husband, wife, and children." This held true for all occupational levels, and even for recent migrants.

A common element in both the Buffalo and Boston studies which may account for family solidarity was the tendency to supplement family income by taking in boarders and lodgers. "Lodgers," wrote one author describing Buffalo in 1911, "are in some sections almost the rule rather than the exception." Boarding expanded the household unit and altered the relationships among family members, but it also brought in much-needed money. For ethnic groups like the Italians, who objected to women working outside the house, it helped relieve the financial pressure, while preserving traditional male authority in the household.

These few recent examples of historical research challenge long-held views of working-class family life. Why, then, did traditional accounts view urban conditions as undermining family ties among the poor? The difference is largely one of perspective. The record accumulated over the years has been an impressionistic one. Writers like Riis and Spargo hoped to shock readers into awareness. While their examples were doubtless accurate, there is no way of knowing how representative they were. Moreover, the reformers who investigated the effects of slum life on family were middle-class people. They may have overestimated the degenerating effects of the slum because the lifestyle they saw was so different from their own. Modern middle-class reformers often take a jaundiced view of lower-class life which causes them to misinterpret what they see. Even such so-called sophisticated studies as the Moynihan Report on black family life badly miss the mark because of a middle-class bias. Then, too, the family as a subject of investigation is relatively new to historians. Perhaps the raw statistics will give us fresh insights into the tenements and the people behind their dingy doors. The question remains open.

As these last three chapters suggest, the family has proven a durable institution. Yet no study of its longevity or conclusions about its remaining intact can eradicate the burdens industrialization placed upon it. Statistical analysis may disclose general patterns, but they cannot capture the pain and hardship, the stench in the hallway, the rats in the kitchen, the emotional turmoil, and the tragedy of stunted lives that were the daily trial of lower-class families.

The Assimilation Mill

As with the middle class, the new economic order reshaped parent-child relations among the working class. Mandatory school attendance created problems for poor families. While education offered the promise of upward mobility, it also robbed the family of potential wage-earners. Since most workers were immigrants, the schools became battlegrounds for cultural disputes. Parents were torn between the desire to see their children "Americanized" and a longing for them to hold onto Old World traditions. In America the balance between pluralism and assimilation has always been delicate, and nowhere did it grow more unstable than in the industrial city. Children became pawns in a battle among adults that achieved its clearest lines in the classroom. Administrators and teachers viewed the school as the ideal chrysalis for transforming immigrants into Americans.* Parents desired education, but wanted their own brand of assimilation for their children.

The battle began with the first large wave of Irish immigration before the Civil War. Catholics naturally chafed at offensive references to their religion in school systems. In 1840 Bishop John Hughes fought the Public School Society in New York to get secular courses instituted in the public schools. He objected especially to the use of Protestant prayers, songs, and the King James Bible, but his plea for secularism failed. During an 1841 city referendum, the bishop's house windows were smashed as Protestants mobbed Irishmen on the streets. The Hughes fight presaged a long era of tension between Protestants and Catholics in the public schools. Once large numbers of Catholics from Italy and Eastern Europe joined the Irish, the Church had to act because the public schools would not satisfy its demand for a religious education. The logical answer was segregation. In 1884 the Third Plenary Council meeting in Baltimore decreed that all parishes throughout the country should provide education for their children.

It was a monumental task the Catholic Church set before itself. Parishes would have to finance, construct, administer, and staff an entire educational operation parallel to the public system. The first facilities

---

* By "American" they meant, of course, children who were inculcated with the values, attitudes, and behavior standards of White Anglo-Saxon Protestant culture.

were shabby and deficient even in the basic rudiments, but gradually the
system grew and matured. By 1903 nearly 4,000 institutions served
1,000,000 children in 95 communities. On the secondary level, Philadelphia Catholics opened a high school in 1890; 300 similar institutions
soon followed. The establishment of a network of parochial schools lifted
an enormous burden off the public's shoulders while providing Catholic
parents with a favorable alternative to public education. The Church's
stupendous effort in setting up the system was in many ways testimony
to the inability of public education to fill the needs of all Americans.
The segregated system has worked, although conflicts, tensions, and
financial crises still remain. Jews in many cities also sought to follow the
Catholic example. Most children of Jewish immigrants attended public
schools and received after-school instruction in Hebrew and Torah
reading.

The most nefarious type of school segregation was that imposed upon
black Americans. Even where housing patterns did not create segregated
schools, blacks were relegated to the city's worst educational facilities and
given substandard buildings, out-of-date textbooks, and worn-out supplies. Black parents had little political clout to improve conditions. School
boycotts in Alton, Illinois; Springfield, Ohio; East Orange, New Jersey;
and other cities during the period of pre-1920 northern migration
brought temporary relief in some places, but the failure to assimilate
Negroes into public school systems is another legacy of the industrial era
which remains unresolved.

Those students who did attend regular public schools may have
wondered why anyone else wanted in. While many cities operated fine
educational facilities, these were usually reserved for the upper and
middle classes. Workers who sent their children to school more often than
not did so under intolerable conditions. The swollen population of
industrial cities overtaxed facilities and, coupled with the mixture of
backgrounds, created virtual chaos in most classrooms. An 1895 survey
of a Brooklyn public school reported:

For one person to teach 150 children is an impossible task and that the
city of Brooklyn requires some poor woman to attempt it shares an ignorance
of human powers and an indifference to human suffering that would be
incredible of the Dark Ages. If a parent were offered the alternative of having
his child go to school in a cellar, or of sharing in the one hundred and
fiftieth part of the time of a tired, over worked teacher, he might well
hesitate before he decided. . . .

Most schools in working-class districts were jungles of disorder in
which the rewards seldom seemed worth the effort, especially when jobs

beckoned. With child labor flourishing and city schools floundering, the choice seemed obvious; but abandoning school for work had serious consequences. Reformer Jane Addams warned that the child laborers of today would be the paupers of tomorrow and that boys and girls with little education soon became "dull, shift-less drifters." United States Commissioner of Labor Charles P. Neill attacked the "honored" profession of newspaper selling as "a training in either knavery or mendicancy."

Critics insisted that child labor added little to the betterment of children or society. Most young people learned nothing to prepare them for a better life or job and merely added ten years or so to their working career. Far worse, those who dropped out of school frequently dropped out of work and joined the ranks of thieves, pimps, gamblers, or tramps who roved the streets alone or in gangs. In Jacob Riis's *A Ten Years' War,* we meet Jacob Bereshein, who

did not go to school, and nobody cared. There was a law directing that every child should go, and a corps of truant officers to catch him if he did not; but the law had been a dead letter for a quarter of a century. There was no census to tell what children ought to be in school, and no place but a jail to put those in who shirked. Jacob was allowed to drift.

Riis used Jacob as an example of the thousands of school dropouts who ran with the pack as kids and trained with the gang as teen-agers.

Those children who did stay in school and managed to avoid child labor or gang life faced difficulties that went beyond the inadequacies of inner-city schools. Foremost among these was the program for assimilating the child into American society. The public school became the key instrument used by assimilationists to break down ethnic solidarity. As one New York high school principal put it, "Education will solve every problem of our national life, even that of assimilating our foreign element." Samuel Bates, chairman of the Boston public school Visiting Committees, stated flatly that "our Public School System is a branch of the Government itself; as much so as our courts, our police, criminal, and charitable regulations for the poor." Bates also believed city schools should "train up all the children within its jurisdiction, to be intelligent, virtuous, patriotic, American citizens." The Daughters of the American Revolution, the Society of Colonial Dames, and other equally vigilant groups pressed the schools toward patriotic work with promises of scholarships, publication of literature, and sponsorship of civics classes. Many individual schools resisted, but pitched battles occurred in large cities over instructional methods and prayer requirements.

The attitudes of assimilationists grated against parents who wished Americanization for their children, yet also desired the preservation of family customs. Jane Addams, whose allies pressed this issue many times, poignantly captured this conflict in her address to the National Educational Association in 1908:

And yet in spite of the fact that the public school is the great savior of the immigrant district, and the one agency which inducts the children into the changed conditions of American life, there is a certain indictment which may justly be brought, in that the school too often separates the child from his parents and widens the old gulf between fathers and sons which is never so cruel and so wide as it is between the immigrants who came to this country and their children who have gone to the public school and feel that they have learned it all. The parents are therefore subjected to certain judgment, the judgment of the young which is always harsh and in this instance founded upon the most superficial standard of Americanism.

The conflict Addams saw was never resolved. The public schools, haltingly and sometimes ineptly, took the working-class poor and educated them. The process was never perfected, but it offered a vehicle for some to better themselves or at least to avoid the more ominous pitfalls that awaited young people in the slums.

The Bending Spire

Far more than the other classes, the workers became alienated from their religion. Some washed away the hardships of urban life with prayer, but the majority found small consolation in the church itself. Most urban churches were slow to comprehend the effects of industrialization upon their worshipers, especially those from the lower class. Clergymen, many of them with rural backgrounds, lost contact with their poorer congregants by failing to adjust their outlook to new conditions. Gradually, however, organized religion realized that it, too, must bend under the onslaught of the urban-industrial order lest its benedictions echo off the walls of empty sanctuaries.

Change struck the Catholic Church hardest. Always a minority, ever on the defensive, the Church had not yet settled upon its own role when the factory whistle called millions of new Catholics to America. Catholic communicants in America leaped from 9,000,000 in 1890 to over 18,-000,000 in 1920, when one out of every six Americans was Catholic. Peasants and unskilled workers from Italy, Poland, Hungary, and other countries seated themselves next to the Irish and Germans already here. Sharing the same religion, yet separated by ethnic backgrounds, the new immigrants felt out of place in their own church. The mass sounded different, the priest looked strange, and their co-worshipers eyed them warily. Gone was the warmth and familiarity of the old village cathedral, and it would be a long time before the church hierarchy assimilated priests of their own kind.

The Church had moved vigorously to meet the crisis in education; its response to the problems posed by new congregants was neither as swift nor as drastic. In major Catholic urban centers like Boston, New York, Baltimore, Cincinnati, and St. Louis, individual churches established programs to aid their members and ease the sufferings of poverty, but it was difficult for so conservative a church to accept the connection between poverty and personal deprivation. Because the Church regarded sin and suffering as personal rather than societal questions, it was attacked for appearing "oblivious to the bearing of civil legislation on the course of moral and social reform."

Although change was slow in coming, Catholics did begin to mobilize. Some work was done on a cooperative basis, like the Society for the Protection of Destitute Catholic Children and the Homes of the Good Shepherd, but in general Catholics responded on a parish basis. Each church determined its social welfare priorities—an orphanage, young adult group, adult evening classes—and then provided them. The extensiveness and effectiveness of programs to aid the working class always depended on the resources and personality of the neighborhood priest. After 1891, however, when Pope Leo XIII issued the historical encyclical *Rerum Novarum,* liberal clergymen were encouraged to increase the social welfare programs of their parishes. By 1920 Catholics had weathered the worst of the storm in dealing with their new members and had extensive social programs operating in most large cities.

The situation facing Jews paralleled that of Catholics. About 2,000,000 Jews—nearly a third of those in Eastern Europe—migrated to America, most of them to New York City. Their huge numbers and Eastern European origins alienated them from the Jews already in America. The well-assimilated, often wealthy German Jews viewed the newcomers with disdain and feared their presence would generate a new wave of anti-Semitism. In addition, their brand of Judaism had cold, formal overtones which seemed bland to the passionate "davening" arrivees. Moses Rischin described the tension between established "uptown" New York Jews and the downtown immigrants:

Nothing in the newcomers seemed worthy of approval. Yiddish, or Jeudo-German, "a language only understood by Polish and Russian Jews," though intelligible to non-Jewish Germans, was denounced a "piggish jargon." Immigrant dress, ceremonials, and rabbinical divorces were anathema. Yiddish theaters were barbarous; Yiddish newspapers, collectively stigmatized as "socialistic", even worse. Furthermore, "dangerous principles" were "innate in the Russian Jew."

Despite rancorous early differences, Jews of all backgrounds gradually banded together. Robert Rockaway's study of Detroit's Jewish ghetto offers a good prototype of how native Jews handled the immigration question. When Russian Jews began to arrive in Detroit in the 1880s, the German Jews already there established the Beth El Hebrew Relief Society to help find jobs, housing, and money for destitute newcomers. They also stressed moral uplift through programs in English and citizenship. Other groups like the Ladies Auxiliary Society and the Self Help Circle visited the homes of poor immigrants with clothing, food, and advice on domestic matters. By 1890 the flow of arrivees became so great that a special Russian Refugees Committee affiliated with the B'nai Brith, Kesher Shel Barzel, Free Sons of Israel, and Sons of Benjamin lodges was formed to coordinate relief, employment, and educational efforts. Finally, in 1898, the ten charity agencies in the city set up the United Jewish Charities of Detroit, which built its own headquarters in 1903. The new building operated as a settlement house where incoming Jews could take classes in English, dancing, stenography, domestic science, and manual training. It also housed a library, model kitchen, day nursery for working mothers, summer camp, legal offices, gymnasium, and bathing facilities which serviced over 5,000 persons a year. In similar ways did Jews in other American cities aid their incoming brethren.

At the national level, wealthy industrialist Baron Maurice de Hirsch founded two organizations: the Baron de Hirsch Fund in 1890 and the Jewish Colonization Association in 1891. The latter's attempt to settle Jews in rural areas failed, but de Hirsch trustees did manage to shift over 64,000 Jewish immigrants out of New York's crowded Lower East Side to 1,400 other locales during the 1900s. The fund's industrial training program succeeded to a great extent by giving local groups grants for the vocational training of newly arriving immigrants.

American Jews responded well to the urgent needs of their poorer brethren in part because ties of religious and cultural kinship were closer among Jews than among Catholics, and because there existed in America a prosperous Jewish community to provide the resources for such work. Yet even these advantages did not prevent ethnic antagonisms between uptown and downtown Jews from arising.

The poverty of the industrial city knew no religious or ethnic barriers.

While Catholics and Jews endured the ordeal of immigration and assimilation, Protestant newcomers found their churches coldly unresponsive to the problems of adjustment. In *Protestant Churches and Industrial America*, Henry May maintained that "until they were shocked by a series of violent social conflicts, most Protestant spokesmen continued to insist that all was well." Indeed, many church leaders believed "greed at the top could be ignored or accepted as a tool of progress," while "misery at the bottom could be waved aside as inevitable." But the abundance of misery coupled with a rising climate of social unrest goaded some theologians into formulating a revised concept of Christian responsibility. From their desire to alleviate the burden of poverty for their Christian brethren came that brand of social Christianity known as the Social Gospel.

The Social Gospel movement drew much of its impetus from Washington Gladden, an ardent minister who attuned himself to the social effects of the industrial system. Appalled by what he found, Gladden was moved to challenge the blind faith of American Protestants in industrial progress. He admitted that he

could not help wondering whether in liberating the force which gathers men into cities, and equipping it with steam and electricity, a power had not been created which was stronger than the intelligence which seeks to control it; whether such aggregations of humanity, with wills no better socialized than those of the average nineteenth-century American, are not by their own action self-destructive.

Through his writings and church work, Gladden inspired other clergymen to take up the Social Gospel. He helped organize labor and management conferences in Columbus and Toledo, urged widespread participation in local service clubs, and even ran for the common council in opposition to the local political machine. Gladden's credo, set down in his book *Applied Christianity* (1896), stressed participation. The Social Gospel sought to become relevant by bringing the kingdom of God to earth in this life rather than the next. Saving souls was an important part of the church's work but, Gladden insisted, it was not enough. The clergy had to extend a helping hand to those it had hitherto ignored: the poor, the homeless, the hungry, those living in misery and squalor.

Walter Rauschenbusch, a young Baptist preacher who had been assigned a small congregation near Hell's Kitchen in New York, saw his faith in the conventional wisdom of his church evaporate amidst the evils of slum life. The depression of the 1890s stirred him to apply the principles of the Social Gospel. Through his charitable efforts and writ-

ings he stressed the notion that environmental forces—not personal weak-
ness—had forced the poor into their state of misery. Later Rauschenbusch went to the Rochester Theological Seminary where he imbued
young clergymen in his philosophy. His pamphlets and books were
widely read, especially *Christianity and the Social Crisis* (1907), in
which he outlined the truths he had discovered from his service in the
slums. In vivid terms he captured the image of city as arena:

Competitive commerce exalts selfishness to the dignity of a moral principle.
It pits men against one another in a gladiator game in which there is no
mercy, and in which ninety per cent of the combatants finally strew the
arena. It makes Ishmaels of our best men and teaches them that their hands
must be against every man, since every man's hand is against them. It makes
men who are the gentlest and kindliest friends and neighbors relentless taskmasters in their shops and stores who will drain the strength of their men
and pay their female employees wages on which no girl can live without
supplementing them in some way.

Rauschenbusch's efforts made him the theological dean of the Social
Gospel. Although he believed that "the church and money power are
not friends," he was in no way the most radical Protestant practitioner.
Congregational minister William D. P. Bliss of Boston moved far closer
to a socialist position than either Gladden or Rauschenbusch. Bliss was
a welfare-state advocate who embraced the utopian dream of Edward
Bellamy's *Looking Backward*. In 1889 he founded the Society of Christian Socialists and then edited a radical journal entitled *The Dawn*, in
which he advocated his plans for nationalizing industry, municipal
ownership of utilities, public housing, unemployment relief, and an array
of other schemes to aid the poor. Bliss, along with his colleagues George
D. Herran and Philo W. Sprague, worked tirelessly "to prepare people for
the co-operative Commonwealth."

The Social Gospel had a wide impact on Protestantism. Rauschenbusch recalled that in the beginning "we were few, and we shouted in
the wilderness. It was always a happy surprise when we found a new
man who had seen the light." But the movement grew. Henry May
observed that "the relative strength of the Social Gospel in the various
churches depended on a great many special factors, geographical, traditional, and perhaps personal." But "in each of the major denominations,"
he added, "the new doctrines were alive and growing."

The popularity of Charles M. Sheldon's novel *In His Steps* (1896)
reflected this rising interest. One of the most widely read books ever
published in the United States, *In His Steps* sold well over a million

copies. Using the God's Kingdom on Earth theme, Sheldon set his story in the imaginary town of Raymond, where the leading citizens are awakened to the needs of the poor in a slum district called the "Rectangle," a place "too dirty, too coarse, too sinful, too awful for close contact." But once the good people undertake to clear the slums and launch a crusade against drunkenness and vice, all goes well in both the "Rectangle" and Raymond. The regenerative effects of the Social Gospel as portrayed by Sheldon did occur on a smaller scale all over the country, and usually inspiration came from the top. According to May, the movement "did not grow out of actual suffering but rather out of moral and intellectual dissatisfaction with the suffering of others. It originated not with 'disinherited' but rather with the educated and pious middle class."

Middle-class reform clergymen were not the only ones seeking to bend Protestantism toward the working poor. Labor leaders and workers themselves meshed Christ's teachings with their striving for better conditions. As one Louisville cigarmaker proclaimed, "The toilers are coming out of darkness into light and . . . have dared to organize, to come closer in touch with our Lord's will and the teachings of Jesus Christ." Labor reformers used religious ideology to urge their followers onward. In many cases these individuals, being closer to the working poor, had more impact than disciples of the Social Gospel. George E. McNeil, an ardent A.F.L. trade unionist and Christian socialist, invoked Christ's message at organizational rallies:

The influence of the teachings of the Carpenter's Son still tends to counteract the influence of Mammon. . . . Though the Mammon-worshipers may cry, "Crucify Him! Crucify Him!", the promise of the prophet and the poet shall be fulfilled . . . by the free acceptance of the Gospel that all men are of one blood. Then the new Pentecost will come, when every man shall have according to his needs.

The adoption of Christ's message by labor leaders and the blending of Protestantism with the rights of workers attracted the working poor to both unions and the church. This brand of social Christianity, along with the Social Gospel's message of practical Protestantism, offered the poor at least a ray of hope that their belief in God had some meaning even in the harsh environs of the slums.

On a quasi-religious level there appeared the Salvation Army. Patterning itself after the English group begun in 1880 by William and Catherine Booth, the American evangelical Army organized into paramilitary units to preach to the city's "rumdom, slumdom, and bumdom."

To those untouched by the message of the church, the Salvation Army ministered (sometimes by song) a credo of uplift that borrowed heavily from the scriptures. Its missions and soup lines included an auxiliary called the Slum Brigade headed by "Slum Brothers and Sisters" who visited the homes of the poor and held special meetings in local neighborhoods. One such meeting drew mixed although optimistic reviews:

The bright, lively songs of the Salvation Army, the ever-changing phases of the meetings, and the thorough bond of sympathy between the speakers on the platform and the roughs in the hall make these meetings a source of great power and interest. Of course, there are occasional fights among the audience, chairs are upset every now and then, windows are broken . . . and yet through it all a deep, powerful wave of influence carries into the hearts of the people the sincerity and truth of things spiritual.

The Salvation Army, its ranks filled with dedicated and sincere soldiers, helped fight the first war on poverty. For many of the city's down-and-outers, it was a straw to clutch which no one else—including organized religion—had bothered to offer.

Poverty's Perils

Industrial society produced the foulest environment yet known to man. Every city had its own peculiar stench. Coal-burning smokestacks blackened everything, including lungs. Animal waste, piles of garbage, outhouses, and overflowing septic systems made some streets virtually impassable. A newspaper report in 1874 labeled Cincinnati a "hideous" place because "an atmosphere heavy with the odors of death and decay and animal filth and steaming nastiness of every description, hangs over it like the sickly smoke of an ancient holocaust." It complained of rats that "propagate undisturbed and grow fat and gigantic among the dung-piles and offal-dumps" and blamed "mammoth slaughter-houses, enormous rendering establishments, vast soap and candle factories, immense hog-pens and gigantic tanneries" for most of the vileness.

Cincinnati was not unique; most American cities had similar problems. The unsanitary conditions that festered, aggravated by overcrowding, made action imperative, for while the disease generated by filth usually began in the districts of the poor and struck them hardest, it knew no neighborhood boundaries. H. L. Mencken remembered a Baltimore that smelled "like a billion polecats" in which there raged "a great epidemic of typhoid fever every Summer, and a wave of malaria every Autumn, and more than a scattering of smallpox, especially among the colored folk in the alley, every Winter."

Bad health was the handmaiden of poverty in the industrial city. Overcrowded tenements, lack of sanitation facilities, and communal water supplies enabled disease to spread rapidly in slum districts. Newcomers to the city, especially those from rural areas, had to run a gauntlet of unfamiliar infections which took a large toll of lives. Long working hours, poor diet, and ignorance of even rudimentary health practices lowered resistance to illness. Public services were inadequate in most cities. In Washington, D. C., for example, there existed an area of indigent blacks, not far from the White House, known as "Murder Bay," where police and health officials watched Negro families pick their dinners out of leavings in garbage cans and dumps. Households were riddled with sickness; an 1891 report described "a one-room shanty in which beside a dead infant lay five adults and six children stricken with influenza." Mortality figures here were always twice as high as among whites, and in 1900 infant mortality still ranged as high as 317 per thousand. Occasionally the tenement alleys of poor black districts were washed out with barrels of lime, but the disinfectant did little more than prevent large-scale epidemics of typhoid and dysentery.

Every major city faced such conditions. New York had one of its neighborhoods dubbed "the lung block" because of the prevalence of tuberculosis. Garment workers gasped for breath in their sweatshops and the prayer of the tenement district became "air—give me air," as Robert Hunter reported:

"Luft—giebt mir luft." He spoke only Yiddish. The new country had given him the Plague before the language. For the sweatshop and the closet had made him weak; his weakened body could make no fight; the Plague had come in and fed swiftly. Still on through the winter he had worked over the machine in the sweatshop, infecting the garments he sewed—feverish, tired, fearful—to buy food and coal, to keep his "home" alive.

In Chicago observers cringed at "the presence of three hundred children in the Chicago Stock Yards, scores of them standing ankle-deep in blood and refuse, as they do the work of butchers. . . ." During plagues Los Angeles "vaccinated school children, quarantined infected homes, closed streets to the stricken, and placed the destitute ill in a pest house," but still the epidemics came.

As with housing, the attack on urban disease came from above. A procession of medical advances during the late nineteenth century aided the city's fight against pestilence. After Pasteur and Koch confirmed the germ theory in the 1870s, several diseases were brought under control in rapid succession: typhoid, leprosy, and malaria in 1880, tuberculosis in

1882, cholera in 1883, diptheria and tetanus in 1884, plague in 1894, and dysentery in 1898. While the public eagerly accepted the novel idea of little microorganisms causing particular diseases, some American doctors shunned the notion. As late as 1892 one prominent doctor stated flatly: "We may drink contaminated water, breathe impure air and live on a polluted soil without getting typhoid . . . or other contagious disease."

The bacteriological revolution gained support in cities for preventive medicine programs. Health boards were established in Massachusetts, Michigan, and Providence, Rhode Island. By 1890 the sanitary technique of cleansing particular areas had given way to the more sophisticated preventive approach of studying the personal factor in the spread of disease. New York City's Board of Health led the way by establishing the first modern diagnostic laboratory. During the 1890s municipal boards of health in other cities shifted their emphasis to diagnostic laboratory work.

Promoting these activities became the concern of a growing corps of doctors entering the new field of public health. Charles V. Chapin of Providence and Hermann Biggs of New York exemplify these medical reformers. Biggs joined the New York City Board of Health in 1892 and introduced diagnostic tests for cholera. The next year, as head of the new Bacteriological Division, he reported on preventive measures that could be taken to avoid the spread of tuberculosis. Circulars printed in several languages were distributed throughout the tenement districts. Biggs later experimented with diptheria vaccine, pioneered in the treatment of "white plague," and developed the Board's programs for checking the purity of milk supplies, attending to the needs of school children, and improving the efficiency of quarantines. So effective was Biggs's work in lowering mortality and disease figures that Tammany boss Charles F. Murphy declared public health a "hands-off" field for politics.

Officials like Hermann Biggs transformed the fledgling field of public health into a highly regarded and effective city service in a short period of time. They did it by abandoning the sanitarian method of sweeping out dead rats and dumping lime for the diagnostic approach of treating disease and preventing its transmission. Educational programs supplemented diagnostic work. Tenement residents received short pamphlets on such topics as infant feeding, transmission of infectious disease, and care of consumptives. City Health Boards concentrated on child care. Many created "Summer Corps" of physicians to visit children in the tenement districts. Nurses were specially trained for these summer visits and for work with children at school. Public health officials aided charities which sponsored "fresh air funds" to allow poor children a summer jaunt in the country. One report testified to the beneficial effects these vacations had on the health and outlook of the children:

As [the train] leaves the dingy town behind, and goes shrieking across green fields, and trees begin to appear, and pretty white houses, a change comes on. Faces brighten, eyes look interested, tongues loosen, and every window is full of heads; . . . for the children, begin a new life. Fresh air, plenty of food of the sweet country sort, green grass, trees, fruits, milk, and flowers everywhere.

The public health movement achieved more success than most campaigns against urban problems. Private doctors developed cures for disease, the city established a vehicle for their work, poor people gained a measure of protection, and the entire city benefited.

Crime also plagued the industrial city. Like disease it threatened the welfare of all citizens but preyed most heavily on the poor. The lower class, in fact, suffered double jeopardy as crime rates increased. The most victimized of all citizens, they were also denounced as the source of criminal behavior.

The presence of poor people has always created tension in cities. People are afraid of the poor; they clutch their purses or wallets, walk a little faster, and sidestep them whenever possible. On a larger scale, the presence of a sizable underclass in any city produced social frictions which often ignited into riots and other forms of violence. The fear generated by the poor was to some extent valid. It was true that the streets of slum districts were less safe than those of fashionable areas. Tenement life spawned more thieves, murderers, and rapists than did more genteel surroundings, and the ghetto harbored more desperate men than any other part of the city. Moveover, the mass influx of newcomers to the city raised tensions higher than ever before and helped force municipalities to create professional police departments.

But the issue was not so simple or clear-cut. While the lower class was certainly not responsible for all urban crime, it was blamed for most of it. Then as now, the legal system exacted its harshest toll from those least able to defend themselves. Petty criminals were dealt with sternly while higher and more subtle acts of criminality like embezzlement or swindling, usually indulged in by the middle and upper classes, received less severe punishment. Much lower-class crime could be seen as the last acts of desperate men; city life imposed hardships upon the poor which drove some to criminal behavior. Finally, the vast majority of poor people were not criminals and were in fact the principal victims of urban crime.

The ghetto riots of the 1960s and the histrionics of the 1970s over "crime in the streets" have prompted historians to take their first systematic look at the incidence of crime in American cities. Their findings reveal that current fears about crime have deep roots in the past. Cities have always been volatile places, to which the emerging immigrant slums merely added a new dimension of social violence. As early as the 1830s, in the older cities on the Atlantic Coast, nativist groups beat and clubbed incoming Irishmen. Ethnic and religious conflicts flared like brush fires; between 1830 and 1860 urban riots were a common spectacle. Gangs roamed the streets with torches, windows were shattered and houses set afire, drunken brawls broke out, and blood poured. In this, probably the worst period of urban violence, over thirty-five major riots occurred, Baltimore leading with twelve; Philadelphia had eleven, New York eight, and Boston four. Northeastern cities were hit hardest because they were older and affected first by immigration, but the riots soon spread to midwestern cities like Cincinnati, which had four. Although nativist-immigrant clashes were the major source of violence, rioting also erupted over "labor disputes, election outcomes, abolitionist activity, anti-Catholic and Negro sentiment, and competing volunteer firemen's units engaging in fierce (and usually drunken) scuffles."

By the 1850s rioting and criminal activity had become part of every city's social fabric. That this date coincides with the onset of industrialization is no accident. By then the pace of economic and population growth had already created a turmoil of social dislocation upon which crime and urban violence fed. Here as elsewhere city governments, with their limited philosophies of responsibility, were simply not prepared for the onslaught that followed. James W. Gerard, a New York lawyer, surveyed the criminal scene of the 1850s in his pamphlet *London and New York: Their Crime and Police*. His findings have a familiar ring:

Look any and *every* day in the week, at your morning paper, and see what a black record of crime has been committed in your public streets the day and the night before, what *stabbings*, what shootings, what knocking down, what assaults by slung shots and otherwise: insults to women and other disgusting details of violence! . . . Look also at our sister city of Philadelphia, which used to be called the city of brotherly love, from the quiet of its streets, and the order and propriety of its population. And what has Philadelphia been for the last ten years? Misrule and riot have reigned there, to the defiance of its magistrates, and have made its streets hideous. Assaults, and shootings, and murders. . . . Look at Baltimore, and what scenes have been presented there for the last six months? Violence of the most savage kind, so frequent, so daring, and by such powerful gangs, as to overawe, openly and publicly, the magistrate and police of the city; and the citizens, to protect themselves go armed; and if they are compelled to go out at night, do so with a fair chance of dismal encounter.

Even after earlier rioting had forced most cities into supporting full-time police forces in the 1850s, there followed tumultuous draft riots in the 1860s. The new policemen did not halt or even control the insurgence of crime. Bostonians wailed that "in the North End each night dozens of spectators, 'pickpockets,' 'petty knucks,' and 'females with vermillion cheeks' gathered in fetid rooms to make bets on the contestants in rat pits and dogfights." During the depression-riddled 1870s street violence escalated again. The railroad strike of 1877—the first on a national scale—created havoc in every major city. Uprisings in Pittsburgh and Baltimore featured the type of rioting, burning, and looting that later befell Detroit, Newark, and Washington. It is ironic that some of the architectural gems of the Gilded Age were armories built to house the National Guard, a new state militia formed to help cities quell lower-class unrest.

Spectacular incidents like the Haymarket Affair in Chicago (1886) whipped up popular fears over the threat of anarchy. Blame for the rising tenor of violence was laid squarely on the invasion of foreigners with their alien ideas. Lower-class districts did indeed contribute a disproportionate number of criminals to the prisons, but that had little to do with the presence of foreign ideologies. Once workers organized to challenge the inequities of the industrial system, some violence was bound to result. Nor could "strange ideas" account for the criminal activity which was a natural by-product of slum life. It was no accident that the worst parts of the city—"Murderer's Row," "Poverty Lane," the "Tenderloin" —spawned the worst crime. New York, Chicago, Boston, Philadelphia, Pittsburgh, Buffalo, Detroit, Cleveland, St. Louis, and San Francisco all gained notoriety as centers of crime. When during the 1880s the number of prison inmates rose by 50 percent, the *Chicago Tribune* was able to show why: In 1881 the increase in murders and homicides was 1,266, or 24.7 per million people. That figure leaped to 4,290 in 1890 (68.5 per million) and then 7,840 (107.2 per million) in 1898. These statistics compared unfavorably with other industrial nations like England and Germany which had declining homicide rates. As Arthur Schlesinger has pointed out, "students of the subject were agreed in placing the fundamental blame on unhealthy urban growth, unrestricted immigration, the saloon, and the maladjusted Negro." Others argued that the lawlessness of the frontier had never really died in America but had merely shifted its locus to the city.

Organized crime also appeared in the industrial city. In Chicago, Michael Cassius McDonald put together an organization during the 1870s. Later syndicates under Mont Tennes, James O'Leary, and Johnny Rogers absorbed immigrants, particularly Italians looking for employment. "The ethnic cohesion and group loyalty exhibited by the Italian criminal element in its struggle to dominate Chicago's organized crime formed a more significant factor than the Sicilian origin of some gangsters," wrote Humbert Nelli. "The 'Southern' background of most of the city's Italians included a deep loyalty to clan traditions held to be sacred from 'outside interference.' . . . these traditions and connections provided a ready-made nucleus for criminal gangs in the new world and ensured a fierce partisanship toward the group's laws and rituals rather than to 'outside' rules and regulations."

Although organized gangs menaced the city (and did considerable damage to each other), they offered some benefits to the immigrant poor. The close clan connections in the mob were often the only such ties available to newcomers. Like a political machine, the organization provided an avenue of social and economic mobility for people who lacked access to more legitimate channels.* In that sense organized crime became still another part of the social overhead costs paid by the industrial city for its neglect of the immigrant poor.

Young people often followed their elders into criminal organizations. Pushed out of overcrowded apartments and alienated by schools, city boys developed a street life all their own. They found jobs as telegraph boys, shoeshine boys, errand and delivery boys, fruit peddlers, and newsboys. Some went about their duties with iron discipline before and after school, but others fell into gangs which prowled the streets, fought one another, and amused themselves with acts of vandalism and petty larceny. In the slums, the doorway to crime and dissipation yawned wide and inviting. John Spargo found that the typical telegraph boy

smokes, drinks, gambles, and, very often, patronizes the lowest class of cheap brothels. In answering calls from houses of ill-repute messengers cannot avoid being witnesses of scenes of licentiousness more or less frequently. By presents of money, fruit, candy, cigarettes, and even liquor, the women make friends of the boys, who quickly learn all the foul slang of the brothels. The conversation of a group of messengers in such a district will often reveal the most astounding intimacy with the grossest things of the underworld. . . .

* See Chapter 10.

The drinking, smoking, and gambling of street gangs were offensive, but not all that dangerous. But some gangs developed into packs of pickpockets and thieves and later organized more sophisticated burglary operations. The plight of these young men moved civic-minded people—especially women—to establish Protective Associations to work for delinquency prevention. Citizens feared the street gangs as much as the hardened criminal, yet recoiled in disgust and sympathy upon reading accounts like the following one from Chicago:

It even became the common thing for men wanting the boys for homosexual practices to come to the news-alley to get them. Many boys added greatly to their income in this way as well as securing better sleeping quarters for the night. Many of these boys were not even ten or twelve years old.

The street life of boys outraged middle-class mores and spurred reformers to find ways of saving the young from corrupting influences. Unfortunately, those concerned with juvenile delinquency too often treated its symptoms rather than its causes. Efforts to clean up street life had little lasting effect.

If the corruption of boys disturbed middle-class sensibilities, the fate of young girls appalled them. Prostitution thrived in lower-class districts. Some girls worked the brothels and others walked the streets; in both cases, most of the recruits came from the ranks of the poor. Working-class mothers struggling to maintain family respectability fought desperately to protect their daughters from "going bad." The temptation was a strong one where life was lived so close to the margin. It is impossible to compile reliable data on how many women and girls resorted to prostitution. In any given city, full-time practitioners were joined by working girls who supplemented their pitiful incomes by part-time street-walking. David Graham Phillips depicted their plight well in *Susan Lenox:*

She knew these girls were either supporting themselves by prostitution or were held up by their families. . . . If to live decently in New York took an income of fifteen dollars a week, what did it matter whether one got five or ten or twelve? Any wages below fifteen meant a steady downward drag—meant exposure to the dirt and poison of poverty tenements—meant the steady decline of the power of resistance, the steady oozing away of self-respect, of the courage and hope that give the power to rise. To have less than the fifteen dollars absolutely necessary for decent surroundings, decent clothing, decent food—that meant one was drowning. What matter whether . . . the waters of destruction were twenty feet deep or twenty thousand?

For many girls the line between prostitution and being "taken care of" by men friends was thin and easily crossed; no such ambiguities troubled those who worked the brothels. Houses of prostitution ranged from bordellos of luxury and style to sordid back-alley dives. Owned by men and women of both races, the houses operated through payoffs to neighborhood policemen and were often patronized by the very men who publicly condemned their existence. Although Americans liked to believe that girls were seduced or "trafficked" into the brothels, most probably came of their own free will. According to Mrs. Charles Lowell, a longtime foe of prostitution:

The immoral women in the houses directly tempt young girls to join them. They also indirectly present the strongest temptations, for they are the only women who have good food, fine clothes, and an easy life in these houses. A girl who is earning $2 or $3 a week by standing behind a counter, running errands 10 hours a day (and 14 or 15 hours at what is called the 'holiday season') cannot but compare her own life with that of one of these girls, who seems to have all she wants and to do nothing to earn it.

Yet no matter how inviting the prospect looked, prostitution was but another trap imprisoning lower-class women in a role of subservience and degradation from which few escaped.

Most brothels, along with gambling and other "pleasure" joints, were confined to that part of the industrial city known as the vice district.* New York's "Tenderloin," Chicago's "Levee," and San Francisco's "Barbary Coast" flourished in part because many people believed that if vice could not be entirely suppressed, the next best solution was to restrict it to one area. The vice district, with its brothels, saloons, pool halls, cabarets, gambling dens, and dance halls, was the only section of town that knew no racial or ethnic bounds. As William Tuttle has observed, that fact in itself disturbed middle-class citizens:

Guides to Chicago's night life boasted of the city's " 'black-and-tan' cabarets," where "promiscuous dancing and the intermingling of the races may be observed . . . freely." Reformers, on the other hand, castigated these biracial houses of amusement, bemoaning that "the patrons were negroes and whites who danced together in a most immoral way."

All these activities were presided over by colorful criminal bosses like "Teenan" Jones, "Red Dick" Wilson, "Yellow Bill" Bass, "Mexican Frank," "Billy" Lewis, and Isadore Levin.

Those who observe the deserted nocturnal caverns of today's down-

* See Chapter 10.

towns may mourn the passing of vice districts. They did provide color and fascination to the drab face of the industrial city. But while the gaiety of night life excited visiting pleasure-seekers, it carried a different message for inhabitants of the district. Those who longed for family stability and social respect found little joy in activities that threatened their children and offended their sense of decency. Others made their living from some angle of the pleasure business. For one, the vice district was a fact of life; for the other, it was a way of life.

Gaiety Amidst the Gloom

The poor were no less partial to pleasure than other classes; it was only that they had less time and money for it. If their amusements seemed simple or mundane to more refined tastes, they were enjoyed with great gusto by those for whom rollicking offered a rare escape from routine.

The immigrant lodge provided a center for many festive occasions. Originally established to aid newcomers, the lodges operated as mutual aid societies furnishing money, insurance, and other services in times of unemployment, sickness, old age, and death. In the process the society's headquarters also become a gathering spot for card playing, chess, newspaper reading, drinking, or just chatting. Dances and parties enlivened special occasions and during the holidays the benefit society usually aided the local church or synagogue. On those festive days the merrymaking sometimes spilled into the streets with songs or carnivals or parades in honor of a devoted saint or the Madonna, all embellished with costumes and decorations of the Old Country.

For many lower-class people, the amusement park became a special mecca of pleasure. Trolley cars carried them by the hundreds to Coney Island, Revere Beach, Riverside, or the countless Paradise Parks to enjoy the rides, shooting galleries, fun houses, games of chance, dance floors, restaurants, and beer gardens. Whole families escaped the city on a day's excursion to swim in the ocean or dip in the pool. "Trolley parks," with their colored lights, noisy excitement, and music shows existed on the outskirts of many large and small cities. The crowds who flocked to the amusement parks also enjoyed new taste treats like soft drinks and chewing gum. Ginger beers, carbonated water, and a multitude of new syrups helped make the soda fountain a national institution. A night out also called for a new cigar or fresh plug of chewing tobacco, both of which grew more popular as the cost of manufactured tobacco products declined.

Sporting events also drew enthusiastic followings. Working men filled the stands of the new baseball teams like their middle-class brethren, but their hearts belonged more to the boxing ring than to the diamond. Indeed, interest in boxing, and the betting that accompanied it, became a national mania by century's end. In 1897 Australian Robert Fitzsimmons took the heavyweight crown away from "Gentleman Jim" Corbett in Carson City, Nevada. Two years later, James J. Jeffries won the championship and defended his title against Fitzsimmons, Corbett, and a covey of other heavyweights until he retired in 1905. While the title was vacant, a black fighter named Jack Johnson rose to prominence. The boxing world, appalled that a Negro might become world champion, lured Jeffries out of retirement as the only remaining "white hope." The bout took place in Reno, Nevada, in 1910, and Johnson pummeled Jeffries back into retirement. So great was interest in the fight that the *New York Tribune* gave it six columns on the front page.

Theater, too, provided enjoyment to lower-class audiences. A peculiar hybrid of entertainment emerged from the urban arena with its varied tastes and cultures. During the 1880s the touring minstrel shows gave way to vaudeville with its crude mélange of dancing, songs, and comedy. By the turn of the century, vaudeville enjoyed immense popularity among ethnic audiences and also offered opportunities for talented immigrant children to advance in show business. Vaudeville routines thrived on ethnic material. Here is an excerpt from a bit by Weber and Fields, two of vaudeville's most popular comics:

"The captain is my ideal of a hero," Uneida told her father.

"A hero! Is dot a business? A tailor is a business, a shoemaker is a business, but a hero? Better you should marry a bookkeeper," Warfield exclaimed.

"A bookkeeper? I suppose you think the pen is mightier than the sword," the girl sneered.

"You bet you my life," said Papa Cohenski. "Could you sign checks with a sword?"

For a time it appeared that the cabaret might rival the popularity of vaudeville among the lower class. Dismissing the cabaret as "that latest importation from the slums of Europe," one critic conceded that "From the Cafe Boulevard on the South, to the Campus restaurant on the North, from the 'Morgue' on the West to Joe Blaney's riverfront cafe on the East, the cabaret is the rage." Cabarets sprung up like mushrooms in the poor districts, offering food, cheap wine, and entertainment.

Some ethnic groups developed their own brand of theater. Like vaudeville, ethnic theater provided both entertainment and an outlet for ambitious immigrant writers and actors. Of the many versions that appeared, none approached the Yiddish theater in quality or popularity. Hutchins Hapgood, in his classic work *The Spirit of the Ghetto* (1902), captured the vibrant mood of Yiddish theater life:

In the three Yiddish theaters on the Bowery is expressed the world of the Ghetto—that New York City of Russian Jews, large, complex, with a full life and civilization. In the midst of the frivolous Bowery, devoted to tinsel variety shows, "dive" music halls, fake museums, trival amusement booths of all sorts, cheap lodging houses, ten-cent shops and Irish-American tough saloons, the theaters of the chosen people alone present the serious as well as the trivial interests of an entire community. Into these three buildings crowd the Jews of all the Ghetto classes—the sweat-shop woman with her baby, the day-laborer, the small Hester street shopkeeper, the Russian–Jewish anarchist and socialist, the Ghetto rabbi and scholar, the poet, the journalist. The poor and ignorant are in the great majority, but the learned, the intellectual and the progressive are also represented, and here, as elsewhere, exert a more than numerically proportionate influence on the character of the theatrical productions, which, nevertheless, remain essentially popular. The socialists and the literati create the demand that forces into the mass of vaudeville, light opera, historical and melodramatic plays a more serious art element, a simple transcript from life or the theatric presentation of a Ghetto problem. But this more serious element is so saturated with the simple manners, humor and patterns of the life of the poor Jew, that it is seldom above the heartfelt understanding of the crowd.

The lower class also found enjoyment and a bond of communal feeling in newspapers. Although foreign-language presses offered an ethnic slant on national and international affairs with particular attention to the mother country, many readers preferred the local coverage. Organizational meetings, gossip, marriages, births, and deaths all furnished grist for the neighborhood's conversation mill. In the Italian community, for instance, *Il Progresso Italo-Americano* reached thousands of immigrants who craved a feeling of community (at least in print) and the latest news from the homeland. While *Il Progresso* informed a large national audience, smaller papers filled in the local news. In Chicago, according to Humbert Nelli, the local *L'Italia* had 38,000 subscribers in 1921 compared to 111,000 for *Il Progresso*.

Besides keeping immigrants informed about community affairs, the local press also served as an instrument of assimilation. Nelli recounted that Italian papers admonished their readers to act like "Americans" by keeping their children in school, not drinking excessively, and staying clean. Nursing babies on the streets was declared a "shameful spectacle" and "not a nice thing to do" because it gave Americans "another point on which to jeer at Italians." The nursing question raised such a hue and cry that *L'Italia* on August 4, 1894 pleaded, "When will Italian parents stop making such a disgraceful show of themselves for American amusement and condemnation?"

The large Jewish population in New York City supported perhaps the liveliest immigrant press in America. The massive influx of immigrants, coupled with the lowered cost of newsprint in the 1890s, spawned a proliferation of newspapers. Earlier weeklies with a socialist or radical bent had attracted a wide audience; the Yiddish daily press prospered by reporting on civic and labor affairs and fanning the debate on radical reform. The first Jewish daily, the *Tageblatt (Jewish Daily News)*, appeared in 1885. Later the *Taglicher Herold (Daily Herald)*, formed in 1891, merged into the *Varheit (Truth)* which in turn merged with *Tag (The Day)*. A third liberal trade-union daily, the *Vorwarts (Forward)*, grew to become the largest foreign-language paper in the English-speaking world. In addition, the Lower East Side also gave birth to countless other publications devoted to literature, humor, politics, labor, *Landsmannschaften,** Zionism, and cultural pursuits.

The *Vorwarts* achieved its mass appeal through the genius and leadership of Abraham Cahan, who edited the paper from 1902 until his death in 1951. No immigrant editor rivaled Cahan's influence or talent. Before joining *Vorwarts,* he wrote editorals for the socialist *Workmen's Advocate* and contributed articles to the *Sun,* the *World, Century,* and *Forum.* His first novel, *Yekl, a Tale of the Ghetto* (1896), and a collection of stories (1898) received critical acclaim but brought Cahan little income. In 1917 he published his masterpiece, *The Rise of David Levinsky.***

Cahan's literary and journalistic talents caught the eye of Lincoln Steffens, then city editor of the *Commercial Advertiser.* In 1897 Steffens hired Cahan as police reporter for the paper. From that experience, which included tutelage from Jacob Riis, Cahan gained exposure to the city as a whole. After joining *Vorwarts,* he transformed it from a local journal with a circulation of about 5,000 to a modern newspaper with a national following of more than 250,000 readers. Cahan attracted readers by concentrating on human-interest stories. The hopes and fears, foibles and insecurities of individuals and families were staples of the foreign-language press, but none rivaled Cahan's ability to move, amuse, and inform his readers. *Vorwarts* featured a unique letter-to-the-

---

* *Landsmannschaften* were fraternal societies formed by immigrants from the same part of Europe.
** See Chapter 6.

editor column ("Bintel Brief") which, as the following excerpts show, reveal much about both the writers and the importance they attached to the newspaper:

My little girl wants to pierce her ears for earrings. She says all the girls here have pierced ears, but my husband says no, that in America you do not pierce ears any more, but the girl is crying, and tell my husband in the letter what is best to do.

My son is against my marriage, but I have left my second husband and I am getting a divorce. My son reads the *Vorwarts*, and I plead with him to forgive me. I am lonely as a stone.

Is it a sin to use face powder? Shouldn't a girl look beautiful? My father does not want me to wear face powder. Is it a sin?

My husband reads the *Vorwarts*, but where does he read it? In the barbershop where he goes all the time with those other card players. Let him see this letter.

The writer of the last letter might well have been grateful that her husband dallied at the barbershop instead of the saloon, which was the premier social center for working-class men. To its mahogany bar, wooden tables, and sawdust-littered floor they came to gulp steins of beer, help themselves to the free lunch, joke with their friends, play cards, sing boisterous and sentimental songs, read newspapers, and argue politics, unionism, and the merits of the city's ball teams. Since the district or ward boss often made his headquarters in the saloon, it was also the place for seeking out jobs or favors. The saloon was above all a man's world, a haven from the grind of work, domestic tribulations, and the day's accumulation of tensions and anxieties. It offered pleasure, escape, and fellowship to men hungry for them.*

Civic reformers despised the saloon and were alarmed that working men spent so much of their time there. In their eyes the saloon was not a social center, but a den of corruption which housed nearly all the evils of urban society: the political boss, the prostitute, the gambler, the social revolutionary, the criminal, and the drunkard. Women reformers especially deplored its effects upon family life and laid every vice at its doorstep.

The concern over drink had a long history among American reformers, who for decades had regarded alcohol as the root of every social malady. During the late nineteenth century, this view gained renewed popu-

---

* It should be noted that lower-class women had no comparable institution to ameliorate the drudgery of their lives. Most saloons did not formally exclude women; it was rather social propriety that kept them away. Any woman found drinking with men in a saloon was assumed to be "of low repute."

larity as an explanation for a whole network of urban ills. In 1907 *McClure's* magazine found the source of a crime wave infesting Chicago, San Francisco, and Pittsburgh in "a population of hundreds of thousands of rough and unrestrained male laborers, plied, with all possible energy and ingenuity, with alcoholic liquor," who could "be counted on, with the certainty of a chemical experiment, for one reaction—violent and fatal crime. . . ." As the crusade against alcohol gained momentum, it singled out the saloon as its chief target. The Anti-Saloon League, founded in 1895, came ultimately to dominate the drive for prohibition.

The visibility of saloons made them an inviting target. Reformers loved to draw up maps comparing the large number of bars in a tenement district to the relatively few churches there. In this respect the maps were accurate: a 1905 survey revealed that Chicago had as many saloons as it did grocery stores, meat markets, and dry-goods stores combined. Houston had one saloon for every 298 persons, and San Francisco one for every 218 citizens.

But as often happened in reform crusades (and perhaps particularly in the antisaloon drive), well-intentioned people looked at the problem from the outside. For if saloons did corrupt young boys and dissipate their fathers (and that point remains controversial), they still served important social functions to which most reformers were blind. The saloon thrived because it fulfilled human needs that could not find other satisfactory outlets in the industrial city. It was more than a sociable watering-hole:

For slum residents, especially in immigrant ghetto and tenement, the neighborhood saloons were inevitably more attractive than their own overcrowded, dirty, noisy, ugly, poorly lighted and ventilated flats. For many immigrants their new homes in America were merely places to sleep and eat—life moved out of the flats into the streets and saloons.

Every neighborhood saloon, be it "Al's," "Tom and Mick's," "The Club," or "The Poor Man's Retreat," had its own atmosphere and peculiar clientele. Behind its swinging doors tensions dissolved into gaiety and loud camaraderie. Sometimes drink inflamed tempers into brawls or converted despondency into a sullen violence that exploded at home. The saloon crowd was a rough one, unfit for the society of the morally squeamish. No other institution better reflected the emotions of working-class men or their hunger for relief from the drab monotony of their lives. No other issue divided the lower and middle classes so bitterly as the controversy over the saloon. By 1900 it had become a potent political symbol for many of the social cleavages that infested the industrial city.

CHAPTER 10

The Business of Politics: Government in the Industrial City

> Without the slightest exaggeration we may assert that, with very few exceptions, the city governments of the United States are the worst in Christendom—the most expensive, the most inefficient, and the most corrupt. No one who has any considerable knowledge of our own country and of other countries can deny this. . . . The difference between foreign cities and ours is that all these well-ordered cities . . . accept this principle—that cities are corporations and not political bodies; that they are not concerned with matters of national policy; that national parties as such have nothing whatever to do with city questions. . . .
>
> —ANDREW D. WHITE
> *The Government of American Cities* (1890)

EVERYBODY KNOWS THAT industrial cities were run by bosses and their political machines. Probably most people share the same image of the boss as that held at the turn of the century: a florid heavy-set Irishman with a colorful nickname who, dressed in a business suit, made his headquarters in the back room of a downtown saloon. From there he ruled his ward or the entire city, receiving at a table the steady stream of supplicants for jobs, favors, or deals. Chomping thoughtfully on a fat cigar, the boss was a man of few words who issued directives to his lieutenants in terse sentences, meaningful grunts, or a simple wave of his hand. Some portray him as a cold dictator with a heart of stone; others see him as a kindly soul whose gruff exterior concealed a wellspring of humanitarianism. Few question his absolute authority over his realm.

Like most stereotypes, that of the political boss contains enough truth to seem plausible and enough falsehood to be misleading. In truth, urban bosses were no less varied than members of any other profession.

Although many did share some common characteristics, it is impossible to construct a composite of the political boss that is accurate or meaningful. They came in all sizes, shapes, and types. Their origins, habits, styles, and techniques differed greatly, as did the circumstances in which they operated.

Unlike zoologists, historians tend to use generic labels like "machine" and "boss" without bothering to define exactly what they mean. In fact, there were as many different kinds of machines as there were different types of bosses.* They operated on many levels and served a wide range of functions. In most cases their nature and purposes depended upon the unique conditions of the city in which they arose. To understand these differences, one must know something about a less glamorous subject: the origins and development of American municipal government.

The City as Corporation

We often forget that as a legal entity the city is but another form of corporation, although the municipal charter has a very different history from its business counterpart. During the nineteenth century private corporations gained increasing immunity from interference by the state while municipal corporations grew more subservient to state legislatures. The significance of these divergent paths requires a brief glimpse into the legal antecedents of American cities.

Frank J. Goodnow, an early authority on municipal government, wrote in 1904, "The term 'city' has two meanings: the one sociological, the other legal or political." The first meaning defined the city as "an aggregation of people living within a comparatively small area"; the second implied that "the city constitutes a political unity—that it has specific political duties to perform, and for that purpose is endowed by the state with more or less definite legal powers." Early American cities derived their legal authority from England. Where English cities (or boroughs) secured charters from the crown, Americans obtained theirs from the provincial governor.

The English inheritance extended to government as well. Colonial municipalities usually had a common council composed of recorder, aldermen, councilmen (elected by qualified voters), and mayor (appointed by the colonial governor). In most cases, the mayor lacked either veto or appointing power but did exercise some judicial and police

---

* By this we mean that there were state, county, city, and ward machines. Not only were the types different from one another, but machines of the same type differed from each other as well.

authority. The council could enact local legislation so long as it did not conflict with English or colonial law. The Revolution left this system mostly intact, except that state legislatures replaced provincial governors as the source for granting municipal charters.

There were in fact few municipal corporations in America prior to 1820. As long as cities remained relatively small, the form found little favor. New England relied upon the township as a form of local government while the southern and mid-Atlantic states favored the county or some combination of town and county. Since these forms provided considerable freedom of government, there was little reason to seek a municipal charter until growth swamped the ability of townships to respond to demands for more services. Of the ten largest American cities in 1890, only four—New York, Philadelphia, Baltimore, and New Orleans—possessed municipal charters in 1820.

These early municipalities had few powers beyond judicial and police authority. Limited taxing power prevented them from providing what later came to be regarded as essential services. Few cities supplied water to their inhabitants, and fewer still undertook charitable or educational work. Until the nineteenth century municipal corporations remained little more than organizations serving a narrow range of local needs. Rarely did their functions extend beyond judicial and police work to social services.

Prior to the Civil War, two important and ultimately conflicting developments occurred. The nation's steady growth created many new cities and increased the size of old ones. Growth compelled cities to regularize and professionalize services formerly left to individuals or volunteer groups. These added responsibilities required changes in government which led many cities to seek municipal charters. At the same time, the federal Constitution had become so popular that many Americans wished to incorporate its principles into state constitutions. As that practice spread, legislatures in turn extended it to municipal charters. Efforts were made to graft the doctrine of separation of powers onto city governments. Often the common council was replaced by a bicameral council. The mayor received the veto power and was elected rather than appointed. In effect, he was made to resemble a governor or president while the common council paralleled the state legislature and national congress.

As J. Allen Smith observed in 1907, these changes "may be attributed to the influence of the Constitution rather than to any intelligent and carefully planned effort to improve the machinery of municipal government." Whatever the defects in the old council system, the new arrangement did not improve upon it. As cities expanded, so did complaints about the inefficiency of their operations. By 1850 cities of every size were groping for new ways to administer their enlarged responsibilities.

By 1850, too, important changes in the structure of national politics had occurred. The major parties, their strength and cohesion increasingly sapped by the sectional controversy, fastened upon the cities as a resource for repairing their weakened state (and national) organizations. Municipalities offered several enticements to state political chieftains. They possessed large numbers of voters in a compact area, which meant they could be organized with relative ease. More important, fast-growing cities had both an abundance of needs and the sources of wealth to pay for them. By extending the state's role in municipal government, the parties could seize a lucrative share of the action for their own purposes. Smith depicted the prospect in acid tones:

The city offered a rich and tempting field for exploitation. It had offices, a large revenue, spent vast sums in public improvements, let valuable contracts of various kinds and had certain needs for water, light, rapid transit, etc., which could be made the pretext for granting franchises and other privileges on such terms as would insure large profits to the grantees at the expense of the general public. That the political machine in control of the state government should have yielded to the temptation to make a selfish use of its powers in this direction, is only what might have been expected.

Thus, on one side, city dwellers clamored for more efficient government; while on the other, state party leaders sought to feed their anemic organizations with the plasma of municipal domination. The historic prejudice of rural folk against the city complicated matters even further. In an agrarian society, cities were widely regarded as dens of sin and corruption which nourished vice, bad habits, and dangerous ideas. Even during the early industrial era, the rise of cities as centers of wealth and power inflamed these dark suspicions. When Josiah Strong asserted, "It is the city where wealth is massed; and here are the tangible evidences of it piled many stories high. Here the sway of Mammon is widest, and his worship the most constant and eager," he was but echoing an old complaint of rural America.

Farm families could not prevent their children from running off to the city in search of better prospects, and the tale of a departed son or daughter sure to "go wrong" became a familiar household sorrow. Nor could they change the wicked ways of the city. They had but one recourse to the urban menace: politics. Rural representatives dominated most state legislatures, and through them could exert great influence in governing cities. That influence was not apt to be either sympathetic or well-informed.

These diverse forces produced changes in urban government which were to shape the destiny of the industrial city. Although the scenario varied in detail from place to place, the overall pattern was a relentless extension of state control over municipalities.

This trend marked a significant departure from past practices and ultimately set the course of municipal corporations on a different track from that of private corporations. Prior to 1850 state legislatures had interfered little in municipal affairs. The courts tended to sustain the view expressed by the New York Supreme Court in *Mayor* v. *Ordrenan* that legislatures rarely if ever intervened in the internal affairs of a corporation without the latter's consent. So long as legislatures subscribed to this viewpoint, cities were free to manage their business like any other corporation.

But this freedom existed wholly at the state's pleasure; nothing in the Constitution granted any inherent right of local government. In effect, this meant that municipalities were entirely the creatures of their state legislature which, in the words of Frank Goodnow, had "absolute legal right to regulate municipal affairs as it sees fit." Municipal charters were, after all, mere legal statutes subject to revision like any other statute. The legislature could create, repeal, or amend charters in any way it chose and could even force incorporation upon the people of a locality against their wishes.

Legal theory and court decisions upheld the legislatures' authority in a related realm by insisting that the city possessed no powers not enumerated in its charter.* Legislatures could of course grant broad powers to a city, but virtually none did so. The typical municipal charter, according to Edward C. Banfield and James Q. Wilson, "fixes the form of its organization, lists the powers that it may exercise, and prescribes the manner in which it may exercise them." That basic

---

* The force of this point may be seen in the following extract from one of the foremost legal authorities on the subject, Judge John F. Dillon:

"It is a general and undisputed proposition of law that a municipal corporation possesses and can exercise the following powers, and no others. First, those granted in express words; second, those necessarily or fairly implied in or incident to the powers expressly granted; third, those essential to the accomplishments of the declared objects and purposes of the corporation—not simply convenient, but indispensable. Any fair reasonable doubt concerning the existence of power is resolved by the courts against the corporation and the power is denied."

John F. Dillon, *Commentaries on the Law of Municipal Corporations* (Boston, 1911), I, 448.

condition remains unchanged to this day. In 1923 the United States
Supreme Court, in *Trenton* v. *New Jersey,* delivered a sweeping opinion
on the issue:

The city is a political subdivision of the state, created as a convenient
agency for the exercise of such of the governmental powers of the state as
may be entrusted to it. . . . the state may withold, grant, or withdraw powers
and privileges as it sees fit. . . . In the absence of state constitutional provisions safeguarding it to them, municipalities have no inherent right of
self-government which is beyond the legislative control of the state.*

Around 1850 state legislatures began to exercise this control by installing in several cities a system of government based upon independent
departments or boards which administered particular functions such as
education, police, water, utilities, and maintenance. In some cases,
board members were appointed by the state; in others, they were appointed by the mayor or elected to the position. In every instance the
boards were independent of both the city council and the mayor, even
when he had the power to appoint. Within a decade, most major
American cities adopted some version of the board system which
stripped city councils of their administrative functions and confined
them to legislative duties.

For most cities separation of powers meant decentralization run
rampant. It kept power from accumulating in one place by scattering
it across a maze of officials and boards. City·fathers found their capacity
to govern eroded on every side. The legislative function had been
separated from the administrative and the latter parceled out among
the mayor, city officials, and diverse boards. Since the boards operated
independently of both the city council and each other, the left hand
seldom knew what the right hand was doing. Through this administrative morass wandered the mayor, a creature endowed with varying
powers ranging from the veto to the appointive. And above the confusion
loomed the state legislature, which might rearrange the whole structure
at any time.

A few examples illustrate the legislature's protean role in municipal
affairs. In 1886 the New York legislature passed 681 bills, 280 of which
bore directly on "the affairs of some particular county, city, village, or
town, specifically and expressly named." Cleveland discovered in 1911

---

* The contrast between American and European cities is striking here. Goodnow
observed that "The Anglo-American local corporation may do only those things which
the legislature of the state says plainly it may do; the European local corporation may
do everything which the legislature of the state has not plainly forbidden it to do."
Frank J. Goodnow, *City Government in the United States* (New York, 1904), 76.

that its council lacked authority to perform such functions as controlling the subsurface of public highways as a means for obtaining revenue; providing public lectures and entertainments; requiring the isolation of tuberculosis patients; regulating the architectural appearance of buildings fronting upon public highways; banishing dogs, chickens, and other noise-making animals from the city; or manufacturing ice for charitable distribution.

When the Pennsylvania legislature decided that Philadelphia required a new city hall, it commissioned buildings denounced by one critic as "projected upon a scale of magnificence better suited for the capitol of an empire than the municipal buildings of a debt-burdened city" and then compelled the city to pay for them. State party leaders routinely expanded their patronage rolls by adding new positions to the city's payrolls, and retiring state politicians often found rewarding positions upon specially created bureaus or commissions which demanded little of their time.

Legislators could punish as well as reward. They wielded authority not only over the city's basic services, such as transportation and utilities, but over its taxing power and thus its revenues as well. More than once legislatures stripped local officials of their authority. In the notorious "ripper" bills of 1901, the Pennsylvania legislature removed the mayor of Pittsburgh from office and directed the governor to appoint his successor for the next two years. A legislative act placed the Boston police under state control in 1885.

In short, municipalities lacked any semblance of real self-government. Their citizens could not determine their own taxation rates, the uses to which their moneys would be put, their election procedures, the educational system, public works priorities, or other basic functions. Every new action required a special enabling act by the legislature, whether it be a new sewer or a restriction upon billboards. The city could not borrow money or raise taxes or feed beggars without applying to the legislature.

To a large extent, city hall had become more an agent of the state than a servant of local interests. Its officers assessed and collected taxes for the state as well as the municipality. In several areas—notably election laws, educational standards, health, safety, and welfare—the state retained the power to impose uniform legislation upon the whole of its population. But in practice, the boundary line between legitimate and dubious state intervention in municipal affairs was difficult to draw. State politicians thrived upon this shadow realm by passing special legislation in the guise of general acts.

Between 1870 and 1920 efforts to restore "home rule" to cities took several forms. Some cities tried to centralize responsibility by strengthening the authority of the mayor, particularly by giving him absolute power to appoint and remove most higher municipal officers. Brooklyn pioneered in this scheme with its new charter of 1882. "In other words," wrote Seth Low, the first mayor to serve under this charter:

with quite unimportant exceptions, the charter of Brooklyn . . . makes the mayor entirely responsible for the conduct of the city government on its executive side and, in holding him to this responsibility, equips him fearlessly with the necessary power to discharge his trust.

Philadelphia adopted a similar plan, as did numerous other cities.

One force behind the "strong mayor" system was the belief among certain reformers that a strong executive should run the city like an efficient business. As Chapter 11 indicates, urban reformers of this stripe valued efficiency above all else in government. They proposed to replace the politicians with businessmen who possessed the two qualities most esteemed by reformers: integrity and executive ability. They succeeded in a few instances, notably William Strong in New York and Percy Jones in Minneapolis, but the results were usually disappointing. Of Strong's mayoralty, Lincoln Steffens wrote:

Mayor Strong, the good man in business, was a bad man in politics. Some critics put it that the good businessman was a bad politician, and that, too, was true. Mr. Strong tried to play the political game; he was pledged not to, but he found that he had to, and—he could not. His moves were technically wrong. But what struck me was that this businessman and his business ethics were immoral in politics; his word was not good; his resistance to pressure was so weak that he sought by compromise to satisfy everybody; and his ideas of integrity, ethical perhaps in a merchant, were downright dishonest in government.

On the "strong mayor" system Seth Low drew the obvious conclusion: "It has been found to have precisely the merits and the defects which one might expect of such an instrument. A strong executive can accomplish satisfactory results; a weak one can disappoint every hope."

A more promising avenue lay in persuading state legislatures to curb their excessive meddling in municipal affairs. This could be done in several ways. The most liberal approach was to allow cities above a certain size the right to frame their own charters.* Missouri was the first

* Of course, these charters had to be consistent with existing state laws.

state to adopt this device through a constitutional amendment in 1875; California, Washington, Minnesota, and Colorado soon followed; but by 1912 only nine states had amended their constitutions to give their cities such broad powers of self-government.

Other states sought to avoid the onus of special legislation by dividing their cities into several classifications and then passing statutes which applied to all cities in a given class.* Some reached a similar position by amending their constitution to forbid the passing of special acts with regard to cities. New York added an extra wrinkle by attempting to give city dwellers a voice in legislation which affected them. Having divided the state's cities into three classes, the law stipulated that any act affecting less than an entire class must first be submitted to the mayor of each city (and the city council for the two smaller classes). If approved by the municipal authorities, the bill went to the governor; if disapproved, it went back to the legislature, which could still enact it into law by repassing it with a majority vote of both houses.

The special act proved an elusive target because it could be hedged to infinity. No state constitution defined what was meant by a "special act," and judges usually upheld the state's position when conflicts arose. The most common subterfuge was to transform a general act into a special act. It was simple enough to do: the Pennsylvania legislature passed a law applying to all cities with 300,000 or more people at a time when only Philadelphia qualified. Ohio did likewise for Cincinnati, and Illinois for Chicago, while other states contrived even more subtle distinctions.

In 1904 the Illinois legislature gave this technique a more positive twist. Having already written a provision against special acts into the Constitution, the legislature inserted a new amendment which permitted it to pass "all laws which it may deem requisite to effectually provide a complete system of local municipal government in and for the City of Chicago." But the legislature also stipulated that no such law could go into effect until the city approved it by a majority vote. In one early instance (1907), Chicago's electorate rejected a new charter passed by the legislature.

In general the attempts to eliminate special acts helped curb some of the worst legislative abuses, but the twentieth century found the industrial city a long distance from home rule. Local government remained the black sheep of American democracy, the pawn of more

---

* The classifications were usually based on population.

than forty separate legislatures. Of this crazy-quilt arrangement, Lord Bryce complained:

not only has each State its own system of laws for the government of cities, but within a State there is . . . little uniformity in municipal arrangements. Larger cities are often governed differently from the smaller ones; and one large city is differently organized from another.

Goodnow agreed with this verdict, declaring that "It cannot, therefore, be said that up to the present time the United States has developed a peculiar type of municipal organization."

Thus did tradition hang like a millstone upon the neck of urban government. Unable to control their own affairs free of outside influence or to clarify their internal lines of authority, most cities were helpless to chart their destinies in an era of rapid expansion. They grew by a process of drift and default in a manner which made them not only the ultimate marketplace but the most conspicuous victims of its workings. It was this spectacle of administrative shambles that prompted Bryce's classic statement:

There is no denying that the government of cities is the one conspicuous failure of the United States. . . . The faults of the State governments are insignificant compared with the extravagance, corruption, and mismanagement which mark the administration of most of the great cities.

But one man's misery is another man's opportunity. Where the institutional defects of local government denied the cities efficient administration, there arose a new breed of men eager to provide services in their own way. Like other businessmen of the industrial era, the political entrepreneurs developed a knack for turning structural weaknesses to their own advantage. Like other entrepreneurs, too, they possessed a talent for bringing order out of chaos, for organizing the disparate materials at hand into a coherent system that satisfied the needs if not the scruples of their clientele. In the urban marketplace they erected political monopolies, profit-making organizations whose inner workings were no less disciplined than the great corporations. What the trust and holding company were to the industrial economy, the political machine became to municipal government.

The rise of municipal machines cannot be understood apart from this tradition of failure in urban government. The machines flourished because they got things done when no one else could. Circumstances had created a power void which had to be filled if the industrial city was to endure. In the immortal phrase of George Washington Plunkitt, the machine politicians "seen their opportunities and they took 'em."

The Municipal Machines

It is scarcely possible to exaggerate the degree of political disorder which characterized most industrial cities in this period of rapid growth. To grasp the extent of this chaotic state of government we must recall the forces which produced it. Foremost among them was the tangled and ineffective heritage of power relationships described in the previous section. At best, this legacy left most cities powerless to control their internal affairs; at worst, it jumbled their political apparatus into a tangled maze that obscured lines of authority and responsibility. The Fassett Committee of the New York Senate, in an 1891 report, itemized this confusion in blunt language:

[That] it is frequently impossible for the legislature, municipal officers, or even for the courts to tell what the law means; . . . it is impossible for any one, either in private life or in public office, to tell what the exact business condition of any city is, and that municipal government is a mystery even to the experienced; . . . that municipal officers can escape responsibility for their acts or failure by securing amendments to the law; that municipal officers can escape responsibility to the public on account of the unintelligibility of the laws and the insufficient publicity of the facts relative to municipal government; . . . that the conflict of authority is sometimes so great as to result in a complete or partial paralysis of the service; that our cities have no real local autonomy; that local self-government is a misnomer; and that consequently so little interest is felt in matters of local business that in almost every city in the state it has fallen into the hands of professional politicians. . . .

From this dismal account, the Committee concluded:

These are conditions which if applied to the business of any other corporation would make the maintenance of a continued policy and a successful administration as impossible as they are today in the government of our municipalities, and produce waste and mismanagement such as is now the distinguishing feature of municipal business as compared with that of private corporations.

This structural vacuum occurred just when the forces of expansion were generating urgent new demands for services and facilities. The industrial city groaned beneath the weight of economic and social change. In an era that required the leadership of giants, urban politics attracted little more than pygmies. The old native elite had abandoned their traditional civic roles and fled to the suburbs, soon to be followed by much of the upper and middle classes. Little semblance of a ruling class remained to staff municipal offices, and few of those who stayed approached politics from a disinterested sense of duty.

To their vacated neighborhoods swarmed thousands of newcomers who required jobs, food, shelter, clothes, water, heat, transportation, amusements, medical care, legal assistance, and a host of other services. No industrial city possessed adequate political mechanisms for fulfilling these needs. Businessmen large and small also had pressing needs. Some wanted franchises or contracts, others licenses or waivers or special regulations. Industrialists had one set of demands, bankers another, and real estate developers still another. Small proprietors, newsstands, fruit stands, saloons, cigar stores, clothiers, demanded services ranging from police protection to loading and storage permits.

The industrial city was a turbulent sea of interests and ambitions, needs and demands, whose waves lapped incessantly at city hall. To stay afloat, urban politicians had to find new ways of doing their business and maintaining themselves in power. The old township model seemed hopelessly antiquated; the industrial city lacked both a small homogeneous population and a disinterested ruling elite willing or able to build a base of political support among such diverse constituencies. The businessmen and the "best people," especially the reformers among them, all wanted "good government," by which they usually meant a small, passive operation offering few services with low tax rates and run efficiently on "sound business principles." But this model fit the realities of life in the industrial city no better than did the township ideal. Both were reactions against the raw vitality of the changing urban environment. Dismissing the possibility that something constructive might emerge from that inchoate spectacle, these models tried to reincarnate the political utopia of an earlier, simpler America.

The industrial city rejected these attempts at political transplant. It required a new type of political organization, one which could weld disparate elements of the city into some cohesive form capable of acquiring power, maintaining order, and satisfying the demands of enough constituencies to transform their agitation into support. Above all, the new organizations had to find ways of enabling the city to surmount the obstacles posed by its tradition of government and the repercussions of uncontrolled growth.

In these needs lay the origins and purposes of the political machines which dominated the politics of nearly all industrial cities. What was a machine? Edward C. Banfield and James Q. Wilson, two political scientists, offer the following scholarly definition:

A political "machine" is a party organization that depends crucially upon inducements that are both *specific* and *material*. . . . a *specific* inducement is one that can be offered to one person while being withheld from others. A *material* inducement is money or some other physical "thing" to which value attaches. *Nonmaterial* inducements include especially the satisfactions of having power or prestige, doing good, the "fun of the game," the sense of enlarged participation in events and a pleasant environment. . . . it is distinguished from other types of organization by the very heavy emphasis it places upon specific, material inducements and the consequent completeness and reliability of its control over behavior, which, of course, account for the name "machine."*

Put another way, the political machine can be seen as the product of ambitious men applying the principles of organizational revolution to the politics of the industrial city. The application of these principles to politics transformed political power into a market commodity to be sold for profit to the highest bidder. The result was a more blatant tendency to identify politics not with ideals or principles, but with material self-interest. "A political machine is a business organization in a particular field—getting votes and winning elections," wrote Banfield and Wilson. "The machine, therefore, is apolitical: it is interested only in making and distributing income—mainly money—to those who run it or work for it. Political principle is foreign to it, and represents a danger and threat to it."

Contemporary observers, bosses and critics alike, shared this view. To the question "How is the Machine run?" Lord Bryce replied that "the source of power and the cohesive force is the desire for office, and for office as a means of gain. . . . Those who in great cities form the committees and work the machine are persons whose chief aim in life is to make their living by office." Tammany politician George Washington Plunkitt put the case with his usual eloquence. He recalled his start in politics:

After goin' through the apprenticeship of the business while I was a boy by workin' around the district headquarters and hustlin' about the polls on election day, I set out when I cast my first vote to win fame and money in New York City politics. . . . What I did was to get some marketable goods before goin' to the leaders. . . . I had a cousin, a young man who didn't take any particular interest in politics. I went to him and said: "Tommy, I'm goin' to be a politician, and I want to get a followin'; can I count on you?" He said:

* Italics are in the original. One could, of course, argue that this same definition could be applied with little change to the business corporations of the late nineteenth century.

"Sure, George." That's how I started in business. I got a marketable commodity—one vote. . . .

Before long I had sixty men back of me, and formed the George Washington Plunkitt Association. . . . I had marketable goods and there was bids for them from all sides, and I was a risin' man in politics.

Lincoln Steffens, who probably knew more bosses on personal terms than any other American, declared flatly:

Politics is business. That's what's the matter with it. That's what's the matter with everything,—art, literature, religion, journalism, law, medicine,—they're all business. . . . The politician is a business man with a specialty.

Richard Croker, a Tammany boss, told Steffens, "Like a business man in business . . . I work for my own pocket all the time." In Alfred Henry Lewis's unjustly neglected novel, *The Boss* (1903), Big John Kennedy, a Tammany chieftain, elaborated on Croker's remark:

Now notice: I've got no office; I'm a private citizen same as you, an' I don't owe no duty to the public. Every man has his pull—his influence. . . . In this case, my pull is bigger than all th' other pulls clubbed together. You get that franchise or you don't get it, just as I say. In short, you get it from me—get it by my pull, d'ye see! Now why shouldn't I charge for th' use of my pull, just as a lawyer asks his fee, or a bank demands interest when it lends? . . . There's my doctrine: I'm a private citizen; my pull is my capital, an' I'm as much entitled to get action on it in favor of myself as a bank has to shave a note.

The parallels between business and political organizations ran deeper. Like the trust or giant combinations, the machine arose in an environment characterized by disorder and instability. Its creators sought to amass wealth and power by supplying important services which existing institutions failed to provide. To do this, political entrepreneurs had to devise new mechanisms for organizing their raw materials (voters), production equipment (political office), and the marketplace. The machine became this new mechanism. In most cases, machines arose on a local (district or ward) basis and confined their business to that market. Often competition within that market remained keen among rival political leaders.

As cities grew and opportunities multiplied, the more ambitious political entrepreneurs moved to extend their control over a larger share of the market. By defeating rivals, absorbing competitors, and forging coalitions, the bigger fish swallowed the smaller fry until the strongest among them wielded enough influence to control an entire city. At that point the machine monopolized the political marketplace and remained in power until some rival combination overthrew it.

In politics as in business, success often proved harder to maintain than to achieve. Changing conditions, no less than ambitious rivals, posed a threat to the dominant machine. Sometimes internal strife weakened the machine's hold; sometimes its masters overstepped the bounds of prudence and aroused a storm of public wrath which toppled the machine—at least temporarily. The more intelligent political entrepreneurs were sensitive to changing conditions and adjusted their operations to fit them; similarly, their political savvy alerted them to any sign of internal friction or rivalry. In some cases, the triumphant city machine extended its influence into county and state government; in others, the urban bosses were content to strike agreements with their state counterparts for an orderly division of markets.

For business and political entrepreneurs alike, efficient organization held the key to success. At every level the leaders were those who combined vision and savvy with close attention to detail. To deliver his product the political boss needed "pull"; to obtain pull he had to elect men loyal to him, which meant that his organization had to start with control over some reliable electoral base. Hard work and personal ability created that "safe" base; possession of it provided the boss with patronage and funds to dispense as rewards to the rank-and-file. Many urban bosses launched their careers as masters of a single ward; a fortunate handful were able to utilize existing party or social organizations, like New York City's Tammany Hall, as a foundation for control of several wards or an entire city.

The most common power base for bosses lay in the "river" wards. Usually nestled against a river, these wards were originally the core of the old "walking city." Formerly prosperous districts, they were the first casualties of growth and the exodus to the suburbs. Warehouses, railroads, tracks and yards, stockyards, factories, flophouses, and the decayed remains of once-tidy neighborhoods lined the streets of these wards. To these shabby streets came the poor and the wretched of the city: the immigrants, the drunks, the toughs, the vice merchants, and those just down on their luck. In dismal alleys the dregs of society rubbed elbows with greenhorns struggling to rise above the refuse heaps that were their first homes in the new land.

New York had its Hell's Kitchen, Tenderloin, and the Bowery; Chicago, its Levee; Kansas City, its Bottoms and the North End; and Cincinnati, its Basin (especially the Over-the-Rhine district). Every city had its slum and vice districts even if they lacked catchy nicknames.

The river wards collected all who could find refuge nowhere else in the industrial city. Upon this humble rock the ward boss built his organization. The fact that "decent" citizens shunned the inhabitants of these districts like lepers only made the politician's work easier. What the genteel folk repulsed, the boss embraced as the raw material of his machine.

To achieve those goals, the boss organized his faithful into a disciplined army. The base of his political pyramid extended far beyond the party organization. It included social clubs, athletic groups, fire companies, and various lodges, all of which served political as well as social purposes. Through these groups and a network of loyal party lieutenants—the district captains, "heelers," runners, block captains—the boss mobilized the vote for his slate of candidates in local elections.* The faithful were herded to the polls to vote the party ticket, while gangs of bully boys and cooperative policemen chased off supporters of the opposition or detained them until the polls closed.

Usually this straightforward program insured an easy victory. If a reform element or internecine rivals posed a threat, the boss resorted to other methods. The party foot-soldiers might vote several times each, usually in place of some duly registered person long dead or departed. It was a standing joke in Chicago that the "cemetery vote" alone could carry close elections in certain wards. When this was not enough, ward bosses could import hundreds of drifters as temporary residents until election time. Michael "Hinky Dink" Kenna, the mastermind of Chicago's notorious First Ward along with "Bathhouse" John Coughlin, refined this technique into an art. Lloyd Wendt and Herman Kogan described the simplicity of it all:

Into the ward from all parts of the city had poured the grateful dregs. They were housed and fed and supplied with plenty of beer. . . . Into The Bath's own precinct Kenna piled 300 additional voters to be registered. Some slept in Coughlin's bathhouse, on the benches or in the steam rooms. Precinct captains like Mike Lawler and Joe Friedman rounded up hundreds of others and transformed their saloons into lodging houses. Cheap hotels, flop joints, deserted buildings, brothels, saloons, empty warehouses, even freight stations—these were the forts where Hinky Dink marshaled the Coughlin voting

---

* In his book *The Tweed Ring* Alexander B. Callow observed:

"The ward captain was to Tammany what the sergeant was to the army—the backbone of the organization. He was responsible, and held to strict account, for the vote of his election district. If the Democratic vote fell off without reasonable explanation, or through his own lack of skill, he was removed with dispatch." (New York, 1966)

forces, to wait the time when they should march out in the interests of their benefactor. When registration day was over, the First Ward had 8,397 voters on the books—almost twice the number that had balloted in the previous mayoralty election.

Of course a boss could always resort to stuffing the ballot box directly, but a good machine seldom had to go that far. The regular party organization, firmly rooted in the ward and district political clubs, the social and fraternal societies, normally had the strength to rout most opposition. This intricate structure, tended by its army of workers, was the machine. While no two machines were alike, nearly all followed a common organizational pattern. Even critics marveled at their disciplined efficiency. The hostile *New York Times* once described Boss Tweed's Tammany Hall as "a wonderfully and admirably-constructed and conducted machine . . . the wheels work smoothly, the pulleys run without a jar, the cogs slip into one another perfectly while everything is kept well oiled and greased from the public funds of our wealthy citizens."

The mortar that cemented this political army together went beyond material rewards. It included personal prestige and ambition, loyalty, tradition, and a sense of participation. Above all, the machine was an instrument of personal politics which served basic human needs. At its heart lay a network of close personal ties among people who had few other avenues for personal advancement. To inhabitants of the industrial city's cold netherworld, the machine stood as a beacon of warmth and hope. For immigrants in particular, this combination of material gain and personal attention proved irresistible.

If a ward boss could extend his control into neighboring wards, or if he could bring other ward bosses into his camp through patronage or other inducements, he might capture city hall. Most urban bosses seem to have followed some version of this route to the top. A few were bold and lucky enough to utilize a citywide organization (such as Tammany Hall) without advancing from ward leadership, but even these men served their apprenticeship in the party ranks. In an early piece of political fiction, *Solid for Mulhooly: A Sketch of Municipal Politics under the Leaders of the Ring and the Boss* (1881), Rufus Shapley summarized the art of mastering the party machine:

When one man owns and dominates four wards . . . he becomes a Leader. Half a dozen such Leaders constitute what is called a Ring. When one Leader is powerful enough to bring three or four such Leaders under his yoke he becomes a Boss. . . .

Under the tutelage of a Leader named Blossom Brick, Mulhooly makes rapid strides in his political career. His saloon becomes the party headquarters for both the precinct and the ward, and he is put on both the ward committee and the city committee:

From this vantage ground he could . . . study the party organization in all its divisions and subdivisions. . . . He saw that the party organization was composed primarily of Precinct Committees, Ward Committees and the City Committee, and secondarily, of Conventions to place in nomination candidates for various offices. . . ; and . . . this perfect party organization . . . placed the entire control of the whole machinery in a central head or master-spirit, composed of one man, or two men, or half a dozen men . . . in other words, of the Leaders, the Ring, and the Boss.

By this system the Ring nominated nearly all candidates. Since nomination was tantamount to election, the Ring in effect named the public officials under the guise of an election. Mulhooly learned that the system was founded upon several key premises:

(a) the tendency of every voter to . . . vote for any man ostensibly nominated by the party; (b) the strict enforcement of the Party Rules; and (c) the judicious distribution of the 4,036 regularly salaried offices in the various departments of the city government . . . ; the various municipal, State and national offices . . . ; and of the various contracts for public work . . . given to contractors who are willing not only to Rebate, but also to properly control at all times the thousands of workmen whom they employ in the public service.

These material rewards were the lubricant that oiled the machine and kept its every part running smoothly. Although there never seemed enough "gravy" to go around, the amount available was staggering in both scope and variety. A vital link in the system was the boss's power to appoint policemen. "As any modern expert on crime knows," Alexander B. Callow noted, "machine rule in American municipalities has been made possible only through control of the police." The politically astute father of Big John Kennedy in *The Boss* put the case more bluntly: " 'They're the foot-stones of politics,' said Old Mike. 'Kape th' p'lice, an' you kape yourself on top.' "

Every boss kept his police as prized foot-soldiers. By appointing ambitious Irishmen or other immigrants as patrolmen, he provided valued jobs to men willing to stand loyally by the party. Police assistance ranged from election-day duties to protection to graft payoffs. The sensational Lexow Committee investigation in New York during the 1890s uncovered an organized police graft system which returned about $7,000,000 a year from saloons, bawdyhouses, and gambling dens. Of this take, 20 percent went to the patrolmen (who served as collectors), about 35 to 50 percent to the precinct commanders, and the rest to the inspector. The testimony also disclosed that policemen paid anywhere from $300 to $15,000 for the privilege of being hired or promoted.

The same pattern, with only minor variations, prevailed elsewhere. In Chicago ward chieftains like Hinky Dink and Bathhouse John used the police in identical fashion. In Minneapolis Albert "Doc" Ames re-organized the city's police force to make it a more perfect engine for graft. After purging honest or "unreliable" officers (those who remained were charged a fee for the privilege) and appointing accomplices to head the department, Ames directed the police to organize the city's vice on an efficient, paying basis. Everyone from burglars and pick-pockets to prostitutes and gamblers worked with the police under what amounted to a kind of license system. Less brazen systems operated in Boston, Kansas City, Philadelphia, and most other large cities.

Important as the police were, they comprised only a small part of the patronage available to the boss. Every municipal service had positions to fill: police and fire, waterworks, garbage collection, and thousands of jobs for laborers. Every office needed clerks, assistants, or other "staff" just as every public building required attendants or maintenance people. If positions were not available, the boss created them at the taxpayers' expense. Some favored public works projects which employed hundreds at a time. More venal leaders like William Tweed invented jobs which were filled either by nonexistent workers or "regulars" who pocketed the salary without performing any services. In his heyday Tweed was esti-mated to have about 12,000 people on the city's payroll. The City Comptroller's office was listed for 131 clerks, the Street Commissioner for 60. The city also had 12 "manure-inspectors," a small army of health wardens, assistant health wardens, street inspectors, meat inspectors, inspectors of encumbrances, and 20 pump inspectors for 3 water pumps.

Every municipal office had its own harvest of patronage which no boss neglected to reap. For those of higher rank, the stakes went up. Leaders and their lieutenants bestowed upon themselves a variety of posts with honorific titles, fat salaries, and untaxing duties. Relatives, too, found places on the staff or in some other department. Lawyers were retained as counsel or given official positions. Some were elevated to judgeships to serve the machine's legal needs on the bench. A privileged few took their reward in the form of high office, as mayor, alderman, legislator, congressman, or in some other state post.

Through this network of patronage the machine rewarded its faithful, and from them it extracted a profit in the form of loyalty and kickbacks. No municipal department escaped the taint of political jobbery; education boards no less than other services were riddled with graft and patronage, especially in Detroit, New York, and San Francisco. The stench of corruption that emanated from this practice drove Lord Bryce to conclude that "The Spoils System reminds us of the Machine and the whole organization of Rings and Bosses. This is the ugliest feature in the current politics of the country."

The spoils system did more than provide offices for the party faithful. Control of offices meant domination of municipal government, which in turn enabled the machine to perform other functions that brought its members revenue. As a business organization, the machine possessed a product—political power—which it dispensed for a profit to a variety of customers. In broad terms, its sources of revenue fell into three categories: salaries, supplies, and services.

As noted earlier, the machine's leadership garnered part of their income by holding real or invented positions within city government. These posts usually tendered large salaries for few if any duties; seldom did a boss hold a "working" office, preferring instead to delegate such responsibilities to loyal underlings while he tended to party affairs. In addition, the machine exacted a tithe from those it installed in city jobs. From some it demanded a percentage of their annual salaries; to others, especially police, judges, and similar posts, it sold places for a flat fee with the understanding that the buyer would do the party's bidding when asked and contribute regularly to its campaign chests.

Supplies offered an even more lucrative source of income. The city needed everything from soap to stationery to horses. From the throng of businessmen eager to sell goods to the city, the machine had little difficulty in extracting "commissions" for a contract. Payment might be a percentage of the contract or a flat fee. If this "rebate" seemed too crude or obvious, the business firm might instead make a generous contribution to the party at a later date. The variations on this theme were endless and often ingenious. Part of the payoff went to officials in the department involved, part to the party, and the rest to the boss and his circle. Sometimes enterprising leaders organized their own company to sell the city supplies at breathtaking prices, a notable example being the New York Printing Company which had Boss Tweed as its president.

Profitable as salaries and supplies were, they paled before the bonanza offered by services. The machine was by nature a service organization which, like Big John Kennedy, charged a stiff fee for its pull. Here, too, the sources of income seem infinite, but in general they may be divided into two groups; protection and privilege.

Protection usually involved the sanctioning of illegal activities in exchange for either a flat fee payoff or a percentage of the take. Brothels, free-lance prostitutes, gambling joints, poolrooms, faro banks, saloons, and other establishments paid the machine for the privilege of operating outside the law on a regular basis. Control of the police made this possible; in fact, patrolmen often served as collectors for the machine. Upton Sinclair, in *The Jungle* (1906), described the threads of connection:

> The law forbade Sunday drinking; and this had delivered the saloon-keepers into the hands of the police, and made an alliance with them necessary. The law forbade prostitution; and this had brought the "madames" into the combination. It was the same with the gambling-house keeper and the pool-room man, and the same with any other man or woman who had a means of getting "graft" and was willing to pay over a share of it: The green-goods man and the highwayman, the pickpocket and the sneak thief, and the receiver of stolen goods . . . the proprietor of unsanitary tenements, the fake doctor and the usurer, the beggar and the "push-cart man," the prize fighter and the professional slugger, the race-track "tout," the procurer, the white-slave agent, and the expert seducer of young girls. All of these agencies of corruption were banded together, and leagued in blood brotherhood with the politican and the police.

This arrangement offered two civic advantages rarely appreciated by the morally squeamish: it tended to restrict vice establishments to one section of town (the river wards), and it stabilized urban crime by "normalizing" relations between criminals and police. New York seems to have pioneered in the latter system, which flourished during the tenure of Superintendent Thomas F. Byrnes. By agreement with the detective bureau, a certain number of each type of criminal were allowed to operate in the city so long as they kept their "practice" within reasonable bounds. Each group in turn divided the city among themselves, giving each member an area to monopolize. Lincoln Steffens recounts what the city received:

> In return . . . the groups were to defend their monopoly from outsiders, report the arrival in town of strangers from other cities, and upon demand furnish information (not evidence) to the detectives and return stolen goods. This was called regulation and control, and it worked pretty well; more to the glory of the police, who could perform "miracles of efficiency" when the victim of a robbery was worth serving, but of course it did not stop stealing; it protected only citizens with pull, power, or privilege.

These arrangements amounted to a kind of social control which had at least tacit approval from some of the "best" citizens. Of course it appalled moral crusaders and reformers who wished to eradicate vice rather than merely keep it out of their neighborhood. Those resigned to accepting the presence of some vice as inevitable, and those who were not above occasional indulgence, found this type of control a reasonable compromise.

Where protection involved the shielding of illegal activity, privilege normally involved the sale of something legal. Like protection, it came in all sizes and made no distinction between shady operators and legitimate businessmen. Unlike protection, the sale of privilege routinely involved the largest and most respected financial interests in the city. The need for privilege bound a critical part of the business community to the machine and thereby undercut the cry for reform. While the "best" people might applaud a moral crusade against the river wards, many shrank from inquiring too closely into the system of privilege. When Joseph W. Folk in St. Louis did exactly that, he discovered that the tracks of corruption led to some of the best thresholds in town.

Privilege covered a wide assortment of venal activities. For individuals and small operators it might involve the sale of a liquor license or building permit, a low tax assessment, a favorable zoning ruling, a waiver of some existing regulation, or any one of a hundred different "favors" available for a price. On a larger scale it involved the most lucrative prizes the city had to offer: the sale of franchises for gas or electric lines, street lights, telephone lines, and street railways. The profits to be gleaned from these franchises spurred businessmen to invest lavish sums in bribes to those having the authority to award them. In many cities the traction and utilities magnates dominated the local machines not through force of leadership, but by the sheer weight of dollars. Rare was the city whose boss did not forge with the traction or utilities interests an alliance similar to that in Chicago, where Charles T. Yerkes fed the notorious "gray wolves" of the city council a steady diet of bribes to build his traction empire.

Nor was this all. Swarms of hungry contractors flocked to the machine, seeking business and willing to pay handsomely for it. The city had much more than franchises to offer; streets had to be constructed and paved, public buildings and parks constructed, sewers laid, bridges built, garbage collected, bond issues sold, and money loaned—the list seemed endless to eager applicants and disgusted reformers alike. In some cities the machine permitted banks to hold municipal funds at no interest, loan the money out at interest, and pocket the difference. The sale of these privileges, which enriched the machine and contractor alike at the taxpayers' expense, differed in degree but not in kind from the dispensing to smaller fry of a permit for street improvement, wharfage or warehouse space, or permission to use sidewalk space for storage or to erect an awning.

While no machine cared to keep too accurate accounts of its revenue sources, it is likely that privilege in all its many guises provided the largest share of gravy. Reformers certainly thought so; more than one believed privilege to be the ultimate source of corruption. Lincoln Steffens blamed the evil not upon the politician who took bribes, but upon the businessman who offered them:

He is the chief source of corruption. . . . I found him buying boodlers in St. Louis, defending grafters in Minneapolis, originating corruption in Pittsburgh, sharing with bosses in Philadelphia, deploring reform in Chicago, and beating good government with corruption funds in New York.

Steffens later had his view refined by Tom Johnson, a onetime traction magnate who switched sides to become a tough reform mayor in Cleveland. From his unique vantage point Johnson told Steffens:

Oh, I could see . . . that you did not know what it was that corrupted politics. First you thought it was bad politicians, who turned out to be pretty good fellows. Then you blamed the bad business men who bribed the good fellows, till you discovered that not all business men bribed and that those who did were pretty good business men. . . . Hell! Can't you see that its privileged business that does it? . . . It's those who seek privileges who corrupt, it's those who possess privileges that defend our corrupt politics. . . . It is privilege that causes evil in the world, not wickedness; and not men.

From salaries, supplies, and services, the machine obtained the income which enabled it to reward its workers and remain in power. Like other business organizations, the machines that did this work best lasted longest, grew richest, and were in optimum position to extend their power. Like corporations, too, the machines performed social services beyond their sphere of self-interest and inflicted social costs of many kinds upon the city. Although much has been written on this subject, no one has succeeded in constructing a satisfactory balance sheet for the sum total of this social overhead—even for a single machine.

Writing in the 1950s, sociologist Robert K. Merton addressed this complex question of estimating social costs against social gains. Leaving aside moral evaluations of the machine's operations, he found that most of them performed four important functions. They organized, centralized, and maintained in sound working order "the scattered fragments of power" in the industrial city; they served the electorate "by elaborate networks of personal ties," providing social welfare services through a process by which "politics is transformed into personal ties"; for business-men large and small they provided "those political privileges which entail immediate economic gains"; and, finally, the machine itself offered "al-ternative channels of social mobility for those otherwise excluded from the more conventional avenues for personal 'advancement.'" This last point should not be neglected, for most of the men who achieved wealth and power through the machine could not otherwise have gone as far. A majority were immigrants or sons of immigrants from poor backgrounds who lacked access to "proper" society and the opportunities it afforded.

However roundly reformers condemned the machine for its venality and vulgarity, however savagely they denounced it as a blight upon dem-ocratic government, they could not deny that it performed useful and important functions more efficiently than other agencies or institutions. If the machine was evil, it was also indispensable until some better system was devised. It could be replaced but not simply eliminated. On this point Richard Croker, a Tammany boss, had the final word. Once again it was the persistent Lincoln Steffens, ever in search of fresh insights, who prodded Croker with the obvious question:

> "Well, about this boss-ship," I began. "Why must there be a boss, when we've got a mayor and—a council and—"
> "That's why," he broke in. "It's because there's a mayor *and* a council *and* judges *and*—a hundred other men to deal with. A government is nothing but a business, and you can't do business with a lot of officials, who check and cross one another and who come and go, there this year, out the next. A business man wants to do business with one man, and one who is always there to remember and carry out the—business."

The Boss as Broker

As noted earlier, there exist two conflicting stereotypes of the boss. The first is that of the rogue with the heart of gold. All warmth and charm, he is the political father figure, attending to the needs of his underprivileged flock. That he wields political power ruthlessly or lines his pocket with graft or resorts to unsavory practices makes him a more complex but rarely less attractive figure. At best he is a modern Robin Hood who can persuade one that the ends do justify the means; at worst he is a lovable rascal whom one finds impossible to dislike no matter how nefarious his deeds. Like Frank Skeffington in Edward O'Connor's *The Last Hurrah,* he is a man you like despite his worst side and your better judgment.

The second stereotype is more sinister. Like the cartoons of Thomas Nast, whose savage caricatures fixed Boss Tweed as the prototype of the species for an entire generation, this image portrays the boss as a political dictator. Usually squat in stature and gross in manner, his stubby fingers bristling with gems and his tie harpooned by a diamond stickpin above his protruding belly, clutching an enormous cigar between cruel lips, the boss presides over his town like an Oriental despot. His word is law: he rewards and punishes at will, and without explanation. To defy his command is foolish; the sources of his power run to the darkest and most mysterious corners of the city. To those who decry his outrages he replies, like Tweed, "What are you going to do about it?"

If one puzzles over these stereotypes and disputes their accuracy, a number of questions arise: Who were the bosses and what kind of men were they? Were most of them Irish and poor? Did they rule as dictators with an iron hand? How real was their benevolence, and how sincere? Did their good deeds outweigh their venality and perversion of the democratic process? What qualities made one a good boss? What characteristics did American bosses have in common?

These are all fundamental questions for which few satisfactory answers exist. Surprisingly little is known about American bosses as a group; that is one reason why our two stereotypes have maintained their hold for so long. The second image gained its currency not only from Nast's vivid drawings but also from the observations of other contemporary critics. One memorable description came from Lord Bryce:

> An army led by a council seldom conquers: it must have a commander-in-chief, who settles disputes, decides in emergencies, inspires fear or attachment. The head of a Ring is such a general. He dispenses places, rewards the loyal, punishes the mutinous, concocts schemes, negotiates treaties. He generally avoids publicity, preferring the substance to the pomp of power, and is all the more dangerous because he sits, like a spider, hidden in the midst of his web. He is a Boss.

Bryce's portrait left a deep impression upon observers then and later. How accurate is it when applied to a large group of political bosses? Is it possible to draw a composite picture of the "typical" boss?

In seeking answers to these questions, we propose a third image: the boss as broker. This view does not reject the characteristics found in the other two images; rather, it subordinates them to a quality we think is more important and more common to most bosses. To see the boss as broker is to catch the essence of his function, which in turn suggests what attributes one needed to be a successful boss.

Before developing this notion, let us first see what truths can be extracted from the other two images. In 1930 Harold Zink published a study of twenty municipal bosses, all but one of whom held sway during the period 1860 to 1920.* After a careful survey of these men, Zink concluded that his findings did not square with the prevailing stereotypes:

A consideration of twenty city bosses does not bolster up the theory of the "typical" boss. One would have a difficult time identifying any appreciable number of them were he to go forth into the highways and byways with any single preconception. . . . Political bosses are not a distinct species of human beings but possess the physical, mental, and moral variations of men in general.

According to Zink, only eight of the nineteen were Irish Catholics. Five others had parents or ancestors who lived in Ireland, but of these three were Scotch-Irish, one English, and one Northern Ireland Protestant. The remaining bosses included an Englishman, a Swede, two Jews, and two whose families had resided in America for several generations. Only five were born in Ireland. The Irish may have produced more urban bosses than other ethnic groups, but they had no monopoly in the field. Nor did either party dominate; the machines divided fairly evenly between the parties, and in some cities—notably St. Louis—managed to work both sides of the political street.

Zink found the physical characteristics and personalities of his sample even more diverse than their ethnic origins. In size they ranged from brawny six-footers like Cox and McLaughlin to the diminutive Vare, who barely reached five feet five inches and weighed less than half of the porcine Tweed's 300-pound bulk. Some bosses were handsome, some plain, and a few were considered downright ugly. Curiously, neither personal attractiveness nor charm appeared to be common traits among the bosses. Zink estimated that less than half his group possessed what could be called a magnetic personality. A few—notably Croker, Cox, and Murphy—actually repelled people with their cold, reserved manner. While most of Zink's bosses were genial good-humored men, a surprising minority were cold fish with the sort of unbending demeanor usually

---

* Zink's group included Martin Lomasney (Boston), William Tweed (New York), Tim Sullivan (New York), John Kelly (New York), Richard Croker (New York), Charles F. Murphy (New York), Hugh McLaughlin (Brooklyn), James McManes (Philadelphia), Israel W. Durham (Philadelphia), Edwin H. Vare (Philadelphia), Christopher L. Magee (Pittsburgh), William Flinn (Pittsburgh), George B. Cox (Cincinnati), Fred Lundin (Chicago), Roger Sullivan (Chicago), Edward Butler (St. Louis), Martin Behrman (New Orleans), Albert A. Ames (Minneapolis), and Abraham Reuf (San Francisco). The twentieth, George W. Olvany (New York), replaced Murphy as head of Tammany in 1924.

associated with blue-blooded reformers. Nor did any common pattern of personal habits emerge. A few drank, gambled, or wenched to excess, an equal minority abstained from vices with puritanical correctness, and the remainder fell somewhere in between.

Career patterns also defied easy summary. Prior to drifting into politics, the bossses earned their livings in various ways. Cox, Murphy, and Sullivan all ran saloons, a business which produced many a ward leader; among the bosses not in Zink's study, "Hinky Dink" Kenna and the Pendergast brothers (Kansas City) began as saloon operators. But there is no one early profession shared by most bosses. Once into politics, bosses tended to rise slowly through the party ranks, reaching the top only after a lengthy apprenticeship. At the top few of the bosses shared a common style. While most images depict the boss as a man of infinite craft and stealth, Zink found the opposite to be true: a majority of his sample tended to pursue their objectives in aggressive and unsubtle fashion. Only a handful made a regular practice of reaching their goals by a roundabout route.

If Zink's conclusions are accurate—and they appear to hold up fairly well when applied to some other bosses—what remains of the stereotypes? Though battered, they are not entirely broken; the bosses do, in fact, share some interesting characteristics. Nearly all were born in the town which they were later to rule or moved there at an early age. Most came from poor or at least humble origins, and thirteen of the nineteen got at best a grammar-school education. A surprising number lost their father and were forced to become the family breadwinner at an early age.

Circumstances forced most of these men to become self-reliant in their youth. Long residence in the neighborhood bred a network of acquaintances and contacts upon which they later capitalized. Although their careers followed no common path, most went into politics as a normal neighborhood activity. From this familiar milieu they rose gradually to the top. While the reasons for their success varied, nearly all earned a reputation for being honest and steadfast; they never betrayed a friend or went back on their word. Most were personally generous to their followers and often to worthy causes. Only Croker and Reuf gained a reputation for being tightfisted.

The bosses also shared some qualities of temperament. Zink found most of them to be shrewd, stubborn men with a talent for staying calm under pressure. They displayed a strong grain of common sense, a sure grasp of practical affairs. Yet, surprisingly, they were not always good judges of men. The stereotypes usually portray the boss as uncanny in his understanding of people, especially since much of his work involved dealing with other persons. But of the nineteen bosses, Zink rated only four as being superior judges of character. "Nine possessed good judgment where men were concerned," he added, "and six had no more than fair ability."

A survey of other urban bosses beyond Zink's sample seems to confirm his central point, that there exists no clear-cut prototype which one can designate as a "typical" boss. There are similarities and shared characteristics but no overall image dominant enough to be called archetypal. If one adds state and county bosses to the list, the picture becomes even more confusing. An instructive example is Charles R. Brayton, the political boss of Rhode Island for about two decades. Born in Apponaug, Rhode Island, of an old Yankee family, Brayton had a mixed career as pension agent, postmaster, and chief of state police before gaining admittance to the bar in 1891 at the age of fifty-one. His rural and small-town-based Republican machine dominated the state legislature and thwarted every effort by Democrats in the city of Providence and reformers alike to break his political stranglehold. In Rhode Island, which Steffens characterized as "a State for sale, and cheap," the "interests" seeking favors ignored the city politicians and went directly to Brayton:

General Brayton received in the sheriff's office the lines of visitors who had business with the State, openly. And openly he did that business. He ran the legislature across the hall. He said so; everybody knew it; and he ran it for business men. . . . It was the best-established, most accepted, most shameless system that I had seen, and it was a State thing, of State, not of city, origin. . . . The Legislature was not the scene of corruption, and the cities were not the origin or the foundation of it. The reformers of Rhode Island, a licked lot, were city men. The legislators came from the country, and they came bought. They had no power, low salaries; they took orders absolutely. . . . The good old American stock sold out. And their price was low.

Having clouded the old stereotypes, there still remains the image of the boss as a benevolent figure who ran his own private social welfare program for the city's deprived. To many people, then and now, the boss was the man who did things or got them done for people who had nowhere else to turn. Whatever his sins, he was an angel to those whom the city ignored or despised, and much of his support came from their gratitude. Martin Lomasney of Boston put it best when he told Steffens, "I think . . . that there's got to be in every ward somebody that any bloke can come to—no matter what he's done—and get help. Help, you understand; none of your law and your justice, but help."

How valid was this image? The evidence on this point is so abundant as to be confusing. There is no doubt that the machine, from the boss on down, performed a wide range of social services for people within every ward. The deeds are a matter of record; it is their interpretation that divides observers. Some have noted correctly that the motives behind these charities were a blend of humanitarianism and political calculation, but no one has devised a formula for determining the exact mixture in each case. Others have charged that the machine exploited the city for far more in riches and human misery than it repaid in good works. This, too, may be true but we also lack a calculus for measuring these effects. The result has been that in most cases the debate over machines as welfare agencies sounds less like a problem in social science than one in moral philosophy.

Some points can be stated with reasonable certainty. Virtually all machines engaged in social-welfare services as a routine part of building reliable support at the grassroots. The nature and extent of this work depended upon the machine, the people who ran it, and local circumstances. The services rendered were nearly always personal, arranged through face-to-face contact. Most of these good works could not otherwise be obtained through existing municipal agencies. The prevailing philosophy of government frowned upon such expenditures as wasteful or extravagant while the dominant social creed among the "best" people viewed them as an immoral and unwise coddling of the lazy and unfit classes.

Normally it was not the boss but his lieutenants who performed these services. The boss might be a philanthropist in his own right, and in his early political career he may have earned a reputation for good works; but once in power, he had little time for personal charities. Instead the machine delegated that responsibility to ward and district leaders, aldermen, and other party officers at the local level. These men were the true dispensers of charity. Most became well-schooled in the classroom of human needs and worked incredibly long hours at the job of helping their constituents. They were the "somebody" in every ward referred to by Lomasney. Needless to say, their work was crucial to the machine's success. Undoubtedly their motives were mixed and their rewards often handsome, but this does not detract from the help they gave. Perhaps others could have done it better or at less cost; the point is that there were no others willing or able to perform the variety of services they did in the manner they did it.

One may look to almost any large city for illustrations. In Chicago "Hinky Dink" Kenna, the elfin political genius of the Levee, cared for the down-and-out of his ward to a degree that went beyond the need for votes. "Hinky Dink had a simple and basic political philosophy," wrote Wendt and Kogan; "favors and benevolence produced votes; organization brought them out." Yet the Dink viewed his luckless charges as more than grist for the political mill:

For all his hard-lipped demeanor, Kenna, like Coughlin, was a benevolent man. In the dire depression that swept the entire country that winter, the whole of Chicago was beset with the jobless, and the First Ward was particularly troubled. . . . great hosts of the unemployed roamed the streets, begging jobs and food. . . . Hinky Dink fed more than any other. In one week . . . he cared for 8,000 destitute men and he fired a bartender who demanded five cents from a vagrant who had helped himself too freely from the [free lunch] counters.

In another part of Chicago, Jane Addams regarded similar activities as the true source of strength for the local ward boss. Her article "Why the Ward Boss Rules" in *The Outlook* (April 1898), reminded reformers that corrupt aldermen survived by fulfilling human needs the "better" people ignored or dismissed:

Primitive people, such as the South Italian peasants who live in the Nineteenth Ward, deep down in their hearts admire nothing so much as the good man. The successful candidate must be a good man according to the standards of his constituents. He must not attempt to reform or change the standard. If he believes what they believe, and does what they are all cherishing a secret ambition to do, he will dazzle them by his success and win their confidence.

The benevolences practiced by the alderman in the Nineteenth Ward were typical of his breed. He furnished food, clothing, coal, and pocket money to the destitute. He found work for the unemployed and once boasted of having 2,600 of his constituents on the city's payroll, prompting Addams to observe that "An Italian laborer wants a job more than anything else, and quite simply votes for the man who promises him one."

But there was much more. He found lodging for the homeless and carried the rent for those threatened with eviction. He bailed out drunks, paid fines for those guilty of petty offenses, and procured legal assistance for those in serious trouble with the law. His influence with the police helped many a man out of a close scrape. He helped bury the dead and faithfully attended funerals, weddings, christenings, and confirmations. No social function escaped his attention or his generosity:

At a church bazaar, for instance. . . . When others are spending pennies he is spending dollars. Where anxious relatives are canvassing to secure votes for the two most beautiful children . . . he recklessly buys votes from both sides, and laughingly declines to say which he likes the best, buying off the young lady who is persistently determined to find out, with five dollars for the flower bazaar, the posies, of course, to be sent to the sick of the parish.

In New York the activities of that irrepressible Tammany wheelhorse, George Washington Plunkitt, confirm that Chicago was not an isolated case. Plunkitt's daily schedule, as recorded by journalist William L. Riordan in 1905, closely resembles that of the Chicago alderman:

This is a record of a day's work by Plunkitt:

2 A.M.: Aroused from sleep by the ringing of his door bell; went to the door and found a bartender, who asked him to go to the police station and bail out a saloon-keeper . . . arrested for violating the excise law. Furnished bail and returned to bed at three o'clock.

6 A.M.: Awakened by fire engines passing his house. Hastened to the scene of the fire, according to the custom of the Tammany district leaders, to give assistance to the fire sufferers, if needed. Met several of his election district captains who are always under orders to look out for fires, which are considered great vote-getters. Found several tenants who had been burned out, took them to a hotel, supplied them with clothes, fed them, and arranged temporary quarters for them until they could rent and furnish new apartments.

8:30 A.M.: Went to the police court to look after his constituents. Found six "drunks." Secured the discharge of four by a timely word with the judge, and paid the fines of two.

9 A.M.: Appeared in the Municipal District Court. Directed one of his district captains to act as counsel for a widow against whom dispossess proceedings had been instituted and obtained an extension of time. Paid the rent of a poor family about to be dispossessed and gave them a dollar for food.

11 A.M.: At home again. Found four men waiting for him. One had been discharged by the Metropolitan Railway Company for neglect of duty, and wanted the district leader to fix things. Another wanted a job on the road. The third sought a place on the Subway and the fourth, a plumber, was looking for work with the Consolidated Gas Company. The district leader spent nearly three hours fixing things for the four men, and succeeded in each case.

3 P.M.: Attended the funeral of an Italian as far as the ferry. Hurried back to make his appearance at the funeral of a Hebrew constituent. Went conspicuously to the front both in the Catholic church and the synagogue, and later attended the Hebrew confirmation ceremonies in the synagogue.

7 P.M.: Went to district headquarters and presided over a meeting of election district captains. Each captain submitted a list of all the voters in his district, reported on their attitude toward Tammany, suggested who

might be won over and how they could be won, told who were in need, and who were in trouble of any kind and the best way to reach them. District leaders took notes and gave orders.

8 P.M.: Went to a church fair. Took chances on everything, bought ice-cream for the young girls and the children. Kissed the little ones, flattered their mothers and took their fathers out for something down at the corner.

9 P.M.: At the club-house again. Spent $10 on tickets for a church excursion and promised a subscription for a new church-bell. Bought tickets for a base-ball game to be played by two nines from his district. Listened to the complaints of a dozen pushcart peddlers who said they were persecuted by the police and assured them he would go to Police Headquarters in the morning and see about it.

10.30 P.M.: Attended a Hebrew wedding reception and dance. Had previously sent a handsome wedding present to the bride.

12 P.M.: In bed.

There is, of course, no way of knowing how typical a day this was for Plunkitt. It may have been an exceptional one, and Plunkitt was in many respects an exceptional man. Yet there is plenty of evidence that the activities were typical of those undertaken by ward and district leaders in many cities, all of whom were accustomed to working long hours. Politics was a full-time profession in the industrial city. For these efforts, and through what he called "honest graft," Plunkitt made himself a millionaire. From his headquarters—a bootblack stand at the county courthouse—he transacted business and philosophized on party politics and reform. On one occasion he boasted of holding four public offices in one year and drawing salaries from three of them at the same time.

All these welfare activities took place under the boss's approving eye but without his direct participation. They were considered a routine part of the district or ward leader's organizational work. Without a reliable means for measuring their social costs and benefits, we cannot strike an overall balance sheet for what the city's people gained and what they lost. Nor does it seem worthwhile to flog the politicians for the self-serving motives behind this kind of personalized philanthropy. The recipients seldom cared about questions of motive. They were grateful for the favors rendered and attention given, and they expressed their thanks in the only useful coin available to them—the ballot box.

So long as the city shirked from providing these services in some acceptable form, the machine's hold on its flock remained unshaken. Neither reformers nor "decent" citizens could cut into that loyalty merely by preaching for virtue and against corruption in tones that were superior, alien, cold, and above all lacking in humanity. One young student of politics, Walter Lippmann, himself an ardent reformer, preferred human corruption to sterile civic purity. In his book *A Preface to Politics* (1914), Lippmann warned:

> You cannot beat the bosses with the reformer's taboo. You will not get far on the Bowery with the cost unit system and low taxes. . . . I am aware of the contract-grafts, the franchise-steals, the dirty streets, the bribing and the blackmail, the vice-and-crime partnership, the Big Business alliances of Tammany Hall. And yet it seems to me that Tammany has a better perception of human need, and comes nearer to being what a government should be, than any scheme yet proposed by a group of "uptown good government" enthusiasts.

If the boss was not personally the great urban philanthropist, neither was he the omnipotent dictator that legend has often made him out to be. To get a sense of that legend, one need only scan the periodicals of the era. Here is one complaint from an article entitled "Bossism" in *The Outlook* (January 1897):

> Despotism dies hard. The present enemy to free institutions in this country is neither a king, an oligarchy, nor a landed aristocracy, which were eminently respectable foes as compared with the "boss" and his ally, corporate greed, who unite in an endeavor to control the commonwealth for what they can jointly make out of it.

To their critics most bosses seemed like perfect juggernauts, able to exert their will through the slightest of gestures and exact a huge tribute from an unwilling municipality.

It is tempting to see the boss in this light, and easy to understand why he cast such a long shadow to his critics. He appeared to control the police, the courts, the city council, and many if not most of the municipal boards. His allies ranged from the mightiest businessman to the meanest slumlord or vice merchant. Above all, he dominated the party machinery in a system which, complained *The Outlook*, gave the boss "the power to nominate all candidates, and the people only power to veto his choice at a general election."

From what they observed, and even more from what they did not see but imagined took place behind the scenes, critics concluded that on anything that mattered the boss's word was law. On the surface they were correct in what they saw. As Lord Bryce put it, "The aim of a Boss is not so much fame as power, and not so much power over the conduct of affairs as over persons." Like all businessmen, the boss had a product de-

manded in the urban marketplace. That product was his "pull" or influence, his ability to deliver what could not be obtained through other
channels.

It is important to grasp this point because critics often missed its underlying assumption: that political power was a commodity which the boss
bought as cheaply as possible and sold at the highest price. Some may
have relished power for its own sake, but that is only to say they enjoyed their work. The boss was a businessman, not a dictator. In the end,
he ruled not by force, but by satisfying his customers. Unlike many businessmen, he had to please not only his customers, but also those who
worked with him. It was this need to satisfy so many diverse clienteles
that made the business of politics so intricate and complex. Joel Tarr has
written:

> The typical urban boss was a man who regarded politics as a business and
> who used his power for personal and party gain. He was a businessman
> whose chief stock in trade was the goods of the political world—influence,
> laws, government grants, and franchises—which he utilized to make a private
> profit.

Perceptive as this passage is, it misleads in one sense: it describes how
the boss made his own fortune but confuses his function as a businessman. In most of his dealings the boss acted not only as an entrepreneur
but also as a broker.

As a political leader, his power depended upon the ability to satisfy the
needs of clients both within and without the machine. Within the machine, the work consisted largely of allocating offices and "gravy" in some
equitable fashion and in resolving differences among conflicting factions.
His commission for these services was the preservation of the machine
which kept him in power and thereby enabled him to enhance his own
fortune. Outside the organization, he acted as agent for those seeking
services of many kinds, from franchises to licenses to waivers of the law.
For all these transactions he exacted a fee—whether it was a flat sum, a
percentage commission, or simply the intangible capital of "favors" owed
for later collection. In each case he acted as a broker among diverse and
often conflicting interests, handling transactions, mediating disputes, and
establishing fee schedules. If the boss slipped in his ability to deliver
these services or got too greedy in the price he asked for them, his customers soon undertook to replace him with someone else.

Observant critics understood his system and accepted the fact that all
politicians must act as brokers among the welter of interests pressing demands upon them. They complained not about the function, but about

the abuses of it that cropped up in machine politics. Specifically they charged boss rule with creating a loaded game that worked against the larger public interest. As Frederic C. Howe put it:

We say we want a business men's government. We already have a business men's government, supplied through the agency of the boss. But he is the broker of unseen principals who own or control the privileged interests which have identified themselves with the government through the aid of the party.

The boss as broker ruled not by force, but through a clever mixture of persuasion, manipulation, and satisfaction rendered. While he might use "muscle" to thwart an enemy or achieve some limited gain, he could not maintain himself in power that way for very long. That is why most bosses tended to dismiss the charge of despot or dictator as so much rubbish. As Jim Pendergast of Kansas City said:

I've been called a boss. All there is to it is having friends, doing things for people, and then later on they'll do things for you. . . . You can't coerce people into doing things for you—you can't make them vote for you. I never coerced anybody in my life. Wherever you see a man bulldozing anybody he don't last long.

Pendergast may have overstated the gentleness of his methods, but his main point was sound. In Cincinnati a similar situation prevailed. George B. Cox fashioned a machine upon a series of delicate alliances which required careful tending and dedication to detail. Of Cox's methods, Zane Miller wrote:

Instead . . . of trading one ally for another, or selling out, Cox pyramided them with the cement of personal favors and party loyalty. He had not created an organization, rather he pasted it together from pre-existing elements. As a leader then, he managed a diverse coalition, serving each of its interests. He saw himself, moreover, as an honest broker.

Of the notorious Boss Tweed—usually denounced as the worst urban tyrant of all—Seymour Mandelbaum has written, "Tweed was a master of the strategy of the leadership which succeeds because it allows men to do as they please." Similarly Zink said of Edward Butler of St. Louis, "He was not a very harsh master. He ruled his forces by the favors he dispensed rather than standing whip in hand as a Simon Legree over the backs of minions." For most urban bosses it could not be otherwise; their position as head of the machine, upon which their power rested, depended upon keeping the organization intact and functioning smoothly. That, in turn, required the talents not of a czar but of a diplomat who retreated to the use of force only as a last resort.

It is possible that this function as broker was the one quality more bosses shared than any other. The way in which they exercised it depended, of course, upon the personality of the boss and the circumstances peculiar to his city. Each man had his own style and his own methods of forging and maintaining an organization. Differences in style and local circumstances make it difficult to generalize about bosses as a species of political leader unless we concentrate upon the functions they performed. Those functions are best understood by regarding the boss as a businessman who organized politics as a commodity within the urban marketplace.

One virtue of this approach is that it gets around the shopworn images and emotion-laden rhetoric that cloud the historical dialogue about bosses. One can always make a moral appraisal of the boss and his machine, wrapping it either in sentimentalism or invective; but this approach is not very helpful until one comprehends who these men were, what they did, why they did it, and how they did it. When this exploration is made, the bosses turn out to be no less immune to easy generalizations than any other complex group of people.

In *The Boss*, Big John Kennedy, on the brink of death, endeavored to instruct his successor in "the whole science of leadership." Among the principles he laid down are some worth repeating because they account for the manner in which the successful boss adjusted to changing conditions:

Always go with th' current; that's th' first rule of leadership. It's easier; an' there's more water down stream than up. . . . remember: while you're Boss, you'll be forced into many things ag'inst your judgment. The head of Tammany is like th' head of a snake, an' gets shoved forward by the tail. Also, like th' head of a snake, th' Boss is th' target for every rock that is thrown. . . . An' the last of it is, don't get sentimental—don't take politics to heart. Politics is only worth while so long as it fills your pockets. Don't tie yourself to anything. A political party is like a street car; stay with it only while it goes your way. A great partisan can never be a great Boss.

As the next chapter suggests, these were principles the successful boss learned far better than his perennial adversary, the urban reformer.

CHAPTER 11

The Endless Seesaw:
Urban Political Reform

I can't tell just how many of these movements I've seen started in New York during my forty years in politics, but I can tell you how many have lasted more than a few years—none. . . . They were mornin' glories—looked lovely in the mornin' and withered up in a short time, while the regular machines went on flourishin' forever, like fine old oaks.

—George Washington Plunkitt (1905)

"IT MUST NOT be supposed that the inhabitants of Ring-ruled cities tamely submit to their tyrants," wrote Lord Bryce. "The Americans are indeed, what with their good nature and what with the participation of the most active men in their private business, a long suffering people. But patience has its limits, and when a Ring has pushed paternal government too far, an insurrection may break out."

Insurrections did indeed break out everywhere. Between 1880 and 1920 American cities were hotbeds of reform. The reform impulse followed no orderly or logical pattern; it was rather a series of discrete, piecemeal attacks upon the whole catalog of municipal ills by people whose goals and methods differed widely and often conflicted with one another. Occasionally some of these swirling currents converged for a time and flowed in unison toward some common objective, but in general the channels they cut through the urban landscape were seldom uniform. In most cases they fertilized the city's institutions without radically altering its topography.

The floodtide of urban reform came during the so-called Progressive era between 1900 and 1920. During those two decades the effort to regenerate society reached a level of coherence and energy unmatched before or since. Armed with blueprints for repairing the city's defective machinery, determined reform armies, their eyes ablaze with visions of that ideal urban community which had somehow always eluded the American experience, marched off to do battle with their enemies much as earlier Christians had gone forth to smite the infidels. Like all crusaders, the reformers were often more earnest than effective. Many were lost along the way; some were exhausted by the struggle while others fought on to their inevitable reward, a varying mixture of success and disappointment. A few suffered what Steffens called "the American reformer's story, a modern tragedy of defeat, humiliation, martyrdom."

Like all crusaders, too, they were a motley, ill-fitting lot with backgrounds as varied as their schemes. Their ranks included sober businessmen, righteous clergy, utopian visionaries, veteran do-gooders, journalists, social workers, ordinary citizens whose consciences had been stabbed by some social ill, and politicians who had sniffed the winds of change. No plan or program united them; they were concerned with many different problems and disagreed bitterly over the best approach to the concerns they did share. Leaving radical crusaders aside, one still searches in vain for some common ground upon which to identify urban progressive reformers other than their general desire to make the city a better place in which to live.

Urban reform was a rainbow of many hues, some blending and some clashing violently. For that reason, the reform crusade was a campaign waged on many fronts. A few scored significant gains while others made little or no headway. In general, those with the most conservative instincts and modest objectives achieved the most success. The overall result was predictable, though elusive to those caught up in the heat of battle: reformers changed the industrial city without transforming it, improved its operation without deflecting its momentum or solving its most basic problems.

The modern metropolis bears distressing witness to this conclusion. Its most intractable problems are but an echo of those which haunted the industrial city. They persist because the generation of progressive reformers failed to alter the fundamental conditions, values, and assumptions which defined the city as marketplace instead of community. To some extent, they improved the quality of life, beautified the city, rationalized its organization, and cleansed its tarnished character; but rarely did they manage to get at those essentials which made the industrial city what it was.

N̪or have their successors gotten much further at the task. Perhaps the job was too big for them or anyone else. Perhaps the city was but a reflection of the larger American experience that could not easily be reversed or deflected from its course. Had the urban industrial network become the modern Leviathan, incapable of being harnessed by those whose lives it dominated? If that is the case, it speaks ominously to the future of American cities.

The Reform Rainbow

Like other aspects of urban life, reform seems a crazy-quilt because so many different people wanted so many different things. It is impossible to give a simple definition of who the reformers were and what they wanted. Even when we say that they all wished "to make our city better," the fact is that few reformers agreed on the meaning of "better" and fewer still on how "better" could be achieved. This diversity of ends and means made the reform marketplace a lively one in which adherents of change competed for support against not only their enemies but each other as well.

Some distinctions can be made among urban reformers. Few lower-class people belonged to their ranks. As staunch supporters of the machine, inhabitants of the river wards were a natural target of political reform; as the city's poor, they were the logical subject for social reform. It was the middle and upper classes who spearheaded the reform drives. Samuel P. Hays has argued that the primary impetus for political reform came from "business, professional, and upper-class groups" involved in the "rationalization and systemization of modern life" who wanted a form of government "more consistent with the objectives inherent in these developments." This desire pitted them directly against the interests of those farther down the social scale:

The movement for reform in municipal government, therefore, constituted an attempt . . . to take formal political power from the previously dominant lower and middle-class elements. . . . These two groups came from entirely different urban worlds, and the political system fashioned by one was no longer acceptable to the other. . . . Reformers, therefore, wished not simply to replace bad men with good; they proposed to change the occupational and class origins of decision-makers.

If Hays's argument is sound, it suggests that *what* reformers wanted depended greatly upon *who* they were. To some extent class values and biases did determine the perception of social and political evils and thereby transformed much of urban reform into a clash of competing interests so typical of the urban arena. But the reform impulse was not only an extension of self-interest; for many upper- and middle-class people, it sprang from a desire to improve conditions of urban life which did not directly affect them but which touched them deeply. This humanitarian impulse cut across class lines and defeats efforts to define reformers by the simple mechanism of class or self-interest.

A more fruitful approach is to examine not who the reformers were, but what they wanted and how they went about getting it. While reformers usually attacked more than one problem, their concerns may be separated into four broad categories: political reform, social reform, moral reform, and city planning. The rich variety of issues within these areas shaded subtly—even imperceptibly—into one another to form what we have called the reform rainbow. The first of these categories, political reform, will be taken up here; the rest will be considered in the next chapter.

Political reform was the first area to attract wide public attention, partly because the excesses of machine corruption were so blatant and offended upper- and middle-class sensibilities so directly. The boss epitomized the industrial city. Like his business counterpart, the financier, he was the lightning rod which money struck to energize urban society. Both fed off cash, contracts, and influence, and both were essentially self-serving. Although criticized as arrogant and corrupt, they were tolerated because their activities made the city run. Their very success helped set in motion forces of revolt which unleashed a torrent of outrage upon their heads. In the crusade launched against them, the boss and the financier were more than targets; they became symbols for the whole spectrum of urban life.

The shower of reform fell first upon the boss. Because his activities were local, they were easier to scrutinize and attack. As political reformers took up the fight against the greed and corruption of the machine, they were joined by other urbanites ready to do battle with countless other inequities in the city. Local progressives mobilized first into bands of guerrilla fighters, then into marching armies, to stalk the boss at the ballot box and fight the inhumanity of the slums and sweatshops, the immorality of prostitution, the poisonous environs of the saloons, the specter of poverty and disease, the greed of the landlord and the utility magnate, the chaos of unregulated housing, and the ugly blight of unrestrained physical growth. The crusade swelled beyond the city into state politics and, after 1900, dominated the national political arena for more than a decade in the turbulent era of Theodore Roosevelt and Woodrow Wilson.

While the tactics used by local reformers varied widely, Melvin G. Holli has suggested an important distinction between two broad patterns which he called *structural* and *social* reform. According to Holli, structural reform involved "the effort to change the structure of municipal government, to eliminate petty crime and vice, and to introduce the business system of the contemporary corporation into municipal government." Structuralists tended to concern themselves with "charter tinkering, elaborate audit procedures, and the drive to impose businesslike efficiency upon city governments." Between 1880 and 1920 it was this stripe of reform that dominated the crusade to purify urban politics.

In contrast, social reform sought to democratize municipal government and to broaden the base of urban social services. Holli wrote:

The whole tone of the social reform movement was humanistic and empirical. It did not attempt to prescribe standards of personal morality nor did it attempt to draft social blueprints or city charters which had as their goals the imposition of middle-class morality and patrician values upon the masses. Instead it sought to find the basic causes of municipal corruption.

Social reformers, though inclined to be more visionary, were nevertheless dedicated to practical goals. Especially did they seek an extension of municipal services for the poorer classes while trying to free government from the stranglehold of privilege.

The difference between these approaches can be seen in the contrary views of Lord Bryce and Frederic Howe on the ultimate source of urban corruption. Bryce listed four conditions which produced "rings and bosses":

The existence of a Spoils System (= paid offices given and taken away for party reasons).
Opportunities for illicit gains arising out of the possession of office.
The presence of a mass of ignorant and pliable voters.
The insufficient participation in politics of the "good citizens."

Howe thought otherwise. To him the boss and his machine were but symptoms of a more corrosive influence, that of privilege:

An examination of the conditions in city after city discloses one sleepless influence that is common to them all . . . the privileges of the street railways, the gas, the water, the telephone, and electric lighting companies. The connection of these industries with politics explains most of the corruption; it explains the power of the boss and the machine; it suggests the explanation of the indifference of the "best" citizen and his hostility to democratic reform.

Howe's last point hit home especially hard because it was the "best people" who controlled the companies that corrupted the city with their insatiable appetite for privilege. As Chapter 10 suggested, the boss was but the intermediary who waxed fat as the broker of privilege. "The boss came in through political apathy," Howe asserted. "He has grown powerful through privilege. . . . He is the link which unites the criminal rich with the criminal poor." This was the revelation unearthed by Lincoln Steffens in his study of St. Louis: the ultimate source of corruption lay not in the river wards or the boss's headquarters but in the best homes in the suburbs. Some conservative "good people" shared this view, including Mayor William J. Gaynor of New York who denounced the "so-called 'leading' citizens" because they "get a million dollars out of the city dishonestly while the 'boss' gets a thousand."

Needless to say, agreement on this indictment was less than universal. The result was a conflicting welter of views which often led reformers to work at cross-purposes with each other. Half a century later, historians have yet to unravel the tangle of their activities to anyone's satisfaction. Through our four broad categories we hope to depict at least the primary colors of the elusive reform rainbow.

The Conservative Revolution

The revolt against urban political corruption began not with the structural reformers but with their precursors, the "mugwumps" or "best men" who surfaced after the Civil War. Appalled by the gauche politics of the Grant administration and the brazen plundering of the Tweed Ring at the local level, the mugwumps made a futile bid to recapture the leadership held by their class prior to industrialization. They pushed reluctant "good men" forward as candidates to retrieve the machinery of government from bossism and corruption. The results of this "retreat to reform," as John G. Sproat called it, were rarely satisfactory. Few mugwumps had the grit or the talent for slugging it out in the political arena. "We have been terribly beaten," groaned Horace Greeley after his unsuccessful campaign for the presidency in 1872. "I was assailed so bitterly that I hardly knew whether I was running for the presidency or the penitentiary."

The mugwumps believed that the chief problem of municipal government was not a flawed system but the presence of corrupt politicians. Their solution was to throw the rascals out and replace them with good honest men. The formula was not quite as simplistic as it sounds, for it rested upon a more elaborate notion of how historical circumstances had driven the "best" people from office and brought in a new breed of narrow, self-serving politicians who drew their strength from lower-class elements. James Russell Lowell summarized this belief in a few lines of verse (1876):

> Is this the country that we dreamed in youth,
> Where wisdom and not numbers should have weight,
> Seed-field of simpler manners, braver truth,
> Where shams should cease to dominate
> In Household, church, and state?

In effect the formula proposed a simple solution to a complex network of problems wrought by radical changes in the character of the city. Some reformers never abandoned the formula; others came to regard it as a mark of their political virginity. Frederic Howe recalled in his autobiography that

> The principal issue in my mind . . . was corruption. The old gang should be cleaned out, a new kind of men put in. The kind of men I had in mind were business men, trained university men. The others, the bad ones, lived principally down under the hill. They were immigrants. . . . The risk of being dirtied by politics had to be taken; the sacrifice involved in running for office had to be made.

The structural reformers shared several assumptions with the "good men" enthusiasts. Both singled out the boss and his machine as the chief source of urban evil and were usually slow to acknowledge that respectable businessmen bore any of the blame. Both believed that municipal government should be simple, clean, and efficient, run by businessmen on sound business principles to provide effective but limited services. Both distrusted the mass of voters and by implication the democratic process itself as it operated in the industrial city. They insisted that the duties of government should fall to that class made superior by lineage or commercial success, however distasteful the burden might be to men distracted by larger affairs and loath to enter the grimy political arena. Government was a civic obligation which, having been allowed through neglect to fall into unfit hands, must be reclaimed by its rightful possessors.*

---

* Contemporary journals and novels abound with illustrations of this attitude. In Paul Leicester Ford's turgid but interesting novel, *The Honorable Peter Stirling* (1894), the hero, who is everything his name implies, reflects upon what he must sacrifice if he runs for governor:

"He saw alienation of friends, income, peace, and independence, and the only return a mere title, which to him meant a loss, rather than a gain of power. Yet this was one of the dozen prizes thought the best worth striving for in our politics. Is it a wonder that our government and office-holding is left to the foreign element?"

The concept of government as a form of business enterprise brought these reformers closer to the bosses they despised than they cared to recognize. Bosses and reformers alike viewed the city as a business organization; they disagreed principally over who should run it, what kind of business should be transacted, and who should benefit. The boss regarded municipal government as a private business to be operated for the unabashed self-interest of those involved. Ironically this vision was more true to the individualist, free-enterprise ethos revered by most businessmen. Reformers believed that the city should be run as an efficient, economical public corporation serving the public interest. By the public they meant, of course, not everyone but rather the "good people" who paid taxes, did honest work, and were sober, upright citizens.

The initial experience of "good men" in politics led structural reformers to conclude that the problem went beyond individual character to the system itself. A strong, honest mayor like Seth Low of Brooklyn (and later New York), William F. Havemeyer of New York, or Grover Cleveland of Buffalo might improve conditions for a time; but sooner or later the reform impulse waned and the machine reclaimed its place. Frequently it was the people themselves who voted the reformers out of office. As Richard Croker told Lincoln Steffens, "Our people could not stand the rotten police corruption. They'll be back at the next election; they can't stand reform either." The hero of *The Boss* reached the same conclusion:

> Now the natural conditions of New York are machine conditions. Wherefore, I realized . . . that no gust of reformation could either trouble it deeply or last for long, and that the moment it had passed, the machine must at once succeed to the situation.

Structural reformers reasoned that if the machine was the heart of the matter, it must be not merely displaced but destroyed. This meant razing its base of support, which in turn required some new structure of government that severed the electoral strength upon which the machine rested. Several critics including Bryce and Josiah Strong thought the answer was to limit voting rights. Abram S. Hewitt, another New York businessman turned reform mayor, proposed that "ignorance should be excluded from control" and asserted that "the city business should be carried on by trained experts selected upon some other principle than popular suffrage." Distrusting the lower-class electorate that maintained the boss and his machine, structural reformers sought to replace the professional politician with businessmen and trained experts. In effect, they proposed to supplant one ruling class with another, not by broadening the base of government but by concentrating it in the hands of those deemed more competent and reliable. As Holli summarized this approach:

The structural reform movement . . . represented . . . the first wave of prescriptive municipal government which placed its faith in rule by educated, upper class Americans and, later, by municipal experts rather than the lower classes. The installation in office of men of character, substance, and integrity was an attempt to impose middle class and patrician ideals upon the urban masses.

For all their vigor and earnestness, reform mayors like Havemeyer, Cleveland, John D. Phelan of San Francisco, and Percy Jones of Minneapolis failed to leave a permanent imprint on their cities. Attempts to purge the city of vice and corruption lasted until their terms expired or the reform impulse was spent. The economy drives were more successful, but were usually done in so ruthless a manner as to antagonize everyone. City employees howled at budget and job cuts. Politicians bemoaned the loss of patronage and graft while businessmen protested that reform disrupted their usual working relationship with city hall without offering new channels for obtaining the "favors" they required. Lower-class people suffered worst as pennypinching administrations slashed expenditures on everything from charities to education to city contracts which provided jobs.

Economy-minded administrations showed little interest in the plight of the poor; nor, surprisingly, did they always run an efficient operation. Efforts to watchdog every dollar spent often ensnarled the administration in a hopeless tangle of red tape, which eventually drove the electorate to turn in wrath upon the reformers and restore the machine. This muddled state of affairs prompted Lincoln Steffens in 1908 to suggest to Boston reformers that the bosses themselves be put in charge of the drive for civic uplift. After all, he reasoned,

. . . good people and the best men had been tried through the world's history and especially in Boston; and they had failed. The clergy had governed Boston once, then the aristocracy, then the leading businessmen. All these forms of goodness had had their day. Let's give up the good men and try the strong men.

For most reformers, however, this was much too advanced a political science. Structuralists tended to be captives of both the new concept of scientific efficiency and the older notions of political economy and social morality. This curious combination led them to seek new forms of urban government which might effect an orderly transfer of power from the machine to themselves without violating the orthodoxy of their social, political, and economic canons. Once convinced of the need for structural reform, their problem became one of finding effective structures.

During the 1890s structural reformers launched a massive national campaign which. followed a logical course for middle- and upper-class reform. Local supporters formed Good Government Leagues, municipal leagues, and reform or city clubs. The organizational thrust moved to the national level in 1894, when the First National Conference for Good City Government and the National Municipal League were established. The movement spread so rapidly that in 1895 the secretary of the National Municipal League reported an upsurge in local groups from 16 to 180. As these organizations gained national attention, other professionals joined their ranks. Journalists published more articles on the city in the 1890s than during all the rest of the nineteenth century. In 1897 the first journal dealing exclusively with urban affairs appeared. Educators began to institutionalize the concept of public service careers when the University of Pennsylvania created its first lectureship in municipal government in 1894. Engineers began looking at water, paving, drainage, and other technical problems in a particularly urban context and formed the American Society of Municipal Engineers to exchange ideas. This organizational drive and the publicity it generated established structural reformers—or "goo-goos," as critics called them—on a firm national footing.

By 1899 the debate over what form city government should take produced a model charter which the National Municipal League promoted as the plan for the twentieth-century city. The model charter contained all the elements of government held dear by structural reformers. It advocated a strong mayor with a unicameral council elected at large for six-year terms and recommended that the number of councilmen range from nine to fifty. To keep the ballot short, only the mayor and the council would be elected. The charter increased the number of appointive offices on the assumption that civil-service reform went hand in hand with good government. Partisanship would decline with the abolition of ward and district representation and the separation of municipal elections from state and national ones. The model also advocated more home rule for the cities, including the power to adopt and amend their charters and control their own bonding and taxing.

While the model charter was never implemented wholesale in any American city, it represented a practical goal toward which all structural reformers looked. Portions were adopted piecemeal wherever the opportunity arose, and the model was occasionally refined to meet new exigencies. But the values inherent in the model—nonpartisanship, professionalism, economy, and efficiency—were the goals which structuralists strove to realize throughout the progressive era.

One of the most successful attempts at institutionalizing these values came in 1906, when New York City established the first Municipal Bureau of Research. No other agency on the state or national level resembled the bureau. Designed to modernize the government, it offered advice and expertise for employing practical business methods in every department. The bureau studied the budget, accounting and auditing systems; experimented with time-and-motion studies; and promoted inventory controls, unified management, and personnel efficiency measures. When one staff specialist declared in 1907, "To be efficient is more difficult than to be good," he summarized the spirit behind the bureau. It tried to move beyond the old concept of "good" versus "bad" men by institutionalizing business techniques in urban government, and was copied throughout the country.

The quest for scientific efficiency led structural reformers to develop two major new approaches to municipal government: the city commission and city manager systems. The commission arose in the wake of a great tidal wave that demolished Galveston, Texas, in 1900. Out of the confusion there emerged an organization of businessmen who fashioned a new plan of government to deal with the emergency. As James Weinstein observed, the plan embodied a concept expressed in 1896 by John H. Patterson, founder of National Cash Register Company, that "a city is a great business enterprise whose stockholders are the people." Patterson entertained the hope that "municipal affairs would be placed on a strict business basis" and be run "not by partisans, either Republican or Democratic, but by men who are skilled in business management and social science." Patterson's ideal approached realization in Galveston when the businessmen's committee, pressed to devise a government capable of rebuilding the city quickly and efficiently, turned to the model most familiar to them: the business corporation.

Galveston's new charter vested all governmental power in the hands of five commissioners, three of whom were to be appointed by the governor and two elected by the people at large. When the courts ruled the appointive provision unconstitutional, a revised version mandated the election of a mayor and four commissioners. Significantly, the "at-large" method of election remained; the old ward system gave way to one in which all the voters elected all the commissioners. By this one stroke, the tradition of ward politics, which had sustained the machine, was abolished. Equally important, the mayor operated as little more than one of the commissioners. In Weinstein's words, the commissioners were "vested with the combined powers of mayor and board of aldermen. Each commissioner headed a city department and functioned as legislator and administrator." The charter divided city administration into four departments: police and fire, streets and public property, waterworks and sewage, and finance and revenue. The mayor was assigned no department to oversee but instead exercised a "general coordinating influence over all." In effect, Galveston was to be run not by politicians, but by a board of directors.

The commission form of government attracted national attention and spread rapidly. By 1912 over 200 cities had adopted some version of it, including Birmingham, Memphis, Oakland, Dallas, Omaha, St. Paul, Spokane, Des Moines, Trenton, Springfield (Illinois), and Kansas City (Kansas). Businessmen, chambers of commerce, boards of trade, and other civic groups gave it glowing endorsements. To these enthusiasts its advantages were many. It centralized authority and responsibility in a few hands and thereby disentangled decision-making from the paralysis wrought by corruption, evasion, and red tape. Fewer officials also meant a shorter ballot for voters to ponder. This was no small point. Charles A. Beard observed that in 1911 the voters of a large Ohio town had to confront a ballot loaded with candidates for twenty-one municipal and thirty state offices.* A shorter ballot enabled voters to become more familiar with each candidate.

Elimination of the ward system, coupled with the concentration of authority, struck a blow at machine politics which enthusiasts hoped would attract more "good men" to political office. Men could be elected on a nonpartisan basis; once in power, the lines of their responsibility were unmistakably clear. The plan, in short, offered businessmen much easier access to control of the city's government. In Weinstein's phrase, "it was a plan to make government more businesslike and to attract more businessmen to government."

Despite its widespread popularity, the commission plan soon betrayed weaknesses of its own. Critics complained that so complete a concentration of power actually made it easier for corrupt interests to control a municipal government. Some cities attempted to meet this objection by instituting such devices as the initiative, referendum, recall, and vigorous

* The municipal offices included the mayor, city council president, auditor, treasurer, solicitor, three at-large councilmen, three justices of the peace, three constables, five positions on the board of education, and one assessor. The state offices covered the gamut from governor to constable. That same year voters in Cleveland confronted seven separate ballots, one of which listed seventy-four candidates for city offices.

corrupt practices acts; but these reforms neither removed the danger nor assuaged the uneasiness.

Nor did combining the legislative and administrative functions prove an unmixed blessing. The commission plan may have attracted more "good men" to office, but it did not eliminate incompetents, and it did not free municipal affairs from political logrolling. The ageless dilemma of American politics remained intact: the men popular enough to win elections were not necessarily those equipped with the skills to administer their office. Successful candidates frequently proved better as politicians than as civil servants; once in office, some commissioners played politics with no less adroitness in the new system than the professionals had in the old one. Logrolling among commissioners on key policy and appropriation votes became a common practice. Where favors were not traded, political rivalries arose as each commissioner tried to build his own power base around his department. The result was often the rise of what one critic called "five separate governments," each centered around a commissioner.

To overcome this tendency, H. S. Gilbertson drew up a refined version of the commission which became the genesis of the city manager plan. Under this proposal the commission retained its legislative powers but transferred all administrative functions to an appointed city manager. As chief administrator, the manager presided over the city's day-to-day affairs and hopefully removed them from direct political pressure. Under Gilbertson's plan the manager had authority over the expenditure of city funds and most departmental appointments. Sumter, South Carolina (1911), and Dayton, Ohio (1913), were the first to adopt the new plan; between 1913 and 1923 some 240 cities followed their lead.

The city-manager plan refined the analogy between municipal government and the business corporation. The manager served as president of the corporation with the commission as his board of directors charged with making the policies which he implemented. To the delight of chambers of commerce and other business groups, the commission and manager plans seemed to reward their booster efforts. City after city reported improved services at reduced costs, bolstered municipal credit, and an extended range of services. In many cities, businessmen did run for the office of commissioner; and even where businessmen did not dominate the commission, they strongly influenced its members. Most business and civic leaders would probably have agreed with the city manager of Manistee, Michigan, who wrote: "You cannot make any mistake in adopting this business form of government."

Outside the business community, however, this favorable consensus

dissolved. In many cities the new forms had achieved the objectives demanded of them: local machines had been routed, businessmen and other
"good men" installed in office, and government made more efficient.
But there were people who believed that a city should be more than a
business organization and who argued that the social costs of a business
government outweighed its benefits. These critics included professional
politicians, labor representatives, socialists, and a wide variety of social
reformers. This debate also divided structural and social reformers. The
latter asserted that the goal of municipal reform should be not more
efficient government or a lower tax rate, but the creation of better living
conditions for all the city's people.

Opponents of the commission-manager system recognized that the
goals of efficiency and economy in government were incompatible with
the desire for social services which cost money and required an enlarged
administrative apparatus. They charged business governments with
showing little concern for interests beyond the commercial and economic
pale. Problems of social welfare and the plight of the poor, the stock-
in-trade of machine politicians, won little sympathy and less attention
from most managers and commissioners. This insensitivity to the larger
needs of the city prompted one Iowan to comment tartly in 1913 that
"Good health is more important than a low tax rate." That same year
a Spokane official bemoaned the growing tendency to run municipal
government from a "cold-blooded business standpoint."

The new forms revolutionized the basis of urban politics. Whatever
its other defects, the ward system had assured the lower class a voice,
usually a powerful one, in city hall. The new system of citywide elections did more than muffle that voice; it eliminated the mechanism by
which workingmen, immigrants, and other minorities had traditionally
entered politics at the neighborhood level. Few working-class candidates
possessed the resources to wage a citywide campaign. Where once they
commanded solid support from wards peopled with their own kind, they
now faced the discouraging task of soliciting votes from the upper and
middle classes whose aim was to purge the political process of the corrupt ward politician and the uninformed rabble who supported him.
When Wichita, Kansas, elected a former street laborer to its commission,
H. S. Gilbertson inquired whether this admittedly "honest calling" gave
the man "quite the preparation for managing one of the departments of
a city?"

The much-acclaimed nonpartisan ballot reinforced this discriminatory
effect. Lower-class candidates had always relied heavily on ward-based
party machinery to organize and finance campaigns. Thrown into a city-

wide arena, they found these traditional resources inadequate for reaching an enlarged, often hostile public without the support usually conferred by party endorsement. Among upper- and middle-class voters a candidate who "represented the people" got nowhere against one with the proper background and experience. As Weinstein put the case, "The nonpartisan ballot was a boon to the well-known man, and the well-known man, more often than not, was a leading merchant, manufacturer, or the lawyer of one or the other."

For those outside the fashionable and comfortable neighborhoods, the new system replaced something with nothing. City hall had, in effect, been improved at their expense. Where the machine had at least provided social services, had ameliorated the adjustments faced by newcomers to the city, and had offered opportunities for ambitious young men to climb above their station, the commission and manager plans sacrificed all these in the name of efficiency, honesty, and "good government." The triumph of businessmen and civic uplifters brought to power a group who by class prejudice or principle were indifferent if not hostile to the social functions inherent in the old system. Believing that government belonged to those with the largest stake in it, they shared the belief of C. E. Picard that "The trouble with leaving our cities to govern themselves, at least along purely democratic lines" was that "they are utterly unworthy of trust." This antidemocratic attitude, so prevalent among structural reformers, prompted Brand Whitlock of Toledo to reflect in 1914:

The word "reformer" like the word "politician" had degenerated, and, in the mind of the common man, come to connotate something very disagreeable. In four terms as mayor I came to know both species pretty well, and, in the latter connotations of the term, I prefer politician. He, at least, is human.

The commission and manager plans reached the height of their popularity during the 1920s. That their zenith came during the era of Harding, Coolidge, and Hoover only underscored what Holli called "the basically conservative nature of the structural-reform tradition." With their triumph, the city as corporation came of age. The industrial city had created a government in the image of its dominant institution, the large business enterprise.

The commission-manager system adapted nicely to small and medium-sized cities, but not to larger ones. No commission could cope with the complex affairs and diverse constituencies of the great cities. In 1912 Charles A. Beard singled out the election of commissioners by citywide vote as "a practice which, of course, substantially excludes minority representation, and is so highly undesirable as to constitute a serious objection to the adoption of the scheme in large cities." Practical politics reinforced this conclusion. The ward system had set down deep roots in the major cities; reformers would find it desperate work to budge— much less abolish—these well-entrenched power structures. The great cities had many more immigrants and minorities than smaller ones had, and the scale of their public affairs defied any proposal to combine legislative and administrative functions in one body.

Structural reformers in the large cities were therefore obliged to try two time-honored tactics. The first was simply to gain control of city hall and clean it up. In Chicago the Municipal Voters' League achieved some success by finding men like George E. Cole, Hoyt King, and Walter L. Fisher who were willing to enter the political arena and beat the politicians at their own game. Reported an admiring Lincoln Steffens:

> Chicago has . . . a reform ring. Political reform, politically conducted, has produced reform politicians working for the reform of the city with the methods of politics. They do everything that a politician does, except buy votes and sell them. They play politics in the interest of the city.

But few cities could uncover reformers able or willing to be pitted against the professionals. In most cases the gains achieved, impressive as they were, ebbed away once the reformers left the scene. On the political seesaw the machine usually had the most weight and always the greatest endurance.

Predictably, the second tactic was to revise the structure of municipal government. The creation of a model charter and bureaus of research were important steps in this direction. Reformers also sought to weaken the city council (which was most susceptible to public influence), strengthen the mayor's office, simplify the overall administrative structure, and bring more positions under civil service examinations.*

Here, too, New York led the way. Its mayor received veto power over all ordinances and resolutions passed by the board of aldermen. He could also appoint and remove at will all department heads; earlier, they had been elected officials beyond his control. In addition, he was made head of the board of estimate and apportionment, which prepared the city's budget, and was given three of the board's sixteen votes.

Boston incorporated a similar arrangement in its charter of 1910 and movements were launched in other cities, notably Minneapolis and Denver, to strengthen the mayor and reorganize municipal offices. Num-

---

* See also Chapter 10.

erous cities created civil service commissions or extended the jurisdiction
of their state commission to cover some municipal offices. In 1911 the
United States Civil Service Commission's report included a list of 217
cities which were applying the merit system to some or all branches
of their administrations.

Thus structural reform veered in two directions. While many small
and medium-sized cities revolutionized their political structures, their
giant cousins continued to grapple with what Van Wyck Brooks called
"the old endless unfruitful seesaw of corruption and reform."

A small minority of urban politicians abandoned the traditional seesaw
and followed the more radical trail of social reform. Tom Johnson and
Newton D. Baker in Cleveland, Samuel M. "Golden Rule" Jones and
Brand Whitlock in Toledo, Hazen S. Pingree in Detroit, and Mark
Fagan in Jersey City were among those who sought to restore genuinely
democratic government. "I have come to lean upon the common people
as the real foundation upon which good government must rest," Pingree
proclaimed in 1897. In their own fashion most social reformers reached
conclusions similar to those of Frederic Howe:

> Business had succeeded in America and it worked with very simple ma-
> chinery. It was not bothered by a constitution; it was not balked by checks
> and balances; it was not compelled to wait for years to achieve what it
> wanted. . . . The freedom of a private corporation was close to license; what
> its officials wanted done was done. Mayors, governors, legislatures, city
> councils had no such power. . . . Taking the private corporation as a model,
> I evolved three basic principles; they were: Government should be easily
> understood and easily worked; it should respond immediately to the decision
> of the majority; the people should always rule.

The City as Servant

With few exceptions, structural reformers labored under one supreme
handicap: they were a dull, colorless lot whose sincerity was rarely
leavened by warmth or personal magnetism. Their elitist notions and
personal reserve won them few friends in the forum of public opinion,
and their disdain for the common rabble alienated the city's largest class
of people. Most structuralists cut a poor figure in the political arena.
Unlike the professional politician, they did not usually know how to
build enduring constituencies, much less excite them. Seth Low, a man
of great integrity and ability, deserves an honored niche in the pantheon
of urban reform. He worked hard for New York, won respect, established a clean record, and earned a national reputation. But Low was

not a dynamic personality or even a moderately exciting one; he was incapable of arousing the public enthusiasm necessary for sustaining a prolonged reform crusade.

Lack of popular appeal was not the only serious handicap for structural reformers. They were more than bland; they possessed too limited a vision of the city as community. Their brand of reform was too cold and mechanical, their sense of humanitarianism too abstract. Human needs figured too little in their calculus of uplift. Even worse, they regarded the lower classes not as potential allies in the redemption of the city, but as enemies whose influence must be removed if good government were to be realized. Their programs betrayed a narrowness of vision that seldom transcended their own class interests. In that sense, most structural reformers never conceived of their task as much more than a reordering of power relationships within the city. That is why they focused so intently upon the area of political reform and showed little interest in social measures which rubbed their political and economic orthodoxies the wrong way.

Social reformers possessed none of these limitations. They tended to be colorful, magnetic individuals whose stock-in-trade was the human touch. Unlike structuralists, they were not merely reformers but reform politicians, men with a gift for attracting staunch followings and a groundswell of popular support that overflowed traditional political bounds. Within the political arena they fought with a gusto that inspired fierce loyalty or hatred but never indifference. Above all, the social reformers were men of deep humanitarian impulses whose vision of the city embraced people of every class. In practice they became champions of the urban underdogs, defending the rights of "the people" against the vested interests of the corporation and the machine. This course aligned social reformers against virtually every element of the urban power structure and makes their accomplishments all the more remarkable. It also locked them in perpetual struggles which wore them out before their time.

Social reform mayors changed the nature of urban government by stamping reform with the imprint of their own personalities. Their individual flamboyance, coupled with the humane quality of their programs, offered electorates a meaningful alternative to machine politics that escaped structuralists entirely. Social reformers cared more about people than about the mechanics of government, and this concern led them to concentrate upon economic and social betterment rather than efficiency and economy. It was not ideology that separated them from structural reformers. Some were captivated by Henry George's single-tax notion and receptive to the economic views of Richard T. Ely and John R. Commons, but in general they were political pragmatists who dealt in fundamental issues which affected the entire citizenry. These included transit fares, utility rates, municipal ownership, schools, free lunch programs, parks, playgrounds, public baths, housing, streets, lighting, public health, social welfare programs, and, of course, political corruption.

It would be fascinating to know just why some individuals approach problems in different ways. Most social-reform mayors did not start with advanced views on these matters; it was the play of experience upon receptive minds that brought them to positions deemed radical by most civic leaders. What seems to have distinguished these political mavericks was their capacity for growth, their ability to shed the blinders of tradition and observe conditions about them with fresh eyes. It was as if they harbored some hidden seed of originality which, after long germination, burst forth to carry them beyond the conventional wisdom. Once circumstance nourished this talent to full flower, most social reformers broke sharply with the political past and embarked upon a perilous course set by their enlarged vision of the city's possibilities.

No single description can encompass the careers of these distinctive individuals, but several of them did follow a fairly common pattern. They began as successful businessmen who were coaxed into politics usually as compromise candidates during some time of civic or party stress. Once in office, their response to problems soon offended entrenched interests and transformed their original supporters into political enemies. Forced to seek a new power base, the social reformers turned inevitably to the lower classes and thereby became champions of "the people" against "the interests." With the backing of their new constituencies, liberal mayors altered the prevailing do-nothing social philosophy of city government and waged vigorous campaigns to establish public interests over private ones. In taking forthright stands for positive action they became the precursors of the twentieth-century liberal mayor.

A brief glimpse at the careers of three social-reform mayors will illuminate some variant strains of this general pattern. Hazen S. Pingree rose from humble origins to become a prosperous shoe manufacturer in Detroit. By the 1880s he lived in a fashionable neighborhood, belonged to the best social clubs, served as a director of the Preston National Bank and the Detroit Board of Trade, and was a staunch Republican. When his circle of upper-class friends asked him to run for mayor in 1889, he agreed reluctantly as a concession to civic duty. Pingree had never displayed any political ambitions and seemed an unlikely choice to lead a reform crusade, but his victory soon unveiled to him the sordid depths of political corruption in Detroit politics.

Appalled by the spectacle, Pingree came gradually to understand that his own class bore much of the responsibility for the graft and bribery that outraged him. He experienced firsthand what Steffens later reported—that city governments were corrupt because city business interests were corrupt. As Steffens said of St. Louis, "the stock-in-trade of the boodler is the rights, privileges, franchises, and real property of the city, and his source of corruption is the top, not the bottom, of society." Pingree also learned in Detroit what Steffens was to find in St. Louis: "when the leading men began to devour their own city, the herd rushed into the trough and fed also."

These insights did not come at once. During his first term Pingree acted out the classic structural reform saga, rooting out dishonesty, eliminating inefficiency, emphasizing economy, and improving municipal services. His record gladdened the hearts of Detroit's civic uplifters but left Pingree unsatisfied. Ultimately it was his confrontation with the powerful street railway companies that pushed Pingree toward a broader conception of reform. In 1891 he vetoed a franchise renewal bill and denounced private ownership of such lines as "the chief source of corruption in city governments."

As Pingree's stand against the transit companies hardened, his original business support, and many of his personal friends, deserted him. In their place came a new coalition of lower-class elements dominated by German, Polish, and other ethnic voters, who kept Pingree in office for three more terms. During that time Pingree fought tirelessly for a three-cent transit fare and municipal ownership, instituted relief measures to ease the blight of depression after 1893, attacked the tax-exempt status of large corporations, and embarked upon numerous social programs. His crusade endeared him to lower-class voters and won him a national reputation. In the late 1890s a Buffalo newspaper described him as "the most talked-of Mayor in the United States."

In his eight years as mayor, Pingree transformed himself from a businessman who believed in clean government and low taxes to an advocate of municipal regulation, public ownership of utilities, and extended social services. Through such programs he hoped to redress the balance of economic and political power within the city. While this lofty ideal was never realized, Pingree did achieve enormous success in implementing specific reforms. Holli summarized Pingree's record:

Pingree had reconstructed the sewer system, brought Detroit to the first rank as a well-paved city, inaugurated a conduit system for unsightly and dangerous overhead wires, constructed schools, parks, and a free public bath, exposed corruption in the school board and bribery by a private light company, broken the paving "combine," implemented his equal-tax policies in the city, forced down the cost of ferry, gas, telephone, and streetcar rates, sponsored the entry into the city of a competitive street railway company and a telephone company, established a municipal light plant, forced the adoption of electrified rapid transit, ousted the toll roads, and initiated a work-relief program that had as its goals both aid to the unfortunate and a change in the climate of public opinion towards "paupers."

Pingree changed the concept of the office of mayor in Detroit. More important, he was hailed throughout urban America in the 1890s as proof that the industrial city could be governed effectively in the interests of the people and not merely the privileged few.

In Toledo the career of Samuel M. "Golden Rule" Jones closely paralleled that of Pingree. The son of a Welsh peasant, Jones was a big, horny-handed, sandy-complexioned man with a warm, captivating smile. His family migrated to America where his father became a tenant farmer, but Jones left home at nineteen to try his luck in the oil fields of Pennsylvania and later Ohio. He invented an all-metal sucker rod for use on oil rigs and in 1894 established the Acme Sucker Rod Company in Toledo. The device made a fortune for Jones and enabled him to experiment with some of the most extraordinary labor practices in the country.

Jones was at heart a simple man with a simple philosophy. On the wall of his factory he nailed a tin sign which read, "And as ye would that men should do to you, do ye also to them likewise." Repelled by the amoral competitive industrial ethic, Jones abided by his faith in the Golden Rule. He gave his employees an eight-hour day, a one-week paid vacation, a joint employer-employee health insurance fund, and a Christmas bonus of 5 percent of their wages. He organized picnics and outings, created a company band, and paid for the instruments and music lessons. For his workers Jones built a company dining hall which provided hot meals at low cost; most of the time he ate there himself. Next to the plant he established Golden Rule Park for his "family," complete with playground and Sunday lectures and band concerts for which Jones sometimes composed special songs.

At one point Jones even abolished his time clock and advised his workers to keep their own time. His passion for liberty and belief in the goodness of all men was deep and genuine. "Jones's point of view was always and invariably the human point of view," Brand Whitlock recalled; "he knew no such thing as murderers or criminals, or 'good' people, or 'bad' people, they were all to him men and, indeed, brothers." Lacking formal education—he did not discover literature until he was fifty—Jones practiced his humanitarian ethic with the burning zeal of an evangelist. In his autobiography he explained what had led him to hang the Golden Rule on his factory wall:

It was the reaction that came from the contemplation of the outrageous justice that was practiced upon my fellow-men by the iron-clad rules to which they are made abject slaves in order to gain the right to a bare living. At that time . . . I did not know that the competitive system of industry was calculated to bring out everything that is bad and to suppress all that is good in us, as I now know it is.

This credo was a far cry from the practical benevolence of the ward boss or the cold efficiency of the structural reformers. Yet, like Pingree, Jones was lured into politics as a compromise mayoralty candidate by a band of Republican "best men" seeking to clean up Toledo's politics. As a dark horse, Jones won election in 1897 by only 564 votes. At once he disavowed any pretense of partisan politics and alienated his supporters by refusing to allot patronage in the customary manner. Instead he set out to realize the ideal community described in his autobiography: "In the co-operative commonwealth that is to be realized, in the kingdom of Heaven *that is to be set up here on this earth,* there will be no patents, no railway passes, no reserved seats, no 'free list,' no franchises, or contracts or special privileges of any sort to enable a select few of the people to live off the toil of others."

As mayor, Jones did not realize this heaven on earth, but he came closer than most. He opened lodging homes for tramps; instituted free kindergartens, night schools, and playgrounds; set a minimum wage of $1.50 (the prevailing wage was about $1.00) per day for municipal labor; fought the street railway franchises; introduced the merit system in the police and public works departments; and worked to abolish capital punishment.* Proclaiming that the city and its government belonged

---

* Whitlock records a revealing incident when Jones vetoed a street railway franchise and helped organize a huge demonstration which frightened the city council out of passing the bill over his veto. At that tumultuous meeting an attorney for the railway company sneered at Jones, "I suppose, Mr. Mayor, that this is an example of government under the Golden Rule."

"No," replied Jones in a flash, "it is an example of government under the rule of gold."

to the people, Jones stripped the police of their clubs and replaced them with sticks. He ordered park officials to remove "Keep off the Grass" signs and put up markers reading "Citizens Protect Your Property." In every way he sought to bring the city's people together as "members of the family."

Naturally these actions infuriated the business community, regular politicians, and most of the "best people." Press and pulpit thundered against him, and both parties contrived endlessly to oust him from office. In 1903 the three Toledo newspapers refused even to carry his acceptance of an endorsement by a group of independents. But Jones could not be touched because the lower classes rallied unflaggingly to his cause. Declaring himself "a Man Without a Party," he campaigned from the back of a horse-drawn wagon while his son Paul played the saxophone to announce his arrival. He won the election of 1903, as he had three others, died in office, and was succeeded by his reform disciple, Brand Whitlock.

Ohio produced another giant of social reform, Tom L. Johnson, who by most contemporary accounts turned Cleveland into "the best governed city in America." A short, heavy-set man with a bull neck and indomitable energy, Johnson resembled the worst caricature of the overstuffed capitalist. His early career was an astounding march to business success in the Alger tradition. From a modest childhood in Kentucky he drifted to Cleveland, where he locked horns with Mark Hanna over streetcar franchises. Johnson won that battle, built up his traction company, and sold out his holdings. He then went to Brooklyn, Philadelphia, and Detroit, and repeated the operation; in Detroit he found himself pitted against Hazen Pingree. He bought steel mills in Ohio and Pennsylvania and sold them out. Not yet forty, Johnson had amassed a fortune, and settled into a palatial home on Euclid Avenue in Cleveland.

At first glance Johnson seemed nothing more than another financial success story. But there was something different about him. His fellow magnates were troubled by what Frederic Howe called "the apparent discrepancy between his social position and the things he advocated." Johnson was a Democrat and believed devoutly in free trade. Iron and steel was a powerful industry in Cleveland, yet he won election to Congress by advocating free trade. Even worse, Johnson professed a belief in municipal ownership of traction lines, a cause he was to plead before the very city councils from which he had once extracted franchises.

Johnson's wholehearted conversion to social reform seems to have been triggered by his reading Henry George's *Social Problems,* a book he bought and read to pass time on a train ride. Staggered by George's arguments, he read the book a second time and then took it to a business partner, Arthur Moxham, saying, "Arthur, you know more about books than I do. I haven't read much. But if this book is right, then your business and mine are all wrong." Moxham tried to refute the arguments but after four readings admitted that "the book is sound. Henry George is right." Meanwhile Johnson read *Progress and Poverty* and took it to his lawyer, L. A. Russell. Handing Russell a $500 retainer, he asked for a considered opinion on George's argument. To himself Johnson admitted that "If this book is really true, I shall have to give up business. . . . I must get out of the business or prove that this book is wrong." After a lengthy session disposed of Russell's objections, Johnson went looking for George himself. He found his prophet in Brooklyn, and according to Johnson it was George who persuaded him to run for mayor of Cleveland.

It is an extraordinary tale, but quite possibly a true one. Whatever the case, Johnson ran for mayor on a platform stressing the three-cent fare, municipal ownership, home rule, and just taxation. He won in 1901 and was reelected three more times by an adoring electorate which did not include many of Cleveland's "better people." Johnson resembled "Golden Rule" Jones in his ability to inspire love or hate and in his capacity to attract talented disciples. Frederic Howe, one of those loyal followers, admitted that he "had greater affection for Tom Johnson than for any man I have ever known. He was as dependent upon those he loved as he was indifferent to the hostility of his enemies. He had as much time for affection as he had for work, and he was greedy for both."

Unlike Jones, Johnson was a superb municipal technician. He grasped not only the ethics but the mathematics of government. He knew the business mind, understood lawyers and the law, and was well schooled in the intricacies of the utility industries and street railways. More than any other businessman-turned-reformer, Johnson knew the game, how it was played, and what weapons were in the arsenals of both sides. His own experience made him a formidable champion of public rights, and to it he added a flair for showmanship. Johnson needed no conversion time; he took up the cause of social reform the day he entered office, and he entered office the day the election returns were officially announced. To prevent the incumbent mayor from signing an ordinance that would turn valuable lakefront property over to the railroads, Johnson strode into his office and declared that he had just been sworn in.

Between 1901 and 1909 Cleveland enjoyed a renaissance in municipal government. Johnson's administration resembled a revival meeting in civics when he pitched a huge tent in different parts of the city to hold forums on public affairs. Like Pingree and Jones, he responded to the need for parks, playgrounds, public baths, and social welfare programs. The editor of Johnson's autobiography has recounted his handling of the city's garbage problem:

When Mr. Johnson became mayor the city was disposing of its garbage under the contract plan at an annual cost of $69,000. When the contract expired the city bought the plant, and the very first year under municipal ownership and operation, reduced 10,000 more tons of garbage than under the contract method, and at a cost of $10,000 less and this, notwithstanding a reduction in the hours of employees and an increase of their wages.

Johnson also instituted a municipal electrical plant which reduced the city's cost for light by over one-third. He put in meters for water consumption which saved over 90 percent of the people money on their water bill, pushed through a model building code, established meat and dairy inspection, paved hundreds of miles of road, and implemented new street-cleaning operations. His fight for municipal ownership, lower fares, and home rule locked him in battle with Ohio's political giants, Mark Hanna and Joseph B. Foraker. Against their opposition Johnson fought to obtain a constitutional amendment giving Cleveland home rule. At home he won the fight for a three-cent fare but lost the long and bitter struggle for municipal ownership of the streetcar lines.

Johnson's domineering personality, his frequent pronouncements on liberal reforms like nationalization of railroads and women's suffrage, and the dedication of his protégés, Newton D. Baker and Frederic Howe, helped earn him a national reputation. To the end he retained his faith in Henry George's single-tax principle. Of his philosophy of government he said with characteristic directness:

I believe in municipal ownership of all public services for the same reason that I believe in the municipal ownership of water works, of parks, of schools. I believe in the municipal ownership of these monopolies because if you do not own them they will in time own you. They will rule your politics, corrupt your institutions, and finally destroy your liberties.

Johnson died in 1911, his fortune dissipated and his health broken by the long years of struggle. His faith in the people and his belief that privilege was the root of urban evil never wavered. He left behind him perhaps the most remarkable record achieved by any social-reform mayor.

The careers of Pingree, Jones, and Johnson suggest how social reformers arrived at bolder and more orignal visions of the city's possibilities. In hammering away at measures to equalize the balance of political and economic power, their genuine concern for the social welfare of their constituents gained them a loyal following among the working class. At times it seemed as if no one supported the social reformers but the people. This warm backing from below refutes the notion that immigrant and lower-class elements did not appreciate good government and could not be lured away from their ties to the machine. By sustaining men like Pingree, Jones, and Johnson, they actually formed the backbone of the social-reform movement. No such groundswell of support rallied to the banner of the colder, more aloof structural reformers, who interpreted this as further proof that the lower classes were politically ignorant and dangerous.

It is interesting that all three mayors started life relatively poor and became successful businessmen without forgetting the lean years of their youth. Their interest in civic affairs stemmed from concern over corruption until events shocked their sense of decency and stirred them to a larger vision of service. Jones absorbed the golden rule into his very marrow and tried to instill the Christian ethic into politics. Johnson was converted by Henry George and came to regard free streetcar rides as "the most perfect device I had ever encountered for getting rid of the evils arising from the collection of fares." Experience in office gave Pingree his shock of recognition, and the Depression of 1893–97 moved him to fight for the rights of the unemployed and to establish municipal "potato patches" to grow food for the poor. All three men deserted their class, and were ostracized for doing so, to serve what they regarded as a higher calling. In effect they transcended the vision of the city as marketplace, something that structural reformers never achieved.

Social reform arose in the great industrial cities of the midwestern states. The movement against powerful corporations and corrupt machines began in these cities when political improprieties became so gross they could no longer be ignored. As George Mowry observed, "In 1896 less than half of the waterworks were owned by municipalities. By 1915 almost two-thirds of them were owned and operated by city governments. New but still significant progress was made in the field of gas, electricity, and public transportation." The results, as Mowry reminds us, went beyond the city limits: "To a larger degree than has been recognized, it was the city that both blazed the way and supplied the pressure for much of the state regulatory enactments in the new century."

Social-reform politicians like Pingree, Jones, and Johnson led a renaissance which many believed would lift the city from the morass of the nineteenth century to become "the hope of democracy." That promise has not been fulfilled. Perhaps we would be nearer that goal if there had been more such men, but there were not. They had pushed urban government into a new realm of possibilities, but their structural counterparts proved more enduring. The latter brand of reform was less humanistic and relied on the more mechanical notions of efficiency and bureaucratization. Structural reform dominated the twentieth century because it challenged fewer interests, caused less radical change, and enshrined the false idol of scientific management as an adequate cure for urban ills. Professionals and experts abound in city governments today and are necessary, but a sprinkling of Tom Johnson or "Golden Rule" Jones might do wonders for the human landscape.

The Reform Riddle

The struggle for political reform in the industrial city was a prominent part of that national reform phenomenon known as the progressive movement. Historians have long been at loggerheads over the question of defining progressivism, its objectives, ideology, and membership.* The ambiguities and disagreements that cloud their appraisal of national progressivism apply with equal force to the municipal level. Urban progressives were of many stripes in backgrounds, objectives, and reform concerns. After sixty years of hindsight no one has improved much on the description of progressivism as a political movement written by Benjamin P. DeWitt in 1915. In *The Progressive Movement*, DeWitt traced the origins and development of political progressivism and outlined its principles and programs in the national, state, and urban arenas. His description of municipal progressivism is worth examining because it embodies a fatal contradiction which tormented those reformers who recognized it and thwarted the efforts of those who overlooked it: the irresolvable conflict between the desire for greater efficiency in government and the desire for a more democratic government.

Like many social reformers, DeWitt believed that "the city is the workshop, the experiment station of democracy."** At the state and national levels, progressivism passed through three phases: it sought to remove corrupt influence from government, to modify the structure of government to make it more responsive to the people, and finally to use this

* One historian, Peter G. Filene, in an article entitled "An Obituary for the Progressive Movement," *American Quarterly* (Spring 1970): 20–34, has argued persuasively that Progressivism cannot even be called a "movement" in any meaningful sense of the term.
** This attitude contrasted sharply with that of structural-reform theorists whose gloomy descriptions of urban politics prompted Frederic Howe to complain that "Distrust of democracy has inspired much of the literature on the city."

restored government to relieve social and economic distress. The urban
version of this agenda differed in certain respects. It began with the fight
for home rule. "The first problem of the city . . . that would be progressive," wrote DeWitt, "is to become free. . . . To realize itself fully, a
city must . . . be free from the domination of the state legislature—must,
in other words, have municipal home rule."

Once free of "domination of special influence and from the interference of the state legislature," the city should "adopt that form of city
charter that will afford to its voters the largest opportunity for direct and
effective participation in municipal affairs." The third phase was what
DeWitt termed "the so-called efficiency movement":

> The thesis of the rapidly increasing body of men who support the efficiency
> movement in city government is that running a city is like running a business
> and that the success of the one, as the success of the other, depends very
> largely on efficient and economical organization and methods.

Finally DeWitt added a fourth phase, "the socialization, so far as is
practicable, of the city's activities." Asserting that the first three phases
were "not ends in themselves, but merely means to an end," and that the
true end of government was "to serve the people," DeWitt saw progressives as endeavoring "to extend the functions of city government to promote the welfare and comfort of its inhabitants."

As we have seen, it was precisely on this last phase that structural and
social reformers parted company. DeWitt himself ignored this fissure in
his survey of the reform terrain. Having made no distinction between
different stripes of reformers, he insisted that efficiency was compatible
with, indeed a necessary prelude to, any extension of social services. "The
efficiency movement is concerned merely with improving government,
the tool of democracy," he declared; "it has no part in directing its use."

Structural reformers thought otherwise. They came to believe that
efficiency and economy in government were not means but ends in
themselves. DeWitt's scheme fit them only halfway. Structuralists applauded home rule and the fight against corruption. To that end they
enthusiastically supported charter reform, but for very different reasons
than DeWitt supposed. Whether advocating the commission-manager
plan in smaller cities or charter revisions in larger ones, they wished to
narrow rather than broaden the base of urban democracy. They wanted
not government by all the people, but government by the right people;
their goal was not to democratize municipal politics, but to supplant one
ruling class with another.

Obviously structural reformers eagerly supported what DeWitt called the "efficiency movement." This was the central canon in their reform creed. Obviously, too, they balked at "socializing" the city beyond the level of improving basic services. Businessmen were not social ogres; they wished to make their city a better place to live, but only to a point where the effort did not undermine their primary goals of efficiency, reduced costs, lower taxes, and government run on sound business principles. According to Weinstein, the quest for these goals sometimes compelled structuralists to adopt the very programs demanded by social reformers:

> Business leaders did not intend to share with other classes in their cities any more than was necessary. They were willing to make concessions on programs, however, particularly since many of the programs supported or demanded by reformers and working men made for greater efficiency and lessened class antagonisms. This led them, perhaps unknowingly in some instances, in the direction of municipal ownership, of increased planning, and, especially where the competition from radicals was keen, even toward social reform.

No amount of concession could ultimately bridge the chasm between structural and social reformers. Their diagnosis of the city's ills differed too radically to allow urban reform the luxury of a united front. Partly because of their class and cultural biases, structuralists identified urban corruption with bossism and political machines which fed on the rising tide of foreign and lower-class elements in the city. Social reformers attributed the urban malaise to the cancerous growth of privilege, the major source of which was the business community that often spearheaded campaigns for structural reform.

Urban reform never found a viable middle ground between these positions, probably because none existed. In the final analysis they were radically opposite visions of what the city should be, and one could not be realized without sacrificing much of the other. The city as community was incompatible with the city as marketplace. Businessmen gave economic growth priority over social development while genteel reformers and social theorists both preferred government by an elite to any democratization of urban politics. These orthodoxies had the weight of tradition on their side along with the tacit approval of those people who had come to the city in search of a new life and new opportunities. For most urbanites the vision of utopia remained a private and individual one devoted to self-betterment rather than a new community founded upon changed social ideals.

Thus it was primarily the structuralists who shaped the course of urban reform and not the social reformers with their more radical and visionary schemes. In the long run the structuralists' victory has proved a Pyrrhic one. Their "conservative revolution in city government," as Holli called it, never got at the basic social needs of urban America. The crusades against political machines crippled the one important institution which took heed of the immigrant's presence and helped assimilate him into a strange new world. Confident that they had touched the heart of the urban dilemma, structuralists had, in fact, only scratched the surface. Blinded by their conviction, they remained little more than moral plumbers forever tinkering with and adjusting the pipes of the political system in hopes of flushing out their clogged residues of evil. While they tinkered, the city's social wounds continued to fester, bursting occasionally into ugly open sores to which were applied the latest reform balm. The "old endless unfruitful seesaw" went on, and with its static undulations persisted those problems that continue to plague the modern city.

CHAPTER 12

Cleansed Cities:
Social Welfare and Moral Purity

It is hardly likely that any social revolution, by which hereafter capitalism may be overthrown, will cause more injustice, more physical suffering, and more heartache than the industrial revolution by which capitalism rose to power.

That such an evil turn could be given to an event that held such a power for good, is a crushing demonstration that the moral forces in humanity failed to keep pace with its intellectual and economic development.

—WALTER RAUSCHENBUSCH
Christianity and the Social Crisis (1907)

WHILE URBAN POLITICAL reform usually received the most publicity, thousands of other individuals crusaded for causes so numerous and diverse as to defy easy summary. The more important of these fell into three categories: social welfare, moral purity, and city planning. Advocates of these causes were not oblivious of politics or the need for political reform; many of them eventually got embroiled in politics to attain their goals. They differed from political reformers in that their main concern was not reform of the political system, but use of it to procure other changes they deemed more important. While this need led some to support political reform drives, it prompted others to make their peace with the prevailing machine and work within the system at hand.

At first glance these three stripes of the reform rainbow appear to have little in common. Their objectives varied widely, and their practitioners held sharply contrasting philosophies of reform. Frequently they came into open conflict with one another. Yet, despite their differences, they shared some important characteristics. All three groups were appalled by the deranged social order of the industrial city and sought to correct its worst features. They disagreed in their diagnoses of the major ills and therefore adopted different remedies. To the first group, the city's worst symptoms revolved around the social and economic plight of the poor. The second group was disturbed by the city's deteriorating moral climate, and the third by its physical blight.

In a sense, the crusades to improve social conditions, the moral climate, and physical blight were but different means to the same end. All three wished to cleanse the city of its worst impurities, to make it a better place to live by scrubbing away the excrescences of evil and disorder which rampant economic growth had nourished. Although their efforts did not bring about the social regeneration they desired, the new institutions, professions, and lobbying groups they established helped push society to the recognition that it bore a large measure of responsibility for the conditions of life in the industrial city. Slowly and painfully this concept of social responsibility eroded the traditional individualist ethos which had allowed government to remain officially indifferent to vast realms of human need and suffering.

Houses of Hope

Of all the city's reformers, none dealt with more fundamental human wants than those engaged in social-welfare work. Their brand of concern took them out of the parlor and into the city's streets, tenements, factories, and schools, where they ministered directly to the needs of the poorer classes. While some social-welfare reformers remained practicing amateurs all their lives, others helped transform charitable work from a part-time activity of volunteer "do-gooders" to a full-time occupation dominated by trained specialists. The emergence of social work as a profession signified among other things that the welfare of the city's poor was becoming the legitimate responsibility of public agencies rather than private charities.

Tradition had made urban benevolence a creature of the marketplace. With few exceptions, charitable work was relegated to private agencies. Public almshouses or poorhouses existed throughout the nineteenth century, but only the most desperate paupers sought asylum in them. The almshouse was a chamber of horrors into which the refuse of suffering humanity was indiscriminately piled. Its degraded state was a deliberate attempt to discourage applicants who might be tempted to seek permanent support from the taxpayers. In Robert Bremner's terse words,

"The aim of public relief in the nineteenth century was to prevent starvation and death from exposure as economically as possible."

Americans frowned upon public relief because they regarded it as a corrupting influence. It ran directly against their ideological grain. The individualist ethos, reinforced by the stern dictums of Social Darwinism, held every individual responsible for his own destiny. Government might provide relief for the insane, the feeble, and the handicapped, but not for the poor, whose distress sprang from economic origins. Unemployment compensation, old-age pensions, or aid to those disabled on the job were not deemed proper public business. Not even a major depression could shake this prevailing faith in the individual's ability to care for himself. Grover Cleveland expressed this sentiment succinctly during the 1890s when he stated in a veto message that "while the people should patriotically and cheerfully support their Government, its functions do not include the support of the people."

This attitude of official indifference prevailed at all levels of government. To some extent it seemed a reasonable one until the rapid march of industrialization transformed the urban environment and created dimensions of poverty and misery so vast that they could no longer be safely ignored. The social dislocation that characterized the rise of the industrial city did more than provide a spectacle of human distress; it posed the more ominous threat of social upheaval. It was the depression of the 1870s that first threw these problems into sharp relief and galvanized concerned citizens into action.

Predictably, the response came from private rather than public agencies. During the 1870s and 1880s the charity organization movement emerged in Buffalo, New Haven, Cincinnati, Boston, Philadelphia, Brooklyn, New York, and elsewhere. Borrowing an English idea, American philanthropists formed charitable organization societies which dispensed no aid but rather served as bureaus of investigation and information. According to Robert Bremner, the societies sought to "coordinate the work of the numerous and occasionally competing philanthropic organizations already in existence, encourage the investigation of appeals for assistance, prevent duplication of effort by different groups, discover imposters, and suppress mendicancy."

In time the charitable organization societies got into the business of providing direct aid, but even then they continued to stress the twin objectives of making relief programs more efficient and eliminating fraud which encouraged indolence. Their work drew upon the earlier experience of the New York Association for Improving the Conditions of the Poor (established in 1843) and some experimental relief programs in

Europe. The organization movement marked an important step in a growing drive to make philanthropy more scientific. It reflected a desire not only to systematize relief work, but also to exert proper supervision over the poor, "to help them avoid the snares of intemperance, indolence, and improvidence."

Supervision took the form of "friendly visits" by volunteer workers to those seeking aid. This notion of personal service gave relief work an unavoidable air of paternalism; it also served as a means of social control. Charity organizers like Josephine Shaw Lowell of New York, Robert Treat Paine of Boston, Mary Richmond of Baltimore, S. Humphreys Gurteen of Buffalo, and Oscar McCulloch of Indianapolis, understood this dual function. They and others like them were not only "missionaries, in the most literal sense, of a new benevolent gospel," as Lubove put it, but also people engaged in work which Paine called the "only hope of civilization against the gathering curse of pauperism in great cities." On this point Lubove concluded that "charity organization represented, in large measure, an instrument of urban social control for the conservative middle class."

During the next three decades, volunteer charitable work gave way to a growing corps of professional social workers administered by bureaucratic agencies. Private charitable organizations and volunteer workers never disappeared, but their role diminished and was profoundly altered by the rise of trained specialists who claimed the field as their own expert domain. Through this process social-welfare work endured growing pains and dislocations similar to those wrought by specialization and bureaucratization in business and other areas.

In the realm of social welfare, the charity organization movement resembled the drive for structural reform in the political sphere. Both sought to solve complex problems by applying scientific techniques of organization. Both made efficiency a primary goal and sought to bring about change without seriously disturbing social, political, and economic orthodoxies. If structural reform had its parallel in social welfare, so did social reform. While the latter existed in numerous forms, the most conspicuous was that band of middle-class men and women who shed their comfortable surroundings to live and work in tenement districts. No institution symbolized the thrust of urban social reform more dramatically than the settlement house. So influential were the settlement-house workers that historian Allen F. Davis has labeled them the "spearheads" of progressive reform in the city.

Inspired by Toynbee Hall (1884), the first settlement house in the slums of East London, several groups of idealistic young Americans established similar institutions in their own cities. To their credit, they plunged into the worst districts the city had to offer. Stanton Coit, Charles Stover, and Edward King located their Neighborhood Guild, the country's first settlement house, on the Lower East Side. In 1887 some graduates of Smith, Vassar, Wellesley, Bryn Mawr, and Radcliffe, headed by Vida Scudder, rented a dilapidated tenement and opened the College Settlement a few blocks from the Neighborhood Guild.* Of this venture a New York paper sneered, "Seven Lilies have been dropped in the mud, and the mud does not seem particularly pleased."

Nevertheless, the girls remained and the settlement idea flourished. Lillian Wald and Mary Brewster opened their Henry Street Settlement (1893) on the Lower East Side. In Chicago, Jane Addams and Ellen Gates Starr converted an old mansion on Halsted Street into what became the nation's best known settlement, Hull House (1889). Three years later, Robert A. Woods began his South End House in Boston. According to Davis, the number of settlements rose from 6 in 1891 to 74 in 1897. During the next decade the increase was even more spectacular, jumping from about 100 in 1900 to more than 400 in 1910.

This record becomes even more impressive when one considers the work involved and the probability of success. Settlement workers sought nothing less than regeneration of the slum neighborhood. That meant abandoning their own middle-class lifestyles. As Lillian Wald stated in *The House on Henry Street* (1915), "We were to live in the neighborhood . . . identify ourselves with it socially, and, in brief, contribute to it our citizenship." The goal was to forge a sense of community spirit among the most desperate people of the city. "We gradually became acquainted with the people of the neighborhood," Robert Woods explained, "and are able to exercise influence on family life, and also on the general social life."

The work covered a broad range of community service. The settlement house served as a social center; immigrants came to regard it as a community club and made it a gathering spot. To keep youngsters off the streets, settlement workers created special clubs; organized classes in art, music, crafts, manual arts, and language; built playgrounds, gymnasiums, and other recreational facilities; served low-cost meals; and provided enter-

* Allen F. Davis recounts the introduction of these young women to slum life: "Their first visitor was a policeman, who could not imagine what the well-dressed young women were doing in the slums if not opening another house of prostitution. He stopped by to let them know that he would leave them alone if they made a regular monthly contribution to his income."

tainment with theater groups. Some settlements stressed educational programs, but all fostered a sense of closeness and community pride.

For all their noble efforts, the settlement workers soon discovered that the services they offered were not enough. They ameliorated the worst excesses of the slums, but could not get at the underlying conditions which perpetuated slum life. Frederic Howe recalled his uneasiness with social and educational work:

My activities at the settlement, as I recall them, were anything but fruitful. As a friendly visitor to the tenements, I was uncomfortable. When I organized clubs, I felt that I had little in common with the boys. I did not enjoy dancing with heavy-footed mothers of many children who were lured from the tenements to our parties. When asked to teach politics, I remembered my experience on the East Side of New York, and felt that my philosophy was somehow out of joint. On the edge of the red-light district, the settlement was expected to investigate and see what could be done to improve the morals of the women who lived there. To that end, I collaborated in making out meaningless charts which nobody read but which we exhibited from time to time at meetings of the boards of trustees.

This disenchantment with purely community-oriented programs led some settlement workers to adopt a more ambitious role as lobbyists for their "constituents." They backed local drives against utility companies, arbitrated labor disputes which affected neighborhood residents, fought for tenement regulations, better schools, and improved health facilities, hounded local ward bosses when city services did not reach the slums, and campaigned for laws restricting child and woman labor. As Jane Addams depicted this new role:

We early found ourselves spending many hours in efforts to secure support for deserted women, insurance for bewildered widows, damages for injured operators, furniture from the clutches of the installment store. The Settlement is valuable as an informative and interpretive bureau. It constantly acts between the various institutions of the city and the people for whose benefits these were enacted.

The motives that inspired this generation of settlement workers are varied, but Davis has offered a profile of their backgrounds which suggests why they undertook such work. Obviously they were an idealistic lot, and usually this idealism sprang from a religious (primarily Calvinist) upbringing. Most were young, came from old-stock families, had grown up in cities, and were moderately well-to-do. Nearly 90 percent had attended college, and a good number were the sons and daughters of ministers. On the whole, they were an intellectually exciting group whose enthusiasm attracted others to settlement work.

It was no accident that many of the settlement workers were women. This first generation of college-trained women were eager to put theory into action. Given the limited options available to middle-class young women, settlement work offered the more idealistic among them a way to attack social problems in a manner that took them outside the parlor and into the "real" world. Davis concluded that "there were many influences that molded a generation of young men and women to make them want to change things. Some became settlement workers for very practical reasons, but as a group they were idealists who believed they were help- ing to solve the problems of urban and industrial America."

In addition to their own activities, settlement workers lent support to other reformers working in related areas of social uplift. Housing reform offers a good example. To some extent, the housing reform movement grew out of the settlement movement. Although some model tenements— notably Alfred T. White's projects in Brooklyn—were built by philan- thropists in the 1870s and 1880s, the main thrust for better housing came during the 1890s under the leadership of Lawrence Veiller, who began his career at University Settlement in New York. After working to aid the poor during the Depression of 1893, Veiller realized that "the im- provement of the homes of the people was the starting point for every- thing." This discovery launched him on his career of fact-finding (usually aided by settlement workers), propagandizing through exhibitions and publications, and pressing for restrictive legislation and housing codes.*
Veiller did much to secure the passage of New York's innovative 1901 code which eliminated the worst abuses of tenement construction and established a Tenement House Department to enforce the new code. His organization of the National Housing Association in 1910 offered models for cities to follow in this area of mass housing improvement.

Settlement workers also aided, indeed inspired, the drive for recreation facilities. At Hull House, Florence Kelley established Chicago's first public playground in 1893, whereupon settlement workers in other cities began pressing landowners and municipal governments to provide and maintain plots of land for outdoor recreation. Jacob Riis took up the cause and led a lengthy campaign which finally demolished a row of tenements at the notorious Mulberry Bend and replaced them with Co- lumbus Park. In 1898 Riis joined with Felix Adler, Nicholas Murray

---

* See Chapter 9.

Butler, Richard Watson Gilder, William Dean Howells, and others, to begin the Outdoor Recreation League in New York. Led by Lillian Wald, the group managed to have a plot of land cleared for a park.* Private donations supplied the equipment, but the League pressed the city to create its own playgrounds with play equipment, sandboxes, and basketball courts. At length the lobbying helped move the city from its position of maintaining only formal parks to one which also provided recreational facilities.

Recognition of the need for play areas in poor areas sparked similar drives in all major cities. By 1910 some 80 cities maintained public playgrounds while nearly 100 more operated privately sponsored facilities. The Playground Association of America, founded in 1906, was dominated by settlement workers, including Jane Addams, who promoted the goal of healthful outdoor play to improve the urban environment. The cry "Playgrounds for the people" struck a vital nerve in the slums, and the open space secured was one of the most tangible assets of the reform crusade.

The fight for playgrounds was part of the larger battle to improve health standards. The revolution in bacteriology enabled urban governments to establish diagnostic clinics which placed preventive medicine on a firm footing.** Some cities, goaded by settlement workers and others, went even further in promoting reform of sanitation and health departments. New York offers an instructive example. While Hermann Biggs campaigned to introduce diagnostic testing in city laboratories, George E. Waring, Jr. transformed the neglected field of urban sanitation.

Waring, a farmer, writer, and engineer, had been appointed head of the Department of Street Cleaning by reform Mayor William Strong. Accepting with glee the free hand given him by Strong, Waring launched a vigorous crusade against urban filth. With reformers cheering him on and Riis promoting his efforts with dramatic "before and after" photographs, Waring purged his department of politics and set his men to work. He outfitted them in snappy white uniforms intended to bring new respect to the sanitation cause. "Waring's White Angels" soon became a sensation in New York and prompted other cities to adopt the device. To publicize his crusade for cleanliness, Waring paraded his Angels through the city's streets like a conquering army come home. Richard Skolnik describes what happened on May 26, 1896, when

New Yorkers lined the streets to watch what surely must have been one of the most bizarre processions to pass through the city's thoroughfares. Amidst

* This playground became known as Seward Park.
** See Chapter 9.

the strains of martial band music, Waring, on horseback with the 2,700-man Department marshaled smartly behind him, acknowledged the cheers of the spectators. Column after column of Department equipment and white-garbed street cleaners, pushing their garbage carts before them, passed the reviewing stand where Mayor Strong and other municipal officials watched approvingly. Newspaper opinion unanimously acclaimed the unusual display for its success in lifting the Department to the level of public acceptance.

One observer noted that "the politicians denounced the outrage and ridiculed the act, but the actor triumphed." Waring even organized children's leagues as auxiliaries to the department. In his campaign against waste, he helped move the city away from traditional sea-dumping toward increased use of incinerator burning. For all its flamboyance, Waring's sanitation corps represented honest, efficient government service. The white uniforms of the Angels symbolized the purity of purpose and "clean broom" image Strong and his fellow reformers wished to project. Other mayors like Pingree and Jones hastened to create their own battalions of White Angels.

Social-welfare reform thus ran the whole gamut of urban ills: housing, recreation, sanitation, health, work, family life, crime, and dozens more. The settlement workers, with their enormous energy and insatiable appetite for the good cause, stood at the intersection of all these issues. Sooner than most social-welfare reformers, they learned the painful truth: none of the city's problems could be treated effectively apart from the others. If nothing else, and there was much else, settlement workers helped demonstrate how all urban problems were interrelated. They were not long at the task of building a sense of community in the slums before realizing the connections between poverty, low wages, long hours in the factory, the need for cheap housing, congestion, health and sanitation, crime, lack of recreation, retarded education, family disintegration, and collapsed moral values.

Having witnessed the process firsthand, social-welfare reformers understood all the elements that made up what we have come to call the poverty cycle. This recognition impelled them to lash out at many of the problems at the same time and thereby to dilute their overall effectiveness. Their dilemma—and ours—was how to find an effective handle on that complex and vicious cycle. No approach seemed entirely satisfactory. Some persisted in a scattergun manner which accomplished little; others burrowed so deeply into one particular area that their expertise encouraged a vested interest in perpetuating the problem and led to a loss of perspective upon the larger picture.

Paradox and irony bedeviled the best efforts of these well-intentioned reformers. To see the whole panoply of urban ills, to grasp their threads of connection, did not unveil clear and fruitful avenues of attack. Their experience taught them the futility of going at problems on a piecemeal basis even while it made them despair that wholesale change could ever be achieved. Knowledge proved to be not power but frustration. Some succumbed to weariness and despondency, while others were content to amass their minor victories and hope for a better day.

Those who attempted to tackle urban problems on a larger scale encountered yet another cruel irony. In carrying their crusade to the national arena, they removed themselves from their cities and created a leadership vacuum at the local level. Yet the temptation to expand the front was irresistible. Jane Addams understood this when she lamented that "Private beneficence is totally inadequate to deal with the vast numbers of the city's disinherited." Historian John Garraty summarized the plight of those who struggled to contain the problem at the local level:

As a tropical forest grows faster than a handful of men armed with machetes can cut it down, so the slums, fed by an annual influx of hundreds of thousands, blighted additional areas more rapidly than the intrepid settlement house workers could clean up old ones. It became increasingly apparent that the wealth and authority of the state must be brought to bear in order to keep abreast of the problems.

Gradually a pattern emerged. Ensnarled in a maze of social problems that creaky, reluctant municipal governments could not or would not attack vigorously, social-welfare reformers moved to the national front. Florence Kelley, Julian Lathrop, Grace Abbott, and Lillian Wald fought for child-labor legislation; Louis Brandeis worked for laws to protect working women; Seth Low pressed for workmen's compensation; and Judge Ben Lindsay labored for humane treatment of juvenile delinquents. These campaigns and others stirred the nation's conscience and contributed much to national progressive reform. The legislation that resulted from the national activities of these reformers surely aided the masses in the cities.

But the vigor of national progressive reform eventually waned. The cities remained essentially unchanged, and their residents, while better off in some respects, never saw the wholesale revamping of their social environment which was so urgently needed. The social-welfare reformers who plunged into the arena of national politics did not find there that road to the better world which had eluded them so persistently in their own cities.

Purification Rites

While social-welfare reformers struggled to improve the city's living conditions, another group devoted itself to purifying the minds and bodies of urbanites. Moral reform embraced many causes: prohibition, abolition of prostitution, suppression of the white-slave traffic, social hygiene, campaigns against venereal disease, sex education, age-of-consent legislation, censorship of literature, child rearing, and many others. Toward the century's end, many of these drives converged into what has been called the "purity crusade," the purpose of which was nothing less than regeneration of the social environment.

No brief account can do justice to the kaleidoscope of causes that comprised moral reform. The movements were so numerous and so intertwined with one another that few historians have braved the thicket. It has always been easier to caricature the moral reformers as Victorian or neo-Puritan prigs who attributed all social ills to a weakening moral fiber and believed the social order could be made whole simply by making it wholesome. Actually, moral reformers were a complex group whose views and intentions went far beyond the mere curbing of physical appetites or suppressing of vice. This more refined conception of moral reform can be illustrated by surveying two major areas of concern: purity and prohibition.

The purity movement sprang from the confusion wrought by changing sex relationships in the industrial urban environment. Americans have always been uneasy in their official attitudes toward sexual behavior, the extremes ranging from the clichés of Victorian prudery to the early nineteenth-century advocacy of free love by John Humphrey Noyes and others to the polygamy practiced by Mormons which drew ferocious censure. In actuality, sexual behavior varied widely. Prostitution and other forms of vice flourished in all the major cities—especially in Boston, of all places—but not on the scale or organized commercial basis it assumed in the industrial city.

In general, Americans dealt with problems of sex simply by refusing to acknowledge or discuss them. This "conspiracy of silence" prevailed throughout much of the nineteenth century until the forces pressing against it could no longer be ignored. The seamy underside of commercialized vice in the industrial city, which deeply offended the dominant middle-class morality, could not be waved aside, if only because of its close connections with political corruption. Moreover, eager bands of reformers were publicizing the doctrines of Freud and pushing such issues as prostitution, birth control, white slavery, and free love into the arena of public discussion. The plight of young girls new to the city and living alone aroused widespread concern. The result was a change in American attitudes toward sexual matters which seemed more abrupt than it was. As David J. Pivar has observed, "For decades, reformers had been conducting a continuing debate among themselves, and occasionally with the public, on numerous sex issues."

A series of exposés on the more lurid aspects of urban life helped shock the public into awareness. Two books—B. E. Lloyd's *Lights and Shades in San Francisco* (1876) and George W. Waring's *Recollections of a New York Chief of Police* (1887)—unveiled sordid portraits of crime, prostitution, and drug addiction. Riis's *How the Other Half Lives* reinforced this impression, but it was Benjamin O. Flower who, after tagging along with the Boston police in the slums, catalogued the horrors he saw with a mixture of concern, disdain, and moralism in *Civilization's Inferno* (1893). Here is his description of one den of inequity:

We have now reached a nest of old buildings with an unsavory record. Here we find negroes and whites mingling together. The creaking stairways are worn and carpeted with filth; the walls and ceilings blistered with the foul accretions of months and perhaps years. It is a noisy spot; snatches of low songs, oaths, coarse jests, and the savage voices of poor wretches whose brains are inflamed and tongues made thick with rum, meet our ears on every side. The air is heavy with odors of spoiled fish, decayed vegetables, smoke from old pipes, stale beer. From one room loud and angry voices proceed, a note of fear mingled with a threatening tone; the room seems perfectly dark. With a quick movement the officer lifts the smoking lamp from a stool in the hall, and opens the door. The scene is sickening in the extreme, one of the most disgusting spectacles in the underworld, none the less terrible because it is common. A filthy den, occupied by a young girl . . . her companion a low-browed, thick-necked negro. . . . Ah! poor Ishmaelites of our 19th century civilization; terrible is your fate!

Civilization's Inferno aroused middle-class awareness to the degradation that befell society's poorest people and would have had an even greater impact had it not been upstaged within a year by William T. Stead's *If Christ Came to Chicago* (1894). Blessed with an eye-catching title, the book enjoyed skyrocketing popularity because of Stead's sensational account of Chicago's netherworld and his pinpoint location of the city's red-light districts. A British journalist-reformer imbued with evangelical religion, Stead itemized the corrupt business-political alliance which allowed vice to flourish in Chicago. By including lists of prominent citizens who owned property being used for criminal purposes, his exposé helped prompt the formation of the Civic Federation as a pressure group for moral uplift.*

As the growing popularity of these exposés attests, the purity movement had come a long way by the 1890s. It had begun in the late 1860s as an attack upon prostitution, the white-slave traffic, and commercialized vice. According to David Pivar, this drive was spearheaded by a variety of women reformers, especially a small band of former abolitionists who after the Civil War "became moral educationists and interested themselves in sex reform, child rearing, sexual criminality, and prostitution. They addressed themselves to seemingly dissimilar reform interests, developed action programs, and infused the women's movement with their spirit of opposition to legalized prostitution in American cities."

The fight against prostitution gradually attracted an assortment of reformers including radical feminists, more conservative groups such as the WCTU and General Federation of Women's Clubs, women physicians, philanthropists, moral education societies, public health officials, prison reformers, working-girl associations, health reformers, social hygienists, and a sprinkling of genteel reformers and moral watchdogs. Indeed, the most remarkable feature of the movement was the panoply of reform elements who lent it support for one reason or another. By the mid–1880s the campaign against prostitution had given way to a much broader crusade for social purity which crested during the years after 1900.

Pivar has delineated this transformation from a relatively modest movement to a national reform phenomenon. Much of its impetus came from the fuel of moral indignation unleashed in the long battle against prostitution. After the Civil War most major American cities veered toward reglementation as a means of dealing with prostitution.** Those who dealt with the problem on a regular basis—the police, physicians, and public health officials—naturally favored a practical solution. The prospect of abolishing prostitution appeared unlikely—there were reasons why it was called "the world's oldest profession"—and meanwhile it posed a health menace if allowed to run unchecked. In practice reglementation amounted to a kind of quasi-license system which permitted prostitutes to practice if they submitted to regular inspections for venereal disease. The result would be a form of regulated vice which protected the innocent from disease.

---

* Stead himself met an unjust reward for his work: he went down with the *Titanic* in 1912.
** Pivar defines reglementation as "the segregation and quarantine of the ill and the compulsory medical inspection of prostitutes."

Reglementation was a practical solution to a sticky problem at a time when the incidence of venereal disease was rising at an alarming rate. Of necessity it remained neutral on the moral dimension of the issue, a fatal stance in a nation where the reform impulse sprang largely from a tradition of religious and moral evangelicism. Reglementation amounted to sanction—if not approval—in the eyes of moral reformers who demanded nothing less than total abolition of prostitution. In the clash that ensued, those favoring reglementation learned the bitter lesson of Stephen A. Douglas in the 1850s: a morally neutral stance on an explosive issue, however sensible, could not withstand concerted attacks grounded in moral and emotional fervor.

For more than a decade the fight went on, with reglementation losing ground steadily in most cities. Between 1877 and 1885 the force of events and emotions broadened the thrust of attack. "Prostitution, as an issue, was subsumed by the larger concern for social purification," Pivar observed, as the various reform elements behind abolition gradually realized that prostitution was but one aspect of a morally flawed social environment. This dawning awareness shifted the reform emphasis from protection of the individual woman to rehabilitation of the environment that threatened her virtue. Prostitution became an intersection at which numerous reform interests met and discovered that their diverse concerns were but different pieces of a much larger puzzle.

As this recognition spread, various reform elements closed ranks to forge what Pivar called "the social purity alliance." The changing environment of the industrial city presented reformers with a choice: "Moralists could respond to new urban conditions . . . by prohibiting specific behavioral deviations, or by constructing social environments that eliminated the potential for that behavior." The one was remedial and tried to tackle difficult problems in isolation from the factors underlying their persistence; the other was preventive and sought to purify urban life by confronting its whole spectrum of evil influences. Clearly the latter offered a more positive and ambitious approach.

Symptoms of this changed emphasis appeared everywhere. During the 1880s vigilance societies, which had been formed to oppose reglementation, regrouped along social purity lines to deal with numerous issues including moral education, child rearing, sex education, the protection of women travelers and working women, social hygiene, and prostitution and the white-slave traffic. As reformers grasped the linkages between their separate concerns, they joined forces to attack several issues simultaneously. Prison reformers recoiled in disgust from the sexual practices they found among prisoners and demanded radical

changes in the penal system. The attack upon white slavery led other reformers to seek changes in "age-of-consent" legislation.* In 1886 the
age of consent was twelve in four states, ten in twenty-five states, and
seven in Delaware. A decade later, twenty-one states had increased the
age of consent, although by 1895 only four had raised it as high as
eighteen.

The protection of single women became the primary mission of
YWCAs, girls' friendly societies, legal aid and traveler societies, and
some church agencies. In New York, Grace Hoadley Dodge prodded the
Working Girls' Society into preventive purity work through lectures
and pamphlets. The Society taught sex education to provide "a training
school for the home" and to prevent innocent girls from going astray
through sheer ignorance. The White Cross Society, modeled on the
English organization, popularized purity objectives through the tireless
efforts of propagandists like Frances Willard of the WCTU. In the
process, it also enlisted many clergymen in the purity crusade. Other religious organizations—especially the Society of Friends—also plunged
into the campaign.

By the 1890s the social purity crusade had emerged as a national movement seeking both remedial solutions to specific problems and the general
purification of social morality. In the latter role, according to Pivar,
"they adopted the principle of prevention popular in public health and
medicine. In so doing they became social hygienists." To preserve stability
in the flux of urban life, they sought to construct a "social religion"
which strengthened family ties and adapted traditional ethical values to
the changed conditions of the city. Child rearing became crucial in this
work because, in Pivar's words, "it focused on character formation. . . .
Character formation, the internalization of values . . . was, above all,
the history of man. Social purists believed they had the key to the future.
Social perfection depended upon the formation of social character."
Proper sex education played an important part in this development by
dispelling ignorance and instilling in children the correct spiritual and
moral attitudes toward sex. If love was to triumph over lust, young people
must learn to regard sex not as mere bestial pleasure, but as the noble
expression of devotion which procreated the species.

In much of their work, social purists faced the same dilemma that
haunted social-welfare reformers. Their experience with specific problems
led them to higher ground where the footing was treacherous and the
task all but insuperable. Particular issues like prostitution did not yield

* The age of consent was that at which a girl could legally have "carnal relations
with the other sex."

to local solutions, yet the totality of social purity reform seemed too vast
to be encompassed or treated effectively. Even worse, purity reformers,
while seeking the positive goal of regenerating society, had of necessity
to fall back upon negative tactics to achieve that end. By its very nature,
moral reform involved the suppression of evil, and the task of suppression
often invited ridicule and bitter opposition. The most sensitive of purity
reformers never resolved this dilemma; the more obtuse went at the work
with a heavy-handed vengeance that distorted their cause into a caricature of its original ideals.

No issue heaped more scorn on the purity movement than censorship.
Any attempt to purify the social environment required the suppression of
unwholesome influences, and the industrial city with its emerging mass
culture abounded in unwholesome influences. Censorship sought to
purge the mind and spirit of poisons just as prohibition and dietary reforms sought to cleanse the body. The common ground between these
types of purity reform went beyond the sharing of metaphors to the
passionate conviction that the individual could not be purified until
society was washed clean of filth and evil. Josiah Leeds of Philadelphia—
an important figure in the censorship campaign who began his career
with an attack on billboard advertising for the 1876 Centennial—referred
to obscene literature, art, and entertainment as "germs of licentiousness."*

The censorship drive extended into every area of urban life which
threatened purity, including ballet and social dancing, photography and
films, clothing, violent sports like football and boxing, and nudity in
art. Determined to eliminate brutalizing influences from society, Frances
Willard once proposed as a debate question, "Resolved, that the
differences between Harvard and Yale be settled by arbitration, without
resort to football." The main thrust of censorship was directed against
reading matter, especially newspapers and literature. Although Josiah
and Deborah Leeds played a major role in this crusade, the man who
became synonymous with antiobscenity was Anthony Comstock.

A rural columnist nurtured on fire-and-brimstone religion, Comstock
moved to New York after the Civil War and was shocked by what he
considered the city's low moral standards. In 1873 he formed the New
York Society for the Suppression of Vice and pressed writs on local
booksellers for carrying lewd reading materials. That same year he
authored and helped steer through Congress the so-called "Comstock

* Both social and health purists thrived on health metaphors. Pivar quotes Dr. J. H.
Kellogg's remark that "As a man eateth, so he thinketh." Kellogg, who ran a sanitarium
in Battle Creek, Michigan, and was an ardent temperance advocate, is best remembered
as the inventor of breakfast cereals.

Law" which banned from the mails any matter "designed to incite lust." As special agent to the Postmaster General, he saw to it that the law was rigorously enforced and was quick to veto advertisements for quack medicines and contraceptives.

For over four decades Comstock stood vigil as guardian of those conventional values clung to by many Americans in a time of turbulent change. He rode herd over printed matter because he believed obscene literature incited sinful actions in its readers. Unfortunately, his definition of obscenity was so indiscriminate that it made no distinction between art and pornography. As a result, Comstock terrorized publishers, artists, and advertisers alike. In helping to form Boston's Watch and Word Society and serving as its "Roundsman of the Lord," he encouraged the Hub City to outstrip all others in banning publications. Balzac, Flaubert, Voltaire, Aristophanes, Ovid, and Whitman led the long list of authors suppressed. Comstock's name became a household word in urban America. As Arthur Schlesinger observed, "His square, stocky figure, bald head and ginger-tinted side whiskers became for many the symbol of a licensed bigotry destructive of much that was choice in art and letters." In a single decade he confiscated an estimated fourteen tons of books and sheet stock and about 1,500,000 circulars, poems, and pictures.

The censorship crusade spread rapidly. Suppression groups were formed in Cincinnati, Chicago, St. Louis, and elsewhere, and the Leedses and Comstock succeeded in persuading several states to enact anti-obscenity legislation. In his relentless campaign, Comstock practiced to the hilt his conviction that "art is not above morals." For other watchdogs with less fixed minds, the distinction between art and pornography was not always so clear-cut, especially among those charged with enforcing the law. Ray Ginger recounted the solution hit upon by a Chicago police sergeant whose job was to ferret out salacious paintings. "If a picture or statue costs $50," he declared, "it is beyond all question a work of art. If an artist devoted sufficient time to make it cost $50 it stands to reason that his motive was high."

Censorship invited ridicule and fierce opposition because it threatened civil and artistic liberties and imposed the tastes of a few as the standard for all. Moreover, it sought to achieve purity through mere suppression rather than through an attempt to get at underlying causes. This shortcoming plagued much of the work done by social purists. In a more subtle fashion, it weakened the movement against the crusade's original objective—prostitution and white slavery—which crested during the 1900s with the activities of the vice commissions.

The parade of shocking exposés like those of Flower and Stead,

coupled with mounting public indignation, prompted several cities to
create blue-ribbon commissions to investigate the problem. After laborious fact-finding, the commissions usually published lengthy reports
which depicted in massive detail the sociology of vice in their cities. As
might be expected, the Chicago Commission and the New York Committee of Fifteen led the field. A brief glimpse at the Chicago report reveals the strengths and limitations of this approach.

Published in 1911, *The Social Evil in Chicago* was a monument to the
techniques of the "factual generation."* It included elaborate studies of
existing conditions, the social evil's relationship to the saloon and the
police, sources of supply, connections to crime, child protection and
education, rescue and reform, medical aspects, law and legislation, and
literature and methods. The commission found that prostitution was
"a *Commercialized Business* of large proportions with tremendous profits
of more than Fifteen Million Dollars per year, controlled largely by
men, not women."

Several factors helped explain this flourishing trade. The commission
concluded that existing laws were not being enforced by the police. It
singled out the saloon and the large number of hotels used as assignation
houses as primary havens of prostitution. Too many children were exposed to immoral conditions and influences. Sex education was woefully
lacking among all classes, but the commission warned that "while intelligence regarding sexual matters, if dictated by moral sentiment, is a
safeguard to the youth of the community, yet the indiscriminate circulation of sexual information among children by means of books and
pamphlets suggests a danger which ought not to escape attention." It
also deplored the unequal burden borne by black citizens who resided in
areas where vice flourished and recommended that "Any effort . . . to
improve conditions in Chicago should provide more wholesome surroundings for the families of its colored citizens who now live in communities of colored people."

In looking at the problem of supply, the commission singled out the
immigrant girl as a major source "because there is no adequate protection
and assistance given her after she reaches the United States," poor home
conditions, the seduction of ignorant young girls by white slavers,
and the desperation of poverty as conditions which brought young women
to prostitution. The commission stressed the importance of rescuing

* The Commission, chaired by Episcopal Dean Walter T. Sumner, included eight
clergy of all denominations, five medical people, five academicians, four businessmen,
three judges and lawyers, the House of Correction superintendent, and representatives
of the Federation of Women's Clubs and Chicago Society of Social Hygiene.

and reforming "immoral girls and women." Its tone toward such women was patronizing but not condemnatory; the main thrust of its criticism was directed at men:

To one who hears the ghastly life story of fallen women it is ever the same—the story of treachery, seduction and downfall . . . the ruin of a soul by man.

It is a man and not a woman problem which we face today—commercialized by man—supported by man—the supply of fresh victims furnished by men— men who have lost that fine instinct of chivalry and that splendid honor for womanhood where the destruction of a woman's soul is abhorrent, and where the defense of a woman's purity is truly the occasion for a valiant fight.

As this passage reveals, the commission viewed prostitution as an outrage, a menace to middle-class values and ideals. Reports from other cities rang with the same indignant tone, which suggests that the commissions, for all their painstaking efforts, filtered their study through the prism of middle-class morality. While their sociology was honest and thorough, it was grounded in a set of moral assumptions that distorted or at least colored much of what the investigators saw.

The tone of the report also reflected how completely the commission embraced the gospel of social purity. Its first recommendation, emblazoned in boldface capital letters atop the first page, read: CONSTANT AND PERSISTENT REPRESSION OF PROSTITUTION THE IMMEDIATE METHOD: ABSOLUTE ANNIHILATION THE ULTIMATE IDEAL. Admitting the problem to be a difficult one, the commission proclaimed:

The Social Evil in its worst phases may be repressed. So long as there is lust in the hearts of men it will seek out some method of expression. Until the hearts of men are changed we can hope for no absolute annihilation of the Social Evil. Religion and education alone can correct the greatest curse which today rests upon mankind. For this there is a mighty work for agencies and institutions of righteousness in our land.

That mighty work was precisely the purpose of the purity crusade. The drive against prostitution achieved modest local victories everywhere, and in 1910 Congress passed the Mann Act forbidding interstate traffic in white slaves.* Yet, as the tide of moral fervor ebbed, it left little permanent imprint. The Social Evil survived and continued to flourish. What had gone wrong? The commission insisted it had "squarely faced the problem," and from its own vantage point it had; but that vantage point

* To get a sense of what the agitation over white slavery was about and why it aroused so much attention, one need only read Reginald Kauffman's *House of Bondage* (1910), a novel based upon the author's research in the white-slave traffic.

was anchored in a middle-class morality which looked at the world through purity-colored glasses.

In *A Preface to Politics* (1913), Walter Lippmann laid bare the shortcomings of this perspective. Dismissing the commission report as "well meaning but unmeaning," Lippmann complained that it "studied a human problem and left humanity out." In regarding lust itself as inherently evil, the commission shut itself off from any alternative to a repressive or negative approach. "Vice issues in pain," Lippmann insisted, and in human need; it could not be dealt with successfully unless those underlying needs were also accommodated. Mere repression treated only symptoms, which prompted Lippmann to complain that "the Commission did not face the sexual impulse squarely. The report is an attempt to deal with a sexual problem by disregarding its source."

The commission itself, Lippmann emphasized, "realized vaguely that repression is not even the first step to a cure," yet it could find nothing more positive to do than issue a string of taboos wrapped around a modest package of moral and educational palliatives. "The millennial goal was one thing; the immediate method quite another. For ideals, a pious phrase; in practice, the police." But increased reliance upon the police created problems of its own. Lippmann recited the experience of the previous generation:

Yet of all the reeds that civilization leans upon, surely the police is the frailest. Anyone who has had the smallest experience of municipal politics knows that the corruption of the police is directly proportionate to the severity of the taboos it is asked to enforce.

Some moral reformers had already learned that lesson from their effort to cleanse the city of crime. In various cities, citizen groups, usually led by clergy, formed Committees of Safety to fight criminal activity. None attracted more attention than New York's Society for the Prevention of Crime. Founded in 1878, the group labored in relative obscurity until Reverend Charles H. Parkhurst of The Madison Square Presbyterian Church assumed its leadership in 1891. Unlike many genteel reformers, Parkhurst had no qualms about plunging into the vice districts to see things for himself. Nor did he hesitate to report what he found in loud and insistent tones. Parkhurst used his pulpit to lambaste Tammany Hall for its collusion with unsavory elements. When city officials, whom Parkhurst denounced as "polluted harpies," pressed him for evidence, the minister hired his own squad of detectives to help him gather it.

It was Parkhurst's crusade that prompted state senator Clarence Lexow to push the legislature into sponsoring an investigating committee.

Amidst a fanfare of publicity, the Lexow Committee, headed by Chief Counsel John Goff, vigorously pursued Parkhurst's allegations. Police, politicians, and businessmen followed prostitutes, madams, and gamblers to the witness stand. From their testimony Goff forged a network of connections that scandalized the Police Department. The ensuing public outcry routed Tammany at the polls and installed William Strong as a reform mayor. Choosing Theodore Roosevelt as his police commissioner, Strong cleaned up police corruption for a time, but the effort proved fleeting. An ineffective, colorless reformer, Strong failed to build a political following. In 1897 Tammany recaptured city hall with the jubilant yell, "Well, well, well! Reform has gone to hell!"

Parkhurst's crusade and the Lexow disclosures exemplified the ephemeral nature of this approach to urban reform. It did generate excitement, especially when muckraking journalists like Steffens publicized the work, and it often brought honest men like Strong and Roosevelt into office. But moral crusaders and politicians rarely joined forces to create a popular following which could maintain them in power long enough to bring about significant change; nor did their structural approach to reform get at the underlying conditions which bred much of urban crime. The moralistic and elitist tone of their campaigns, coupled with their dim view of the lower classes, isolated them from both the insight and support needed to fashion enduring change.

A similar fate befell the temperance and prohibition movements even though their efforts appeared to be crowned with success by 1920. The crusade against drink held center stage in the great moral reform drama. All moral uplifters, whatever their major concern, identified the saloon as the sink of urban evil and alcohol as a potent factor behind vice, crime, violence, family stress, and most other social problems. It was the source from which the vast flood of urban misery and social distress issued. A passage from Frederic Howe's autobiography offers a glimpse into the reform mentality on the importance of the drink question:

A Johns Hopkins friend offered to introduce me to Dr. Parkhurst, who was engaged in one of his many crusades to clean up the morals of New York City. His organization had agents, mostly unpaid, whose business it was to watch the saloons, to report . . . violations of the numerous regulatory laws of the city and the state. . . . The saloon was the source of political power. It bred the gang, was the training-school of the boss. It gathered in tribute from the underworld and provided a club for the immigrant and Irish leaders who ruled the City of New York. The saloon was the root of our political evils, that was clear.

The saloon's influence extended beyond politics to the entire fabric of lower-class society. It offered a haven for prostitutes and corrupted the morals of young women and men alike. It harbored pimps, cadets, thieves, criminals, and rowdies of the worst sort. As the social center for the working class, it bred improvident habits and contributed to family degeneration. Alcohol dulled the senses, undermined health, corroded work habits, and thereby fueled the poverty cycle. Since drink and the saloon lay at the crossroads of so much urban evil, it was tempting to conclude that it was the primary cause of them. Like the "free silver" issue in the 1890s, the antisaloon campaign attracted a wide range of reformers who saw it as the panacea for a whole spectrum of social problems.

Temperance had long been a concern of American reformers, but pre-Civil War crusaders had attacked drinking primarily as an individual rather than a social problem: they concentrated upon reforming individual drinkers instead of seeking to eliminate it through institutional change. The shift in emphasis after the war was led by three organizations: the Women's Christian Temperance Union, founded in 1874 and headed for decades by Frances Willard; the Anti-Saloon League (1895), which ultimately dominated the prohibition crusade; and the Methodist Church. As with other moral reforms, clergymen and women provided much of the movement's leadership and support.*

The efforts of these groups met with greatest success in rural areas. On the national level, therefore, prohibition turned into the sort of urban vs. rural issue that characterized much of American reform after the Civil War. Because the saloon was so visible a target, and because it was related to so many other vices, country folk naturally regarded the social evils of drinking as a product of urban life. As one prohibitionist put it, "Our nation can only be saved by turning the pure stream of country sentiment and township morals to flush out the cesspools of cities and save civilization from pollution."

Some prohibitionists realized that they had been least effective in the

---

* The elaborate network of interrelationships among the various reform movements is a fascinating subject worth a book in itself. The ties between the women's movement and other stripes of the reform rainbow are especially important although outside the scope of this volume. Pivar's *Purity Crusade* traces the connections between that reform drive and the women's movement. Similarly, Ross Evans Paulson, *Women's Suffrage and Prohibition* (Glenview, Ill.; 1973), is a provocative interpretation of the relationship between those two reform crusades. Another work, Joseph R. Gusfield, *Symbolic Crusade* (Urbana, Ill.; 1963) relates the temperance movement to status politics. James H. Timberlake, *Prohibition and the Progressive Movement, 1900–1920* (Cambridge, Mass., 1963), discusses the role of prohibition in the broader framework of progressive reform. Timberlake also provides a useful summary of the different arguments—political, economic, religious, and scientific—advanced by prohibitionists.

areas which counted most. The failure to curb the evil of demon rum only illustrated again why efforts to deal with prostitution, crime, gambling, pornography, and other vices proved ineffective. Moral reformers like Comstock, Stead, even Parkhurst, never related to the people who were the target of their good intentions. In trying to impose middle-class values and the attitudes of an older, more rural America upon the urban masses, moralists tended to confuse cause and effect. They understood, for example, that drink caused undisciplined work habits, but seldom recognized that the nature of work drove people to drink.

As Lippmann said of the Chicago Commission, moralists were wont to indict symptoms rather than causes. Even when they realized that domestic reforms were not sufficient, they could find no suitable alternatives. The result was a tendency to attack the immediate problem in the most obvious way. If the saloon were abolished and alcohol banned, the problems would somehow disappear along with the symptoms. But tackling evils from a lofty moral plane permitted no shadings between right and wrong; if distinctions were recognized in theory, they were obliterated in practice. If the saloon were a menace, it had to be eradicated, its good features thrown out with the bad. Few moralists offered practical suggestions for replacing its social functions through other devices; most refused to concede that the saloon served any worthwhile purpose. So, too, with the anti-smut campaign. To protect the masses from corrupting filth, Comstock wielded an indiscriminate ax against pornography, fine literature and art, and useful manuals on sex or anatomy.

The closed-minded smugness of most moral reformers, the determination to impose their own value system upon the lower classes, made them the least effective of all uplifters. Few made any significant dent into the undeniably real problems they attacked. They were expert at generating smoke, inept at handling fires. Yet their influence upon urban reform was considerable. Although they represented the outer extremes of reform thinking, all of progressive reform suffered from the smugness born of a righteous cause. For zealous crusaders it was as natural an attitude as it was harmful to their work. For moral reformers, though they differed from others in degree, not kind, it proved fatal. Like social-welfare reformers, they groped futilely with the dilemma that modest reforms on the local level failed to achieve their grand objectives while more ambitious schemes—even when enacted into law—were frustrated or evaded into extinction. More than most reformers, the moralists learned by bitter experience that the grander the vision, the harder it fell.

EPILOGUE

Imaginary Cities:
The City-Planning Movement

Before I came to this country, and in all the time I have been here, it never has occurred to me to think of New York as being beautiful. Therefore all this talk of beautifying New York seems strange to me. . . . We expect of her power and magnificence, but not beauty. If a European came over here and found that New York was beautiful in the same way as the European cities, he knew he would be very much disappointed. I do not see how you can make New York beautiful in that way, with the laws and democratic spirit that you have here. The kind of beauty that makes Paris charming can only exist where private rights and personal liberty are or have been trampled on.

—NIELS GRON
Danish consul to London (1900)

D REAMS WERE THE stock-in-trade of all reformers. In the mind's eye of every uplifter glimmered a vision of urban utopia washed clean of blight and corrupting influences. For many reformers, the perception of what was wrong with cities and what could be done to improve them sprang from some vision of what the city ought to be. That ideal, however vague or incomplete, separated devout reformers from mere carpers or critics, infusing them with a zeal that complaint alone could not enlist.

There were, of course, as many imaginary cities as there were dreamers. If no two visions were identical, neither were the roads leading to them. In our survey of the reform rainbow, a common pattern has unfolded. Every issue—be it police corruption, housing, or sex education —may be likened to a lonely country road which attracted a hardy band of reformers determined to know its source. In time, some grew weary of the journey or were constrained by conservative instincts not to go too far, but those who persisted found that their lonely road converged with other roads whose travelers had begun their journey at equally remote points.

418

At these intersections, the avenue of reform broadened into a great thoroughfare which gathered traffic from numerous connecting arteries. Those who entered upon this avenue often had little in common except the hope that it would lead them to their destination. In this way, scattered bands of fellow travelers swelled into a heavy traffic flowing toward the imaginary city. But as the highway drew near the outskirts, the going got rougher. Obstructions slowed traffic, then snarled it into hopeless jams. Detours shunted part of the flow onto side streets and dead ends. Bumpy surfaces stalled progress and caused breakdowns.

Even worse, it turned out that not all the travelers had the same destination in mind. Since reformers had different notions of where they were heading, no one road could take them there. This discrepancy, coupled with the obstacles they encountered, broke up the flow of traffic and scattered it onto a maze of streets which seemed to take them everywhere but where they wished to go. The more ambitious travelers never reached their destination and despaired that it could ever be found even with the best of road maps. Those with less lofty ambitions were content to stop somewhere along the way and accept the most suitable accommodations they could find.

As this metaphor suggests, urban reform was an endless journey, an odyssey beset with frustration, delay, and disappointment, partly because the final destination seemed unapproachable regardless of what route one took. The imaginary cities of most reformers defied realization because their essence differed so radically from that of the industrial city. The vast array of forces that created the industrial city, which this book has tried to describe, were deeply rooted in the bedrock of American experience and values. Any major change of direction challenged the most basic national traditions as well as the institutions which served them. To attempt this challenge meant nothing less than to recast the fundamental mold of our civilization, a formidable task made even more difficult by the fact that most Americans considered their civilization to be both superior and astoundingly successful.

Reformers thus confronted an impossible dilemma: they could try to alter or overthrow the existing framework of values and institutions, or they could work to bring about change within it. Wholesale attacks on such sacred cows as private property, individual liberty, and corporate capitalism had little chance of success. Yet efforts to work within the system also fell short because the more important problems were rooted deep within the framework itself; ameliorative reforms could not get at the underlying conditions that bred them. Any effective solution to housing and congestion problems, for example, required a radical shift in the

prevailing notions of property rights, personal liberty, and use of governmental power.

Neither approach got very far in the long run. Unable to find a way
around this dilemma, reformers found themselves locked into a frustrating
cycle. They attacked specific problems only to discover that social ills did
not exist in isolation from one another. Once aware of this seamless web,
they broadened their base of concern and joined other uplifters in a
wholesale assault. From this experience they learned that most problems
were firmly embedded in the prevailing economic structure and could
not be dislodged without dismantling the system itself. At that point the
reform crusade began to fall apart. A few diehards continued to hurl
frontal attacks against the system in hopes of bringing about fundamental
change. Most shrank from going that far and retreated to working within
the restricted medium of the existing order. Some buried themselves in
structural change and were ironically co-opted by the very forces they had
once opposed.

While all the reformers discussed earlier followed some variant of this
cycle, none illustrate it quite so well as does the city-planning movement.
In little more than a generation, urban planning emerged as a profession
whose practitioners had begun as audacious dreamers and wound up as
narrow technicians in league with the dominant business interests. Few
urban dreamers advanced bolder schemes or were carried further from
them. Their experience offers a final insight into the tenacity of the
marketplace tradition as the dominant force in the industrial city.

The City Beautiful

Grandiose schemes came naturally to those reformers who believed that
the physical environment held the key to urban regeneration. Convinced
that unrestrained growth within the marketplace tradition had rendered
cities formless, inefficient, and polluted, they concluded that problems like
poverty, housing, sanitation, and congestion could be solved through planning. Cast a beautiful container and the mold would emerge true; function would follow form. The trick was to design the form rather than
to leave it to the whims of individual decision-making.

Because the notion of urban planning runs directly counter to the
marketplace tradition, it is hardly surprising that the concept emerged
after the industrial city had already taken shape. In effect, planning was
a response to existing social chaos; its origins lay in a scattering of movements which arose during the 1890s. Part of its theoretical framework was
supplied by conservationists like John Wesley Powell and Elwood Mead

who had been pushing for an end to the exploitative waste of resources so prevalent during industrialization. Although principally concerned with large unsettled areas, their work anticipated land-use objectives which planners later applied to urban areas.

The first tentative steps toward planning occurred during the 1890s when several cities created boards of survey to control the rampant platting of homesites that characterized much of urban growth. In their quest for profits, developers threw up subdivisions with little concern for problems of drainage, traffic flow, sanitation, or utility installation. In trying to restrain these abuses, boards of survey foundered at once on the shoals of property rights and individual liberty. Landowners bitterly opposed any municipal interference with the right to do what they wished with their property, and more often than not the courts sustained their position.

Through the period 1870–1920, the courts stood as a major barrier to municipal reform. The industrial city arose during an era of judicial conservatism, the primary thrust of which was to maximize individual liberty and defend the sanctity of property rights from encroachment by government. During these years the courts relentlessly narrowed the sphere of municipal power over land use at the very time that such authority was most urgently needed. Even after 1900 most judges remained staunchly immune to the virus of progressivism. As a result, municipal reformers in many fields struggled to push legislation through city and state governments only to have their work undone by the courts. Since planners dealt primarily in land use and relied heavily upon the right of eminent domain to carry out their schemes, they were perhaps the hardest hit by adverse legal decisions.

Landscape architects were among the first to drift into planning. As critics began to set aside some land for open space, a handful of innovative landscapers seized the opportunity to design not only parks, but park systems linked by wide boulevards swathed in greenery. As early as the 1850s, New York created a park commission to plan Central Park. In designing Central Park, Frederick Law Olmsted and Calvert Vaux created a pastoral idyll where one might enjoy a day in the country without leaving the city. Similar efforts like Lincoln Park in Chicago, Fairmount in Philadelphia, and later Swope in Kansas City ushered in a new era of breathing space for the crowded city.

But a single park—usually on the outskirts of town—could not provide "lungs" for the whole city. Some landscape architects, unhappy with lonely parks stranded in a sea of urban congestion, won commissions to design park systems in which several patches of green would be connected with attractive tree-lined parkways. Horace W. S. Cleveland created systems for Minneapolis, which developed twenty-nine parks covering 1,200 acres, and for Chicago and Omaha. In Kansas City, George E. Kessler produced a comprehensive plan which, coupled with the extensive lands donated to the city by Thomas H. Swope in 1896, led to the creation of a park and boulevard system that won national acclaim. Charles Eliot helped fashion a metropolitan park system for Boston that by 1902 included 15,000 acres, ten miles of ocean shoreline, and twenty-two miles of right-of-way for parkways. Impressed by these systems, other cities gave these landscape architects the opportunity to duplicate their feats elsewhere. The establishment of parks did more than improve the urban landscape and provide charming recreational retreats; it also fostered the creation of park commissions which became prototype planning agencies.

Architects also turned their expertise toward planning. For many of them, the Columbian World's Fair of 1893 served as both catalyst and point of departure. The exposition was awarded to Chicago, which had put on a vigorous campaign to win it. Having become the nation's second largest city, Chicago intended to honor not only the quadricentennial of Columbus's landing, but also its own emergence as a booming urban giant. After Chicago's premier architects invited leading eastern designers to help plan the fair, a blue-ribbon commission headed by Daniel Burnham, Charles McKim, and Charles Eliot approved a proposal made by the easterners to cast all major buildings in classical and renaissance styles. The result was a fairyland city whose clean, white, monumental lines overwhelmed the more than 21,000,000 visitors who flocked to Chicago to see this new wonder of the world.*

The beauty and unity of the "White City" excited people's imaginations as nothing had before. Its huge white buildings and fountains reflected a classicism filtered through the Beaux Arts tradition then the current rage among leading New York and Boston architects. A stroll along the broad walkways, clear lagoons, and symmetrical lawns inspired Henry Adams to exclaim:

As a scenic display, Paris had never approached it, but the inconceivable scenic display consisted in its being there at all—more surprising, as it was, than anything else on the continent, Niagara Falls, the Yellowstone Geysers, and the whole railway system thrown in. . . .

* Typically, Louis Sullivan alone departed from the classical theme. His Transportation Building, a marvelously ornate structure, was banished to an inconspicuous site and drew its loudest praise from foreign critics.

Less sophisticated tourists shared this sense of wonder, as Mel Scott has depicted:

Here was an enthralling amalgam of classic Greece, imperial Rome, Renaissance Italy, and Bourbon Paris, as improbable in the Midwest as a gleaming iceberg would be in the Gulf of Mexico, yet somehow expressive of the boastfulness, the pretentions [sic], the cultural dependence, the explosive energy, and the ingenuous optimism of industrial America. . . . the millions gaped and admired and almost disbelieved that so much beauty and splendor had sprung up in Chicago, city of grain and lumber and meat, city of railroads and smoke and grime.

The spectacle of the Fair impressed upon people the revelation that there could be beautiful cities, that there were alternatives to the drab, nondescript dinginess of a Cleveland or Pittsburgh. It was not a new lesson, but one that had never before been demonstrated so strikingly. "Chicago was the first expression of American thought as a unity," declared Henry Adams, and this vision of unity suggested to thoughtful observers, perhaps for the first time, that the city was a whole entity whose parts could not be separated from one another. Even more, it was a unity born of careful planning. The usefulness of planning as a tool did not go unnoticed; people left the Fair convinced that its lessons could be applied to their own cities with equally rewarding results.

The vehicle used to advance this conviction in most cities was the Municipal Art Society. Usually funded by members of the cultural elite, these groups spread the gospel of the Fair by lobbying for more attractive parks, statues, municipal buildings, fountains, bridges, and lampposts. Other groups pushed for the planting of street trees and even the creation of municipal forestry agencies. While these campaigns drew much of their impetus from the inspiration of the White City, they had been in the wind for several years. Charles M. Robinson, a prolific writer on urban affairs, stressed this point in 1910:

It is common to hear it spoken of as "the white city" and even "the dream city." In these terms was revealed a yearning toward a condition which we had not reached. To say that the world's fair created the subsequent aesthetic effort in municipal life were therefore false; to say that it immensely strengthened, quickened, and encouraged it would be true. The fair gave tangible shape to a desire that was arising . . . but the movement has had a special impetus since 1893.

From this surge of activity emerged the first major phase of the planning movement. Known as the City Beautiful, it conceived of urban regeneration primarily in aesthetic terms. Those who fought to improve the appearance of cities were not insensitive to the practical and social benefits of their work. Beautiful cities could also be efficient cities in which, as Robinson put it, "the utilitarian lion lies down with the artistic lamb, and in which all things are as they should be." But these considerations took a back seat to the goal of creating a unified physical environment which, through public buildings, railroad stations, grand esplanades, boulevards, malls, parks, and open vistas, expressed the city's vision of its future and might forge a new sense of community among its disparate peoples.

During the next decade, City Beautiful advocates labored to implement the lessons of the Fair in their own cities. Their efforts produced the first comprehensive planning schemes for numerous American cities. Washington, D. C. was a logical place to begin. As the nation's capital, it was already a city of monuments and it already had a plan, the celebrated design prepared by Pierre L'Enfant in 1791 and later ignored until its "rediscovery" in 1894. In 1901 Senator James McMillan of Michigan got Congress to create a commission for unifying and improving the capital's parks. With McMillan's approval, a distinguished committee of Daniel Burnham, Frederick Law Olmsted, Jr., Charles McKim, and sculptor Augustus St. Gaudens went beyond the parks to the more ambitious task of reviving the L'Enfant plan.

As work progressed, the project evolved away from L'Enfant's design into a new plan which included a grandly classical railroad station, a new axis for the mall between the Capitol and the Washington Monument, a triangle of neoclassical federal buildings, the Lincoln Memorial, a memorial bridge to Arlington, and a superb park system proposal done by Olmsted. The McMillan Commission's general plan of 1902 attracted national attention. Although the plan was only partially realized, Washington remained the major showcase of City Beautiful planning. As John Reps has written,

The influence exerted on city planning by the Senate Park Commission for Washington and its gradual implementation was enormous. The wide and overwhelmingly favorable publicity given to the plan helped to make its chief features known throughout the country.

Other cities scrambled to acquire beautification plans of their own. New York created an Improvement Commission in 1903 and demanded a comprehensive plan for the entire city within one year. After four years of tangling with New York's intractable physical limitations (such as its rectangular street plan), the commission submitted a final report bristling with bold proposals. Despite Mayor George McClellan's avowal that "it is the city beautiful that compels and retains the love of her people. It is in the city beautiful that civic spirit is at its best," the report was virtually ignored. Philadelphia's City Parks Association presented a report embodying a long-desired parkway between City Hall and Fairmount Park; after a series of delays the parkway opened in 1919 and was finally completed several years later.

Cleveland enlisted the services of Burnham for a group of public buildings. Completed in 1903, Burnham's design restated the familiar classical motif of the Fair. Unlike most other cities where the civic center rage produced only an isolated city hall or courthouse before enthusiasm waned, Cleveland labored for over two decades to construct a post office, courthouse, public library, city hall, and even a Federal Reserve Building and public auditorium not included in the original plan. Burnham went on to provide San Francisco with a plan, only to have it undone by political enmity, despite the rare opportunity afforded by the earthquake and fire which devastated the city in 1906. Kansas City, Boston, St. Louis, Baltimore, Buffalo, and San Diego were among the many other cities which pursued the grail of the City Beautiful.

Here, too, lusty Chicago outdid all rivals in its ambitions. For that exploding city, the indefatigable Burnham prepared his masterpiece. His *Plan of Chicago* (1909) was a colossal work which organized the lakefront into a system of harbors and beaches, and created a civic center complex, an elaborate boulevard system, and a transportation network for the entire city. Covering an area of 4,000 square miles from Kenosha, Wisconsin to Michigan City, Indiana, the report followed the City Beautiful blueprint in its proposals for buildings, streets, and parks. But it went further by dealing with practical matters of transportation in obeisance to the business elements that underwrote the work. Unlike most plans, Burnham's *Chicago* was not consigned to the file cabinet. During the next fifteen years Chicagoans, who rarely undertook anything small, spent nearly $300,000,000 on projects related to the plan. No other plan rivaled it in scope, daring, or comprehensiveness. Even so, it is hard to dispute Mel Scott's judgment that the plan embodied the worst as well as the best of the City Beautiful movement:

In many respects the Chicago of the Burnham plan is a city of a past that America never knew, notwithstanding the facilities for transportation and transit, the network of roadways for automobiles, and the generous provision of recreation areas for the people. It is an essentially aristocratic city, pleasing to the merchant princes who participated in its conception but not meeting some of the basic economic and human needs.

The City Beautiful represented the apotheosis of utopian planning. It envisioned a pure city, clean and symmetrical—but alas, essentially without people. Few of the grand plans bothered with such questions as housing, sanitation, congestion, pollution, or transportation. A civic center disguised as the Parthenon might unify the city's focus, but it could do nothing to arrest the forces which had pulled the city and its people apart in the first place. A static, orderly plan could not easily be imposed upon the dynamic urban arena. In the end, City Beautiful resembled a literalist version of structural reform which never touched the heart of the matter. The rage for City Beautiful faded before most of the plans it spawned were completed; the majority gathered dust in forgotten file cabinets.

Like other structural reformers, the City Beautiful advocates drew fire from journalists and social-welfare reformers for their neglect of the city's poorest classes and most pressing problems. These critics appreciated the value of planning but objected to the form it had taken. Their concern brought into the planning movement a corps of fresh recruits whose presence diversified the ranks and sent them marching in new directions.

The drive to extend planning to social problems had already attracted those seeking more parks, playgrounds, and open space for recreation. Jacob Riis had earlier advanced the notion of the neighborhood unit in which each neighborhood would utilize its public school to serve as a sort of mini-civic center for activities of all kinds. In 1907 the Committee on Civic Centers in St. Louis discarded the City Beautiful concept of the monumental city in favor of a bold proposal for clusters of neighborhood centers. The committee's report suggested that such centers include schools (public and parochial), parks, playgrounds, a branch library, public bath, model tenements, a settlement house, churches, police and fire stations, and headquarters for social and athletic organizations. Unlike City Beautiful, the St. Louis proposal concentrated upon the social needs of the lower classes. It did not ignore the other classes but warned that

The indiscriminate herding together of large masses of human beings ignorant of the simplest laws of sanitation, the evils of child labor, the corruption in political life, and, above all, the weakening of the ties which bind together the home—these are dangers which strike at the very roots of society.

To combat these evils, the report insisted that "the government must employ every resource in its power." These were strong words in an age reluctant to concede to government any powers that restricted individual property rights or transferred some economic decision-making from the private to the public sector. The St. Louis plan was, in fact, the rarest of species: a set of concrete proposals designed to graft a sense of community onto city life. In its pages the ideal of city as community challenged the prevailing reality of city as marketplace, but it proved to be no contest. Neither the public officials nor citizens of St. Louis made any concerted effort to implement it.

If nothing else, the St. Louis report helped wrench planning free from the City Beautiful concept and converted it into an instrument of social reform. As City Beautiful declined, the notion that some form of urban planning was desirable—indeed necessary—grew stronger. Hartford, Connecticut set a precedent in 1907 by establishing the nation's first city-planning commission. That same year, a more ambitious effort was launched in New York when Florence Kelley, Mary Simkhovitch, Lillian Wald, and other social-welfare reformers founded the Committee on Congestion of Population (CCP). The purpose of the new organization was to collect data on the congestion problem and present exhibits to arouse public awareness.

CCP was galvanized into prominence by the vigor of its young executive secretary, Benjamin C. Marsh. A crusading lobbyist for various reform causes, Marsh was a fiery infighter, a bantam rooster who poked at establishment shibboleths with obvious relish. He combined a missionary zeal with a radical social philosophy grounded in Henry George's single-tax philosophy, the doctrines of Fabian socialism, and the bold dictums of economist Simon Patten, whose writings were a requiem to laissez-faire dogma and a call for economic planning. Marsh offended devotees of the conventional wisdom with both his ideas and his abrasive personality. Early in his career with CCP, he drew a warning from Robert W. DeForest that "if you touch the land problem in New York, you probably won't last here two years."

After touring Europe to gather information on housing and city planning, Marsh helped organize a CCP exhibition which opened in March 1908. Along with unusually impressive maps, charts,* and diagrams, the exhibition stressed the importance of urban planning and offered three bold proposals to ease overcrowding. The first of these recognized that improved transportation only worsened congestion, and recommended spacing factories out in scattered industrial sites each with its own

---

* It was a chart at this exhibition which stated that "The population of the world could be contained in Delaware if they were as congested as the people in eleven New York City blocks, at the rate of twelve hundred per acre."

cluster of lower-class housing. A second plan advocated removal of whole families to less densely populated areas, and a third proposed a model village for creating whole new communities where land was still cheap. The Congestion Exhibition did its work well—perhaps too well. Several years later, Mary Simkhovitch recalled that "many superficial observers horrified at the evils of overcrowding felt that the problem was of such magnitude that it was hardly worthwhile to have brought the public to a realization of evils which . . . could be remedied or prevented only in the course of years and after a prolonged struggle."

Marsh rendered a more succinct verdict. He declared the Exhibition "a distinct success from every point of view—except producing action to remedy the condition shown!" A year later Marsh published privately a short volume entitled *An Introduction to City Planning: Democracy's Challenge & the American City* (1909). Atop the first page in bold type blared the dictum: "A CITY WITHOUT A PLAN IS LIKE A SHIP WITHOUT A RUDDER." Earlier Marsh had already dismissed the City Beautiful approach as irrelevant to social needs:

The grouping of public buildings and the installation of speedways, parks and drives, which affect only moderately the daily lives of the city's toilers, are important; but vastly more so is the securing of decent home conditions of the countless thousands who otherwise can but occasionally escape from their squalid, confining surroundings to view the architectural perfection and to experience the aesthetic delights of the remote improvements.

Drawing upon European examples, especially Frankfurt, Marsh outlined the features of a model city and discussed the ways in which planning was vital to realizing it. That this first manual on planning came not from an architect but from a social reformer suggests how diffused the planning movement had grown by 1909.

The first National Conference on City Planning and Congestion, held in 1909, also betrayed this diffusion of interests. The delegates included government officials, architects, landscape architects, social workers, housing reformers, public health people, and engineers. The conference proceedings revealed that the planning movement had reached a crossroads; its diverse participants, having come to that juncture by their separate routes, were uncertain as to what road to follow next. Everyone understood that the power of the state was necessary to guide urban development and restrict practices harmful to the larger community. As keynote speaker John Nolen declared, "We should no longer be content with more increases in population and wealth. We should insist upon asking, 'How do the people live, where do they work, what do they play?' "

But how far should that impulse be carried? The movement's first phase, City Beautiful, had already faded into disrepute. Cities continued to grow and problems to multiply. Everywhere cities and towns were beginning to appreciate the value of planning but were unsure of what it entailed and what course it should take. The National Conference symbolized the emergence of city planning as a permanent feature of the urban environment, but its role remained undefined. For that brief moment, a harmony born of shared aspirations reigned within the planning movement; during the next decade, the quest for clear definitions of purpose splintered its unity and relegated many of the ideals of 1909 to the ash heap of utopian possibilities.

The City Functional

No sooner had the planning movement coalesced than it began to fall apart. The first casualties were the more radical reformers like Marsh. In 1910 New York created a City Commission on Congestion of Population, of which Marsh became secretary. In his work with the commission, Marsh aroused widespread antagonism, especially with his taxation proposals. The commission's report in 1911 documented a steadily worsening congestion crisis and thereby indicted the city for neglect of its citizens' well-being. But the commission, dominated by aldermen and real estate men, ventured only modest recommendations, the import of which was that urban overcrowding would somehow have to solve itself.

Marsh countered this timidity with an attack on the prevailing economic structure as the true source of evil. He viewed congestion as the product of "protected privilege and exploitation" stemming from the high cost of land, low wages, congestion of factories, and rampant speculation in real estate. Arguing that "with expensive land no remedy for congestion among unskilled workers can permanently be found," he denounced existing conditions as "the outcome of a system of laissez-faire" and insisted that "the police power of the state must be extended and enlarged to deal with it."

This argument won Marsh few friends and legions of enemies. Most planners and conservative reformers shrank from so radical a notion, especially one that alienated businessmen whose support was so desperately needed by planning advocates. Charles M. Robinson complained that radical taxation schemes "immediately put the average man on the defensive. He feared he was getting into something socialistic. . . ." In 1910 DeForest and Veiller shattered the hope for a unified movement by forming the National Housing Association. That same year the second meeting of the National Conference dropped the word "congestion" from its title. Thereafter fewer social workers and civic reformers attended as the National Conference on City Planning gradually evolved into a professional organization concerned with planning techniques, data gathering, statistical method, management standards, and efficiency.

George B. Ford, a prime mover in this shift, had anticipated the wave of the future in writing the technical chapter for Marsh's book. Stressing the necessity of "scientific management," Ford argued that planning had to become systematized if it were to develop as a legitimate profession and gain the support of the businessman "who has to pay the bills." Not social uplift but professional competence became the flag around which the planning movement rallied during the 1910s. The nobler ends which had brought together the patchwork quilt of early planners gave way to a concern for means, for techniques which could be applied to the objectives of whatever interests required their services.*

And in the dynamic arena of the urban marketplace there was little doubt as to which interests those would be. Planning enthusiasts had thrown themselves into battle against the social ills of the city and, like other reformers, were repulsed by the unyielding redoubts of the "system," of "things as they are." They discovered that utopia required more drastic change than some could achieve and others were willing to make. Unable to realize their dreams, they fell back upon their technique. The social impulse that had sparked City Beautiful veered naturally toward the creation of the City Functional. City planners redefined their mission as the changing of spatial relationships to achieve efficiency.

The City Functional was in part the legacy of dreamers made wiser by their experience. Having failed to realize their ideal city, they abandoned dreams for more practical goals with the admission that, in young Olmsted's words, planners were "dealing . . . with the play of enormously complex forces which no one clearly understands and few pretend to." This confession that the city was a maze of bewildering and contradictory forces chastened planners into lowering their sights while spurring them to develop more sophisticated techniques. Above all, planners sought to become more "scientific" and "systematic" in their work. The virus of Taylorism, of which Taylor and his disciples were by no means the only carriers, infected planning no less than other professions.

---

* In 1917 the American Institute of Planners, an even more narrowly professional organization than NCCP (it required two years experience in city planning activities to be eligible for membership), was formed. By that time Marsh's isolation from the mainstream of city planning was complete, though he remained a vigorous reformer for over thirty years.

By 1920 city planning had firmly established itself as a profession on this new basis. On one hand, the quest for the City Functional embodied an echo of the progressive conservation movement in its ambition to promote efficiency and eliminate waste. As the Pittsburgh Civic Commission proclaimed in 1910, "City planning is municipal conservation." A well-planned city conserved resources, saved money, and provided better services at lower costs. Development, once a wasteful, haphazard process, could proceed in an orderly, systematic fashion.

On the other hand, the City Functional brought planners into close alliance with the business community and thereby legitimatized their work. In the years after 1920, planning devoted itself overwhelmingly to problems of zoning and circulation. Zoning emerged as the planner's favorite tool because it was effective and comprehensible and because businessmen favored it. Originally tinged with radicalism, zoning won conservative support when businessmen realized it stabilized the uncertain real estate market while offering a sop to those concerned about congestion. This realization prompted most real estate operators to support New York's comprehensive zoning law of 1916, which became a model for statutes enacted elsewhere.* By outflanking the agitation over congestion, zoning became the conservative tool for tempering the reformer's ardor. In his plan for Dallas (1910), George Kessler sounded the note that would guide planners for over two decades:

Regard for the people at large means that a city should be divided into areas and zones, each devoted to its own particular purpose. The greatest possible accessibility for all should be provided in ample and direct connecting thoroughfares and all barriers, such as railroad grade crossings, narrow congested streets and excessively long blocks, should be removed and corrected.

While important, these concerns were a far cry from the larger ambitions of earlier planning enthusiasts. By 1920 the cycle had played itself out. Urban planners had soared to lofty heights in their visions for transforming the industrial city. When these schemes proved unrealistic or encountered stiff opposition, their designers began groping for some new role to play. After their fling with utopia, planners ended up as utilitarian co-partners with business to make the city more efficient. Instead of directing what type of growth should take place, they began designing for growth to accommodate more business expansion. Ironically, then, the movement which sought to liberate the city from the fetters of the

---

* See Chapter 4.

marketplace tradition evolved into one which chained urban growth more firmly to that tradition.

This transformation of the planning movement within a few short years speaks volumes to the point of why reform failed to alter the on-rushing course of the industrial city. Its brief history offers insight into our continuing inability to deal with urban problems. The imaginary city never came into being not because it lacked dreamers, but because the dreamers seldom got their way for very long. The best of them challenged the essence of the industrial city, which was the marketplace tradition. It was a grossly uneven battle, a tragic mismatch of good intention against the leviathan of forces which brought the industrial city into being and which, a century later, have scarcely slowed their momentum.

Citation Sources

CHAPTER 1

Alfred D. Chandler, Jr., "Anthracite ·Coal and the Beginnings of the Industrial Revolution in the United States," *Business History Review* (Summer 1972):141–81.

Alfred D. Chandler, Jr., (ed.), *The Railroads: The Nation's First Big Business* (New York, 1965).

Robert Dorfman, *The Price System* (Englewood Cliffs, N.J., 1964).

Jacques Ellul, *The Technological Society* (New York, 1964).

Hannah Josephson, *The Golden Threads: New England's Mill Girls and Magnates* (New York, 1949).

Curtis P. Nettels, *The Emergence of a National Economy, 1775–1815* (New York, 1962).

Gilman M. Ostrander, *American Civilization in the First Machine Age, 1890–1940* (New York, 1970).

Karl Polanyi, *The Great Transformation* (New York, 1944).

Arthur M. Schlesinger, *The Rise of the City 1878–1898* (New York, 1933).

George R. Taylor, *The Transportation Revolution 1815–1860* (New York, 1954).

William A. Williams, *The Contours of American History* (Cleveland, 1961).

CHAPTER 2

Rowland Bertoff, *An Unsettled People: Social Order and Disorder in American History* (New York, 1971).

Kenneth Boulding, *The Organizational Revolution* (New York, 1953).

Thomas C. Cochran, *The American Business System* (Cambridge, 1957).

Ray Ginger, *Age of Excess* (New York, 1965).

Gerald Grob, *Workers and Utopia* (Evanston, 1961).

Samuel P. Hays, *The Response to Industrialism 1885–1914* (Chicago, 1957).

Ralph L. Nelson, *Merger Movements in American Industry, 1895–1956* (Princeton, 1959).

Nettels, *Emergence of a National Economy*.

Arthur M. Schlesinger, Jr., *The Age of Jackson* (Boston, 1945).

CHAPTER 3

Louis D. Brandeis, *Other People's Money* (New York, 1914).

Alfred D. Chandler, Jr., *Strategy and Structure* (Cambridge, 1962).

Thomas C. Cochran and William Miller, *The Age of Enterprise* (New York, 1945).

Lewis Corey, "Problems of the Peace: IV. The Middle Class," *Antioch Review* (March 1945):68–87.

Eric E. Lampard, "The History of Cities in the Economically Advanced Areas," *Economic Development and Cultural Change*, III, no. 2 (January 1955):81–136.

C. Wright Mills, *White Collar* (New York, 1951).

Sam H. Schurr, Bruce C. Netschert, et al., *Energy in the American Economy, 1850–1975* (Baltimore, 1960).

Edward G. Stockwell, *Population and People* (Chicago, 1968).

David Ward, *Cities and Immigrants* (New York, 1971).

Sam Bass Warner, Jr., *The Urban Wilderness* (New York, 1972).
Bernard Weisberger, *The New Industrial Society* (New York, 1969).

CHAPTER 4

Albert Bush-Brown and John Burchard, *The Architecture of America* (Boston, 1966).
Lord James Bryce, *The American Commonwealth* (New York, 1889). 2 vols.
Sidney Ratner, *New Light on the History of Great American Fortunes: American Millionaires of 1892 and 1902* (New York, 1953).
Warner, *The Urban Wilderness.*

CHAPTER 5

Wayne Andrews, *Architecture, Ambition, and Americans: A Social History of American Architecture* (New York, 1964).
Nelson M. Blake, *Water for the Cities: A History of the Urban Water Supply Problem in the United States* (Syracuse, 1956).
Daniel J. Boorstin, *The Americans: The National Experience* (New York, 1965).
Roger Burlingame, *Machines That Built America* (New York, 1953).
Bush-Brown and Burchard, *The Architecture of America.*
Carl Condit, *American Building Art: The Nineteenth Century* (New York, 1960).
Carl Condit, *American Building: Materials and Techniques from the Beginning of the Colonial Period to the Present* (Chicago, 1968).
Carl Condit, *The Chicago School of Architecture: A History of Commercial and Public Buildings in the Chicago Area, 1875–1925* (Chicago, 1964).
Herbert G. Gutman, "Work, Culture, and Society in Industrializing America, 1815–1919," *American Historical Review* 78 (1973):531–88.
Melvin G. Holli, *Reform in Detroit: Hazen S. Pingree and Urban Politics* (New York, 1969).
Glen E. Holt, "The Changing Perception of Urban Pathology: An Essay on the Development of Mass Transit in the United States," in Kenneth Jackson and Stanley K. Schultz (eds.) *Cities in American History* (New York, 1972), pp. 324–43.
Homer Hoyt, *One Hundred Years of Land Values in Chicago: The Relationship of the Growth of Chicago to the Rise in its Land Values, 1830–1933* (Chicago, 1933).
Lawrence H. Larsen, "Nineteenth-Century Street Sanitation: A Study in Filth and Frustration," *Wisconsin Magazine of History,* LII (1969):239–47.
David McCullough, *The Great Bridge* (New York, 1972).
Blake McKelvey, *The Urbanization of America 1860–1915* (New Brunswick, 1963).
John Anderson Miller, *Fares Please! From Horsecars to Streamliners* (New York, 1941).
Zane Miller, *The Urbanization of Modern America: A Brief History* (New York, 1973).
Lewis Mumford, *The Culture of Cities* (New York, 1938).
Lewis Mumford, *Sticks and Stones* (New York, 1924).
Schlesinger, *The Rise of the City.*
Montgomery Schuyler, *American Architecture and Other Writings,* (ed.) by William H. Jordy and Ralph Coe (Cambridge, 1961).
Bayrd Still, *Mirror for Gotham: New York as Seen by Contemporaries from Dutch Days to the Present* (New York, 1956).
Bayrd Still, *Urban America: A History with Documents* (Boston, 1974).
Joel A. Tarr, "From City to Suburb: The 'Moral' Influence of Transportation

Technology," in Alexander B. Callow, Jr. (ed.), *American Urban History: An Interpretive Reader with Commentaries* (New York, 1973).

Joel A. Tarr, "Urban Pollution—Many Long Years Ago," *American Heritage,* XXII (October 1971), pp. 65–106.

George R. Taylor, "The Beginnings of Mass Transportation in Urban America," *Smithsonian Journal of History,* I (Summer 1966):35–50; (Autumn 1966):31–54.

Alan Tractenberg, *Brooklyn Bridge, Fact and Symbol* (New York, 1965).

Christopher Tunnard and Henry Hope Reed, *American Skyline* (Boston, 1955).

James Blaine Walker, *Fifty Years of Rapid Transit in New York, 1864–1917* (New York, 1918).

Sam Bass Warner, Jr., *Streetcar Suburbs: The Process of Growth in Boston, 1870–1900* (Cambridge, 1962).

Adna F. Weber, *The Growth of Cities in the Nineteenth Century: A Study in Statistics* (Ithaca, 1963 [first published in 1899]).

CHAPTER 6

Jane Addams, "Hull House, Chicago: An Effort toward Social Democracy," *Forum* 14 (1892):226–41.

Lewis Atherton, *Main Street on the Middle Border* (Bloomington, 1954).

Charles Loring Brace, *The Dangerous Classes of New York and Twenty Years' Work Among Them* (New York, 1872).

David Brody, *Steelworkers in America: The Nonunion Era* (Cambridge, 1960).

Howard P. Chudacoff, "A New Look at Ethnic Neighborhoods: Residential Dispersion and the Concept of Visibility in a Medium-Sized City," *Journal of American History,* 60 (1973):76–93.

Alexander DeConde, *Half Bitter, Half Sweet: An Excursion into Italian-American History* (New York, 1971).

Benjamin O. Flower, *Civilization's Inferno: or, Studies in the Social Cellar* (Boston, 1893).

Madison Grant, *The Passing of the Great Race* (New York, 1916).

John Higham, *Strangers in the Land: Patterns of America Nativism, 1860–1925* (New York, 1963).

Frederic Howe, *The Confessions of a Reformer* (New York, 1925).

Michael Lesey, *Wisconsin Death Trip* (New York, 1973).

Stefan Lorant, *Pittsburgh: The Story of an American City* (New York, 1964).

Zane Miller, "The Black Experience in the Modern American City," in Raymond A. Mohl and James F. Richardson, ed., *The Urban Experience: Themes in American History* (Belmont, Cal., 1973).

Gilbert Osofsky, *Harlem: The Making of a Ghetto: Negro New York, 1890–1930* (New York, 1966).

Jacob Riis, *How the Other Half Lives* (New York, 1890).

Kenneth L. Roberts, *Why Europe Leaves Home* (Indianapolis, 1922).

Josiah Strong, *Our Country: Its Possible Future and Its Present Crisis* (New York, 1885).

Philip Taylor, *The Distant Magnet* (New York, 1971).

Ward, *Cities and Immigrants.*

Carl Wittke, *We Who Built America* (New York, 1939).

CHAPTER 7

Andrews, *Architecture, Ambition and Americans.*

Thomas Beer, *The Mauve Decade* (New York, 1926).

Andrew Carnegie, *The Gospel of Wealth* (Boston, 1892).

Cochran and Miller, *Age of Enterprise.*

Robert E. Dahl, *Who Governs: Democracy and Power in an American City* (New Haven, 1961).

Finley Peter Dunne, *Dissertations by Mr. Dooley* (New York, 1906).

Michael H. Frisch, *Town into City: Springfield, Massachusetts and the Meaning of Community, 1840–1880* (Cambridge, 1972).

Ginger, *Age of Excess.*

Herbert G. Gutman, "The Reality of the Rag-to-Riches 'Myth': The Case of the Paterson, New Jersey, Locomotive, Iron, and Machinery Manufacturers, 1830–1880", in Stephan Thernstrom and Richard Sennett (eds.), *Nineteenth-Century Cities: Essays in the New Urban History* (New Haven, 1969).

Oscar Handlin, *Boston's Immigrants, 1790–1865: A Study in Acculturation* (Cambridge, 1941).

James A. Henretta, "Economic Development and Social Structure in Colonial Boston," *William and Mary Quarterly,* 3d. ser., XXII (1965):75–92.

Frederic C. Jaher, "The Boston Brahmins in the Age of Industrial Capitalism," in Frederic C. Jaher (ed.), *The Age of Industrialism in America: Essays in Social Structure and Cultural Values* (New York, 1968).

Howard Mumford Jones, *The Age of Energy* (New York, 1970).

Edward C. Kirkland, *Men, Cities, and Transportation: A Study in New England History, 1820–1900,* 2 vols. (Cambridge, .1948).

Russell Lynes, "Chateau Builder to Fifth Avenue," *American Heritage* 6 (1955): 20–26.

Russell Lynes, *The Tastemakers* (New York, 1949).

Ward McAllister, *Society as I Have Found It* (New York, 1890).

William Miller, "American Historians and the Business Elite," *Journal of Economic History* IX (1949): 184–208.

Lloyd Morris, *Postscript to Yesterday: American Life and Thought 1896–1946* (New York, 1947).

Edward Pessen, *Riches, Class, and Power before the Civil War* (Lexington, Ky., 1973).

Stephan Thernstrom, *Progress and Poverty: Social Mobility in a Nineteenth-Century City* (Cambridge, 1964).

Thorstein Veblen, *The Higher Learning in America* (New York, 1918).

Richard C. Wade, *The Urban Frontier: The Rise of Western Cities, 1790–1830* (Cambridge, 1959).

Sam Bass Warner, Jr., *The Private City: Philadelphia in Three Periods of Its Growth* (Philadelphia, 1968).

Dixon Wecter, *The Saga of American Society: A Record of Social Aspiration, 1607–1937* (New York, 1937).

Irvin G. Wyllie, *The Self-Made Man in America: The Myth of Rags to Riches* (New Brunswick, 1954).

CHAPTER 8

Aaron I. Abell, *The Urban Impact on American Protestantism, 1865–1900* (Cambridge, 1943).

Arthur W. Calhoun, *A Social History of the American Family,* 3 vols. (Cleveland, 1917).

Russell H. Conwell, *Acres of Diamonds* (New York, 1915).

Robert D. Cross (ed.), *The Church and the City, 1865–1910* (Indianapolis, 1967).

Jacob H. Dorn, *Washington Gladden: Prophet of the Social Gospel* (Columbus, 1966).

Frank F. Farstenberg, Jr., "Industrialization and the American Family: A Look Backward," *American Sociological Review* XXXI (1966):326–37.

James F. Findlay, Jr., *Dwight L. Moody: American Evangelist, 1837–1899* (Chicago, 1969).

Charles H. Hopkins, *The Rise of the Social Gospel in American Protestantism, 1865–1915* (New Haven, 1940).

Kenneth T. Jackson, "The Crabgrass Frontier: 150 Years of Suburban Growth in America," in Raymond A. Mohl and James F. Richardson (eds.), *The Urban Experience: Themes in American History* (Belmont, Cal., 1973).

Michael Katz, *The Irony of Early School Reform: Educational Innovation in Mid-Nineteenth Century Massachusetts* (Cambridge, 1968).

Paul Underwood Kellogg, *The Pittsburgh Survey*, 6 vols. (New York, 1909–14).

Roy Lubove, *The Progressives and the Slums: Tenement House Reform in New York City, 1890–1917* (Pittsburgh, 1962).

Mabel Dodge Luhan, *Intimate Memories . . .* 2 vols. (New York, 1933).

Arthur Mann, *Yankee Reformers in the Urban Age: Social Reform in Boston, 1880–1900* (New York, 1954).

Henry F. May, *Protestant Churches and Industrial America* (New York, 1949).

James R. McGovern, "The American Women's Pre-World War I Freedom in Manners and Morals," *Journal of American History* 55 (1968):315–33.

William G. McLoughlin, *Modern Revivalism: Charles Grandison Finney to Billy Graham* (New York, 1959).

Mills, *White Collar.*

Allan Nevins, *The Emergence of Modern America, 1865–1878* (New York, 1927).

William L. O'Neill, *Divorce in the Progressive Era* (New Haven, 1967).

Ostrander, *American Civilization in the First Machine Age.*

David M. Potter, *People of Plenty: Economic Abundance and the American Character* (Chicago, 1954).

Stanley K. Schultz, *The Culture Factory: Boston Public Schools, 1789–1860* (New York, 1973).

Richard Sennett, *Families Against the City: Middle Class Homes of Industrial Chicago, 1872–1890* (Cambridge, 1970).

Mark Sullivan, *Our Times: The Turn of the Century* (New York, 1926).

William Graham Sumner, "The Forgotten Man" in Stow Persons (ed.), *Social Darwinism: Selected Essays of William Graham Sumner* (Englewood Cliffs, 1963).

Time-Life Editors, *This Fabulous Century: Volume 1 1900–1910* (New York, 1969).

Selwyn K. Troen, "Education in the City," in Raymond A. Mohl and James F. Richardson (eds.), *The Urban Experience: Themes in American History* (Belmont, Cal., 1973).

Robert H. Wiebe, *The Search for Order, 1877–1920* (New York, 1967).

Larzer Ziff, *The American 1890s: Life and Times of a Lost Generation* (New York, 1966).

CHAPTER 9

Jane Addams, *Twenty Years at Hull House* (New York, 1910).

Robert Bremner, *From the Depths: The Discovery of Poverty in the United States* (New York, 1956).

James H. Cassedy, *Charles V. Chapin and the Public Health Movement* (Cambridge, 1962).

Clarke A. Chambers, *Paul U. Kellogg and the Survey: Voices for Social Welfare and Social Justice* (Minneapolis, 1971).

Robert D. Cross, *The Emergence of Liberal Catholicism in America* (Cambridge, 1959).

Robert W. DeForest and Lawrence Veiller (eds.), *The Tenement House Problem Including the Report of the New York State Tenement House Commission of 1900*. 2 vols. (New York, 1903).

Emily W. Dinwiddie, *Housing Conditions in Philadelphia* (Philadelphia, 1904).

W. E. B. DuBois, *The Philadelphia Negro* (New York, 1967).

Harold U. Faulkner, *Politics, Reform and Expansion 1890-1900* (New York, 1959).

Philip S. Foner, *History of the Labor Movement in the United States* (New York, 1947).

John A. Garraty, *The American Nation* (New York, 1966).

Constance M. L. Green, *The Secret City: A History of Race Relations in the Nation's Capital* (Princeton, 1967).

Herbert G. Gutman, "Protestantism and the American Labor Movement: The Christian Spirit in the Gilded Age," *American Historical Review*, 72 (1966):74–101.

Gutman, "The Reality of the Rag-to-Riches 'Myth'."

Gutman, "Work, Culture, and Society in Industrializing America."

Mark H. Haller, "Urban Vice and Civic Reform: Chicago in Early Twentieth Century" in Kenneth T. Jackson and Stanley K. Schultz (eds.), *Cities in American History* (New York, 1972).

Hutchins Hapgood, *The Spirit of the Ghetto: Studies of the Jewish Quarter in New York* (New York, 1910).

Higham, *Strangers in the Land*.

Robert Hunter, *Poverty* (New York, 1904).

Robert Hunter, *Tenement Conditions in Chicago. Report by the Investigating Committee of the City Homes Association* (Chicago, 1901).

Kellogg, *The Pittsburgh Survey*.

Roger Lane, *Policing the City: Boston, 1822-1885* (Cambridge, 1967).

Josephine Shaw Lowell, *Public Relief and Private Charity* (New York, 1884).

Roy Lubove, *Twentieth-Century Pittsburgh: Government, Business, and Environmental Change* (New York, 1969).

Mann, *Yankee Reformers in the Urban Age*.

May, *Protestant Churches and Industrial America*.

Virginia Yans McLaughlin, "Patterns of Work and Family Organization: Buffalo's Italians," *Journal of Interdisciplinary History*, II (1971):299–314.

Samuel Eliot Morison, Henry Steele Commager, and William E. Leuchtenberg, *The Growth of the American Republic*, 2 vols. (New York, 1969).

Humbert S. Nelli, *The Italians in Chicago, 1880-1930, A Study in Ethnic Mobility* (New York, 1970).

Mary White Ovington, *Half a Man: The Status of the Negro in New York* (New York, 1911).

Elizabeth H. Pleck, "The Two-Parent Household: Black Family Structure in Late Nineteenth-Century Boston," *Journal of Social History*, VI (1972):1–31.

Jacob A. Riis, *The Children of the Poor* (New York, 1892).

Riis, *How the Other Half Lives*.

Jacob Riis, *The Making of an American* (New York, 1903).

Jacob Riis, *A Ten Years' War: An Account of the Battle with the Slum in New York* (New York, 1900).

Moses Rischin, *The Promised City: New York City's Jews, 1870-1914* (Cambridge, 1962).

Robert Rockaway, "Ethnic Conflict in an Urban Environment: The German and

Russian Jew in Detroit, 1881–1914," *American Jewish Historical Quarterly* (December 1970):133–147, 150.

Stanley K. Schultz, "Breaking the Chains of Poverty: Public Education in Boston, 1800–1860" in Kenneth T. Jackson and Stanley K. Schultz (eds.), *Cities in American History* (New York, 1972).

Thernstrom, *Poverty and Progress.*

William M. Tuttle, Jr., "Contested Neighborhoods and Racial Violence: Chicago in 1919," in Kenneth T. Jackson and Stanley K. Schultz (eds.), *Cities in American History* (New York, 1972).

Edith Elmer Wood, *The Housing of the Unskilled Worker* (New York, 1919).

Robert A. Woods, *The City Wilderness: A Settlement Study, South End, Boston* (Boston, 1899).

Robert A. Woods, et al., *The Poor in Great Cities* (New York, 1895).

CHAPTER 10

Edward C. Banfield and James Q. Wilson, *City Politics* (Cambridge, 1963).

Charles A. Beard, *American City Government* (New York, 1912).

James Bryce, *The American Commonwealth* (New York, 1889), 2 vols.

Alexander B. Callow, *The Tweed Ring* (New York, 1966).

Frank J. Goodnow, *City Government in the United States* (New York, 1904).

Robert K. Merton, *Social Theory and Social Structure* (New York, 1957).

Seymour Mandelbaum, *Boss Tweed's New York* (New York, 1965).

Zane Miller, *Boss Cox's Cincinnati* (New York, 1968).

William L. Riordan, *Plunkitt of Tammany Hall* (New York, 1905).

J. Allen Smith, *The Spirit of American Government* (New York, 1907).

Lincoln Steffens, *The Autobiography of Lincoln Steffens*, 2 vols. (New York, 1931).

Joel A. Tarr, "The Urban Politician as Entrepreneur," *Mid-America* (January 1967): 55–67.

Lloyd Wendt and Herman Kogan, *Bosses in Lusty Chicago* (Bloomington, 1967).

Harold Zink, *City Bosses in the United States* (Durham, 1930).

CHAPTER 11

Van Wyck Brooks, *America's Coming-of-Age* (New York, 1934).

Robert M. Crunden, *A Hero in Spite of Himself: Brand Whitlock; in Art, Politics and War* (New York, 1969).

Samuel P. Hays, "The Politics of Reform in Municipal Government in the Progressive Era," *Pacific Northwest Quarterly* 55 (1964):157–69.

Melvin G. Holli, *Reform in Detroit* (New York, 1969).

Frederic C. Howe, *Confessions of a Reformer* (New York, 1925).

Frederic C. Howe, *The City: The Hope of Democracy* (New York, 1905).

Tom L. Johnson, *My Story* (New York, 1911).

George E. Mowry, *The Era of Theodore Roosevelt* (New York, 1958).

John G. Sproat, *"The Best Men": Liberal Reformers in the Gilded Age* (New York, 1968).

Steffens, *Autobiography.*

Jack Tager, *The Intellectual as Social Reformer; Brand Whitlock and the Progressive Movement* (Cleveland, 1968).

James Weinstein, *The Corporate Ideal in the Liberal State 1900–1916* (Boston, 1968).

Brand Whitlock, *Forty Years of It* (New York, 1914).

CHAPTER 12

Jane Addams, *Twenty Years at Hull House* (New York, 1910).

Bremner, *The Lower Depths*.

Heywood Broun and Margaret Leech, *Anthony Comstock* (New York, 1927).

Allen F. Davis, *Spearheads for Reform: The Social Settlements and the Progressive Movement, 1890–1914* (New York, 1967).

John A. Garraty, *The New Commonwealth, 1877–1890* (New York, 1968).

Ginger, *Age of Excess*.

Howe, *Confessions of a Reformer*.

Roy Lubove, *The Professional Altruist: The Emergence of Social Work as a Career 1880–1930* (Cambridge, 1965).

David J. Pivar, *Purity Crusade: Sexual Morality and Social Control, 1868–1900* (Westport, Conn., 1973).

Schlesinger, *The Rise of the City*.

Richard Skolnik, "George Edwin Waring, Jr.," *New-York Historical Society Quarterly* LII (1968):354–78.

EPILOGUE

Henry Adams, *The Education of Henry Adams* (Boston, 1918).

Civic League of St. Louis, *A City Plan for St. Louis* (St. Louis, 1907).

Herbert Croly, "What Is Civic Art?," *Architectural Record* XVI (1904):47–52.

Harvey A. Kantor, "The City Beautiful in New York," *The New-York Historical Society Quarterly* LVII (1973):149–71.

Harvey A. Kantor, "Benjamin C. Marsh and the Fight over Population Congestion," *Journal of American Institute of Planners* (November 1974):422–29.

George E. Kessler, *A City Plan for Dallas* (1910).

Benjamin C. Marsh, *Lobbyist for the People* (Washington, 1953).

Benjamin C. Marsh, "City Planning in Justice to the Working Population," *Charities and the Commons* XIX (1908):1514–18.

Frederick Law Olmsted, "Introductory Address on City Planning," *Proceedings of the Second National Conference on City Planning and the Problems of Congestion* (1909).

John Reps, *Monumental Washington* (Princeton, 1967).

Mel Scott, *American City Planning* (Berkeley, 1969).

General Bibliography

Howard P. Chudacoff, *The Evolution of American Urban Society* (Englewood Cliffs, 1975).

Thomas C. Cochran and William Miller, *The Age of Enterprise* (New York, 1945).

Harold U. Faulkner, *Politics, Reform, and Expansion, 1890–1900* (New York, 1959).

John A. Garraty, *The New Commonwealth, 1877–1890* (New York, 1968).

Ray Ginger, *Age of Excess* (New York, 1965).

Charles N. Glaab and A. Theodore Brown, *A History of Urban America* (New York, 1967).

Charles N. Glaab, *The American City: A Documentary History* (Homewood, Illinois, 1963).

Edward C. Kirkland, *Industry Comes of Age* (New York, 1961).

Blake McKelvey, *The Urbanization of America: 1860–1915* (New Brunswick, 1963).

Zane Miller, *The Urbanization of Modern America: A Brief History* (New York, 1973).

George E. Mowry, *The Era of Theodore Roosevelt and the Birth of Modern America, 1900–1912.* (New York, 1958).

Lewis Mumford, *The Culture of Cities* (New York, 1938).

Arthur M. Schlesinger, *The Rise of the City 1878–1898* (New York, 1933).

Bayrd Still, *Urban America: A History with Documents* (Boston, 1974).

Sam Bass Warner, Jr., *The Urban Wilderness: A History of the American City* (New York, 1973).

Robert H. Wiebe, *The Search for Order, 1877–1920* (New York, 1967).

William A. Williams, *The Contours of American History* (Cleveland, 1961).

Index

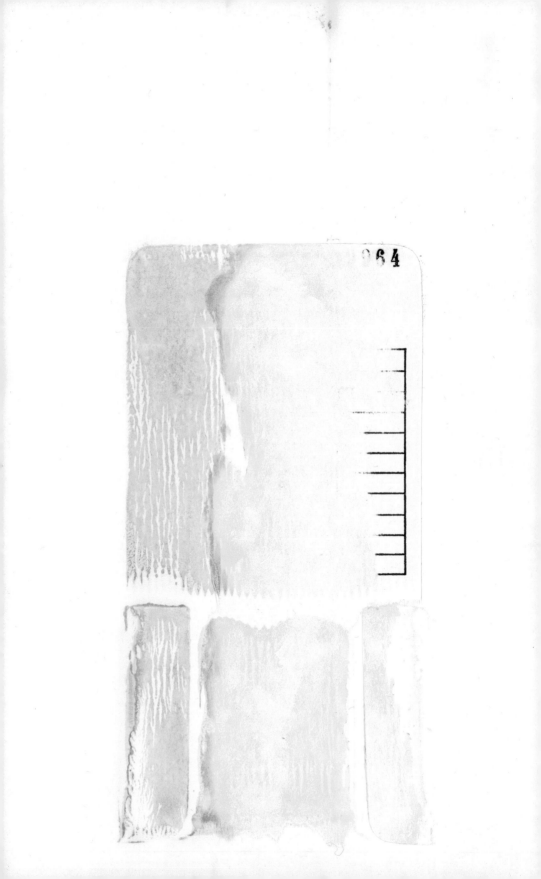